• STATISTICS FOR PSYCHOLOGY

Second Edition

William Mendenhall
University of Florida

James T. McClave
University of Florida

Madelaine Ramey
Matteo Ricci College

DUXBURY PRESS • North Scituate, Massachusetts

Library of Congress Cataloging in Publication Data

Mendenhall, William.
   Statistics for psychology.

   Includes bibliographical references and index.
   1. Psychometrics. I. McClave, James T., joint
author. II. Ramey, Madelaine, joint author.
III. Title.
BF39.M45 1977   519.5'02'415   77-23194
ISBN 0-87872-126-6

Duxbury Press

A Division of Wadsworth Publishing Company, Inc.

Statistics for Psychologists, 2nd ed. was edited and prepared for composition by Carol Beal. Interior design was provided by Walter Williams and the cover was provided by Joseph Landry.

L.C. Cat. Card No.: 77-23194

ISBN 0-87872-126-6

Printed in the United States of America

1 2 3 4 5 6 7 8 9 10—81 80 79 78 77

• Contents

5 The Binomial Probability Distribution   78

6 Some Nonparametric Statistical Tests   116

7 The Normal Probability Distribution   155

8 Parametric Statistical Inference   192

9 Small-Sample Parametric Inference 236

10 The Design of Psychological Experiments 275

11 The Analysis of Variance 298

12 Linear Regression and Correlation 368

13 The Analysis of Enumerative Data   408

14 Nonparametric Analysis of Variance   432

15 A Summary and Conclusion   446

• Preface

An introduction to statistics for psychology students must focus simultaneously on an understanding of the theory and techniques of statistics and on the particular day-to-day uses of statistics in psychology. For these reasons we believe that an effective text for this purpose should be written jointly by statisticians and psychologists. By synthesizing these complementary points of view, we feel we have produced a text that is more valuable than the typical general introductory statistics book. The latter cannot show the psychology student how statistical methods and techniques can be applied to psychological experimentation specifically. We also hope to have overcome the weaknesses of some introductory-statistics-for-psychology books, which may *inform* the student about statistics but do not *teach* the subject.

The basic objective of the present text is to stress the role of statistical inference in the scientific method. This theme, carried by the chapter introductions and summaries, relates one body of material to another and produces a connectivity that aids the student in understanding and learning statistics. By concentrating on applications within a single discipline—psychology—the student's familiarity with the language and experimental techniques of the field is reinforced while learning statistics.

The mathematical difficulty associated with an introductory statistics course can be increased or decreased by including or excluding material on the theory of probability. We can explain the role that probability plays in inference making by teaching the student how to calculate the probability of certain events for the discrete case, or we can simply assume that approximate values for required probabilities can be obtained by observing the relative frequencies of the events in many repetitions of an experiment. This text takes the latter approach, thus substantially reducing the mathematical level of the content without sacrificing an explanation of the role that probability plays in making inferences. The ordering of topics has been directed specifically at the type of experimentation common in psychological research. Specifically, we introduce nonparametric statistics early in the text (chapter 6) because of the frequent occurrence of ordinal data in psychological experimentation. This alteration to the usual ordering of topics—presenting nonparametric before parametric statistical methods—is of particular value to students in psychology. It provides them with statistical techniques that are easy to comprehend, easy to apply, and applicable for analyzing both ordinal and measurement data. Because the techniques are intuitively easy to comprehend, they provide an excellent vehicle for conveying the notions involved in a statistical test of an hypothesis. Tests of hypotheses, a topic of considerable difficulty to the beginning student, are presented early in the text and are reinforced in later chapters.

CHANGES IN THE SECOND EDITION

Our aims in writing the present revision have been threefold:

• To make the book easier and simpler.

• To make it as up-to-date and modern as possible.

• To make it interesting and motivating to psychology students.

To achieve the first objective—that of making the book easier and simpler—we have introduced the following improvements in this second edition. (1) A great deal more verbal explanation appears in this edition than was in the first edition. (2) The number of worked-out examples is roughly double that of the earlier version of the book. (3) The number of graphic illustrations has been doubled. (4) The exercise sets have been thoroughly revised and many more simple exercises introduced. (5) The probability chapter has been carefully rewritten. (6) Hypothesis testing has been rewritten and its presentation made simpler and more consistent. (7) The chapter introducing nonparametric methods has been similarly simplified. (8) The chapters on small-sample inference, experimental design, and analysis of variance have also been thoroughly reworked and made clearer and more consistent with the rest of the book. (9) The sections on contingency tables have been rewritten.

A number of changes in this revision reflect our second aim, that of making the book as up-to-date and modern as possible. Especially significant are the following. (1) The coverage of *descriptive statistics* has been expanded, in particular through the addition of a new chapter 3 covering *correlation*. (2) Greater attention has been given to the discussions of significance levels when testing hypotheses, since the reporting of significance levels has become an accepted practice among many behavioral scientists. (3) The concept of experimental design has been introduced through the matched pairs experiment in chapter 6. This is followed by an elementary, but careful, discussion of experimental design in chapter 10. (4) Because it is often encountered in psychological research, the analysis of repeated measures design has been added to chapter 11. This chapter also includes an explanation of the important concept of factor interaction, as well as the analyses of the completely randomized and the randomized block designs. (5) A new chapter 14 has been added, covering nonparametric analysis of variance.

The third objective of this edition—to make it interesting and motivating to psychology students—has caused the addition of many exercises and examples which are motivated by actual research in the behavioral sciences. References to journals are included where appropriate. We think that this feature emphasizes the relevance and utility of statistics for psychologists and that it provides realistic exercises for the student to work. In another effort to provide motivation, the chapter openings now refer explicitly to the chapter outlines, thus listing for the reader the specific organization of each chapter.

While we believe that all these changes make for a more teachable, more motivating, and more modern introduction to statistics for psychologists, we wish to emphasize again that our primary goal is to present a cohesive view of statistics, with each topic, section, and chapter an integral part of the unit, and with statistical inference as the theme.

ACKNOWLEDGEMENTS

The authors of the second edition wish to acknowledge the valuable comments and the encouragement of the manuscript reviewers, John E. Holmgren, University of Maryland,

Arthur D. Kirsch, George Washington University, James A. McMartin, California State University—Northridge, and S. H. Revusky, Memorial University of Newfoundland. Cheryl Stanley provided the solutions to the exercises, as well as a valuable line-by-line review. Thanks are also due to Professor E. J. Pearson; the Biometrika Trustees; Professors Beyer, Friedman, Kruskal, and Hald; and the Editors of the *Journal of the American Statistical Association* and the *Annals of Mathematical Statistics* for material included in the statistical tables in appendix II. We are also indebted to our typist, Ellen Evans, for her excellent typing and for her patience. Particular thanks are due to Carol Storer, secretary of the Department of Statistics, for her help in coordinating the work and the typing. Finally, we acknowledge the assistance of numerous friends who have helped in many ways to make this text a reality.

1 • Statistics and the Behavioral Scientist

INTRODUCTION

In recent years, statistics has come to play an increasingly important role in the behavioral sciences. Indeed, an experimental plan or research report that does not include some statistical method is fast becoming a rarity. This state of affairs has not come about by accident. Statistics supplies a methodology that is particularly well suited to the needs of behavioral research. What these needs are and how statistics meets them become more apparent when we consider the essential features of a scientific investigation, pointing out some of the specific problems involved and indicating how statistics can be used in dealing with these problems.

Scientific inquiry is essentially a three-step procedure. First, a relationship is formulated, or hypothesized; that is, the problem is defined. Then, relevant information is obtained. Finally, the relationship is tested.

The relationships of interest in the behavioral sciences are those between given behaviors or behavioral properties and their modifiers or determinants. For example, an investigator observes that when an unfamiliar object, such as a doll, is placed in its cage, a young chimpanzee shows a reaction very similar to curiosity in humans. The chimp circles the object, sniffs at it, nudges and pokes it. Yet when an identical object is placed in the cage of an older but still active chimp, the response is seemingly one of indifference. On the basis of this comparison, the investigator hypothesizes (predicts) that "curiosity" in chimpanzees decreases with age. He or she selects a number of chimps of different ages, introduces the unfamiliar object to each, and records the amount of time spent by each in curiosity behavior—operationally defined as circling, sniffing, nudging, poking, and so on. The researcher then uses these recorded values as evidence for (or against) the hypothesized relationship.

In this example, the relationship hypothesized is that between curiosity—

1

defined in terms of particular behaviors—and age. More specifically, the investigator predicts that curiosity decreases with increasing age. To bring his prediction out of the realm of mere speculation, the investigator next obtains relevant information. Here he or she obtains measures of the amount of curiosity shown at each age level. The final or testing stage of the investigation consists in showing that the data—the collected information—support or refute the predicted relationship. Here the investigator determines whether that the observed curiosity measurements bear out the prediction that curiosity decreases as age increases.

This description of scientific investigation as a sequence of three distinct and readily identifiable steps is, of course, oversimplified. In practice, good researchers do not move blindly from hypothesizing a relationship to obtaining information and then to testing the relationship. Rather, researchers define the phenomena and specify the relationships of interest. They realize that they must collect data that are accurate, representative of the phenomena, and can be meaningfully described and analyzed. They know they must collect and analyze the data in such a way that the results can be used in testing the relationships under investigation.

Nevertheless, a representation of scientific inquiry as a stepwise process serves two useful purposes: It summarizes the essential features, and it provides a convenient framework for discussing some of the specific problems associated with scientific research.

1.1 • THE POPULATION AND THE SAMPLE

Implicit in the preceding discussion is a restriction that the relationship being investigated applies to some defined *population*. In the example in the Introduction, the prediction of an age-curiosity relationship might, for instance, be limited to male chimpanzees raised in captivity whose ages fall within a specific range. Measurements of curiosity on all animals fitting this description comprise the population of interest.

However, it is not possible ordinarily to observe every member of the population. The set of measurements actually obtained is usually a *sample* from the population. The investigator of chimpanzee behavior cannot observe every chimp in the prescribed experimental setting, so he or she obtains measurements of curiosity on a limited number of chimps. The obtained measurements comprise a sample. The investigator then uses these sample measurements to make a general conclusion—an **inference**—about the population: curiosity in captive male chimpanzees does (or does not) decrease with increasing age.

The terms **population** and **sample** can be defined quite simply.

Definition 1.1

A **population** is a set of measurements of interest to the experimenter.

The population associated with the chimpanzee experiment is the set of curiosity measurements made on all captive male chimpanzees whose ages fall within a specific range. In this example, the population is a large set of measurements that exists conceptually; that is, the measurements that *could be* acquired on all these male chimpanzees have not been made, but we can conceive of their existence in our imagination.

In contrast, suppose that we wish to determine the fraction of students at a particular university that favors Sam Smith for student body president. Each student in favor could be counted as a 1; each opposed or having no opinion, as a 0. Thus the population of measurements is a set of 1s and 0s associated with the entire student body. Unlike the conceptual chimpanzee population, this population exists in reality and the number of measurements in the population is equal to the number of students enrolled in the university.

Now we examine the term **sample.**

Definition 1.2

A **sample** is a subset of measurements selected from the population.

For example, the measurements actually obtained in the chimpanzee curiosity experiment represent a sample selected from the conceptual population of all chimpanzee curiosity measurements. Similarly, a sample of the opinions of 200 students is a subset of measurements selected from the population of all opinions of students.

In both examples, and in general, the statistical problem involves sampling from a population with a very definite objective in mind. We wish to use the information contained in a subset of measurements—the sample—to infer the nature of the larger set—the population from which the sample was selected. That is, we wish to make an *inference,* a statement about the population based on information in the sample.

1.2 • WHAT IS STATISTICS? WHAT IS ITS ROLE IN THE SCIENTIFIC METHOD?

The scientific method has been described as a three-step inference-making procedure in which inferences (decisions or predictions) are made about the population on the basis of sample information. Statistics, a branch of applied mathematics, provides the methodology for making inferences. To illustrate where and how statistical methods enter into the process of scientific investigation, consider our chimpanzee example.

To decide whether or not curiosity decreases with age, the investigator must obtain measurements on a number of chimps at various ages. Questions that immediately arise are these: How many measurements should be obtained? How should we sample the age range of interest? Questions such as these, concerning **experimental design** or **sampling procedure**, can be answered by using statistical methodology. **Statistics provides the strategy and methods for gathering the maximum amount of information for a given expenditure of time and other resources.**

Once the relevant information is obtained, the investigator requires methods to describe and summarize the data so that the results can be interpreted and communicated. **Statistics supplies these methods of data analysis—techniques for extracting the essential features of a data set.**

The final stage of the investigation is that of testing an hypothesized relationship. The investigator must decide whether or not the sample data support the hypothesis that curiosity in captive chimpanzees decreases with increasing age. **Statistics offers procedures for making the inference from sample data to the population. Moreover, these statistical inference procedures are based on a rationale that permits error evaluation.** Not only do these procedures supply the principles and methodology for making inferences, but they give information about the chance of error in the decision or prediction. If it is decided that curiosity does indeed decrease with age, what is the chance that this decision is incorrect? Statistical inference procedures provide an answer to this question.

In short, statistics is a science concerned with inference. We select a sample of measurements from a larger set, a population, in order to make an inference about the population. The sampling procedure involves the collection of a quantity of **information** at a specified cost. Hence we think of statistics as a *theory of information* concerned with inference. The *objective of statistics* is stated as follows.

Objective of Statistics

The **objective of statistics** is to make an inference about a population based on information contained in a sample.

SUMMARY

Investigation in the behavioral sciences is a three-step process in which a behavioral relationship is hypothesized, relevant information is collected, and the hypothesized relationship is tested. This process is necessarily one of inference. The information collected is a *sample* from the *population* of interest, and these sample data are used to make inferences (decisions, predictions) about the population relationship. Statistics provides the vehicle for making inferences about the population on the basis of sample data. The behavioral scientist also relies upon statistical procedures for the *experimental design* and *data analysis* aspects of information collecting. He or she uses the principles and methodology of *statistical inference* to test behavioral relationships and to control the chance of error in the decision or prediction.

REFERENCES

Hyman, R. 1964. *The nature of psychological inquiry.* Englewood Cliffs, N.J.: Prentice-Hall.

Kerlinger, F. 1973. *Foundations of behavioral research: Educational and psychological inquiry.* 2d ed. New York: Holt, Rinehart and Winston.

2·Description of the Data

INTRODUCTION

An important step in the inference-making process is that of collecting relevant information. But what kind of data are relevant? Having observed the behavior of interest, how do we translate that observation into a measurement? What categorization or numbering scheme best represents a set of behavioral observations? Then, given a set of measurements, whether it be the entire population or the sample at hand, how will we describe that set?

The two problems, measurement and description, are related. The kind of categorization or numbering system adopted determines in large part the methods that are appropriate for describing a set of observations. In this chapter we will first briefly consider different kinds of measurement. As shown in the chapter outline, this discussion is found in section 2.1. Then we will turn to methods for describing a set of measurements, sections 2.2 through 2.7 and section 2.9.

Throughout these discussions, and especially in section 2.10, we will emphasize those methods which are useful not only for descriptive purposes but also for statistical inference. Since an inference is a descriptive statement about a population, and since a population is a set of measurements, you can see that methods for describing sets of measurements are essential for making inferences about populations.

2.1 • KINDS OF MEASUREMENT

Measurement may be broadly defined as the process of classifying or assigning numbers to observations in order to differentiate these observations with respect to some criterion or property. It is convenient to distinguish three kinds of measurement frequently used in the behavioral sciences: categorization, rank ordering, and numerical scoring.

Categorization is measurement at its most primitive level. Observations are simply grouped into mutually exclusive categories which may be either qualitatively different or ordered with respect to some property. If, for example, we wish to classify individuals on the basis of marital status, we might form the categories Single, Married, Separated, Divorced, and Widowed. Similarly, we might assign individuals to the categories High, Medium, and Low socioeconomic status. In the first case, the categories are qualitatively different; in the second, the categories are ordered with respect to the property of interest—socioeconomic status. In either case, measurement consists in assigning each individual to that category which best locates him or her with respect to the criterion or property.

Rank ordering consists in assigning whole numbers to observations in a conventional sequence, 1, 2, 3, . . . , so as to reflect the empirical ordering within a set of observations. This technique is particularly useful in the behavioral sciences for measuring properties not otherwise quantifiable. For example, an attribute such as popularity is difficult to quantify. However, we can rank-order individuals with respect to popularity and in this fashion generate a measurement on each individual in a group.

Numerical scoring consists in assigning to each observation a number which indicates the magnitude of the measurement. Scores may be anything from measurements of chronological age to the number of items endorsed on an attitude questionnaire. Scores depend, of course, on the property being measured. Since magnitude as well as order is preserved in numerical scoring, this is usually the most desirable kind of measurement.

2.2 • FREQUENCY DISTRIBUTIONS

Once a measurement procedure has been adopted, the next problem is how to describe the sets of measurements. Two complementary approaches to data description can be taken: frequency distributions are convenient for examining and displaying an entire set of data; **summary numerical methods,** which focus on specific features of the data, are useful for comparing two or more sets of data.

To introduce the notion of a frequency distribution, it is useful to consider a sample set of measurements. The data in table 2.1 give the political affiliations of 16 office employees. The list of name-affiliation pairs contains all the required information, but it is difficult to see a picture of the group as a whole. If, instead, each category is paired with the total number of persons in that category, the relevant information is retained and a more readily interpretable picture of the entire group emerges. This method of summarizing the raw data is displayed in table 2.2.

Table 2.1 • Political affiliation classifications of 16 registered voters

Betty C.	Dem	Donald W.	Dem
John F.	Rep	Karen B.	Dem
Peggy M.	Dem	Steven T.	Rep
Mary McB.	Ind	John S.	Rep
George S.	Dem	James H.	Dem
Ann L.	Ind	Susan W.	Rep
Fred L.	Dem	Fran R.	Rep
Jean R.	Rep	Bill C.	Dem

The second column of table 2.2 illustrates a convenient way to obtain a count of the number of persons in a category. Each name is recorded by a tally mark opposite the appropriate category. **The first and third columns taken together form a *frequency distribution*—a pairing of each measurement class with its frequency, the number of measurements in that class. The first and last columns taken together form a *relative frequency distribution*—a pairing of each measurement class with its relative frequency, the fraction of the total number of measurements in that class.**

Table 2.2 • Tabulation of political affiliation classification frequencies

Political Affiliation	Tally	Frequency	Relative Frequency
Democrat	ⵜ |||	8	$\frac{8}{16} = .500$
Republican	ⵜ		6	$\frac{6}{16} = .375$
Independent	||	2	$\frac{2}{16} = .125$
		16	1 1

Frequency distributions for numerical scoring data are constructed in a similar manner. To illustrate, consider the data given in table 2.3, which represent the reaction times (in seconds) of 30 adults subjected to the same visual stimulus.

Table 2.3 • Reaction times (in seconds) of 30 adults subjected to a visual stimulus

14.5	24.4	13.6	18.8	13.6
17.2	19.9	24.4	19.0	15.4
22.6	23.5	20.8	19.2	18.1
20.8	19.0	18.1	23.5	27.1
19.9	21.7	19.0	20.9	22.6
20.8	21.7	16.3	20.7	15.4

Unlike the preceding example, the measurements do not fall into natural categories. Instead, measurement classes are formed by grouping the scores into equal intervals. The interval size is determined by dividing the range of the scores—the highest score minus the lowest score—by the desired number of measurement classes. To avoid the possibility of measurements falling on interval boundaries, we determine the lower boundary of the first class as the lowest score minus one-half of the minimum possible difference between two scores. The upper boundary of the last class is the highest score plus one-half of the minimum possible difference between two scores.

The time scores in table 2.3 are rounded to the nearest tenth of a second, so the minimum possible difference between two scores is .1. Since the lowest and highest scores are 13.6 and 27.1, respectively, the scores will range from 13.55 to 27.15, or over an interval of length 13.6. Using 8 measurement classes, the interval size is then 1.7 (13.6 divided by 8) and the intervals are 13.55 to 15.25, 15.25 to 16.95, 16.95 to 18.65, and so on. In general, the number of measurement classes may vary from 5 to 20, depending on the amount of data available.

Having defined our measurement classes, we can construct a frequency distribution in the same manner as for categorical data. Table 2.4 represents the frequency and relative frequency distributions for the reaction time data. Note in table 2.4 that the sum of the decimal forms of the relative frequencies is .999 and not 1. This is due to the rounding errors involved in converting fractions to decimals.

Table 2.4 • Tabulation of reaction time frequencies

Class Interval	Tally	Frequency	Relative Frequency	
13.55–15.25	|||	3	$\frac{3}{30}$ = .100	
15.25–16.95	|||	3	$\frac{3}{30}$ = .100	
16.95–18.65	|||	3	$\frac{3}{30}$ = .100	
18.65–20.35	ℕ ||	7	$\frac{7}{30}$ = .233	
20.35–22.05	ℕ ||	7	$\frac{7}{30}$ = .233	
22.05–23.75	||||	4	$\frac{4}{30}$ = .133	
23.75–25.45	||	2	$\frac{2}{30}$ = .067	
25.45–27.15			1	$\frac{1}{30}$ = .033	
		30	1	.999

Figure 2.1 • Relative frequency histogram

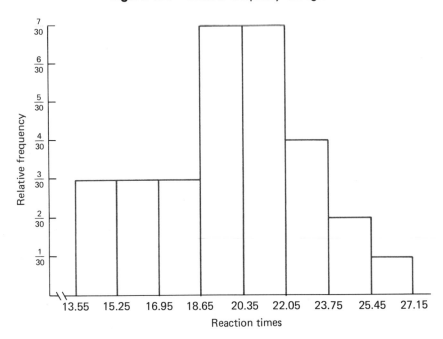

Frequency distributions may be displayed graphically as well as in a table. Graphic representations are, in fact, often preferred, since it is thought that they give a more immediate and readily interpretable picture of the entire data set. Although many methods of graphic display are available, we will consider just one of these, the **histogram,** which is not only one of the most popular but also one of the most useful tools for statistical inference.

In a histogram, rectangles are constructed over each class or class interval with a height equal to the frequency (or relative frequency) for that particular class. Figure 2.1 shows the histogram for the relative frequency distribution in table 2.4. It should be pointed out that the figure is scaled so that the vertical axis is roughly three-fourths of the length of the horizontal axis. This scaling adheres to a convention adopted in the behavioral sciences to minimize possible distorting effects. A summary of rules for constructing histograms is given in the box.

Rules for Constructing Histograms

1. Arrange the data in increasing order, from the smallest to the largest measurement.
2. Divide the interval from the smallest to the largest measurement into subintervals. The number of subintervals should be somewhere from 5 to 20. The widths of the subintervals should be equal. Make sure that
   (a) each measurement falls into one and only one measurement class, and

(b) no measurement falls on a measurement class boundary.
Use a small number of measurement classes if you have a small amount of data; use a larger number of classes for larger amounts of data.
3. Compute the frequency (or relative frequency) of measurements in each measurement class.
4. Using a vertical axis of about three-fourths the length of the horizontal axis, plot each frequency (or relative frequency) as a rectangle over the corresponding measurement class.

Whichever method of display is used for the data of table 2.4, tabular or graphic, we have at hand a basis for making inferences about the population as well as a way of describing the set of sample data. Although we are interested in describing the set of 30 measurements, the main purpose of the experiment is to draw a general conclusion about reaction times. We wish to use these sample data to make an inference about the population of potential measurements. For example, we might ask what proportion of all adults would have a reaction time to this visual stimulus exceeding 22 seconds. If we had reaction time measurements for all adults, we could construct the relative frequency distribution of the population and give the exact answer to this question; we could find the relative frequency of reaction times greater than 22 seconds. Since such a distribution is not available, we use the sample relative frequency distribution to estimate this population proportion. Our most reasonable estimate would be the proportion of sample measurements greater than 22 seconds.

Using table 2.4, we find this proportion to be $\frac{7}{30}$—the sum of the relative frequencies for the class intervals 22.05–23.75, 23.75–25.45, and 25.45–27.15. We could also find this value by using figure 2.1 and calculating the proportion of the total area of the histogram lying to the right of 22.05. This estimate, $\frac{7}{30}$, is our best guess of the population proportion. However, we do expect error in our estimate, since it is based on a single sample from the entire population. As we will see in chapter 8, it is possible—and usually desirable—to determine the magnitude of this estimation error. This error lets us know how good our estimate is.

The concept of relative frequency is an important one in applied statistics. As used so far, it denotes the fraction of measurements falling in a given class or classes. However, when relative frequencies are used to describe a population of measurements, we call them *probabilities*. Thus if the fraction of all adult reaction times that exceed 22 seconds is $\frac{7}{30}$, we say that the *probability* of this event is $\frac{7}{30}$. We will, however, defer a formal definition and a more extensive development of probability until chapter 4.

EXERCISES

1. At the conclusion of a group therapy program, 15 clients were asked to rate themselves as either not improved (A), somewhat improved (B), or greatly improved (C). Two clients rated themselves A, 7 rated themselves B, and 6 rated themselves C.

Construct a frequency distribution to describe the results of the program as assessed by the clients' self-ratings.

2. The following scores represent the grade point averages of 25 college freshmen (the maximum grade point average is 4.0).

2.6	1.8	3.7	1.9	2.6
2.1	2.7	2.4	2.3	3.0
3.1	2.6	2.5	2.7	2.6
2.7	2.9	1.9	2.3	3.5
3.3	2.2	3.0	2.5	3.5

Construct a relative frequency histogram for these data by using 5 measurement classes of length .4.

2.3 • COMMENTS CONCERNING HISTOGRAMS

The relative frequency histogram represents a most important graphical descriptive technique. It is also important to note that we can, in theory, construct a frequency histogram for *any* set of measurements, any sample, or any population. Since our objective is to describe or to make inferences about a population, and since we will never actually have in hand all the measurements for a population, we will not be able to construct a complete frequency histogram. However, it is important to be able to picture the shape a frequency histogram would have if we were to increase the sample size indefinitely.

Since populations usually contain a very large number of measurements, the number of measurement classes can be made so large that the frequency histogram almost becomes a smooth curve. For example, consider the reaction time experiment introduced in section 2.2, in which adults' reaction times to a visual stimulus were recorded. The histogram corresponding to the actual sample of 30 adult reaction times (table 2.3) is repeated for convenience in figure 2.2(a). The histogram in figure 2.2(b) describes a sample of 100 reaction times from the same population. Note that both the scale of the relative frequency (the y-axis) and the endpoints of the class intervals change when the histogram describes a larger sample. Also, the shape of the histogram for a sample size $n = 100$ has a more regular shape, a smoother look, than that for $n = 30$ because we have decreased the size of the class intervals. Figure 2.2(c) is the frequency histogram for the entire population. Notice that the frequency histogram of figure 2.2(c) looks somewhat like a mound or a bell. Frequency histograms for large populations often have this form, and consequently they are known as *bell-shaped* or *mound-shaped* distributions.

We have previously stated that we will never know all the measurements in a population. But if we did, the frequency histogram would be an excellent way to describe a population of measurements because the area under the histogram tells us that fraction of the total number of measurements which fall in each interval. The population frequency histogram also tells us the largest and the smallest measurements in the set.

Figure 2.2 • Relative frequency histograms for the reaction time data

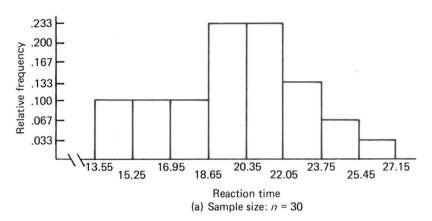

(a) Sample size: $n = 30$

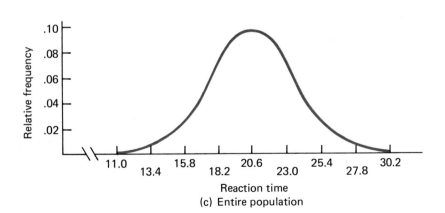

(b) Sample size: $n = 100$

(c) Entire population

2.4 • SUMMARY NUMERICAL METHODS

Frequency distributions, represented either in tabular form or graphic form, are useful in providing an overall picture of an entire data set. However, they are not particularly convenient when our purpose is to compare two or more sets of data. If, for example, we wish to assess the effectiveness of a new teaching method, we might administer an achievement test to two groups, those taught by the standard method and those taught by the new method, and then compare achievement test scores for the two groups. We may, of course, construct histograms to describe the two score distributions, but what would we look for as points of comparison? In what respects do they differ and how much do they differ? Assessment of the degree of similarity between two or more distributions requires summary numerical methods that summarize the relevant information in each.

In addition to noting the difficulty of using graphical methods to compare data sets, we also note that there is a degree of subjectivity in the choice of measurement classes. Different choices of interval boundaries could result in histograms leading to different opinions about the same data set. This fact makes us reluctant to use graphical methods as inference-making tools. We therefore need more precise methods of describing data sets. These methods are presented in the next two sections.

2.5 • MEASURES OF CENTRAL TENDENCY

Faced with the problem of finding a single value that best characterizes an entire distribution of measurements, we would probably turn first to the center of the distribution. However, there are at least three ways we can specify what is meant by the central value: we can use the mode, the median, or the mean.

The first of these measures of central tendency is the **mode.**

Definition 2.1

The **mode** of a set of measurements is the midpoint of the class interval containing the maximum frequency or, in the case of categorical data, the name of the most frequent measurement class.

For the political affiliation data of table 2.2, the mode is the category Democrat, since it is the class with the highest frequency. For the reaction time scores tabulated in table 2.4, the maximum frequency of 7 is the same for two class intervals, 18.65 to 20.35 and 20.35 to 22.05. Since the two intervals are adjacent, the mode would be taken as 20.35, the midpoint of the entire interval 18.65 to 22.05. If the two intervals with a common maximum frequency were not adjacent, we would consider the distribution to be **bimodal,** that is, as having two modes.

A second measure of central tendency is the **median.**

Definition 2.2

The **median** of a set of measurements is that value that falls in the middle when the measurements are arranged in order of magnitude.

To illustrate how we find the median, consider the set of five measurements

$$9, 2, 7, 11, 14$$

Arranging the measurements in order of magnitude, 2, 7, 9, 11, 14, the median is 9, since 9 falls in the middle of the ordered series. If another observation were added, so that the number of measurements is even, we would take the median as the value halfway between the two middle measurements. For example, arranging the set of measurements

$$9, 2, 7, 11, 14, 6$$

in order of magnitude, 2, 6, 7, 9, 11, 14, we find the median to be 8, which is halfway between the two middle measurements, 7 and 9.

Measurements must be arranged in order of magnitude to locate the median. For a large set of data, the task is simplified by making use of the frequency distribution. To illustrate, consider the reaction time scores already arranged in order of magnitude, by intervals, in table 2.4. Since there are 30 measurements, the median is taken as the value halfway between the fifteenth and sixteenth in order of magnitude. From the frequency column, we can see that this value must fall in the interval 18.65 to 20.35, since the total frequency below this interval is 9 (3 + 3 + 3) and the total frequency including this interval is 16 (9 + 7). From table 2.3 we find the 7 measurements between 18.65 and 20.35 to be

$$19.9, 19.9, 19.0, 19.0, 18.8, 19.0, 19.2$$

Arrange these in order of magnitude: 18.8, 19.0, 19.0, 19.0, 19.2, 19.9, 19.9. The last two are the fifteenth and sixteenth in an ordering of all 30 measurements. Thus the median is taken to be 19.9.

The third measure of central tendency is the **arithmetic mean,** usually referred to simply as the **mean.**

Definition 2.3

The **arithmetic mean** of a set of n measurements is the sum of the measurements divided by n.

This definition can be written more compactly by introducing some notation we will find useful in other contexts as well. Let a set of n sample measurements be denoted by

$$y_1, y_2, y_3, \ldots, y_n$$

where y_1 is the measurement on the first observation or individual, y_2 is the measurement on the second observation, and so on. In general, y_i is the measurement on the ith observation; the subscript i is simply a position index designating the location of a measurement in the set. Then by using the letter Σ (capital Greek sigma) to indicate "the sum of," the operation of adding the n measurements, $y_1, y_2, \ldots, y_n$, is represented as

$$\sum_{i=1}^{n} y_i$$

That is,

$$\sum_{i=1}^{n} y_i = y_1 + y_2 + y_3 + \cdots + y_n$$

Finally, using the symbol $\bar{y}$ to denote the *sample mean*, we can write

$$\bar{y} = \frac{\sum_{i=1}^{n} y_i}{n}$$

as the arithmetic mean for a set of n sample measurements, $y_1, y_2, y_3, \ldots, y_n$. To distinguish between the sample and the population, we will use the letter μ (Greek mu) to designate the population mean.

$\bar{y}$ is the sample mean
μ is the population mean

To illustrate the calculation of the mean, consider the sample of five measurements 2, 9, 11, 5, 6. The mean is

$$\bar{y} = \frac{\sum_{i=1}^{n} y_i}{n} = \frac{2 + 9 + 11 + 5 + 6}{5} = 6.6$$

In addition to being a descriptive measure, $\bar{y}$ also serves an important function in statistical inference as an estimator (predictor) of μ, the unknown population mean. For example, the mean of the reaction time data in table 2.3 is equal to

$$\bar{y} = \frac{\sum\limits_{i=1}^{n} y_i}{n} = \frac{592.5}{30} = 19.75$$

The mean of the entire population of reaction times is unknown to us, but if we were to estimate its value, our estimate of μ would be 19.75. We again note the importance of assessing the error associated with this estimate, but we will defer further discussion of this important point until chapter 8.

You should note that we have not specified symbols for the population or sample median and mode. This is because the sample mean has, as we will see, certain desirable properties for making inferences that are not shared by the sample median or mode. Although for some kinds of data the median or mode may be preferred for descriptive purposes, the sample mean is distinctly superior for purposes of statistical inference. Because this text is primarily concerned with making inferences based on sampling, we will henceforth use the sample mean exclusively as a measure of central tendency.

EXERCISES

1. Find the median and mean values of the following sample.

    3, 6, 1, 5, 20, 2, 5, 8

2. Find the median and mean values of the following sample.

    9, 4, 4, 7, 2, 6, 1

3. Social scientists use personal income as one index of an individual's socioeconomic status. For instance, Cahalan, Cisin, and Crossley (1969) compiled a breakdown of the percentage of drinkers and abstainers by socioeconomic status. Since there will probably be differences among the different measures of central tendency, it is advisable for researchers to compute more than one measure.

    Respondents in a survey noted their yearly income. For the given set of income values, compute the mean, the median, and the mode.

12,000	10,000	10,000	90,800	9,800
12,000	5,600	9,000	9,000	10,200
15,000	17,000	11,500	13,000	8,000
9,500	13,500	12,200	17,000	11,400

    Now drop the highest value and again compute the mean, the median, and the mode. What effect does dropping this large measurement have on the measures of central tendency?

4. Refer to exercise 1 of section 2.2. Find the mode of this distribution.

5. Refer to exercise 2 of section 2.2. Find the mode, the median, and the mean of this distribution.

2.6 • MEASURES OF VARIABILITY

It would be incorrect to conclude that two data sets are the same because they have the same mean, median, or mode; they may differ markedly in the variation about their centers. The importance of data variation is illustrated by a story that a friend of ours, a law professor, always tells at cocktail parties. Gathering a group of listeners about him and casting a mischievous glance in our direction, he asks, "Have you ever heard the story about the statistician who couldn't swim and drowned in a river with an average depth of three feet?" While we admit to some discomfort every time we hear the joke, it does stress the importance of data variation. The mean (or any other measure of central tendency) only tells part of the story; that is, it only partially describes a distribution of measurements.

Does the average (mean) tell us all we need to know about a distribution for a set of measurements?

Suppose a psychologist is comparing two different test procedures which purport to measure IQ. Suppose that both tests have been extensively used and that the distributions of measurements for the two tests are described by figure 2.3. We note that both tests have a "center" score of 100, and yet the score distributions are very different. The difference lies in the amount of *variability*, or dispersion, of the two distributions.

Figure 2.3 • Relative frequency distributions for two IQ tests

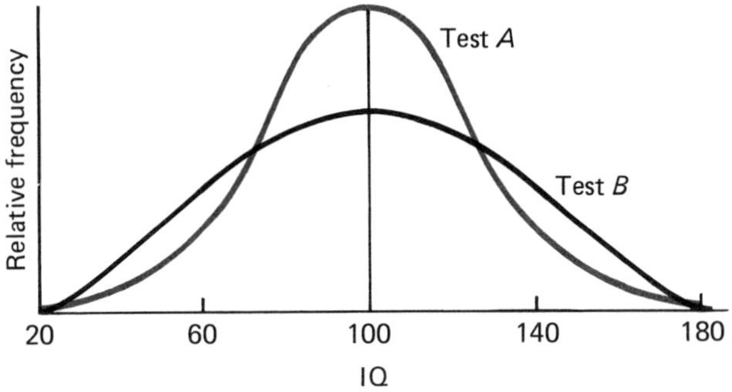

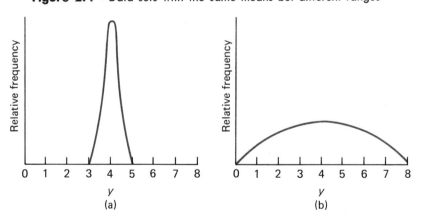

The simplest measure of variation is the **range.**

Definition 2.4

The **range** of a set of measurements is the difference between the largest and the smallest measurement.

Figure 2.4 shows two data sets with identical means (and medians) of 4, but their difference in variability is clearly indicated by their ranges. The data set in figure 2.4(a) has a range of $5 - 3 = 2$, and the data set in figure 2.4(b) has a range of $8 - 0 = 8$.

Figure 2.4 • Data sets with the same means but different ranges

However, the IQ data sets in figure 2.3 indicate that the range is not a completely satisfactory measure of variability. Both data sets vary from 20 to 180, giving a range of $180 - 20 = 160$. But clearly Test B has more variable measurements.

The limitation of the range is overcome to some extent by introducing the notion of quartiles. Remember that if we specify an interval along the horizontal axis of our histogram, the percentage of area under the histogram lying above the interval is equal to the percentage of the total number of measurements falling in that interval. Since the median is the middle measurement when the data are arranged in order of magnitude, the median is the value of y such that half the area of the histogram lies to its left, half to its right. Similarly, we define **quartiles** as the values of y that divide the area of the histogram into quarters.

Definition 2.5

Let $y_1, y_2, \ldots, y_n$ be a set of n measurements arranged in order of magnitude. The **lower quartile (first quartile)** is the value of y that exceeds $\frac{1}{4}$ of the measurements and is less than the remaining $\frac{3}{4}$. The **second quartile** is the median. The **upper quartile (third quartile)** is the value of y that exceeds $\frac{3}{4}$ of the measurements and is less than the remaining $\frac{1}{4}$.

Locating the lower quartile on a histogram, figure 2.5, we note that $\frac{1}{4}$ of the area lies to the left of the lower quartile, $\frac{3}{4}$ to the right. The upper quartile is the value of y such that $\frac{3}{4}$ of the area lies to the left, $\frac{1}{4}$ to the right.

Figure 2.5 • Location of quartiles

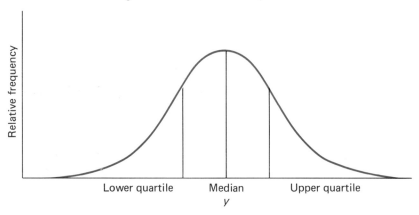

Lower quartile   Median   Upper quartile

y

For very large data sets, we may wish to use **percentiles** for descriptive purposes.

Definition 2.6

Let $y_1, y_2, \ldots, y_n$ be a set of n measurements arranged in order of magnitude. The **pth percentile** is the value of y such that p percent of the measurements are less than that value of y and $(100 - p)$ percent are greater.

For example, if the 90th percentile of the IQ Test A is a score of 130, the implication is that 90 percent of all IQs measured by Test A are less than 130, with only 10 percent exceeding 130. Examination of figure 2.3 indicates that the 90th percentile for Test B is larger than 130 (about 150).

Quartiles and percentiles may be grouped under the general heading of **measures of relative standing.** They are used when it is important to determine the location of a particular measurement with respect to the rest of that data set, that is, its relative standing. The reporting of Scholastic Aptitude Test (SAT) scores and Graduate Record Examination (GRE) scores by the Educational Testing Service is a prime example of measures of relative standing. All scores are reported both as numbers on a scale from 200 to 800 and as percentile rankings within various groups who took the test. For example, suppose you scored 576 on the verbal section of the GRE. Then your score may be reported as being in the 68th percentile of all females who took the exam, in the 75th percentile of all males taking the exam, and in the 72nd percentile of all examinees.

Measures of relative standing are useful in locating a specific measurement relative to the remainder of the data set. However, we still need a measure of variability that can be expressed as a single number yet is more sensitive than the range. Consider, as an example, the sample of five measurements 5, 7, 1, 2, 4. We can depict these data graphically, as in figure 2.6, by showing the measurements as dots falling along the y-axis. Figure 2.6 is called a **dot diagram**.

Figure 2.6 • Dot diagram

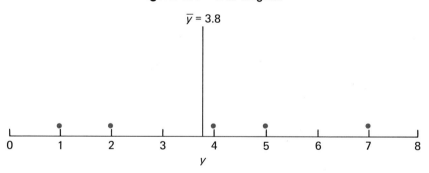

Calculating the mean as the measure of central tendency, we obtain

$$\bar{y} = \frac{\sum\limits_{i=1}^{n} y_i}{n} = \frac{19}{5} = 3.8$$

and locate it on the dot diagram. We can now view variability in terms of the distance between each dot (measurement) and the mean $\bar{y}$. If the distances are large, we can say that the data are more variable than they would be if the distances were small. The values of y and the distances, or deviations, from the mean $\bar{y}$ for our example are shown in table 2.5.

Table 2.5 • Deviations of the 5 measurements from their mean ($y = 3.8$)

Measurement y_i	Deviation $(y_i - \bar{y})$	Squared Deviation $(y_i - \bar{y})^2$
5	1.2	1.44
7	3.2	10.24
1	−2.8	7.84
2	−1.8	3.24
4	.2	.04
$\sum_{i=1}^{5} y_i = 19$	$\sum_{i=1}^{5} (y_i - \bar{y}) = 0$	$\sum_{i=1}^{5} (y_i - \bar{y})^2 = 22.80$

If we now agree that deviations contain information about variation, our next step is to construct a formula, based upon the deviations, which will provide a good measure of variation. As a first possibility we might choose the average of the deviations. However, this will not work because some of the deviations are positive and some are negative, and the sum is equal to zero. This is shown in the second column of table 2.5 and can be shown to be true in general.

A second possibility would be to ignore the minus signs and compute the average of the absolute (positive) values of the deviations. This quantity is easy to compute but difficult to use in making inferences about the population.

A third possibility, and the one we will employ, makes use of the sum of the squared deviations of the measurements from their mean. As we will subsequently show, a meaningful measure of variability, called the variance, can be calculated using this sum.

The deviation of a measurement y from the sample mean $\bar{y}$ is expressed as $(y - \bar{y})$. The square of a deviation can then be represented as $(y - \bar{y})^2$. We use the sum of these squared deviations in the definition of the *sample variance*.

Definition 2.7

The **sample variance** of a set of n measurements is the sum of the squared deviations of the measurements from their mean divided by $(n - 1)$.

You may wonder why we use the divisor $(n - 1)$ rather than n in defining sample variance. (Note that if the sum of the squared deviations was divided by n, the resulting quotient would be the average of the squared deviations.) The divisor $(n - 1)$ is used instead of n because it yields a more accurate estimate of the corresponding population variance.

We will use the symbol s^2 to represent the sample variance. Thus

$$s^2 = \frac{\sum_{i=1}^{n} (y_i - \bar{y})^2}{n - 1} = \frac{SS_{yy}}{n - 1}$$

where we abbreviate

$$\frac{\sum_{i=1}^{n} (y_i - \bar{y})^2}{n-1}$$

by SS_{yy}. The corresponding population variance will be denoted by σ^2 (σ is the Greek letter sigma).

---

s^2 is the sample variance

σ^2 is the population variance

Example 2.1

Calculate the variance of the $n = 5$ measurements, 5, 7, 1, 2, 4, given in table 2.5.

Solution: Using the information in the third column of table 2.5, we find the sample variance to be

$$s^2 = \frac{\sum_{i=1}^{5} (y_i - \bar{y})^2}{5 - 1} = \frac{22.80}{4} = 5.70$$

The basic problem with using the variance as a measure of variability is that it is difficult to interpret. For example, what can we say about the spread of a set of measurements with a variance of 5.7? The greater the variability or spread in a set of measurements, the larger will be the variance; but how large is large? Although we can compare variances of sets of measurements to compare variability, it is difficult to interpret the variance for a single set of measurements.

We will now consider a measure of variability that is useful not only for comparison purposes but also for describing a single set of measurements. This measure is called the **standard deviation.**

Definition 2.8

The **standard deviation** of a set of measurements is the positive square root of the variance.

The sample standard deviation will be denoted by s and the corresponding population standard deviation by the symbol σ.

---

s is the sample standard deviation

σ is the population standard deviation

$s = \sqrt{\text{variance}}$ or $s^2 = \text{variance}$

If you know s (standard dev) you can square it to get variance.

standard deviation is the square root of it to get variance you can take the square root of variance if you

As an aid to remembering the notation, note that the letter s is the first letter of "standard" in standard deviation and of "sample" in sample variance. (Remember not to confuse s and σ, the symbols for standard deviations, with s^2 and σ^2, the symbols for variances.)

Having defined the standard deviation, you might wonder why we bothered to define the variance in the first place. Actually, both the variance and the standard deviation play an important role in statistics, a fact that will become evident as we proceed.

EXERCISES

1. Cashen and Leicht (1973) predicted that subjects who did well in a general psychology course would be better able to correctly answer questions testing their knowledge of principles than low-scoring students would be able to do. As the first part of the study, the researchers had to choose the top and bottom students in the grade distribution. For the following sample of scores, find the upper and lower quartiles.

89	54	93	73	98
87	97	90	87	84
83	72	84	76	70
67	82	68	94	81
83	91	86	90	78

Find the range for this set of measurements.

2. Find s^2 and s for the following sample.

$$3, 0, 4, 1, 1, 5, 0$$

3. Find s^2 and s for the following sample.

$$6, 4, 7, 10, 7, 2$$

2.7 • THE EMPIRICAL RULE

We now state a rule that describes accurately the variability of a bell-shaped distribution and describes reasonably well the variability of other mound-shaped distributions of data. The frequent occurrence of mound-shaped and bell-shaped distributions of data in nature and hence the applicability of our rule leads us to call it the Empirical Rule.

The Empirical Rule

For a distribution of measurements that is approximately bell-shaped (see figure 2.7), the interval

1. ($\mu \pm \sigma$) will contain approximately 68 percent of the measurements;
2. ($\mu \pm 2\sigma$) will contain approximately 95 percent of the measurements;
3. ($\mu \pm 3\sigma$) will contain all or almost all of the measurements.

The bell-shaped distribution, figure 2.7, is commonly known as the *normal distribution* and will be discussed in detail in chapter 7. The point we wish to make here is not only that the Empirical Rule applies to normal distributions but that it provides an excellent description of variation for many types of data. Although the rule is stated in terms of population values (μ and σ), it also applies to sample data that yield approximately mound-shaped distributions.

Figure 2.7 • The normal distribution

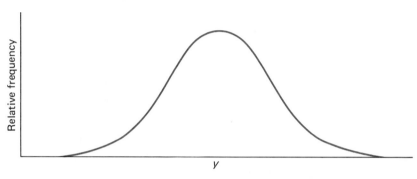

For example, a study is conducted to determine the degree of physical separation preferred by persons in a social situation. Each of $n = 40$ subjects is introduced into a room with the experimenter, and the distance between the two, at the time the subject stops his approach, is noted. The mean and standard deviation of these distance measurements are found to be 5.9 feet and 1.1 feet, respectively. To describe the data, we calculate the following intervals:

$$\bar{y} \pm s = 5.9 \pm 1.1 \quad \text{or} \quad 4.8 \text{ to } 7.0$$

$$\bar{y} \pm 2s = 5.9 \pm 2.2 \quad \text{or} \quad 3.7 \text{ to } 8.1$$

$$\bar{y} \pm 3s = 5.9 \pm 3.3 \quad \text{or} \quad 2.6 \text{ to } 9.2$$

If the distribution is mound-shaped, we would expect, by the Empirical Rule, that approximately 68 percent of the measurements will fall in the interval 4.8 to 7.0, 95 percent in the interval 3.7 to 8.1, and all or almost all in the interval 2.6 to 9.2.

Example 2.2

Consider the reaction times of 30 adults to a visual stimulus. The data were given in table 2.3. The mean for these measurements was found to be $\bar{y} = 19.75$, and we will show in section 2.8 that the standard deviation is $s = 3.34$. The frequency distribution of the 30 measurements in figure 2.1 indicates an approximately mound-shaped distribution. Use the Empirical Rule to describe the variability of this sample.

Solution: We use the sample mean $\bar{y}$ and the standard deviation s to form $k = 1, 2,$ and 3 standard deviation intervals around $\bar{y}$. We then calculate the

Table 2.6 • Frequency of measurements lying within
k standard deviations of the mean
for the reaction time data in table 2.3

k	Interval $(\bar{y} \pm ks)$	Frequency in Interval	Relative Frequency
1	16.41–23.09	19	.63
2	13.07–26.43	29	.97
3	9.73–29.77	30	1.00

frequency and the relative frequency of the sample measurements within each
interval. The results are presented in table 2.6.

It is evident that the observed relative frequencies, .63, .97, and 1.00, do
not agree exactly with those expected from the Empirical Rule, namely,
.68, .95, and all or almost all, respectively. This is because the distribution
for the set of measurements is not exactly bell-shaped, as we see from the
histogram of figure 2.1. However, the approximation given by the Empirical
Rule is still fairly close. There is a possibility that an increase in sample size
would result in a more nearly bell-shaped distribution and a correspondingly
closer approximation by the Empirical Rule. This would be the expectation if
the population distribution were itself bell-shaped.

EXERCISES

1. Two thousand examinees were administered an ability test and the mean $\bar{y}$ and the
   standard deviation s were calculated to be 52.0 and 9.8, respectively. Assuming that
   the distribution of test scores was approximately bell-shaped, 68 percent of the
   examinees could be expected to score between _____ and _____ ; 95 percent
   between _____ and _____ ; and almost all between _____ and _____ .
   (Round to the nearest integer.)
2. One thousand high school students were administered Rotter's Internal-External Locus
   of Control Scale, which measures the tendency to see reinforcement as following one's
   own behavior or as a result of luck. The obtained mean was 8.5 and the standard
   deviation was 3.41 (Franklin 1963). Assuming that the distribution of test scores was
   approximately bell-shaped, 68 percent of the examinees would be expected to score
   between _____ and _____ ; 95 percent between _____ and _____ ; and
   almost all between _____ and _____ . (Round to the nearest integer.)

2.8 • A SHORT METHOD FOR CALCULATING THE SUM OF SQUARES OF DEVIATIONS

The calculation of the variance and the standard deviation of a set of measurements is no small task, regardless of the method employed. It is particularly
tedious if we proceed, according to the definition, by calculating each deviation
individually, as shown in table 2.5. A shorter method for calculating the sum of
the squares of the deviations follows.

Computing Formula for the Sum of Squares of Deviations

$$SS_{yy} = \sum_{i=1}^{n} (y_i - \bar{y})^2 = \sum_{i=1}^{n} y_i^2 - \frac{\left(\sum_{i=1}^{n} y_i\right)^2}{n}$$

The first expression for SS_{yy} is the sum of the squares of the deviations needed in the formula for the variance and standard deviation. The second expression gives a simpler method of calculating this sum of squares.

To illustrate this shorter method of calculation and to compare our results with those obtained by using the definition formula, we will again use the data of table 2.5. The tabulations are presented in table 2.7 in two columns, the first containing the individual measurements and the second containing the squares of the measurements.

Table 2.7 • Table for simplified calculations of SS_{yy}

y_i	y_i^2
5	25
7	49
1	1
2	4
4	16
19	95

We now calculate

$$\sum_{i=1}^{n} y_i^2 - \frac{\left(\sum_{i=1}^{n} y_i\right)^2}{n} = 95 - \frac{(19)^2}{5} = 95 - \frac{361}{5}$$

$$= 95 - 72.2 = 22.8$$

and notice that it is exactly equal to the sum of the squares of the deviations,

$$\sum_{i=1}^{n} (y_i - \bar{y})^2$$

given in the third column of table 2.5.

The data of table 2.5, manufactured to illustrate a method, are somewhat more easily handled than the kind of data usually encountered in the behavioral sciences. It is for the less tidy real life data that the advantages of a computational shortcut become most apparent. The following example is a case in point.

Example 2.3

Use the shortcut formula to compute the standard deviation of the 30 reaction time measurements given in table 2.3.

Solution: First, we find that

$$\sum_{i=1}^{30} y_i = 592.5$$

$$\sum_{i=1}^{30} y_i^2 = 12{,}024.49$$

(On many calculators these two quantities may be accumulated simultaneously.) Then, using the shortcut formula,

$$SS_{yy} = \sum_{i=1}^{30} (y_i - \bar{y})^2 = \sum_{i=1}^{30} y_i^2 - \frac{\left(\sum\limits_{i=1}^{30} y_i\right)^2}{30}$$

$$= 12{,}024.49 - \frac{(592.5)^2}{30} = 12{,}024.49 - 11{,}701.875 = 322.615$$

and so the standard deviation is

$$s = \sqrt{\frac{\sum\limits_{i=1}^{30} (y_i - \bar{y})^2}{30 - 1}} = \sqrt{\frac{322.615}{29}} = \sqrt{11.125} = 3.34$$

EXERCISES

1. Use the shortcut formula to compute the standard deviation for the following measurements.

$$3, 6, 1, 4, 0, 1, 5$$

2. Use the shortcut formula to compute the standard deviation for the following 20 sample measurements.

$$4, 3, 2, 2, 3, 1, 0, 2, 2, 1, 5, 3, 1, 2, 4, 0, 1, 3, 2, 1$$

Calculate the mean for this data and construct the interval $(\bar{y} \pm 2s)$. What percentage of the 20 measurements fall in this interval? Is this percentage consistent with the Empirical Rule?

3. A study was conducted to see if subjects showed consistency in pain response when exposed to two kinds of pain-producing stimuli (Brown, Fader, and Barber, 1973). This is important for physiological psychologists who study the generality of response to pain. Find the mean, variance, and standard deviation for the pain-responsivity scores.

10	13	20	15	13
16	13	21	19	11
12	16	11	15	16

2.9 • ANOTHER MEASURE OF RELATIVE STANDING: THE z SCORE

In section 2.6 we introduced quartiles and percentiles as measures of the *relative standing* of a measurement in the data set. Another measure of relative standing that is commonly used in the behavioral sciences is the z score.

Definition 2.9

The sample z score for a measurement y is

$$z = \frac{y - \bar{y}}{s}$$

The population z score for a measurement y is

$$z = \frac{y - \mu}{\sigma}$$

As seen in definition 2.9, the z score is calculated by subtracting $\bar{y}$ (or μ) from y and dividing by s (or σ). The result is a z score, which represents the number of standard deviations between the measurement and the mean.

Example 2.4

Suppose a sample of 100 scores on the Advanced Psychology Graduate Record Examination produces the following mean and standard deviation.

$$\bar{y} = 560$$
$$s = 50$$

Suppose your score is 640. What is your sample z score?

Solution: Looking at figure 2.8, we see that your score lies to the right of (above) the average score of 560.

Figure 2.8 • Advanced psychology GRE

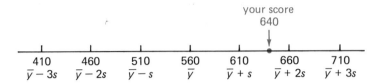

We compute

$$z = \frac{y - \bar{y}}{s} = \frac{640 - 560}{50} = \frac{80}{50} = 1.6$$

which tells us that your GRE score is 1.6 standard deviations above $\bar{y}$, or, in short, your sample z score is 1.6.

Note that if a measurement y lies to the right of (above) the mean, the z score is positive. If a measurement lies to the left of (below) the mean, the z score is negative. If a measurement is equal to the mean, then the z score is zero.

The z scores of measurements above the mean are positive.

The z scores of measurements equal to the mean are zero.

The z scores of measurements below the mean are negative.

The numerical size of the z score reflects the relative standing of the measurement. A large positive z score implies that the measurement is greater than almost all other measurements. A large negative z score indicates that the measurement is less than almost all other measurements. If the z score is zero or near zero, the measurement is located somewhere in the midsection of the sample or population.

We can be more specific if we have additional information about the shape of the frequency distribution of the measurements. For example, if the distribution of measurements is mound-shaped, we can use the Empirical Rule to give some meaning to a z score. Then the following interpretation of z scores can be obtained from the Empirical Rule.

Interpretation of z Scores for Mound-shaped Distributions of Data

1. Approximately 68 percent of the measurements will have a z score between −1 and 1.
2. Approximately 95 percent of the measurements will have a z score between −2 and 2.
3. All or almost all of the measurements will have a z score between −3 and 3.

Note that the above interpretation of the Empirical Rule is identical to the interpretation given at the beginning of section 2.7. The statement that a measurement falls in the interval $(\mu \pm \sigma)$ is identical to the statement that a measurement has a population z score between -1 and 1, since all measurements between $(\mu - \sigma)$ and $(\mu + \sigma)$ are within one standard deviation of μ. See figure 2.9.

Figure 2.9 • Population z score for a bell-shaped distribution

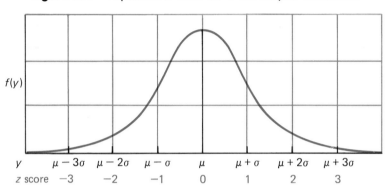

y	$\mu - 3\sigma$	$\mu - 2\sigma$	$\mu - \sigma$	μ	$\mu + \sigma$	$\mu + 2\sigma$	$\mu + 3\sigma$
z score	-3	-2	-1	0	1	2	3

We end this section with an example which indicates how the Empirical Rule and z scores may be used to accomplish our main objective: the use of sample information to make inferences about the population.

Example 2.5

Suppose, as a part of a course in psychological research, a student keeps very extensive records on a single laboratory rat. The student determines that the rat's average heartbeat rate is 100 beats per minute, with a standard deviation of 10 beats per minute. As part of an experiment, the student administers an hallucinogenic drug to the rat and, after a specified time, measures the heartbeat rate, finding it to be 135 beats per minute. Should the student conclude that the drug causes an increase in heartbeat rate?

Solution: A careful analysis might proceed as follows. First we calculate the z score for the single measurement of heartbeat rate taken after the drug was administered, as if it were taken from the original sample. Thus

$$z = \frac{135 - 100}{10} = 3.5$$

Then the student has observed a heartbeat rate 3.5 standard deviations above the mean in terms of the ''before drug'' distribution. If a check of the data set shows that this distribution is mound-shaped, the student can use the Empirical Rule to infer that very few of the heartbeat measurements taken on this rat should have a z score exceeding 3, as shown in figure 2.10. Therefore, a z score of 3.5 *either* represents a measurement from a distribution different from that describing the ''before drug'' heartbeat rate *or* it represents a very unusual (highly improbable) measurement from the ''before drug'' distribution.

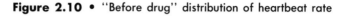

Figure 2.10 • "Before drug" distribution of heartbeat rate

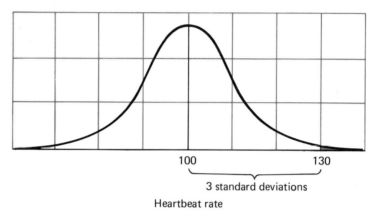

100   130

3 standard deviations

Heartbeat rate

Well, which of the two situations do you think prevails? Do you think we have observed a heartbeat rate that should rarely occur, or do you think the drug affected the heartbeat rate distribution? Most people would probably conclude that the heartbeat rate distribution has been altered, recognizing that there is a very small risk that this conclusion is unwarranted. However, even in reaching the conclusion that the "after" heartbeat rate distribution is different from the "before" distribution, we are not necessarily answering the research question affirmatively.

In an experiment concerning the effects of a drug on the heartbeat rate of rats, a student studies a single rat. After the drug is administered, the student observes a heartbeat rate measurement that is 3.5 standard deviations above the mean of the hypothesized distribution. What should the student conclude? (Photo courtesy of Photo Researchers, Inc.)

The student wished to know whether the drug increases heartbeat rate. We have concluded that the distribution is *changed* by the drug, but there are several changes which may have occurred. The mean heartbeat rate may have been increased by the drug. The standard deviation may have been increased (note that the measurement of 135 becomes much more probable if the standard deviation is increased from 10 to 30). Or some combination of mean and standard deviation changes may have taken place. Another possibility is that the process of administering the drug, rather than the drug itself, causes a change in the heartbeat rate distribution. A much more extensive experiment with a large number of rats would be needed before we could make more specific inferences.

Example 2.5 illustrates an approach to statistical inference which might be called the "rare event" approach. An experimenter hypothesizes that a specific frequency distribution describes a population of measurements. Then a sample of measurements is drawn from the population. If the experimenter finds it unlikely that the sample came from the hypothesized distribution, the hypothesis is concluded to be false. Thus in the example, the student hypothesized that the drug would not affect the frequency distribution of heartbeat rates. However, it was so unlikely that the sample (of one measurement) came from the "before drug" distribution that the student rejected that hypothesis and concluded that the distribution had changed in some way.

This rare event approach to inference making will be further explored in later chapters. However, proper application of the rare event approach requires a knowledge of probability, the subject of chapter 4.

EXERCISES

1. For a sample of $n = 50$ measurements with a mean and a standard deviation given by $\bar{y} = 10.0$ and $s = 2.0$, respectively, find the sample z score for the following measurements.
   (a) $y = 14.0$
   (b) $y = 8.0$
   (c) $y = 11.2$
2. For a population with a mean and a standard deviation given by $\mu = 25.0$ and $\sigma = 3.0$, respectively, find the population z scores for the following measurements.
   (a) $y = 20.0$
   (b) $y = 35.0$
   (c) $y = 24.5$
3. Suppose a sample of 50 undergraduate psychology majors is taken. The grade point average (GPA) of each is recorded, and the mean and standard deviation are $\bar{y} = 2.86$ and $s = .35$, respectively. Assume that the distribution of GPAs is mound-shaped.
   (a) Use the Empirical Rule to describe the data. That is, about how many sample z scores are between -1 and $+1$? Between -2 and $+2$? Between -3 and $+3$?
   (b) Suppose your GPA is 3.60. Calculate your sample z score.

(c) Using the sample z score found in part (b) and the assumption that the distribution is mound-shaped, estimate your standing in this sample (about how many students in the sample have GPAs less than yours?).

2.10 · ESTIMATING POPULATION PARAMETERS

You will recall that we introduced the symbols μ and σ to represent the population mean and standard deviation, respectively. They represent examples of **population parameters**.

Definition 2.10

A **population parameter** is a numerical descriptive measure of a population.

Usually the only information that we will have concerning the true values of population parameters will be the information contained in a sample of the population. It is natural to use the sample mean $\bar{y}$ to estimate μ and the sample standard deviation s to estimate σ.

The use of sample statistics to estimate population parameters is a dangerous technique unless we can associate some measure of accuracy with our estimate. We avoid making inferences without including "statements of goodness." The tools for measuring the precision of our estimates are discussed in later chapters.

SUMMARY

In the data-collecting stage of any scientific investigation, we are concerned with two related problems, measurement and description. In the behavioral sciences, particularly, we make use of a wide range of measurement procedures, including categorization, rank ordering, and numerical scoring. The methods appropriate for describing sets of such measurements are correspondingly varied, but they may be regarded as falling into one of two general classifications: frequency or relative frequency distributions and summary numerical methods.

The relative frequency distribution, displayed either in tabular or histogram form, gives an overall picture of the entire data set. Summary measures focus on specific aspects of the data and are particularly useful for the purposes of comparison and inference. Among these summary measures, special emphasis was placed on the mean and variance. The mean has intuitive descriptive significance. The variance gains descriptive significance through its positive square root, the standard deviation, particularly when used in conjunction with the Empirical Rule. Moreover, the sample mean $\bar{y}$ and the sample variance s^2 are extremely useful in view of our main objective—statistical inference. They provide us with estimators of the population mean μ and the population variance σ^2.

Measures of relative standing describe the position of a particular measurement with respect to the rest of the data set. The z score accomplishes this by giving the number of standard deviations between the measurement and the mean of the data set. The Empirical Rule gives approximations for the fractions of measurements to be found within certain z-score limits when the data distribution is mound-shaped.

Many descriptive methods and numerical measures have been presented in this chapter, but they constitute only a small percentage of those that might have been discussed. In addition, many special computational techniques usually found in elementary texts have not been included. This was necessary because of the limited time available in an elementary course and because of the advent and common use of electronic computers, which has minimized the importance of special computational formulas. But, more important, the inclusion of such techniques would tend to detract from and obscure the main objective of modern statistics and this text: statistical inference.

SUPPLEMENTARY EXERCISES

1. Conduct the following experiment. Toss 10 coins and record y, the number of heads observed. Repeat this process $n = 50$ times, thus providing 50 values of y. Construct a relative frequency histogram for these measurements and find the mode of the distribution.

2. For the set of $n = 6$ measurements, 5, 7, 2, 1, 3, 0, calculate $\bar{y}$, s^2, and s.

3. Calculate $\bar{y}$, s^2, and s for the data in exercise 1.

4. Refer to the histogram constructed in exercise 1 and find the fraction of measurements lying in the interval $(\bar{y} \pm 2s)$. (Use the results of exercise 3.) Is the frequency histogram of exercise 1 relatively mound-shaped? Does the Empirical Rule adequately describe the variability of the data in exercise 1?

5. Refer to the grade point data in exercise 2, section 2.2. Find the fraction of measurements falling in the intervals $(\bar{y} \pm s)$ and $(\bar{y} \pm 2s)$. Do these results agree with the Empirical Rule?

6. Since the nineteenth century when Wilhelm Wundt, the founder of modern experimental psychology, conducted his research, reaction time has been an important and sensitive measure in psychology. In one experiment, reaction times in response to a visual stimulus were recorded for five subjects and the following measurements were obtained: .148, .153, .143, .158, .143. Calculate $\bar{y}$, s^2, and s.

7. Refer to exercise 6. Calculate the fraction of measurements in the intervals $(\bar{y} \pm s)$ and $(\bar{y} \pm 2s)$. Why is the Empirical Rule inappropriate for describing the variability of these data?

8. One of the classic topics of research in social psychology is conformity to social influence, or whether individuals agree with a majority opinion even though they know it to be incorrect. In a study on forced deviation and conformity (Slatin 1974), the number of conforming responses of each subject was observed. Construct a frequency distribution for the data.

1	6	14	0	1
13	15	8	3	1
0	2	0	6	2
2	1	4	1	3

9. An experiment was conducted to determine whether performance of movement can be caused by the central nervous system without the participation of the peripheral nervous system (Taub, Bacon, and Berman, 1965). Below are listed the number of days it took monkeys with and without peripheral feedback to learn to flex their limb in order to avoid shock. Calculate $\bar{y}$, s^2, and s for each group.

Without Feedback	19	31	19	50	27	15	12
With Feedback	5	15	10	6	18	2	

10. In contrast to aptitude tests, which are predictive measures of what one can accomplish with training, achievement tests tell what an individual can do at the time of the test. Mathematics achievement test scores for 400 students were found to have a mean and a variance equal to 600 and 4900, respectively. If the distribution of test scores was bell-shaped, approximately how many of the scores would fall in the interval 530 to 670? Approximately how many scores would be expected to exceed 740?

11. After 20 generations of selective breeding for high locomotor activity, a strain of mice is found to have a mean of 23 revolutions per minute and a standard deviation of 4.5 revolutions per minute in an activity wheel. If the distribution of activity scores is bell-shaped and if the experimeter regards "high activity" as more than 18.5 revolutions per minute, what percentage would have activity scores between 18.5 and 32 revolutions per minute?

12. The intelligence quotient (IQ) expresses intelligence as a ratio of the mental age to the chronological age, multiplied by 100. Thus the average (when mental age equals chronological age) is 100. Construct a relative frequency histogram for the following IQ scores.

100	103	99	101	100	120	109	82
101	112	95	118	118	89	114	113
92	137	130	94	87	93	111	96
93	98	101	96	84	86	89	90

13. Refer to exercise 12. Find the number of scores in the intervals $(\bar{y} \pm s)$ and $(\bar{y} \pm 2s)$ and compare your findings with the Empirical Rule.

14. Find the range for the data in exercise 12. Find the ratio of the range to s. If we possessed a large amount of data possessing a bell-shaped distribution, the range would be expected to equal how many standard deviations? (Note that this provides a rough check for the computation of s.)

15. Find the ratio of the range to s for the data in exercise 1.

16. The rule of thumb found in exercise 14 for a large amount of data (more than 25 measurements) can be extended to smaller amounts of data obtained in sampling from a bell-shaped distribution. The calculated s should not be far different from the range divided by the appropriate ratio in the following table.

No. Measurements	5	10	25
Expected Ratio of Range to s	2.5	3	4

Use this extended rule of thumb to estimate s for the data in exercise 2 and compare your estimate with the calculated value of s.

17. Use the table given in exercise 16 to estimate s for the sets of measurements in exercises 1 and 12. Compare these estimates with the calculated values for s.

18. Acquisition refers to the stage during which a new response is learned and is gradually strengthened. The following data, obtained from a learning experiment, represent rates of acquisition as measured by the number of trials it took subjects to successfully perform a memory task.

12	10	16	7	18
13	14	20	9	23
8	13	14	6	19
6	11	15	10	16

Computing s for these data, the experimenter obtained a value of 8.90. Use the range approximation for s as a check on this computation. Do these estimated and computed values for s appear to differ excessively?

19. An industrial concern uses an employee screening test with average score μ and standard deviation $\sigma = 10$. Assume that the test score distribution is approximately bell-shaped and that a score of 65 qualifies an applicant for further consideration. What is the value of μ such that approximately 2.5 percent of the applicants will qualify for further consideration?

20. Two researchers studied test anxiety in students to see if there had been an increase from 1965 to 1971 (Bronzaft and Epstein 1973). Students in both years at three colleges took the Alpert-Haber Achievement Anxiety Test. The scores for College A in 1971 were as follows:

26.7	17.8	22.4	30.1	21.0
22.6	29.3	24.2	20.6	24.3

Calculate $\bar{y}$, s^2, and s for these data.

21. The Repression-Sensitization Scale, which measures psychological defense reaction to threatening stimuli, relates to compliance with experimental demands. Berquist and Klein (1973) divided subjects into High, Medium, and Low groups based on this scale and rated their acquisition of verbal concepts. These acquisition ratings are given below for the three groups.

High	22.80	24.00	23.60	21.75	24.11
Medium	25.17	24.97	26.10	25.40	25.90
Low	26.90	25.00	25.90	27.00	26.40

(a) Calculate and compare the means and variances of the three samples.
(b) Suppose a subject receives a verbalization rating of 22.00. Calculate the sample z score of this measurement for each of the three samples.
(c) Use the sample z scores calculated in part (b) to predict which class (High, Medium, or Low) the subject belongs to on the Repression-Sensitization Scale.

REFERENCES

Berquist, W. H., and Klein, H. D. 1973. Acquisition of verbal concepts as a function of explicit and implicit experimental demands and repression-sensitization. *Journal of General Psychology* 89:67–80.

Bronzaft, A. L., and Epstein, G. F. 1973. Is test anxiety increasing? *Journal of Psychology* 85:17–19.

Brown, R. A.; Fader, K.; and Barber, T. X. 1973. Responsiveness to pain: Stimulus specificity versus generality. *Psychological Record* 23:1–7.

Cahalan, D.; Cisin, I. H.; and Crossley, H. 1969. *American drinking practices.* Monograph no. 6. New Brunswick, N.J.: Rutgers Center of Alcohol Studies.

Cashen, V. M., and Leicht, K. L. 1973. Class performance as a function of student achievement and type of learning material. *Psychology Reports* 33:157–158.

Franklin, R. D. 1963. Youth's expectancies about internal versus external control of reinforcement related to N variables. Unpublished doctoral dissertation, Purdue University.

Hays, W. L. 1963. *Statistics for psychologists.* New York: Holt, Rinehart and Winston. Chapter 3.

Mendenhall, W. 1975. *Introduction to probability and statistics.* 4th ed. N. Scituate Mass.: Duxbury Press.

Morlock, G. W.; Erspamer, R. T.; and Meyer, M. E. 1971. The effect of arousal on exploration in the rat. *Psychonomic Science* 25:43–44.

Slatin, G. T. 1974. Forced deviation, conformity and commitment. *Journal of Psychology* 86:341–353.

Taub, E.; Bacon, R. C.; and Berman, A. J. 1965. Acquisition of trace-conditioned avoidance response after deafferentation of the responding limb. *Journal of Comparative and Physiological Psychology* 59:275–279.

3•Description of Data: Two Variables

3.1
* **The Scattergram**
3.2
* **The Correlation Coefficient**

Note to the instructor: This chapter can be deferred and presented in conjunction with chapter 12.

INTRODUCTION

In chapter 2 we presented various graphical and numerical methods for describing a set of data collected on a single variable. However, many experiments in the behavioral sciences are designed to explore the relationship between two (or more) variables. For example, we might be interested in the relationship between activation and performance in humans; the relationship between the therapist's and the client's assessment of the client's adjustment due to therapy; the relationship between an aggressive behavior measurement and the latency of response to a stimulus for a strain of rats; or the relationship between IQ and the score on a self-assessment test. When experiments are performed to examine the relationship between two variables, the set of data which results cannot be sufficiently described by the methods presented in chapter 2. We need graphical and numerical measures of the relationships between the two variables in addition to the single-variable descriptions given in the previous chapter.

In this chapter we present a graphical method and a numerical method for describing a set of data on two variables. The graphical method, the *scattergram*, discussed in section 3.1, plots the data on a plane, allowing us to see visually any simple relationships between the variables. A numerical measure, the *correlation coefficient*, discussed in section 3.2, provides a measure of the *colinearity* between the variables, that is, how closely a straight line fits the data.

Although in this chapter we are only presenting the tools for describing samples of two variables, we must be careful not to forget our ultimate objective. We wish to use these sample quantities to make inferences about the population from which the sample is taken. We are examining the relationships between two variables in the sample so that we can make inferences about the true or population relationship between the variables.

3.1 • THE SCATTERGRAM

A simple but informative graphical description of a data set on two variables is the **scattergram.** A scattergram consists of a two-dimensional plot of the data points in the sample, with one dimension for each variable measured. The scattergram allows us to observe obvious sample relationships between the two variables and obtain a basic understanding of the population relationship between the variables.

Suppose, for example, that we are interested in the relationship between an individual's undergraduate grade point average (GPA) in psychology courses and his or her score on the Graduate Record Examination (GRE) advanced test in psychology. Shand (1970) studied this relationship over a period of several years. Table 3.1 contains a sample of 10 individuals' scores on both variables.

Table 3.1 • Sample of psychology
GPAs and GREs

GPA	GRE
2.96	529
2.43	506
3.36	591
3.40	610
2.43	474
2.12	509
2.85	550
3.12	600
3.20	575
2.75	540

We can calculate the sample descriptive statistics for the two variables separately. For example, the mean GPA of the 10 students is 2.86, while the mean GRE is 548.4. However, these measures do not contain information about the relationship between the variables, and yet this relationship is our main concern.

To construct a scattergram for this sample, we first assign one of the variables to the horizontal or x-axis and the other to the vertical or y-axis. In figure 3.1 we have used the x-axis to represent the psychology undergraduate GPA and the y-axis to represent the advanced psychology GRE score. The second and final step is to plot each pair of sample values on the graph.

To illustrate, first consider only the first pair of values in the sample (table 3.1). The first pair of sample values is (2.96, 529), where by convention we always list the x-value (GPA) first and the y-value (GRE) second in the pair. To plot the point (2.96, 529) on the graph, we begin at the origin (0, 0) and move to the point 2.96 on the horizontal (x) axis. We then move 529 units in the vertical (y) direction. This is the point to be marked or plotted, as illustrated in figure 3.1. Note that the dotted line in color first traces the distance 2.96 units from the

Figure 3.1 • Plotting the point (2.96, 529)

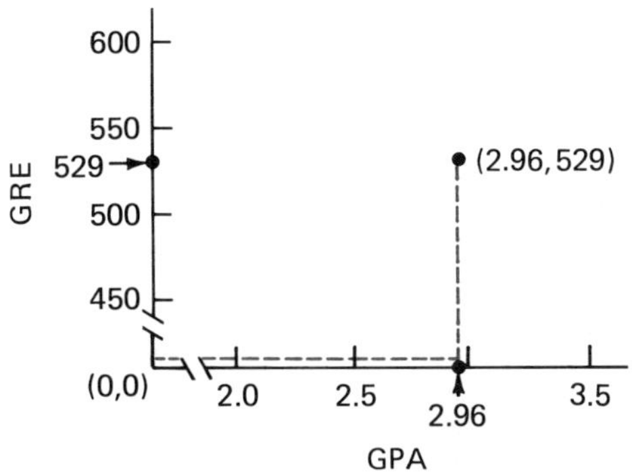

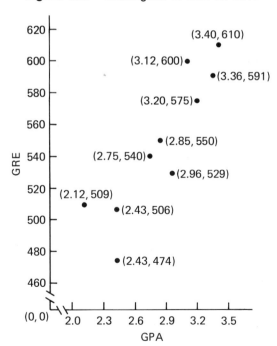

origin along the x-axis, then moves vertically until reaching the point 529. The point is then marked by a large black dot and labeled as (2.96, 529).

Note in figure 3.1 that we have shown a break on each axis to denote a skip or omission of values not needed in the plot. The scale need only be large enough to include all the sample x- and y-values.

We now plot the other 9 points in the sample to complete the scattergram. The completed scattergram is shown in figure 3.2. We have labeled each point so that you may check our plotting, but this labeling is usually omitted in scattergrams.

Figure 3.2 • Scattergram of GRE vs. GPA

To get an idea of the sample relationship between the two variables, GPA and GRE, let your eyes quickly scan the points, paying little attention to detail (the labels, the precise location on the axes, etc.). Focus only on the black dots in figure 3.2. You should note a general positive straight-line (linear) relationship between GPA and GRE—that is, as GPA increases in this sample, GRE also tends to increase.

Student's test results, such as the results of the Graduate Record Examination in advanced psychology, could be plotted in a scattergram against their undergraduate grade point averages. What would this graphic representation of the data tell us about our sample? (Photo courtesy of Nancy Palmer/Ron Sherman.)

Example 3.1

Burgess and Hokanson (1964) examined the relationship between activation and performance by recording subjects' heart rate and digit symbol improvement score. The digit symbol task is a subtest of the Wechsler Adult Intelligence Scale and is used as a measure of performance. Construct a scattergram using the set of 25 measurements in table 3.2.

Solution: We arbitrarily assign heart rate to the x-axis and improvement score to the y-axis. The 25 data points are then plotted, resulting in the scattergram shown in figure 3.3. We have not labeled the points here because we did not want the scattergram to look cluttered.

A scan of the points indicates no simple increasing or decreasing linear relationship between the variables. Instead, we get an impression of an inverted U-shape. Performance (improvement score) seems optimal at some intermediate level of activation (heart rate); performance seems lower at low or high activation. This is an important relationship in psychology; for more detail and background see Burgess and Hokanson (1964).

Table 3.2 • Data for heart rate and improvement score

Heart Rate	Improvement Score	Heart Rate	Improvement Score
72	5.0	95	7.8
77	8.0	98	7.7
85	7.5	70	5.3
99	8.9	105	6.1
107	7.3	88	8.1
110	5.3	78	7.4
82	8.0	103	6.7
73	5.2	95	7.9
92	8.3	70	5.1
92	8.6	83	7.4
104	6.5	94	8.8
74	6.0	115	5.2
80	8.4		

Example 3.1 illustrates both the basic strength and the basic weakness of the scattergram. The primary purpose of a scattergram is to provide a descriptive picture of the sample when two variables are measured. This is accomplished in figure 3.3 since we are able to gain information about a sample relationship at a glance. However, we are ultimately interested in making inferences about the true relationship, if any, between the two variables. To accomplish this requires more precise tools than the scattergram. Thus, if we wish to determine whether

Figure 3.3 • Scattergram of improvement score vs. heart rate

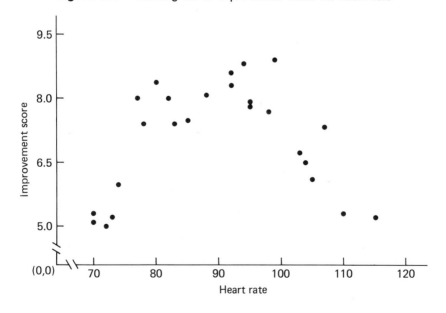

activation and performance really have an inverted U-relationship, we must collect more sample data and use numerical techniques for determining variable relationships. (This topic will be discussed in chapter 12.) **The fact remains, however, that the first thing we usually do in examining even the most complex relationship is construct a simple plot of the sample values—the scattergram.**

EXERCISES

1. Kidd (1964) investigated the possibility of dysfunction in monocular depth perception in schizophrenics. Subjects had to align images at different distances from the light. Draw a scattergram of the distances and scores given below.

Distance from Light (in feet)	4	6	4	8	10	10	12	6	12	8
Coded Score	25	22	26	17	16	21	13	18	19	22

2. Refer to exercise 2. In another part of the same study, Kidd (1964) used two ways (A and B) of measuring monocular depth perception. Draw a scattergram showing their relationship.

A	25	15	15	17	17	23	23	20	22	16
B	28	13	18	16	17	29	22	18	24	18

3. Ausubal and Schiff (1955) obtained teachers' ratings of adolescents and sociometric ratings of the same students by their classmates. The sociometric ratings were obtained by having each student rate the other students. Given below are the two scores for 25 students. Draw a scattergram of the data.

Teacher Rating	20	22	27	18	10	13	24	21	18	18	23	16	27
Sociometric Rating	5	3	4	5	1	2	4	3	3	4	3	1	5

Teacher Rating	21	19	23	18	24	19	26	20	19	22	16	21
Sociometric Rating	2	1	4	2	4	3	5	2	4	3	1	3

3.2 · THE CORRELATION COEFFICIENT

The most popular numerical measure of the strength of the relationship between two variables is the **correlation coefficient.** The correlation coefficient provides a measure of the linear (straight-line) relationship between two variables. That is, when two variables have a positive relationship (y tends to increase as x increases) or a negative relationship (y tends to decrease as x increases), the correlation coefficient will reflect this.

Consider the two hypothetical data sets whose scattergrams are shown in figures 3.4(a) and 3.4(b). The data set shown in figure 3.4(a) illustrates a strong positive linear relationship. All the data points lie on a straight line whose slope is positive—that is, the line goes upward as we move from left to right along the x-axis. Figure 3.4(b), on the other hand, exhibits no readily recognizable relationship between x and y. But how do we *numerically* describe the difference between the relationships illustrated by these data sets?

Figure 3.4 • Scattergrams of two hypothetical data sets

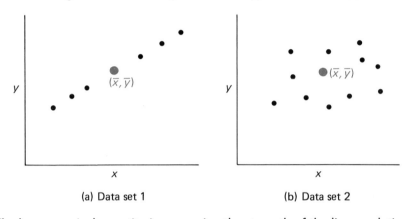

(a) Data set 1   (b) Data set 2

The key numerical quantity in measuring the strength of the linear relationship between two variables x and y is the product $(x - \bar{x})(y - \bar{y})$. Some possible values of this product are shown in figure 3.5. Keep in mind that the quantities $(x - \bar{x})$ and $(y - \bar{y})$ are deviations, that is, numbers.

Parts (a), (b), (c), and (d) in figure 3.5 show the point $(\bar{x}, \bar{y})$, and it is in the same position in each figure. Now look at figure 3.5(a) and note that the particular point (x, y) lies to the *right and above* $(\bar{x}, \bar{y})$. The horizontal line segment to the right of $(\bar{x}, \bar{y})$ corresponds to the deviation $(x - \bar{x})$ and is shown in black because the deviation is positive. Similarly, the vertical line segment corresponds to the deviation $(y - \bar{y})$ and is also shown in black, since $(y - \bar{y})$ is positive. Therefore, you can see that both $(x - \bar{x})$ and $(y - \bar{y})$ will be positive when a point is located to the *right and above* $(\bar{x}, \bar{y})$. It follows that the product $(x - \bar{x})(y - \bar{y})$ will also be positive.

Now examine figure 3.5(b), where we show a point to the *left and below* $(\bar{x}, \bar{y})$. Note that both the horizontal line segment corresponding to $(x - \bar{x})$ and the vertical line segment corresponding to $(y - \bar{y})$ are shown in color to signify that both these deviations are negative. However, because the product of two negative numbers is a positive number, we find that the product $(x - \bar{x})(y - \bar{y})$ is positive when the point (x, y) is to the *left and below* $(\bar{x}, \bar{y})$.

Figures 3.5(c) and (d) show that if the point (x, y) is to the *right and below* or

Figure 3.5 • Some possible values for the product $(x - \bar{x})(y - \bar{y})$

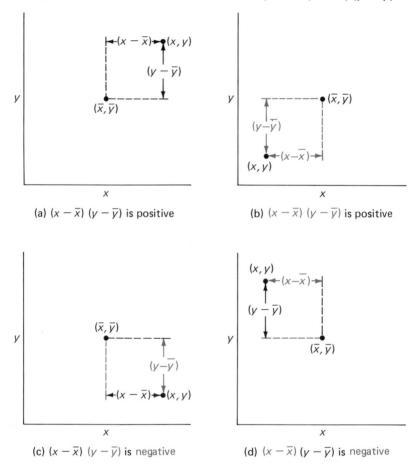

(a) $(x - \bar{x})(y - \bar{y})$ is positive

(b) $(x - \bar{x})(y - \bar{y})$ is positive

(c) $(x - \bar{x})(y - \bar{y})$ is negative

(d) $(x - \bar{x})(y - \bar{y})$ is negative

to the *left and above* the point $(\bar{x}, \bar{y})$, the product $(x - \bar{x})(y - \bar{y})$ will be negative. You will note that we continue to show positive deviations in black and negative deviations in color.

Now, refer again to the hypothetical examples in figure 3.4. Note that if we simply average the products $(x - \bar{x})(y - \bar{y})$ for the data points shown in figure 3.4(a), we would get a positive number since all the points lie either to the *right and above* or to the *left and below* $(\bar{x}, \bar{y})$. However, for the data points in figure 3.4(b), the products $(x - \bar{x})(y - \bar{y})$ are positive and negative since there are some points in each of the four positions defined above (right and above, right and below, etc.) around $(\bar{x}, \bar{y})$. Since the negative and positive products tend to cancel, we would expect the average product to be close to zero. Thus the average of the products $(x - \bar{x})(y - \bar{y})$ provides a measure of the straight-line relationship between x and y. The average will be positive when a positive-slope relationship exists, negative when a negative-slope relationship exists, and near zero when no relationship exists.

In calculating our numerical measure of linear relationship, the correlation coefficient, we still have one problem—the problem of scale. If we simply compute the average product $(x - \bar{x})(y - \bar{y})$, the scale of the data will greatly influence this average, thus making it difficult to interpret and compare data measured on different scales. We therefore divide the sum of these products not by n to get an average but by a quantity which solves the scaling problem.

Definition 3.1

The **correlation coefficient** r is a measure of the strength of the linear (straight-line) relationship between two variables. It is computed by

$$r = \frac{\Sigma (x - \bar{x})(y - \bar{y})}{\sqrt{\Sigma (x - \bar{x})^2 \, \Sigma (y - \bar{y})^2}} = \frac{SS_{xy}}{\sqrt{SS_{xx} SS_{yy}}}$$

where

$$SS_{xy} = \Sigma (x - \bar{x})(y - \bar{y}) = \Sigma xy - \frac{(\Sigma x)(\Sigma y)}{n}$$

$$SS_{xx} = \Sigma (x - \bar{x})^2 = \Sigma x^2 - \frac{(\Sigma x)^2}{n}$$

$$SS_{yy} = \Sigma (y - \bar{y})^2 = \Sigma y^2 - \frac{(\Sigma y)^2}{n}$$

Using definition 3.1 for the correlation coefficient assures us of always obtaining a number r which is between -1 and $+1$ no matter what the scale of the variables. It should be emphasized that by using the denominator $\sqrt{SS_{xx} SS_{yy}}$ in the calculation of r, we do not change the sign of the correlation coefficient. Since the quantity $\sqrt{SS_{xx} SS_{yy}}$ is always positive, r has the same sign as the sum of the products SS_{xy}.

Example 3.2

Calculate the correlation coefficient r for the following hypothetical data set.

x	1	3	0	4
y	5	2	5	0

Solution: We first calculate $\bar{x}$ and $\bar{y}$.

$$\bar{x} = \frac{\Sigma x}{n} = \frac{1 + 3 + 0 + 4}{4} = \frac{8}{4} = 2$$

$$\bar{y} = \frac{\Sigma y}{n} = \frac{5 + 2 + 5 + 0}{4} = \frac{12}{4} = 3$$

We then construct a scattergram showing the relationship of each point (x, y) to the point $(\bar{x}, \bar{y}) = (2, 3)$. This is shown in figure 3.6.

Figure 3.6 • Scattergram for hypothetical data set of example 3.2

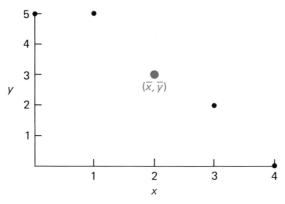

Note that all points lie in the "negative quadrants," that is, to the right and below $(\bar{x}, \bar{y})$ or to the left and above $(\bar{x}, \bar{y})$. What do you expect the sign of the correlation coefficient r to be, positive or negative?

We calculate the following.

$$\Sigma\, xy = (1)(5) + (3)(2) + (0)(5) + (4)(0) = 11$$

$$\Sigma\, x^2 = (1)^2 + (3)^2 + (0)^2 + (4)^2 = 1 + 9 + 0 + 16 = 26$$

$$\Sigma\, y^2 = (5)^2 + (2)^2 + (5)^2 + (0)^2 = 25 + 4 + 25 = 54$$

$$SS_{xy} = \Sigma\, xy - \frac{(\Sigma\, x)(\Sigma\, y)}{4} = 11 - \frac{(8)(12)}{4} = -13$$

$$SS_{xx} = \Sigma\, x^2 - \frac{(\Sigma\, x)^2}{4} = 26 - \frac{(8)^2}{4} = 10$$

$$SS_{yy} = \Sigma\, y^2 - \frac{(\Sigma\, y)^2}{4} = 54 - \frac{(12)^2}{4} = 18$$

Then

$$r = \frac{SS_{xy}}{\sqrt{SS_{xx}SS_{yy}}} = \frac{-13}{\sqrt{(10)(18)}} = -.97$$

The negative value for r indicates that the data set shows a negative-slope linear relationship between x and y, that is, y tends to decrease as x increases. This numerically based conclusion thus agrees with the graphical description in figure 3.6. However, making an inference about the population relationship between x and y would be risky, since the sample size is very small.

Table 3.3 provides a summary of the various possible values for r and their implications. Of course, the term "near" is vague.

Table 3.3 • Summary of r values and their implications

$r = 1$:	All the data points lie on a positive-slope straight line.
r near 1:	Almost all the data points lie in the positive ($+$) quadrants of $(x - \bar{x})(y - \bar{y})$ (see figure 3.7); y tends to increase as x increases.
r near 0:	Data points are evenly distributed around $(\bar{x}, \bar{y})$; no apparent linear relationship exists between x and y.
r near -1:	Almost all the data points lie in the negative ($-$) quadrants of $(x - \bar{x})(y - \bar{y})$ (see figure 3.7); y tends to decrease as x decreases.
$r = -1$:	All the data points lie on a negative-slope straight line.

Figure 3.7 • Sign quadrants of $(x - \bar{x})(y - \bar{y})$

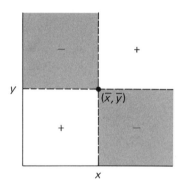

How do we decide when a value is "near" 1 or "near" 0? The answer is not simple, for we are really asking: "How large must r be before we can infer that the two variables are positively related in the population?" That is, we would like to know the numerical value of the population correlation coefficient, which we will denote as ρ (Greek rho). We will discuss the accuracy of r as an estimate or approximation to ρ in chapter 12. For now, we simply use r as a numerical descriptive measure of the linear relationship between two sample variables. We temporarily accept the fact that the implications of some r-values will be unclear.

One final caution concerns the use of the correlation coefficient to infer causal relationships between variables. The correlation coefficient does not imply or measure cause and effect between two variables. Even if two variables are perfectly correlated in the population, so that $\rho = 1$ or $\rho = -1$, it is incorrect to assume that x causes y or vice versa. It may be that both x and y are caused by some third unidentified variable z, which causes both x and y to lie on a straight line, yielding a correlation coefficient $\rho = 1$ or $\rho = -1$, depending on whether the slope of the line is positive or negative. You should be wary of researchers who claim to have discovered that changing some variable x **causes** another variable y to change. Such a claim is often the result of a misuse of the correlation coefficient.

Example 3.3

Refer to the experiment in which the undergraduate GPA (x) and advanced psychology GRE (y) were recorded for 10 psychology majors. The data are repeated here in table 3.4. Compute the correlation coefficient r between GPA and GRE for the 10 students.

Table 3.4 • Sample of psychology
GPAs and GREs

GPA	GRE
2.96	529
2.43	506
3.36	591
3.40	610
2.43	474
2.12	509
2.85	550
3.12	600
3.20	575
2.75	540

Solution: First we compute $\bar{x}$ and $\bar{y}$.

$$\bar{x} = \frac{\Sigma x}{n} = \frac{2.96 + 2.43 + \cdots + 2.75}{10} = \frac{28.62}{10} = 2.862$$

$$\bar{y} = \frac{\Sigma y}{n} = \frac{529 + 506 + \cdots + 540}{10} = \frac{5484}{10} = 548.4$$

The scattergram for these 10 data points is shown in figure 3.8 with $(\bar{x}, \bar{y})$ included. Note again the general positive-slope relationship indicated by the presence of most of the data points in the two positive $(x - \bar{x})(y - \bar{y})$ quadrants (see figure 3.7).

We now calculate

$$\Sigma xy = 2.96(529) + 2.43(506) + \cdots + 2.75(540) = 15850.58$$

Then

$$S_{xy} = \Sigma xy - \frac{(\Sigma x)(\Sigma y)}{n} = 15850.58 - \frac{(28.62)(5484)}{10} = 155.372$$

Next,

$$SS_{xx} = \Sigma x^2 - \frac{(\Sigma x)^2}{n}$$

$$= (2.96)^2 + (2.43)^2 + \cdots + (2.75)^2 - \frac{(28.62)^2}{10}$$

$$= 83.5748 - 81.91044 = 1.66436$$

Figure 3.8 • Scattergram for GRE vs. GPA, $(\overline{x}, \overline{y})$ included

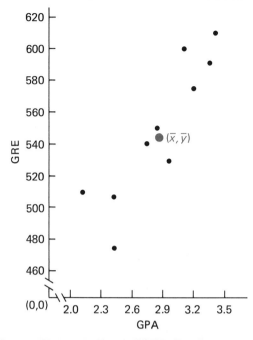

Warning: Performing calculations like those in example 3.3 without the use of a calculator may be hazardous to your mental health!

and

$$SS_{yy} = \Sigma\, y^2 - \frac{(\Sigma\, y)^2}{n}$$

$$= (529)^2 + (506)^2 + \cdots + (540)^2 - \frac{(5484)^2}{10}$$

$$= 3{,}025{,}740 - 3{,}007{,}425.6 = 18{,}314.4$$

Finally,

$$r = \frac{SS_{xy}}{\sqrt{SS_{xx}SS_{yy}}} = \frac{155.372}{\sqrt{(1.66436)(18314.4)}} = \frac{155.372}{174.590} = .89$$

Example 3.4

Refer to example 3.1. We examined the relationship between activation and performance by recording heart rates and digit symbol improvement scores for 25 subjects. The data are repeated in table 3.5. Calculate the correlation coefficient r between heart rate and improvement score for these 25 subjects.

Table 3.5 • Data for heart rate and improvement score

Heart Rate	Improvement Score	Heart Rate	Improvement Score
72	5.0	95	7.8
77	8.0	98	7.7
85	7.5	70	5.3
99	8.9	105	6.1
107	7.3	88	8.1
110	5.3	78	7.4
82	8.0	103	6.7
73	5.2	95	7.9
92	8.3	70	5.1
92	8.6	83	7.4
104	6.5	94	8.8
74	6.0	115	5.2
80	8.4		

Solution:

$$\bar{x} = \frac{\Sigma\, x}{25} = \frac{72 + 77 + \cdots + 115}{25} = \frac{2241}{25} = 89.64$$

$$\bar{y} = \frac{\Sigma\, y}{25} = \frac{5.0 + 8.0 + \cdots + 5.2}{25} = \frac{176.5}{25} = 7.06$$

We repeat the scattergram for this data in figure 3.9, with the point $(\bar{x}, \bar{y})$ plotted in color. Note that the inverted U-shape of the scattergram causes the points to fall in all four $(x - \bar{x})(y - \bar{y})$ quadrants.

Figure 3.9 • Scattergram for improvement score vs. heart rate, $(\bar{x}, \bar{y})$ included

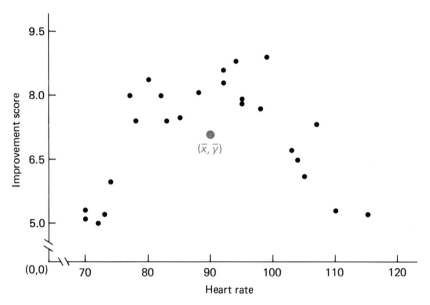

Now we calculate the following.

$$\Sigma\, xy = (72)(5.0) + (77)(8.0) + \cdots + (115)(5.2) = 15{,}875.2$$
$$\Sigma\, x^2 = (72)^2 + (77)^2 + \cdots + (115)^2 = 205{,}227$$
$$\Sigma\, y^2 = (5.0)^2 + (8.0)^2 + \cdots + (5.2)^2 = 1{,}286.89$$

Thus

$$SS_{xy} = \Sigma\, xy - \frac{(\Sigma\, x)(\Sigma\, y)}{n} = 15{,}875.2 - \frac{(2241)(176.5)}{25} = 53.74$$

$$SS_{xx} = \Sigma\, x^2 - \frac{(\Sigma\, x)^2}{n} = 205{,}227 - \frac{(2241)^2}{25} = 4343.76$$

$$SS_{yy} = \Sigma\, y^2 - \frac{(\Sigma\, y)^2}{n} = 1{,}286.89 - \frac{(176.5)^2}{25} = 40.8$$

Finally,

$$r = \frac{SS_{xy}}{\sqrt{SS_{xx}SS_{yy}}} = \frac{53.74}{\sqrt{(4343.76)(40.8)}} = .13$$

No strong linear relationship between heart rate and improvement score is indicated by this correlation coefficient. However, this fact does *not* imply that no relationship exists between the variables. On the contrary, our graphical techniques indicate that an inverted U-relationship exists. This further emphasizes the fact that *r* measures only the *linear* relationship between two variables.

EXERCISES

1. Given the following data points (corresponding values of x and y).

x	2	5	3	2	4
y	3	1	3	5	2

    (a) Construct a scattergram for this data.
    (b) Calculate $\bar{x}$ and $\bar{y}$ and locate the point $(\bar{x}, \bar{y})$ on the scattergram.
    (c) Examine the scattergram and deduce the sign of the correlation coefficient.
    (d) Calculate the value of the correlation coefficient r. Interpret your result.
2. Repeat the instructions of exercise 1 for the following data points.

x	3	5	2	1	3	1
y	4	5	3	1	3	2

3. Repeat the instructions of exercise 1 for the following data points.

x	3	1	4	2	0	1	1	0
y	5	3	5	4	2	4	2	1

4. Refer to exercise 1, section 3.1. Ten measurements were made on monocular depth perception in schizophrenics at various distances from a light. The data are repeated below for your convenience.

Distance from Light (in feet)	4	6	4	8	10	10	12	6	12	8
Coded Score	25	22	26	17	16	21	13	18	19	22

    Calculate the correlation coefficient r between the two variables—distance from the light and the coded score for depth perception. Comment on their sample relationship.
5. Refer to exercise 2, section 3.1. We compared two ways (A and B) of measuring monocular depth perception. The 10 measurements on methods A and B are repeated below.

A	25	15	15	17	17	23	23	20	22	16
B	28	13	18	16	17	29	22	18	24	18

    Calculate the correlation coefficient r between methods A and B. Comment on their sample relationship.

6. Refer to exercise 3, section 3.1. A scattergram was constructed for teacher and sociometric ratings of 25 students. The data is repeated below.

Teacher Rating	20	22	27	18	10	13	24	21	18	18	23	16	27
Sociometric Rating	5	3	4	5	1	2	4	3	3	4	3	1	5

Teacher Rating	21	19	23	18	24	19	26	20	19	22	16	21
Sociometric Rating	2	1	4	2	4	3	5	2	4	3	1	3

Calculate the correlation coefficient r between teacher rating and sociometric rating. Comment on their sample relationship.

SUMMARY

In this chapter we presented sample descriptive measures that can be used with an experiment for investigating the relationship between two variables. Both graphical and numerical techniques were discussed.

The scattergram provides a graphical measure of a two-variable relationship. The correlation coefficient r is a numerical measure of the linear relationship between two variables. Since r is always between -1 and $+1$, the correlation coefficient provides information about both the strength and the nature (positive or negative) of the relationship, regardless of the scale on which the variables are measured.

Our ultimate objective is to use these sample descriptive measures to make inferences about the true or population relationship between the two variables. We will discuss this type of inference in chapter 12.

SUPPLEMENTARY EXERCISES

1. Consider the following sample data collected on two variables (x and y).

x	4	2	4	5	7	6
y	7	3	6	7	9	6

   (a) Construct a scattergram for this sample.
   (b) Calculate $\bar{x}$ and $\bar{y}$ and plot the point $(\bar{x}, \bar{y})$ on the scattergram.
   (c) Examine the scattergram and deduce the sign of the correlation coefficient.
   (d) Calculate the value of the correlation coefficient r. Interpret your result.
2. Repeat the instructions of exercise 1 for the following sample.

x	0	5	2	7	3	4	1	0
y	8	3	6	0	4	4	9	6

3. Repeat the instructions of exercise 1 for the following sample.

x	4	8	5	2	0	7	1	5	0	8
y	3	0	5	1	0	2	2	6	1	3

4. Lane and Albee (1963) studied intellectual development of adult schizophrenics. Included among the measures were two administrations of an intelligence test, at different time periods. Given below are each subject's scores for the two test administrations. Draw a scattergram of the data.

Time I	81	100	90	94	110	105
Time II	69	102	88	89	105	103

5. Refer to exercise 4. Calculate the correlation coefficient between the subjects' scores on the two test administrations. Comment on the sample relationship.

6. An experiment was conducted (Mukherjee 1969) to study the role of verbal factors in a test of achievement. Two of the measures of subject verbal ability were scores on the Sentence Completion Test and on a vocabulary test. The experimenter tested whether there was a relationship between these two measures of verbal ability. For the data below, draw a scattergram.

SCT	15.46	20.88	22.73	12.36	18.35
Vocabulary lest	40.63	40.09	29.12	45.67	51.74

7. Refer to exercise 6. Calculate the correlation coefficient between the Sentence Completion Test score and the vocabulary test score. Comment on the sample relationship.

8. Desor, Maller, and Andrews (1975) studied ingestive responses of human newborns to see if they differed in intake of salty, sour, and bitter liquids. Given below are the data for the intake of two of the liquids. Draw a scattergram to show the relationship between the two variables.

Liquid A	9.4	21.0	2.9	10.5	12.6	8.7	15.8	19.0	18.8	11.9
Liquid B	17.6	20.6	3.4	9.6	14.0	9.7	13.7	17.6	20.2	9.8

9. Refer to exercise 8. Calculate the coefficient of correlation between the measurements for liquids A and B. Comment on the sample relationships.

10. In a study of cage size as a factor in environmental enrichment, Manosevitz and Pryor (1975) took several behavioral measures to see if they were related to each

other. Given below are running wheel scores and exploration scores for each rat. Calculate the correlation coefficient between the two scores. Comment on the sample relationship. Note: Even though the scales of the scores are large, the value of r is still between -1 and 1.

Running Wheel Score	4192	3312	3021	4213	4635	4006	5723	4674
Exploration	964	907	970	921	1218	990	1074	1009

REFERENCES

Ausubal, P., and Schiff, H. H. 1955. Some intrapersonal and interpersonal determinants of individual differences in socioempathic ability among adolescents. *Journal of Social Psychology* 41:39–56.

Burgess, M., and Hokanson, J. E. 1964. Effects of increased heart rate on intellectual performance. *Journal of Abnormal and Social Psychology* 68:85–91.

Desor, J. A.; Maller, O.; and Andrews, K. 1975. Ingestive responses of human newborns to salty, sour and bitter stimuli. *Journal of Comparative Physiological Psychology* 89:966–970.

Kidd, A. H. 1964. Monocular distance perception in schizophrenics. *Journal of Abnormal and Social Psychology* 68:100–103.

Lane, E. A., and Albee, G. W. 1963. Childhood intellectual development of adult schizophrenics. *Journal of Abnormal and Social Psychology* 67:186–189.

Manosevitz, M., and Pryor, J. B. 1975. Cage size as a factor in environmental enrichment. *Journal of Comparative and Physiological Psychology* 89:648–654.

Mukherjee, B. N. 1969. The role of verbal factors in a forced choice test of achievement value. *Journal of Psychology* 72:119–124.

Shand, S. 1970. The GRE advanced test in psychology in relation to undergraduate academic standing. *Journal of Psychology* 76:85–90.

4·Probability

INTRODUCTION

As stated in chapter 1, the objective of statistics is to make inferences about a population based on information contained in a sample. Since the sample provides only partial information about the population, we need a mechanism that will allow us to accomplish this objective. Probability is such a mechanism and enables us to use the information contained in a set of sample data to infer the nature of the larger set of data, the population.

How we use probability to make inferences is best illustrated by considering an example. A marital counseling center conducts an experiment to determine whether it is husbands or wives who are more apt to seek outside help in solving marital problems. Suppose that it is widely held that wives and husbands are equally likely to seek such help, that is, that the population proportion of "wife responsible" couples is $\frac{1}{2}$. To test this assumption, 20 couples participating in the center's program are randomly sampled and each is asked which partner was initially responsible for the couple's participation. In this sample, all 20 couples indicate that the husband was initially responsible. What would you conclude about the original assumption? Clearly, 0 out of 20 "wife responsible" couples is highly improbable if the population proportion is $\frac{1}{2}$.

But let us take an example where the probability of the sample result is less obvious. For example, suppose that 5 of 20 couples in the sample were "wife responsible." Does this result contradict our theory that 50 percent of all couples are "wife responsible"?

To answer this question, we need to know how improbable it is to observe 5 or fewer couples in our sample when our hypothesis is that 50 percent of the couples in the population are "wife responsible." That is, we need to know the probability of obtaining a particular sample outcome. Once we know this probability, we can decide whether our hypothesis is reasonable or should be rejected as untrue. Thus it is *probability* that allows us to make inferences about the population on the basis of sample evidence.

In chapters 2 and 3 we discussed methods for describing sets of measurements, a necessary subject since we will want to make statements about a population when we make an inference. Thus chapters 2 and 3 are concerned with how to phrase an inference. In this chapter we will study the mechanism for making inferences.

How probability plays a role in inference making and how we find probabilities are discussed in sections 4.1 and 4.2. You will learn that the measurements of chapters 2 and 3 are made on random variables. These variables, their types, and the probabilities associated with them are discussed in sections 4.3, 4.4, and 4.5. Descriptive measures of populations are presented in section 4.6. Random sampling and how it relates to inference making is the subject of section 4.7.

4.1 • THE MEANING OF PROBABILITY

So far we have employed the term "probability" as it might be used in ordinary conversation. Since probability plays such an important role in making inferences, we now proceed to examine the concept in more detail. Before we can define probability, however, we must consider what is meant by an experiment.

Data are obtained by observing uncontrolled events in nature or by controlled experimentation in the laboratory. To simplify our terminology, we seek a word that will apply to either method of data collection, and hence we define an experiment as follows.

Definition 4.1

An **experiment** is the process by which an observation (or measurement) is obtained.

Note that the outcome of an experiment, the observation actually obtained, may be either numerically valued—as when an observation is assigned a number that represents the magnitude of some property—or categorical—as when an observation is merely assigned to one of two or more categories. Even in the latter case it may be useful to assign numbers to represent qualitatively different categories. Referring to the example in the Introduction, a simple experiment consisted of interviewing a single couple and noting whether the wife or the husband was responsible for seeking help. Suppose we let a 1 denote the outcome "wife responsible" and a 0 denote the outcome "husband responsible." This amounts to assigning numbers to represent qualitatively different categories.

Other typical examples of experiments are given in the list below.

1. Making a measurement of reading rate.
2. Counting the number of lever presses for a food reward.
3. Measuring the latency of response to a given stimulus.
4. Tossing a coin and observing the face that appears.
5. Recording an examinee's response to a multiple-choice test item.
6. Measuring a chimpanzee's curiosity.
7. Recording whether or not a student favors Sam Smith for student body president.

You may recall that the last two experiments were used in chapter 1 to help define the objective of statistics. There we pointed out that the populations associated with these experiments were the sets of data obtained by performing the experiment a very large number of times. In the case of the chimpanzee curiosity measurements, the population only exists conceptually. In the case of the student body presidency, the population is real and can actually be produced by determining whether or not each member of the student body favors Sam Smith.

Crucial to our definition of probability is the concept of a population as the collection of data generated by repeating an experiment a very large number of times, conceptually or in fact.

Definition 4.2

The **probability** of a particular experimental outcome is the fraction of times the outcome will occur in an indefinitely long series of repetitions of the experiment.

Thus the probability that a chimpanzee's curiosity measurement decreases with age is the actual fraction of experiments in which such an event would occur if we could somehow measure the curiosity of all captive male chimpanzees in a specific age range. Similarly, the probability that a randomly selected student favors Sam Smith for president is the fraction of the student body who favor Smith. In the marital counseling example presented in the Introduction, the population consists of all couples who have sought or will seek marital counseling. The probability that the couple indicates that the husband is responsible for seeking help is the fraction of this population of couples who indicate the husband's responsibility. Finally, the probability of observing a head when a coin is tossed is the fraction of heads in the population, where the population would be created by tossing the coin *ad infinitum.*

Definition 4.2, known as the relative frequency definition of probability, is easier to accept when the population is real. If you buy 5 tickets in a 100-ticket lottery, there is little argument that the probability of your winning the grand prize is $\frac{5}{100}$, assuming that the draw is random. This conforms precisely with our relative frequency definition, since the fraction of tickets in the population that you own is $\frac{5}{100}$.

However, the definition is harder to accept if we have a vaguely defined conceptual population. For example, if we are trying to determine the probability of rain tomorrow, the conceptual population might consist of all days, past and future, whose atmospheric conditions match those of today. Then the probability of rain tomorrow would be the fraction of rainy days which followed or will follow the days in our population. However, there is really no clearly defined and repeatable experiment associated with this population. Some refuse to accept a relative frequency definition of probability because of its doubtful applicability to examples like the latter. They prefer instead to define the probability of an outcome as a quantity determined personally by each individual (the *subjective definition* of probability).

In psychological research requiring statistical methods, the experiment must be clearly defined and repeatable in order to generate a sample of outcomes. This being the case, we can at least conceptually define the population by *imagining* that the sample size is increased indefinitely. It is then reasonable to apply the relative frequency definition for determining the probability of a particular outcome of the experiment. Under these conditions, an empirical method for estimating or approximating a probability follows logically from definition 4.2, as we will now show.

If we are interested in the probability of some event A, we repeat the experiment N times and count the number of times A occurs, $n(A)$. Our estimate of the probability of A is the sample relative frequency of event A, that is

$$P(A) \approx \frac{n(A)}{N}$$

(The $\approx$ sign means "approximately equal to" or "is estimated by.") As with all inferences, we would like to have some measure of goodness or precision for our estimate. But let it suffice here to note that our estimate will improve as N is increased, since we will be examining a larger portion of the population.

Example 4.1

Suppose a marital counseling center randomly selects 20 couples and determines that 17 husbands were responsible for seeking help. Estimate the probability that the husband is responsible when a couple seeks help. Can we conclude on the basis of our sample that this probability is greater than $\frac{1}{2}$?

Solution: Let A represent the event that the husband is responsible for seeking help. Then we estimate the probability of A by the sample relative frequency,

$$P(A) \approx \frac{n(A)}{N} = \frac{17}{20}$$

However, this result does not indicate that the value of $P(A)$ is exactly $\frac{17}{20}$, or even greater than $\frac{1}{2}$, since only 20 measurements (couples) have been sampled from the population. To infer that $P(A)$ exceeds $\frac{1}{2}$, we need a measure of precision for our sample estimate. However, we do know that if we increase our sample size until it becomes very large and then find that the sample relative frequency remains greater than $\frac{1}{2}$, our inference that $P(A)$ exceeds $\frac{1}{2}$ becomes increasingly credible.

The use of a very large sample for finding probabilities is illustrated in the next section.

4.2 · FINDING THE PROBABILITY OF AN EXPERIMENTAL OUTCOME

To illustrate the empirical method for finding the probability of an outcome, consider an experiment of tossing two coins. Letting H denote a head and T denote a tail, four possible outcomes may be distinguished, as shown in table 4.1.

Table 4.1 · Possible outcomes of toss of two coins

First Coin	Second Coin	Outcome
H	H	HH
H	T	HT
T	H	TH
T	T	TT

Suppose that the experiment is repeated $N = 1000$ times, with results as shown in table 4.2. Suppose further that we want to find the probability of the outcome "observe exactly one head." Calling this outcome A, we note that the number of occurrences of A is $n(A) = 241 + 255 = 496$, so that

$$P(A) \approx \frac{n(A)}{N} = \frac{496}{1000} = .496$$

If we had two "fair" (unweighted) coins, and if we tossed them infinitely many times, we would expect each outcome listed in table 4.1 to be equally likely to occur. Hence we would expect the probability of each outcome to be exactly $\frac{1}{4}$, or .25. Similarly, we would expect the probability of the outcome "observe exactly one head" to be exactly $\frac{1}{4} + \frac{1}{4} = \frac{1}{2}$, or .5. Note that the approximate

Table 4.2 • Results of $N = 1000$ tosses of
two coins

Outcome	Frequency	Relative Frequency
HH	246	.246
HT	241	.241
TH	255	.255
TT	258	.258

probability found above, based on a finite number of repetitions of the coin-tossing experiment, is very close to the value we would expect.

We will discuss this notion of exact or expected probability in more detail in section 4.4 and in chapter 5.

EXERCISES

1. Consider the experiment of drawing one card at random from an ordinary deck of 52 cards. Suppose we are interested in the probability that the card drawn will be a face card.
   (a) Find the approximate probability of drawing a face card by repeating the experiment 100 times (shuffling before each draw) and observing the fraction of times a face card is drawn.
   (b) Because there are 12 face cards in the deck, we know the probability of drawing a face card is $\frac{12}{52}$. Compare the results of part (a) with this known probability.
   (c) To obtain a more accurate estimate of the probability of drawing a face card, combine your experimental results with others in your class. Note that this combined estimate is (most probably will be) closer to the known probability, $\frac{12}{52}$.
2. Consider the experiment of rolling a pair of dice and observing the sum of the two numbers showing on the upper faces of the dice. Suppose we are interested in the probability that this sum is 7.
   (a) Find the approximate probability of rolling a sum of 7 by repeating the experiment 100 times and observing the fraction of times a sum of 7 is rolled.
   (b) Because there are 6 ways to roll a sum of 7 ($1 + 6, 2 + 5, 3 + 4, 4 + 3, 5 + 2, 6 + 1$) and 36 possible outcomes on each roll (list these), we deduce that the probability of rolling a sum of 7 is $\frac{6}{36} = \frac{1}{6}$. Compare this known probability with the results of part (a).
   (c) Combine your experimental results with others in your class to obtain a better estimate of the probability of rolling a sum of 7.

4.3 • RANDOM VARIABLES

In section 4.1 we defined an experiment as the process by which an observation (or measurement) is obtained. Then we noted that the population associated with an experiment is the collection of outcomes for infinitely many repetitions of the experiment. The observations in this population need not be numerically valued.

However, most experiments in the behavioral sciences either produce quantitative data or can be quantified by assigning numbers to represent categories. For example, rather than noting whether an individual favors, opposes, or has no opinion on some issue, we could record a 0 for "favors," a 1 for "opposes," and a 2 for "has no opinion." As a result, our population would consist of a collection of 0s, 1s, and 2s with the relative frequency of each being its probability, by definition 4.2. We will find that quantifying the outcomes of experiments allows us to construct probability models more consistently than we could if we permitted verbal descriptions to be members of the population.

Usually, the quantified variable measured in an experiment is denoted by the symbol y. The variable y should be defined so that it can assume all the possible numerical values corresponding to the various experimental outcomes. When the variable is defined in this way, it is called a random variable.

Definition 4.3

A random variable y is a numerically valued variable whose values correspond to the various outcomes of an experiment.

For example, consider the sampling of 20 couples who are participating in a marital counseling program and who are asked whether the wife or the husband was responsible for their participation. The number of couples who indicate that the wife was responsible may be regarded as a variable y that assumes any of the values 0, 1, 2, . . . , 20. Each of these values corresponds to a particular experimental outcome. The experiment consists of drawing a sample of 20 couples' responses and noting how many indicate that the wife was responsible. The variable y is a *random* variable since the value that y assumes is an outcome that cannot be predicted with absolute certainty before the experiment. That is, the particular value that y takes is the result of a chance or random event.

Random variables are classified as one of two types: discrete or continuous.

Definition 4.4

A discrete random variable is one that can assume a countable number of values.

Typical examples of discrete random variables are shown below.

1. The number of errors made on a multiple-choice test.
2. The number of brain-damaged individuals in a group of 10 mental retardates.
3. The number of trials needed to reach a certain criterion in a learning task (the number of trials to and including the trial at which learning occurs).

4. The number of responses indicating that the wife was responsible for a couple's participation in a marriage counseling program.

A discrete random variable may be identified by noting the number of values that it can assume. If a random variable can assume only a finite number or a countable infinity of values, it is discrete. For example, if y represents the number of errors made on a multiple-choice test, y can assume a finite number of values, 0, 1, 2, . . . , n, where n is the number of items on the test. The number of trials y to reach a certain criterion in a learning task could conceivably be infinite if the task is so difficult that some subjects never reach the criterion. However, the number of values that y can assume is countably infinite, since we can imagine a count that is continued indefinitely.

A *continuous random variable* is defined as follows.

Definition 4.5

A continuous random variable is one that can assume the infinitely many values corresponding to the points on a line interval.

For example, suppose that we measured the physical distance between two individuals in a social situation and represented this distance by the random variable y. If a tape measure were used, each value that y could assume would correspond to a point on the tape measure that, in turn, might be viewed theoretically as a point on a line. With a sufficiently fine measuring instrument, we could associate each value of y with one of infinitely many points on a line interval.

Typical examples of continuous random variables are shown below.

1. The weight of a laboratory rat after experiencing stress for some specified time period.
2. The length of time a subject requires to complete a specific task.
3. The blood pressure of an individual after being subjected to a stimulus.
4. The maximum reading level attained by an individual taking a polygraph examination.

The distinction between discrete and continuous random variables is an important one, since different probability models are required for each. The probabilities associated with each value of a discrete random variable can be assigned in such a way that the probabilities add up to 1. This is not possible with continuous random variables, since they can assume infinitely many (and uncountable) values. Accordingly, we shall consider the probability distributions for discrete and continuous random variables separately in the following two sections.

The length of time a subject needs to complete a specific task is frequently a topic of concern in psychology. What kind of variable would be used for such a measurement? (Photo by Susan Szasz for Photo Researchers, Inc.)

EXERCISES

1. Identify the following random variables as discrete or continuous.
   (a) The number of children in a classroom who grasp a new concept.
   (b) The difference in response times to two stimuli.
   (c) A score on an IQ test.
   (d) The number of trials needed to reach a criterion for laboratory monkeys.
   (e) The distance between two subjects in a social interaction experiment.
2. Identify the following random variables as discrete or continuous.
   (a) The length of time needed to respond to a stimulus.
   (b) An individual's pulse rate.
   (c) The number of respondents in a survey who favor capital punishment.
   (d) The number of movements in one minute by a one-day-old infant.

4.4 • DISCRETE RANDOM VARIABLES AND THEIR PROBABILITY DISTRIBUTIONS

The probability distribution for a discrete random variable y is a pairing of each value of y with its probability p(y), and it may be represented by a table, a graph, or a formula. Viewing probability as population relative frequency, p(y) represents the fraction of times that a particular value of y is observed when the experiment is repeated an unlimited number of times. Thus the probability distribution of y can be approximated by repeating the experiment a large number of times, noting the value that y assumes on each repetition, and then pairing each value of y with the fraction of times it occurs.

To illustrate, we consider the coin-tossing experiment of section 4.2. Defining the random variable y as the number of heads observed in a toss of two coins, y can take the value 0, 1, or 2. From table 4.2 we obtain approximate probabilities for each of these values of y. We present the resulting distribution in table 4.3.

Table 4.3 • Approximate probability distribution for y, the number of heads in a two-coin toss (N = 1000 tosses)

y	Frequency	Relative Frequency
0	258	.258
1	496	.496
2	246	.246

Note that the relative frequencies are very close to the values that would be expected if we assume that heads and tails are equally likely for both coins. The corresponding known, or expected, probabilities, which can be derived mathematically (we will do this in chapter 5), are p(0) = .25, p(1) = .50, and p(2) = .25.

Granted that this model is appropriate, so that these expected probabilities can be taken as actual probabilities, the exact probability distribution for y is as shown in table 4.4 and in the histogram in figure 4.1.

Table 4.4 • Probability distribution for y, the number of heads in a two-coin toss

y	p(y)
0	$\frac{1}{4}$ = .25
1	$\frac{1}{2}$ = .50
2	$\frac{1}{4}$ = .25

Figure 4.1 • Probability histogram for y, the number of heads in a two-coin toss

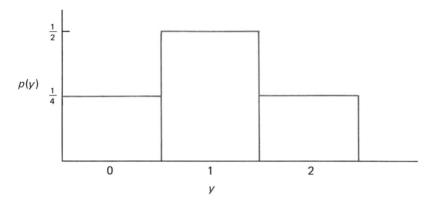

This simple coin-tossing experiment illustrates three important properties of probability distributions for discrete random variables.

Important Properties of Discrete Random Variables

1. The probability associated with each value of y must be greater than or equal to 0 and less than or equal to 1. Stated more briefly,

$$0 \le p(y) \le 1$$

2. The probabilities for discrete random variables can be added. For example, if the probability that y assumes the value 1 is $\frac{1}{2}$ and the probability that y assumes the value 2 is $\frac{1}{4}$, then the probability that y assumes either the value 1 or the value 2 is equal to $p(1) + p(2) = \frac{1}{2} + \frac{1}{4} = \frac{3}{4}$.

3. The sum of the probabilities for all values of y must equal 1. Stated more briefly,

$$\sum_{\text{all } y} p(y) = 1$$

We use all available information about an experiment to assign a probability function that satisfies these rules. When, as is most often the case, the information available does not permit us to assign a credible probability distribution to y, the problem becomes statistical. We then use the information in a sample from the population to make an inference about the probabilities in question.

To illustrate the problems associated with assigning discrete probability distributions, again consider the marital counseling problem in the Introduction (see also example 4.1). The experiment consists of selecting 20 couples from among those who are participating in a marriage counseling program and asking each whether the wife or the husband was responsible for the participation. If we let y be the number of couples out of 20 who indicate that the husband is responsible for seeking help, then y is a discrete random variable that can assume any of the values 0, 1, 2, . . . , 20.

The available information which may help us to determine the probability distribution of y is scarce. We may assume that the trials of the experiment are independent, that is, that the response for each couple is unaffected by other couples' responses. (We would be sure to interview the couples separately to avoid any social pressure which might lead to false responses.) However, if we let p represent the probability that each couple declares the husband is responsible, all we know about p is that it must be a number between 0 and 1. However, suppose we *assume* that $p = \frac{1}{2}$, which implies that the fraction of *all* "husband responsible" couples in the population equals the fraction of *all* "wife responsible" couples in the population. Then the experiment becomes analogous to tossing 20 fair coins. We may then extend the reasoning which led to the probability distribution for tossing 2 coins (table 4.4) to an experiment using 20 coins. The resulting probability distribution would appear as in figure 4.2.

Figure 4.2 • Probability distribution for y, the number of couples in which the wife seeks marital counseling; $n = 20$, $p = \frac{1}{2}$

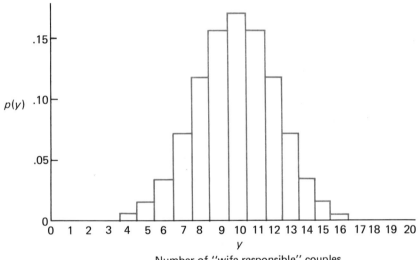

y

Number of "wife responsible" couples

Suppose we perform this experiment and 17 of the 20 couples indicate that the husband was responsible for seeking help. Does such an outcome cast doubt upon or even disprove our assumption that $p = \frac{1}{2}$? Examination of figure 4.2 indicates that we are very unlikely to observe 17 or more "husband responsible" couples if $p = \frac{1}{2}$ (the exact probability that $y \geq 17$ is .001). The occurrence of such an event would imply that either we have observed a very rare event in the $p = \frac{1}{2}$ distribution, or our assumption that $p = \frac{1}{2}$ is false. The rare event approach to statistical inference, introduced in section 2.9, would lead to the conclusion that more than $\frac{1}{2}$ of the couples in the population are "husband responsible," that is, that $p > \frac{1}{2}$. However, we must remember that the event $y \geq 17$ is not *impossible* in the $p = \frac{1}{2}$ distribution, but it is very *unlikely*. Thus the occurrence of the event *does not disprove* our assumption that $p = \frac{1}{2}$, but it does cast doubt upon its validity.

EXERCISES

1. Consider a discrete random variable with the following probability distribution.

y	0	1	2	3
$p(y)$	$\frac{1}{10}$	$\frac{3}{10}$	$\frac{3}{10}$	? $\frac{3}{10}$

(a) Find $p(3)$.
(b) Draw a probability histogram similar to figure 4.2.
(c) What is the probability that y is 0 or 2?
(d) What is the probability that y is at least 1?
2. Consider the experiment of tossing three coins and observing the number of heads y.
   (a) Find the approximate values of $p(0)$, $p(1)$, $p(2)$, and $p(3)$ by repeating the experiment 100 times and recording the fraction of times y equals 0, 1, 2, and 3 in the 100 tosses of the three coins.
   (b) Combine your experimental results with others in your class to obtain a more accurate estimate of the probability distribution of y.
   (c) As we will subsequently show in chapter 5, the probability distribution (assuming three fair coins) is given by

y	0	1	2	3
$p(y)$	$\frac{1}{8}$	$\frac{3}{8}$	$\frac{3}{8}$	$\frac{1}{8}$

Compare these values with your experimental results.

4.5 • CONTINUOUS RANDOM VARIABLES AND THEIR PROBABILITY DISTRIBUTIONS

As indicated in section 4.3, continuous random variables can assume the infinitely many values corresponding to points on a line interval. It is not possible to assign a probability to each of infinitely many points and have these probabilities sum to 1, as for discrete random variables. Thus a different approach is used to generate the probability distribution for a continuous random variable.

The approach that we adopt uses the concept of a relative frequency histogram such as shown in figure 4.2. Recall that the relative frequency histogram becomes a smooth curve when we have a population of measurements made on a continuous scale (see section 2.3).

The relative frequency associated with a particular class in the population is the fraction of measurements in the population falling in that interval and also is the probability of drawing a measurement in that class. If the total area under the relative frequency histogram were adjusted to equal 1, areas under the frequency curve would correspond to probabilities. Indeed, this was the basis for the application of the Empirical Rule in chapter 2.

Let us construct a model for the probability distribution for a continuous random variable. Assume that the random variable y may take values on a real line as in figure 4.3. We will then distribute 1 unit of probability along the line much as a person might distribute a handful of sand, each measurement in the population corresponding to a single grain. The probability, grains of sand or measurements, will pile up in certain places, and the result will be the probability distribution as in figure 4.4.

Figure 4.3 • Relative frequency histogram for a continuous random variable y

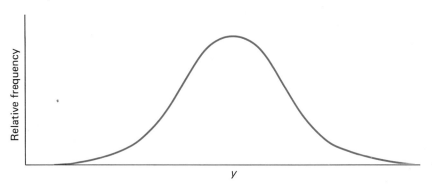

The depth or density of the probability, which varies with y, may be represented by a mathematical function f(y), called the probability distribution (or the probability density function) for the random variable y. The function f(y), represented graphically in figure 4.4, provides a mathematical model for the population relative frequency histogram that exists in reality. The total area under the curve f(y) is equal to 1. The area lying above a given interval will equal the probability that y will fall in that interval. Thus the probability that a < y < b (a is less than y and y is less than b) is equal to the shaded area under the density function between the two points a and b.

A question remains. How do we choose the model—that is, the probability distribution f(y)—appropriate for a given physical situation? Fortunately, we will find that most data collected on continuous random variables have mound-shaped frequency distributions, often very nearly bell-shaped. A probability model that provides a good approximation to such population distributions is the normal probability distribution, which we will study in detail in chapter 7.

The practice of adopting a model f(y) that can only be expected to approximate the population relative frequency curve requires some comment. It is, of course, a

Figure 4.4 • Probability distribution f(y)

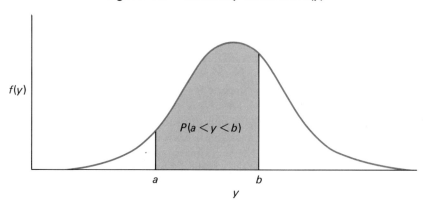

practice that could lead to an invalid conclusion—if an inappropriate model is chosen out of poor judgment or insufficient knowledge of the phenomenon under study. On the other hand, it represents a strategy which, when appropriately applied, has been found highly successful in scientific research.

The equations, formulas, and various numerical expressions used in all the sciences are simply mathematical models that provide approximations to reality, the goodness of which are evaluated through experimental application. In the behavioral sciences, our criterion for a successful technique is that it leads to good inferences concerning behavior and its determinants.

A model is evaluated in terms of the results of its application: decisions or predictions about behavior. Necessarily, such an evaluation is made outside the immediate application of the model, through comparison with the other lines of evidence and by further experimentation. Do the resulting inferences fit in with the body of accumulated evidence? Are the deductions that follow from these inferences verified experimentally? If so, the model has proved its worth.

4.6 • PARAMETERS OF POPULATIONS

Recall that numerical descriptive measures of populations are called parameters. Thus the population mean μ and the population standard deviation σ are parameters of a population in the same way that a median, percentiles, and other numerical descriptive measures defined in chapter 2 are parameters of a population.

To illustrate, refer again to the probability distribution for y, the number of heads in two coin tosses, shown in figure 4.5. Note that the center of the distribution is at $y = 1$. It is easy to show that the average value of y is $\mu = 1$. Similarly, it can be shown that the standard deviation of y is $\sigma = 0.71$.

In most practical problems we will not know the precise form of the population relative frequency distribution as we did for the toss of two coins. Hence we will

Figure 4.5 • Probability distribution for the number of heads in a two-coin toss

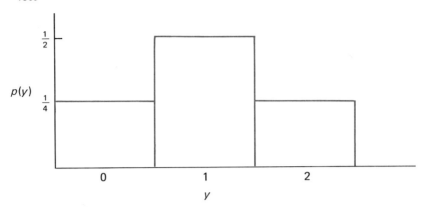

not know the values of μ, σ, or any other parameters. Since the objective of statistics is inference, and since we wish to describe a population based on information contained in a sample, it is reasonable that we would wish to make inferences about μ, σ (or σ^2), and other parameters of the population. In fact, it is quite logical that we would use the sample mean $\bar{y}$ to estimate μ and that we would use other sample numerical descriptive measures to estimate their population counterparts. To do this we must select a random sample from the population of interest.

4.7 • RANDOM SAMPLING

The Environmental Protection Agency (EPA) recently announced that Alachua County, along with nine other Florida areas, had been tentatively designated as an Air Quality Maintenance Area. This designation means that local officials in the affected areas must develop a ten-year master plan to improve the air quality.

Upon receiving the EPA announcement, the Alachua County Engineer stated that he planned to fight the EPA designation because the sampling stations used were ill placed and did not provide accurate readings of the air quality. Further investigation showed that at least one of the stations was located near a dusty clay road. This alone could have accounted for the poor air quality of the samples taken at that location.

Additional information was acquired to substantiate the claim that the sampling was biased and tended to show a much higher rate of pollution than actually existed. Then an appeal was sent through proper channels, and the air quality maintenance designation for Alachua County was lifted by the EPA. This example illustrates the important role that sampling plays in statistical inferences. In particular, it shows that statistical inferences depend on how the sample is selected.

Careful sampling is important because of biases that might be introduced

in the procedure. Careful sampling is also important because the sample selection procedure is the key to making inferences.

To make an inference in the Sam Smith political survey, we must calculate (or at least be able to approximately evaluate) the probability of the observed sample. To do this we need to know precisely how the sample was selected. We loosely referred to the sampling in Smith's survey as random, but we will now define the meaning of this term.

Definition 4.6

A **random sample of one measurement** from a population of N measurements is one in which each of the N measurements has an equal probability of being selected.

The notion of random sampling can be extended to the selection of more than one measurement, say n measurements. For purposes of illustration, we will take a population that contains a very small number of measurements, say $N = 4$, the 4 measurements being 1, 2, 3, and 4. We will further assume that we wish to select a random sample of $n = 2$ from the 4. How many different and distinct samples could we select? The 6 possible samples are listed in table 4.5. A sample of $n = 2$ measurements taken from the population of $N = 4$ measurements would be a random sample only if each of the 6 different samples listed in table 4.5 had an equal chance of being selected.

Table 4.5 • Six possible samples from a population of four measurements

Possible Samples	Measurements in Sample
1	1, 2
2	1, 3
3	1, 4
4	2, 3
5	2, 4
6	3, 4

Definition 4.7

A **random sample of n measurements** from a population is one in which every different sample of size n in the population has an equal probability of being selected.

It is unlikely that we would ever be confronted with measurements that can be sampled in a perfectly random manner. But practical random sampling can be achieved by thoroughly mixing the measurements prior to the selection. (For example, card shuffling is an attempt to distribute a random sample of cards to each player.) Populations are often conceptual in nature, and it is impossible to "mix" the measurements prior to sampling. For example, in measuring the heartbeat of a laboratory rat, there is no way to be certain that the sample of heartbeat readings for the rat is selected in a random manner. However, by carefully avoiding any bias in the selection of the sample measurements, the experimenter hopes to approximate random sampling.

What is the importance of random sampling? We must know how the sample was selected so that we can determine its probability. The probabilities of samples selected in a random manner can be determined, thus enabling us to make valid inferences about the population from which the sample was drawn. Nonrandom samples may have unknown probabilities associated with them and hence may be useless for purposes of statistical inferences.

SUMMARY

The objective of statistics is to make inferences about a population based on information contained in a sample. Probability is the mechanism that enables us to make inferences about the population on the basis of sample evidence. In the marital counseling example, we examined the probability distribution for y, the number of couples who indicated that the husband was responsible for seeking help in a sample of 20 couples. Using the probability of the observed sample outcome $y = 17$, we made an inference about the population of couples. The knowledge of probability enabled us to make our inference and to assess its goodness, or validity.

Most experiments in the behavioral sciences either result in numerically valued outcomes or have outcomes which are easily assigned numerical values. These values can be represented by a random variable. We discussed two types of random variables in this chapter: discrete and continuous. The only difference between the probability distributions for the two types is that we assign probabilities to intervals for continuous random variables and to individual values for a discrete random variable. Probability distributions for random variables can be derived mathematically by using the theory of probability. They also can be approximated empirically by repeating the experiment a large number of times and constructing a relative frequency histogram of the results. Each probability distribution is a model for the population relative frequency histogram, and each can be described by a mean, a standard deviation, or any of the other numerical descriptive measures discussed in chapter 2.

Numerical descriptive measures of the population are called parameters.

In future chapters we will attempt to describe populations by estimating, or making decisions about, these parameters.

In order for our inference about the population parameters to be valid, the sample must be drawn from the population in a random manner.

SUPPLEMENTARY EXERCISES

1. Consider an experiment of drawing one marble from each of two boxes, both of which contain two green and two yellow marbles. Carry out this experiment $N = 100$ times, each time noting which of the outcomes, GG, GY, YG, YY, occurs and each time replacing the marbles drawn and shaking the box before the next draw. Construct a relative frequency distribution similar to that shown in table 4.2. What is the relative frequency of the outcome "observe exactly one green marble"? Compare your results with those found for the two-coin-toss experiment described in section 4.2.

2. Refer to exercise 1. Let y denote the number of green marbles observed on a single repetition of the experiment. Construct a relative frequency histogram for y.

3. Suppose that the experiment described in exercise 1 is altered so that each box contains one green and three yellow marbles. Again, draw one marble from each of the two boxes and repeat the experiment $N = 100$ times. Construct a relative frequency distribution similar to that shown in table 4.2. What is the relative frequency of the outcome "observe exactly one green marble"?

4. Refer to exercise 3. Let y denote the number of green marbles observed on a single repetition of the experiment. Construct a relative frequency histogram for y. Compare this distribution with the distribution found in exercise 2. How do they differ?

5. Class Exercise: Have each student perform the following experiment 20 times.

Experiment Toss 5 coins and observe the number of heads.

The possible values of y, the number of heads in 5 coin tosses, are 0, 1, 2, 3, 4, 5. Each student should keep track of the number of times each outcome is observed and combine his or her results with the rest of the class to construct a table of the form shown here.

y	Frequency	Relative Frequency (Approximate Probability)	$p(y)$
0			.031
1			.156
2			.313
3			.313
4			.156
5			.031

You will note that the exact probability $p(y)$ associated with each value of y is listed in the last column of the table. Your relative frequencies computed from this procedure should be approximately the same as the exact probabilities. As mentioned previously, the degree of accuracy increases as the number of repetitions of the experiment increases.

6. Identify the following random variables as discrete or continuous.
   (a) The length of time a subject spends in Stage 1 (very light) sleep.
   (b) The number of errors a subject makes in a multiple-choice examination.
   (c) The body temperature of a laboratory rat after the administration of a drug.
7. Given the following probability distribution for the random variable y:

y	0	1	2	3
p(y)	?	$\frac{2}{10}$	$\frac{4}{10}$	$\frac{3}{10}$

   (a) Find $p(0)$.
   (b) What is the probability that y is 0 or 3?
   (c) What is the probability that y is at least 2?
8. What are the similarities and differences between the probability distributions for discrete and continuous random variables?
9. What is the importance of random sampling?

REFERENCES

Mendenhall, W. 1975. *Introduction to probability and statistics.* 4th ed. N. Scituate, Mass.: Duxbury Press. Chapter 4.

Mendenhall, W., and Ott, R. L. 1976. *Understanding statistics.* 2d ed. N. Scituate, Mass.: Duxbury Press. Chapter 4.

Mood, A. M., et al. 1974. *Introduction to the theory of statistics.* 3d ed. New York: McGraw-Hill. Chapter 1.

5 • The Binomial Probability Distribution

INTRODUCTION

In chapter 4 we discussed the role that probability plays in making inferences. We find the probability associated with a sample outcome and use that probability to make an inference about the population from which the sample was drawn. In this chapter we consider the probability distribution for a discrete random variable that is frequently encountered in behavioral experiments and in sample surveys. This distribution is called the binomial probability distribution.

We shall be concerned in this chapter with developing what is meant by a binomial probability distribution—sections 5.1 and 5.2—how it is described—section 5.3—and how its use as a model for a physical situation enables us to make inferences—sections 5.4 and 5.5.

5.1 • THE BINOMIAL EXPERIMENT

One of the most elementary and yet most useful discrete random variables is associated with a coin-tossing experiment such as that described in chapter 4. In an abstract sense, numerous coin-tossing experiments of practical importance are conducted daily in the behavioral sciences.

To illustrate, consider the marriage counseling example of chapter 4. There, a simple experiment consisted in asking a single couple whether the husband or the wife first sought counseling. Recording a single couple's response bears a similarity, in many respects, to tossing a single coin and recording the result as either a head—"wife"—or a tail—"husband." Likewise, a series of such observations on a number of couples is similar to the repeated tossing of a coin, so that noting the number of couples in which the wife first sought assistance is similar to noting the number of heads in a series of tosses.

Other examples may be readily found. Answering a multiple-choice test item is similar to a coin-tossing experiment if a correct response and an incorrect response are regarded as a head and a tail, respectively. A new drug will prove either effective or ineffective when administered to a single patient; a single message relay may result in a change in content or no change; and an experimental subject may either choose a synonym or not choose a synonym in response to a given word stimulus.

Although dissimilar in some respects, the experiments described above all often exhibit, to a reasonable degree of approximation, the characteristics of a *binomial experiment.*

Definition 5.1

A binomial experiment is one that possesses the following properties.

1. The experiment consists of n identical trials.
2. Each trial results in one of two outcomes. For lack of a better nomenclature, we will call one outcome a success, S, and the other a failure, F.
3. The probability of success on a single trial, p, remains the same from trial to trial. The probability of a failure is $(1 - p) = q$.
4. The trials are independent; that is, the outcome of one trial does not influence the outcome of any other trial.
5. We are interested in y, the number of successes observed during the n trials.

Very few real life situations will perfectly satisfy these requirements, but this is of little consequence as long as the lack of agreement is moderate and does not affect the end result. For instance, the probability of drawing a patient for whom a particular drug will be effective remains approximately constant from trial to trial as long as the population of patients is relatively large in comparison with the sample. If the drug is effective for 50 percent of a population of 1000 patients, the probability that the first patient drawn is one for whom the drug is effective will be $\frac{1}{2}$. For the second patient drawn, the probability will be $\frac{499}{999}$ or $\frac{500}{999}$, depending upon whether the outcome of the first draw was "effective" or "ineffective." Both numbers are near $\frac{1}{2}$, for all practical purposes, and would continue to be so for the third, fourth, and succeeding trials as long as the number of trials is not too large in comparison with the population. Thus we can regard the trials as being independent.

On the other hand, suppose that the number of patients in the population is 10 and that the drug is effective for 50 percent of the population. Then the probability that the drug is effective for the first patient drawn is $\frac{1}{2}$. The probability that the drug is effective on the second trial will be $\frac{4}{9}$ or $\frac{5}{9}$, depending upon whether the outcome of the first draw was "effective" or "ineffective." That is, for small populations, the probability of obtaining the "effective" outcome will vary appreciably from trial to trial. Thus the trials are dependent, and the resulting experiment will not be a binomial experiment.

"You mean you're going to test it on a guinea pig <u>now</u>?"
(Cartoon by S. Hams, *Changing Times*.)

5.2 • THE BINOMIAL PROBABILITY DISTRIBUTION

Having defined the binomial experiment, we now present the probability distribution for the random variable y, the number of successes observed in n trials. Although proof is omitted, the probability distribution for y is given by the formula shown in the box.

Binomial Probability Distribution

$$p(y) = \frac{n!}{y! \, (n-y)!} \, p^y q^{n-y}$$

where y may take the values 0, 1, 2, 3, . . . , n.

The notation "!" is called *factorial notation,* where n!, called "n factorial," is equal to $n(n - 1)(n - 2) \cdots (2)(1)$, and 0! is defined to be 1. [Thus $5! = (5)(4)(3)(2)(1)$.] Readers interested in the derivation of the binomial probability distribution should consult the references at the end of the chapter.

Returning to the marital counseling example, let us assume that the probability of drawing a "wife responsible" couple is $p = \frac{1}{2}$. Then the probability of drawing $y = 2$ "wife responsible" couples in a sample of $n = 3$ is

$$p(2) = \frac{3!}{2!\,(3 - 2)!} \left(\frac{1}{2}\right)^2 \cdot \left(\frac{1}{2}\right)^1$$

$$= \frac{3 \cdot 2 \cdot 1}{(2 \cdot 1)(1)} \left(\frac{1}{4}\right) \cdot \left(\frac{1}{2}\right) = 3 \cdot \left(\frac{1}{8}\right) = \frac{3}{8}$$

Similarly, the probability of drawing $y = 3$ "wife responsible" couples in a sample of $n = 3$ is

$$p(3) = \frac{3!}{3!\,0!} \left(\frac{1}{2}\right)^3 \cdot \left(\frac{1}{2}\right)^0 = \frac{1}{8}$$

(Recall that $a^0 = 1$ for any a.) We could also calculate $p(0) = \frac{1}{8}$ and $p(1) = \frac{3}{8}$ to obtain the complete probability distribution, shown in figure 5.1.

Figure 5.1 • Binomial probability distribution for $n = 3$ and $p = \frac{1}{2}$

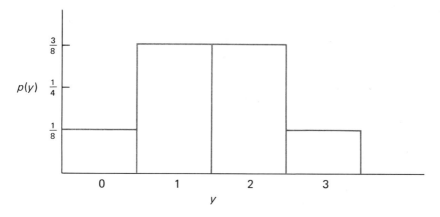

Although knowledge of the following is not essential for use of the formula for $p(y)$, you may wonder where statisticians obtained the term "binomial probability distribution." It comes from the fact that $p(0), p(1), \ldots, p(n)$ are terms of the *binomial expansion*

$$(q + p)^n \qquad \text{where} \qquad q = 1 - p$$

(A binomial is an algebraic expression consisting of two terms. For our example, q and p are the two terms.) For example, for $n = 3$,

$$p(0) = \frac{3!}{0! \, 3!} \, p^0 q^3 = q^3$$

$$p(1) = \frac{3!}{1! \, 2!} \, p^1 q^2 = 3pq^2$$

$$p(2) = \frac{3!}{2! \, 1!} \, p^2 q^1 = 3p^2 q$$

$$p(3) = \frac{3!}{3! \, 0!} \, p^3 q^0 = p^3$$

Now, by noting that

$$(q + p)^3 = q^3 + 3pq^2 + 3p^2 q + p^3$$

we see that the terms of $(q + p)^3$ are the values of $p(y)$ for $n = 3$. This result holds in general, so the expansion of $(q + p)^n$ gives the values of $p(y)$ for a given number of trials n.

As may be anticipated, the computations involved in generating the probability distribution for the binomial experiment can become quite tedious if n is very large, even when the preceding general formula is used. For this reason you may find it helpful to refer to table 1 in appendix II, which gives the cumulative binomial probabilities for $n = 5, 10, 15, 20, 25$ and for p, the probability of success on a single trial, equal to .01, .05, .10, .20, . . . , .90, .95, .99. Thus the tabulated quantities are the probability sums

$$\sum_{y=0}^{a} p(y)$$

rather than the probabilities $p(y)$.

To illustrate the use of the binomial probability distribution and the table, we will consider several examples.

Example 5.1

In the marital counseling example, the experiment consisted of randomly sampling 20 couples' responses and recording y, the number of wives who first sought counseling assistance.

(a) What is the probability that 5 or fewer of the 20 wives first sought assistance?

(b) What is the probability that *exactly* 5 couples are "wife responsible"?

Solution: We can think of the sampling of the 20 couples' responses as $n = 20$ trials, each of which results in one of two outcomes: "wife responsible" or "husband responsible." If the population (all the couples seeking marriage counseling) is sufficiently large so that the trials can be considered independent, then the experiment or survey can be considered a binomial experiment.

(a) Assuming that the fraction of "wife responsible" couples in the population is $p = \frac{1}{2}$, we have

$$P(5 \text{ or fewer}) = p(0) + p(1) + p(2) + p(3) + p(4) + p(5)$$

Each of the six terms on the right-hand side can be computed using the formula for the binomial probability distribution with $n = 20$ and $p = \frac{1}{2}$. However, from table 1(d) in appendix II, we find the entry for $p = .5$ and $a = 5$. (See figure 5.2 for a partial reproduction of this table). The letter a in the table represents the largest y-value to be included in the summation of the probabilities.

Figure 5.2 • Table 1(d) of appendix II and the probability distribution for $p = .5$

(d) $n = 20$

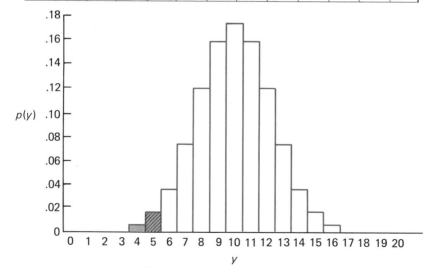

a	0.01	0.05	0.10	0.20	0.30	0.40	0.50	0.60	0.70	0.80	0.90	0.95	0.99	a
0	.818	.358	.122	.002	.001	.000	.000	.000	.000	.000	.000	.000	.000	0
1	.983	.736	.392	.069	.008	.001	.000	.000	.000	.000	.000	.000	.000	1
2	.999	.925	.677	.206	.035	.004	.000	.000	.000	.000	.000	.000	.000	2
3	1.000	.984	.867	.411	.107	.016	.001	.000	.000	.000	.000	.000	.000	3
4	1.000	.997	.957	.630	.238	.051	.006	.000	.000	.000	.000	.000	.000	4
5	1.000	1.000	.989	.804	.416	.126	.021	.002	.000	.000	.000	.000	.000	5
6	1.000	1.000	.998	.913	.608	.250	.058	.006	.000	.000	.000	.000	.000	6
7	1.000	1.000	1.000	.968	.772	.416	.132	.021	.001	.000	.000	.000	.000	7
8	1.000	1.000	1.000	.990	.887	.596	.252	.057	.005	.000	.000	.000	.000	8

The entry for $p = .5$ and $a = 5$ is

$$P(5 \text{ or fewer}) = \sum_{y=0}^{5} p(y) = .021$$

This is shown as the shaded area in the probability histogram in figure 5.2. Thus if $p = \frac{1}{2}$, the probability of observing 5 or fewer "wife responsible" couples in a sample of 20 couples is only about 2 in 100.

(b) To determine the probability that *exactly* 5 couples are "wife responsible," we again make the assumption that $p = \frac{1}{2}$. We can use the binomial probability distribution to calculate

$$p(5) = \frac{20!}{5! (20 - 5)!} \left(\frac{1}{2}\right)^5 \left(\frac{1}{2}\right)^{20-5}$$

However, the calculation is tedious, so we again make use of table 1(d). Note that we want to include only the crosshatched area of figure 5.2. This can be obtained by subtraction

$$p(5) = p(y \le 5) - p(y \le 4)$$

$$= \sum_{y=0}^{5} p(y) - \sum_{y=0}^{4} p(y)$$

The last two summations are entries in the table at $a = 5$ and $a = 4$, respectively, for $p = .5$. Thus

$$p(5) = .021 - .006 = .015$$

The numerical values for the entire probability distribution of this experiment can be obtained in the way shown in example 5.1. These values are displayed in table 5.1. You can check your understanding of the binomial tables in appendix II by verifying several of the probabilities found in table 5.1.

Example 5.2

Numerous replications of a "rumor transmission" study indicate that a given message undergoes content change in a single relay with a probability equal to .2. Suppose four relays occur.

(a) What is the probability that exactly two relays result in a content change?

(b) What is the probability that no more than two relays result in a content change?

(c) What is the probability that none of the relays results in a content change?

Solution: We can think of the relays as trials, each of which results in two outcomes: "change in content" or "no change in content." Assume that the trials are independent and that p remains constant from trial to trial. We may think of y, the number of content changes, as having a binomial probability distribution with $p = .2$ and $n = 4$. Thus

Table 5.1 • Probability distribution for y,
the number of couples in which
the wife seeks marital
counseling; $n = 20$, $p = \frac{1}{2}$

y	p(y)
0	.000
1	.000
2	.000
3	.001
4	.005
5	.015
6	.037
7	.074
8	.120
9	.160
10	.176
11	.160
12	.120
13	.074
14	.037
15	.015
16	.005
17	.001
18	.000
19	.000
20	.000

$$\sum_{y=0}^{20} p(y) = (.5 + .5)^{20} = 1$$

$$p(y) = \frac{4!}{y! \, (4 - y)!} \, (.2)^y (.8)^{4-y}$$

(a) The probability that exactly two relays (trials) result in a content change is

$$p(2) = \frac{4!}{2! \, 2!} (.2)^2 (.8)^2 = \frac{4 \cdot 3 \cdot 2 \cdot 1}{(2 \cdot 1)(2 \cdot 1)} (.04)(.64)$$

$$= 6(.04)(.64) = .1536$$

(b) The probability that no more than two relays result in a content change is

$$P(\text{no more than 2}) = p(0) + p(1) + p(2) = 1 - p(3) - p(4)$$

$$= 1 - \frac{4!}{3! \, 1!} (.2)^3 (.8) - \frac{4!}{4! \, 0!} (.2)^4 (.8)^0$$

$$= 1 - \frac{4 \cdot 3 \cdot 2 \cdot 1}{(3 \cdot 2 \cdot 1)(1)}(.008)(.8)$$

$$- \frac{4 \cdot 3 \cdot 2 \cdot 1}{(4 \cdot 3 \cdot 2 \cdot 1)(1)}(.0016)(1)$$

$$= 1 - .0256 - .0016 = .9728$$

(c) The probability that none of the relays results in a content change is

$$p(0) = \frac{4!}{0! \, 4!}(.2)^0(.8)^4 = .4096$$

Note that these probabilities would be incorrect if a content change on one relay altered the probability of a subsequent content change. In that case, the trials would be dependent and p would not be constant from trial to trial.

Example 5.3

"Standardization group" refers generally to a sample of subjects who are used to provide preliminary data on some measure, such as a scale or test, so that norms of performance can be established. Suppose a complex problem is constructed so that only 5 percent of the standardization group reaches the solution. The problem is to be used to evaluate the effectiveness of a program designed to promote creative thinking. The program is to be judged favorable if 2 or more in a group of 10 trainees solve the problem. If, in fact, the trainees are no more creative than the standardization group, what is the probability that the program will be judged favorably? Unfavorably?

Solution: The experiment possesses the characteristics of a binomial distribution, where the $n = 10$ trainees are trials and the number of successes y equals the number of trainees who solve the problem. If we assume that the trainees are no more creative than the standardization group, the probability of success p is .05, since the problem is designed so that only 5 percent of the standardization group can solve it. Thus

$$p(y) = \frac{10!}{y! \, (10 - y)!}(.05)^y(.95)^{10-y}$$

Now an *unfavorable* judgment of the program will be made if less than 2 trainees solve the problem, that is, if $y = 0$ or 1. Therefore,

$$P(\text{unfavorable judgment}) = p(0) + p(1)$$

$$= \frac{10!}{0! \, 10!}(.05)^0(.95)^{10} + \frac{10!}{1! \, 9!}(.05)^1(.95)^9$$

Rather than calculating these probabilities, we use table 1(b). The entry under $p = .05$ at $a = 1$ is

$$P(\text{unfavorable judgment}) = p(0) + p(1) = .914$$

The probability of mistakenly judging the program favorably is the probability that 2 or more trainees solve the problem when in fact each trainee has only a 5 percent chance of solving it. That is,

$$P(\text{favorable judgment}) = P(y = 2, 3, \ldots, 10)$$

We may calculate this by noting that

$$P(\text{favorable judgment}) = 1 - P(\text{unfavorable judgment})$$

$$= 1 - .914 = .086$$

Example 5.4

In a maze-running study, each rat of a given strain is run twice in a T-maze. The result of the two runs is recorded as either "repeat" or "alternate," depending on whether the animal chooses the same arm on both runs or an alternate arm on the second run. Suppose that 8 out of 10 animals make the same choice on both runs. If, in fact, the probability of the "repeat" category is .5, what is the probability of obtaining 8 or more repeaters?

In a maze-running study, each rat is run through the maze twice to see whether the animal chooses the same path in both runs or different paths. Would this study fit the definition of a binomial experiment? (Photo courtesy of Monkmeyer Press Photo Service.)

Solution: This experiment exhibits the characteristics of a binomial experiment, with the $n = 10$ rats representing the trials, and y being the number of "repeaters." If the choice of arms is random on each run, the probability a rat "repeats" is .5. Then

$$p(y) = \frac{10!}{y! \, (10 - y)!} (.5)^{y} (.5)^{10-y}$$

and

$$P(8 \text{ or more}) = p(8) + p(9) + p(10)$$

$$= \frac{10!}{8! \ 2!}(.5)^{10} + \frac{10!}{9! \ 1!}(.5)^{10} + \frac{10!}{10! \ 0!}(.5)^{10}$$

Again, rather than calculate this quantity, we prefer to use table 1(b). The probability is the shaded area in figure 5.3, which is not directly obtainable from table 1(b). However, the unshaded area is the table entry under $p = .5$ at $a = 7$, that is,

$$P(7 \text{ or less}) = .945$$

Since the total area in the probability histogram must equal 1, we find the shaded area by subtracting the unshaded area from 1. Then

$$P(8 \text{ or more}) = 1 - P(7 \text{ or less}) = 1 - .945 = .055$$

Figure 5.3 • Probability of obtaining 8 or more "repeaters" in the maze-running study

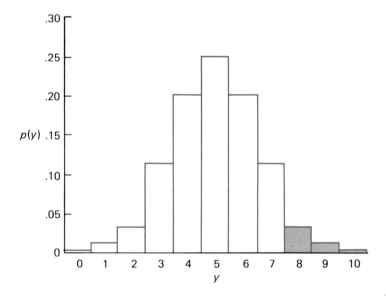

If this event were to occur, that is, if 8 or more rats were "repeaters," could we infer that the choice of arms is nonrandom (i.e., $p > .5$)? Since such an event occurs rarely (only about 55 times in 1000) under the random choice assumption, the sample evidence indicates a nonrandom choice of arms in the T-maze.

Examples 5.1, 5.2, 5.3, and 5.4 illustrate the use of the binomial probability distribution in calculating the probability associated with values of y, the number of successes in n trials defined for the binomial experiment. We note that the probability distribution

$$p(y) = \frac{n!}{y!(n-y)!} p^y q^{n-y}$$

provides a simple formula for calculating the probabilities of numerical events y, applicable to a broad class of experiments that occur in everyday life. This statement must be accompanied by a word of caution. The important point, of course, is that each physical application must be carefully checked against the defining characteristics of the binomial experiment, section 5.1, to determine whether the binomial experiment is a valid model for the application of interest.

EXERCISES

1. List the five identifying characteristics of the binomial experiment.
2. The probability of the attainment of a goal is important in theories on motivation (for example, Atkinson 1964) since it is a factor that is used to assess a subject's need or desire to attain the goal. Assume that the probability of attainment of a goal is .4, and that four subjects try to attain the goal. Let y be the number who attain the goal.
   (a) Construct a graph of $p(y)$ similar to figure 5.3.
   (b) What is the probability that none of the four will attain the goal?
   (c) What is the probability that more than one will attain the goal?
3. Researchers in the area of learning often assume that the probability of a correct response on a given trial is known (Estes 1964). In one matched pairs learning experiment, the probability of a correct response on a given trial is assumed to be .8. Suppose $n = 10$ subjects participate in a study, and let y be the number of the 10 giving a correct response. (Use table 1 in appendix II.)
   (a) What is the probability that 5 or fewer make a correct response?
   (b) More than 5?
   (c) More than 8?
   (d) Exactly 8?
4. Suppose that 5 percent of undergraduates can give advanced phenomena of hypnosis, such as visual hallucination with the eyes open (Hilgard 1965). Suppose 20 students are tested for hypnotic susceptibility. (Use table 1 in appendix II.)
   (a) What is the probability that none of the students can give advanced phenomena of hypnosis?
   (b) Three or fewer?
   (c) More than 3?

5.3 • THE MEAN AND VARIANCE FOR THE BINOMIAL RANDOM VARIABLE

Having presented the theoretical frequency distribution for the binomial random variable y, it would seem desirable to find formulas for its mean and standard deviation. Specifically, we would like to describe this theoretical distribution by using the mean and standard deviation as measures of central tendency and variation.

The population mean, the variance, and the standard deviation of a binomial random variable are given by the following formulas.

Mean, Variance, and Standard Deviation for a Binomial Random Variable

$$\mu = np$$

$$\sigma^2 = npq$$

$$\sigma = \sqrt{npq}$$

where p is the probability of success in a given trial, $q = 1 - p$, and n is the number of trials in the binomial experiment.

To give an example, we refer again to the probability distribution for the binomial experiment involving the sampling of 20 couples' responses in the marital counseling survey. This distribution is presented in table 5.1 and in histogram form in figure 5.4. For this experiment, $n = 20$ and p was assumed equal to .5. The mean value of y, the number of "wife responsible" couples, is

$$\mu = np = 20(.5) = 10$$

The mean is shown in figure 5.4.

Figure 5.4 • Mean and standard deviation of y, the number of "wife responsible" couples, when $p = .5$

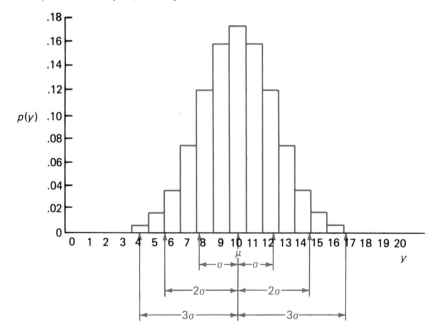

The standard deviation of y, σ, measures the spread or variability of the probability distribution. For the binomial experiment consisting of $n = 20$ trials with $p = .5$, the standard deviation of y, the number of successes or "wife responsible" couples, is

$$\sigma = \sqrt{npq} = \sqrt{20(.5)(.5)} = 2.236$$

One, two, and three standard deviations from μ are shown on figure 5.4.

Example 5.5

Refer to the marital counseling probability distribution in figure 5.4. Verify that the Empirical Rule gives reasonable approximations for the fraction of measurements in the intervals $(\mu \pm \sigma)$, $(\mu \pm 2\sigma)$, and $(\mu \pm 3\sigma)$.

Solution: We first calculate

$$(\mu \pm \sigma) = (10 \pm 2.236) = (7.764, 12.236)$$

Then we determine the fraction of the probability distribution in this interval by using table 1(d) in the appendix and finding

$$p(8) + p(9) + p(10) + p(11) + p(12) = P(y \le 12) - P(y \le 7)$$
$$= .868 - .132 = .736$$

The Empirical Rule approximation for this interval is .68.
Similarly,

$$\mu \pm 2\sigma = 10 \pm (2)(2.236) = (5.528, 14.472)$$

The fraction of measurements in this interval is

$$\sum_{y=6}^{14} p(y) = P(y \le 14) - P(y \le 5) = .958$$

The Empirical Rule approximation is .95.
Finally,

$$\mu \pm 3\sigma = 10 \pm 3(2.236) = (3.292, 16.708)$$

The fraction of measurements in this interval is

$$\sum_{y=4}^{16} p(y) = .998$$

The Empirical Rule states that all or almost all of the measurements will fall in this interval.

It is not surprising that the Empirical Rule approximations are rather good, since figure 5.4 shows that the distribution of y is mound-shaped.

EXERCISES

1. It has been estimated (Goldhammer and Marshall 1953) that one of every ten babies born will be hospitalized for mental illness at some time during his or her life. Let y be the number in a sample of 5000 babies who are eventually hospitalized for mental illness. Find the mean and standard deviation for y.
2. Refer to exercise 4 at the end of section 5.2, in which 5 percent of the undergraduates were assumed to give advanced phenomena of hypnosis. Again let y be the number of tested students who can give advanced phenomena.
   (a) If $n = 20$ students are tested, what are the mean and standard deviation of y?
   (b) If $n = 200$ students are tested, what are the mean and standard deviation of y?
3. Refer to exercise 2. Assuming that $n = 20$ students are tested, verify that the Empirical Rule does *not* give reasonable approximations for the fraction of students in the intervals $(\mu \pm \sigma)$ and $(\mu \pm 2\sigma)$. Why not?
4. In an investigation of the effect of social mobility on suicide rate, Lipset and Bendix (1959) found that 3 percent of the United States nonfarm sample was upwardly mobile (fathers were manual workers while their sons were nonmanual workers). In a sample of 600 father-son pairs, let y be the number of upwardly mobile pairs. Find the mean and variance of y.

5.4 · TEST OF A RESEARCH HYPOTHESIS

Let us now reverse a procedure followed in the earlier sections of this chapter. Up to this point we have been interested in calculating the probabilities of certain numerically valued outcomes. We assumed that we knew the composition of a dichotomous (two-class) population—or, equivalently, that we knew p, the probability of a success on a single trial of a binomial experiment. Now let us assume that we possess a single sample from the population and wish to use this sample to test an hypothesis concerning p.

The maze-running problem of example 5.4 provides an excellent illustration, since its solution can be viewed as such a statistical test. The experimenter is actually interested in stereotyped maze behavior as defined by persistence in an initial choice. He or she wishes to use the sample data as evidence for the presence of this behavior in a particular rat strain. That is, the experimenter wishes to use the sample to test the research hypothesis that the rats will exhibit stereotyped behavior. As a result of the manner of defining stereotyped behavior and the nature of the measurements, the experimenter's argument rests on a test of an hypothesis concerning p, the probability that an observation falls in the "repeat" category.

A statistical test of an hypothesis can be likened to a court trial. The research hypothesis, the hypothesis that we wish to verify, is that the defendant is guilty. (If the grand jury did not think the defendant guilty, he or she would not have been indicted.) However, the burden of proof is on the prosecution, since the court assumes the defendant is innocent until proven guilty, that is, until the prosecution presents sufficient evidence to convince the court that the research hypothesis is true. The antithesis of the research hypothesis—in this case, the defendant's innocence—is called the **null hypothesis** in statistical tests.

In the maze-running example, the experimenter plays the role of the prosecutor, trying to prove the research hypothesis that the strain's behavior is stereotyped. The experimenter hopes that the evidence contained in the sample will be sufficient to reject the null hypothesis that the strain's behavior is not stereotyped.

Definition 5.2

The **research hypothesis** (or **alternative hypothesis**) is the hypothesis that the experimenter wishes to verify. We denote the research hypothesis by the symbol H_a.

Definition 5.3

The **null hypothesis** is the antithesis of the research hypothesis. The experimenter starts with this hypothesis and hopes to use the sample data to show that the null hypothesis is false and hence that the research hypothesis is true. We denote the null hypothesis by the symbol H_0.

The evidence in a statistical test is a quantity computed from the sample measurements, called the **test statistic.** Because of the manner in which stereotyped behavior is defined and measured in the maze-running example, the number of repeaters y is an intuitively appealing test statistic. A large value of y would indicate that most rats chose the same arm of the maze both times. We would tend to reject the null hypothesis and accept the research hypothesis when presented with this evidence.

On the other hand, a small value of y would provide no support for our research hypothesis. Such evidence would not disprove our research hypothesis any more than a "not guilty" verdict disproves guilt. The implication in each case is simply that insufficient evidence has been presented to establish the truth of the research hypothesis. In the case of a court trial, double jeopardy laws prevent the prosecution from further attempts to establish the defendant's guilt. Fortunately, the research scientist is bound by no such law and may decide to collect more sample evidence in an attempt to establish the research hypothesis.

Definition 5.4

A **test statistic** is a quantity computed from the sample measurements and functions as a decision maker. Certain values of the test statistic will imply rejection of the null hypothesis and support for the research hypothesis.

Earlier we said that a large value of y would lead us to accept the research hypothesis. But how large is large? That is, how many of the 10 rats must choose the same arm in both runs before we accept the research hypothesis? In most trials by jury, all members of the jury must vote "guilty" before the research hypothesis is accepted as valid. This rigorous requirement attempts to minimize the chance of finding an innocent defendant guilty, that is, of concluding that the research hypothesis is true when in fact the null hypothesis is true. As you may have guessed, there is a similar requirement in statistics.

In statistical tests, the error that is made by concluding that the research hypothesis is true when it is really false is called a **type I error**. The probability of making such an error is denoted by α.

Definition 5.5

$\alpha = P(\text{type I error})$

$= P(\text{researcher concludes the research hypothesis is true when the null hypothesis is actually true})$

In the court case, α represents the probability that all jurors vote "guilty" when the defendant is actually innocent. We expect α to be small since all jurors must make an error in judgment before a type I error occurs. In the maze-running example, the experimenter can control the α-value by the choice of the **rejection region**, those values of y for which the null hypothesis is rejected and the research hypothesis is accepted.

Definition 5.6

The **rejection region** in a statistical test consists of those values of the test statistic that imply rejection of the null hypothesis and support for the research hypothesis.

We have reasoned that if a large number of rats choose the same path of the maze both times, we will have sufficient evidence to reject the null hypothesis that the strain's behavior is not stereotyped. Specifically, suppose we decide to reject the null hypothesis if 8 or more rats choose the same path on both runs. That is, we choose as our rejection region $y = 8, 9, 10$, as shown in figure 5.5.

Figure 5.5 • Rejection region for the maze-running study

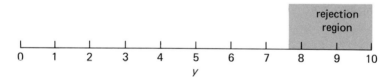

What is the value of α for this rejection region? Or, asking this question in another way, what is the probability that 8 or more of the 10 rats will choose the

same path in both runs if, in fact, the strain's behavior is not stereotyped, that is, $p = .5$? To answer this question, we must compute

$\alpha = P(\text{concluding the strain's behavior is stereotyped when it is not})$

Remember that if the null hypothesis is true, that is, the strain is *not* stereotyped, then the probability that a single rat chooses the same arm on both runs is $p = .5$. Then for the rejection region $y = 8, 9, 10$, we compute

$$\alpha = P(y = 8, 9, 10 \text{ when } p = .5)$$

$$= p(8) + p(9) + p(10) = 1 - \sum_{y=0}^{7} p(y)$$

This sum can be found in table 1(b), appendix II, for $p = .5$ and $a = 7$. Then

$$\alpha = 1 - .945 = .055$$

This is the shaded area shown in figure 5.6(a).

The implication of this α-value is that if the strain's behavior *is not* stereotyped, and thus $p = .5$, we would expect to see a y-value of 8, 9, or 10 about five times out of one hundred. Thus we would make the incorrect decision that the behavior *is* stereotyped about five times in one hundred.

You may well wonder why we do not choose rejection regions which have zero or near zero α-values so that we may be almost sure that we won't incorrectly accept our research hypothesis. In the maze-running example we could have chosen a smaller rejection region, say $y = 9, 10$. Then we would have an α-value given by

$$\alpha = P(\text{test statistic falls in the rejection}$$
$$\text{region when the null hypothesis is true})$$

$$= P(y = 9, 10 \text{ when } p = .5)$$

$$= 1 - \sum_{y=0}^{8} p(y) = 1 - .989 = .011$$

This α-value is shown in figure 5.6(b).

We could even specify a smaller rejection region, say $y = 10$. The value of α would be further reduced, since now

$$\alpha = P(y = 10 \text{ when } p = .5)$$

$$= 1 - \sum_{y=0}^{9} p(y) = 1 - .999 = .001$$

This α-value is shown in figure 5.6(c).

Surely it must be better to infer the truth of the research hypothesis incorrectly one in a thousand times ($\alpha = .001$) than one in twenty times ($\alpha = .05$).

Figure 5.6 • α-values for various rejection regions in the maze-running study

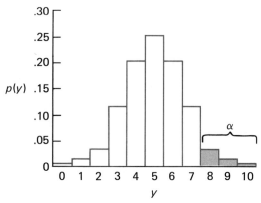

(a) Rejection region: y = 8, 9, 10

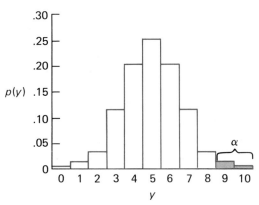

(b) Rejection region: y = 9, 10

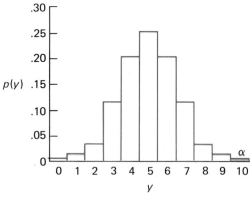

(c) Rejection region: y = 10

However, we have omitted one important consideration from our previous discussion. If the research hypothesis is actually true, we want the probability that our experiment leads to its acceptance to be as near 1 as possible. The probability that our test leads to an acceptance of a true research hypothesis is called the *power* of the test. We want to choose a rejection region which yields a maximum power.

Definition 5.7

The **power** of a statistical test is the probability that the test statistic assumes a value in the rejection region when the research hypothesis is true, that is, the probability that we accept the research hypothesis when it is true.

Note the distinction between α and the power of a test. The probability α is the probability of accepting the research hypothesis when it is false. The power of the test is the probability of accepting the research hypothesis when it is true.

In the maze-running example, $p = .5$ corresponds to nonstereotyped behavior (null hypothesis). Values of p exceeding .5, for example, $p = .7$, represent stereotyped behavior (research hypothesis). That is, $p = .7$ implies that 70 percent of the rats in this strain will choose the same arm in both runs. Thus the research hypothesis is true if $p = .7$. To find the power of the test when $p = .7$ and the rejection region is $y = 8, 9, 10$, we find the probability that $y = 8, 9, 10$ when $p = .7$. Denoting the power associated with this region by Power $(8, 9, 10)$, we find that

$$\text{Power}(8, 9, 10) = P(8, 9, 10 \text{ when } p = .7) = .383$$

This power is shown by the shaded area in figure 5.7(a).

Note the difference between finding the power of the test and finding the α-value. To find the α-value associated with a rejection region, we use the value of p associated with the null hypothesis, $p = .5$. To find the power associated with the same rejection region, we use a value of p associated with the research hypothesis, $p = .7$. Thus to find the α-value for a test, we use the probability associated with the null hypothesis. To find the power for a test, we use a probability associated with the research hypothesis.

To find the power of the test when $p = .7$ and the rejection region is $y = 10$, we find the probability that $y = 10$ when $p = .7$,

$$\text{Power}(10) = P(10 \text{ when } p = .7) = .028$$

This power is shown by the shaded area in figure 5.7(b).

The implication of the value of the power is that we would correctly identify the $p = .7$ stereotyped behavior only about three times in one hundred using $y = 10$ as our rejection region. We would correctly accept the research hypothesis about four times in ten using $y = 8, 9, 10$ as the rejection region. The larger rejection region will always have the greater power.

Figure 5.7 • Powers for different rejection regions in the maze-running study, $p = .7$

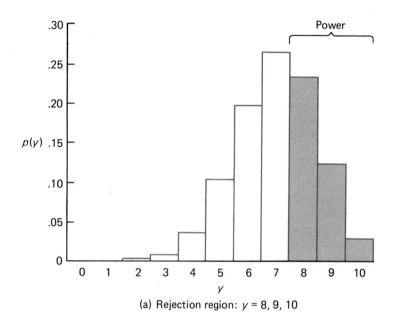

(a) Rejection region: $y = 8, 9, 10$

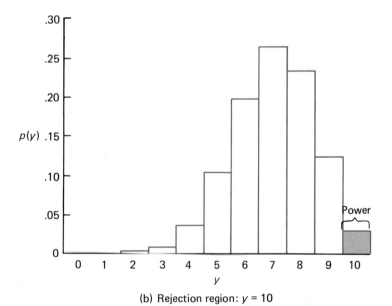

(b) Rejection region: $y = 10$

Remember that the power of the test not only depends upon the size of the rejection region but also depends upon p. We stated that values of p larger than $p = .5$ imply that the research hypothesis is true. The larger the value of p, the greater the degree of stereotyped behavior. Therefore, we could calculate the power of the test to detect any value of p larger than .5. We illustrated the calculations only for $p = .7$.

Our objective, then, is to choose a rejection region with balance. On the one hand we want a value of α which is small enough to make us reasonably sure we will not be accepting a high percentage of incorrect research hypotheses. On the other hand we want a rejection region which is large enough to make us reasonably sure it contains our test statistic when our research hypothesis is true. In other words, we want to choose a rejection region whose probability of a type I error is small, but not so small that the power of the test is very low. Typical α-values chosen for experiments are .01, .05, and .10. The value of α chosen for a particular test depends on the nature of the experiment and the personal philosophy of the experimenter.

Key Quantities in Testing Research Hypotheses

$\alpha = P(\text{type I error})$

$\quad = P(\text{accepting the research hypothesis when it is false})$

$\text{Power} = P(\text{accepting the research hypothesis when it is true})$

Assume the researcher now performs the experiment with $n = 10$ rats. The researcher observes a value of y, the number of rats who choose the same arm of the T-maze both times, in the $\alpha = .055$ rejection region, $y = 8, 9, 10$. The conclusion made is to accept the research hypothesis of stereotyped behavior. This decision is consistent with the rare event philosophy introduced in section 2.9. If a y-value of 8, 9, or 10 is observed, the experimenter knows that one of two things is true: either the null hypothesis is true and a rare event (probability $= .055$) has occurred, or the research hypothesis is true.

A statement which may help clarify the rare event philosophy is the following: If a researcher conducts all the statistical tests with rejection regions having $\alpha = .05$, he or she will falsely reject only 5 percent of all true null hypotheses.

What happens if the maze-running experiment results in a y-value less than 8? Since our test statistic is not in the rejection region, the conclusion is that this particular experiment did not establish the truth of the research hypothesis when conducted at a .055 α-level. If the experimenter still believes that the strain's behavior is stereotyped, he or she will have to conduct additional experiments to statistically validate this hypothesis.

Example 5.6

An experiment is to be conducted to show that an acclaimed psychic has extrasensory perception (ESP). A referee will thoroughly shuffle five different cards and then choose one at random. The psychic will then try to identify which card was drawn without seeing it. This experiment is to be repeated 20 times, and then the number of correct decisions y is to be computed. (The psychic will not be told whether his decision was right or wrong after each trial.) The experimenters agree to accept the psychic's claim of ESP if he is correct on 9 or more trials, that is, if $y = 9, 10, 11, \ldots, 20$.

(a) Set up the statistical test of an hypothesis by stating the null hypothesis H_0, the research hypothesis H_a, the test statistic, and the rejection region.

(b) Calculate α for the test.

(c) Suppose the experiment is conducted using the rejection region $y = 9, 10, 11, \ldots, 20$. Assume that the psychic makes 7 correct decisions in 20 trials, that is, $y = 7$. What could be concluded?

Solution: (a) Since the psychic receives no feedback after each trial, it is reasonable to assume that the experimental trials are independent and that his probability of success will remain the same from trial to trial. We thus have a binomial experiment with $n = 20$ and an unknown p.

Now, if the psychic has no ESP and is guessing on each trial, the probability of guessing correctly is one in five, or $p = .2$. His claim of possessing ESP (the research hypothesis) may be stated like this: p, his probability of making a correct decision on each trial, exceeds .2.

Note that a p-value less than .2 has no realistic meaning in this experiment, since such a value would imply that his decisions were somehow worse than guesses. We therefore will only reject the null hypothesis when an unusually large value of y is observed. In this case, the term "unusually large" has been agreed upon to mean any y-value *greater than* 8.

When a rejection region consists *only* of large or small values, we refer to the test as a *one-tailed test* of an hypothesis. That is, we reject the null hypothesis only when the test statistic assumes a value in one extreme, or one tail, of its range.

The one-tailed test is constructed as follows.

Null hypothesis H_0: The psychic is guessing; that is, $p = .2$.

Research hypothesis H_a: The psychic has ESP; that is, $p > .2$.

Test statistic: y = number of correct decisions in 20 trials.

Rejection region: $y = 9, 10, 11, \ldots, 20$.

The one-tailed rejection region is shown in figure 5.8.

Figure 5.8 • Rejection region for the ESP experiment

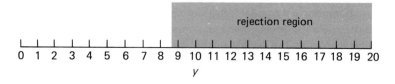

(b) We calculate the α-value for this test as follows:

$\alpha = P(\text{type I error})$

= P(accepting the research hypothesis when

the null hypothesis is true)

For our rejection region,

$$\alpha = P(y = 9, 10, 11, \ldots, 20 \text{ when } p = .2)$$

We can use the binomial probability formula to find this probability, or we can use table 1(d) in appendix II. First, note that

$$\alpha = 1 - P(y = 0, 1, \ldots, 8 \text{ when } p = .2)$$

This latter probability is the entry in table 1(d) at $a = 8$ and $p = .2$, so

$$\alpha = 1 - .990 = .01$$

This α-value is shown by the shaded area in figure 5.9.

Figure 5.9 • α-value for the ESP experiment of example 5.6

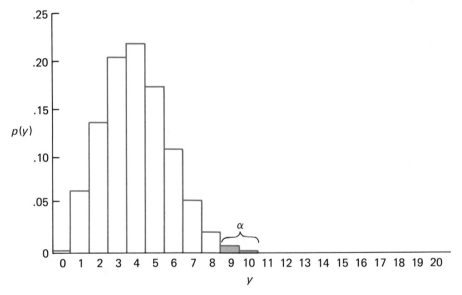

The implication of this α-value is that if the psychic possesses no ESP and is guessing, his chance of correctly guessing on nine or more trials is $\frac{1}{100}$. Or, stated another way, the chance that the experimenters will accept the psychic's claim of ESP when he is, in fact, only guessing is one in one hundred.

If the experimenters were willing to accept a greater risk of making a type I error, they could enlarge the rejection region, thereby increasing α. For example, you can check that if the rejection region were $y = 7, 8, 9, \ldots, 20$, then α would equal .087. By enlarging the rejection region, we have increased the chances of a guesser convincing us he possesses ESP. A guesser will get 7 or more correct responses about nine times in one hundred. However, if the psychic really does possess ESP, that is, $p > .2$, we are more likely to accept the research hypothesis if we are using the larger rejection region, $y = 7, 8, 9, \ldots, 20$. That is, the power of the test is greater for the rejection region $y = 7, 8, \ldots, 20$ than it is for the rejection region $y = 9, 10, \ldots, 20$.

For example, if $p = .5$, the psychic has a 50-50 chance of making the correct decision on each try, much better than if he were guessing ($p = .2$). You can check that the probability of rejecting the null hypothesis that $p = .2$ when, in fact, $p = .5$ is .942 for the rejection region $y = 7, 8, \ldots, 20$. That is, Power $(7, 8, \ldots, 20) = .942$. The chance of making the correct decision for the smaller rejection region, $y = 9, 10, \ldots, 20$, is only .748. These powers are shown in figures 5.10(a) and 5.10(b), respectively.

(c) If we use the rejection region $y = 9, 10, \ldots, 20$, conduct the experiment, and find that the psychic makes 7 correct decisions in 20 trials, then the test statistic y does not fall in the rejection region. We can conclude that this experiment did not establish the psychic's claim of possessing ESP at the .01 α-level. Note that this result does not *force* us to accept the null hypothesis and say that the psychic is only guessing. Our test was constructed to place the burden of proof on the psychic, and the sample evidence did not support his claim.

Note that if we had used the larger rejection region of $y = 7, 8, 9, \ldots, 20$, the result of the experiment would have caused us to accept the psychic's claim of possessing ESP at the .087 α-level. The fact that we would decide to accept the research hypothesis in this case does not contradict our decision not to accept it using the smaller rejection region. The example simply reflects the fact that the use of the larger rejection region will result in an acceptance of the research hypothesis more often than the use of the smaller one will. This happens both when the null hypothesis is true—thus leading to a type I error—and when the research hypothesis is true—thus leading to a correct decision.

If we wish to resolve the question of which hypothesis is true, we must determine the true probability of a correct decision being made by the psychic. To do this, we could use the relative frequency estimate of probability introduced in section 4.1. We could conduct a very large number of trials and use the approximation

$$p \approx \frac{\text{number of correct decisions}}{\text{number of trials}}$$

Example 5.7

Two therapists, A and B, have been trained at the same university, at the same time, and by the same instructors. From tape recordings of actual therapy sessions, 20 trained observers independently rate the two therapists on a 10-point "empathy" scale, and the number y of observers rating B higher than A is recorded. We wish to test the research hypothesis that the observers will rate the therapists differently with regard to their "empathy," in spite of the therapists similar backgrounds.

Suppose we let p be the probability that an observer rates B higher than A

Figure 5.10 • Powers for the ESP experiment in example 5.6 when $p = .5$

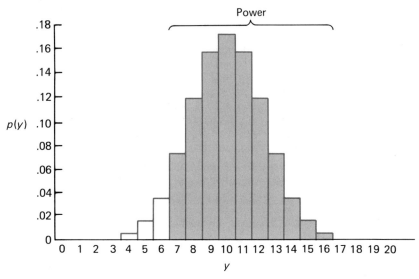

(a) Rejection region: $y = 7, 8, \ldots, 20$

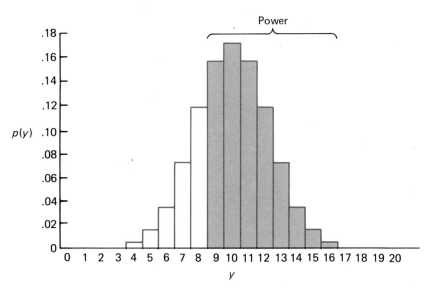

(b) Rejection region: $y = 9, 10, \ldots, 20$

on the "empathy" scale. Then our research hypothesis implies that p is different from $\frac{1}{2}$. This follows from the fact that if the empathy of the therapists seems identical to the observers, there should be a 50-50 chance ($p = \frac{1}{2}$) of B receiving the higher rating.

The rejection region for this test should consist of both unusually small and unusually large values of y, since we wish to detect departures from $p = \frac{1}{2}$ in either direction. That is, we are interested in $p < \frac{1}{2}$ or $p > \frac{1}{2}$. If $p < \frac{1}{2}$, indicating A has a greater chance of receiving a high "empathy" rating than does B, we expect to see small y-values. If $p > \frac{1}{2}$, we expect to see large values of y, since $p > \frac{1}{2}$ indicates that B is likely to be rated higher than A.

A test which has a rejection region consisting of both small and large values of the test statistic is called a *two-tailed test*. Suppose that in this example we decide to reject the null hypothesis when $y = 0, 1, 2, 3, 4, 5, 15, 16, 17, 18, 19, 20$. Note that we have included y-values in both extremes, or both tails, of the range of y.

(a) Set up the statistical test by stating the null hypothesis H_0, the research hypothesis H_a, the test statistic, and the rejection region.
(b) Calculate α for the two-tailed test in part (a).
(c) Suppose the experiment is performed, and 3 of the 20 observers rank B higher than A on the "empathy" scale. What could we conclude?

Solution: (a) We set up the statistical test as follows.

Null hypothesis H_0: Observers rate the therapists the same on "empathy"; that is, $p = .5$.

Research hypothesis H_a: The observers rate the therapists differently on "empathy"; that is, $p \neq .5$, or p is either greater than or less than .5.

Test statistic: $y = $ the number of observers who rate B higher than A on the 10-point "empathy" scale.

Rejection region: $y = 0, 1, 2, 3, 4, 5, 15, 16, 17, 18, 19, 20$.

Figure 5.11 shows that the rejection region is two-tailed.

Figure 5.11 • Rejection region for the "empathy" rating experiment of example 5.7

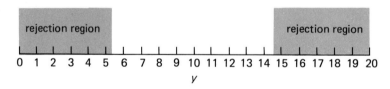

(b) Since the rejection region is two-tailed, we must compute α by calculating the probabilities of both tails, assuming the null hypothesis is true.

$\alpha = P(\text{rejecting } H_0 \text{ when } H_0 \text{ is true})$

$= P(y = 0, 1, 2, 3, 4, 5 \text{ when } p = .5)$
$\qquad + P(y = 15, 16, 17, 18, 19, 20 \text{ when } p = .5)$

We can use table 1(d) by writing

$\alpha = P(y = 0, 1, \ldots, 5 \text{ when } p = .5)$
$\qquad + [1 - P(y = 0, 1, \ldots, 14 \text{ when } p = .5)]$

Now we find the entries in table 1(d) for $a = 5$, $p = .5$, and $a = 14$, $p = .5$, respectively. Then

$$\alpha = .021 + [1 - .979] = .021 + .021 = .042$$

This α-value is shown by the shaded area in figure 5.12.

Figure 5.12 • α-value for the "empathy" rating experiment of example 5.7

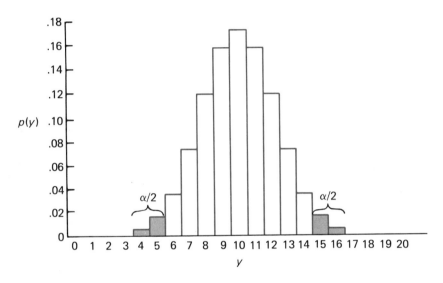

(c) Since $y = 3$, we have observed a value of the test statistic in the lower tail of the two-tailed rejection region. The sample has provided sufficient evidence to reject the null hypothesis at the $\alpha = .042$ level. We therefore infer that $p \neq .5$. More specifically, we infer that p is less than .5 (since our test statistic fell into the lower tail). We understand that it is possible for this event $(y = 3)$ to occur even when H_0 is true. But our α-value tells us this event will occur only about four times in one hundred if $p = .5$.

In making our decision to reject H_0, we should be wary of concluding that empathy will differ in *all* equally trained therapists. Or even of concluding that A exhibits more empathy than B in *all* therapy sessions. We only conclude that Therapist B is likely to receive a lower "empathy" rating than Therapist A when trained observers view the films of the two selected sessions.

EXERCISES

1. Define a type I error for a statistical test. What happens to α, the probability of a type I error, when the size of the rejection region is increased? When it is decreased? What happens to the power in each case?

2. Jordan (1933) administered an intelligence test to a sample of mill-worker's children to see how they compared with established norms. Suppose the probability p that any child scores in the "normal" intelligence range is .6. To test the research hypothesis that this probability is less than .6 for mill-worker children, we randomly sample $n = 10$ mill-worker children and administer the test. We decide to accept the research hypothesis if y, the number of the 10 who score in the "normal" range, is 0, 1, 2, or 3.
   (a) Set up the statistical test by stating the null and research hypotheses, the test statistic, and the rejection region. Is this a one-tailed or a two-tailed test?
   (b) Calculate α for this test.
   (c) Suppose the test is administered, and $y = 2$ mill-worker children score in the "normal" range. What is your conclusion?
3. Suppose you wish to test the research hypothesis that subjects' scores on a vocabulary test will tend to improve on a second administration of the test. You select a random sample of $n = 20$ subjects. You reason that if there is no effect of the first administration on the second, then the probability p that the second score is higher than the first is .5. However, if the research hypothesis is true and the first administration does tend to improve performance on the second, p will exceed .5. With this in mind, you decide to reject the null hypothesis in favor of the research hypothesis if more than 13 of the 20 subjects score higher on the second administration of the test.
   (a) Set up the statistical test by stating the null and research hypotheses, the test statistic, and the rejection region. Is this a one-tailed or a two-tailed test?
   (b) Find α for this test.
   (c) Suppose the test is conducted and $y = 12$ subjects score higher on the second administration then they did on the first. What is your conclusion?
4. Two educational films dealing with the same subject matter are shown to a random sample of 20 instructors to determine whether there is a preference. If no preference exists, the probability p that an instructor ranks Film B higher than Film A is .5. If Film B is preferred, p would exceed .5. A preference for Film A would imply that p is less than .5. It is decided to reject the hypothesis that no preference exists if y, the number of the 20 instructors who prefer Film B, is 0, 1, 2, 3, 4, 16, 17, 18, 19, 20.
   (a) Set up the statistical test by stating the null and research hypotheses, the test statistic, and the rejection region. Is this a one-tailed or a two-tailed test?
   (b) Find α for this test.
   (c) Suppose the 20 instructors are shown the two films, and 5 prefer Film B over Film A. What is your conclusion?

5.5 ● SIGNIFICANCE LEVELS

The structure developed in section 5.4 for testing a research hypothesis may be summarized as follows.

Structure of a Statistical Test

1. State the null and research hypotheses.
2. Choose a test statistic.

3. Choose a value of α and establish a one- or two-tailed rejection region, depending on the nature of the hypotheses.
4. Perform the experiment, observe the value of the test statistic, and state a conclusion based on the results of the experiment.

You probably have noted that there is a degree of rigidity inherent in step 3 above. Once the rejection region is established to agree with the chosen α, the researcher need only report whether the test statistic falls into or out of the rejection region. The conclusion follows automatically. But the selection of an α-value is primarily a matter of the researcher's personal preference or tradition. Another researcher may be critical of the decision about the research hypothesis simply because he or she disagrees with the choice of α.

The problems introduced by a rigid choice of an α-value have led to another method of reporting the results of the test of a research hypothesis. Rather than fixing an α-value prior to performing the experiment, we can simply establish the null and research hypotheses and perform the experiment. We observe the value of the test statistic and pose the following question: Assuming that the null hypothesis is true, what is the probability that we would observe a value of the test statistic *as contradictory* to the null hypothesis as that which we observed? That is, having observed the test statistic, what is the smallest value of α that would lead us to reject the null hypothesis? We call this smallest α-value the **significance level** of the observed outcome and denote its value by P.

Definition 5.8

The **significance level** P for an observed value of the test statistic is the smallest α-value that would lead to the rejection of the null hypothesis.

Example 5.8

Recall the maze-running experiment introduced in example 5.4 and discussed at length in section 5.4. We tested the null hypothesis that the strain of rats was not stereotyped against the research hypothesis that their behavior was stereotyped. In terms of the probability p that a rat of this strain will choose the same arm of a T-maze in two different runs, we tested

$$H_0: p = .5$$
$$H_a: p > .5$$

As a test statistic we used y, the number of rats who choose the same arm twice in a sample of $n = 10$ rats of the strain. What is the significance level P corresponding to the test statistic value of $y = 9$.

Solution: The first step in determining the significance level is to specify the smallest rejection region containing the observed value of the test statistic. Recall that this is a one-tailed test. We will reject the null hypothesis of unstereotyped behavior for large values of the test statistic. Therefore, the smallest rejection region containing $y = 9$ is that of $y = 9, 10$, as shown in figure 5.13.

Figure 5.13 • Smallest rejection region containing $y = 9$ for the maze-running study

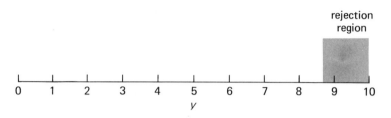

Now, the value of P is the α-value corresponding to this smallest rejection region. This value is shown by the shaded area in figure 5.14. P is calculated by using table 1(b) in appendix II:

$$P = P(y = 9, 10 \text{ when } p = .5)$$
$$= 1 - P(y = 0, 1, \ldots, 8)$$
$$= 1 - .989 = .011$$

Figure 5.14 • P-value for the smallest rejection region containing $y = 9$ in the maze-running study

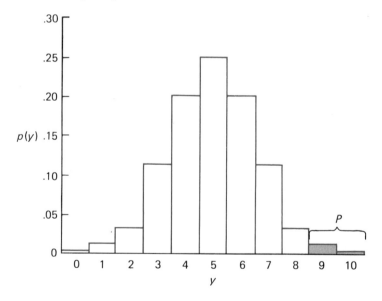

Therefore, the significance level associated with the test statistic value $y = 9$ is $P = .011$. The implication of this P-value is that any researcher who would be willing to specify an α-value greater than or equal to .011 to test the

hypothesis of unstereotyped behavior would reject this hypothesis when $y = 9$ is observed. Researchers desiring an α-value smaller than .011 would not reject the null hypothesis of unstereotyped behavior when $y = 9$ is observed.

The rejection region of $y = 8, 9, 10$ is larger than necessary in finding the significance level, since it contains the extra value $y = 8$. The region consisting of only $y = 10$ is too small, since it does not contain the value of interest, $y = 9$. You may well be asking: Why isn't the smallest rejection region simply $y = 9$, the specific value of the test statistic? The answer lies in the rare event philosophy, which says that we should reject an hypothesis when an event occurs such that the total probability of this event and *any rarer events* is small. Thus we use this philosophy and always include the specified value *and any rarer values* of the test statistic in the rejection region.

Example 5.9

Consider again example 5.6. A psychic's claim of ESP is to be tested by counting the number of correct decisions he makes in 20 trials, each trial consisting of a choice among 5 cards. We let p represent the probability of a correct choice on each trial, and we test

$$H_0: p = .2$$
$$H_a: p > .2$$

What is the significance level P corresponding to the test statistic value of $y = 7$?

Solution: Recall that we decided to reject H_0 when unusually large values of y occur. The smallest rejection region for this one-tailed test containing the value $y = 7$ is $y = 7, 8, 9, \ldots, 20$. The α-value corresponding to this rejection region [using table 1(d)] gives us the significance level:

$$P = P(y = 7, 8, 9, \ldots, 20 \text{ when } p = .2)$$
$$= 1 - P(y = 0, 1, \ldots, 6)$$
$$= 1 - .913 = .087$$

Only those willing to use an α-value of .087 or larger for testing the research hypothesis would reject the null hypothesis of no ESP upon observing $y = 7$ correct decisions in 20 trials.

Example 5.10

In example 5.7 we compared "empathy" ratings given to two therapists by $n = 20$ trained observers. We wished to test the null hypothesis that the probability of Therapist B being ranked higher than Therapist A by an observer is $\frac{1}{2}$. The research hypothesis was that there would be an "empathy" rating difference, that is, p is not equal to $\frac{1}{2}$. We set up the test

$$H_0: p = .5$$
$$H_a: p \neq .5$$

What is the significance level P for the test statistic value of $y = 3$?

Solution: The calculation of the significance level for a two-tailed test of an hypothesis is performed in three steps. First, we determine whether the test statistic value is an upper- or lower-tail value. We use all the values *in that tail* as rare as or rarer than the specified value. In our example, the value $y = 3$ is clearly in the lower tail of the distribution when the null hypothesis is true. Then the collection of values *as rare as or rarer than* $y = 3$ in the *lower tail* of the distribution when the null hypothesis is true is $y = 0, 1, 2, 3$, as shown in figure 5.15.

Figure 5.15 • P-value for $y = 3$ in the "empathy" rating experiment

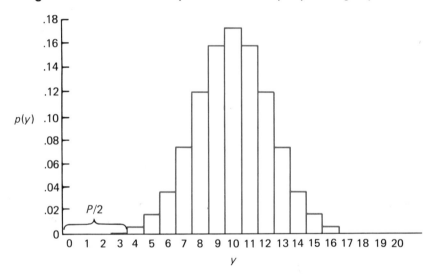

The second step in the calculation of P is to determine the probability associated with the test statistic values found in the first step. We calculate this probability assuming that the null hypothesis is true. In this example, we find, using table 1(d),

$$P(y = 0, 1, 2, 3 \text{ when } p = .5) = .001$$

The third and final step is to calculate the significance level by doubling the one-tailed probability found in the second step:

$$P = 2(.001) = .002$$

The rationale for this procedure is this: we consider rejecting the null hypothesis for rare or unusual values of the test statistic in *both tails* of the null hypothesis distribution. Thus we should calculate the significance level for two-tailed tests by calculating the probabilities for values of the test statistic in both tails which are *as rare as or rarer than* the specified test statistic value. We did this by first calculating the probability in the tail of the distribution which contains the specified test statistic value. Then we doubled that probability to compensate for equally rare events in the other tail of the distribution.

The significance level $P = .002$ corresponding to $y = 3$ indicates that anyone willing to use an α-value equal to or greater than .002 for testing the hypothesis of equal "empathy" ratings for the two therapists would reject that hypothesis upon observing $y = 3$.

Reporting the significance level with a given experimental outcome means that we do not have to make an arbitrary selection of α which must be acceptable to all. Even if we wish to conduct a test of an hypothesis at a fixed α-level, reporting the significance level lets others know more precisely the rarity of the observed outcome. Then they may make their own decisions about the research hypothesis. The steps for calculating a significance level are summarized below.

Steps for Calculating P-values

1. List all the values of the test statistic that are as rare as or rarer than the specified value in the same tail (upper or lower) of the null hypothesis distribution.
2. Calculate the probability of observing a test statistic value in the collection of values found in step 1, assuming the null hypothesis to be true. If the test is one-tailed, this probability is the P-value corresponding to the specified test statistic value.
3. If the test is two-tailed, the P-value is twice the probability calculated in step 2.

EXERCISES

1. What is the difference between testing a research hypothesis at a fixed α-level and testing a research hypothesis by reporting the significance level of the observed test statistic?
2. Refer to exercise 2 in section 5.4. We tested the null hypothesis that the probability p of mill-worker children scoring in the "normal" range of an intelligence test is .6. The research hypothesis was that p is less than .6. The test was administered to a random sample of 10 mill-worker children, with y representing the number scoring in the "normal" range.
   (a) Find the significance level P for the test statistic value of $y = 2$.
   (b) Discuss the implications of the P-value found in part (a).
3. Refer to exercise 3 in section 5.4. The null hypothesis that subjects would not tend to improve on a second administration of a vocabulary test was tested against the

research hypothesis that they would tend to improve. We let p be the probability of improvement on the second administration and tested

$$H_0: p = .5$$
$$H_a: p > .5$$

Our test statistic was y, the number of $n = 20$ subjects who improved on a second administration.

(a) Find the significance level P associated with the test statistic value of $y = 12$.

(b) Discuss the implications of the P-value found in part (a).

4. Refer to exercise 4, section 5.4. We wished to determine whether instructors had a preference for either of two educational films on the same subject. We let p represent the probability that an instructor prefers Film B to Film A. We tested the null hypothesis of no preference against the research hypothesis that a preference exists by showing the films to 20 instructors. That is, we tested

$$H_0: p = .5$$
$$H_a: p \neq .5$$

Our test statistic was the number of instructors (of $n = 20$) who prefer Film B.

(a) What is the significance level P associated with the test statistic value of $y = 5$?

(b) Discuss the implications of the P-value calculated in part (a).

SUMMARY

A wide variety of experiments conducted in the behavioral sciences satisfy, to a reasonable degree, the five defining characteristics of a binomial experiment. The single measurement of interest in such an experiment is y, the number of successes observed in n trials. The observation y is a discrete random variable with a probability distribution

$$p(y) = \frac{n!}{y! \, (n - y)!} \, p^y q^{n-y}$$

where $q = (1 - p)$ and $y = 0, 1, 2, \ldots, n$. The population mean and standard deviation for this probability distribution are

$$\mu = np \quad \text{and} \quad \sigma = \sqrt{npq}$$

In practical situations, the true value of p, the probability of success on each trial, will usually be unknown. Research hypotheses about p may be tested by performing a binomial experiment, using y as the test statistic. An hypothesis test may be performed by using a fixed α-value and a corresponding rejection region, or by reporting the significance level associated with the observed value of y.

SUPPLEMENTARY EXERCISES

1. A balanced coin is tossed three times. Let y be the number of heads observed.
   (a) Use the formula for the binomial probability distribution to calculate the probabilities associated with $y = 0, 1, 2, 3$.
   (b) Construct a probability distribution similar to figure 4.5.
   (c) Find the mean and standard deviation of y, using the formulas

$$\mu = np \quad \text{and} \quad \sigma = \sqrt{npq}$$

   (d) Using the probability distribution in part (b), find the fraction of the population measurements lying within one standard deviation of the mean. Repeat for two standard deviations. How do your results agree with the Empirical Rule?
2. Suppose that a coin is definitely unbalanced and that the probability of a head is $p = .1$. Follow instructions (a), (b), (c), and (d) of exercise 1. Note that the probability distribution loses its symmetry and becomes skewed when p is not equal to $\frac{1}{2}$.
3. Several types of mental and behavioral deficiencies have direct chromosomal and metabolic antecedents and are therefore of interest to developmental psychologists in the study of human behavior. Consider a metabolic defect that occurs in approximately 1 out of every 100 births. Suppose 4 infants are born in a particular hospital on a given day.
   (a) What is the probability that none has the defect?
   (b) What is the probability that no more than one has the defect?
4. Referring to exercise 3, what are the mean and standard deviation of y, the number of infants of every 4 who are born with the defect? Would the Empirical Rule be applicable in describing the distribution of y?
5. The Swiss psychologist Piaget has presented four stages of intellectual development. During the preoperational thought period, children gradually develop the concepts of conservation of mass, weight, and volume. It has been found that approximately 1 of every 10 children between the ages of five and six have acquired the concept of conservation of mass, as evidenced by their knowledge that the amount of a substance is not changed when only its shape is changed. In a testing situation, 10 five and six year olds are observed.
   (a) What is the probability that exactly one will make the correct choice?
   (b) What is the probability that at least one will make the correct choice?
   (c) What is the probability that at least two will make the correct choice?
6. Refer to exercise 5. Suppose a special preschool training program is designed to develop the concept of conservation of mass in very young children. It is desired to test the research hypothesis that more than one-tenth of these specially trained children will acquire this concept by age six. A random sample of 10 children are placed in this training program. Let y be the number who acquire the conservation of mass concept by age six, and let p represent the true probability that a child in this program acquires the concept of mass by age six. Suppose the researchers decide to reject the hypothesis that p equals .1 and conclude that p exceeds .1 when $y = 3, 4, 5, 6, 7, 8, 9, 10$.
   (a) Set up the statistical test by stating the null hypothesis, the research hypothesis, the test statistic, and the rejection region.
   (b) Calculate α for this test.

(c) Suppose the 10 specially trained children are tested at age six, and $y = 5$ have acquired the concept of mass. What is your conclusion?

7. Refer to exercise 6. What is the significance level associated with the observed test statistic of $y = 5$? Discuss the implications of this P-value.

8. Public opinion polling has gained much prominence in the last few years. At first it was used primarily before national elections, but now these polls are conducted to determine public opinion about a wide variety of issues.

   Suppose the people in a random sample of 400 adults are asked whether or not they favor capital punishment. Let y be the number sampled who favor capital punishment, and suppose that 50 percent of the adult population favor it.
   (a) Find μ, the mean of y.
   (b) Find σ, the standard deviation of y.
   (c) Construct the intervals $(\mu \pm \sigma)$, $(\mu \pm 2\sigma)$, and $(\mu \pm 3\sigma)$. Use the Empirical Rule to approximate the fraction of the probability distribution in each interval. Do you expect the approximations to be accurate?

9. Refer to exercise 8. Suppose a citizens' group that favors capital punishment wishes to test the research hypothesis that a majority of adults favor capital punishment. They plan to randomly sample 25 adults and to observe the number y who are in favor of capital punishment. Let p represent the true probability that an adult favors capital punishment. The group wishes to test

$$H_0: p = .5$$
$$H_a: p > .5$$

Suppose the rejection region chosen by the group is $y = 16, 17, 18, \ldots, 25$.
   (a) Calculate α for this rejection region.
   (b) Discuss the implications of choosing a rejection region with the relatively large α-value found in part (a).
   (c) Suppose the poll of 25 adults is taken, and $y = 17$ favor capital punishment. What is your conclusion?

Note: You will have noticed that the sample sizes we use in our examples and exercises are, in most cases, unrealistically small. Our purpose is to use the small binomial experiments to establish the methodology of hypothesis testing. The large-sample case will be considered in later chapters.

10. Refer to exercise 9. What is the significance level associated with the test statistic value of $y = 17$? Discuss the implications of the P-value.

11. Dmitruk (1973) studied the probability that children will yield to temptation in a laboratory study of situational influences on behavior. From control group response it was learned that the probability of yielding to the temptation to look at answers to a guessing task is .2. An experimental group of 25 children is trained to please the experimenter. The research hypothesis is that children so trained will yield to temptation with a probability greater than .2. This hypothesis will be accepted if y, the number of the 25 who yield to temptation, is $9, 10, 11, \ldots, 25$.
   (a) Set up the statistical test by stating the null hypothesis, the research hypothesis, the test statistic, and the rejection region.
   (b) Calculate α for this test.
   (c) Suppose the experiment is conducted and $y = 7$ children yield to the temptation. What is your conclusion?

12. Refer to exercise 11. What is the significance level associated with the test statistic value $y = 7$? Discuss the implications of this P-value.
13. Schachter's (1959) original study of stress and affiliation showed that 60 percent of the people expecting painful shock (high-stress group) desired to affiliate. Only 30 percent of the people expecting nonpainful shock (low-stress group) wanted to affiliate. This is the "misery loves company" effect. Later studies examined how birth order influences the relationship between stress and affiliation.

    Suppose, in particular, that we wish to test the research hypothesis that the fraction of firstborns who would want to affiliate under high stress differs from .6. We examine $n = 20$ firstborns and record the number y who desire to affiliate under high stress. Suppose we decide to reject the null hypothesis that p, the true population fraction of first borns who want to affiliate under high stress, differs from .6 if $y = 0, 1, 2, \ldots, 7, 17, 18, 19, 20$.

    (a) Set up the statistical test by specifying the null hypothesis, the research hypothesis, the test statistic, and the rejection region.
    (b) Calculate α for this test.
    (c) Suppose the 20 firstborns are subjected to the high stress, and $y = 16$ desire to affiliate. What is your conclusion?
14. Refer to exercise 13. What is the significance level associated with the test statistic value of $y = 16$? Discuss the implications of this P-value.
15. Refer to exercise 13. Suppose that 200 firstborns had been included in the study.
    (a) Assume that p, the fraction of firstborns who desire affiliation under high stress, is .6. What are the mean μ and the standard deviation σ of y, the number of the 200 who desire affiliation under high stress?
    (b) Binomial populations become mound-shaped when n is large. Use the Empirical Rule and the rare event philosophy to construct a set of y-values for which the assumption that $p = .6$ seems doubtful.

REFERENCES

Atkinson, J. W. 1964. *An introduction to motivation.* Princeton, N.J.: Van Nostrand.
Dmitruk, V. M. 1973. Intangible motivation and resistance to temptation. *Journal of Genetic Psychology* 123:47–53.
Estes, W. K. 1964. Probability learning. In *Categories of human learning*, edited by A. W. Melton. New York: Academic Press.
Goldhammer, H., and Marshall, A. W. 1953. *Psychosis and civilization.* Chicago: Free Press of Glencoe, Illinois.
Hilgard, E. R. 1965. *Hypnotic susceptibility.* New York: Harcourt, Brace and World.
Jordan, A. M. 1933. Parental occupation and children's intelligence scores. *Journal of Applied Psychology* 17:103–119.
Lipset, S. M., and Bendix, R. 1959. *Social mobility in the industrial society.* Berkeley, Calif.: University of California Press.
Mendenhall, W. 1975. *Introduction to probability and statistics.* 4th ed. N. Scituate, Mass.: Duxbury Press. Chapter 6.
Parzen, E. 1960. *Modern probability theory and its applications.* New York: Wiley. Chapters 2–5.
Schachter, S. 1959. *The psychology of affiliation.* Stanford: Stanford University Press.

6·Some Nonparametric Statistical Tests

INTRODUCTION

Testing research hypotheses, which we introduced in section 5.4, is one important way we can accomplish our statistical objective—to make inferences about populations based on information contained in a sample. In chapter 5 we introduced the procedures of testing by using relatively straightforward hypotheses about a binomial probability of success, p. However, most of the research in the behavioral sciences is much more involved than this. Consequently, we need to develop techniques to deal with these more complex investigations.

In this chapter we consider experiments whose ultimate objective is to compare two populations. Such experiments are quite common in behavioral research. We first present a few comments about the design of psychological experiments in section 6.1. We follow this in section 6.2 with a brief overview of two experimental designs for comparing two populations: the **independent sampling design** and the **matched pairs design**. Then we discuss the distinctions between two inference-making tools for comparing two populations—nonparametric and parametric comparisons—in section 6.3. Finally, we present several statistical procedures for making nonparametric comparisons in sections 6.4 through 6.6.

6.1 • EXPERIMENTAL DESIGNS IN PSYCHOLOGY: AN INTRODUCTION

To acquire a sample from a population, an experiment must be performed. However, before an experiment can be performed, the researcher must consider and plan its design. Designs, of course, vary considerably depending on the purpose of the experiment. But one element that stays the same, no matter what the specific application, is this goal: to obtain a specified amount of information about the population parameters of interest at a minimum cost. (Recall that population parameters are numerical descriptive measures of the population—for example, the population mean μ, the population variance σ^2, and the like.)

Experimental design has evolved from this simply stated objective into a very important aspect of research. Designs now can range anywhere from extremely simple to incredibly complex. In this section we present a very brief introduction to this important topic. Our main purpose is to acquaint you with the basic terminology of experimental design. It should be stressed that this is only an introduction. We will use these concepts and develop them further throughout the rest of the text.

At the core of every experiment are the experimental units, the objects on which the measurements are taken.

Definition 6.1

The objects on which measurements are taken are called experimental units.

If an experimenter subjects a set of $n = 10$ rats to a stimulus and measures the response of each, a rat is the experimental unit. The collection of $n = 10$ measurements is a sample. Similarly, if a set of $n = 10$ therapy patients is selected from the files of a particular clinic, each of the 10 selected patients is an experimental unit. The observation made on each experimental unit might be a score on some scale of a personality inventory.

What one does or what has been done to the experimental units that makes them differ from one population to another is called a treatment.

Definition 6.2

The treatments in an experimental design are the things done to the experimental units that make them differ from one population to another.

To illustrate the kinds of experiments we are talking about here, we will briefly describe a few of the many possible experimental situations.

Suppose we wish to study the pupillary dilation of subjects administered $x = 10$, $x = 15$, and $x = 20$ milligrams (mg) of a certain drug. An experimental unit is a single subject observed at a given time. The three dosage levels,

$x = 10, 15$, and 20 milligrams, represent three treatments. The thousands of subjects that conceptually *could* be administered the 10-mg dose generate a population of pupillary response measurements. We could similarly generate populations corresponding to 15 mg and 20 mg. The objective of the experiment is to compare the pupillary dilation y for the three populations. Or, we might wish to study the effect of drug dosage level x on pupillary dilation by fitting a linear or curvilinear function to the data points, as will be discussed in chapter 12.

In another experiment we might wish to compare activity scores of two inbred strains of mice, A and B. Each individual mouse tested at a particular time represents an experimental unit. Each of the two inbred strains corresponds to a treatment. Note that we do not physically treat the mice to make them different. They receive two different treatments because they have been developed as two genetically distinct strains through successive generations of inbreeding.

As a third example, consider an experiment conducted to investigate two different teaching methods, A and B, as well as the age of the child, as these variables affect a child's reading ability. An experimental unit is a single child. A treatment is a particular combination of teaching method and age of child (for example, Method A applied to a seven-year-old child). Note that there are as many different treatments as there are possible combinations of teaching method and age of child.

It usually will help us to understand what is involved in an experiment if we summarize the basic elements of the experiment. To do this we specify the experimental units, the response to be measured on each experimental unit, and the treatments. For example, in an experiment involving two methods of teaching reading to seven year olds, we might have the following summary.

Elements of the Teaching Experiment

Experimental units: Children seven years old.

Response: Score on a reading achievement test.

Treatments: Teaching Method A
Teaching Method B.

The design of an experiment involves one final problem after we have selected the treatments to be used. We must decide how the treatments should be assigned to the experimental units. Should the treatments be randomly assigned to the experimental units or should a semirandom pattern be employed? For example, should the children receiving teaching methods A and B be randomly assigned to the two teaching methods? Or should they be pair-matched on the basis of a preexperimental measure of reading ability?

There are two basic quantities in an experiment which affect the way we answer these questions and the information we obtain. You will probably have already guessed the first of these: sample size. Once we decide on the experi-

A group of seven year olds participate in a study to determine the relative merits of two teaching methods. How would you summarize the elements of this experiment? (Photo by Bruce Roberts for Rapho/Photo Researchers, Inc.)

mental procedure, we obtain more information from a large number of repetitions than we do from a small number of repetitions.

The second quantity which affects information in an experiment is the variability of the experimental units. Refer to table 6.1 in which we present three hypothetical examples of experimental results. Each experiment compares two treatments and uses six experimental units for each treatment.

Table 6.1 • Results from an experimental design: Three hypothetical examples

	Treatment A							Treatment B						
Example 1	6	6	6	6	6	6	6	8	8	8	8	8	8	8
Example 2	6	7	6	5	5	7	6	9	7	7	8	9	8	8
Example 3	4	9	10	3	6	2	8	14	5	8	11	4	5	9

Note that example 1 poses no problem in making an inference about the difference between the treatments A and B. There is no variation in the measurements for a given treatment. So we would infer that a difference of $8 - 6 = 2$ units exists between responses to Treatment B and Treatment A.

However, the picture is cloudy in example 2. The variation in response, though small, gives rise to some doubts about the true difference between Treatments A and B.

Example 3 in table 6.1 is most confusing, since the variability of experimental units is large. We would be wary of making any inferences about the difference between treatments when presented with this data.

In the next section we discuss two methods for assigning treatments to experimental units. One of these methods allows us to have some control over the variability in the experimental units.

6.2 · COMPARING TWO POPULATIONS:
THE INDEPENDENT SAMPLING DESIGN AND
THE MATCHED PAIRS DESIGN

When the experimental objective is to compare two treatments or two populations, the researcher is faced with one basic decision in designing the experiment: How should the treatments be assigned to the experimental units? Two experimental designs which can be employed are the *independent sampling design* and the *matched pairs design*.

The *independent sampling design* involves assigning the treatments to the experimental units in a completely random, independent manner. That is, experimental units are selected randomly, as described in section 4.7. Then the two treatments are assigned to the experimental units so that the measurements are independent from unit to unit. By independence of measurements we mean that the outcome on one trial of an experiment in no way affects the outcomes of other trials.

An experimenter wishing to compare male and female reaction times to a visual stimulus could employ the independent sampling design by separately selecting a random sample of males and a random sample of females from the two populations. The random choice of experimental units would result from the selection of random samples. The independence would result from performing the selection from the two populations separately. (An example of dependent sampling in this case would be the selection of husband-wife pairs.)

Similarly, the independent sampling design could be employed to compare the two methods of teaching reading to seven year olds. A random sample of seven year olds (experimental units) would be selected from the population. Then the experimenter would randomly assign each child (experimental unit) to one teaching method (treatment) or the other. The assignment of the experimental units to the two treatments is usually one-half to each treatment, but it could be made in any specified ratio.

An alternative experimental design for comparing two populations is the matched pairs design. The *matched pairs design* consists of selecting the experimental units in pairs, with each pair being relatively homogeneous (i.e., having little variability). Then the experimenter randomly chooses an experimental unit in each pair to receive Treatment A. The other experimental unit in the pair will receive Treatment B. The samples generated for each treatment are no longer independent, since the pairs of experimental units were specifically chosen because they were alike in some way. Thus the response on one experimental unit in a pair will be related to that on the other unit in the pair. Therefore, rather than analyzing the two samples independently, the experimenter analyzes the *difference between the responses* for each pair of experimental units.

For example, suppose we wish to use a matched pairs design to compare male and female reaction times to a visual stimulus. One way we might do this is by selecting male-female pairs (i.e., pairs of experimental units) whose eyesights are identical. Or, an even more precise comparison might result if we gave each subject a sensory pretest. Then the male-female pairs could be formed by matching their scores on the pretest as closely as possible. We would then analyze the difference in visual reaction times to the stimulus for each pair.

Similarly, a matched pairs design could be used to evaluate the two methods of teaching reading by selecting pairs of seven year olds whose IQs are identical, or nearly so. Or, if this is possible, the experimenter could select a set of seven-year-old identical twins and randomly assign one member of each pair to each teaching method. The differences in designing this experiment by using an independent sampling design and by using a matched pairs design may be schematically represented as shown in figure 6.1. Note the homogeneity of the experimental units in each pair of the matched pairs design. But there is no control of experimental unit variability inherent in the independent sampling design.

Figure 6.1 • Comparison of independent sampling design and matched pairs design

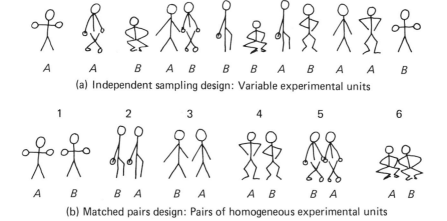

(a) Independent sampling design: Variable experimental units

(b) Matched pairs design: Pairs of homogeneous experimental units

The experimenter hopes that by employing a matched pairs design to compare two populations, the experimental unit variability will be reduced. The reduction is obtained by analyzing the response differences within pairs of experimental units that are very much alike. The hope is that any variability that shows up within pairs is due to differences in response to the treatments and not to differences in the experimental units.

Of course, in practice we will rarely know the degree of variability in the experimental units before actually performing the experiment. But in general, we should try to control for variability by employing a matched pairs design if much variability is suspected and a small sample is dictated. Even if little variability is present between pairs, you can still make the treatment comparison. The only disadvantage is that there is a slight loss in information caused by pairing when pairing is not really needed.

On the other hand, suppose we use an independent sampling design and find much experimental unit variability. In this case the population information is likely to be obscured. Is the observed difference between treatments real—or is it due to some unknown differences in the experimental units—or to some combination of both? Since no meaningful population inference can be made, the experiment is a failure. The objective of the experiment is to make inferences about the difference between the populations based on information in the two samples. Large experimental unit variability prevents us from accomplishing this objective.

Example 6.1

An investigation of the difference in visual scanning behavior between deaf children and hearing children is to be made by measuring eye movement rates of subjects selected from each population.

(a) Summarize the elements of this experiment.

(b) What type of experimental design seems more appropriate for this comparison, an independent sampling design or a matched pairs design?

Solution: (a) From a careful reading of the experimental description, we have the following summary.

Elements of the Visual Scanning Experiment

Experimental units: Children.

Response: Eye movement rates.

Treatments: Deaf Children
Hearing Children.

Note here that the treatments are not something we do to the children. The children receive two different treatments because they have two different physical characteristics.

(b) For this experiment the design is primarily dictated by the nature of the treatments being compared. Since the development of deaf and hearing children is very different in almost every respect, we would probably have much difficulty forming pairs, no matter how "pairs" might be defined (a problem in itself).

We could probably make the best use of our resources by selecting the samples of hearing and deaf children independently from the respective populations. The measurement of eye movement is probably not a difficult one to make, so we may be able to examine a rather large sample from each population. Then, even if there is much variability in eye movement among the children in each population, the large number of measurements will allow the comparison to be meaningful.

Table 6.2 shows part of an independent sampling design for this experiment, with some simulated data.

Table 6.2 • Eye movement measurements in an independent sample design for example 6.1

Deaf Children ($n_1 = 30$)		Hearing Children ($n_2 = 25$)	
1	2.75	1	0.89
2	2.14	2	1.75
3	3.23	3	1.49
4	2.07	4	2.13
.	.	.	.
.	.	.	.
.	.	.	.
30	3.0	25	1.64

Example 6.2

A researcher wishes to compare the effects of two different diets, A and B, on aggressive behavior in a strain of rats. The plan is to measure the number of aggressive overtures made by each rat during a 30-minute interval after being on the diet for 14 days. There are 12 rats of this strain available for experimentation.

(a) Summarize the elements of this experiment.

(b) How should this experiment be designed?

Solution: (a) The elements of the experiment are summarized below.

Elements of the Aggressive Behavior Experiment

Experimental units: Rats.

Response: Number of aggressive overtures made in a 30-minute interval.

Treatments: Diet A
　　　　　　Diet B.

(b) Since the sample size $n = 12$ is fixed and small, the experimenter should be especially concerned that high variability in aggressive behavior may obscure the comparison of diets. That is, if aggressive behavior is to be measured by the number of aggressive overtures made by a rat in a given time period, this number may vary widely among the 12 rats, even if their diets are identical. This concern prompts the experimenter to consider a matched pairs design.

To employ the matched pairs design, the experimenter could observe the behavior of the 12 rats *before* beginning the experiment. Some preliminary observations about the aggressive behavior of each could be made. Then the rats could be ranked according to their observed behavior, with a rank of 1 denoting the most aggressive, 2 denoting the second most aggressive, and so on. Then the experimenter pairs rat 1 with rat 2, 3 with 4, and so forth, forming 6 pairs. Each pair can be considered as having shown relatively homogeneous behavior.

The next step is to choose randomly one rat from each pair to receive Diet A, with the other to receive Diet B. Then, after administering the diets for a specified period, a measurement of aggressive behavior is made on each of the 12 rats. The differences in these measurements for each of the 6 pairs is analyzed. Then the researcher makes an inference about the difference in the two diets A and B with respect to aggressive behavior.

More resources have been used in employing the matched pairs design than would have been needed for an independent sampling design. However, if there is great variability in aggressive behavior among the rats of this strain, more information will be obtained using the matched pairs design.

Simulated data for this matched pairs experiment are presented in table 6.3.

Table 6.3 • Aggressive behavior measurements in a matched pairs design for example 6.2

Pair	Diet A	Diet B	Difference (A — B)
1	127	115	12
2	104	95	9
3	90	87	3
4	84	77	7
5	86	75	11
6	80	73	7

A final comment about matched pairs designs should be made here. The experimenter should not form the pairs after the experiment by using the data collected for making the comparison of the two populations. Pairing in this manner could bias the results of the comparison. The pairing of experimental units should be done before performing the experiment, by using either historical data or some preliminary observations on the subjects.

EXERCISES

1. An experiment is conducted to compare the scores of schizophrenics and nonschizophrenics on a personality index.

(a) Summarize the elements of this experiment.

(b) What type of experimental design should be employed, independent sampling or matched pairs?

2. Wegener (1965) was interested in whether animals could readily form discrimination principles allowing them to differentiate between different amounts of some stimulus. Suppose we have available 22 monkeys for experimentation. We plan to compare the effects of positive and negative reinforcement methods on the number of trials it takes a monkey to learn an auditory stimulus.

(a) Summarize the elements of this experiment.

(b) What type of experimental design should be employed, independent sampling or matched pairs?

6.3 • NONPARAMETRIC AND PARAMETRIC POPULATION COMPARISONS

Two distinct types of statistical inference-making tools are available for comparing two populations: *nonparametric* and *parametric methods*. *Nonparametric comparisons of two populations use the information in the samples to make inferences about the differences between the population frequency distributions. Parametric comparisons use the sample information to compare corresponding parameters (numerical descriptive measures) of the populations, such as their means or their variances.*

We defer discussion of the relative merits of nonparametric and parametric techniques until both have been presented in some detail (see chapter 9). The nonparametric methods lend themselves to easy calculations and may be applied to a very general class of populations. Thus we consider several nonparametric techniques in the following sections of this chapter. Parametric comparisons of populations will be discussed in chapters 8 and 9.

6.4 • THE SIGN TEST FOR COMPARING POPULATIONS

One of the simplest nonparametric techniques for comparing the frequency distributions of two populations (or treatments) is the *sign test*. Suppose we employ a matched pairs design to obtain sample information about the populations. To use the sign test to compare treatments, we use as a test statistic the number of times the numerical response on an experimental unit in Sample *A* exceeds the numerical response of the paired experimental unit in Sample *B*. Paired measurements that result in a tie are omitted.

The sign test gets its name because we only look at the *sign* of the difference between *A* and *B*, rather than at the actual numerical value. A sample calculation of the test statistic *y* appears in table 6.4 with some hypothetical data from a matched pairs design.

Recall the five characteristics of the binomial distribution (see section 5.1). We see that *y* is a binomial random variable, where a "success" corresponds to a pair

Table 6.4 • Computation of the test statistic for a sign test

Pair	Sample A	Sample B	A exceeds B? ($+$ if yes, $-$ if no)
1	76	65	$+$
2	83	79	$+$
3	64	66	$-$
4	101	89	$+$
5	54	60	$-$
6	79	63	$+$
7	82	82	tied

$$y = \text{number of plus signs} = 4$$

of experimental units for which the response of Treatment A exceeds that of Treatment B. We would like to know the value of p, the probability of "success" on each trial, that is, the probability that A exceeds B on a given pair of experimental units.

If the population frequency distributions are the same, as depicted in figure 6.2(a), an observation from A should have a 50-50 chance of exceeding an observation from B, that is, $p = .5$. If the frequency distribution corresponding to population A lies mostly below or to the left of the frequency distribution for B [figure 6.2(b)], then a randomly selected measurement from A is not likely to exceed one from B, so $p < .5$. How much smaller p is than .5 depends on how much difference exists between the location of the frequency distributions. The situation for which $p > .5$ is depicted in figure 6.2(c).

Figure 6.2 • Frequency distribution relationships

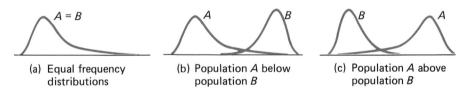

| (a) Equal frequency distributions | (b) Population A below population B | (c) Population A above population B |

Since y, the number of experimental unit pairs for which A's response exceeds B's, is a binomial random variable, we may use the testing methods introduced in section 5.4. That is, we can test research hypotheses about the true probability p that a Treatment A measurement exceeds a Treatment B measurement. In particular, we may test the research hypothesis that populations A and B have different frequency distributions ($p \neq .5$) against the null hypothesis that there is no difference between their frequency distributions ($p = .5$).

Example 6.3

Refer to example 6.2. A matched pairs design was recommended to compare the effects of two different diets, A and B, on aggressive behavior in a certain strain of rats. Suppose that 20 rats (experimental units) are available. The researcher forms 10 pairs by monitoring their behavior before the diets are administered (see example 6.2 for a more complete discussion of the experimental design). After diets A and B are administered for a specific time period, a measurement of aggressive behavior is made on each rat. The data in table 6.5 result.

Table 6.5 • Data for aggressive behavior experiment of example 6.3

Pair	Diet A	Diet B	A exceeds B? ($+$ if yes, $-$ if no)
1	127	116	$+$
2	104	95	$+$
3	86	91	$-$
4	74	62	$+$
5	91	92	$-$
6	62	54	$+$
7	113	99	$+$
8	95	88	$+$
9	73	64	$+$
10	81	78	$+$
			y = number of plus signs = 8

Do these data provide sufficient evidence to indicate that the rats of this strain exhibit different degrees of aggressive behavior when on Diet A than when on Diet B? Use the sign test.

Solution: The research hypothesis is that aggressive behavior is dependent on the diet that is administered. In the statistical terminology of a nonparametric test, the research hypothesis is that the frequency distribution corresponding to the conceptual population of aggressive behavior measurements for rats on Diet A is different from the frequency distribution corresponding to the population of aggressive behavior measurements for rats on Diet B. That is, the frequency distribution for Diet A lies either to the right of that for Diet B or to the left of that for Diet B. The null hypothesis, always the antithesis of the research hypothesis, is that the frequency distributions are the same.

Suppose we define p as the probability that an aggressive behavior observation on a rat from Diet A exceeds the paired aggressive behavior observation on a rat from Diet B. Then we wish to test

$$H_0: p = .5$$
$$H_a: p \neq .5$$

using the test statistic

$$y = \text{the number of pairs for which A exceeds B}$$

You will note that this is a two-tailed test (section 5.4) because we wish to detect whether $p > .5$ or $p < .5$. The two-tailed research hypothesis is depicted in figures 6.3(a) and 6.3(b). The general two-tailed rejection region is shown in figure 6.3(c).

Figure 6.3 • Two-tailed research hypothesis

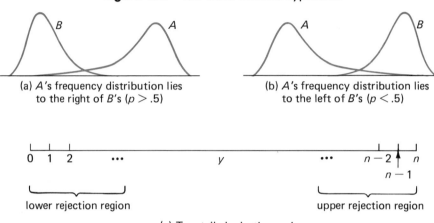

(a) A's frequency distribution lies to the right of B's ($p > .5$)

(b) A's frequency distribution lies to the left of B's ($p < .5$)

(c) Two-tailed rejection region

Let us now calculate the significance level P for the observed test statistic value $y = 8$. First note that 8 is a relatively large value of y in the null hypothesis distribution, shown in figure 6.4. We therefore calculate the probability that y assumes the value 8 or *greater*, assuming the null hypothesis to be true, that is, $p = .5$. So we calculate

$$p(8) + p(9) + p(10) = .055$$

using table 1(d) in appendix II. Recall that the probabilities in the table are of the form $p(0) + p(1) + \cdots + p(a)$, so that

$$p(8) + p(9) + p(10) = 1 - [p(0) + p(1) + \cdots + p(7)]$$
$$\vdots \qquad = 1 - .945 = .055$$

Since the research hypothesis is two-tailed, we calculate P by doubling the above probability to allow for equally rare events in the lower tail of the null hypothesis distribution. Thus

$$P = 2(.055) = .11$$

The implication of the significance level of .11 is that any researcher who would choose a value of α, the type I error probability, greater than .11 for this test would reject the hypothesis of identical frequency distributions of aggressive behavior of rats on the two diets. A researcher not willing to assume a risk level as high as .11 would require more evidence before concluding that a difference exists. A researcher who decides to reject H_0 at this significance level would expect that the frequency distribution of aggressive behavior for rats on Diet A lies to the right of the distribution for Diet B, since a relatively large value of y was observed.

Figure 6.4 • P-value for aggressive behavior experiment when $y = 8$

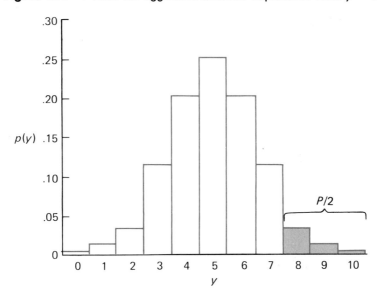

Example 6.4

An innovative method of teaching reading to six year olds is to be tested using a matched pairs design. The researcher randomly selects 34 six year olds and then forms 17 pairs by matching their IQs as closely as possible. Then one child from each pair will be taught to read using Method A, the standard method, and the other child in the pair will be taught to read by Method B, the new method. At the end of a specified period, a reading achievement test will be given to each of the 34 children.

Suppose the results are those given in table 6.6. Here y represents the number of pairs for which the achievement test score is higher for the standard method (A) than it is for the new method (B).

Is there evidence to indicate that the new method of teaching reading (Treatment B) to six year olds is better than the old method (Treatment A)? Use the sign test.

Solution: The research hypothesis is that the frequency distribution of reading achievement test scores for Method A lies to the left of that for Method B, as shown in figure 6.5. The research hypothesis does not imply that the relationship between the two populations is exactly as depicted in figure 6.5. However, it does imply that the probability is less than .5 that a child taught by the old method will score higher on the reading achievement test than a child taught by the new method.

The null hypothesis is that the two distributions are the same or, equivalently, that p, the probability that an A score exceeds the corresponding B score, is equal to .5. If the research hypothesis is true, p will be less than .5.

Table 6.6 • Reading achievement test scores for example 6.4

Pair	Standard Method A	New Method B	A exceeds B? (+ if yes, − if no)
1	75	79	−
2	57	69	−
3	72	71	+
4	89	93	−
5	45	58	−
6	67	67	tied
7	63	75	−
8	93	95	−
9	56	64	−
10	90	97	−
11	85	89	−
12	94	93	+
13	57	67	−
14	79	85	−
15	83	87	−
16	74	74	tied
17	82	89	−

$$y = \text{number of plus signs} = 2$$

Thus we test

$$H_0: p = .5$$
$$H_a: p < .5$$

using the test statistic

$$y = \text{the number of pairs for which A exceeds B}$$

After throwing out the ties in the pairs of observations in table 6.6, we are left with $n = 15$ pairs of measurements. We will reject H_0 in favor of H_a if an unusually *small* value of y is observed for these pairs. The smallest

Figure 6.5 • Research hypothesis for the reading experiment

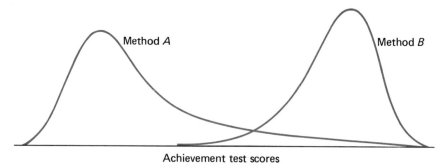

Achievement test scores

rejection region containing the observed value of the test statistic, $y = 2$, is shown in figure 6.6.

Figure 6.6 • Smallest rejection region containing $y = 2$ for the one-tailed sign test of example 6.4

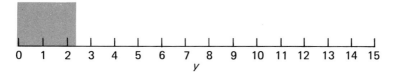

The significance level P corresponding to this test statistic value is therefore

$$P = p(0) + p(1) + p(2)$$

when $p = .5$. From table 1(c) in appendix II for $p = .5$ and $a = 2$, we find

$$P = .004$$

This very small significance level implies that it is extremely unlikely to observe 2 or fewer pairs on which the A score exceeds the B score if the two treatments have the same frequency distribution of achievement test scores. This event, $y = 2$, provides strong evidence that the new method of teaching reading is better than the standard method, at least as measured by this achievement test. In other words, we have strong evidence to indicate that if the population of six year olds is taught to read by the new method, they are likely to score higher on this achievement test than they would if they were taught by the standard method.

The sign test can be adapted to independent sampling experiments *providing the sample sizes are equal.* The test still requires a comparison of pairs of measurements, one from population A and one from population B. However, there is no natural pairing in an independent sampling experiment, and, in fact, all measurements are independent. Thus we form pseudo pairs by randomly choosing one measurement from each sample. Once these pairs are chosen, we conduct the test exactly as we would a sign test for a matched pairs experiment.

Example 6.5

In a comparison of visual acuity of deaf and hearing children, eye movement rates were taken on 10 deaf and 10 hearing children. The resulting data are shown in table 6.7. Use the sign test to determine whether the data provide sufficient evidence to conclude that deaf children have greater visual acuity, as measured by eye movement rates, than hearing children.

Solution: The research hypothesis is that deaf children have greater visual acuity than hearing children and, more specifically, that the frequency distribution of eye movement rate for deaf children (A) lies to the right of that for hearing children (B). See figure 6.7.

Table 6.7 • Eye movement rates for visual acuity experiment of example 6.5

Deaf Children (A)	Hearing Children (B)
2.75	1.15
3.14	1.65
3.23	1.43
2.30	1.83
2.64	1.75
1.95	1.23
2.17	2.03
2.45	1.64
1.83	1.96
2.23	1.37

Since we plan to use the sign test, we define the binomial parameter p as the probability that a randomly chosen eye movement rate from the deaf children's frequency distribution exceeds a randomly chosen eye movement rate from the hearing children's frequency distribution. Then our test structure is as follows:

Null hypothesis H_0: $p = .5$.

Research hypothesis H_a: $p > .5$.

Test statistic: $y =$ the number of times A exceeds B in $n = 10$ randomly formed pairs.

We will tend to reject H_0 when y is unusually large.

The first step in computing the test statistic y is to randomly pair the sample observations. A simple way to do this is to place the numbers from 1 to 10 on separate slips of paper and then draw the numbered slips one at a time and

Figure 6.7 • Research hypothesis: The eye movement rate frequency distribution for deaf children (A) lies to the right of (above) that for hearing children (B)

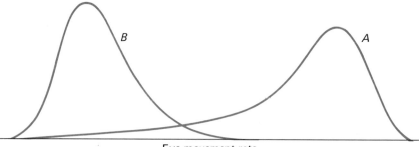

Eye movement rate

record the numbers. We did this and obtained the second column in table 6.8. We leave the column for the deaf children data in this example unchanged, but we rearrange the column for the hearing children to correspond to the random number column. Thus, since the number 5 was drawn first, we use as our first observation what was originally the fifth observation in the hearing children data, 1.75 (see tables 6.7 and 6.8). The second number drawn is 8, so the original eighth measurement, 1.64, is now second; and so on.

Table 6.8 • Random pairing of measurements and calculation of y for visual acuity experiment, example 6.5

Deaf Children (A)	Random Numbers	Hearing Children (B)	A exceeds B? (+ if yes, − if no)
2.75	5	1.75	+
3.14	8	1.64	+
3.23	2	1.65	+
2.30	9	1.96	+
2.64	7	2.03	+
1.95	4	1.83	+
2.17	1	1.15	+
2.45	10	1.37	+
1.83	3	1.43	+
2.23	6	1.23	+

$$y = \text{number of plus signs} = 10$$

For this particular matching, we get a test statistic value of $y = 10$. That is, the A observation exceeds the B observation for every randomly formed pair. Therefore, the significance level P is the probability of observing $y = 10$ plus signs when $p = .5$. Then

$$P = P(y = 10 \text{ when } p = .5)$$

$$= 1 - p(0) - p(1) - \cdots - p(9) = 1 - \sum_{y=0}^{9} p(y)$$

Checking table 1(b) in appendix II, we read the value for $p = .5$ and $a = 9$. Thus

$$P = 1 - .999 = .001$$

Since this significance level is so small, we conclude that p exceeds .5. That is, we conclude that the frequency distribution of eye movement rate for deaf children lies above that for hearing children.

Note than a different selection of random numbers may lead to a different y-value and hence to a different significance level, perhaps one so large that we would be unwilling to reject the null hypothesis. You may conduct the same test with your own random pairing and compare the results with ours.

A final comment about using the sign test for independent sampling experiments should be made here. The sign test is based on a probability structure which requires *random* pairing of the observations for each treatment. By a nonrandom and precalculated choice of pairs, an experimenter could make the significance level smaller than would be obtained for a random selection. Thus the experimenter could force the test to lend greater support to the research hypothesis. However, this practice is highly unethical, and the significance level of the resulting test would no longer be valid. The sign test is applicable only if the pairing is done randomly.

EXERCISES

1. To compare two junior high schools, A and B, in academic effectiveness, an experiment was designed using 12 sets of identical twins, each twin having just completed the sixth grade. In each case the twins in the same set had obtained their schooling in the same classrooms at each grade level. The experimenters were thus fortunate in having a good control for genetic influence on intelligence and temperament and for educational background. One child was selected at random from each set and assigned to School A; the other twins were sent to School B. Near the end of the ninth grade, an achievement test was given to each child in the experiment. The results were as follows.

Twin Pair	1	2	3	4	5	6	7	8	9	10	11	12
School A	67	80	65	72	70	86	50	63	56	81	86	60
School B	39	75	69	72	55	74	52	56	56	72	89	47

   (a) Set up the structure for testing the research hypothesis that the two schools differ in academic effectiveness. Assume the sign test is to be used.
   (b) Calculate the significance level P associated with the observed test statistic. What is your conclusion?

2. Validity refers to the degree to which a scale measures what it is supposed to measure. One strategy of determining validity uses the known-groups method. For instance, to validate a measure of marital adjustment, two groups, consisting of 10 married couples each, were identified as "well-adjusted" (A) and "poorly adjusted" (B) on the basis of interviews and self-reports. Then a score was obtained for a new marital adjustment scale for each couple to see if the scale discriminated between the two groups. The scores are presented below, with A representing the well-adjusted group and B the poorly adjusted group.

A	11	42	37	39	26	21	45	33	40	43
B	41	22	32	36	19	25	29	33	28	39

(a) What test structure would you use to test the research hypothesis that the frequency distribution of scores on the new scale for well-adjusted couples lies to the right of that for poorly adjusted couples? Assume the sign test is to be used.

(b) Establish a rejection region such that α is as close to .05 as possible.

(c) Calculate the test statistic and state your conclusion.

6.5 • THE MANN-WHITNEY U TEST FOR AN INDEPENDENT SAMPLING EXPERIMENT

The main advantage of the sign test in comparing frequency distributions is that it is simple to apply. The price paid for this simplicity is the loss of sample information. Note that the actual differences between pairs (whether randomly or naturally formed) of measurements are not used or even computed. We only compute the number of times "A exceeds B," without considering the magnitude of the differences. This results in a loss of sample information.

Nonparametric tests which are based on the *ranks* of the measurements employ more sample information because they utilize the relative magnitudes of the observations. A rank test for comparing populations using an *independent sampling design* is the *Mann-Whitney U test*. The computation of the U statistic is best introduced by an example.

Consider a hypothetical independent sampling experiment resulting in the data shown in table 6.9. Assume that $n_1 = n_2 = 4$ measurements are randomly selected from each population and that the two samples are selected independently.

Table 6.9 • Independent sampling experiment data for a Mann-Whitney U test

Sample A	Ranks	Sample B	Ranks
27	3	31	6
25	1	28	4
29	5	35	8
26	2	32	7
	$T_A = 11$		$T_B = 25$

The first step in calculating U is to rank all $n_1 + n_2 = 8$ observations. The number 1 denotes the smallest measurement, 2 the next smallest, and so forth, with the rank $(n_1 + n_2)$ denoting the largest measurement. The ranks for our hypothetical example appear in the columns next to the sample measurements. Note that the smallest measurement, 25, receives rank 1, the next smallest, 26, receives rank 2, and so on to the largest measurement, 35, which receives rank 8.

The second step in calculating U is to compute the sum of the ranks for each sample. That is, we compute T_A, the sum of the ranks of the Sample A measurements, and T_B, the sum of the ranks of the Sample B measurements.

The final step in the computation of U is given by the rules shown in the box.

Computing the U Statistic for a Two-tailed Test

If T_A is larger,

$$U = n_1 n_2 + \frac{n_1(n_1 + 1)}{2} - T_A$$

If T_B is larger,

$$U = n_1 n_2 + \frac{n_2(n_2 + 1)}{2} - T_B$$

Computing the U Statistic for a One-tailed Test

If the research hypothesis is that the frequency distribution of A is above (to the right of) that of B [figure 6.8(a)],

$$U = n_1 n_2 + \frac{n_1(n_1 + 1)}{2} - T_A$$

If the research hypothesis is that the frequency distribution of A is below (to the left of) that of B [figure 6.8(b)],

$$U = n_1 n_2 + \frac{n_2(n_2 + 1)}{2} - T_B$$

Figure 6.8 • Possible one-tailed research hypotheses in computing the U statistic

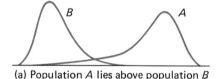

(a) Population A lies above population B   (b) Population A lies below population B

Assume that our hypothetical example is a two-tailed test. The larger rank sum is $T_B = 25$. Thus

$$U = n_1 n_2 + \frac{n_2(n_2 + 1)}{2} - T_B$$

$$= (4)(4) + \frac{4(4 + 1)}{2} - 25$$

$$= 16 + 10 - 25 = 1$$

The steps in computing the Mann-Whitney test statistic U for independent sampling experiments are summarized below.

---

1. Rank all $n_1 + n_2$ sample measurements in the experiment.
2. Compute the rank sums T_A and T_B for each sample.
3. Calculate U according to the rules given in the previous box.

The slightly more complex calculations of the Mann-Whitney test yield a test statistic which contains more information than the statistic for a sign test. This is because the Mann-Whitney U statistic uses the relative magnitude (the rank) of each observation.

To give you an idea of how the Mann-Whitney U statistic works, consider the case where the two sample sizes are equal (i.e., $n_1 = n_2$). If the frequency distributions for the two populations are the same, there should be little difference between the two sample rank sums T_A and T_B. If, however, we find that one rank sum is much larger than the other, we will get a small value of U and reject the hypothesis that the frequency distributions are the same. If T_B is much larger than T_A, the implication is that A's frequency distribution lies to the left of (below) B's [figure 6.9(a)]. If T_A is much larger than T_B, we conclude that the frequency distribution for population A lies to the right of (above) that for population B [figure 6.9(b)].

Figure 6.9 • Inferences from the Mann-Whitney U test

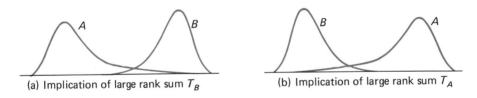

(a) Implication of large rank sum T_B (b) Implication of large rank sum T_A

In either case, the value of U will be small if one of the rank sums is much larger than the other. Table 2 in appendix II contains one-tailed significance levels associated with various U-values for all sample sizes n_1 and n_2 up to and including 10. The entry in the table corresponding to a value U_0 represents the probability that we observe a value of U as small as or smaller than U_0 when the two population frequency distributions are the same (the null hypothesis). Thus if we want to determine the significance level associated with our observed $U = 1$ in the hypothetical example, we consult table 2, appendix II, for $n_1 = 4$ and $n_2 = 4$. This table is reproduced here in table 6.10 for your convenience. We then find the entry corresponding to $U_0 = 1$, which is .0286. If the test were two-tailed, the significance level corresponding to $U = 1$ would be $P = 2(.0286) = .0572$.

Table 6.10 • Mann-Whitney U test one-tailed
significance levels for
$n_1 = 1, 2, 3, 4$ and $n_2 = 4$;
from table 2, appendix II

	n_1	$n_2 = 4$			
		1	2	3	4
	0	.2000	.0667	.0286	.0143
	1	.4000	.1333	.0571	.0286
	2	.6000	.2667	.1143	.0571
	3		.4000	.2000	.1000
U_0	4		.6000	.3143	.1714
	5			.4286	.2429
	6			.5714	.3429
	7				.4429
	8				.5571

The implication of this significance level is that the probability is .0572 that the U statistic is 1 or less when the two frequency distributions are the same. Thus there is some evidence that the two population frequency distributions are different. Since the larger rank sum is T_B, the inference we would draw is that the frequency distribution for population A lies to the left of (below) that of population B. See figure 6.10.

Figure 6.10 • Inference that population A is to the left of population B in our hypothetical example

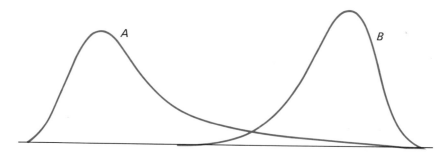

If the preceding test were one-tailed with the research hypothesis as depicted in figure 6.9(a), the significance level would be the number found in table 2, appendix II, which is .0286 in this case.

Before presenting some examples, several additional comments should be made here. If any measurements result in ties, we compute the average of the ranks which would have been assigned to these measurements and assign this average to each. Also, if the number of measurements in either sample exceeds 10, then table 2 in appendix II is no longer applicable. We will show you how to conduct large-sample Mann-Whitney U tests in chapter 7.

Example 6.6

Refer to example 6.5. We conducted an independent sampling experiment to compare the visual acuity of deaf and hearing children by measuring eye movement rates for 10 deaf and 10 hearing children. The data is repeated here in table 6.11.

Table 6.11 • Eye movement rates for visual acuity experiment, example 6.6

Deaf Children	Ranks	Hearing Children	Ranks
2.75	18	1.15	1
3.14	19	1.65	6
3.23	20	1.43	4
2.30	15	1.83	8.5
2.64	17	1.75	7
1.95	10	1.23	2
2.17	13	2.03	12
2.45	16	1.64	5
1.83	8.5	1.96	11
2.23	14	1.37	3
	$T_A = 150.5$		$T_B = 59.5$

Use the Mann-Whitney U test to determine whether these data provide sufficient evidence to conclude that the visual acuity of deaf children, as measured by eye movement rate, is greater than that of hearing children.

Solution: The research hypothesis is that the frequency distribution for deaf children's eye movement rate (A) lies to the right of that for hearing children (B), as shown in figure 6.11.

The null hypothesis is that no difference exists between the distributions. Thus we have the following test structure.

Figure 6.11 • Research hypothesis that the eye movement frequency distribution for deaf children (A) lies above that for hearing children (b)

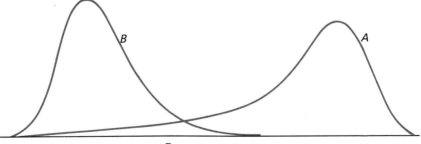

Eye movement rate

H_0: The eye movement rate frequency distributions for deaf and hearing children are the same.

H_a: The eye movement rate frequency distribution for deaf children lies to the right of (above) that for hearing children.

Test statistic: The Mann-Whitney U statistic.

To compute U, we first rank all 20 measurements and then compute the rank sum for each sample. This is shown in table 6.11, where we find that $T_A = 150.5$ and $T_B = 59.5$. Since the test is one-tailed with the research hypothesis that A's frequency distribution lies above B's, we use T_A in computing U. Thus

$$U = n_1 n_2 + \frac{n_1(n_1 + 1)}{2} - T_A = (10)(10) + \frac{10(11)}{2} - 150.5$$

$$= 155 - 150.5 = 4.5$$

To determine the significance level associated with $U = 4.5$, we consult table 2, appendix II, for $n_1 = n_2 = 10$. The entries corresponding to $U_0 = 4$ and $U_0 = 5$ are both .0001. Thus, since this is a one-tailed test, the significance level corresponding to $U = 4.5$ is .0001, to four decimal places. See figure 6.12.

Figure 6.12 • Significance level for the observed $U = 4.5$ in example 6.6

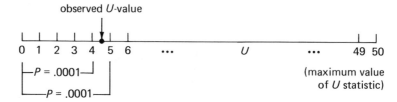

The implication of this significance level is that we would observe a test statistic U-value of 4.5 or less only 1 in 10,000 times if the deaf and hearing children's frequency distributions were the same. There is strong evidence that the visual acuity of deaf children, as measured by eye movement rate, is greater than that of hearing children.

The Mann-Whitney U test is computationally more cumbersome than the sign test. However, we have more confidence in our inference because we obtained a smaller significance level using the Mann-Whitney test.

Example 6.7

Each monkey in a sample of 11 monkeys is taught to respond to a certain stimulus. Two different reinforcement schedules are developed to extinguish the response to the stimulus. Five of the monkeys are randomly selected to receive Schedule A, while the other 6 receive Schedule B. The number of trials until the response is extinguished is given in table 6.12.

Do these data present sufficient evidence to indicate that the two schedules have different population frequency distributions of the number of trials until

Table 6.12 • Number of trials until response is extinguished, example 6.7

Schedule A	Ranks	Schedule B	Ranks
8	4	14	9
13	8	11	7
6	2	16	11
5	1	10	6
9	5	7	3
		15	10
	$T_A = 20$		$T_B = 46$

response is extinguished? Use the Mann-Whitney *U* test and a fixed α-level of .05.

Solution: Our test structure is as follows:

H_0: The frequency distributions of number of trials until response is extinguished for Schedules A and B are the same.

H_a: The frequency distributions of number of trials until response is extinguished for Schedules A and B are different.

Test statistic: The Mann-Whitney *U* statistic.

To find the rejection region corresponding to the fixed $\alpha = .05$, we consult table 2, appendix II, for $n_1 = 5$ and $n_2 = 6$. Remember that the table entries will have to be doubled since the test is two-tailed. In the table for $n_2 = 6$, we look at the column under $n_1 = 5$ and try to find a value which, when doubled, will be close to our fixed α-value of .05. In the column under $n_1 = 5$, we find the value .0260. This value doubled is .0520—so this is the closest we can come to our α-value of .05. Reading across the table from the value .0260, we see this corresponds to a U_0-value of 4. Then our rejection region, for an α-value of .052, is $U \leq 4$. This rejection region is shown in figure 6.13.

Figure 6.13 • Rejection region for the Mann-Whitney *U* test in example 6.7

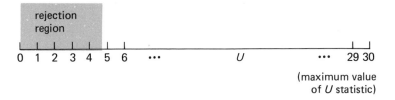

(maximum value of *U* statistic)

To compute the test statistic *U* for this two-tailed test, we use the larger of the two rank sums. This is shown in table 6.12 to be $T_B = 46$. Then

$$U = n_1 n_2 + \frac{n_2(n_2 + 1)}{2} - T_B = (5)(6) + \frac{6(7)}{2} - 46$$

$$= 30 + 21 - 46 = 5$$

Since $U = 5$ is not in our rejection region (see figure 6.13), we conclude that the data do not provide sufficient evidence to reject the null hypothesis that the frequency distributions are the same.

The test statistic value $U = 5$ is very close to being in the rejection region. So we may be interested in computing the corresponding significance level. The entry at $U_0 = 5$ in table 2, appendix II, for $n_1 = 5$ and $n_2 = 6$ is .0411. For this two-tailed test, we find $P = 2(.0411) = .0822$. Thus if we had chosen an α-value exceeding .0822, we would have concluded that the frequency distributions were different, that is, we would have rejected H_0. But in doing so we also would have assumed a greater risk of committing a type I error, that is, of rejecting H_0 when it is really true.

In summary, the Mann-Whitney U test provides a procedure for making a nonparametric comparison of two frequency distributions using an independent sampling design. The Mann-Whitney test requires more complex calculations than the simpler sign test. However, we have more confidence in the results of a Mann-Whitney test than a sign test because the Mann-Whitney test uses more sample information.

EXERCISES

1. Refer to exercise 2 in section 6.4. A validity study was done on a new marital adjustment scale. Recall that Sample A represents 10 well-adjusted couples and Sample B represents 10 poorly adjusted couples. The scores are repeated below for convenience.

A	11	42	37	39	26	21	45	33	40	43
B	41	22	32	36	19	25	29	33	28	39

   (a) Use the Mann-Whitney procedure to test the nonparametric research hypothesis that the frequency distribution of scores on the new scale for well-adjusted couples lies to the right of that for poorly adjusted couples.
   (b) State your conclusion and compare it to that obtained using the sign test. In which test do you have more confidence?

2. In a study of individual versus multiple therapy, two groups of therapy clients were compared. Group A consists of 8 clients in contact with a single therapist; Group B consists of 7 clients in contact with a male-female therapist pair. Each client was administered a "personal improvement" scale after a fixed number of therapy sessions, and the following scale scores were obtained.

A	16	20	13	8	5	12	15	7
B	17	7	16	22	18	10	12	

Do the data present sufficient evidence to indicate a difference in "personal improvement" between individual (A) and multiple (B) therapy clients? Use a Mann-Whitney U test with α as close as possible to .10.

6.6 • THE WILCOXON RANK SUM TEST FOR A MATCHED PAIRS EXPERIMENT

The Wilcoxon rank sum test is a rank test which uses more sample information than the sign test for comparing populations using a matched pairs experiment. To conduct the Wilcoxon rank sum test, we first compute the differences between each pair in the two samples, $A - B$. We then find the *absolute values* of these differences. (In computing absolute values, we simply make all signs positive.) Then we rank the absolute values of the differences. Next we compute two rank sums: the sum of the ranks of the negative differences, T_B, and the sum of the ranks of the positive differences, T_A. The hypothetical example shown by the data of table 6.13 will help to clarify these computations. The experimental information and the calculation of the rank sums are shown in table 6.13.

Table 6.13 • Example of computations for the Wilcoxon rank sum test

Pair	Sample A	Sample B	Difference (A − B)	Absolute Value of Difference	Rank of Absolute Value
1	76	65	11	11	4
2	83	79	4	4	2
3	64	66	−2	2	1
4	101	89	12	12	5
5	54	60	−6	6	3
6	79	63	16	16	6

T_A = Sum of positive ranks (in black) = 17
T_B = Sum of negative ranks (in color) = 4

Finally, we compute the test statistic T according to the rules given in the box.

Computing the Wilcoxon T Statistic for a Two-tailed Test

T = the smaller of the positive and negative rank sums, T_A and T_B, respectively

Computing the Wilcoxon T Statistic for a One-tailed Test

If the research hypothesis is that the frequency distribution for A is above (to the right of) that for B [figure 6.14(a)],

$$T = T_B \quad \text{(negative rank sum)}$$

If the research hypothesis is that the frequency distribution for A is below (to the left of) that for B [figure 6.14(b)],

$$T = T_A \quad \text{(positive rank sum)}$$

Figure 6.14 • Possible one-tailed research hypotheses in computing the *T* statistic

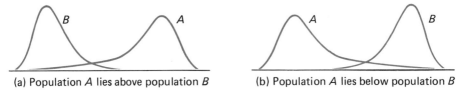

(a) Population *A* lies above population *B*   (b) Population *A* lies below population *B*

For our hypothetical example, assume that the research hypothesis is two-tailed. Then we calculate

$$T = \text{smaller rank sum} = T_B \text{ (negative rank sum)} = 4$$

We summarize in the next box the steps in computing the Wilcoxon *T* statistic for a matched pairs experiment.

Computing the Wilcoxon Test Statistic

1. Compute the differences $(A - B)$ for each pair in the sample.
2. Rank the absolute values of the differences.
3. Compute two rank sums:

$$T_A = \text{rank sum of the positive differences}$$

$$T_B = \text{rank sum of the negative differences}$$

4. Compute the Wilcoxon test statistic *T* according to the rules given in the preceding box.

If the frequency distributions for the two populations are the same, there should be little difference between the sum of the ranks of the negative differences (the ranks shown in color in table 6.13) and the sum of the ranks of the positive differences (the ranks shown in black in table 6.13). If, however, we observe a value of *T*, the smaller rank sum, which is very small compared to the larger rank sum, we will tend to reject the hypothesis that the frequency distributions are the same. A very small negative rank sum T_B would imply that A's frequency distribution lies to the right of B's [figure 6.15(a)]. In this case there would be only a *few small negative* $(A - B)$ differences in the sample. On the

Figure 6.15 • Inferences from the Wilcoxon rank sum test

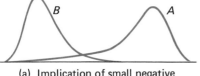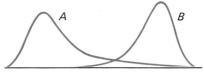

(a) Implication of small negative rank sum T_B (b) Implication of small positive rank sum T_A

other hand, a very small positive rank sum T_A would indicate that A's frequency distribution lies to the left of B's [figure 6.15(b)]. In this case only a few *small positive* $(A - B)$ differences would be present in the sample.

Rejection regions corresponding to some commonly used significance levels $(P = .10, .05,$ etc.) are given in table 3 in appendix II for both one-tailed and two-tailed tests. To use this table, we first note that n refers to the number of *pairs* of experimental units used in the experiment. Thus, for the hypothetical example, we used $n = 6$ pairs of experimental units. Table 3 of appendix II is partially reproduced in table 6.14 for your convenience.

Table 6.14 • Wilcoxon T statistic significance levels for one-tailed and two-tailed tests; from table 3, appendix II

One-tailed	Two-tailed	$n = 5$	$n = 6$
$P = .05$	$P = .10$	1	2
$P = .025$	$P = .05$		1
$P = .01$	$P = .02$		
$P = .005$	$P = .01$		

If we were testing the two-tailed research hypothesis that the frequency distributions differ, the table value corresponding to $n = 6$ and $P = .05$ (two-tailed) is $T_0 = 1$. The implication is that if the test statistic T is 1 or less, that is, 1 or 0, we will accept the hypothesis of different frequency distributions at the $\alpha = .05$ significance level. Figure 6.16(a) shows the rejection region corresponding to the two-tailed test with $\alpha = .05$.

If, however, we wished to conduct a one-tailed test, the rejection region given by table 6.14 (the partial reproduction of table 3, appendix II) is $T_0 = 2$ for $P = .05$. We therefore would accept the one-tailed research hypothesis if we observed a test statistic value T of 2 or less. This rejection region is shown in figure 6.16(b).

Figure 6.16 • Rejection regions for one-tailed and two-tailed tests using the Wilcoxon T statistic

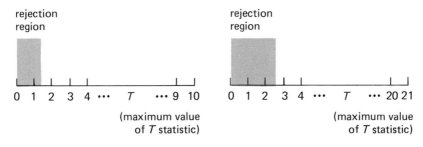

(a) Rejection region for $\alpha = .05$, two-tailed comparison

(b) Rejection region for $\alpha = .05$, one-tailed comparison

Returning to our hypothetical example, where we assumed our test is two-tailed, we calculated $T = 4$. We see that this value does not fall in the rejection region [figure 6.16(a)]. Thus these data do not provide sufficient evidence at the $\alpha = .05$ level to reject the hypothesis that the frequency distributions are the same.

In general, then, we reject the null hypothesis that the frequency distributions corresponding to populations A and B are the same when we observe a value of T that is less than or equal to the value in the table at the desired significance level. If we denote the table entry as T_0, then our rejection region is $T \leq T_0$, as shown in figure 6.17.

Figure 6.17 • Rejection region for the Wilcoxon rank sum test for a paired experiment (reject if $T \leq T_0$)

Several comments should be made before we work some examples. If any sample differences are 0 (both A and B have the same response for a given pair), we eliminate that pair and reduce our sample size (number of pairs) to $(n - 1)$. If any absolute differences result in ties, we compute the average of the ranks which would have been assigned to these measurements and assign this average to each. Finally, if the number of pairs of experimental units exceeds 50, then table 3, appendix II, is no longer applicable for finding rejection regions. We will show you how to conduct large-sample ($n > 50$) Wilcoxon rank sum tests in chapter 7.

Example 6.8

Refer to example 6.3. We compared the effects of two different diets, A and B, on the aggressive behavior of a certain strain of rats. The results of a matched pairs experiment using 10 pairs of rats (matched on preexperiment aggressive behavior) are repeated here in table 6.15.

Do these data provide sufficient evidence to indicate that the rats of this strain exhibit different amounts of aggressive behavior when on Diet A than when on Diet B?

Solution: As in example 6.3, the research hypothesis is that diet affects the frequency distribution of aggressive behavior. However, in calculating the Wilcoxon rank sum test statistic, we are using more information than we did with the sign test. The numerical magnitude of the differences is considered in the Wilcoxon test but not in the sign test. The null hypothesis is that no difference exists between the two aggressive behavior frequency distributions. Thus the test structure is as follows:

H_0: The aggressive behavior frequency distributions for diets A and B are the same.

Table 6.15 • Data and Wilcoxon calculations for the aggressive behavior experiment

Pair	Diet A	Diet B	Difference (A − B)	Absolute Value of Difference	Rank of Absolute Value
1	127	116	11	11	8
2	104	95	9	9	6.5
3	86	91	−5	5	3
4	74	62	12	12	9
5	91	92	−1	1	1
6	62	54	8	8	5
7	113	99	14	14	10
8	95	88	7	7	4
9	73	64	9	9	6.5
10	81	78	3	3	2

T_A = positive rank sum = 51
T_B = negative rank sum = 4

H_a: The aggressive behavior frequency distributions for diets A and B are different.

Since the test is two-tailed, we form the test statistic

T = smaller rank sum (of positive difference rank sum T_A and negative difference rank sum T_B)

The smaller rank sum is seen to be $T_B = 4$ in table 6.15, so the test statistic is $T = 4$.

To determine the significance level of the observed $T = 4$, we consult table 3, appendix II. For a two-tailed test and $n = 10$ pairs, we find a value of $P = .02$ for $T_0 = 5$ and a value of $P = .01$ for $T_0 = 3$. Since the observed $T = 4$ falls between the two values, we conclude that our significance level is between .01 and .02. See figure 6.18.

Figure 6.18 • Significance level for the observed $T = 4$ when $n = 10$ in example 6.8

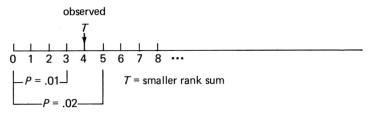

Since an event of such small probability is unlikely to occur when the null hypothesis is *true*, we have strong evidence that the two frequency distributions differ. Since the smaller rank sum is T_B, that of the negative differences, it appears that the aggressive behavior frequency distribution for diet A lies above (to the right of) that for diet B, as depicted in figure 6.19.

Figure 6.19 • Implication of small T_B (negative difference rank sum) in aggressive behavior experiment

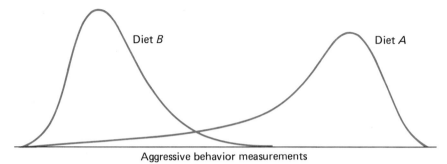

Aggressive behavior measurements

Recall from example 6.3 that the significance level associated with these same hypotheses and identical data when using the sign test is .11. Are the results contradictory? They are not. The two tests use different sample information. So if the significance levels differ, we should not be surprised. Since the Wilcoxon rank sum test uses more sample information, the inferences about the populations will, in general, be more reliable than those drawn from sign test results.

Example 6.9

Measurements of activity level are taken on each of 6 albino mice under two different conditions: White Light A and Red Light B. The resulting activity scores are given in table 6.16. Do the data provide sufficient evidence to conclude that mice are more active under a red light than they are under a white light? Use the Wilcoxon rank sum test and a fixed α of .05.

Table 6.16 • Data and Wilcoxon calculations for activity level experiment

Mouse	White Light A	Red Light B	Difference (A − B)	Absolute Value of Difference	Rank of Absolute Value
1	58	53	5	5	3
2	49	57	− 8	8	5
3	62	65	− 3	3	1.5
4	66	72	− 6	6	4
5	71	74	− 3	3	1.5
6	52	63	− 11	11	6

$$T_A = \text{positive rank sum} = 3$$
$$T_B = \text{negative rank sum} = 18$$

Solution: The research hypothesis is that mice are more active under a red light than they are under a white light. If the research hypothesis is true, then the frequency distribution of activity level measurements for mice under White

Figure 6.20 • Research hypothesis: More activity when under Red Light B than when under White Light A

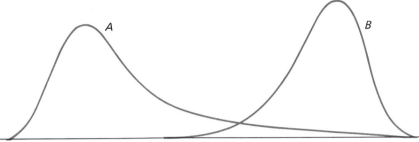

Activity level measurement

Light A should lie to the left of (below) the frequency distribution of activity level measurements for mice under Red Light B. See figure 6.20.

The null hypothesis is, as usual, that the frequency distributions for activity levels under the two conditions are the same. Since the research hypothesis is one-tailed, with A to the left of B, we use the positive rank sum as our test statistic. The test structure is as follows:

H_0: The activity level frequency distributions for White Light A and Red Light B are the same.

H_a: The activity level frequency distribution for A lies to the left of (below) that for B.

Test statistic: $T = T_A$ = positive rank sum.

We wish to test this hypothesis at a fixed α-level of .05. From table 3, appendix II, for $n = 6$, we find the rejection region to be

rejection region ($\alpha = .05$, one-tailed): $T = 0, 1, 2$

This rejection region is shown in figure 6.21.

Figure 6.21 • Rejection region for the activity level experiment when $n = 10$ and $\alpha = .05$ in a one-tailed test

rejection
region

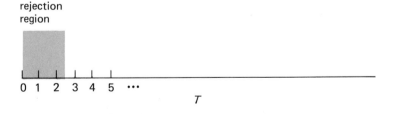

0 1 2 3 4 5 ⋯

T

Referring to table 6.16, we calculate the test statistic $T = T_A = 3$. Since this value is not in the rejection region, we find insufficient evidence to accept the research hypothesis of more activity under a red light than under a white light at the $\alpha = .05$ level. The significance level P associated with $T = 3$ is greater than .05, but more extensive tables would be needed to determine the exact value of P.

EXERCISES

1. Refer to exercise 1 in section 6.4. The level of student achievement for two junior high schools, A and B, were compared using a matched pairs experiment. Twelve sets of twins were used to reduce experimental unit variability, with one child from each twin pair attending School A and the other attending School B. An achievement test was given near the end of the ninth grade; the results are repeated below for your convenience.

Twin Pair	1	2	3	4	5	6	7	8	9	10	11	12
School A	67	80	65	72	70	86	50	63	56	81	86	60
School B	39	75	69	72	55	74	52	56	56	72	89	47

(a) Set up the structure for testing the research hypothesis that the two schools differ in academic effectiveness. Assume the Wilcoxon rank sum test is to be used.
(b) Calculate the test statistic value. Compute the significance level (as closely as possible) of the observed value using table 3 in appendix II. Compare the result with that of the sign test.

2. An experiment was conducted to compare the lengths of response time (in seconds) for two stimuli to determine if individuals exhibit a stable tendency in response time. To remove natural person-to-person variability in the responses, both stimuli were administered to each of 9 subjects in a random order. This permits an analysis of the difference between stimuli *within* each person. The results are given below.

Subject	1	2	3	4	5	6	7	8	9
Stimulus 1	9.4	7.8	5.6	12.1	6.9	4.2	8.8	7.7	6.4
Stimulus 2	10.3	8.9	4.1	14.7	8.7	7.1	11.3	5.2	7.8

(a) Set up the test structure for using the Wilcoxon rank sum test to test the research hypothesis that the frequency distributions for the two stimuli differ. Use a fixed $\alpha = .10$.
(b) Calculate the test statistic and state your conclusion.

SUMMARY

All experimental designs have a common goal: to obtain a specified amount of information from the population(s) within the limitations of the available resources. The basic elements of any experiment are the experimental units, the response measured on each experimental unit, and the treatments to be compared. Many behavioral science experiments involve the comparison of two treatments. Two experimental designs for comparing two treatments or two populations are the independent sampling design and the matched pairs design.

Methods of comparing two populations (or treatments) are either nonparametric or parametric. Nonparametric methods compare the frequency distributions of the populations, while parametric methods compare specific parameters (e.g., means, variances, etc.) of the frequency distributions. In this chapter we presented several nonparametric methods.

The *sign test* is an intuitively appealing, easy-to-apply nonparametric test for comparing populations. It is applicable either to an independent sampling experiment or to a matched pairs experiment. However, more sample information is used with rank tests for nonparametric frequency distribution comparisons. Hence rank tests are more powerful in detecting differences in population relative frequency distributions than the sign test. If an independent sampling design is used, the *Mann-Whitney U test* is appropriate. The *Wilcoxon rank sum test* is applicable to matched pairs experiments.

SUPPLEMENTARY EXERCISES

1. Define the following experimental design terms.
   (a) experimental unit   (b) treatment
2. Should an independent sampling design or a matched pairs design be used to compare two treatments when much experimental unit variability is suspected? Why?
3. In a study of public attitudes toward the mentally disturbed, 12 randomly selected subjects were assigned to one of two conditions. The 6 subjects in Condition A were read the case history of a hypothetical mental patient who had volunteered for hospitalization. The 6 subjects in Condition B were read a case history indicating that the patient had been committed. Each subject was administered a test to assess his or her attitude toward the patient described. The following results were obtained.

Condition A	27	14	11	28	22	19
Condition B	21	18	17	16	10	8

Assume that a higher score indicates a more favorable attitude towards the patient.
   (a) Give the basic elements of the experiment: experimental units, response, and treatments.
   (b) Set up a test structure for using the sign test to determine whether a difference between the frequency distributions of attitude scores exists for the two conditions.
   (c) Calculate the test statistic and the significance level P associated with its value. What is the implication of the P-value?
4. Repeat exercise 3, parts (b) and (c), but use the Mann-Whitney U test. Compare the results of the tests.
5. Haywood and Moelis (1963) used a matched pairs experiment to compare the gain in IQ for two groups of schizophrenics: those who improved in therapy and those who did not. For clinical psychologists, change in intellectual functioning as a result of therapy is an important factor in relation to improvement. The 20 pairs of schizophrenics were formed using pretherapy IQ scores and other psychological measure-

Pair	Improved in Therapy	Not Improved in Therapy	Pair	Improved in Therapy	Not Improved in Therapy
1	+8	−3	11	−3	−3
2	+0	+6	12	+4	−2
3	+7	−6	13	+10	−9
4	+3	+0	14	+8	−6
5	+4	−3	15	+6	−4
6	−3	+3	16	+3	+7
7	−6	−6	17	+1	+1
8	+4	+4	18	+2	−1
9	+4	+0	19	−1	−3
10	+5	−4	20	+0	+0

ments. The IQ score increases were as given (negative numbers indicate a decrease in IQ).

(a) State the basic elements of this experiment.

(b) Establish a structure for using the sign test to test the research hypothesis that the frequency distributions of IQ score changes differ for the two groups. Use a fixed $\alpha = .05$ (or as close as possible).

(c) Calculate the test statistic and state the conclusion.

6. (a) Repeat parts (b) and (c) of exercise 5 but use the Wilcoxon rank sum test.

(b) Compare the results to those of the sign test. In which test do you have more confidence? Why?

7. A study was undertaken to compare two food deprivation schedules, A and B, for their effect on hoarding behavior in rats. Fourteen rats were used in the study. An independent sampling design was employed with 7 rats randomly assigned to each schedule. At the end of the deprivation period, the rats were permitted free access to food pellets. The number of pellets hoarded (taken but not eaten) during a given time period were recorded. The data obtained are given below.

Schedule A	5	1	2	8	2	6	3
Schedule B	15	10	5	7	4	9	7

(a) List the basic elements of this experiment.

(b) Conduct a Mann-Whitney U test to determine at what significance level it can be inferred that a difference exists between the hoarding frequency distributions for the two deprivation schedules.

8. The experiment in exercise 7 might have been designed somewhat more carefully. If, for example, some rats characteristically take more pellets than others, even though never deprived, this kind of subject-to-subject variation could obscure actual treatment effects. An alternate design using paired rather than independent samples might be preferable. That is, prior to the actual experiment, the investigator might record the pellet intake for each potential subject and form pairs of subjects with similar intake records. Then, within each pair, the investigator could randomly assign each subject to one of the two deprivation conditions. Such a design would permit a

comparison of the effects of the two deprivation conditions within relatively homogeneous pairs of subjects.

Suppose that a subsequent experiment was conducted in the fashion described above. The results on the number of pellets hoarded are given below.

Pair	1	2	3	4	5	6	7
Schedule A	2	3	7	4	3	10	6
Schedule B	7	8	6	11	6	12	8

(a) Conduct the test of the same research hypothesis as in exercise 7(b) but use the Wilcoxon rank sum test.

(b) Compare the results of the two tests. Did the change in experimental design pay any dividends?

9. Much research has recently been conducted on prosocial behavior and the conditions under which people help others. Rosenhan, Underwood, and Moore (1974) investigated the influence of mood on sharing. Research like this looks at the influence our moods have on our behaviors.

The following data are measures of sharing obtained in an independent sampling design to compare a control group to a positive affect group. There are 10 subjects in each group.

Control Group	0	3	1	1	2	0	2	4	0	1
Positive Affect Group	3	6	4	2	3	3	3	2	4	0

Use the sign test to determine whether there is sufficient evidence to support the research hypothesis that the sharing measurement frequency distribution for the positive affect group lies above (to the right of) that for the control group. Use $\alpha = .05$ (as close as possible).

10. Repeat exercise 9 but use a Mann-Whitney U test. Compare the results of the two tests.

11. Wegener (1965) was interested in whether animals can readily discriminate between varying amounts of a stimulus. Ten pairs of monkeys were matched for performance on an illumination task. They were trained so that performance on that task either would enhance or would retard learning on an auditory task. The following data give the number of trials to reach criterion for the positively and negatively trained groups.

Pair	1	2	3	4	5	6	7	8	9	10
Positive Training	23	34	27	26	40	35	50	31	51	49
Negative Training	35	30	25	35	27	36	27	48	53	26

(a) List the basic elements of this experiment.
(b) Set up a structure to use the sign test to determine whether the frequency distribution of trials to reach criterion for positively trained monkeys lies below (to the left of) that for monkeys receiving negative training.
(c) Calculate the test statistic and determine its significance level. What is your conclusion?

12. Repeat parts (b) and (c) of exercise 11 but use the Wilcoxon rank sum test. Compare the significance levels for the two tests.

REFERENCES

Haywood, H. C., and Moelis, I. 1963. Effect of symptom change on intellectual function in schizophrenia. *Journal of Abnormal and Social Psychology* 67:76–78.

Rosenhan, D.; Underwood, B.; and Moore, B. 1974. Affect moderates self-gratification and altruism. *Journal of Personality and Social Psychology* 30:546–554.

Savage, I. R. 1953. Bibliography of nonparametric statistics and related topics. *Journal of the American Statistical Association* 48:844–906.

Siegel, S. 1956. *Nonparametric statistics for the behavioral sciences.* New York: McGraw-Hill.

Wegener, J. G. 1965. Cross-modal transfer in monkeys. *Journal of Comparative and Physiological Psychology* 59:450–452.

7•The Normal Probability Distribution

INTRODUCTION

In this chapter we come to a probability distribution of immense importance in statistical inference. This distribution, called the *normal probability distribution,* plays a prominent role in both parametric and nonparametric inference-making procedures. It provides a large-sample approximation to the probability distributions for many estimators and test statistics.

This chapter is linked to chapters 5 and 6 because the probability distributions for the binomial random variable, the Mann-Whitney U statistic, and the Wilcoxon matched pairs statistic can all be approximated by a normal probability distribution when moderate to large samples are used. This chapter is also linked to future chapters because the probability distribution of the sample mean and many other statistics tend to have probability distributions that are approximately normal when the samples are large. Accordingly, we will examine the nature and properties of the normal probability distribution in some detail here.

In section 7.1 we discuss the properties of the normal probability distribution. One of the most important theorems in statistics, the Central Limit Theorem, is the topic of section 7.2. This theorem is one of the major reasons that the normal distribution plays such a key role in statistics. A general discussion of the probability distributions of sample statistics is contained in section 7.3.

In section 7.4 we show you how to use a table to calculate the probabilities

155

associated with the normal distribution. Finally, in sections 7.5 and 7.6 we use the normal distribution to approximate the probability distributions of the binomial random variable and some nonparametric test statistics.

7.1 • PROPERTIES OF THE NORMAL PROBABILITY DISTRIBUTION

Continuous random variables, as we noted in section 4.3, can assume infinitely many values corresponding to the points on a line interval. The heights and weights of people, laboratory experimental measurement errors, and latencies of response to an applied stimulus are typical examples of continuous random variables. Reviewing section 4.5, we note that the probabilistic model for the frequency distribution of a continuous random variable involves the selection of a curve, usually smooth, called the probability distribution (or probability density function). These distributions may assume a variety of shapes. It is interesting to note, though, that a very large number of random variables observed in nature possess a frequency distribution that is approximately bell-shaped or, as the statistician would say, is approximately a normal probability distribution.

A normal probability distribution is shown in figure 7.1. Notice that it is bell-shaped and that it is symmetrical about the mean μ.

Figure 7.1 • Normal probability distribution

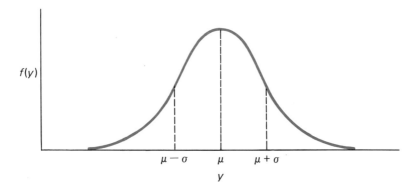

The area under the normal curve, by convention, is equal to 1, half lying to the left of the mean, half to the right. Distances along the horizontal axis of figure 7.1 are measured in units of σ, the standard deviation of y. Consequently, there are many normal curves, one for each pair of values of the mean μ and the standard deviation σ. See figure 7.2. All the curves in figure 7.2 are bell-shaped and possess the properties described above. (Note that the mathematical equation for the normal probability distribution is omitted here. If you are interested in studying the equation, consult the references listed at the end of the chapter.)

Figure 7.2 • Three different normal probability distributions

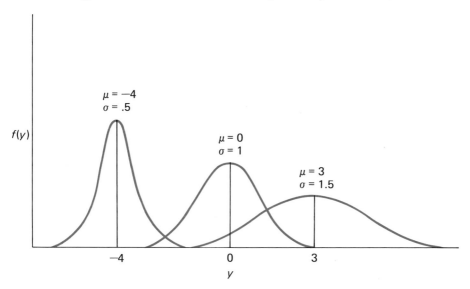

The normal probability distribution has one additional property. Theoretically, the normal random variable can assume any positive or negative value, no matter how large or how small. That means that the normal curves in figures 7.1 and 7.2 never actually touch the horizontal axis. But you can see from figure 7.3 that it is highly improbable that the normal random variable would assume values lying in the tails of the distribution.

Figure 7.3 • The probability that a normal random variable will fall in a certain interval

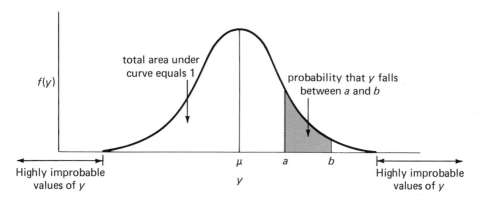

Saying that the normal random variable can assume any value, positive or negative, raises a question. How can it be used to model the probability distributions for random variables that are observed in nature? Certainly the height of

people, the liver weight of laboratory mice, or the latency of responses to a given stimulus cannot assume *any* value. For example, none of these random variables can assume negative values. Nevertheless, frequency histograms plotted for data collected on these random variables, and for many other random variables, often generate a bell-shaped figure which may be approximated by a normal probability distribution. Why this particular phenomenon exists is still unknown. However, one explanation is provided by the Central Limit Theorem, a theorem that may be regarded as one of the most important and pervasive in statistics.

One important point should be noted here. Many random variables possess probability distributions that are not normal. Some are nonsymmetric, some skewing to the right and some to the left. Some tend to be flat, others, peaked. But, surprisingly, many distributions of data will tend to be bell-shaped.

7.2 • THE CENTRAL LIMIT THEOREM

The *Central Limit Theorem* states that under rather general conditions, sums and means of samples of random measurements drawn from a population tend to possess, approximately, a bell-shaped distribution in *repeated sampling*. The significance of this statement is perhaps best illustrated by the following sampling experiment.

Consider a population of die throws generated by tossing a die infinitely many times with the resulting probability distribution given in figure 7.4. We draw a sample of $n = 5$ measurements from the population by tossing a die five times. Then we record each of the five observations, as indicated in table 7.1. Note that the numbers we observed in the first sample were 3, 5, 1, 3, and 2. We calculate the sum of the five measurements as well as the sample mean $\bar{y}$.

Figure 7.4 • Probability distribution for y, the number shown in the toss of a single die

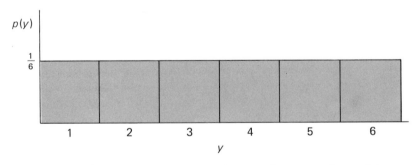

For experimental purposes, we repeat the sampling procedure 100 times, or preferably even more times. The results for 100 samples are given in table 7.1 along with the corresponding values of

$$\sum_{i=1}^{5} y_i \text{ and } \bar{y}$$

Table 7.1 • Sampling from the population of die throws

Sample Number	Sample Measurements	$\sum y_i$	$\bar{y}$	Sample Number	Sample Measurements	$\sum y_i$	$\bar{y}$
1	3, 5, 1, 3, 2	14	2.8	51	2, 3, 5, 3, 2	15	3.0
2	3, 1, 1, 4, 6	15	3.0	52	1, 1, 1, 2, 4	9	1.8
3	1, 3, 1, 6, 1	12	2.4	53	2, 6, 3, 4, 5	20	4.0
4	4, 5, 3, 3, 2	17	3.4	54	1, 2, 2, 1, 1	7	1.4
5	3, 1, 3, 5, 2	14	2.8	55	2, 4, 4, 6, 2	18	3.6
6	2, 4, 4, 2, 4	16	3.2	56	3, 2, 5, 4, 5	19	3.8
7	4, 2, 5, 5, 3	19	3.8	57	2, 4, 2, 4, 5	17	3.4
8	3, 5, 5, 5, 5	23	4.6	58	5, 5, 4, 3, 2	19	3.8
9	6, 5, 5, 1, 6	23	4.6	59	5, 4, 4, 6, 3	22	4.4
10	5, 1, 6, 1, 6	19	3.8	60	3, 2, 5, 3, 1	14	2.8
11	1, 1, 1, 5, 3	11	2.2	61	2, 1, 4, 1, 3	11	2.2
12	3, 4, 2, 4, 4	17	3.4	62	4, 1, 1, 5, 2	13	2.6
13	2, 6, 1, 5, 4	18	3.6	63	2, 3, 1, 2, 3	11	2.2
14	6, 3, 4, 2, 5	20	4.0	64	2, 3, 3, 2, 6	16	3.2
15	2, 6, 2, 1, 5	16	3.2	65	4, 3, 5, 2, 6	20	4.0
16	1, 5, 1, 2, 5	14	2.8	66	3, 1, 3, 3, 4	14	2.8
17	3, 5, 1, 1, 2	12	2.4	67	4, 6, 1, 3, 6	20	4.0
18	3, 2, 4, 3, 5	17	3.4	68	2, 4, 6, 6, 3	21	4.2
19	5, 1, 6, 3, 1	16	3.2	69	4, 1, 6, 5, 5	21	4.2
20	1, 6, 4, 4, 1	16	3.2	70	6, 6, 6, 4, 5	27	5.4
21	6, 4, 2, 3, 5	20	4.0	71	2, 2, 5, 6, 3	18	3.6
22	1, 3, 5, 4, 1	14	2.8	72	6, 6, 6, 1, 6	25	5.0
23	2, 6, 5, 2, 6	21	4.2	73	4, 4, 4, 3, 1	16	3.2
24	3, 5, 1, 3, 5	17	3.4	74	4, 4, 5, 4, 2	19	3.8
25	5, 2, 4, 4, 3	18	3.6	75	4, 5, 4, 1, 4	18	3.6
26	6, 1, 1, 1, 6	15	3.0	76	5, 3, 2, 3, 4	17	3.4
27	1, 4, 1, 2, 6	14	2.8	77	1, 3, 3, 1, 5	13	2.6
28	3, 1, 2, 1, 5	12	2.4	78	4, 1, 5, 5, 3	18	3.6
29	1, 5, 5, 4, 5	20	4.0	79	4, 5, 6, 5, 4	24	4.8
30	4, 5, 3, 5, 2	19	3.8	80	1, 5, 3, 4, 2	15	3.0
31	4, 1, 6, 1, 1	13	2.6	81	4, 3, 4, 6, 3	20	4.0
32	3, 6, 4, 1, 2	16	3.2	82	5, 4, 2, 1, 6	18	3.6
33	3, 5, 5, 2, 2	17	3.4	83	1, 3, 2, 2, 5	13	2.6
34	1, 1, 5, 6, 3	16	3.2	84	5, 4, 1, 4, 6	20	4.0
35	2, 6, 1, 6, 2	17	3.4	85	2, 4, 2, 5, 5	18	3.6
36	2, 4, 3, 1, 3	13	2.6	86	1, 6, 3, 1, 6	17	3.4
37	1, 5, 1, 5, 2	14	2.8	87	2, 2, 4, 3, 2	13	2.6
38	6, 6, 5, 3, 3	23	4.6	88	4, 4, 5, 4, 4	21	4.2
39	3, 3, 5, 2, 1	14	2.8	89	2, 5, 4, 3, 4	18	3.6
40	2, 6, 6, 6, 5	25	5.0	90	5, 1, 6, 4, 3	19	3.8
41	5, 5, 2, 3, 4	19	3.8	91	5, 2, 5, 6, 3	21	4.2
42	6, 4, 1, 6, 2	19	3.8	92	6, 4, 1, 2, 1	14	2.8
43	2, 5, 3, 1, 4	15	3.0	93	6, 3, 1, 5, 2	17	3.4
44	4, 2, 3, 2, 1	12	2.4	94	1, 3, 6, 4, 2	16	3.2
45	4, 4, 5, 4, 4	21	4.2	95	6, 1, 4, 2, 2	15	3.0
46	5, 4, 5, 5, 4	23	4.6	96	1, 1, 2, 3, 1	8	1.6
47	6, 6, 6, 2, 1	21	4.2	97	6, 2, 5, 1, 6	20	4.0
48	2, 1, 5, 5, 4	17	3.4	98	3, 1, 1, 4, 1	10	2.0
49	6, 4, 3, 1, 5	19	3.8	99	5, 2, 1, 6, 1	15	3.0
50	4, 4, 4, 4, 4	20	4.0	100	2, 4, 3, 4, 6	19	3.8

We construct a frequency histogram for

$$\bar{y} \text{ or } \sum_{i=1}^{5} y_i$$

for the 100 samples and observe the resulting distribution in figure 7.5.

Figure 7.5 • Histogram of the sample means for the die-tossing experiments in section 7.2

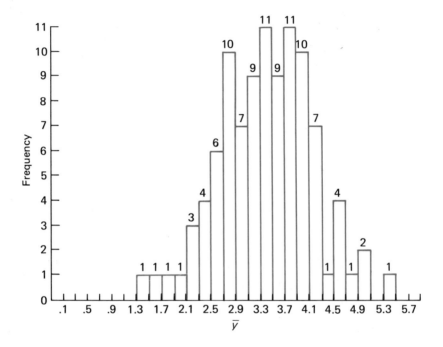

You will observe an interesting result. The values of y in the population (y = 1, 2, 3, 4, 5, 6) are equiprobable and hence have a probability distribution that is perfectly horizontal. However, the distribution of the sample means (or sums) chosen from the population is *mound-shaped*. We will add one additional comment without proof. If we should repeat the experiment outlined above for a larger sample size, say n = 10, we would find that the distribution of the sample means tends to become more nearly bell-shaped.

A proper determination of the form of the probability distribution of the sample means requires infinitely many samples, or, at the very least, far more than the 100 samples contained in our experiment. Nevertheless, the 100 samples illustrate the basic idea involved in the *Central Limit Theorem*, which may be stated as follows.

The Central Limit Theorem

If random samples, each of n observations, are drawn from a population with finite mean μ and standard deviation σ, then when n is large, the sample mean $\bar{y}$ will be approximately normally distributed with mean μ and standard deviation $\sigma/\sqrt{n}$. The approximation will become more and more accurate as n becomes larger.

The Central Limit Theorem can be restated to apply to the *sum* of the sample measurements,

$$\sum_{i=1}^{n} y_i$$

This sum, as n becomes large, also tends to possess a normal distribution in repeated sampling, with mean $n\mu$ and standard deviation $\sigma\sqrt{n}$.

You will note that the mean and standard deviation of the distribution of sample means are definitely related to the mean and standard deviation of the sampled population as well as to the sample size n. We will defer discussion of this point for the moment and consider the relevance of the Central Limit Theorem to our previous work.

The significance of the Central Limit Theorem is twofold. First, it explains why some measurements tend to possess, approximately, a normal distribution. We might imagine the height of a human as being composed of a number of elements, each random, associated with such things as the height of the mother, the height of the father, the activity of a particular gland, the environment, and diet. If each of these effects tends to add to the others to yield the measurement of height, then height is the sum of a number of random variables. Thus the Central Limit Theorem may become effective and yield a distribution of heights that is approximately normal. All this is conjecture, of course, because we really do not know the true situation. Nevertheless, the Central Limit Theorem, along with other theorems dealing with normally distributed random variables, provides an explanation of the rather common occurrence of normally distributed random variables in nature.

The second and most important contribution of the Central Limit Theorem is in statistical inference. Many estimators and decision makers that are used to make inferences about population parameters are sums or averages of the sample measurements. When this is true and when the sample size n is sufficiently large, we would expect the estimator or decision maker to possess an approximately normal probability distribution in repeated sampling according to the Central Limit Theorem. This is particularly important because, for all practical situations you will confront, this result does not depend on the shape of the probability distribution of the individual sample measurements. Then, because of this approximate normality, we can use the Empirical Rule discussed in chapter 2 to describe the behavior of the inference maker. This aspect of the Central Limit Theorem will be used in section 7.5 and in later chapters dealing with statistical inference.

One disturbing feature of the Central Limit theorem, and of most approximation procedures, is that we must have some idea as to how large the sample size *n* must be for the approximation to give useful results. Unfortunately, there is no clear-cut answer to this question. The appropriate value for *n* will depend on the population probability distribution as well as on the use we make of the approximation.

Although the preceding comment sidesteps the difficulty and suggests that we must rely solely upon experience, we may take comfort in the results of the die-tossing experiment discussed previously in this section. Observe figure 7.5 and note that the distribution of $\bar{y}$, in repeated sampling, based upon a sample of only $n = 5$ measurements, tends to be approximately bell-shaped. Generally speaking, the Central Limit Theorem works very well, even for small samples. But this is not always true. We will observe an exception to this rule in section 7.5. The appropriate sample size *n* will be given for specific applications of the Central Limit Theorem as they are encountered in section 7.5 and later in the text.

EXERCISES

1. Give two reasons why the Central Limit Theorem is so important in statistics.
2. Let *y* be the number of dots observed when a single die is tossed. It can be shown (we omit the proof) that the mean and the standard deviation of the probability distribution for *y* in figure 7.4 are $\mu = 3.5$ and $\sigma = 1.71$, respectively. Suppose the sampling experiments of section 7.2 were repeated over and over again infinitely many times, each sample consisting of $n = 5$ measurements. Find the mean and standard deviation for this distribution of sample means. (Hint: Use the information contained in the Central Limit Theorem.) Do these values describe the histogram shown in figure 7.5?

7.3 • STATISTICS AND SAMPLING DISTRIBUTIONS

Recall that numerical descriptive measures of the population are called parameters. Since our objective is to make inferences about the population, it is reasonable that we would wish to make inferences about μ, σ, σ^2, and other parameters of the population. For example, we might use the sample measurements to estimate μ, σ^2, or σ by computing the corresponding sample numerical descriptive measures. These sample measurements are called *statistics*. For example, we might use the sample mean $\bar{y}$ to estimate the population mean μ. Other examples of statistics are the Mann-Whitney *U* statistic and the Wilcoxon rank sum statistic of chapter 6.

> **Definition 7.1**
>
> A statistic is a quantity computed from the sample measurements.

> **Definition 7.2**
>
> The probability distribution for a statistic is called its sampling distribution.

What does this mean?

Recall that the probability distribution for a random variable is the relative frequency histogram that would be obtained if we were to observe the random variable infinitely many times. Here the random variable is a statistic, a quantity computed from the measurements in a sample. Therefore, to be able to observe the statistic over and over again, we must sample repeatedly. For this reason, the relative frequency histogram for a statistic obtained in repeated sampling is called the sampling distribution, or equivalently, the probability distribution for the statistic.

Figure 7.5, the relative frequency histogram for 100 samples of $n = 5$ measurements, is intended to give us an idea of the shape of the sampling distribution for the mean of a sample of five tosses of a die. To obtain the exact form of the sampling distribution, we would have to repeat the process of sampling not 100 but infinitely many times. The point of the Central Limit Theorem is that the resulting distribution will be approximately normal.

We now know that many inference makers—test statistics and estimators—possess sampling distributions that are approximately normal for large samples. Next we must become more familiar with the properties of the normal distribution. You will recall that the area under a probability distribution corresponds to a probability. In the next section we will learn how to find areas under the normal curve.

EXERCISES

1. To give some insight into the nature of the sampling distribution for the mean of a sample of five die tosses, we conducted an empirical sampling experiment (see table 7.1). We obtained the relative frequency histogram for 100 sample means, figure 7.5. If we had sampled over and over again, selecting infinitely many samples of five die tosses each, and had constructed a similar relative frequency histogram, we would have obtained the sampling distribution for the mean of a sample of five die tosses.

   To better understand the notion of a sampling distribution for a statistic, conduct an empirical sampling experiment similar to the one described above but use the median of a sample of five die tosses. To minimize your labor, use the data for the 100 samples presented in table 7.1. Find the median for each of the 100 samples and construct a relative frequency histogram. Compare your histogram with the relative frequency histogram for the sample means in figure 7.5. How could you obtain a more accurate characterization of the sampling distribution of the sample median?

2. Repeat the sampling experiment for die tosses in section 7.2 and combine your 100 samples with the one hundred samples of table 7.1.

   (a) Use the combined collection of 200 sample means to construct a relative frequency histogram. You will probably obtain a better characterization of the sampling distribution of the sample mean than that provided by figure 7.5.

   (b) Repeat the preceding instructions but use the sample medians. Construct a relative frequency histogram for the 200 sample medians.

7.4 · TABULATED AREAS OF THE NORMAL PROBABILITY DISTRIBUTION

In section 7.1 we noted that the normal probability distribution depends on the numerical values of μ and σ. By choosing different values for these parameters, we could generate infinitely many bell-shaped normal distributions. A separate table of areas for each of these curves is obviously impractical. We would like one table of areas applicable to all normal distributions. Then we could calculate any probability associated with a normal distribution. Why? Because for continuous random variables like the normal distribution, areas under the frequency function are probabilities.

The easiest way to do this is to work with areas lying within a specified number of standard deviations of the mean, as was done in the case of the Empirical Rule. For instance, we know that approximately .68 of the area lies within one standard deviation of the mean, .95 within two, and almost all within three. What fraction of the total area will lie within .7 standard deviations, for instance? This question, as well as others, can be answered by table 4, appendix II.

Since the normal curve is symmetrical about the mean, we may simplify our table of areas by listing the areas between the mean μ and a specified number z of standard deviations to the right of μ. The distance from the mean to a given value of y is $(y - \mu)$. Expressing this distance in units of the standard deviation σ, we obtain the z score that was initially defined in section 2.9. Because this z score is associated with the normal probability distribution, we call it a *normal z score*.

Normal z score

$$z = \frac{y - \mu}{\sigma}$$

Note that there is a one-to-one correspondence between the normal z score and the normal random variable y. Particularly, $z = 0$ when $y = \mu$.

The probability distribution for z is often called the *standardized normal distribution* because its mean is 0 and its standard deviation is 1. It is shown in figure 7.6. The area under the normal curve between the mean $z = 0$ and a specified value of z, say z_0, is recorded in table 4, appendix II, and is shown as the shaded area in figure 7.6.

Figure 7.6 • Standardized normal distribution

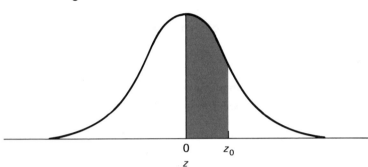

Since the normal distribution is symmetrical and the total area under the curve is 1, half of the area will lie to the right of the mean and half to the left. Areas to the left of the mean can be calculated by using the corresponding, and equal, area to the right of the mean.

Referring to table 4, appendix II, we note that z, correct to the nearest tenth, is recorded in the left-hand column. The second decimal place for z, corresponding to hundredths, is given across the top row. The area between the mean and $z = .7$ standard deviations to the right, read in the second column of the table opposite $z = .7$, is found to be .2580. This value is shaded in table 7.2.

Table 7.2 • Portion of table 4, appendix II, the table of areas under the normal curve

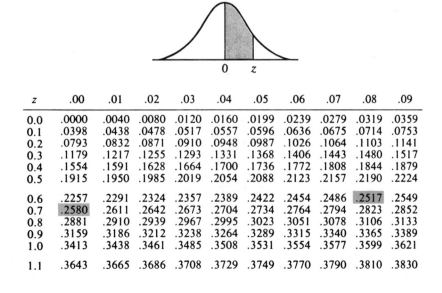

z	.00	.01	.02	.03	.04	.05	.06	.07	.08	.09
0.0	.0000	.0040	.0080	.0120	.0160	.0199	.0239	.0279	.0319	.0359
0.1	.0398	.0438	.0478	.0517	.0557	.0596	.0636	.0675	.0714	.0753
0.2	.0793	.0832	.0871	.0910	.0948	.0987	.1026	.1064	.1103	.1141
0.3	.1179	.1217	.1255	.1293	.1331	.1368	.1406	.1443	.1480	.1517
0.4	.1554	.1591	.1628	.1664	.1700	.1736	.1772	.1808	.1844	.1879
0.5	.1915	.1950	.1985	.2019	.2054	.2088	.2123	.2157	.2190	.2224
0.6	.2257	.2291	.2324	.2357	.2389	.2422	.2454	.2486	.2517	.2549
0.7	.2580	.2611	.2642	.2673	.2704	.2734	.2764	.2794	.2823	.2852
0.8	.2881	.2910	.2939	.2967	.2995	.3023	.3051	.3078	.3106	.3133
0.9	.3159	.3186	.3212	.3238	.3264	.3289	.3315	.3340	.3365	.3389
1.0	.3413	.3438	.3461	.3485	.3508	.3531	.3554	.3577	.3599	.3621
1.1	.3643	.3665	.3686	.3708	.3729	.3749	.3770	.3790	.3810	.3830

Similarly, the area between the mean and $z = 1.0$ is .3413. The area lying within one standard deviation on either side of the mean is twice the quantity .3413, or .6826. The area lying within two standard deviations of the mean, correct to four decimal places, is $(2)(.4772) = .9544$. These numbers correspond to the approximate values, 68 percent and 95 percent, respectively, used in the Empirical Rule in chapter 2. We conclude this section with some examples showing how we find and use areas under the normal curve.

Example 7.1

Find the area under the normal curve between $z = 0$ and $z = .68$.

Solution: The area that we seek is shown in figure 7.7

Figure 7.7 • Area under the normal curve between $z = 0$ and $z = .68$

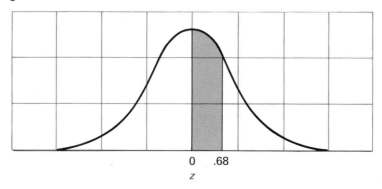

$$0 \quad .68$$
$$z$$

To find this area, move down the left-hand column of table 7.2 until you reach $z = .6$. Then move across the top row of table 7.2 to the .08 column. The desired area is at the intersection of the $z = .6$ row and the .08 column, namely, .2517. This entry is shaded in table 7.2.

Example 7.2

Find the area between $z = -.5$ and $z = 1.0$, as shown in figure 7.8.

Figure 7.8 • Area under the normal curve for example 7.2

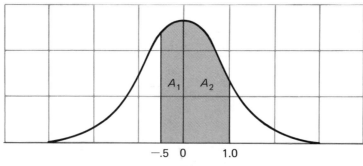

$$-.5 \quad 0 \qquad 1.0$$
$$z$$

Solution The area is equal to the sum of the two areas A_1 and A_2 shown in figure 7.8. From table 4, appendix II, we find $A_2 = .3413$. The area A_1 is equal to the corresponding area between $z = 0$ and $z = .5$, or $A_1 = .1915$. Thus the total area is

$$A = A_1 + A_2 = .1915 + .3413 = .5328$$

Example 7.3

Let y be a normally distributed random variable with mean 10 and standard deviation 2. Find the probability that y lies between 11 and 13.6.

Solution As a first step, we must calculate the values of z corresponding to $y_1 = 11$ and $y_2 = 13.6$. Thus

$$z_1 = \frac{y_1 - \mu}{\sigma} = \frac{11 - 10}{2} = .5$$

$$z_2 = \frac{y_2 - \mu}{\sigma} = \frac{13.6 - 10}{2} = 1.80$$

The desired probability P is therefore the area lying between z_1 and z_2, as shown in figure 7.9. The area between $z = 0$ and z_1 is $A_1 = .1915$, and the area between $z = 0$ and z_2 is $A_2 = .4641$. These values are easily obtained from table 4. The probability P is equal to the difference between A_1 and A_2; that is,

$$P = A_2 - A_1 = .4641 - .1915 = .2726$$

Figure 7.9 • Area under the normal curve for example 7.3

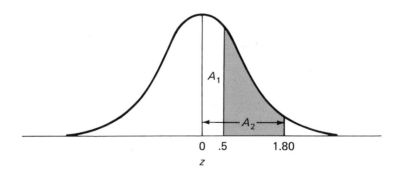

Example 7.4

Find the value of z such that the area to the right of the mean is equal to .4678. See figure 7.10.

Solution: In the preceding examples we found the area under the normal curve over the interval determined by two normal scores. That is, we gave z-values and asked for the corresponding areas. In this problem we will have to reverse the procedure.

We are given an area to the right of the mean $(z = 0)$ of the standard

Figure 7.10 • Area under the normal curve for example 7.4

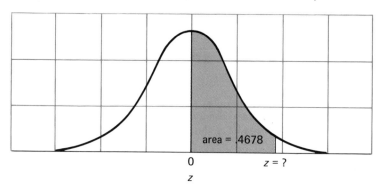

normal distribution and are asked to find the corresponding z score. To do this, we examine table 4 in appendix II. We look for an entry (area) as close as possible to the specified area, .4678. In this case we see that .4678 appears in the row corresponding to $z = 1.8$ and the column corresponding to .05. See figure 7.11. Then the desired value of z (figure 7.10) is 1.85.

Figure 7.11 • Finding the z score corresponding to an area of .4678, example 7.4

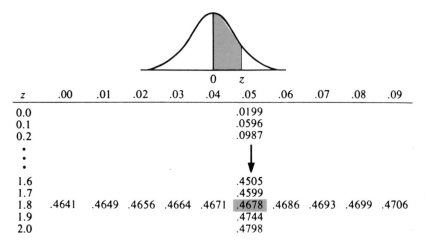

z	.00	.01	.02	.03	.04	.05	.06	.07	.08	.09
0.0						.0199				
0.1						.0596				
0.2						.0987				
•										
•										
•										
1.6						.4505				
1.7						.4599				
1.8	.4641	.4649	.4656	.4664	.4671	.4678	.4686	.4693	.4699	.4706
1.9						.4744				
2.0						.4798				

Example 7.5

Find the value of z such that the area to the right of the mean is equal to .2953. See figure 7.12.

Solution: Just as we did for example 7.4, we search table 4 in appendix II for the area closest to .2953. We find that .2953 falls between the table values of .2939 and .2967 (see figure 7.13). In fact, it falls exactly halfway between these two areas: $\frac{1}{2}(.2939 + .2967) = .2953$.

Figure 7.12 • Area under the normal curve for example 7.5

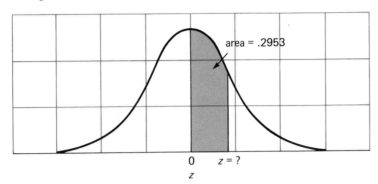

area = .2953

0 z = ?

z

The z scores corresponding to these two areas are .82 and .83, respectively. Thus we would expect the z score corresponding to an area of .2953 to fall halfway between these two scores, or $z = .825$. If we were asked to round to the nearest hundredth, we would give our answer as $z = .83$.

Figure 7.13 • Finding the z score for an area of .2953, example 7.5

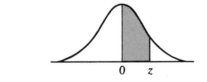

0 z

z	.00	.01	.02	.03	.04	.05	.06	.07	.08	.09
.	.	.	.	.	.	.	.	.	.	.
.	.	.	.	.	.	.	.	.	.	.
.	.	.	.	.	.	.	.	.	.	.
0.6	.2257	.2291	.2324	.2357	.2389	.2422	.2454	.2486	.2517	.2549
0.7	.2580	.2611	.2642	.2673	.2704	.2734	.2764	.2794	.2823	.2852
0.8	.2881	.2910	.2939	.2967	.2995	.3023	.3051	.3078	.3106	.3133
0.9	.3159	.3186	.3212	.3238	.3264	.3289	.3315	.3340	.3365	.3389
1.0	.3413	.3438	.3461	.3485	.3508	.3531	.3554	.3577	.3599	.3621

Example 7.6

Find the value of z, say z_0, such that .95 of the area (to four decimal places) is within $\pm z_0$ standard deviations of the mean. See figure 7.14.

Solution: Half of the total area .95 lies to the left of the mean and half to the right, because the normal distribution is symmetrical. Thus we seek the value z_0 corresponding to an area equal to .475. The area .475 is in the row corresponding to $z = 1.9$ and the .06 column. Hence $z_0 = 1.96$. Note that this is very close to the approximate value $z = 2$ used in the Empirical Rule.

Figure 7.14 • Area under the normal curve for example 7.6

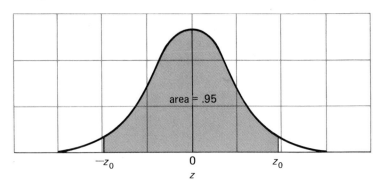

EXERCISES

1. Using table 4 in appendix II, calculate the area under the normal curve between the given values.
   (a) $z = 0$ and $z = 1.4$ (b) $z = 0$ and $z = .96$
2. Repeat exercise 1 for these values.
   (a) $z = 0$ and $z = 1.2$ (b) $z = 0$ and $z = -.9$
3. Repeat exercise 1 for these values.
   (a) $z = 0$ and $z = 1.61$ (b) $z = 0$ and $z = -.24$
4. Repeat exercise 1 for these values.
   (a) $z = 0$ and $z = -1.35$ (b) $z = 0$ and $z = 2.01$
5. Repeat exercise 1 for these values.
   (a) $z = .21$ and $z = 1.5$ (b) $z = .3$ and $z = -.3$
6. Repeat exercise 1 for these values.
   (a) $z = 1.21$ and $z = 1.68$ (b) $z = -1.14$ and $z = 1.4$
7. Using table 4, calculate the area under the normal curve between these values.
   (a) $z = -.22$ and $z = .75$ (b) $z = 1.25$ and $z = 1.83$
8. Using table 4, calculate the area under the normal curve corresponding to these values.
   (a) $-0.8 \le z \le 0.8$ (b) $z < -1.3$ or $z > 1.3$
9. Repeat exercise 8 for these values.
   (a) $-1.6 < z < 1.6$ (b) $z < -.7$ or $z > .7$
10. Repeat exercise 8 for these values.
   (a) $-1.96 < z < 1.96$ (b) $z \le -2.58$ or $z \ge 2.58$
11. Find the probability that z is greater than $-.75$.
12. Find the probability that z is less than 1.42.
13. Find a value z_0 such that $P(z > z_0) = .5$.
14. Find a value z_0 such that $P(z > z_0) = .025$.
15. Find a value z_0 such that $P(z < z_0) = .8051$.
16. Find a value z_0 such that $P(z > z_0) = .2327$.
17. Find a value z_0 such that $P(z < z_0) = .1170$.
18. Find a value z_0 such that $P(z > z_0) = .10$.
19. Find a value z_0 such that $P(z < z_0) = .05$.
20. Find a value z_0 such that $P(-z_0 < z < z_0) = .90$.

21. Find a value z_0 such that $P(-z_0 < z < z_0) = .99$.
22. Let y be a normally distributed random variable with mean 100 and standard deviation 15. If a value of y is chosen at random from the population, find the probability that y falls between $y = 110$ and $y = 120$.
23. The grade point averages of a large population of college students are approximately normally distributed, with mean 2.4 and standard deviation .8. What fraction of the students will possess a grade point average in excess of 3.0?
24. Refer to exercise 23. If students with a grade point average equal to or less than 1.4 are dropped from college, what percentage of the students will be dropped?
25. One dimension of personality that psychologists are interested in measuring is the masculinity-feminity aspect and how it relates to other personality and behavioral indices. Bieliauskas (1974) reports a study in which feminist and nonfeminist college women took two tests: the Gough Feminity Scale and the Drawing Completion Test. The first test measures conscious attitudes and the second test taps unconscious masculine-feminine identity. Below are given the means and standard deviations on both tests for both sets of subjects.

	Feminists		Nonfeminists	
	Mean	Standard Deviation	Mean	Standard Deviation
Gough	32.14	5.59	34.10	4.46
DCT	18.83	3.52	20.69	3.34

    Suppose one feminist obtained a Gough score of 40 and a DCT score of 23. Convert her scores to standard scores. On which scale did she score the highest? If a large number of feminists took the Gough test, what percentage of feminists got higher scores than she did? What percentage scored higher than she did on the DCT test?
26. Refer to exercise 25. If a person got scores of 30 and 15 on the Gough and DCT tests, respectively, what is the person's percentile rank (see def. 2.6) for each test on both feminist and nonfeminist norms?
27. The intelligence quotient is a normally distributed random variable with mean 100 and standard deviation 16. Find the probability that a person's IQ lies between 115 and 95. What fraction of people have an IQ over 120?

7.5 • THE NORMAL APPROXIMATION TO THE BINOMIAL DISTRIBUTION

In chapter 5 we considered several applications of the binomial probability distribution. All of them required that we calculate the probability $p(y)$ that the number y of successes in n trials would fall in a given region. For the most part, we restricted our attention to examples where n is small because of the tedious calculations necessary in the computations of $p(y)$. Let us now consider the problem of calculating $p(y)$, or the probability that y falls in a given region, when n is large, say $n = 1000$.

A direct calculation of $p(y)$ for large values of n is not an impossibility, but it is a formidable task which we would prefer to avoid. Fortunately, the Central Limit Theorem provides a solution to this problem. We may view y, the number of successes in n trials, as a sum that satisfies the conditions of the Central Limit Theorem. Each trial results in either "no success" or "success," with probability q and p, respectively. Therefore, each of the n trials may be regarded as an independent observation drawn from a simpler binomial experiment consisting of one trial. The total number y of successes in n trials is the sum of these n independent observations. Then if n is sufficiently large, the binomial variable y will be approximately normally distributed with mean and standard deviation (given in chapter 5) np and $\sqrt{npq}$, respectively. We may then use areas under a fitted normal curve to approximate the binomial probabilities.

For instance, consider a binomial probability distribution for y when $n = 10$ and $p = \frac{1}{2}$. Then

$$\mu = np = (10)(\tfrac{1}{2}) = 5 \quad \text{and} \quad \sigma = \sqrt{npq} = \sqrt{2.5} = 1.58$$

Figure 7.15 shows the corresponding binomial probability distribution and the approximating normal curve on the same graph. A visual comparison of the figures would suggest that the approximation is reasonably good, even though a small sample, $n = 10$, was used for this illustration.

Figure 7.15 • Comparison of a binomial probability distribution and the approximating normal distribution when $n = 10$ and $p = \frac{1}{2}$

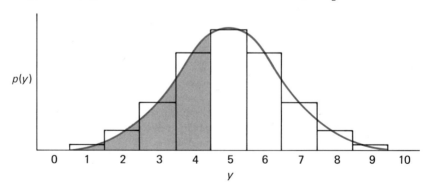

Example 7.7

For the binomial probability distribution illustrated in figure 7.15, calculate the probability that $y = 2$, 3, or 4, correct to three decimal places, using table 1, appendix II. Then calculate the normal approximation to this probability.

Solution: The exact probability P_1 can be calculated using table 1(b). Recall from section 5.2 that the entries in table 1 are the sums of the binomial probabilities from $y = 0$ to whatever value we choose, say $y = a$. Therefore, when $p = .5$,

$$P_1 = \sum_{y=2}^{4} p(y) = \sum_{y=0}^{4} p(y) - \sum_{y=0}^{1} p(y)$$

$$= .377 - .011 = .366$$

The probability that $y = 2, 3,$ or 4 corresponds to the sum of the areas of the three rectangles in figure 7.15 that are over $y = 2, 3,$ and 4. To obtain the normal approximation to this area, we would use the area under the normal curve between $y_1 = 1.5$ and $y_2 = 4.5$, which is shaded in figure 7.15. (Note that we must use 1.5 and 4.5 rather than 2 and 4 so that we include entirely the probability rectangles associated with $y = 2, 3,$ and 4.)

We have noted that for a binomial experiment with $n = 10$ and $p = .5$, we have $\mu = np = (10)(.5) = 5$ and $\sigma = \sqrt{npq} = \sqrt{(10)(.5)(.5)}$ $= 1.58$. Then the z scores corresponding to 1.5 and 4.5 are

$$z_1 = \frac{y_1 - \mu}{\sigma} = \frac{1.5 - 5}{1.58} = -2.22$$

$$z_2 = \frac{y_2 - \mu}{\sigma} = \frac{4.5 - 5}{1.58} = -.32$$

The probability P_2 is shown in figure 7.16. The area between $z = 0$ and $z = 2.22$ is $A_1 = .4868$. The area between $z = 0$ and $z = .32$ is $A_2 = .1255$. It is obvious from figure 7.16 that

$$P_2 = A_1 - A_2 = .4868 - .1255 = .3613$$

Note that the normal approximation is quite close to the binomial probability obtained from table 1.

Figure 7.16 • Area under the normal curve for example 7.7

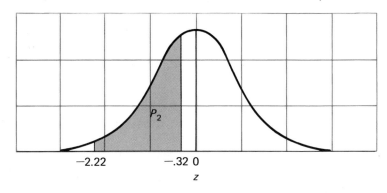

Although the normal probability distribution provides a reasonably good approximation to the binomial probability distribution shown in figure 7.15, this will not always be the case. When n is small and p is near 0 or 1, the binomial probability distribution will be nonsymmetrical. That is, its mean will be located near 0 or n. For example, when p is near 0, most values of y will be small, producing a distribution which is concentrated near $y = 0$ and which tails gradually toward n (see figure 7.17). Certainly when this is true, the normal distribution, symmetrical and bell-shaped, will provide a poor approximation to the binomial probability distribution. How, then, can we tell whether n and p are values that will produce a symmetrical binomial distribution?

Figure 7.17 • Comparison of a binomial probability distribution (shaded) and the approximating normal distribution when $n = 10$ and $p = .1$ ($\mu = np = 1; \sigma = \sqrt{npq} = .95$)

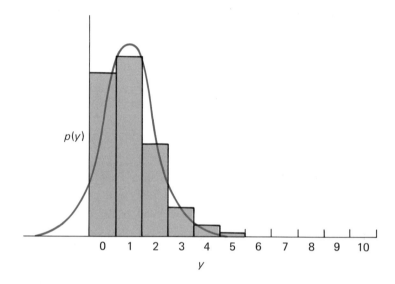

Recalling the Empirical Rule from chapter 2, we know that approximately 95 percent of the measurements associated with a normal distribution lie within two standard deviations of the mean and almost all lie within three. We would suspect that the binomial probability distribution would be nearly symmetrical if the distribution spread out a distance equal to two standard deviations on either side of the mean. This is, in fact, the case. **Hence, to determine when the normal approximation will be adequate, calculate $\mu = np$ and $\sigma = \sqrt{npq}$. If the interval ($\mu \pm 2\sigma$) lies within the binomial bounds 0 and n, the approximation will be reasonably good.**

Note that this requirement is satisfied for the example in figure 7.15, but it is not satisfied for figure 7.17. For figure 7.17, $\mu = np = 1$ and $\sigma = \sqrt{npq} = .95$. Then

$$\mu - 2\sigma = -.9$$

$$\mu + 2\sigma = 2.90$$

This interval does not fall between 0 and 10.

Let us now consider some applications of the normal distribution as an approximation to the binomial probability distribution. We will consider very large samples, where it is no longer feasible to calculate exact binomial probabilities.

Example 7.8

The identical twin concordance rate for a given trait has been defined as the probability that both members of an identical twin pair share that trait. When the identical twin sibling of each of 120 hospitalized schizophrenics is examined, it is found that $y = 31$ twin pairs are discordant (unalike) for schizophrenia. Calculate the probability of observing 31 or more discordant identical twin pairs, assuming that the concordance rate is .80.

Solution: The probability of observing a discordant twin pair when a single pair is examined is $p = .20$, given that the concordance rate is .80. Then

$$\mu = np = (120)(.20) = 24$$
$$\sigma = \sqrt{npq} = \sqrt{(120)(.20)(.80)} = 4.38$$

As a preliminary check on the adequacy of the normal approximation, we calculate

$$(\mu \pm 2\sigma) = (24 \pm 8.76)$$

Since this interval, (15.24, 32.76), lies within the binomial bounds 0 and 120, the approximation should be reasonably close.

The probability of 31 or more discordant twin pairs, given $n = 120$, is

$$P = P(y \geq 31)$$
$$= p(31) + p(32) + p(33) + \cdots + p(119) + p(120)$$

The normal approximation to P is the area under the normal curve to the right of $y = 30.5$. The z-value corresponding to $y = 30.5$ is

$$z = \frac{y - \mu}{\sigma} = \frac{30.5 - 24}{4.38} = \frac{6.5}{4.38} = 1.48$$

The area between $z = 0$ and $z = 1.48$ is .4306, as shown in figure 7.18.

Figure 7.18 • Normal approximation to the binomial distribution in example 7.8

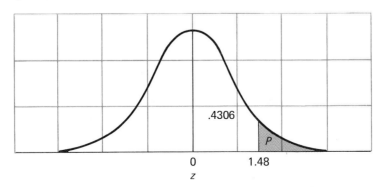

.4306

P

0 1.48
z

Since the total area to the right of the mean is .5, then

$$P = .5 - .4306 = .0694$$

Thus the probability of observing 31 or more discordant identical twin pairs is .0694, or about 7 in 100, assuming that the concordance rate is .80.

Example 7.9

A psychological test battery was employed to select candidates to train for teaching handicapped children. Of the 100 trainees selected on the basis of the test battery, 68 successfully completed the program. Suppose that past records indicate that the probability of successfully completing the program is .5 when the test battery is not used for selecting trainees. On the basis of the results of the testing, what conclusions would you draw regarding the effectiveness of the test battery as a selection device?

Solution: First we translate the question into an hypothesis concerning the parameter of a binomial probability distribution. We wish to test the null hypothesis that p, the probability of successful completion for a trainee selected on the basis of the test battery, is .5. It is hoped that the test battery tends to identify potentially successful candidates, so that the alternative to the null hypothesis, the research hypothesis, is $p > .5$. Then the rejection region consists of large values of y, the number of successful trainees. The test structure is summarized as follows.

Null hypothesis H_0: $p = .5$.

Research hypothesis H_a: $p > .5$.

Test statistic: $y =$ the number of successful trainees.

The normal approximation to the binomial is adequate for this example. So we would interpret a large and improbable value of y to be one that lies several standard deviations away from the hypothesized mean, $\mu = np = (100)(.5) = 50$.

Noting that

$$\sigma = \sqrt{npq} = \sqrt{(100)(.5)(.5)} = 5$$

we find that the observed value of y, 68, lies more than 3σ away from the hypothesized mean $\mu = 50$. Specifically, y lies

$$z = \frac{y - \mu}{\sigma} = \frac{68 - 50}{5} = 3.6$$

standard deviations away from the hypothesized mean.

This result is so improbable, assuming that the test battery is ineffective, that we would reject the null hypothesis. Thus we would conclude that the probability of successfully completing the program is greater than .5 for trainees selected on the basis of the test battery. (You will observe that the area above $z = 3.6$ is so small that it is not included in table 4 in appendix II.)

Rejecting the null hypothesis raises additional questions. How effective is the test battery as a selection device, and is it sufficiently effective, from an economic point of view, to warrant continued use? The first question is an estimation problem, a topic discussed in chapter 8. The latter question is one of economics. To answer it we would utilize the results of our statistical test and would take into consideration such factors as the time, labor, and expense involved in administering, scoring, and interpreting the test battery.

Example 7.10

The probability α of a type I error and the location of the rejection region for a statistical test of an hypothesis are sometimes specified before the data are collected. Suppose that we wish to test the null hypothesis $p = .5$ in a situation identical to the trainee selection example (example 7.9). Find the appropriate rejection region for the test if we wish α to be approximately .05. (See figure 7.19.)

Figure 7.19 • Location of the rejection region for the experiment in example 7.10

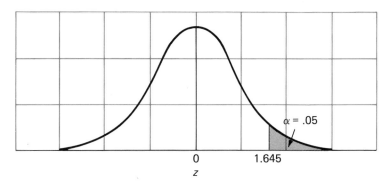

Solution: We previously stated in example 7.9 that y, the number of successful trainees, would be used as a test statistic. The rejection region is located in the upper tail of the probability distribution for y. Desiring α to be approximately .05, we seek a value of y, say y_α, such that

$$P(y \geq y_\alpha) \approx .05$$

(Note: The symbol $\approx$ means "approximately equal to.")
This probability can be determined by first finding the corresponding z_α which gives the number of standard deviations between the mean $\mu = 50$ and y_α. Since the total area to the right of $z = 0$ is .5, the area between $z = 0$ and z_α is .45. Checking table 4, we find that $z = 1.64$ corresponds to an area equal to .4495 and $z = 1.65$ to an area of .4505. Since .45 is halfway between these area values, z_α is halfway between the z-values, or

$$z_\alpha = 1.645$$

Recalling the relation between z and y, we have

$$z_\alpha = \frac{y_\alpha - \mu}{\sigma} \quad \text{or} \quad 1.645 = \frac{y_\alpha - 50}{5}$$

Solving for y_α, we obtain

$$y_\alpha = 5(1.645) + 50 = 58.225$$

Obviously, we cannot observe $y = 58.225$ successful trainees and hence we must choose 58 or 59 as the point where the rejection region begins.

Suppose that we decide to reject when y is greater than or equal to 59. Then the actual probability α of a type I error for the test is

$$P(y \geq 59) = \alpha$$

This probability can be approximated by using the area under the normal curve above $y = 58.5$, a problem similar to that encountered in example 7.8. The z-value corresponding to $y = 58.5$ is

$$z = \frac{y - \mu}{\sigma} = \frac{58.5 - 50}{5} = 1.7$$

The tabulated area between $z = 0$ and $z = 1.7$ is .4554, so α is

$$\alpha = .5 - .4554 = .0446$$

While the method described above provides a more accurate value for α, there is very little practical difference between an α of .0446 and an α of .05. When n is large, time and effort may be saved by using z as a test statistic rather than y. This method was used in example 7.9. We would then reject the null hypothesis when z is greater than or equal to 1.645.

In concluding this section we remind you that although we use the normal probability distribution to approximate the binomial probability distribution for large samples, the two random variables are quite different. The binomial random variable, presented in chapter 5, is discrete and represents the number of successes in a series of n trials. The normal random variable is continuous and possesses the bell-shaped probability distribution discussed in earlier sections of this chapter. Despite these differences, the two variables are related by the Central Limit Theorem. Thus when the number of trials n is large, the probability distribution for the number of successes y will be bell-shaped and can be approximated by the normal probability distribution.

EXERCISES

1. Consider a binomial experiment with $n = 25$ and $p = .4$.
   (a) Calculate $P(9 \leq y \leq 13)$ by using the binomial probabilities in table 1 of appendix II.
   (b) Calculate $P(9 \leq y \leq 13)$ by using the normal approximation to the binomial.
2. Consider a binomial experiment with $n = 25$ and $p = .2$.
   (a) Calculate $P(y \leq 4)$ by using table 1 in appendix II.
   (b) Calculate $P(y \leq 4)$ by using the normal approximation to the binomial.
3. An experimenter has found that, on the average, the probability of a subject failing to appear for an experimental session is .5. If 50 subjects volunteer for the experiment,

what is the probability that at least 30 will appear? Assume that y, the number of subjects who appear, has a binomial probability distribution. Can you think of any circumstances for which y might not have a binomial probability distribution?

4. The probability of a person falling in the superior intelligence range is .15. In Jordan's (1933) study of 578 mill-worker children, what is the probability that at least 95 children will score in the superior range if the probability that a single child will score in this range is .15? Assume that y, the number of children in a sample of 578 who score in the superior intelligence range, possesses a binomial probability distribution.

5. Hamilton (1974) conducted an experiment on risk taking to test a theory of motivation. The dependent measure was performance at a ring-toss task. The probability of success was .5 and $n = 30$ subjects participated. Let y be the number of the 30 subjects who are successful in the ring toss. Calculate $P(y \leq 12)$ using the normal approximation to the binomial distribution.

7.6 • APPROXIMATE NONPARAMETRIC TESTS USING THE NORMAL DISTRIBUTION

In the preceding section we used the fact that y, the number of "successes" in n trials of a binomial experiment, tends to be normally distributed as n increases. We described a rough check to tell whether the sample size is large enough for the approximation to be satisfactory. Thus for large n, we could use the standardized normal distribution as an approximate distribution for

$$z = \frac{y - \mu}{\sigma}$$

with $\mu = np$ and $\sigma^2 = npq$, the mean and variance of the binomial variable y.

The approximate normality of the binomial probability distribution was justified simply by appealing to the Central Limit Theorem. However, mathematical statistics offers other methods for deriving approximate distributions. These methods have been used to show that various other test statistics also tend, as sample sizes increase, to be normally distributed.

In particular, for the Mann-Whitney U statistic of section 6.5, when the null hypothesis is true and the two populations being compared have identical distributions, the mean and variance of U are

$$\mu_U = \frac{n_1 n_2}{2}$$

$$\sigma_U^2 = \frac{n_1 n_2 (n_1 + n_2 + 1)}{12}$$

The distribution of

$$z = \frac{U - \mu_U}{\sigma_U}$$

tends to normality with mean 0 and variance 1 as n_1 and n_2 become large. By "large" we mean that this approximation will be adequate when n_1 and n_2 are both larger than, say, 10, a rule of thumb that has been verified by theoretical statisticians. For a two-tailed test with $\alpha = .05$, we would reject the null hypothesis if $z < -1.96$ or $z > 1.96$ (see figure 7.20).

Figure 7.20 • Rejection region for the two-tailed large-sample U test

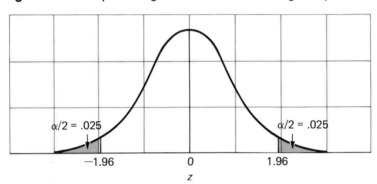

$\alpha/2 = .025$ $\alpha/2 = .025$

-1.96 0 1.96

z

Example 7.11

To investigate possible sex differences in the amount of patient-psychiatrist contact in a mental hospital, the mean number of contacts per week (for ten weeks) is recorded for each of 12 male and 12 female patients. The data for the male and female patients are shown in table 7.3. The male patient scores appear under column A and the female scores under column B. The appropriate rank for each score is also shown in table 7.3. As mentioned in sec-

Table 7.3 • Data and Mann-Whitney U test calculations for example 7.11

A	Rank	B	Rank
2.2	12	2.8	15
.6	3.5	3.2	18
1.2	7	4.8	22
3.0	16.5	2.4	13
.8	5	1.8	10
.2	1	2.0	11
1.0	6	5.6	24
1.6	9	1.4	8
3.0	16.5	3.6	20
2.6	14	.6	3.5
3.4	19	4.2	21
.4	2	5.0	23
	$T_A = 111.5$		$T_B = 188.5$

tion 6.5, scores resulting in ties are assigned a rank equal to the average of the ranks that would have been given to each score if no tie had occurred.
(a) List the basic elements of this experiment.
(b) Do the data provide sufficient evidence to conclude that the frequency distributions of the average number of psychiatric contacts differ for male and female patients?

Solution: (a) The basic elements of the experiment are listed below.

Experimental units: Patients in a mental hospital.

Response: Average number of psychiatric contacts per week over ten weeks.

Treatments: Female patients
Male patients.

(b) For a nonparametric comparison of the two frequency distributions, we use the Mann-Whitney U test to make the best use of sample information. Our test structure is given below.

Null hypothesis H_0: The frequency distributions of the average number of psychiatric contacts are the same for male and female patients.

Research hypothesis H_a: The frequency distributions of the average number of psychiatric contacts are different for male and female patients.

Test statistic: The Mann-Whitney U statistic.

In calculating U, we first note that the research hypothesis H_a is two-tailed. We thus choose the smaller rank sum of T_A and T_B, which is found in table 7.3 to be $T_A = 111.5$. Then

$$U = (n_1)(n_2) + \frac{n_1(n_1 + 1)}{2} - T_A$$

$$= (12)(12) + \frac{12(13)}{2} - 111.5 = 110.5$$

Since n_1 and n_2 both exceed 10, we use the normal approximation for U. To find the z score, we need

$$\mu_U = \frac{n_1 n_2}{2} = \frac{144}{2} = 72$$

and

$$\sigma_U^2 = \frac{n_1 n_2(n_1 + n_2 + 1)}{12} = \frac{(12)(12)(25)}{12} = 300$$

The approximately normal z score is then

$$z = \frac{U - \mu_U}{\sigma_U} = \frac{110.5 - 72}{\sqrt{300}} = 2.22$$

We look up this z score in the normal tables and find the corresponding area is .4868. We are interested in the probability of observing a z score as rare as or rarer than $z = 2.22$. This is shown by the shaded area in figure 7.21 to the right of the mean ($z = 0$). This shaded area is $(.5 - .4868) = .0132$.

Figure 7.21 • Two-tailed significance level for the experiment of example 7.11 for $z = 2.22$

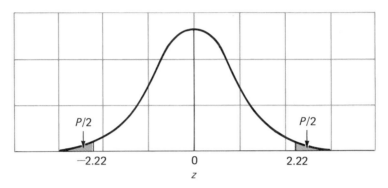

Finally, to determine the significance level for this two-tailed test, we double this probability to allow for equally rare events in the other (lower) tail of the distribution. Thus

$$P = 2(.0132) = .0264 \approx .03$$

We have rounded to two decimal places since the normal distribution is only an approximation to the actual distribution of U.

The implication is that we have observed a value of U which is unlikely to occur if the male and female frequency distributions are the same. We would therefore infer, at the .03 significance level, that the frequency distributions of the number of psychiatric contacts differ for male and female patients. In particular, since the male rank sum T_A is the smaller rank sum, we infer that the frequency distribution for male patients lies to the left of (below) that for female patients. It appears that female patients in this hospital tend to have more psychiatric contact than male patients.

Like the U statistic, the distribution of T in the Wilcoxon rank sum test of section 6.6 may be approximated by a normal distribution if n, the number of pairs, is large. The approximation will be satisfactory if the number of pairs is 25 or more. When the null hypothesis is true and the population distributions for the matched pairs experiment are identical, the mean and variance of T are

$$\mu_T = \frac{n(n + 1)}{4}$$

$$\sigma_T^2 = \frac{n(n + 1)(2n + 1)}{24}$$

Then for large n $(n \geq 25)$, the distribution of

$$z = \frac{T - \mu_T}{\sigma_T}$$

will be approximately normal. Thus for a two-tailed test and $\alpha = .05$, we would reject the hypothesis of identical population distributions when $z < -1.96$ or $z > 1.96$. The rejection region would be located exactly as shown in figure 7.20.

Example 7.12

We would like to compare high school students of average and superior intelligence for their ability to generate unique ideas in response to a series of visual stimuli. To control for individual differences in sheer verbal productivity, each of $n = 25$ average students is paired with a superior student on the basis of the total number of responses. The number of unique ideas generated by each student is given in table 7.4, where each row represents a pair. Column A lists the data for the average students and column B lists the data for the students of superior intelligence.

(a) List the basic elements for this experiment.

(b) Is there evidence to support the research hypothesis that the "unique idea" frequency distribution for students of superior intelligence lies above that for average students? Use $\alpha = .05$.

Solution: (a) The basic elements of the experiment are listed below.

Experimental units: High school students.

Response: Number of unique ideas in response to a visual stimulus.

Treatments: Average intelligence students
  Superior intelligence students.

(b) We will use the Wilcoxon rank sum test for this matched pairs experiment so that the nonparametric comparison makes optimal use of the sample information. The test structure is given below.

Null hypothesis H_0: The "unique idea" frequency distribution is the same for average (A) and superior (B) intelligence students.

Research hypothesis H_a: The "unique idea" frequency distribution for superior intelligence students lies above that for average intelligence students.

Test statistic: $T = T_A$ = average intelligence rank sum.

Since we wish to conduct the test using a fixed $\alpha = .05$, we must establish a rejection region. If the research hypothesis is true, we expect T_A to be small. But how small can T_A be before we can reject at the .05 significance level? Since the sample is large, we can approximate the sampling distribution of T_A

Table 7.4 • Data and Wilcoxon rank sum calculations for example 7.12

Pair	A	B	Difference (A − B)	Absolute Value of Difference	Rank
1	3	6	−3	3	11
2	12	8	4	4	15.5
3	5	10	−5	5	19.5
4	7	6	1	1	3
5	10	11	−1	1	3
6	8	4	4	4	15.5
7	8	10	−2	2	7
8	9	15	−6	6	22
9	7	6	1	1	3
10	4	13	−9	9	25
11	4	7	−3	3	11
12	9	5	4	4	15.5
13	6	10	−4	4	15.5
14	9	8	1	1	3
15	2	10	−8	8	24
16	4	11	−7	7	23
17	6	9	−3	3	11
18	17	12	5	5	19.5
19	12	13	−1	1	3
20	16	14	2	2	7
21	11	16	−5	5	19.5
22	3	1	2	2	7
23	6	11	−5	5	19.5
24	8	5	3	3	11
25	14	11	3	3	11

$$T_A = \text{positive rank sum} = 111$$
$$T_B = \text{negative rank sum} = 214$$

by the normal distribution. Therefore we may use the test statistic

$$z = \frac{T_A - \mu_T}{\sigma_T}$$

For this one-tailed test, all of α is to be placed in the lower tail of the z distribution, since we also expect z to be small if the research hypothesis is true. To find the rejection region, we consult table 4 in appendix II to find the z-value corresponding to an area of .45. See figure 7.22. We previously found (see example 7.10 and figure 7.19) this value to be $z = 1.645$. Since we are rejecting in the lower tail, we make the sign of z negative. Thus we have

Rejection region: $z < -1.645$

Figure 7.22 • One-tailed rejection region for $\alpha = .05$ (lower tail) for example 7.12

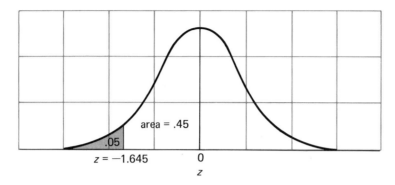

To calculate the approximately normal z score, we first calculate T_A, which is found in table 7.4 to be 111. Then we calculate

$$\mu_T = \frac{n(n+1)}{4} = \frac{(25)(26)}{4} = 162.5$$

and

$$\sigma_T^2 = \frac{n(n+1)(2n+1)}{24} = \frac{(25)(26)(51)}{24} = 1381.25$$

Finally,

$$z = \frac{111 - 162.5}{\sqrt{1381.25}} = -1.39$$

Since the calculated z is not less than -1.645, that is, is not in the rejection region, we cannot reject the hypothesis that the "unique idea" frequency distributions are the same, at least not at the $\alpha = .05$ significance level.

It may be of interest to compute the significance level corresponding to the observed $z = -1.39$. We first find the corresponding area in table 4 to be .4177. Thus

$$P = .5 - .4177 = .0823$$

Note that this area need not be doubled, since the test is one-tailed. A summary of these results is given in figure 7.23.

Only if we are willing to assume a .0823 or higher level of risk of rejecting the null hypothesis when it is actually true do we infer that the research hypothesis is true. We apparently are *not* willing to assume this risk, since we set $\alpha = .05$ prior to performing the test. However, the significance level is close enough to the desired level for α to warrant further investigation of the research hypothesis.

Figure 7.23 • Rejection region, observed z score, and significance level for example 7.12

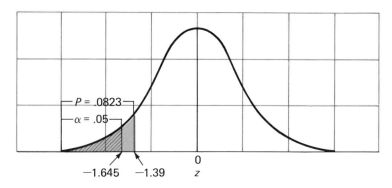

EXERCISES

1. Fourteen males and 12 females participated in a study for investigating the effects of fatigue on visual acuity. All the subjects were awake for 48 hours preceding an experimental session that involved sighting an unfamiliar object (an unknown experimenter who entered the room by another door). Each subject's latency of visual response to the experimenter's entry was recorded and the following results were obtained.

Males				Females		
1.7	2.0	1.0	1.2	1.0	3.0	3.8
.8	.1	1.1	.9	.9	1.0	1.9
.3	.5	.8		2.2	4.1	.9
1.2	1.6	.6		3.2	2.6	3.0

(a) List the basic elements of this experiment.
(b) Use the large-sample Mann-Whitney U test to determine whether we can infer that the frequency distributions of latency of visual response differ for males and females. Use a fixed $\alpha = .05$, but also determine the significance level for the calculated normal z score.

2. Three developmental psychologists (Tigue, Tigue, and Schechter, 1975) studied learning and memory in 32 seven year olds and 32 college students to see if there were age-based differences. Subjects were presented with triads of verbal stimuli and had to state which of the three words had appeared in an earlier learning trial. The number of errors for each subject was recorded and the following results were obtained.

Children	1	1	0	2	0	1	1	2	1	2	2	2	1	1	0	1
	1	1	0	1	0	1	0	1	0	0	1	3	1	1	1	0
Students	2	3	1	2	2	2	1	1	1	3	2	2	0	1	1	2
	2	2	1	3	1	4	1	1	1	2	0	0	3	4	1	0

Using the large-sample Mann-Whitney U test, do the data provide sufficient evidence to support the research hypothesis that the frequency distributions of the number of errors on the memory task differ for the two age groups? If your answer is affirmative, give the level of significance for the test results.

3. In a study comparing therapist and client views on therapy outcome, 28 therapist–client pairs were independently administered a questionnaire designed to evaluate clients' adjustment as a result of therapy. High scores on the questionnaire represent "good adjustment" and low scores represent "poor adjustment." The results are shown below.

Pair	1	2	3	4	5	6	7	8	9	10	11	12	13	14
Therapist	16	8	11	19	16	10	4	9	10	18	14	13	12	10
Client	11	9	13	17	12	8	4	6	9	19	9	6	15	2

Pair	15	16	17	18	19	20	21	22	23	24	25	26	27	28
Therapist	6	11	15	14	18	20	17	12	10	16	4	11	19	17
Client	7	8	18	9	14	16	13	7	15	13	8	13	18	12

(a) Give the basic elements of this experiment.
(b) At what significance level do the data support the research hypothesis that the frequency distributions of questionnaire scores differ for therapists and clients?

SUMMARY

Many continuous random variables observed in nature have a probability distribution which is bell-shaped and which may be approximated by the normal probability distribution.

The common occurrence of normally distributed random variables may be explained partially by the Central Limit Theorem. This theorem states that, under rather general conditions, the sum or the mean of a random sample of n measurements drawn from a population will be approximately normally distributed in repeated sampling when n is large. In addition to random sampling, the only other condition required by the Central Limit Theorem is that the probability distribution of the individual sample measurements possess a finite mean and variance. This condition will be satisfied for all populations sampled in practice. You can assume that the Central Limit Theorem will apply to sums and means, regardless of the shape of the frequency distribution of the population measurements.

As a case in point, the number of successes y associated with a binomial experiment may be regarded as a sum of n sample measurements which will possess, approximately, a normal probability distribution when n, the total number of trials, is large. Consequently, binomial probabilities may be calculated, with reasonable accuracy, by using corresponding areas under the normal probability distribution.

The normal probability distribution also provides an approximate distribution for some nonparametric test statistics. In particular, we can use the normal distribution with the Mann-Whitney U and the Wilcoxon rank sum tests discussed in chapter 6.

Other applications of the Central Limit Theorem and the normal distribution will be encountered in succeeding chapters. Here we particularly note that the Central Limit Theorem provides justification for using the Empirical Rule of chapter 2. Furthermore, the discussions of this chapter provide an extension and refinement of the ideas embodied in the Empirical Rule.

SUPPLEMENTARY EXERCISES

1. A student applying to medical school scored 660 on the basic science portion of a medical aptitude test. If the mean and the standard deviation for scores on the test were 590 and 82, respectively, in what percentile did the score of 660 fall, assuming the scores are normally distributed?

2. Scores on a foreign language placement test are approximately normally distributed with mean and standard deviation equal to 90 and 20, respectively. If a student who scores above 118 is not required to take a language course, for what fraction of students would the language requirement be waived?

3. The scores on standard aptitude tests for graduate student applicants have a mean of 550 and a standard deviation of 95. Suppose you took the test and scored at the 95th percentile. What score did you make on the test, assuming the population of scores is normally distributed?

4. The average length of time required for a rat to escape a noxious experimental situation was found to be 7 minutes, with a standard deviation of 1.2 minutes. When should each trial be terminated if the experimenter wishes to allow sufficient time for 90 percent of the rats to escape? (Assume that the time required to escape is normally distributed.)

5. A sample of 4000 males took the Edwards Personal Preference Schedule (Edwards 1959). Scores were normally distributed with a mean and a standard deviation, on the endurance scale, of 16.97 and 4.3, respectively. If an extreme score is regarded as one that falls in either the upper or lower third of the distribution, what are the two scores that mark the extremes of the distribution? Round to the nearest integer.

6. In certain areas of psychological research, test construction is a major activity. Tests are administered to measure all types of attributes, tendencies, and abilities. Suppose that the difficulty of an ability test item is defined as the probability p that it is answered incorrectly by a potential examinee. On a certain test, 940 out of a sample of 2500 examinees answer a given item incorrectly. Does this contradict the hypothesis that the difficulty of the item is at least $p = .4$? Use the normal approximation to the binomial distribution and thus obtain a normal z score and a corresponding significance level.

7. Fifteen hundred volunteer subjects were administered a standard dose of a new tranquilizing drug and 22 reported experiencing mild but unpleasant side effects. Does the sample present sufficient evidence to indicate more than a 1 percent incidence of undesirable side effects with the new drug? Use a one-tailed test with $\alpha = .05$.

Test construction is a major activity in certain areas of psychological research. What kind of statistical methods might be used in determining the difficulty of a test item? Would a binomial experiment be appropriate? Photo by Van Bucher, Photo Researchers, Inc.

8. A statistical test is conducted to test the hypothesis that p, the parameter of a binomial population, is equal to .1. If the sample size is $n = 400$ and we wish α to be approximately .05 (two-tailed test), locate the rejection region if the test statistic is (a) z, (b) y.

9. A scholastic achievement test is timed so that the examinees are allowed exactly 1 hour to work through the test. Suppose it is known that when no time limit is imposed, the average time required to complete the test is 54.12 minutes, with a standard deviation of 4.20 minutes. Assuming that test completion times are normally distributed, what percentage of examinees would be expected to finish in the allotted 1-hour period?

10. Rutschmann (1973) conducted an experiment comparing normal and schizophrenic subjects. As one of the measures, the subjects took the Taylor Manifest Anxiety Scale, which is widely used in psychological research. The scores of the normal subjects were approximately normally distributed with mean 48.9 and standard deviation 10.4. If normal subjects with scores above 65 and below 30 are excluded from the sample, what percentage of subjects would be excluded?

11. The Matching Familiar Figures Test is used to assess the tendency for children to be reflective or impulsive in problem solving. Six variants of a figure are presented and the subjects must select the one that is identical with the standard picture. The two measures used are the time it takes the child to give an answer and the number of errors on all items. In one study the experimenter was testing the research hypothesis that more than 30 percent of six year olds are impulsive and take less than 40 seconds to answer. In a sample of 50 six-year-old children, 20 answered in less than 40 seconds. Is there sufficient evidence to support the experimenter's research hypothesis at the .05 significance level?

12. American and Austrian students participated in a study on reward allocation to see if there were differences based on nationality and performance outcome (Mikula 1974). Subjects observed one of their own nationality perform a task (which the subjects themselves had previously performed), and then each subject ranked the performance on a scale from 1 to 20. The results of an experiment using 14 American subjects and 14 Austrian subjects are given below.

Americans	12	14	13	20	8	9	10	16	13	10	9	8	7	8
Austrians	10	7	7	6	15	9	11	8	11	9	11	16	17	12

   (a) List the basic elements of this experiment.
   (b) Test the research hypothesis that the frequency distribution of reward allocation differs for the two nationalities using the large-sample Mann-Whitney U test and $\alpha = .05$.

13. Twelve firstborn children were matched on age, sex, and socioeconomic status of parents to 12 laterborn children whose next older sibling was under six years old. Collard (1968) studied their social and play responses in an unfamiliar situation to see if infants receiving stimulation from fewer persons are less exploratory. One measure employed in the research was the latency of response in seconds for picking up the test toy. The data are shown below.

Pair	1	2	3	4	5	6	7	8	9	10	11	12
Firstborn	180	145	31	24	9	4	180	45	31	13	6	0
Laterborn	1	10	0	5	16	0	0	15	20	10	10	8

   (a) If the research hypothesis is that, on the average, infants receiving stimulation from fewer persons are less exploratory, should you use a one-tailed or a two-tailed test?
   (b) At what significance level do these data from a matched pairs design support the research hypothesis given in part (a)? Use a large-sample Wilcoxon rank sum test.

14. Refer to exercise 13. Another dependent measure used was the number of responses to a test toy during a six-minute time period. The results of this experiment are given below.

Pair	1	2	3	4	5	6	7	8	9	10	11	12
Firstborn	60	58	63	55	98	56	57	64	80	52	71	52
Laterborn	96	77	71	52	69	63	63	78	70	98	51	61

   (a) Give the basic elements of this experiment.
   (b) State the research hypothesis you consider relevant for this experiment. Is it one-tailed or two-tailed?
   (c) Conduct the test of your research hypothesis using the Wilcoxon rank sum test at a fixed $\alpha = .10$.

REFERENCES

Bieliauskas, V. J. 1974. A new look at "masculine protest." *Journal of Individual Psychology* 30:92–96.

Collard, R. R. 1968. Social and play responses of first-born and later-born infants in an unfamiliar situation. *Child Development* 39:325–334.

Edwards, A. L. 1959. *Manual for the Edwards personal preference schedule.* New York: The Psychological Corporation.

Hamilton, J. O. 1974. Motivation and risk-taking behavior: A test of Atkinson's theory. *Journal of Personality and Social Psychology* 29:856–864.

Jordan, A. M. 1933. Parental occupation and children's intelligence scores. *Journal of Applied Psychology* 17:103–119.

Mendenhall, W. 1975. *Introduction to probability and statistics.* 4th ed. N. Scituate, Mass.: Duxbury Press. Chapter 7.

Mikula, G. 1974. Nationality, performance and sex as determinants of reward allocation. *Journal of Personality and Social Psychology* 29:435–440.

Rutschmann, J. 1973. Time judgement by magnitude estimations and magnitude production and anxiety: A problem of comparison between normals and certain schizophrenic patients. *Journal of Psychology* 85:187–223.

Siegel, S. 1956. *Nonparametric statistics.* New York: McGraw-Hill.

Tigue, T. J.; Tigue, L. S.; and Schechter, J. 1975. Memory for instances and categories in children and adults. *Journal of Experimental Child Psychology* 20:22–37.

8•Parametric Statistical Inference

INTRODUCTION

As we stated in chapter 1 and in subsequent chapters of this text, the objective of statistics is to make inferences about a population based on information contained in a sample. We discussed one aspect of inference, decision making, at some length in chapter 6 in connection with the testing of nonparametric hypotheses. There each statistical test resulted in a decision to reject or not to reject an hypothesis of identical population frequency distributions.

In this chapter we will consider both the estimation and decision-making aspects of statistical inference. Here, however, our inference will concern the *values* of population parameters. Typical parameters are the population mean and variance, the probability of success for a binomial random variable, and the proportion of the area under the population distribution between two values of a quantitative variable. In many behavioral investigations the question of interest can be best answered either by testing an hypothesis about such a population parameter or by estimating the value of the population parameter.

For example, a researcher may suspect that the lower IQ scores of emotionally disturbed children are related to the difference between verbal abilities and performance abilities. One way of investigating this is to test a research hypothesis about the mean (average) difference between the verbal subscores and the performance subscores for the population of emotionally disturbed children. The null hypothesis is that this mean difference is equal to the mean difference of the norm group. This would be a *parametric* test of an hypothesis since we are comparing specific parameters, the means, of two populations.

In other instances the information sought may be an estimate of the value of a population parameter. For example, suppose that we wish to find the probability p of a premature childbirth, given that the expectant mother exceeds a certain age. To estimate this probability, we might select a random sample of maternity patients who exceed the specified age. Then we would determine the proportion of the sample that give birth prematurely. This proportion would provide an intuitively reasonable estimate of p, the relative frequency of premature childbirth for the population of interest. (As we will see, the sample proportion also possesses certain statistically desirable properties as an estimator of p.)

The two preceding examples illustrate the two aspects of parametric inference, decision making via hypothesis testing and estimation. Together they also illustrate that neither approach necessarily excludes the other. The first example focused on testing an hypothesis about the population mean difference between verbal subscores and performance subscores. But very likely the investigator would also be interested in estimating the actual value of μ. Likewise, in the second example, the sample estimator of the probability p of a premature childbirth might in turn be used to test an hypothesis involving a comparison of probabilities for two different age levels. The behavioral question involved will usually determine whether one inferential approach is more appropriate than the other, or whether a combination of both would yield the required information.

However, we will regard the two aspects of parametric inference—hypothesis testing and estimation—as conceptually distinct. We will retain the distinction in the sections to follow, treating first the topic of estimation and then tests of hypotheses. Thus in section 8.1 we discuss the two different kinds of estimation we can use: point estimation and interval estimation. Each of these types is discussed in more detail in sections 8.2 and 8.3.

In sections 8.4 through 8.7 we present other estimation problems: large-sample techniques; estimating the difference between two means; determining the estimator of a binomial distribution and estimating the difference between two binomial parameters.

Another important question to researchers is how large the sample size should be in order to attain a specified precision of estimation. This topic is discussed in detail in section 8.8.

Finally, in section 8.9 we present the methods involved in parametric tests of hypotheses.

A discussion of the aspects and objectives of parametric inference would be incomplete without reference to a measure of the goodness of an inferential procedure. A good estimation procedure yields results—estimates—that are likely to be close in value to the parameters in question. A good hypothesis-testing procedure yields results—decisions—that are likely to be correct. Certainly a measure of goodness is necessary to compare alternative inferential procedures. Moreover, a statement of the goodness of a particular inference in a specific empirical situation lends credibility to that inference. Thus parametric inference as applied in an empirical situation includes two components: (1) the inference itself and (2) a measure of its goodness. Consequently, for each method presented in this chapter, we will also discuss a measure of its goodness.

8.1 • TYPES OF ESTIMATORS

Estimation procedures may be classified into two types, point estimation and interval estimation. Suppose that we wish to estimate the proportion of adults in the United States who have not completed high school. The estimate might be given as a single number, for instance, .12. Or we might estimate that the proportion is somewhere between .07 and .23. The first type of estimate is called a point estimate because the single number representing the estimate may be associated with a point on a line. The second type, involving two points and defining an interval on a line, is called an interval estimate. We will consider each method of estimation in turn.

A point estimation procedure utilizes information in a sample to arrive at a single number, or point, which estimates the population parameter of interest. The actual estimation is accomplished by using an *estimator*.

Definition 8.1

An estimator is a rule that tells us how to calculate the estimate based on measurements in the sample, and it is generally expressed as a formula.

For example, the sample mean

$$\bar{y} = \frac{\sum_{i=1}^{n} y_i}{n}$$

is an *estimator* of the population mean μ. It explains exactly how the actual numerical value of the estimate may be obtained once the sample values $y_1, y_2, \ldots, y_n$ are known. The numerical value of $\bar{y}$, found by using the sample values, is the *estimate* of μ. On the other hand, an interval estimator is used with the data in the sample to calculate *two points* which are intended to enclose the true value of the parameter estimated.

Point estimation is analogous to firing a revolver at a target. Each time we sample the population and calculate an estimate using the estimator, we are firing a bullet at the target. The bull's-eye of the target is the numerical value of the population parameter. We want our estimator to hit consistently or, at worst, only nearly miss the bull's-eye.

Suppose we have two estimators, that is, two rules, available for estimating a particular population parameter. How should the estimators be compared? One possibility is to conduct an experiment. Draw a random sample from a known population, that is, one for which the population parameter is known. Then calculate the numerical value using each estimator and see which estimate is closer to the value of the population parameter. This is analogous to judging two marksmen (estimators) by allowing each to fire just one shot (estimate) at a bull's-eye (population parameter) and concluding that the better marksman is the one whose shot is closer to the bull's-eye. Clearly, a better comparison could be made if each marksman fires at the target many times.

Similarly, we can better judge the goodness of an estimator if we draw many samples from the known population. Then we calculate the numerical value using our estimator for every sample, and we observe how the estimates are distributed around the population parameter. If we repeat this sampling procedure many times, we generate the sampling distribution (see section 7.3) of the estimator. That is, instead of seeing only a single value, we see a very large number of values before deciding whether the estimator is a good one or not. The better estimator will be the one that gives values which cluster more closely around the parameter value, just as the better marksman is the one whose shots cluster more closely around the bull's-eye.

William Tell was reputedly a good marksman—but his reputation was based on a single shot. Are you convinced that Tell's marksmanship was as good as legend would have it?

More specifically, suppose we wish to estimate some specific population parameter, which we will call θ (Greek theta). Thus θ may be the population mean, median, standard deviation, range, or any other parameter. We are considering two estimators of θ, namely, $\widehat{\theta}_1$ (theta hat 1) and $\widehat{\theta}_2$ (theta hat 2). The "hat" ($\widehat{}$) is a symbol often used to denote estimators. Assume the sampling distribution of $\widehat{\theta}_1$ is as shown in figure 8.1. Here we have calculated a population of $\widehat{\theta}_1$ values by sampling the original population many times, each time getting a new value of $\widehat{\theta}_1$. Notice that the values of $\widehat{\theta}_1$ pile up around θ, certainly a desirable property.

Figure 8.1 • Sampling distribution of $\widehat{\theta}_1$

You may wonder how this repeated sampling is accomplished in practice. Fortunately, mathematical methods are available for deriving the sampling distributions of many estimators without actually drawing samples. However, these methods are beyond the scope of this text, and we will present sampling distributions without giving proof or justification.

Notice that we have constructed the sampling distribution of $\widehat{\theta}_1$, figure 8.1, so that the mean of the sampling distribution is equal to θ, the parameter of interest. This is a desirable property, since it implies that $\widehat{\theta}_1$ does not tend consistently to underestimate or overestimate θ. We call this property *unbiasedness*.

Definition 8.2

An estimator $\widehat{\theta}$ is said to be an **unbiased estimator of** θ if the mean of its sampling distribution equals θ. Otherwise, $\widehat{\theta}$ is said to be biased.

Suppose $\widehat{\theta}_1$ and $\widehat{\theta}_2$ have the sampling distributions shown in figure 8.2. You can see that $\widehat{\theta}_1$ is an unbiased estimator because the mean of the sampling distribution is equal to θ. In contrast, $\widehat{\theta}_2$ is biased because the mean of the sampling distribution for $\widehat{\theta}_2$ lies to the right of θ. Consequently, $\widehat{\theta}_2$ tends to overestimate θ.

Naturally, we prefer unbiased estimators to biased ones. However, we often will find more than one unbiased estimator of a parameter. How, then, should we decide which estimator is the best? We will always prefer that estimator whose values cluster most closely around the parameter θ, that is, the unbiased estimator with the minimum variability.

Suppose $\widehat{\theta}_1$ and $\widehat{\theta}_2$ have sampling distributions as shown in figure 8.3. Now both $\widehat{\theta}_1$ and $\widehat{\theta}_2$ are unbiased. However, the sampling distribution of $\widehat{\theta}_2$ has more

Figure 8.2 • Sampling distributions of $\widehat{\theta}_1$ and $\widehat{\theta}_2$

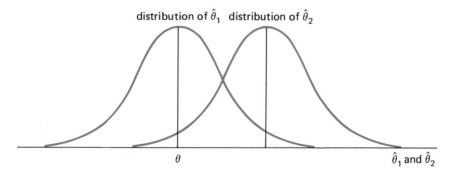

distribution of $\hat{\theta}_1$ distribution of $\hat{\theta}_2$

θ $\hat{\theta}_1$ and $\hat{\theta}_2$

variability than that of $\widehat{\theta}_1$. If we were betting which estimator would provide a closer estimate of θ for a particular sample, $\widehat{\theta}_1$ would be the better bet. Put simply, the variance of $\widehat{\theta}_2$ is larger than that of $\widehat{\theta}_1$.

Figure 8.3 • Sampling distributions of $\widehat{\theta}_1$ and $\widehat{\theta}_2$

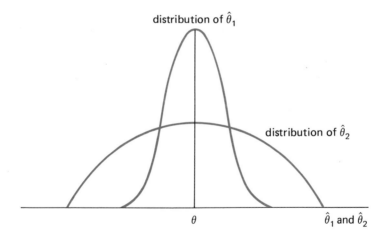

distribution of $\hat{\theta}_1$

distribution of $\hat{\theta}_2$

θ $\hat{\theta}_1$ and $\hat{\theta}_2$

Keep in mind that in a practical situation the true value of a parameter will be unknown. In fact, the objective of experimentation is to make an inference about the value of a parameter based on information contained in a sample. Furthermore, you will not be involved in finding the sampling distribution for an estimator. This will be done for you. All you need to know are the characteristics of the sampling distributions for various estimators, particularly, the means and variances of these distributions. Then you will be inclined to select an estimator in a practical situation that satisfies these two criteria:

1. unbiasedness; and
2. minimum variance.

We realize that if $\widehat{\theta}$ satisfies these two criteria, we are not *guaranteed* that $\widehat{\theta}$ will provide a closer estimate than any other estimator each time we use it. However, we do know that it will outperform other estimators in *repeated applications*, since our choice is based on its repeated sampling properties, that is, its sampling distribution.

8.2 • POINT ESTIMATION OF A POPULATION MEAN

The population mean μ is a measure of central tendency. Therefore, it is very often the parameter of particular interest in the investigation of a behavioral question. For example, suppose we are concerned with the average age at which children begin to use whole sentences, or with the average latency of response to a visual stimulus, or with the average change in voice pitch in a stress situation, or with the average change in IQ scores of mental retardates after treatment for a given biochemical deficiency. Conveniently, the estimation of μ serves as a very practical application of statistical inference as well as an excellent illustration of the principles of estimation discussed in section 8.1.

Many estimators are available for estimating the population mean μ, including the sample median, the average between the largest and smallest measurements in the sample, and the sample mean $\bar{y}$. Each generates its own probability distribution in repeated sampling. Depending on the population and the practical problem involved, each possesses certain advantages and disadvantages. The sample median and the average of the sample extremes are easy to calculate. However, the sample mean $\bar{y}$ is usually superior to them as an estimator because, for most populations, the variance of its sampling distribution is a minimum. Furthermore, regardless of the population, the sample mean $\bar{y}$ is always an unbiased estimator of the population mean μ.

In section 7.2 we introduced the Central Limit Theorem and we stated the following facts about the sampling distribution of $\bar{y}$.

If the mean of the sampled population is μ and the standard deviation is σ, then we have the following:

1. The mean of the sampling distribution of $\bar{y}$ equals μ.
2. The standard deviation of the sampling distribution of $\bar{y}$ equals $\sigma/\sqrt{n}$. We will denote the standard deviation of the sampling distribution of $\bar{y}$ by the symbol $\sigma_{\bar{y}}$. Therefore,

$$\sigma_{\bar{y}} = \frac{\sigma}{\sqrt{n}}$$

where σ is the standard deviation of the sampled population and n is the number of measurements in the sample. The above quantity, $\sigma_{\bar{y}}$, is also called the standard error of the sample mean.
3. When the sample size n is large, the sampling distribution of $\bar{y}$ is approximately normal.

The first fact means that $\bar{y}$ is unbiased. The second tells us that the standard deviation of $\bar{y}$ decreases as the sample size n increases. For most populations, no other unbiased estimator has a standard deviation smaller than the standard error of the sample mean, $\sigma_{\bar{y}} = \sigma/\sqrt{n}$. In general, therefore, we prefer $\bar{y}$ to all other estimators of μ.

The third fact provides information about the form or shape of the sampling distribution. The Central Limit Theorem states that when n is large the sampling distribution of $\bar{y}$ is approximately normal, as shown in figure 8.4.

Figure 8.4 • Sampling distribution of $\bar{y}$ for large n

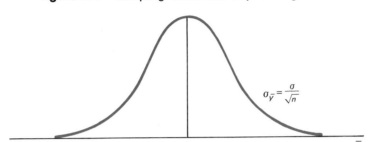

One immediate consequence of the approximate normality of the sampling distribution of $\bar{y}$ is that the Empirical Rule can be applied.

In repeated sampling, when each sample has n observations, and the population has mean μ and standard deviation σ, we have the following:

(a) Approximately 68 percent of the $\bar{y}$'s fall in the interval ($\mu \pm \sigma/\sqrt{n}$).
(b) Approximately 95 percent of the $\bar{y}$'s fall in the interval ($\mu \pm 2\sigma/\sqrt{n}$).
(c) All or almost all of the $\bar{y}$'s fall in the interval ($\mu \pm 3\sigma/\sqrt{n}$).

Note that we use the standard error of the sample mean, $\sigma_{\bar{y}} = \sigma/\sqrt{n}$, rather than the standard deviation of the sampled population, σ, to form our intervals. That is, when describing the variability of $\bar{y}$, we must use the standard deviation of the sampling distribution for $\bar{y}$, which is $\sigma/\sqrt{n}$, not σ.

Example 8.1

Refer to the die-tossing population described in section 7.2. Suppose we draw a single sample of $n = 5$ measurements from the die-tossing population and calculate the sample mean $\bar{y}$. How good will this estimate of μ be; that is, how far will $\bar{y}$ deviate from $\mu = 3.5$?

Solution: We cannot state that $\bar{y}$ will *definitely* lie within a specified distance of μ. However, we saw evidence in section 7.2 that the sampling distribution of $\bar{y}$ is approximately normal, even though our sample size is only

$n = 5$. Therefore, we can state that approximately 95 percent of our sample mean estimates of μ will fall within $2\sigma_{\bar{y}}$ of μ. In exercise 2 of section 7.2 we found $\sigma = 1.71$, so that 2 times the standard error of $\bar{y}$ is

$$2\sigma_{\bar{y}} = \frac{2\sigma}{\sqrt{n}} = \frac{2(1.71)}{\sqrt{5}} = \frac{2(1.71)}{2.24} = 1.53$$

Figure 7.5, repeated below in figure 8.5, shows the results of 100 repetitions of this experiment: toss the die $n = 5$ times and calculate $\bar{y}$. A check of this histogram verifies that 96 of these 100 sample means lie in the interval (3.5 ± 1.53), or $(1.97, 5.03)$.

Figure 8.5 • Histogram of the sample means for the die-tossing experiments in section 7.2

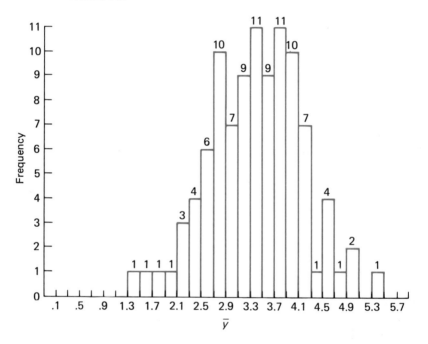

The quantity $2\sigma_{\bar{y}}$ is often used as an approximate bound on the error of estimation. We take this to imply that most of the estimates, approximately 95 percent, will lie within $2\sigma_{\bar{y}}$ of the population mean μ. Although the use of two standard deviations is not sacred, two seems to be a reasonable choice for most practical problems.

Consider the following example of point estimation.

Example 8.2

In a study of susceptibility to perceptual illusions, 50 male subjects judged the length of an illusory figure. When each judgment was scored in terms of the difference between the actual length and the perceived length of the figure, the resultant scores had a mean and standard deviation of

$$\bar{y} = 81 \text{ millimeters}$$
$$s = 12 \text{ millimeters}$$

Estimate the mean perceptual error for the population of all potential male subjects.

Solution: The estimate of the population mean is $\bar{y} = 81$ millimeters. The bound on the error of estimation is

$$2\sigma_{\bar{y}} = \frac{2\sigma}{\sqrt{n}} = \frac{2\sigma}{\sqrt{50}}$$

Although σ is unknown, we may approximate its value by using s, the estimate of σ. Thus the bound on the error of estimation is approximately

$$\frac{2s}{\sqrt{n}} = \frac{(2)(12)}{\sqrt{50}} = \frac{24}{7.07} = 3.39$$

We are fairly confident (about 95 percent sure) that our estimate of 81 millimeters is within 3.39 millimeters of the true mean perceptual error for all male subjects.

A point of interest in example 8.2 concerns the use of s to approximate σ. This approximation is reasonably good when n is large, say 30 or greater. If the sample size n is small, two techniques are available. Sometimes experience or data obtained from previous experiments will provide a good estimate of σ. When this is not available, we may resort to a small-sample procedure to be described in chapter 9. The choice of $n = 30$ as the division between "large" and "small" samples is arbitrary. The reasoning for its selection will be discussed in chapter 9.

EXERCISES

1. A sample of 144 coronary patients' medical records was examined to estimate the mean age of first attack. The sample mean and standard deviation were found to be 43.8 years and 4.5 years, respectively. Estimate the mean age of first attack for the population of coronary patients and place bounds on the error of estimation.
2. An investigator wished to determine the average amount of time individuals take to make their selections on the Matching Familiar Figures Test. A random sample of 130 twelve-year-old children was selected from the population of all twelve year olds in a large city. Each child in the sample was tested, and the result was a sample mean of 9.8 minutes and a sample standard deviation of 3.2 minutes. Estimate the mean response time for all twelve year olds in the city and place bounds on the error of estimation.

8.3 • INTERVAL ESTIMATION OF A POPULATION MEAN

Constructing an interval estimate is like attempting to rope a steer. In this case, the parameter that you wish to estimate corresponds to the steer and the interval corresponds to the loop formed by the cowboy's lariat. Each time you draw a sample, you construct a *confidence interval* for a parameter and you hope to "rope it," that is, include it in the interval. You will not be successful for every sample. The probability that an interval will enclose the parameter is called the *confidence coefficient.*

To consider a practical example, suppose we wish to estimate the mean reaction time μ to a certain stimulus. We draw 10 samples, each containing $n = 20$ observations. For each sample, we construct a confidence interval for the population mean μ. The intervals might appear as shown in figure 8.6. The horizontal line segments represent the 10 intervals and the vertical line represents the location of the true mean reaction time. Note that all but one of the intervals enclose μ for these particular samples.

Figure 8.6 • Ten confidence intervals for mean reaction time (each based on a sample of $n = 20$ observations)

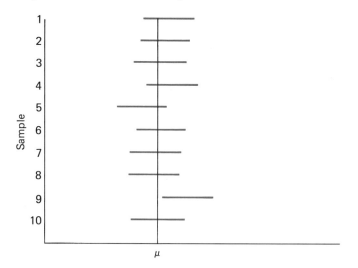

Having examined the concept of a confidence interval, let us now consider how to find the confidence interval for a population mean μ based on a random sample of n observations.

The interval estimator, or **confidence interval,** for a population mean may be obtained from the results of section 8.2. It is possible that a sample mean $\bar{y}$ lies either above or below the population mean. However, we would not expect it to deviate more than approximately $2\sigma_{\bar{y}}$ from μ. Hence we choose $(\bar{y} - 2\sigma_{\bar{y}})$ as the lower point of the interval, called the **lower confidence limit,** or LCL. We choose $(\bar{y} + 2\sigma_{\bar{y}})$ as the upper point, or **upper confidence limit,** UCL. Then we expect, with a high probability, that this interval will enclose the true population mean μ. In fact, if n is large and the distribution of $\bar{y}$ is approximately normal, we would expect about 95 percent of the intervals obtained in repeated sampling to enclose the population mean μ.

The confidence interval described here is called a *large-sample confidence interval* (or confidence limits). That is, n must be large enough for the Central Limit Theorem to be effective and hence for the distribution of $\bar{y}$ to be approximately normal. Since σ is usually unknown, the sample standard deviation must be used to estimate σ. As a rule of thumb, the large-sample confidence interval is appropriate when n is at least 30.

The confidence coefficient .95 corresponds to $\pm 2\sigma_{\bar{y}}$, or, more exactly, $1.96\sigma_{\bar{y}}$. Recall that .90 of the measurements in a normal distribution will fall within $z = 1.645$ standard deviations of the mean (table 4, appendix II). Thus we can construct 90 percent confidence intervals by using

$$LCL = \bar{y} - 1.645\sigma_{\bar{y}} = \bar{y} - \frac{1.645\sigma}{\sqrt{n}}$$

$$UCL = \bar{y} + 1.645\sigma_{\bar{y}} = \bar{y} + \frac{1.645\sigma}{\sqrt{n}}$$

In general, we can construct confidence intervals corresponding to any desired confidence coefficient, say $(1 - \alpha)$, by using the rule given in the box.

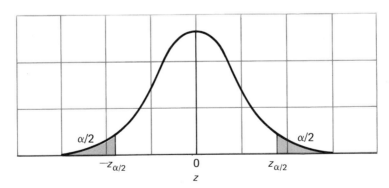

> To construct a confidence interval having a $(1 - \alpha)$ confidence coefficient, we use
>
> $$\left(\bar{y} \pm z_{\alpha/2} \frac{\sigma}{\sqrt{n}}\right)$$
>
> The quantity $z_{\alpha/2}$ is the value in the z table such that the area to the right of $z_{\alpha/2}$ is equal to $\alpha/2$ (see figure 8.7); that is, $P(z > z_{\alpha/2}) = \alpha/2$.

Figure 8.7 • Location of $z_{\alpha/2}$ and $-z_{\alpha/2}$ in constructing a confidence interval

Thus the confidence coefficient of .95 implies that $\alpha = .05$ and $\alpha/2 = .025$. To find $z_{.025}$ in table 4 of appendix II, recall that the areas given in table 4 are areas between 0 and the table z-value. So to find $z_{.025}$, we first calculate the area $(.5 - .025) = .475$. Then we search table 4 for the z-value corresponding to the area .475. This we find to be 1.96, so $z_{.025} = 1.96$. In a similar way we find that the z-value used for a 90 percent confidence interval is $z_{.05} = 1.645$.

Example 8.3

Refer to example 8.2. We wished to estimate the mean perceptual error for a population of male subjects' judgments of the length of an illusory figure. Construct a 90 percent confidence interval for this population mean. Recall that $\bar{y} = 81$ millimeters and $s = 12$ millimeters.

Solution: The 90 percent confidence limits are

$$\left(\bar{y} \pm \frac{1.645\sigma}{\sqrt{n}}\right)$$

Using s to estimate σ, we obtain

$$\left(81 \pm \frac{(1.645)(12)}{\sqrt{50}}\right) = (81 \pm 2.79)$$

Therefore, we estimate that the mean perceptual error μ for the population of all male subjects lies in the interval 78.21 millimeters to 83.79 millimeters. The confidence coefficient .90 implies that in repeated sampling, 90 percent of the confidence intervals, formed by using the above method, would enclose μ.

Note that the width of the confidence interval increases as the confidence coefficient increases, a result that agrees with our intuition. If we wish to be more confident that the interval will enclose μ, we would certainly increase the width of the interval. Confidence limits corresponding to some of the commonly used confidence coefficients are given in table 8.1.

Table 8.1 • Confidence limits for μ

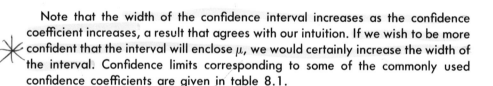

Confidence Coefficient $(1 - \alpha)$	$z_{\alpha/2}$	LCL	UCL
.90	1.645	$\bar{y} - \dfrac{1.645\sigma}{\sqrt{n}}$	$\bar{y} + \dfrac{1.645\sigma}{\sqrt{n}}$
.95	1.96	$\bar{y} - \dfrac{1.96\sigma}{\sqrt{n}}$	$\bar{y} + \dfrac{1.96\sigma}{\sqrt{n}}$
.99	2.58	$\bar{y} - \dfrac{2.58\sigma}{\sqrt{n}}$	$\bar{y} + \dfrac{2.58\sigma}{\sqrt{n}}$

The choice of the confidence coefficient to be used in a given situation is made by the experimenter and depends upon the degree of confidence desired for the estimate. As we pointed out, the larger the confidence coefficient, the wider the interval. As a result of this freedom of choice, it has become the custom of many experimenters to use a .95 confidence coefficient, although there is no logical foundation for its popularity.

The frequent use of the .95 confidence coefficient introduces a question asked by many beginners. Should we use $z = 1.96$ or $z = 2$ in the confidence interval? The answer is that it does not really make much difference which value is used. The value $z = 1.96$ is more exact for a .95 confidence coefficient, but the error introduced by using $z = 2$ is very small. The use of $z = 2$ simplifies the calculations, particularly when the computing is done manually. We will use two standard deviations when placing bounds on the error of a point estimator. But we will use $z = 1.96$ when constructing a confidence interval simply to remind you that this is the z-value obtained from the table of areas for the normal curve.

You may have noted the fine distinction between point estimators and interval estimators. Note also that when we place bounds on the error of a point estimate, for all practical purposes we are constructing an interval estimate. Furthermore, the point estimate falls in the middle of the interval estimate when a population mean is being estimated.

Since this close relationship exists for most of the parameters estimated in this text, we should give a word of explanation about our separate treatment of point and interval estimation here. For instance, it is not obvious that the best point estimate will fall in the middle of the best interval estimate—in many cases it does not. Furthermore, it is not necessarily true that the best interval estimator depends on the best point estimator. Although these are theoretical problems, they are important and worth mentioning. From a practical point of view, the two methods are closely related and the choice between the point and the interval estimators in an actual problem depends upon the preference of the experimenter.

EXERCISES

1. Refer to exercise 2 of section 8.2. An investigator wished to estimate the mean time twelve year olds take to make their selections on the Matching Familiar Figures Test. A random sample of 130 twelve year olds produced a mean of 9.8 minutes and a standard deviation of 3.2 minutes. Construct a confidence interval for the mean of the population, using a confidence coefficient of .99.
2. A random sample of 400 test scores from an introductory psychology course produced a mean of 78 and a standard deviation of 12. Construct a confidence interval for the mean score of the population by using a confidence coefficient of .95.

8.4 · ESTIMATION FROM LARGE SAMPLES

Estimation of a population mean, sections 8.2 and 8.3, sets the stage for the other estimation problems to be discussed in this chapter. A thread of unity runs through all, which, once observed, will simplify the learning process for the beginner. The following conditions will be satisfied for all estimation problems discussed in this chapter.

1. Each point estimator of a parameter, say θ, will be unbiased. That is, the mean of the distribution of the estimates obtained in repeated sampling will equal the parameter estimated.
2. The standard deviation of the estimator will be given so that we may place a two-standard-deviation $(2\sigma_{\hat{\theta}})$ bound on the error of estimation.
3. In each case, when n is large, the point estimator will be approximately normally distributed, as given by the Central Limit Theorem.
4. The probability that the error will be less than the bound $2\sigma_{\hat{\theta}}$ will be approximately .95.

In forming the corresponding interval estimators, we will assume that the sample is large enough for the Central Limit Theorem to apply. Thus we can assume that the distribution of the point estimator of θ is a normal distribution. Also, we assume that the sample is large enough to provide a good estimate of any other unknown (for example, σ). Then the confidence intervals for any confidence coefficient $(1 - \alpha)$ will be as given in the box.

Large-Sample $(1 - \alpha)$ Confidence Interval for θ

$$(\hat{\theta} \pm z_{\alpha/2}\sigma_{\hat{\theta}})$$

8.5 • ESTIMATING THE DIFFERENCE BETWEEN TWO MEANS

In chapter 6 we presented several *nonparametric methods* for comparing two populations. These methods compared the relative frequency distribution of the two populations. In this section we discuss a **parametric comparison** of two populations. In particular, we will compare the means of the two populations.

You will recall that we have examined two different methods of designing experiments to compare populations. One method is the independent sampling design, in which we draw independent random samples from the two populations. The second method is the matched pairs design (see section 6.2), in which we select pairs of homogeneous experimental units and randomly assign one to each treatment (population). Then we examine the set of differences between the responses for each pair. In this chapter we use the independent sampling design for making parametric comparisons.

We assume that population 1 has mean μ_1 and variance σ_1^2. We draw a random sample of n_1 measurements from this population. Then we calculate the sample mean $\overline{x}_1$ and the sample variance s_1^2. Population 2 is assumed to have mean μ_2 and variance σ_2^2. An *independent* sample of n_2 measurements is drawn from the second population, and the sample mean $\overline{x}_2$ and sample variance s_2^2 are calculated. The summary of this method is shown in table 8.2.

Table 8.2 • Summary of notation for population comparison

	Population 1	Population 2
Mean	μ_1	μ_2
Variance	σ_1^2	σ_2^2

	Sample 1	Sample 2
Sample Size	n_1	n_2
Mean	$\bar{y}_1$	$\bar{y}_2$
Variance	s_1^2	s_2^2

As you would guess, the best point estimator of the difference $(\mu_1 - \mu_2)$ between the two population means is, for most populations, the difference $(\bar{x}_1 - \bar{x}_2)$ between the sample means. Some facts about this estimator are listed in the box.

The Sampling Distribution of the Estimator for the Difference Between Two Population Means

1. The mean of the sampling distribution of $(\bar{x}_1 - \bar{x}_2)$ is $(\mu_1 - \mu_2)$.
2. The standard deviation of the sampling distribution of $(\bar{x}_1 - \bar{x}_2)$ is

$$\sigma_{(\bar{x}_1 - \bar{x}_2)} = \sqrt{\frac{\sigma_1^2}{n_1} + \frac{\sigma_2^2}{n_2}}$$

   The above quantity is also called the standard error for the difference between two sample means.
3. When n_1 and n_2 are large, say 30 or more, the sampling distribution of $(\bar{x}_1 - \bar{x}_2)$ is approximately normal.

The sample variances s_1^2 and s_2^2 may be used to estimate σ_1^2 and σ_2^2 when these parameters are unknown. The approximations are reasonable when n_1 and n_2 are each 30 or more.

Example 8.4

Referring to example 8.2, suppose that we desire to compare males and females with respect to susceptibility to perceptual illusions. Accordingly, 50 female subjects judge the length of the same illusory figure and each judgment is scored in terms of the magnitude of its deviation from the actual length. Males are represented as population 1 and females as population 2. The following results are obtained (in millimeters).

$$\bar{x}_1 = 81 \qquad \bar{x}_2 = 74$$
$$s_1^2 = 144 \qquad s_2^2 = 196$$

Estimate the population difference in mean perceptual error, $(\mu_1 - \mu_2)$, and place bounds on the error of estimation.

Solution: The point estimate of $(\mu_1 - \mu_2)$ is

$$\bar{X}_1 - \bar{X}_2 = 81 - 74 = 7 \text{ mm}$$

and

$$\sigma_{(\bar{y}_1 - \bar{y}_2)} = \sqrt{\frac{\sigma_1^2}{n_1} + \frac{\sigma_2^2}{n_2}}$$

$$\approx \sqrt{\frac{s_1^2}{n_1} + \frac{s_2^2}{n_2}} = \sqrt{\frac{144}{50} + \frac{196}{50}}$$

$$= \sqrt{6.8} = 2.61 \text{ mm}$$

The bound on our error of estimation is therefore $2\sigma_{(\bar{y}_1 - \bar{y}_2)} = 2(2.61) = 5.22$ mm. We do not expect our sample mean difference of 7 mm to be farther than 5.22 mm from the true population difference $(\mu_1 - \mu_2)$.

A confidence interval for $(\mu_1 - \mu_2)$ with confidence coefficient $(1 - \alpha)$ is given in the box.

Large-Sample $(1 - \alpha)$ Confidence Interval for $(\mu_1 - \mu_2)$

$$(\bar{X}_1 - \bar{X}_2) \pm z_{\alpha/2} \sqrt{\frac{\sigma_1^2}{n_1} + \frac{\sigma_2^2}{n_2}}$$

Example 8.5

Place a confidence interval on the population difference in mean perceptual error for the problem described in example 8.4. Use a confidence coefficient of .99.

Solution: In table 8.1 we find that $z_{\alpha/2}$ is 2.58 for a confidence coefficient of .99. Thus the confidence interval is

$$(\bar{y}_1 - \bar{y}_2) \pm 2.58 \sqrt{\frac{\sigma_1^2}{n_1} + \frac{\sigma_2^2}{n_2}}$$

Using the results of example 8.4, we find that the confidence interval is

$$7 \pm (2.58)(2.61) \quad \text{or} \quad 7 \pm (6.73)$$

Therefore, LCL $= .27$, and UCL $= 13.73$. The population difference in mean perceptual error is estimated to lie between these two points.

The fact that this confidence interval, $(.27, 13.73)$, is composed entirely of positive numbers allows us to infer with 99 percent confidence that $(\mu_1 - \mu_2)$ is positive. That is, there is strong evidence that $\mu_1 > \mu_2$, which implies that the mean male error in judgment exceeds the mean female error. We might conclude, therefore, that, on the average, males are more susceptible to perceptual illusions than females.

EXERCISES

1. One study compared boys and girls for the age at which the first recognizable word was spoken. From the parents' reports of age, the average for 100 boys was found to be 10.7 months with a standard deviation of 3.1 months. The average for 80 girls was found to be 9.4 months with a standard deviation of 2.6 months. Estimate the difference in mean ages for the two populations from which these samples were drawn. Place bounds on the error of estimation.
2. Construct a confidence interval for the difference between the population means of exercise 1 using a confidence coefficient of .99. Based on this confidence interval, can you conclude that the population means are different?

8.6 • ESTIMATING THE PARAMETER OF A BINOMIAL DISTRIBUTION

In chapter 5 we introduced an important discrete random variable, the binomial. Recall that the binomial random variable y represents the number of successes in n independent trials of an experiment, where only two outcomes (success or failure) are possible on each trial. A good example of a binomial experiment is a coin toss. The probability of success p is the same on each trial. In most practical situations, p will be unknown. Hence in this section we develop an estimator for p.

The best point estimator of the binomial parameter p is also the estimator that would be chosen intuitively. That is, we use the estimator

$$\hat{p} = \frac{y}{n}$$

the total number of successes y divided by the total number of trials n. By "best" we mean that p is unbiased and has a smaller variance than other unbiased estimators.

We recall that, according to the Central Limit Theorem, y is approximately normally distributed when n is large (see section 7.5). Since n is a constant, we would suspect that $\hat{p}$ is also normally distributed when n is large, and this is indeed true. Some facts about the sampling distribution of the estimator $\hat{p}$ are summarized in the box.

The Sampling Distribution of the Estimator for the Parameter of a Binomial Distribution

1. The mean of the sampling distribution of $\hat{p}$ is p.

2. The standard deviation of the sampling distribution of $\hat{p}$ is

$$\sigma_{\hat{p}} = \sqrt{\frac{pq}{n}}$$

The above quantity is also called the standard error of $\hat{p}$.

3. When n is large, the sampling distribution of $\hat{p}$ is approximately normal.

A bound on the error of this point estimate is

$$2\sqrt{\frac{pq}{n}}$$

The $(1 - \alpha)$ confidence interval, appropriate for large n, is given in the box.

Large-Sample $(1 - \alpha)$ Confidence Interval for p

$$\left(\hat{p} \pm z_{\alpha/2} \sqrt{\frac{pq}{n}} \right)$$

The sample size is considered large if it satisfies the conditions discussed in section 7.5.

Note that calculating the standard deviation of $\hat{p}$, $\sigma_{\hat{p}} = \sqrt{pq/n}$, requires that we know p (and $q = 1 - p$). But p is unknown and is, in fact, the parameter we are trying to estimate. However, when n is large, little error will be introduced by substituting $\hat{p}$ for the parameter p in the standard deviation $\sqrt{pq/n}$. As a matter of fact, the standard deviation changes only slightly as p changes. This can be observed in table 8.3, where $\sqrt{pq}$ is recorded for several values of p. Note that $\sqrt{pq}$ changes very little as p changes, especially when p is near .5. We therefore will use $\sqrt{\hat{p}\hat{q}/n}$ to approximate $\sigma_{\hat{p}} = \sqrt{pq/n}$ when forming confidence intervals or calculating a bound on the error of estimation.

Table 8.3 • Some calculated values of $\sqrt{pq}$

p	$\sqrt{pq}$
.5	.50
.4	.49
.3	.46
.2	.40
.1	.30

Example 8.6

A sample of 400 human subjects produced $y = 280$ subjects who were classed as right-eye dominant on the basis of a sighting task.

(a) Estimate the fraction of the entire population who are right-eye dominant and place a bound on the error of estimation.
(b) Form a 95 percent confidence interval for p.

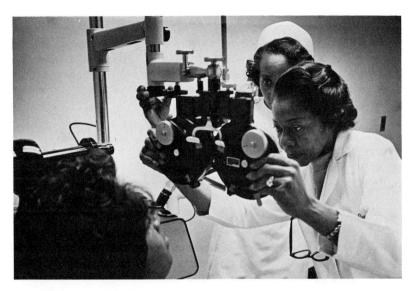

A study is conducted to determine the number of subjects who are classed as right-eye dominant, based on a sighting task. What would the researcher use as a point estimate of p, the fraction of subjects in the population who are right-eye dominant? Photo by Bruce Roberts, Rapho/Photo Researchers, Inc.

Solution: (a) The point estimate is

$$\hat{p} = \frac{y}{n} = \frac{280}{400} = .70$$

The bound on the error of estimation is

$$2\sigma_{\hat{p}} = 2\sqrt{\frac{pq}{n}} \approx 2\sqrt{\frac{(.70)(.30)}{400}} = .046$$

(b) A 95 percent confidence interval for p is

$$\hat{p} \pm 1.96\sqrt{\frac{pq}{n}} = .70 \pm (1.96)(.023)$$

$$= (.655, .745)$$

Thus we estimate that p lies in the interval .655 to .745, with confidence coefficient .95. Since the interval does not include the value .50, it appears that more than half the population are right-eye dominant as defined by the particular sighting task.

EXERCISES

1. Behavior genetics is concerned with the inheritance of behavior rather than the inheritance of physical characteristics. Because of the ethics involved with controlled experimentation on human heredity, animal breeding is the source of the data. To determine whether a given inbred strain of mice can be considered susceptible to audiogenic seizure, a study was conducted to estimate the probability p of seizure response to a loud noise. A sample of 1000 mice was tested and 810 responded with seizures. Estimate p and place bounds on the error of estimation.
2. Place a confidence interval on p of exercise 1, using a confidence coefficient of .90.

8.7 • ESTIMATING THE DIFFERENCE BETWEEN TWO BINOMIAL PARAMETERS

The fourth and final estimation problem considered in this chapter is the estimation of the difference between the parameters of two binomial populations. Assume that the probabilities of success for populations 1 and 2 are p_1 and p_2, respectively. Independent random samples consisting of n_1 and n_2 trials are drawn from the population. The estimates $\hat{p}_1$ and $\hat{p}_2$ are calculated, where $\hat{p}_1$ and $\hat{p}_2$ are the fractions of success in samples 1 and 2, respectively.

The best point estimate (unbiased, with minimum variance) of $(p_1 - p_2)$ is $(\hat{p}_1 - \hat{p}_2)$, as you might intuitively expect. The properties of this sampling distribution of $(\hat{p}_1 - \hat{p}_2)$ are summarized in the box.

The Sampling Distribution of the Estimator for the Difference Between Two Binomial Parameters

1. The mean of the sampling distribution of $(\hat{p}_1 - \hat{p}_2)$ is $(p_1 - p_2)$.
2. The standard deviation of the sampling distribution of $(\hat{p}_1 - \hat{p}_2)$ is

$$\sigma_{(\hat{p}_1 - \hat{p}_2)} = \sqrt{\frac{p_1 q_1}{n_1} + \frac{p_2 q_2}{n_2}}$$

The above quantity is also called the standard error of $(\hat{p}_1 - \hat{p}_2)$.
3. The sampling distribution of $(\hat{p}_1 - \hat{p}_2)$ is approximately normal for large n_1 and n_2.

Therefore, the bound on the error of estimation is

$$2\sqrt{\frac{p_1 q_1}{n_1} + \frac{p_2 q_2}{n_2}}$$

where the estimates $\hat{p}_1$ and $\hat{p}_2$ may be substituted for p_1 and p_2.

The $(1 - \alpha)$ confidence interval, appropriate when n_1 and n_2 are large, is given in the box.

Large-Sample $(1 - \alpha)$ Confidence Interval for $(p_1 - p_2)$

$$(\hat{p}_1 - \hat{p}_2) \pm z_{\alpha/2} \sqrt{\frac{p_1 q_1}{n_1} + \frac{p_2 q_2}{n_2}}$$

Example 8.7

The twin concordance rate for a given trait is the probability that both members of a twin pair share the trait. Suppose that a researcher wishes to compare the concordance rates of identical and fraternal twins with respect to schizophrenia. When the sibling of each of $n_1 = 120$ hospitalized schizophrenics who have identical twins is examined, it is found that 74.2 percent of the pairs are concordant. When the sibling of each of $n_2 = 350$ schizophrenics who have fraternal twins is examined, it is found that 16.0 percent of the pairs are concordant. Estimate the difference in concordance rates between identical and fraternal twins.

Solution: Identical twins and fraternal twins are populations 1 and 2, respectively. The point estimate of the difference between the two concordance rates, p_1 and p_2, is

$$\hat{p}_1 - \hat{p}_2 = .742 - .160 = .582$$

The bound on the error of estimation is

$$2\sqrt{\frac{p_1 q_1}{n_1} + \frac{p_2 q_2}{n_2}} \approx 2\sqrt{\frac{(.742)(.258)}{120} + \frac{(.16)(.84)}{350}} = .089$$

The corresponding confidence interval, using confidence coefficient .95, is

$$(\hat{p}_1 - \hat{p}_2) \pm 1.96 \sqrt{\frac{p_1 q_1}{n_1} + \frac{p_2 q_2}{n_2}}$$

The resulting confidence interval is

$$.582 \pm (1.96)(.0445) = (.495, .669)$$

Hence we estimate that the difference $(p_1 - p_2)$ in concordance rates between identical and fraternal twins falls in the interval .495 to .669. We are fairly confident that this interval estimate actually contains $(p_1 - p_2)$. We know that, if our sampling procedure were repeated over and over again, each time generating an interval estimate, approximately 95 percent of the estimates would enclose $(p_1 - p_2)$.

EXERCISES

1. In developmental and social psychological research, birth order, or ordinal position, as it is called, has come to be an important variable of study. It has been found, for instance that a higher proportion of firstborn children are found in U.S. colleges than would be expected (Warren 1966). In a study of the relationship between birth order

and college success, an investigator found that 126 in a sample of 180 college graduates were firstborn children. In a sample of 100 nongraduates of comparable age and socioeconomic background, the number of firstborn children was 54. Estimate the difference in the proportion of firstborn children for the two populations from which these samples were drawn. Place bounds on the error of estimation.

2. Construct a confidence interval for the difference between the population proportions of exercise 1, using a confidence coefficient of .95. Can you infer from this confidence interval that the population proportions are different?

8.8 • CHOOSING THE SAMPLE SIZE

One of the most important decisions a researcher must make in designing an experiment is in chosing the size of the sample from each population. Indeed, perhaps one of the most frequent questions asked of the statistician is this: How many measurements should be included in the sample? When the purpose of the experiment is to estimate a parameter value, the answer to this question depends on how accurate the experimenter wishes the estimate to be and, of course, on the resources available for experimentation. Often the accuracy is specified by the desired bound on the error of estimation.

For instance, suppose that we wish to estimate the mean perceptual error μ for the judgments of the length of an illusory figure (example 8.2). We wish the error of estimation to be less than 3 millimeters with a probability of .95. Since approximately 95 percent of the sample means will lie within $2\sigma_{\bar{y}}$ of μ in repeated sampling, we are asking that $2\sigma_{\bar{y}}$ equal 3 millimeters (see figure 8.8).* Then

$$2\sigma_{\bar{y}} = 3 \quad \text{or} \quad \frac{2\sigma}{\sqrt{n}} = 3$$

Solving for n, we obtain

$$n = \frac{4\sigma^2}{9}$$

* If the estimator were exactly normally distributed and if σ were known, a more exact value for the sample size could be obtained by using 1.96 in place of 2. Since this situation will rarely, if ever, exist, you lose little accuracy by using 2 rather than 1.96.

You will quickly note that we cannot obtain a numerical value for n unless the population standard deviation σ is known. And certainly this is exactly what we would expect because the variability of $\bar{y}$ depends on the variability of the population from which the sample was drawn.

Lacking an exact value for σ, we would use the best approximation available. We may use an estimate s obtained from a previous sample, or we may have knowledge of the range in which the measurements will fall. Since the population in question represents a large number of measurements, a conservative estimate of σ is one-fourth of the range (see the discussion of the Empirical Rule in chapter 2).

Here we can use the result of our previous sample (example 8.2), $s = 12$,

Figure 8.8 • Approximate distribution of $\bar{y}$ for large samples and the location of $2\sigma_{\bar{y}}$ from μ

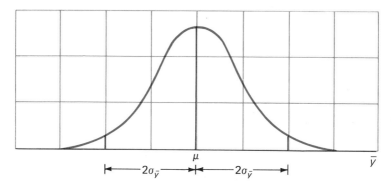

which provides a reasonably accurate estimate of σ. Then

$$n = \frac{4\sigma^2}{9} \approx \frac{(4)(12)^2}{9} = 64$$

Using a sample size of $n = 64$, we would be reasonably certain (with probability approximately .95) that our estimate will lie within $2\sigma_{\bar{y}} = 3$ millimeters of the population mean μ.

Actually, we would expect the error of estimation to be much less than 3 millimeters. According to the Empirical Rule, the error of estimation will be less than $\sigma_{\bar{y}} = 1.5$ millimeters about 68 percent of the time. You will note that the probabilities .95 and .68 used in these statements are inexact. This is because s was substituted for σ and because the sampling distribution of $\bar{y}$ is only approximately normal. So this method of choosing the sample size is only approximate for a desired accuracy of estimation. However, it is the best method available and is certainly better than selecting the sample size intuitively.

The method of choosing the sample size for all the large-sample estimation procedures discussed in the preceding sections is identical to the method described above. The experimenter must specify a desired bound on the error of estimation and an associated confidence level $(1 - \alpha)$. For example, if the parameter is θ and the desired bound is B, we would proceed as follows.

Determination of Sample Size for Large-Sample Estimation Procedures

$$z_{\alpha/2}\sigma_{\hat{\theta}} = B$$

where $z_{\alpha/2}$ is the z-value defined in section 8.3; that is,

$$P(z > z_{\alpha/2}) = \frac{\alpha}{2}$$

This idea is illustrated in figure 8.9.

Figure 8.9 • Choosing the sample size so that $\hat{\theta}$ is within bound B of θ, with a $(1 - \alpha)$ confidence level

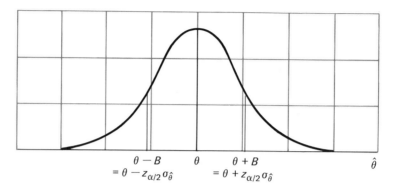

$$\underset{= \theta - z_{\alpha/2}\sigma_{\hat{\theta}}}{\theta - B} \qquad \theta \qquad \underset{= \theta + z_{\alpha/2}\sigma_{\hat{\theta}}}{\theta + B} \qquad\qquad\qquad \hat{\theta}$$

In the following examples we illustrate how the method can be used.

Example 8.8

To establish the difficulty level of an achievement test, an educational testing concern wishes to estimate the probability p that a child in the fifth grade will answer any given item correctly. How may children should be tested if the error of estimation is to be less than .04 with a confidence coefficient of .90? Assume that p is expected to be approximately .6.

Solution: Since the confidence coefficient is $(1 - \alpha) = .90$, α must equal .10 and so $\alpha/2 = .05$. The z-value corresponding to an area of .05 in the upper tail of the z distribution is $z_{\alpha/2} = 1.645$. We then require

$$1.645\sigma_{\hat{p}} = .04 \qquad \text{or} \qquad 1.645\sqrt{\frac{pq}{n}} = .04$$

Since the variability of $\hat{p}$ depends upon p, which is unknown, we must use the anticipated value of $p = .6$ as an approximation. Then

$$1.645\sqrt{\frac{(.6)(.4)}{n}} = .04$$

$$\frac{(.6)(.4)}{n} = \frac{(.04)^2}{(1.645)^2}$$

$$n = \frac{(.6)(.4)(1.645)^2}{(.04)^2} = 406$$

Thus 406 children should be tested if the error of estimation is to be less than .04 at a confidence level of .90.

Example 8.9

An experimenter wishes to compare the effectiveness of two methods of training industrial employees to perform a certain assembly operation. A number of employees are to be divided into two groups of equal size, the first receiving Training Method 1 and the second, Training Method 2. Each employee will perform the assembly operation and the length of assembly time will be recorded. It is expected that the measurements for both groups will have a range of approximately 8 minutes. If the estimate of the difference in mean assembly time is desired correct to within 1 minute with a confidence coefficient of .95, how many workers must be included in each training group?

Solution: Equating $2\sigma_{(\bar{y}_1 - \bar{y}_2)}$ to 1 minute, we obtain

$$2\sqrt{\frac{\sigma_1^2}{n_1} + \frac{\sigma_2^2}{n_2}} = 1$$

Or, since we desire n_1 to equal n_2, we may let $n_1 = n_2 = n$ and obtain the equation

$$2\sqrt{\frac{\sigma_1^2}{n} + \frac{\sigma_2^2}{n}} = 1$$

As noted above, the variability of each method of assembly is approximately the same, and hence $\sigma_1^2 = \sigma_2^2 = \sigma^2$. Since the range of 8 minutes is approximately equal to 4σ, then

$$4\sigma = 8$$

$$\sigma = 2$$

Substituting this value 2 for σ_1 and σ_2 in the equation above, we obtain

$$2\sqrt{\frac{(2)^2}{n} + \frac{(2)^2}{n}} = 1$$

$$\sqrt{\frac{4+4}{n}} = \frac{1}{2}$$

$$\frac{8}{n} = \frac{(1)^2}{(2)^2}$$

$$n = (8)(4) = 32$$

Thus each group should contain $n = 32$ members if we desire our .95 bound on the error of estimation for the difference between the population mean assembly times to be approximately 1 minute.

EXERCISES

1. One topic of concern to educational and school psychologists is the study of performance on school-related abilities and activities. It is desired to estimate the mean score on a reading skills test for a population of reading-disabled children. How large a sample should be administered the test if we wish the sample mean to be within 1 test-score unit of the population mean, with a confidence level of .95? Assume the standard deviation is approximately 15 test-score units.

2. Important research is being conducted on the subject of sleep and dreams. Although

everyone dreams, some people more readily recall their dreams. An experimenter prepared a drug-dose level designed to induce sleep in 60 percent of all cases treated. How large a sample should be treated if the experimenter wishes to estimate the true fraction of those for whom the drug is effective to within .02, with a confidence level of .95?

3. It is desired to estimate the difference in mean grade point average between two groups of college students accurate to within .2 grade points. If the standard deviation of the grade point measurements is approximately .6, how many students must be included in each group? (Assume that the groups will be of equal size.)

4. Given that the two samples in exercise 3 yield mean grade point averages of 2.8 and 3.1 with standard deviations of .62 and .56, respectively, construct 95 percent confidence limits for the difference between the population means.

8.9 LARGE-SAMPLE PARAMETRIC HYPOTHESIS TESTING

The testing of research hypotheses was discussed in chapter 5 in connection with the binomial random variable and in chapter 6 in connection with nonparametric comparisons of two populations. In this section we extend hypothesis testing to include research hypotheses about specific parameters of the population(s).

For example, we may wish to test the research hypothesis that the mean reaction time to a visual stimulus exceeds 2 seconds; or that the average increase in blood pressure for males when subjected to a certain stress exceeds the average increase for females; or that the fraction of firstborn children who attend college exceeds the fraction of secondborn children who attend college. These examples all state research hypotheses about population parameters. In this section we consider large-sample tests of research hypotheses about the parameters discussed in sections 8.2 through 8.8: μ, $(\mu_1 - \mu_2)$, p, or $(p_1 - p_2)$.

We were able to find a minimum-variance unbiased estimator for each of the parameters discussed in sections 8.2 through 8.8. **Each estimator had an approximately normal sampling distribution for large sample size(s).** This fact allows us to treat the four cases in a very general manner.

Employing the notation of previous sections, let θ represent the parameter that is the object of the research, and let $\hat{\theta}$ represent the estimator of θ. Then $\hat{\theta}$ is approximately normally distributed.

You will recall that there are two types of research hypotheses: one-tailed hypotheses and two-tailed hypotheses. In parametric tests, one-tailed parametric research hypotheses will always specify either that the parameter θ is greater than some number θ_0, that is, $\theta > \theta_0$, or that θ is smaller than some number θ_0, that is, $\theta < \theta_0$. Two-tailed research hypotheses will specify that the parameter θ is different from a given number θ_0, that is, $\theta \neq \theta_0$. This is summarized in table 8.4.

In every case the null hypothesis is

$$H_0 : \theta = \theta_0$$

Table 8.4 • One-tailed and two-tailed parametric research hypotheses

One-tailed		Two-tailed
Lower-tailed	**Upper-tailed**	
$H_a: \theta < \theta_0$	$H_a: \theta > \theta_0$	$H_a: \theta \neq \theta_0$

We employ the rare event philosophy to decide whether the research hypothesis is supported or not supported by the data. Our test statistic $\hat{\theta}$ is the best estimator of θ. The sampling distribution of $\hat{\theta}$ when the null hypothesis is true ($\theta = \theta_0$) is shown in figure 8.10.

Figure 8.10 • Sampling distribution of $\hat{\theta}$ when $H_0 : \theta = \theta_0$ is true

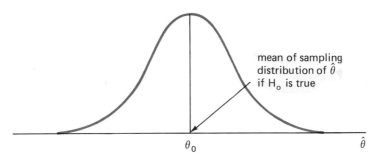

mean of sampling distribution of $\hat{\theta}$ if H_o is true

θ_0

$\hat{\theta}$

Now, what observed values of $\hat{\theta}$ would cause us to disbelieve the null hypothesis, that is, to disbelieve that figure 8.10 depicts the *true* sampling distribution of $\hat{\theta}$? We will doubt that the mean value of $\hat{\theta}$ is θ_0 when we observe rare or unexpected values of $\hat{\theta}$ in the extremes of the sampling distribution in figure 8.10. And the more extreme the value of $\hat{\theta}$, the more we will doubt the null hypothesis.

The nature of the rejection region, those values of $\hat{\theta}$ for which we will reject the null hypothesis H_0, may now be specified for each type of research hypothesis. This is done pictorially in figure 8.11.

As you would expect, if the one-tailed research hypothesis is $H_a : \theta > \theta_0$, then we will favor this research hypothesis when unusually large values of $\hat{\theta}$ are observed [figure 8.11(a)].

If the one-tailed research hypothesis is $H_a : \theta < \theta_0$, the research hypothesis will be supported by extremely small values of $\hat{\theta}$ [figure 8.11(b)].

Finally, if the research hypothesis is two-tailed, both very large values and very small values of $\hat{\theta}$ imply the truth of that hypothesis [figure 8.11(c)].

Notice that in figure 8.11 we have shaded the areas under the null hypothesis distribution that correspond to each rejection region. The shaded areas correspond to the probability α of making a type 1 error, that is, of rejecting the null

Figure 8.11 • Rejection regions for $H_0: \theta = \theta_0$

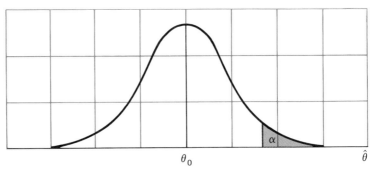

(a) One-tailed research hypothesis $H_a: \theta > \theta_0$

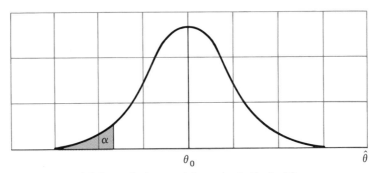

(b) One-tailed research hypothesis $H_a: \theta < \theta_0$

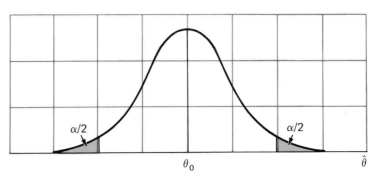

(c) Two-tailed research hypothesis $H_a: \theta \neq \theta_0$

hypothesis when it is true. Actual numerical values of α will be determined by the researcher, and these values in turn specify the exact rejection region.

The sampling distribution of $\hat{\theta}$ is approximately normal. Thus the normal z score is a convenient test statistic to use when determining whether a value of $\hat{\theta}$ is far enough from θ_0 to warrant rejecting the null hypothesis $H_0 : \theta = \theta_0$. This normal z score is the number of standard deviations between $\hat{\theta}$ and θ_0:

$$z = \frac{\hat{\theta} - \theta_0}{\sigma_{\hat{\theta}}}$$

Remember from section 8.3 that the relative frequency distribution of z is as shown in Figure 8.12. Particularly note that the mean of z is 0 and that 95 percent of the z scores fall within 1.96 of the mean 0. For example, suppose we were testing the two-tailed research hypothesis $H_a : \theta \neq \theta_0$. A z-value greater than 1.96 or less than -1.96 would support this research hypothesis at the $\alpha = .05$ level of significance. That is, if we observe a very large value or a very small value of z, we will infer that the statistic

$$z = \frac{\hat{\theta} - \theta_0}{\sigma_{\hat{\theta}}}$$

is not a z score at all, because θ_0, we infer, is not the true mean of the sampling distribution of θ.

Figure 8.12 • Normal z-score frequency distribution showing the areas under the curve for a z-value of 1.96

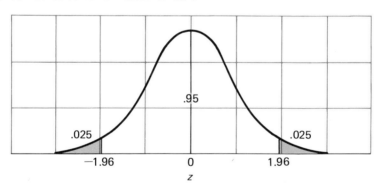

Before presenting some examples, we summarize the steps to be followed in testing a parametric research hypothesis.

Summary of Parametric Hypothesis Testing

1. Null hypothesis $H_0 : \theta = \theta_0$.
2. Research hypothesis
   (a) $H_a : \theta < \theta_0$ (one-tailed, lower tail);
   (b) $H_a : \theta > \theta_0$ (one-tailed, upper tail);
   (c) $H_a : \theta \neq \theta_0$ (two-tailed).

3. Test statistic: $z = \dfrac{\hat{\theta} - \theta_0}{\sigma_{\hat{\theta}}}$.

4. Rejection region, where α is the probability of a type 1 error:
   (a) $z < -z_\alpha$;
   (b) $z > z_\alpha$;
   (c) $z > z_{\alpha/2}$ or $z < -z_{\alpha/2}$.
5. Calculations and conclusion.

Example 8.10

A program of dietary control was developed for mentally retarded children with a known biochemical deficiency. The objective was to increase their intelligence. To test the research hypothesis that the dietary program would result in an increase in the average IQ, a random sample of 40 mentally retarded children is selected. Each child is administered two forms of an IQ test, one before and one after the program of dietary control. The difference ("before" IQ minus "after" IQ) is recorded for each child. The 40 sample differences have a mean $\bar{y} = -3.5$ and a standard deviation $s = 7.5$.
(a) Set up a test of the research hypothesis by specifying the null hypothesis, the research hypothesis, the test statistic, and the rejection region for $\alpha = .05$.
(b) Calculate the test statistic and state your conclusion.

Solution: (a) The research hypothesis concerns the parameter μ, the mean IQ difference ("before" minus "after"). If the dietary program is a success, we expect μ to be negative. That is, we expect the average "after program" IQ score to exceed the average "before program" IQ score. Therefore, our research hypothesis is that the mean difference is less than zero, and the null hypothesis is that the mean difference is zero.

$$H_0: \mu = 0$$
$$H_a: \mu < 0$$

Intuitively, a test statistic for the population mean would involve the distance between the sample mean $\bar{y}$ and the null hypothesis population mean μ_0. Consequently, we will use the normal z score for our test statistic,

$$\text{Test statistic: } z = \frac{\bar{y} - \mu_0}{\sigma_{\bar{y}}} = \frac{\bar{y} - 0}{\sigma_{\bar{y}}}$$

where μ_0 is the value of μ for the null hypothesis.

The rejection region for this one-tailed test would consist of unusually small values of $\bar{y}$, that is, small values of z, as shown in figure 8.13. Thus, for $\alpha = .05$ and a one-tailed (lower-tailed) test, we have

$$\text{Rejection region: } z < -1.645$$

Figure 8.13 • Rejection region for a one-tailed (lower-tailed) test, when $\alpha = .05$ (example 8.10)

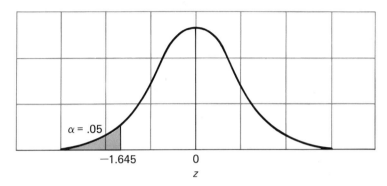

(b) The value of the test statistic is

$$z = \frac{\bar{y} - \mu_0}{\sigma_{\bar{y}}} = \frac{\bar{y} - 0}{\sigma/\sqrt{n}}$$

$$\approx \frac{-3.5}{s/\sqrt{40}} = \frac{-3.5}{7.5/\sqrt{40}} = -2.95$$

Note that we have used s to approximate σ. Since the test statistic z is less than -1.645, we conclude that the dietary control program is effective in increasing the population average IQ, and we make this conclusion at the $\alpha = .05$ level of significance. That is, we understand that the test is con- structed so that the probability of incorrectly rejecting the null hypothesis is $\alpha = .05$.

Note that our test statistic $z = -2.95$ is well into the rejection region. We may naturally inquire about the smallest α-value that would have resulted in a rejection of the null hypothesis. That is, what significance level corresponds to $z = -2.95$? Referring to figure 8.14, we see that the significance level P

Figure 8.14 • Significance level for $z = -2.95$ in example 8.10

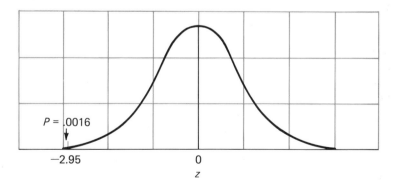

is obtained by determining the area for $z = -2.95$ from table 4 in appendix II and subtracting this value from .5.

$$P = .5 - .4984 = .0016$$

Thus we would have accepted the research hypothesis at any α-value exceeding .0016. The data provides very strong evidence for the research hypothesis.

Example 8.11

A study is to be conducted to examine the research hypothesis that birth order and various personality traits are related. As part of this study, a random sample of 100 firstborn children is selected, and they rate themselves on a social-dominance scale. Independently of this, a second random sample of 100 laterborn children is chosen, and they also rate themselves on the social-dominance scale. You should recognize this as the independent sampling design, with the following basic elements:

Experimental units: Children.

Response: Self-rating score on a social-dominance scale.

Treatments: The conditions of birth order, firstborn and laterborn.

(a) Set up the hypothesis test, using an α-value of .05.
(b) Suppose the experiment is conducted with the following results.

Firstborn	Laterborn
$n_1 = 100$	$n_2 = 100$
$\bar{x}_1 = 5.70$	$\bar{x}_2 = 5.54$
$s_1^2 = .36$	$s_2^2 = .40$

Calculate the test statistic and state your conclusion.

Solution: (a) The research hypothesis for this specific aspect of the study may be stated as a parametric hypothesis involving the means of the two populations (treatments) being sampled. Specifically, the research hypothesis is that the mean self-rating scores on the social-dominance scale differ for firstborn and laterborn children. Let μ_1 represent the mean of the self-rating scores for the population of firstborns, and let μ_2 represent the mean self-rating scores for the population of laterborns.

$$H_0: \mu_1 - \mu_2 = 0$$
$$H_a: \mu_1 - \mu_2 \neq 0$$

We again employ the z score as the test statistic, using the difference in sample means $(\bar{x}_1 - \bar{x}_2)$ as our estimator of $(\mu_1 - \mu_2)$. Also, $(\mu_1 - \mu_2)_0$ represents the null hypothesis value of $(\mu_1 - \mu_2)$.

Test statistic: $z = \dfrac{(\bar{X}_1 - \bar{X}_2) - (\mu_1 - \mu_2)_0}{\sigma_{\bar{y}_1 - \bar{y}_2}} = \dfrac{(\bar{y}_1 - \bar{y}_2) - 0}{\sigma_{(\bar{y}_1 - \bar{y}_2)}}$

Finally, the rejection region corresponding to a two-tailed test for $\alpha = .05$ is, as shown in figure 8.15,

Rejection region: $z > 1.96$ or $z < -1.96$

Figure 8.15 • Rejection region for a two-tailed test, when $\alpha = .05$ (example 8.11)

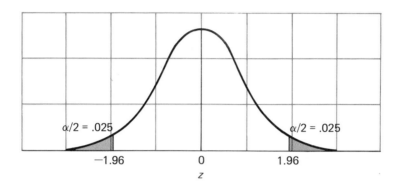

$\alpha/2 = .025$ $\alpha/2 = .025$

-1.96 0 1.96

z

(b) The value of the test statistic is

$$z = \frac{(\bar{X}_1 - \bar{X}_2) - (\mu_1 - \mu_2)_0}{\sigma_{(\bar{y}_1 - \bar{y}_2)}} = \frac{(\bar{y}_1 - \bar{y}_2) - 0}{\sqrt{\dfrac{\sigma_1^2}{n_1} + \dfrac{\sigma_2^2}{n_2}}}$$

$$= \frac{5.70 - 5.54}{\sqrt{\dfrac{\sigma_1^2}{100} + \dfrac{\sigma_2^2}{100}}} \approx \frac{.16}{\sqrt{\dfrac{s_1^2}{100} + \dfrac{s_2^2}{100}}}$$

$$= \frac{.16}{\sqrt{\dfrac{.36}{100} + \dfrac{.40}{100}}} = 1.84$$

Since this z-value is less than 1.96, we cannot conclude that the mean self-rating score μ_1 on the social-dominance scale for firstborn children differs from that for laterborn children (μ_2).

Note that we do not accept the null hypothesis of no difference in population means. The observation of a z score which is not unusual or rare does *not* imply that H_0 is true. All we can conclude from such a z score is that the evidence is not decisive enough to warrant acceptance of the research hypothesis. Thus we are in a position of not rejecting the null hypothesis rather than accepting it as true.

To calculate the significance level for this test, we find the probablity that a z score would exceed the observed $z = 1.84$, as shown in figure 8.16. This probability is .0329. Since the research hypothesis is two-tailed, we double this to obtain the significance level P.

$$P = 2(.0329) = .0658$$

Only a researcher willing to use an α-value of .0658 or greater would conclude that this experiment supports the research hypothesis. Since the z-value is positive, researchers using an α-value greater than .0658 would conclude that μ_1 exceeds μ_2, that is, that the mean self-rating score for the population of firstborns exceeds that for laterborns.

Figure 8.16 • Significance level for $z = 1.84$ in example 8.11

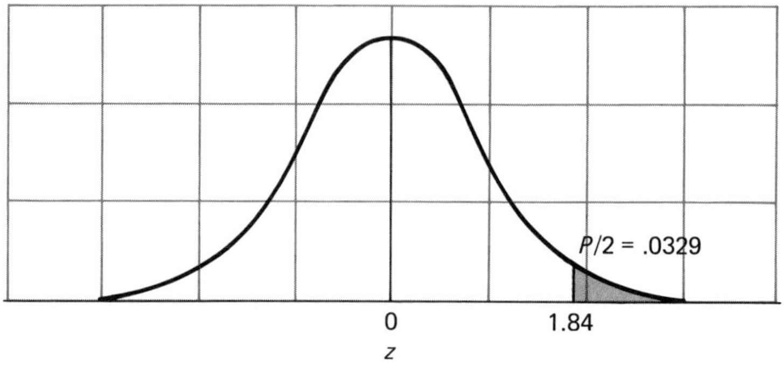

Example 8.12

Jordan (1933) studied a sample of 578 mill-worker children. One of the objectives was to compare their results on an intelligence test to established norms. Suppose we wish to use this sample to test the research hypothesis that the true fraction p of mill-workers' children who fall in the normal intelligence range on this test is less than .6, where .6 represents the norm fraction in this range.
(a) Set up the test of this research hypothesis using $\alpha = .01$.
(b) Suppose that 245 of the 578 children fall in the normal range. What is your conclusion?

Solution: (a) We are testing the research hypothesis that the binomial probability p is smaller than .6. Thus

Null hypothesis H_0: $p = .6$.

Research hypothesis H_a: $p < .6$.

Test statistic: $z = \dfrac{\hat{p} - p_0}{\sigma_{\hat{p}}} = \dfrac{\hat{p} - .6}{\sigma_{\hat{p}}}.$

We use figure 8.17 to illustrate the rejection region for this one-tailed (lower-tailed) research hypothesis.

Rejection region: $z < -2.33$

A sample of mill-worker children was studied to compare their results on an intelligence test to established norms. The result of the statistical test showed the sample fraction to be 8.6 standard deviations below the norm. Would the researcher reject the null hypothesis? Photo by Rohn Engh, Photo Researchers, Inc.

Figure 8.17 • Rejection region for a one-tailed (lower-tailed) test, when $\alpha = .01$ (example 8.12)

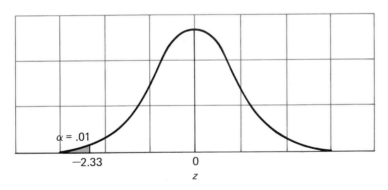

$\alpha = .01$

-2.33 0

z

(b) The value of the test statistic is

$$z = \frac{\hat{p} - p_0}{\sigma_{\hat{p}}} = \frac{\hat{p} - .6}{\sqrt{p_0 q_0 / n}} \qquad \sigma_{\hat{p}}$$

$$= \frac{(245/578) - .6}{\sqrt{p_0 q_0 / 578}} = \frac{.424 - .6}{\sqrt{(.6)(.4)/578}} = -8.6$$

Notice that in calculating $\sigma_{\hat{p}}$, we substitute $p_0 = .6$ for p because this is the value of p under the null hypothesis. Checking the computed value of z, -8.6, you can see that it falls well into the rejection region. There is no question about the conclusion: the fraction of the population of mill-workers' children who fall into the normal intelligence range is smaller than .6.

Although we tested at the $\alpha = .01$ level, our significance level is, for all practical purposes, zero. This is true because our sample fraction .424 is 8.6 *standard deviations* below the norm of .6.

Since such an extreme value occurs, more information may be obtained by forming a confidence interval on the true fraction of the mill-worker children population in the normal range. If we use a confidence coefficient of .99, we find

$$\hat{p} \pm z_{.005}\sigma_{\hat{p}} = .424 \pm 2.58\sqrt{\frac{pq}{n}}$$

$$\approx .424 \pm 2.58\sqrt{\frac{(.424)(.576)}{578}} = .424 \pm .053$$

$$= (.37, .48)$$

(Note that we approximated p in this expression by our best estimate of p, namely, $\hat{p}$.) Thus we are 99 percent confident that the true fraction of mill-workers' children in the normal intelligence range (according to this intelligence test) is between .37 and .48, that is, *well below* the norm value of .6.

Example 8.13

Part of the testing to determine the fitness of prospective astronauts is psychological testing. Suppose we wish to test the research hypothesis that the fraction of prospective male astronauts giving a response to a specific test stimulus differs from the fraction of prospective female astronauts who give a response. Samples of 100 male prospects and 100 female prospects are selected. We observe that 23 of the men respond to the stimulus and 37 of the women respond.
(a) Set up the test with $\alpha = .10$.
(b) What should be concluded?

Solution: (a) Let p_1 and p_2 represent the population fractions of male and female prospective astronauts, respectively, giving responses when subjected to the test stimulus. Then we will test the null hypothesis that p_1 and p_2 are the same against the research hypothesis that they differ.

Null hypotheses H_0: $p_1 - p_2 = 0$.

Research hypothesis H_a: $p_1 - p_2 \neq 0$.

Test statistic: $z = \dfrac{(\hat{p}_1 - \hat{p}_2) - (p_1 - p_2)_0}{\sigma_{(\hat{p}_1 - \hat{p}_2)}} = \dfrac{(\hat{p}_1 - \hat{p}_2) - 0}{\sigma_{(\hat{p}_1 - \hat{p}_2)}}.$

Rejection region: For $\alpha = .10$, our two-tailed rejection region is as shown in figure 8.18. It is

$$z > 1.645 \quad \text{or} \quad z < -1.645$$

Figure 8.18 • Rejection region for the two-tailed research hypothesis in example 8.13

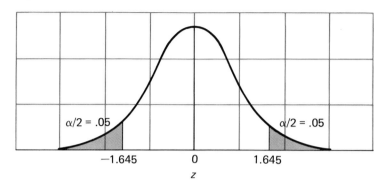

(b) The value of the test statistic is

$$z = \frac{(\hat{p}_1 - \hat{p}_2) - (p_1 - p_2)_0}{\sigma_{(\hat{p}_1 - \hat{p}_2)}} = \frac{(\hat{p}_1 - \hat{p}_2) - 0}{\sqrt{\dfrac{p_1 q_1}{n_1} + \dfrac{p_2 q_2}{n_2}}}$$

$$= \frac{[(23/100) - (37/100)] - 0}{\sqrt{\dfrac{p_1 q_1}{100} + \dfrac{p_2 q_2}{100}}} \approx \frac{.23 - .37}{\sqrt{\dfrac{(.23)(.77)}{100} + \dfrac{(.37)(.63)}{100}}}$$

$$= \frac{-.14}{.064} = -2.19$$

This z-value falls in the lower tail of the rejection region. Thus we should reject the null hypothesis at the $\alpha = .10$ level. We should conclude from the negative z-value ($z < -1.645$) that p_2 exceeds p_1. That is, the fraction of all female prospective astronauts who give a response will exceed the fraction of male prospective astronauts who give a response to the test stimulus.

The significance level P corresponding to the z-value of -2.19 would be determined as shown in figure 8.19. The area below $z = -2.19$ is .0143,

Figure 8.19 • Significance level for $z = -2.19$ in example 8.13

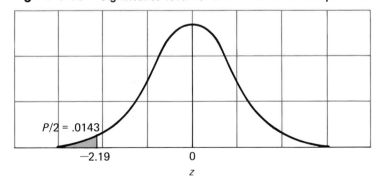

which we double to obtain the significance level associated with the two-tailed test. Thus

$$P = 2(.0143) = .0286$$

So we would accept the research hypothesis at any α-level of .0286 or higher.

EXERCISES

1. The Wechsler Intelligence Scale for Children (WISC), with standard mean of 100, is administered to a sample of 225 children in a school district to determine whether those children differ from the general population of children. The plan is to test the parametric research hypothesis that the population mean μ for this district differs from 100, the general population mean. Suppose the sample mean and standard deviation are 98.6 and 12.0, respectively.
    (a) Set up the test of hypothesis. Include the null and research hypotheses, the test statistic (in terms of a z score), and the rejection region. Use $\alpha = .05$.
    (b) Calculate the test statistic and state your conclusion.
    (c) What is the significance level corresponding to the observed z score?
2. In exercise 1, section 8.6, we estimated the proportion of a population of an inbred strain of mice that are susceptible to audiogenic seizure. In a sample of 1000 mice of this strain, 810 responded with seizures when a loud noise was made.
    Suppose we wish to test the research hypothesis that more than 80 percent of this strain will respond with seizures, that is, that $p > .8$.
    (a) Set up the test with $\alpha = .01$.
    (b) Calculate the test statistic and state your conclusion.
    (c) What is the significance level P associated with the observed z score?
3. Industrial psychologists are interested in business and organizational psychology, and they also do research on consumer behavior. In a study to assess various effects of using a female model in automobile advertising, each of 100 male subjects was shown photographs of two automobiles matched for price, color, and size but of different makes. Both automobiles were shown, one with a female model and one without a model, to 50 of the subjects (Group A); to the other 50 subjects (Group B), both automobiles were shown without the model. In Group A, the automobile shown with the female model was judged as the more expensive one by 37 subjects, while in Group B the same automobile was judged as the more expensive one by 23 subjects. We wish to test the research hypothesis that using a female model influences the perceived expensiveness of an automobile.
    (a) Set up the test with $\alpha = .05$.
    (b) Calculate the test statistic and state your conclusion.
    (c) What is the significance level associated with the observed z score?
4. Rosenthal and Jacobson (1968) have illustrated the effect that teaching expectation can have on student performance. In a similar study, IQ-change scores for two groups of 100 students were compared. Teachers of subjects in the experimental group were told that their students would show large IQ gains during the school year, while teachers of subjects in the control group were given no such information. At the conclusion of the school year, IQ-change scores were calculated, yielding averages

and standard deviations of $\bar{y}_1 = 16.5, s_1 = 14.2, \bar{y}_2 = 7.0$, and $s_2 = 13.1$ for the experimental and control group, respectively. The research hypothesis is that the result of teacher expectation will be a greater average increase in IQ score than if no such expectation existed.

(a) Set up the test of hypothesis using $\alpha = .01$.

(b) Calculate the test statistic and state your conclusion.

(c) What is the significance level P associated with the observed z score?

SUMMARY

Two basic approaches are available for parametric statistical inference: estimation and hypothesis testing. In this chapter we considered various large-sample estimation procedures and statistical tests of hypotheses about specific parameters of the population, along with methods for evaluating the goodness of our techniques.

Estimation procedures may use either a point estimation or an interval estimation. A parameter may be estimated by a single value, a point estimate. Or a parameter may be estimated by specifying an interval within which it will fall, with the width of the interval and the confidence coefficient measuring the goodness of the procedure. Also, given a specific bound on the error of estimation and some desired confidence level to accompany this bound, we can determine the approximate sample size needed to obtain the bound.

A statistical test of a research hypothesis is designed in one of two ways. We may fix α, the probability of incorrectly accepting the research hypothesis. Or we may conduct the test and report the significance level P of the result, letting each individual who reads the report determine the level at which he or she will infer that the research hypothesis is true. In many behavioral experiments, the researcher may wish both to estimate the value of some population parameter and to test an hypothesis about its value.

All the confidence intervals and statistical tests described in this chapter were based upon the Central Limit Theorem and hence apply to large samples. When n is large, each of the respective estimators and test statistics possess, for all practical purposes, a normal distribution in repeated sampling. This result, along with the properties of the normal distribution studied in chapter 7, permits the construction of the confidence intervals and the calculation of α and P for the statistical tests.

SUPPLEMENTARY EXERCISES

1. One example of human behavior that is interesting in terms of changes over the years is the mean age at which people get married. The mean and standard deviation of ages for a random sample of 100 marriage license applicants were calculated to be 27.9 years and 8.7 years, respectively. Estimate the mean marriage age for the

population from which the sample was drawn and place bounds on the error of estimation.

2. What is the Central Limit Theorem? How is the Central Limit Theorem used in exercise 1?

3. Suppose that the population mean in exercise 1 were really 26.6 years with $\sigma = 9.1$. What is the probability that the mean of a random sample of $n = 100$ measurements would exceed 27 years?

4. Using a confidence coefficient of .90, construct a confidence interval for the mean of the population in exercise 1.

5. Social facilitation refers to the fact that in some situations a person's performance will be better if there is an audience. Laughlin and Jaccard (1975) tested this idea with undergraduate students trying to solve problems. Subjects were either alone or observed by one or two persons. The mean score for 36 subjects observed by one person was 11.39 with a standard deviation of 2.9. Estimate the mean score μ for the population of potential undergraduate students and place bounds on the error of estimation.

6. Construct a 95 percent confidence interval for the population mean in exercise 5.

7. In studying attitude change and testing the various relevant theories, it is important to know people's attitudes toward particular issues. In a survey of attitudes toward censorship, 300 of 500 males and 64 of 100 females indicated a favorable attitude toward censorship. Estimate the difference in the population segments favoring censorship and place bounds on the error of estimation.

8. Refer to exercise 7. How many males and females must be included in the survey if we wish to estimate the difference in the population segments correct to within .05? Assume that the samples will be of equal size and that $p = .6$ is the approximation to both segments.

9. Hoffman (1975) studied sex differences in morality and values using samples of children and parents. One variable measured for each subject was the value he or she placed on consideration of other people. The data obtained are given below (a higher score implies a higher rank given this value by the respondent).

Sample Types	n	$\bar{y}$	s
Mothers	210	.70	.19
Fathers	210	.28	.07
Girls	124	.51	.11
Boys	146	.19	.07

Determine a 95 percent confidence interval for the difference between the population mean score for fathers and mothers.

10. Refer to exercise 9. Construct a 99 percent confidence interval for the difference in the population means between girls and boys.

11. Refer to exercise 9. Is there enough evidence in these data to support, at the $\alpha = .05$ level, the research hypothesis that the mean scores differ for fathers and boys?

12. Refer to exercise 9. At what significance level can you infer the truth of the research hypothesis that the mean scores for the populations of mothers and girls are different?

13. Feagin (1972) investigated American attitudes toward poverty and the poor. The

researcher was interested in the degree to which people blamed poverty on the poor people themselves or blamed poverty on social and economic forces. In a sample of 1017 people in 1969, 27 percent said that failure of private industry to provide enough jobs was a very important reason for poverty. Estimate the fraction of the population who would also agree with the statement. Place a bound on the error of estimation.

14. Refer to exercise 13. Place a 95 percent confidence interval on the true fraction who agree that failure of private industry to provide enough jobs is an important reason for poverty (in 1969).

15. As applied to aggression, the notion of catharsis means that once aggressive impulses are aroused, aggression will produce a decrease in tension. Green, Stonner, and Shope (1975) tested this notion. In order to arouse anger and the desire to be aggressive, 45 males received electric shocks. The measure of effectiveness of this manipulation was an anger rating by the subjects. The mean rating was 55.1 with a standard deviation of 6.2.
    (a) Is there evidence, at the $\alpha = .10$ level, that the mean anger rating μ for the population of all male subjects exceeds 50?
    (b) What is the significance level associated with the test statistic calculated in part (a)?

16. Refer to exercise 15. Suppose the objective is to estimate the population mean anger rating for males rather than to test an hypothesis about μ. Construct a 90 percent confidence interval for μ.

17. Santi and Wells (1975) had subjects play a threat-vulnerable game in order to study the effects of communication between players. The dependent measure was the amount of payoff points each subject gave to the other. The mean number of payoff points for 60 subjects in the "communication" condition was 846.05 with a standard deviation of 435.28. For the 30 subjects in the "no communication" condition, the mean and standard deviation were 598.00 and 288.08, respectively.
    Do the data support the research hypothesis that the mean number of payoff points is higher for players in the "communication" condition than for players in the "no communication" condition?

18. An investigator believes that the fraction p_1 of men in favor of capital punishment is greater than the fraction p_2 of women in favor of capital punishment. He acquires independent random samples of 200 men and 200 women, respectively, and finds 46 men and 34 women favoring capital punishment. Does this evidence provide statistical support for the investigator's belief at the 5 percent level of significance?

19. In an article on obese people, Thomas and Mayer (1973) mention a study showing that 35 percent of executives in a sample earning between $10,000 and $20,000 were at least 10 pounds overweight. If $n = 265$, estimate the percentage of the population of such executives who are overweight and place a bound on the error of estimation.

20. Refer to exercise 19. Determine a 90 percent confidence interval for the fraction of executives in the $10,000 to $20,000 range who are overweight by at least 10 pounds.

21. Sixty subjects were administered a syllogistic reasoning test in which half of the items were "emotionally charged" and the other half were "neutral" in content. For each subject, the number of incorrect responses was recorded for each half of the test and a difference score calculated: number of errors on "emotional" items minus number of errors on "neutral" items. Given that the average score was found to be 4.5, with

a standard deviation of 7.8, do the data provide sufficient evidence to indicate that subjects make more errors on the "emotionally charged" items than on the "neutral" items? Use $\alpha = .05$.

Note: When difference scores are used, as in this exercise, a potential two-population problem becomes a one-population problem. In this exercise, one population consists of scores on "emotionally charged" items and the second, of scores on "neutral" items. However, we are only analyzing the differences between these scores. Hence we are making an inference about a single population, the population of differences. Often the reason for analyzing difference scores is that the experimenter employed a matched pairs design, necessitating the use of differences to remove the effect of dependence between pairs of experimental units.

22. Nelson and Kagan (1972) reported on the competitiveness and lack of cooperation among Anglo-American children. They expressed concern about the environment in which American children are raised and about the kinds of behavior they learn. In one study Anglo-American children took toys away from another child on 78 of 100 trials, even when they could not keep the toys themselves. In the same situation, rural Mexican children took toys from another child on 39 of 100 trials.
    (a) Estimate the difference between the true proportions of Anglo-American children and rural Mexican children who would compete in the manner described in this experiment. Use a 95 percent confidence interval.
    (b) Without formally testing a research hypothesis, can you infer from the confidence interval formed in part (a) that there is a difference in the competitiveness proportions for the two populations? Why or why not?

23. Eighty high-IQ subjects and 80 low-IQ subjects participated in a learning experiment in which they had to recall lists of words with different reinforcement value (Rychlak 1975). The mean scores and standard deviations for each group are given below.

	Mean	Standard Deviation
High IQ	88.23	5.34
Low IQ	84.76	6.37

Is there support for the research hypothesis that the mean score for the population of high-IQ subjects exceeds that for the population of low-IQ subjects?

24. Refer to exercise 23. How many subjects would have to be included in the study if the investigator wished to estimate the true difference in average scores for the high-IQ and low-IQ subjects to within .5 points at the 95 percent confidence level?

25. Refer to exercise 1. Suppose that 10 samples of $n = 100$ marriage license applicants were drawn and a confidence interval constructed for the population mean μ for each of the 10 samples. What is the probability that exactly one of the intervals will not enclose the true value of μ? At least one?

REFERENCES

Feagin, J. R. 1972. Poverty: We still believe that God helps those who help themselves. *Psychology Today* 6(6):101–110, 129.

Green, R. G.; Stonner, D.; and Shope, G. L. 1975. The facilitation of aggression by aggression evidence against the catharsis hypothesis. *Journal of Personality and Social Psychology* 31:721–726.

Hoffman, M. L. 1975. Sex differences in moral internalization and values. *Journal of Personality and Social Psychology* 32:720–729.

Jordan, A. M. 1933. Parental occupation and children's intelligence scores. *Journal of Applied Psychology* 17:103–119.

Laughlin, R. R., and Jaccard, J. J. 1975. Social facilitation and observational learning of individuals and cooperative pairs. *Journal of Personality and Social Psychology* 32:873–879.

Nelson, L. L., and Kagan, S. 1972. Competition: The star spangled scramble. *Psychology Today* 6(4):53–56, 90–91.

Rosenthal, R., and Jacobson, L. 1968. *Pygmalian in the classroom: Teacher expectation and pupil's intellectual development*. New York: Holt, Rinehart and Winston.

Rychlak, J. F. 1975. Affective assessment, intelligence, social class and racial learning style. *Journal of Personality and Social Psychology* 32:989–995.

Santi, A., and Wells, R. 1975. Strategy in three variants of a threat-vulnerable game. *Journal of Personality and Social Psychology* 31:776–786.

Thomas, D. W., and Mayer, J. 1973. The search for the secret of fat. *Psychology Today* 7(4):74–79.

Warren, J. B. 1966. Birth-order and social behavior. *Psychological Bulletin* 65:38–49.

9 • Small-Sample Parametric Inference

INTRODUCTION

One of the major advantages of using large samples in statistical inference is that the normal probability distribution provides a good approximation to the sampling distribution of various estimators and test statistics.

However, for many behavioral experiments, it is not possible to obtain large samples. Practical considerations such as time, expense, and subject availability may limit sample sizes. Accordingly, in this chapter we will consider some small-sample methods that can be used in statistical inference.

A test statistic that has proven useful for small-sample experiments that are concerned with population means is the Student's *t* statistic. So to begin our discussion of small-sample methods, we consider the distribution and properties of this test statistic in section 9.1. By using this test statistic, we can make inferences about population means in a variety of ways. These various inference-making techniques are discussed in sections 9.2 through 9.4. (Small-sample tests and confidence intervals for binomial parameters are omitted since a more extensive treatment than that given in chapter 5 is beyond the scope of this text.)

We will also consider a method for comparing two population variances. This method, based on the F distribution, is presented in section 9.5. Our reasons for including this subject are twofold. First, it allows us to test the equality of two population variances. This equality is an important assumption in the small-sample comparison of population means. Secondly, it enables us to introduce an important probability distribution which is extremely useful in other contexts, as we will see in chapter 11.

Finally, in section 9.6, we will consider the question of parametric methods versus nonparametric methods. Now that we have discussed both methods in some detail, we can talk intelligently about their relative advantages and disadvantages—as we promised we would do in chapter 6.

All the methods discussed in this chapter have in common a basic assumption: that the population in question is normally distributed. One justification for this assumption is found in the Central Limit Theorem (section 7.2). That is, we might imagine the variable of interest as influenced by a number of factors, each varying randomly. If we could measure the effect of every such factor, and if each effect tended to add to the others, we could express a given measurement as the sum of a number of random variables. Then, if this number is large, the Central Limit Theorem and other theorems dealing with sums of random variables support our expectation that the distribution of measurements will be approximately normal.

Many phenomena yield measurements that include the effects of numerous sources of random or uncontrolled variation. So perhaps it is not surprising that the normal probability distribution should so often prove to be a reasonable model for the population.

9.1 • THE STUDENT'S *t* DISTRIBUTION

We introduce our topic by considering the following problem. An experiment requiring several weeks of subject participation was conducted to determine the effects of lack of sleep on the performance of various perceptual-motor tasks. After a given period of sleep deprivation, a measurement of reaction time to an auditory stimulus was taken for each of 6 adult male subjects. The resulting reaction times, in seconds, were 1.54, 2.14, 1.78, 1.62, 1.98, and 1.86. Previous data indicate that the average reaction time for non-sleep-deprived subjects is 1.70. Do the 6 measurements given above provide sufficient evidence to indicate that the average reaction time is longer for sleep-deprived subjects?

You will recall that, according to the Central Limit Theorem, the statistic

$$z = \frac{\bar{y} - \mu}{\sigma/\sqrt{n}}$$

has an approximately normal distribution in repeated sampling when n is large. For $\alpha = .05$, we would employ a one-tailed statistical test and reject the null hypothesis when $z > 1.645$. This, of course, assumes that σ is known or that a good estimate s is available and is based on a reasonably large sample (we have suggested $n \geq 30$). Certainly, the latter requirement will not be satisfied for the $n = 6$ reaction time measurements. How, then, can we test the null hypothesis that $\mu = 1.70$ against the alternative that $\mu > 1.70$?

The problem we pose is not new; it received serious attention from statisticians and experimenters at the turn of the century. If a sample standard deviation s were substituted for σ in z, would the resulting quantity possess approximately a standardized normal distribution in repeated sampling? More specifically, would the rejection region $z > 1.645$ be appropriate? That is, would approximately 5 percent of the values of the test statistic, computed in repeated sampling, exceed 1.645?

The answers to these questions, not unlike many of the problems encountered in the sciences, may be resolved by *experimentation*. That is, we could draw a small sample, say $n = 6$ measurements, and compute the value of the test statistic. Then we would repeat this process a very large number of times and construct a frequency distribution for the computed values of the test statistic. The general shape of the distribution and the location of the rejection region would then be evident.

The distribution of

$$t = \frac{\bar{y} - \mu}{s/\sqrt{n}}$$

for samples drawn from a *normally distributed population* was discovered by W. S. Gosset and published (1908) under the pen name of Student. He referred to the quantity under study as t and it has ever since been known as Student's t. We omit the complicated mathematical expression for the frequency function for t but we will describe some of its characteristics.

The distribution of the test statistic

$$t = \frac{\bar{y} - \mu}{s/\sqrt{n}}$$

in repeated sampling is, like the distribution of z, mound-shaped and perfectly symmetrical about $t = 0$. Unlike z, it is much more variable, with larger tail areas than the normal distribution, a phenomenon that may be readily explained.

The variability of z in repeated sampling is due solely to $\bar{x}$; the other quantities (n and σ) appearing in z are nonrandom. On the other hand, the variability of t is due to *two* random quantities, $\bar{x}$ and s. As a result, t will be more variable than z in repeated sampling.

Finally, as you might surmise, the variability of t decreases as n increases, because the estimate s of σ will be based on more and more information. When n is infinitely large, the t and z distributions are identical (see figure 9.1). Thus Gosset discovered that the distribution of t depended upon the sample size n.

Recall that s^2 is computed by dividing the sum of the squared distances from the sample mean by $(n - 1)$. The divisor $(n - 1)$ is called the number of

Figure 9.1 • Standard normal *z* distribution and the *t* distribution, based on $n = 6$ measurements

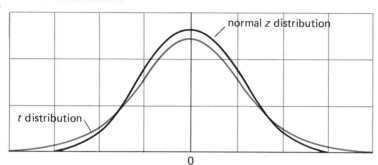

degrees of freedom associated with s^2. The origin of the term "degrees of freedom" is linked to the statistical theory underlying the probability distribution of s^2. We will not pursue this point further except to note that the test statistic *t* is based on a sample of *n* measurements and that it possesses $(n - 1)$ degrees of freedom. (Degrees of freedom is abbreviated d.f.) We will see later that it is important to make this distinction between sample size and degrees of freedom. The *t* statistic used in comparing two populations has its number of degrees of freedom computed by a different formula (section 9.3).

The values for *t* that separate the rejection and acceptance regions for a statistical test are presented in table 5 of appendix II. The table value t_α is that value such that α equals the fraction of the entire area of the *t* distribution to the right of t_α, as shown in figure 9.2. The degrees of freedom (d.f.) are shown in the first and last column of the table and the values of t_α corresponding to various values of α appear in the top row. Table 9.1 gives a partial reproduction of table 5, appendix II.

Suppose we wish to find the value of *t* such that .05 of the *t* distribution lies to its right. We then use the column marked $t_{.05}$ in table 9.1. For our sleep

Figure 9.2 • A tabulated value for the Student's *t*

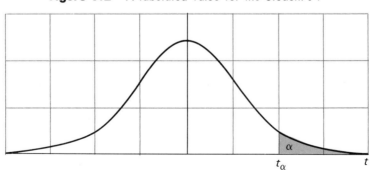

Table 9.1 • Partial reproduction of table 5, appendix II

d.f.	$t_{.100}$	$t_{.050}$	$t_{.025}$	$t_{.010}$	$t_{.005}$	d.f.
1	3.078	6.314	12.706	31.821	63.657	1
2	1.886	2.920	4.303	6.965	9.925	2
3	1.638	2.353	3.182	4.541	5.841	3
4	1.533	2.132	2.776	3.747	4.604	4
5	1.476	2.015	2.571	3.365	4.032	5
6	1.440	1.943	2.447	3.143	3.707	6
7	1.415	1.895	2.365	2.998	3.499	7
8	1.397	1.860	2.306	2.896	3.355	8
9	1.383	1.833	2.262	2.821	3.250	9

deprivation example, the number of degrees of freedom associated with the t statistic is

$$\text{d.f.} = n - 1 = 6 - 1 = 5$$

Then the table value of t corresponding to $\alpha = .05$ and d.f. $= 5$ is $t = 2.015$, shown by the shading in table 9.1. Therefore, we accept the one-tailed research hypothesis $H_a : \mu > 1.70$ at the $\alpha = .05$ level if the computed test statistic t exceeds 2.015. Figure 9.3 shows a comparison of the t-statistic and the z-statistic rejection regions at $\alpha = .05$. The larger t-value reflects the greater variability of the t-statistic.

As the degrees of freedom associated with the t statistic become larger, the shape of the t distribution becomes more and more like that of the z statistic. Finally, when d.f. is infinite, the t distribution and the z distribution are identical. Note in table 5, appendix II, that at d.f. $= \infty$, we have $t_{.05} = z_{.05} = 1.645$.

This explains why we advised a sample size of $n = 30$ or larger before applying the z test of chapter 8. The choice was arbitrary and we could have been more conservative and required $n \geq 35$ or $n \geq 40$. However, you can see from table 5 that, for $n \geq 30$, the z test and the t test are, for all practical purposes, equivalent. We therefore do not distinguish between t and z after the degrees of freedom exceed 29.

As we indicated in the Introduction to this chapter, the Student's t and the corresponding table values are based on the assumption that the sampled population has a normal probability distribution. Although the Central Limit Theorem gives us some basis for this assumption, in most practical situations we have no way of knowing how well it is satisfied. The normal probability distribution is used as a model for the population, and this model may or may not be entirely appropriate in a given situation. Fortunately, our lack of knowledge on this point does not seriously limit the applicability of the t distribution. It can be shown that the distribution of the t statistic is approximately the same when we sample the populations that are nonnormal but possess a mound-shaped frequency distribution. This property of the t statistic and the common occur-

Figure 9.3 • Comparison of t (d.f. $= 5$) and z for $\alpha = .05$

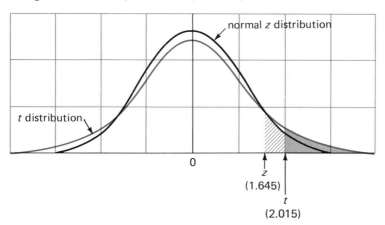

rence of mound-shaped distributions of data in nature enhance the value of using the Student's t in statistical inference.

Having considered the distribution and various properties of the Student's t statistic, we will return in the next section to the sleep deprivation experiment. We want to make an inference about the mean reaction time for sleep-deprived subjects based on our sample of $n = 6$ measurements. Prior to considering the solution, you may wish to test your built-in inference-making equipment by glancing at the 6 measurements and arriving at a conclusion regarding the significance of the data.

9.2 • SMALL-SAMPLE INFERENCES ABOUT A POPULATION MEAN

The types of small-sample inferences about a single population mean that we want to consider are test of hypothesis and estimation. We first consider testing an hypothesis about a population mean. For small samples, this test is constructed as follows.

Small-Sample Test of an Hypothesis About a Population Mean

Null hypothesis H_0: $\mu = \mu_0$.

Research hypothesis H_a: Specified by the experimenter, depending upon the alternative values of μ which he or she wishes to detect. For a two-tailed statistical test, H_a is $\mu \neq \mu_0$.

Test statistic: $t = \dfrac{\bar{y} - \mu_0}{s/\sqrt{n}}$.

Assumption: The sampled population is approximately normally distributed.

Rejection region: See the values of t in table 5, appendix II. For a two-tailed test, reject H_0 if $t < -t_{\alpha/2}$ or $t > t_{\alpha/2}$, where $t_{\alpha/2}$ is based on $(n - 1)$ degrees of freedom.

Note that the null and research hypotheses are constructed exactly as they would be constructed for large-sample tests. However, the test statistic is now a t statistic, which requires the assumption that the sampled population is approximately normal. The rejection region will reflect the additional variability of the t statistic, depending on the degrees of freedom $(n - 1)$ associated with the t.

In the sleep deprivation experiment introduced in section 9.1, the mean and standard deviation for the 6 reaction time measurements are 1.82 and .223, respectively. The elements of the test, as defined above, are as follows:

Null hypothesis H_0: $\mu = 1.70$.

Research hypothesis H_a: $\mu > 1.70$.

Test statistic: $t = \dfrac{\bar{y} - \mu_0}{s/\sqrt{n}} = \dfrac{1.82 - 1.70}{.223/\sqrt{6}} = 1.32.$

Rejection region: For $\alpha = .05$ and $(6 - 1) = 5$ degrees of freedom, our one-tailed rejection region is found in the $t_{.05}$ column of table 5, appendix II, to be $t > 2.015$, as shown in figure 9.4.

Figure 9.4 • One-tailed small-sample rejection region for $\alpha = .05$ and d.f. $= 5$

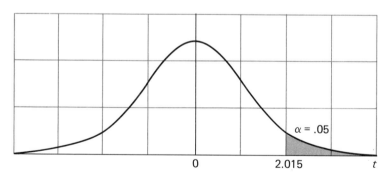

Noting that the calculated value of the test statistic, $t = 1.32$, does *not* fall in the rejection region, we do *not* reject H_0. The data therefore do not provide sufficient evidence to indicate that the mean reaction time for sleep-deprived subjects is greater than 1.70 seconds, the average time given for non-sleep-deprived subjects.

Without extensive t tables it is not possible to find the significance level P associated with $t = 1.32$. However, we can note that we would not have rejected the null hypothesis even at the $\alpha = .10$ level, since the rejection region is $t > 1.476$ for $\alpha = .10$ and d.f. $= 5$. We know, therefore, that the significance level P exceeds $.10$ ($P > .10$).

Is it possible that μ is substantially greater than 1.70 and that our failure to detect this difference is due solely to insufficient data? The answer to this question can only be found by collecting more data from this population. However, a partial answer can be obtained by constructing a small-sample confidence interval for μ.

Recall that the large-sample confidence interval for μ is

$$\left(\bar{y} \pm z_{\alpha/2} \frac{\sigma}{\sqrt{n}} \right)$$

where $z_{\alpha/2} = 1.96$ for a confidence coefficient of .95 ($\alpha = 1 - .95 = .05$). This result assumes that σ is known and simply involves a measurement of $1.96\sigma_{\bar{y}}$ (or approximately $2\sigma_{\bar{y}}$) on either side of $\bar{y}$, in conformity with the Empirical Rule.

When σ is unknown and must be estimated by a small-sample standard deviation s, the z statistic will no longer be appropriate for the confidence interval. In this case, $(\bar{x} \pm 2s/\sqrt{n})$ will *not* contain μ approximately 95 percent of the time in repeated sampling. **A confidence interval must be made that applies to small samples, and this is accomplished by replacing the table z-value by the corresponding t-value with $(n - 1)$ degrees of freedom.** Although we omit the derivation, it seems fairly clear that the corresponding small-sample confidence interval for μ will be as shown in the box.

Small-Sample Confidence Interval for μ

$$\left(\bar{y} \pm t_{\alpha/2} \frac{s}{\sqrt{n}} \right)$$

Assumption: The sampled population is approximately normal.

For our sleep deprivation example, a 95 percent confidence interval for the mean reaction time is

$$\left(\bar{y} \pm t_{\alpha/2} \frac{s}{\sqrt{n}} \right)$$

where $t_{\alpha/2}$, based on 5 degrees of freedom, is $t_{.025} = 2.571$. This t-value is shown in figure 9.5.

Substituting into the formula for the confidence interval, we obtain

$$\left(1.82 \pm 2.571 \frac{.223}{\sqrt{6}} \right) \qquad \text{or} \qquad (1.82 \pm .234)$$

Figure 9.5 • Two-tailed small-sample confidence interval for $\alpha = .05$ and d.f. $= 5$

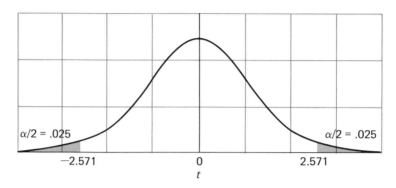

The interval estimate for μ is, therefore, 1.586 to 2.054, with confidence coefficient of .95.

Note that the half-width of the interval is .234 seconds. We can see that it would be difficult with this small sample size to detect departures from the hypothesized mean that are as small as .10, for example. If the experimenter wishes to detect a small increase in mean reaction time from 1.70 seconds (say as small as .10 seconds), the width of the interval must be reduced by obtaining a larger sample of reaction time measurements. This will decrease both $1/\sqrt{n}$ and $t_{\alpha/2}$ and thereby decrease the width of the interval. Or, looking at it from the standpoint of a statistical test of an hypothesis, more information will be available upon which to base a decision.

Example 9.1

Eight sixth-grade schoolchildren are randomly selected to participate in a program using an experimental teaching method. At the conclusion of the program, each child is administered a test designed to assess sixth-grade school achievement and standardized to have a mean of 300. The resulting achievement test scores are

386	311	374	316
303	350	387	285

Do the data provide sufficient evidence to indicate that the average test score for program participants is greater than 300?

Solution: The elements for this statistical test are as follows.

Null hypothesis H_0: $\mu = 300$.

Research hypothesis H_a: $\mu > 300$.

Test statistic: $t = \dfrac{\bar{y} - \mu_0}{s/\sqrt{n}}$.

Assumption: The population of achievement test scores is approximately normal.

Rejection region: For $\alpha = .05$ and d.f. $= (n - 1) = (8 - 1) = 7$, we find the one-tailed table value of $t = 1.895$. We reject H_0 if $t > 1.895$.

The sample mean and standard deviation for the recorded data are

$$\bar{y} = 339 \quad \text{and} \quad s = 40.3$$

Then

$$t = \frac{\bar{y} - \mu_0}{s/\sqrt{n}} = \frac{339 - 300}{40.3/\sqrt{8}} = 2.74$$

Since the observed value of t falls in the rejection region, we will reject H_0 and conclude that the average test score for program participants is greater than 300. Furthermore, we can be reasonably confident that we have made the correct decision. Using our procedure, we would erroneously reject H_0 only 5 percent of the time in repeated applications of the statistical test.

The significance level P can be approximated by referring again to table 5, appendix II. Note that the value $t = 2.74$ also exceeds the $t_{.025}$-value (d.f. $= 7$), which is 2.365. However, the value $t = 2.74$ is less than the table value $t_{.01} = 2.998$. Thus the significance level P associated with the calculated $t = 2.74$ is less than .025 but greater than .01 ($.01 < P < .025$).

We can also obtain additional information by constructing a confidence interval for μ. If we want a confidence coefficient of .95, we use a table t-value corresponding to $\alpha/2 = .025$ and d.f. $= 7$, which is $t_{.025} = 2.365$. Then the confidence interval is

$$\left(\bar{y} \pm t_{\alpha/2} \frac{s}{\sqrt{n}} \right) = \left(339 \pm 2.365 \frac{40.3}{\sqrt{8}} \right) = (339 \pm 33.7)$$

Thus we estimate that the average achievement test score for program participants lies in the interval 305.3 to 372.7. The small sample size has resulted in a rather wide confidence interval for μ. A more accurate estimate can be obtained by increasing the sample size.

EXERCISES

1. Why is the z test usually inappropriate as a test statistic when the sample size is small?
2. What assumptions are made when the Student's t test is employed to test an hypothesis about a population mean?
3. A group of clinical psychologists (Sheppard, Ricca, Fracchia, and Merlis, 1974) tested male heroin addicts on psychological need structure to see if heroin addicts differ in this respect from the general adult male population. A sample of 25 male heroin addicts completed the Edwards Personal Preference Schedule, which measures psychological needs.

(a) On the "need for difference," the mean of the sample scores for the 25 heroin addicts was 11.53 and the standard deviation was 3.65. The general adult population mean is known to be 14.19. Test the research hypothesis that the mean "need for difference" for heroin addicts is lower than the mean for the general population. Use $\alpha = .05$.

(b) The sample of heroin addicts had a mean "need for nurturance" score of 14.51 with a standard deviation of 4.9. The general population mean is known to be 15.67. Do the data support the research hypothesis that the heroin addicts' population mean "need for nurturance" score differs from 15.67? Use $\alpha = .05$.

(c) The EPPS also measures the "need for heterosexuality." The sample of 25 heroin addicts had a mean score of 16.63 with a standard deviation of 5.2. The general male adult population mean is 11.31. Is there evidence, at the $\alpha = .05$ level, that adult male heroin addicts have a greater "need for heterosexuality"?

4. For the above means of the three psychological needs of heroin addicts, construct a 90 percent confidence interval for each.

5. How would your analyses of exercises 3 and 4 change if the sample size is 51 (which it was in the actual study)?

9.3 • SMALL-SAMPLE INFERENCES ABOUT THE DIFFERENCE BETWEEN TWO MEANS: THE INDEPENDENT SAMPLING DESIGN

The independent sampling design for comparing two populations was introduced in section 6.2. In succeeding sections of chapter 6, we considered some nonparametric methods of comparing the frequency distributions of two populations using the independent sampling design. Then in chapter 8 we used the independent sampling design to make large-sample comparisons of two population means.

In this section we consider a small-sample method of comparing two population means. As with the large-sample method, independent random samples of n_1 and n_2 measurements, respectively, are drawn from two populations which have means and variances of μ_1, σ_1^2 and μ_2, σ_2^2. Our objective is to make inferences about the difference between the two population means $(\mu_1 - \mu_2)$.

We are going to consider small-sample methods for testing hypotheses and for placing a confidence interval on the difference between two means. These methods are, like the case for a single mean, based on assumptions regarding the probability distributions of the sampled populations. Specifically, we assume that both populations have a normal probability distribution and also that the population variances σ_1^2 and σ_2^2 are equal. In other words, we assume that the variability of the measurements in the two populations is the same and can be measured by a common variance, which we will designate as σ^2. That is, $\sigma_1^2 = \sigma_2^2 = \sigma^2$. When there are experimental situations for which this assumption is unwarranted, one possible remedy is to use nonparametric techniques for which this assumption is

Figure 9.6 • Assumptions for a small-sample comparison of population means: The populations are normal with equal variances

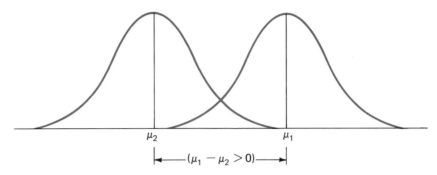

unnecessary. In section 9.5 we will present a method for checking this assumption. These assumptions are shown graphically in figure 9.6.

The point estimator of $(\mu_1 - \mu_2)$ is $(\bar{x}_1 - \bar{x}_2)$, the difference between the sample means. In section 8.5 it was observed that $(\bar{x}_1 - \bar{x}_2)$ is unbiased and has a standard deviation

$$\sigma_{(\bar{x}_1 - \bar{x}_2)} = \sqrt{\frac{\sigma_1^2}{n_1} + \frac{\sigma_2^2}{n_2}}$$

in repeated sampling. This result was used in placing bounds on the error of estimation, in constructing large-sample confidence intervals, and in testing the null hypothesis $H_0\colon (\mu_1 - \mu_2) = D_0$, where D_0 is the hypothesized difference between the population means (often, $D_0 = 0$).

In example 8.11 the test statistic used was

$$z = \frac{(\bar{y}_1 - \bar{y}_2) - D_0}{\sqrt{\dfrac{\sigma_1^2}{n_1} + \dfrac{\sigma_2^2}{n_2}}}$$

Utilizing the assumption that $\sigma_1^2 = \sigma_2^2 = \sigma^2$, the z test statistic can be simplified as follows:

$$z = \frac{(\bar{y}_1 - \bar{y}_2) - D_0}{\sqrt{\dfrac{\sigma_1^2}{n_1} + \dfrac{\sigma_2^2}{n_2}}} = \frac{(\bar{y}_1 - \bar{y}_2) - D_0}{\sigma\sqrt{\dfrac{1}{n_1} + \dfrac{1}{n_2}}}$$

For small-sample tests of the hypothesis $H_0\colon (\mu_1 - \mu_2) = D_0$, it would seem reasonable to use the test statistic

$$t = \frac{(\bar{y}_1 - \bar{y}_2) - D_0}{s\sqrt{\dfrac{1}{n_1} + \dfrac{1}{n_2}}}$$

That is, we would substitute a sample standard deviation s for σ. As it happens, this test statistic will possess the Student's t distribution in repeated sampling when the assumptions for the Student's t are satisfied.

The estimate s to be used in the t statistic could be either s_1 or s_2, the standard deviations for the two samples. The use of either would be wasteful, however, since both estimate σ. Since we wish to obtain the best estimate available, it would seem reasonable to use an estimator that pools the *information* from both samples. This estimator, utilizing the sums of the squares of the deviations about the mean for both samples, is given in the box.

Small-Sample Pooled Estimator for the Population Variance

$$s_p^2 = \frac{\sum_{i=1}^{n_1}(y_i - \bar{y}_1)^2 + \sum_{i=1}^{n_2}(y_i - \bar{y}_2)^2}{n_1 + n_2 - 2}$$

Note that the pooled estimator may also be written as

$$s_p^2 = \frac{(n_1 - 1)s_1^2 + (n_2 - 1)s_2^2}{n_1 + n_2 - 2}$$

We can write s_p^2 as we did in the second expression since

$$s_1^2 = \frac{\sum_{i=1}^{n_1}(y_i - \bar{y}_1)^2}{n_1 - 1} \qquad \text{or} \qquad (n_1 - 1)s_1^2 = \sum_{i=1}^{n_1}(y_i - \bar{y}_1)^2$$

$$s_2^2 = \frac{\sum_{i=1}^{n_2}(y_i - \bar{y}_2)^2}{n_2 - 1} \qquad \text{or} \qquad (n_2 - 1)s_2^2 = \sum_{i=1}^{n_2}(y_i - \bar{y}_2)^2$$

When we pool the two sample variances, we also pool their degrees of freedom. Thus the number of degrees of freedom associated with the pooled estimate s_p^2 is the sum of the degrees of freedom associated with s_1^2 and s_2^2. This sum is

$$(n_1 - 1) + (n_2 - 1) = n_1 + n_2 - 2$$

Therefore our t statistic for comparing two population means, using the independent sampling design, has $(n_1 + n_2 - 2)$ degrees of freedom. In other words, as was true for the single-sample t statistic introduced in the previous section, the degrees of freedom associated with the t statistic is the denominator in the formula for the estimator of the variance σ^2.

Small-Sample Test of an Hypothesis About the Difference Between Two Population Means for an Independent Sampling Design

Null hypothesis H_0: $(\mu_1 - \mu_2) = D_0$.

Research hypothesis H_a: $(\mu_1 - \mu_2) \neq D_0$, for a two-tailed statistical test.

Test statistic: $t = \dfrac{(\bar{y}_1 - \bar{y}_2) - D_0}{s_p \sqrt{\dfrac{1}{n_1} + \dfrac{1}{n_2}}}$.

Assumptions: 1. The two sampled populations are approximately normally distributed.
2. The population variances are equal.

Rejection region: For a two-tailed test, reject H_0 if $t < -t_{\alpha/2}$ or $t > t_{\alpha/2}$, where $t_{\alpha/2}$ is based on $(n_1 + n_2 - 2)$ degrees of freedom.

There is no change from large-sample testing in the construction of the null and the research hypotheses. The test statistic, however, is now a t statistic, necessitating the assumption that the distributions of the populations are normal with equal variances. The rejection region depends on whether the test is one-tailed or two-tailed, on the α-level, and on the degrees of freedom $(n_1 + n_2 - 2)$.

Example 9.2

Scores on a reading comprehension test were recorded for two groups of 9 students enrolled in a remedial reading class. One group read each test passage aloud and the other group read silently. The resulting test scores are given below.

Oral	35	31	29	25	34	40	27	32	31
Silent	41	35	31	28	35	44	32	37	34

Do the data provide sufficient evidence to indicate that the mean comprehension score is different for the oral and silent reading methods? Use $\alpha = .05$.

Solution: The experiment employed an independent sampling design to compare the two methods of teaching reading, since different experimental units (students) were used for the two methods, and no effort was made to pair-match the students. The basic elements of the experiment are as follows.

Experimental units: Remedial reading students.
Response: Reading comprehension test score.
Treatments: The two types of teaching methods, reading orally and reading silently.

Since we wish to make a parametric comparison of the two treatment (population) means, let μ_1 and μ_2 represent the mean reading comprehension scores for the oral and the silent reading populations, respectively. The small-sample parametric test setup for testing the research hypothesis that these mean scores differ is as follows.

Null hypothesis H_0: $(\mu_1 - \mu_2) = 0$.

Research hypothesis H_a: $(\mu_1 - \mu_2) \neq 0$.

Test statistic: $t = \dfrac{(\bar{y}_1 - \bar{y}_2) - 0}{s_p \sqrt{\dfrac{1}{n_1} + \dfrac{1}{n_2}}}$.

Assumptions: 1. The two populations of reading comprehension scores are approximately normal.
2. The variances of the populations of scores are equal.

Rejection Region: The research hypothesis is two-tailed. For $\alpha = .05$ and d.f. $= (n_1 + n_2 - 2) = (9 + 9 - 2) = 16$, we find the table 5 value for $t_{\alpha/2}$ with 16 degrees of freedom. This is $t_{.025} = 2.120$. Thus the rejection region is

$$t < -2.120 \qquad \text{or} \qquad t > 2.120$$

as shown in figure 9.7.

Figure 9.7 • Two-tailed rejection region for example 9.2, with $\alpha = .05$ and d.f. $= 16$

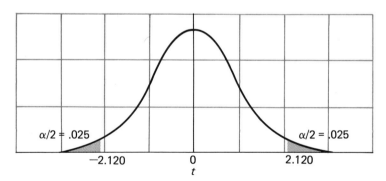

$\alpha/2 = .025$ $\alpha/2 = .025$

-2.120 0 2.120

t

Before we can calculate our test statistic, we need the sample means and the sum of the squares of the deviations about the means. Thus

$$\bar{y}_1 = 31.56$$

$$\sum_{i=1}^{9} (y_i - \bar{y}_1)^2 = 160.22$$

$$\bar{y}_2 = 35.22$$

$$\sum_{i=1}^{9} (y_i - \bar{y}_2)^2 = 195.56$$

Then the pooled estimate of the common variance is

$$s_p^2 = \frac{\displaystyle\sum_{i=1}^{9} (y_i - \bar{y}_1)^2 + \sum_{i=1}^{9} (y_i - \bar{y}_2)^2}{n_1 + n_2 - 2}$$

$$= \frac{160.22 + 195.56}{16} = 22.24$$

The standard deviation is $s_p = 4.72$. We now calculate t:

$$t = \frac{(\bar{y}_1 - \bar{y}_2)}{s_p \sqrt{\dfrac{1}{n_1} + \dfrac{1}{n_2}}} = \frac{31.56 - 35.22}{4.72 \sqrt{\dfrac{1}{9} + \dfrac{1}{9}}} = -1.65$$

Since this t-value of -1.65 is not in the rejection region, we conclude that these data do not support the research hypothesis at the $\alpha = .05$ level. That is, there is insufficient evidence to conclude that the mean reading comprehension scores differ for the oral and the silent reading populations.

To find the approximate significance level associated with the calculated $t = -1.65$, note that at the $\alpha = .10$ level, the rejection region for a t statistic with 16 degrees of freedom is $t > t_{.05} = 1.746$ or $t < -1.746$. With $\alpha = .20$, it becomes $t > t_{.10} = 1.337$ or $t < -1.337$. Since the calculated $t = -1.65$ *would not* be in the $\alpha = .10$ rejection region but *would* be in the $\alpha = .20$ rejection region, we conclude that the significance level P (the smallest α for which rejection is warranted) is between .10 and .20, as shown in figure 9.8.

Figure 9.8 • Significance level associated with $t = -1.65$ for a two-tailed research hypothesis and d.f. $= 16$

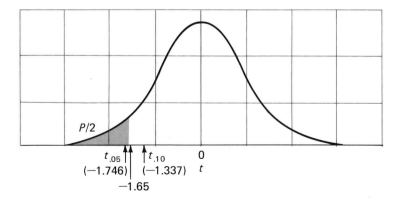

The small-sample confidence interval for $(\mu_1 - \mu_2)$ is based on the same assumptions made for the statistical test procedure. This confidence interval, with confidence coefficient of $(1 - \alpha)$, is given by the formula in the box.

Small-Sample Confidence Interval for $(\mu_1 - \mu_2)$ for an Independent Sampling Design

$$(\bar{X}_1 - \bar{X}_2) \pm t_{\alpha/2} s_p \sqrt{\frac{1}{n_1} + \frac{1}{n_2}}$$

Assumptions: 1. The two sampled populations are approximately normally distributed.
2. The population variances are equal.

Note the similarity in the procedures for constructing the confidence interval for a single mean, section 9.2, and for the difference between two means. In both cases the interval is constructed by using the appropriate point estimator and then adding and subtracting an amount equal to $t_{\alpha/2}$ times the *estimated* standard deviation of the point estimator.

Example 9.3

Find an interval estimate for $(\mu_1 - \mu_2)$ in example 9.2, using a confidence coefficient of .95.

Solution: Substituting into the formula

$$(\bar{y}_1 - \bar{y}_2) \pm t_{\alpha/2} s_p \sqrt{\frac{1}{n_1} + \frac{1}{n_2}}$$

we find the interval estimate (or 95 percent confidence interval) to be

$$(31.56 - 35.22) \pm (2.120)(4.72) \sqrt{\frac{1}{9} + \frac{1}{9}} = -3.66 \pm 4.72$$

Note that $t_{.025} = 2.120$ is based on $(n_1 + n_2 - 2) = 16$ degrees of freedom.

Thus we estimate that the difference $(\mu_1 - \mu_2)$ in mean reading comprehension score falls in the interval -8.38 to 1.06. Since the interval is rather wide, it seems advisable to increase the size of the samples and reestimate if we wish to obtain more information about $(\mu_1 - \mu_2)$.

Before concluding our discussion, it is necessary to comment on the two assumptions upon which our inferential procedures are based. Moderate departures from the assumption that the populations have a normal probability distribution do not seriously affect the distribution of the test statistic and the confidence coefficient for the corresponding confidence interval. On the other hand, the population variances should be nearly equal for the above procedures to be valid.

If there is reason to believe that the population variances are unequal, an adjustment must be made in the test procedure and the corresponding confidence interval. We omit a discussion of these techniques but refer the interested reader to the texts by Li or by Anderson and Bancroft, listed at the end of the chapter.

A procedure will be presented in section 9.5 for testing the hypothesis that two population variances are equal.

EXERCISES

1. What assumptions are made about the populations from which independent random samples are obtained when using the *t* distribution for making small-sample inferences about the difference in population means?

2. In psychological research it is important to determine whether subjects are perceiving the stimuli as the experimenter thinks they are. In one study (Fontaine 1974) the experimenter was testing the extent to which people base their attributions on the judgments of similar people rather than on the judgments of dissimilar people. One group of 15 subjects was exposed to the opinions of "psychology students from this university" while the other group of 15 was exposed to information from "businessmen from Perth." A manipulation check tested to determine if, in fact, the first group perceived their comparison as similar and the second group as dissimilar. Mean ratings of similarity were 5.6 for the first group and 2.3 for the second group. The respective standard deviations were .6 and .3. Do the data support the research hypothesis that the population mean perception of similarity for subjects exposed to similar people's judgments exceeds that for subjects exposed to dissimilar people's judgments? Use $\alpha = .10$.

3. Dutton and Avon (1974) conducted research to see if sexual attractions occur with increased frequency during states of strong emotion. The emotion in this case was anxiety; subjects either anticipated receiving a strong electric shock or a mild electric shock. Mean ratings of anxiety were 3.17 for the "strong shock" group and 2.28 for the "mild shock" group, and the standard deviations were .35 and .40, respectively. Suppose there were 10 subjects in each group. Is there evidence of a significant difference in mean anxiety experienced by the populations from which these samples were drawn? Use $\alpha = .05$.

4. Construct a 99 percent confidence interval for the difference between the two population means in exercise 3.

9.4 • SMALL-SAMPLE INFERENCES ABOUT
TWO POPULATION MEANS:
THE MATCHED PAIRS DESIGN

The matched pairs design for comparing two populations was first introduced in section 6.2. It is employed when the experimenter believes that the high degree of variability among the experimental units may obscure the sample information about the population differences. In chapter 6 we presented several nonparametric methods for comparing population frequency distributions by using the matched pairs design. In this section we consider the use of this design to compare two population means. To illustrate how a parametric inference is made from the data of a matched pairs experiment, we consider the following example.

A program was set up to promote early development of preschool children's reading ability. Participating children spent one hour a day in a room well stocked with toys, most of which were "educational" in nature (alphabet blocks and puzzles, ABC readers, labeled coloring books). To evaluate the program it was desired to compare program participants with a control group of children who spent one hour a day in a "noneducational" toy room. The measurement of interest was the age (in months) when each child began reading at a primary level.

Educators are often involved in evaluating programs designed to promote specific academic abilities in children. Why is a matched pairs design appropriate for this kind of evaluation study? Photo by H. Armstrong Roberts.

Since it was anticipated that IQ differences as well as differences in home environment would contribute considerably to the variability of these reading age measurements, identical twins were used in the evaluation study. Accordingly, 6 pairs of identical twins of preschool age were selected. One twin of each pair was randomly chosen to participate in the program, and the other twin was assigned to the control (no program) group. This assignment of twins to the two conditions (Program *P* and Control *C*) might be as shown here.

Twin Pair

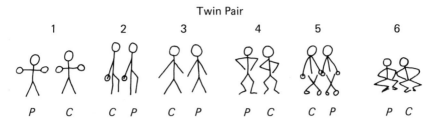

| 1 | 2 | 3 | 4 | 5 | 6 |

P   C   C P   C P   P C   C P   P C

For each twin the age (in months) when he or she began reading at a primary level is shown in table 9.2.

Table 9.2 • Reading age measurements (in months)

Twin Pair	Program y_1	Control y_2	$y_1 - y_2$
1	60	64	-4
2	54	57	-3
3	62	68	-6
4	71	73	-2
5	57	63	-6
6	63	66	-3

We wish to determine whether the data provide sufficient evidence to indicate that program participants begin to read earlier, on the average, than non-participants. We use the 6 *difference* measurements, $(y_1 - y_2)$, to test the null hypothesis

$$H_0: \mu_d = 0$$

against the research hypothesis

$$H_a: \mu_d < 0$$

Here μ_d is the population mean of the difference measurements; or, equivalently, $\mu_d = (\mu_1 - \mu_2)$, where μ_1 and μ_2 are the program and control means, respectively. Note that $\mu_d < 0$ implies that $\mu_2 > \mu_1$, that is, that the average reading age for nonparticipants exceeds that for participants.

By analyzing the differences between experimental unit responses, we effectively turn a two-population problem into a one-population problem. We are now making a parametric inference about the mean of a single population: the population of differences.

The appropriate test statistic is that given in section 9.2—a single-sample t statistic. However, we replace $\bar{y}$ and s by $\bar{d}$ and s_d, the mean and the standard deviation of the sample difference measurements, respectively. That is,

$$t = \frac{\bar{d} - D_0}{s_d/\sqrt{n}}$$

where D_0 is the null hypothesis value of μ_d and n represents the number of *pairs* of measurements.

In using this test statistic, we need only assume that the population of difference measurements is approximately normal. **We need not assume that the two population variances are equal.**

Finally, the rejection region is constructed as though the inference concerned a single population mean with n sample measurements. In our reading age example, we will accept the one-tailed research hypothesis that $\mu_d < 0$ at the $\alpha = .05$ level when $t < -2.015$, the table t-value corresponding to $\alpha = .05$ and $(n - 1) = (6 - 1) = 5$ degrees of freedom. **Note that we have used n to represent the number of difference measurements, since they are the object of our analysis.**

The procedure for testing an hypothesis about two population means by using the matched pairs design is summarized in the box.

Small-Sample Test of an Hypothesis About the Difference Between Two Population Means for a Matched Pairs Design

Null hypothesis H_0: $\mu_d = D_0$ [equivalently, $(\mu_1 - \mu_2) = D_0$].

Research hypothesis H_a: $\mu_d \neq D_0$, for a two-tailed statistical test.

Test statistic: $t = \dfrac{\bar{d} - D_0}{s_d/\sqrt{n}}$.

Assumptions: The population of difference measurements is approximately normally distributed.

Rejection region: For a two-tailed test, reject H_0 if $t < -t_{\alpha/2}$ or $t > t_{\alpha/2}$, where $t_{\alpha/2}$ is based on $(n - 1)$ degrees of freedom and n is the number of *difference* measurements.

For the reading age example, we find

$$\bar{d} = \frac{\sum\limits_{i=1}^{6} d_i}{6} = \frac{-24}{6} = -4.0$$

$$s_d^2 = \frac{\sum\limits_{i=1}^{6} (d_i - \bar{d})^2}{5} = \frac{(14)}{5} = 2.8$$

$$s_d = 1.673$$

Thus the calculated value of the test statistic is

$$t = \frac{\bar{d} - 0}{s_d/\sqrt{n}} = \frac{-4.0}{1.673/\sqrt{6}} = -5.86$$

Since this calculated t is less than -2.015, the rejection value for $\alpha = .05$, we conclude that, at the $\alpha = .05$ level, the data support the research hypothesis that, on the average, program participants begin to read earlier than non-participants. This calculated t-value is smaller than $-t_{.005} = -4.032$ for d.f. $= 5$. Thus the significance level P associated with $t = -5.86$ is less than .005 $(P < .005)$. The evidence in support of the research hypothesis is quite strong.

The small-sample confidence interval for the population mean of the differences μ_d is constructed exactly like that for the single mean, as shown in the box.

Small-Sample Confidence Interval for μ_d (or, Equivalently, $\mu_1 - \mu_2$) for a Matched Pairs Design

$$\left(\bar{d} \pm t_{\alpha/2} \frac{s_d}{\sqrt{n}} \right)$$

Assumption: The population of difference measurements is approximately normal.

Therefore, in our example, a 90 percent confidence interval for the mean difference in beginning reading age of the population of program participants and nonparticipants is

$$\left(\bar{d} \pm t_{.05} \frac{s_d}{\sqrt{n}} \right) = \left(-4.0 \pm 2.015 \frac{1.673}{\sqrt{6}} \right) = (-4.0 \pm 1.38)$$

or from -5.38 to -2.62. The value $t_{.05} = 2.015$ is based on 5 degrees of freedom, since there are $n = 6$ difference measurements.

To demonstrate that extraexperimental or "nuisance" variability (attributed at least in part to differences in IQ, home environment, etc.) is actually reduced in this paired experiment, we consider a design that does not permit direct control of the relevant extraexperimental factors. Suppose that the program evaluation study had been conducted by drawing a random sample of 12 preschool children, 6 of whom were then randomly chosen to participate in the program and the remaining 6 assigned to the control (no program) group. This is an independent sampling design and could be depicted as shown here.

Further suppose, for the sake of comparison, that the same measurements as those in table 9.2 were obtained under the two conditions. However, since the

P   P   C   P   C   C   C   P   P   C   P   C

two samples are independent, the hypothesis of no difference between program participants and nonparticipants in average beginning reading age would be tested by using the *t* statistic of section 9.3. That is,

$$t = \frac{\bar{y}_1 - \bar{y}_2}{s_p \sqrt{\dfrac{1}{n_1} + \dfrac{1}{n_2}}}$$

where s_p is the pooled estimate of σ, the common standard deviation for the two populations. For these data, $s_p^2 = 31.367$ (we won't go through the calculation here), so $s_p = 5.60$ and

$$t = \frac{-4}{5.60 \sqrt{\dfrac{1}{6} + \dfrac{1}{6}}} = -1.24$$

The table value of *t* for this one-tailed test, with $\alpha = .05$ and $(n_1 + n_2 - 2) = 10$ degrees of freedom, is -1.812. Since the observed value of $t = -1.24$ is not less than the table value, the null hypothesis would not be rejected.

The 90 percent confidence interval corresponding to this independent sampling analysis is

$$(\bar{y}_1 - \bar{y}_2) \pm t_{\alpha/2} s_p \sqrt{\frac{1}{n_1} + \frac{1}{n_2}} = -4.0 \pm (1.812)(5.60) \sqrt{\frac{1}{6} + \frac{1}{6}}$$

$$= -4.0 \pm 5.86$$

or from -9.86 to 1.86.

Certainly the two methods of analysis yield markedly different results. When the hypothesis of no difference between the two means is tested, the matched pairs analysis supports the research hypothesis at the .005 level. The analysis for the independent sampling design does not support this hypothesis even at the .10 level (you should check this). Morever, the 90 percent confidence interval for the difference between means for the matched pairs analysis is

$$-5.38 \text{ to } -2.62$$

This is less than one-fourth the width of the 90 percent confidence interval

$$-9.86 \text{ to } 1.86$$

which was based on the independent sampling analysis.

The familiarity we have gained with interval estimation has shown that the width of a confidence interval depends upon the magnitude of the standard deviation of the point estimator of a parameter. The smaller the standard deviation, the better the estimate, and the more likely it is that the test statistic will reject the null hypothesis if it is actually false.

For the independent sampling analysis, the estimated standard deviation of the difference between two sample means,

$$s_p \sqrt{\frac{1}{n_1} + \frac{1}{n_2}} = 5.60 \sqrt{\frac{1}{6} + \frac{1}{6}} = 3.23$$

includes variability attributable to IQ differences, differences in home environment, and so on.

For the matched pairs analysis, the estimated standard deviation of the difference between two means,

$$\frac{s_d}{\sqrt{n}} = \frac{1.673}{\sqrt{6}} = .68$$

is unaffected by those factors producing variability between twin pairs (differences in IQ, home environment, etc.).

Certainly the estimated standard deviation is considerably smaller for the matched pairs analysis. Anticipation of such a reduction in variability would most likely lead an experimenter to choose the matched pairs design as a more sensitive method for comparing the two treatments.

A word of caution should be given here. The foregoing example illustrated the advantages of using a matched pairs rather than an independent sampling design in a particular research situation. In our example, using identical twin pairs enabled the experimenter to eliminate variability due to factors relevant to the measurement of interest (age at which children begin to read). If the factors that are controlled by using matched pairs are not related to the variable being measured, pairing may be disadvantageous.

We observe that the degrees of freedom available for estimating σ^2 are less for the matched pairs design than for the corresponding independent sampling design. If there were actually no differences between the pairs, the reduction in the degrees of freedom would produce a moderate increase in the $t_{\alpha/2}$ employed in the confidence interval and hence would increase the width of the interval. This, of course, did not occur in the reading age experiment because the large reduction in the standard deviation of $\bar{d}$ more than compensated for the loss in degrees of freedom. Thus the advice given in section 6.2 bears repeating: if the experimenter suspects a high degree of variability in the experimental units, a matched pairs design should be employed when comparing two populations.

Example 9.4

Throughout chapter 6 we considered an example (see examples 6.2, 6.3, and 6.8) of a matched pairs design to compare the effect of two different diets on the aggressive behavior in a certain strain of rats. The researcher formed 10 pairs of rats on the basis of similar behavior during a monitoring period prior to the administration of the diets. Then one rat from each pair received Diet A

Table 9.3 • Aggressive behavior experiment data

Puir	Diet A	Diet B	Difference (A − B)
1	127	116	11
2	104	95	9
3	86	91	−5
4	74	62	12
5	91	92	−1
6	62	54	8
7	113	99	14
8	95	88	7
9	73	64	9
10	81	78	3

and the other Diet B, for a period of 14 days. At the end of this time, the researcher recorded the number of aggressive overtures made by each of the 20 rats during a 30-minute interval. The data are repeated in table 9.3.

In examples 6.3 and 6.8 we tested the research hypothesis that the aggressive behavior frequency distributions differ for Diets A and B, using the nonparametric sign test and the Wilcoxon rank sum test, respectively. Do the data support the parametric research hypothesis that the *mean number* of aggressive overtures associated with the populations for Diets A and B differ?

Solution: Let μ_1 and μ_2 represent the mean number of aggressive overtures for the population of rats using Diet A and Diet B, respectively. Also, let $\mu_d = (\mu_1 - \mu_2)$. Then for this matched pairs design, our test setup is as follows.

Null hypothesis H_0: $\mu_d = 0$.

Research hypothesis H_a: $\mu_d \neq 0$.

Test statistic: $t = \dfrac{\overline{d} - 0}{s_d/\sqrt{n}}$.

Assumption: The population of differences between the number of aggressive overtures is approximately normal.

Rejection region: Choosing $\alpha = .05$, the two-tailed research hypothesis may be accepted when $t > 2.262$ or $t < -2.262$. We found the table value $t_{.025} = 2.262$ with $(n - 1) = 9$ degrees of freedom, remembering that n represents the number of difference measurements (or, equivalently, the number of pairs of measurements).

We now find $\overline{d}$ and s_d.

$$\overline{d} = \frac{\sum_{i=1}^{10} d_i}{10} = \frac{67}{10} = 6.7$$

$$s_d^2 = \frac{\sum\limits_{i=1}^{10} (d_i - \bar{d})^2}{9} = \frac{332.1}{9} = 35.789$$

$$s_d = 5.982$$

Then

$$t = \frac{\bar{d} - 0}{s_d/\sqrt{n}} = \frac{6.7}{5.982/\sqrt{10}} = 3.54$$

Since this calculated t-value exceeds 2.262, we conclude that the data support the research hypothesis at the $\alpha = .05$ level. That is, there is sufficient evidence to conclude that the population mean number of aggressive overtures differs for rats on the two diets. The fact that t is positive allows us to infer further that $\mu_d > 0$, that is, that the mean μ_1 for Diet A exceeds the mean μ_2 for Diet B, as shown in figure 9.9.

Note that our conclusion in example 9.4 agrees with the nonparametric Wilcoxon rank sum test (example 6.8), for which we concluded that the frequency distribution of aggressive behavior for Diet A lies to the right of (above) that for Diet B.

What, then, are the differences between the nonparametric and parametric techniques for analyzing this matched pairs experiment? The first difference is rather subtle. The nonparametric test compared the relative frequency distributions, while the parametric test compared only the means of the two distributions. Second, the parametric test requires the assumption that the population of difference measurements is normally distributed, while no such assumption is necessary for the nonparametric test. The decision about which test to use must be based on the specific objective of the experimenter and the validity of the assumptions necessary for the parametric test. A more detailed discussion of parametric versus nonparametric tests will be presented in section 9.6.

Figure 9.9 • Inference that $\mu_d > 0$ in the aggressive behavior experiment

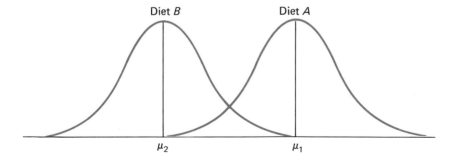

Diet B   Diet A

μ_2 μ_1

EXERCISES

1. Millar (1974) points out that we know little about tactile short-term memory, and yet it is both theoretically important and important for the education of the blind. She conducted research using 9 blind children and 9 sighted children matched on age, sex, and digit span. In addition, the two groups were matched on intelligence and socioeconomic status.

   Subjects were presented with a standard object and then a comparison object, and they had to tell whether each comparison was the same size as the standard. When the delay between withdrawal of the standard and the signal to compare was 10 seconds, the difference mean of the 9 difference measurements ("blind" minus "sighted") was − 1.37 with a standard deviation of .34. Do the data support the hypothesis that the mean latency responses differ for blind and sighted children?

2. Place a 90 percent confidence interval on the difference between blind and sighted children's mean latencies in exercise 1.

3. In addition to physiological interest in asthmatic children, researchers are also interested in psychological factors, such as achievement motivation. Williams (1975) matched asthmatic and control children on sex, age, family characteristics, socioeconomic status, parental birthplace, position in family, and number of siblings. Subjects took an achievement motivation test. Below are the scores for 6 pairs of children. Test the research hypothesis that asthmatic children have stronger mean achievement motivation. Use $\alpha = .05$.

Pair	1	2	3	4	5	6
Asthmatic	18.6	16.3	20.8	15.7	16.8	21.9
Control	13.6	14.8	14.5	15.0	12.9	13.8

4. Refer to exercise 3. Place a 90 percent confidence interval on the difference between asthmatic children's mean score and control children's mean score on achievement motivation.

9.5 · COMPARING TWO POPULATION VARIANCES: THE F DISTRIBUTION

In section 9.3 we considered the small-sample parametric comparison of population means using the independent sampling design. Recall that the use of the t statistic for making this comparison requires the assumption that the population variances are equal. In this section we will present a method of testing this assumption by making a parametric comparison of two *population variances*. We assume that the experiment is an independent sampling design.

In addition to providing a check on the assumption of equal variances when comparing two population means, a parametric comparison of variances may itself be the objective of the experiment. For example, we might wish to compare the variability in task performance under an experimental condition with the task performance under a control condition; or we might wish to investigate the possibility that responses to one stimulus are more variable than responses to a second stimulus; or we might wish to test the research hypothesis that IQs are less variable for children from low socioeconomic backgrounds than for children from high socioeconomic backgrounds.

Intuitively, we could compare two population variances σ_1^2 and σ_2^2 by using the ratio of the sample variances, s_1^2/s_2^2. If the ratio s_1^2/s_2^2 is either very large or very small, the inference is that σ_1^2 and σ_2^2 are unequal. If, however, the ratio of s_1^2/s_2^2 is close to 1, little evidence exists to support such an inference.

In comparing two population variances, our null hypothesis is

$$H_0: \sigma_1^2 = \sigma_2^2$$

and our research hypothesis is

$$H_a: \sigma_1^2 \neq \sigma_2^2$$

Our question is this: How large or small must s_1^2/s_2^2 be to provide sufficient evidence to reject the null hypothesis in favor of the research hypothesis? The answer to this question may readily be found by studying the distribution of s_1^2/s_2^2 in repeated sampling.

When independent random samples are drawn from two normal populations with equal variances, that is, $\sigma_1^2 = \sigma_2^2$, then s_1^2/s_2^2 possesses a probability distribution in repeated sampling that is known to statisticians as an *F* distribution. We need not concern ourselves with the equation of the frequency function for *F* except to state that, as you might surmise, it is quite complex. For our purposes it will suffice to accept the fact that the distribution is well known and that values for it have been tabulated. These appear in tables 6 and 7 of appendix II.

The shape of the F distribution is nonsymmetrical and depends upon the number of degrees of freedom associated with s_1^2 and s_2^2. We will represent these quantities as ν_1 and ν_2, respectively. Figure 9.10 shows the F distributions for selected values of ν_1 and ν_2. Thus tables of values for the F distribution are entered with two quantities, ν_1 and ν_2. The values corresponding to an upper-tail rejection region for $\alpha = .05$ and .01 are presented in tables 6 and 7, appendix II, respectively.

Suppose, for example, that we have drawn independent samples from two populations. Assume that the first sample contains $n_1 = 8$ measurements and the second sample has $n_2 = 10$ measurements. Then the degrees of freedom available for s_1^2 are $\nu_1 = (n_1 - 1) = 7$, and the degrees of freedom associated with s_2^2 are $\nu_2 = (n_2 - 1) = 9$. Suppose we wish to determine the F-value corresponding to $\alpha = .05$. That is, we wish to find the F-value such that only 5 percent of all the ratios s_1^2/s_2^2 will exceed it in repeated sampling when $\sigma_1^2 = \sigma_2^2$. We would then refer to table 6 of appendix II, part of which is shown in table 9.4.

Figure 9.10 • F distributions for selected values of ν_1 and ν_2

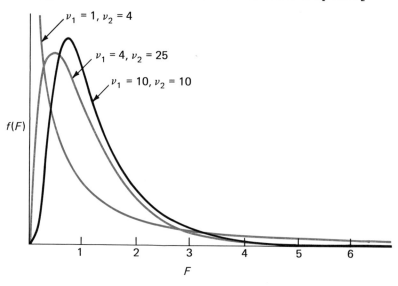

Table 9.4 • Partial reproduction of table 6, appendix II

Degrees of Freedom $\alpha = .05$

ν_1

ν_2	1	2	3	4	5	6	7	8	9
1	161.4	199.5	215.7	224.6	230.2	234.0	236.8	238.9	240.5
2	18.51	19.00	19.16	19.25	19.30	19.33	19.35	19.37	19.38
3	10.13	9.55	9.28	9.12	9.01	8.94	8.89	8.85	8.81
4	7.71	6.94	6.59	6.39	6.26	6.16	6.09	6.04	6.00
5	6.61	5.79	5.41	5.19	5.05	4.95	4.88	4.82	4.77
6	5.99	5.14	4.76	4.53	4.39	4.28	4.21	4.15	4.10
7	5.59	4.74	4.35	4.12	3.97	3.87	3.79	3.73	3.68
8	5.32	4.46	4.07	3.84	3.69	3.58	3.50	3.44	3.39
9	5.12	4.26	3.86	3.63	3.48	3.37	3.29	3.23	3.18
10	4.96	4.10	3.71	3.48	3.33	3.22	3.14	3.07	3.02
11	4.84	3.98	3.59	3.36	3.20	3.09	3.01	2.95	2.90
12	4.75	3.89	3.49	3.26	3.11	3.00	2.91	2.85	2.80
13	4.67	3.81	3.41	3.18	3.03	2.92	2.83	2.77	2.71
14	4.60	3.74	3.34	3.11	2.96	2.85	2.76	2.70	2.65

The keys to locating $F_{.05}$ are the degrees of freedom. First, we locate the *column* corresponding to $\nu_1 = 7$. Then we locate the *row* in this column corresponding to $\nu_2 = 9$. The desired $F_{.05}$-value is 3.29, shown by the shading in table 9.4. We know, therefore, that only 5 percent of the F-values will exceed 3.29 in repeated sampling, as shown in figure 9.11.

Figure 9.11 • The F-value for $\nu_1 = 7$ and $\nu_2 = 9$ when $\alpha = .05$

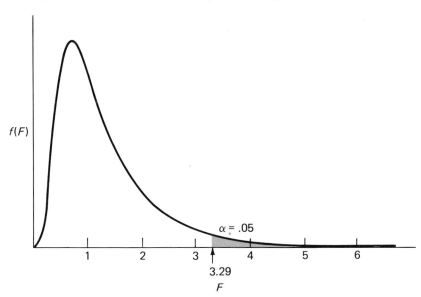

We use table 7 of appendix II in a similar manner to obtain F-values for $\alpha = .01$. You should check that, for $\nu_1 = 7$ and $\nu_2 = 9$, $F_{.01} = 5.61$, which implies that only 1 percent of the F-values exceed 5.61 when the degrees of freedom are 7 and 9, respectively.

To conduct a one-tailed test of the research hypothesis H_a: $\sigma_1^2 > \sigma_2^2$, we will use the test statistic $F = s_1^2/s_2^2$. We will reject the null hypothesis H_0: $\sigma_1^2 = \sigma_2^2$ if F is larger than the upper-tail value shown in table 6 or table 7. Consequently, we may use the tables directly. If we use table 6 for a one-tailed test, the probability of a type I error will be .05; if we use table 7, α will be .01.

For a two-tailed F test of the research hypothesis H_a: $\sigma_1^2 \neq \sigma_2^2$, we would place $\alpha/2$ in the lower tail of the F distribution and $\alpha/2$ in the upper tail of the F distribution. Even though we do not have tabulated lower-tail values of F, we can adjust for this. We always place the larger sample variance in the numerator of the F statistic. Then we double the upper-tail probability associated with the table F-value. For example, if you conduct a two-tailed F test using table 6 (which is computed for an upper-tail probability of .05), you would be using an α-value of

.10. Similarly, the α-value for a two-tailed F test using table 7 would be $\alpha = 2(.01) = .02$.

The statistical test of a null hypothesis about the equality of two population variances may be summarized as follows.

Test of an Hypothesis About the Equality of Two Population Variances for an Independent Sampling Design

Null hypothesis H_0: $\sigma_1^2 = \sigma_2^2$.

Research hypothesis H_a: $\sigma_1^2 \neq \sigma_2^2$, for a two-tailed statistical test.

Test statistic: $F = s_1^2/s_2^2$, where s_1^2 is the larger sample variance. You will need to place the larger sample variance in the numerator because tables 6 and 7 give only upper-tail values for the F distribution.

Assumption: The two populations are approximately normal.

Rejection region: For a two-tailed test, reject H_0 if $F > F_{\alpha/2}$, where $F_{\alpha/2}$ is based on $(n_1 - 1)$ and $(n_2 - 1)$ degrees of freedom and the value $\alpha/2$ is doubled to obtain the correct value for the probability of a type I error, α. Thus if we use table 6 for a two-tailed test, the probability of a type I error will be $\alpha = .10$.

Example 9.5

Refer to example 9.2. We used an independent sampling design to compare the mean reading comprehension scores when two methods were used to teach remedial reading classes: the oral reading method and the silent reading method. You will notice that in conducting the t test to compare the means, we made the assumption that the two populations of reading scores have equal variances.

Use the F test to determine whether the data imply that this assumption is false, that is, that the variances are unequal. Use $\alpha = .10$. The data of the experiment, the resulting test scores, are repeated here for your convenience.

Oral	35	31	29	25	34	40	27	32	31
Silent	41	35	31	28	35	44	32	37	34

Solution: Let σ_1^2 and σ_2^2 represent the variances for the silent and the oral reading populations, respectively. We wish to test

$$H_0: \sigma_1^2 = \sigma_2^2$$
$$H_a: \sigma_1^2 \neq \sigma_2^2$$

In setting up the test statistic, we always place the larger sample variance in the numerator. Referring to the calculations in example 9.2, we found

$$s_1^2 = \frac{195.56}{8} = 24.45$$

$$s_2^2 = \frac{160.22}{8} = 20.03$$

You may have noticed that we have switched the subscript notation from that used in example 9.2. We want sample 1 (and population 1) to refer to the sample that has the larger sample variance so that we can use our F tables. Thus we peeked at the data, noticed that the sample variance for the silent readers is larger than that for the oral readers, and we numbered our subscripts accordingly. The numbering, of course, has no effect on our conclusions.

Our test statistic is

$$F = \frac{s_1^2}{s_2^2} = \frac{24.45}{20.03} = 1.22$$

We assume that both our populations are approximately normal. Is this ratio, 1.22, sufficiently larger than 1.0 to support the research hypothesis at the $\alpha = .10$ level? To answer this, we consult table 6, corresponding to $\alpha/2 = .05$, with the degrees of freedom of $\nu_1 = (n_1 - 1) = 8$ and $\nu_2 = (n_2 - 1) = 8$, respectively. We find that

Rejection region: $F > F_{.05} = 3.44$

Thus the data provide no support for the conclusion that the variances are unequal. This does not imply that the null hypothesis is necessarily true, that is, that the variances are equal. Rarely, if ever, do sample data prove the equality of two population parameters. However, we take some solace in knowing that the data do not indicate, even at the .10 level, that our assumption of equal variances is unfounded.

Example 9.6

In a strain comparison study, $n_1 = 25$ mice of Strain A and $n_2 = 30$ mice of Strain B were measured for the amount of time elapsed before leaving an opened cage. The mean elapsed time was approximately the same for the two samples. The sample variances differed, however. They were

$$s_1^2 = 104 \text{ (seconds)}^2$$

$$s_2^2 = 51 \text{ (seconds)}^2$$

Do the data provide sufficient evidence to indicate, at the $\alpha = .05$ level, that the variability in elapsed time is greater for Strain A than for Strain B?

Solution: Let σ_1^2 and σ_2^2 represent the variances of the elapsed-time distributions for the populations of Strain A and Strain B, respectively. Our research hypothesis is that $\sigma_1^2 > \sigma_2^2$, that is, the variance associated with the Strain A population exceeds the variance associated with the Strain B population. Our test is set up as follows.

Null hypothesis H_0: $\sigma_1^2 = \sigma_2^2$.

Research hypothesis H_a: $\sigma_1^2 > \sigma_2^2$.

Test statistic: $F = s_1^2/s_2^2$.

Assumption: The two elapsed-time populations are approximately normal.

Rejection region: For the one-tailed test with $\alpha = .05$ and degrees of freedom $\nu_1 = (25 - 1) = 24$ and $\nu_2 = (30 - 1) = 29$, we reject the null hypothesis when

$$F > F_{.05} = 1.90$$

We now calculate F:

$$F = \frac{s_1^2}{s_2^2} = \frac{104}{51} = 2.04$$

which exceeds 1.90. The data support, at the $\alpha = .05$ level, the research hypothesis that the variability in elapsed time is greater for Strain A than for Strain B.

EXERCISES

1. Under what assumptions may the F distribution be used in making inferences about the ratio of population variances?
2. Schachter and Wheeler (1962) gave one group of subjects an injection of a drug and one group a placebo, then showed both groups a comedy film and measured their reactions. They were testing the theoretical notion that cognitive factors as well as physiological factors influence our emotional reactions. This experiment was conducted to see what degree of reaction must still be attributed to physiological (in this case, drug-induced) behavior. The response consisted of each subject's rating of the film. The mean and variance for the drug group were 17.79 and 6.5, respectively, and were 14.31 and 2.6, respectively, for the placebo group. Do the data indicate a significant difference in variability between reactions for the drug and the placebo conditions? Use a two-tailed test, with $\alpha = .10$, and assume that there were 10 subjects in each group.
3. Refer to exercise 2, section 9.3. We compared the mean perceptions of similarity for subjects exposed to similar people's judgments with that for subjects exposed to dissimilar people's judgments. Recall that this comparison uses a t statistic that requires the assumption of equal population variances. The sample standard deviations were .6 and .3, respectively. Both samples consisted of 15 subjects. Test the research hypothesis that the assumption of equal population variances is unwarranted, that is, that the variances are unequal. Use $\alpha = .10$.
4. Sidney Jourard developed a self-disclosure scale, which refers to the process of making the self known to other persons. He and Lasakow (1958) administered the scale to undergraduates and tested for differences between males and females in willingness to disclose the self to others. The means and the standard deviations were 185.90 and 36.10, respectively, for males and 215.00 and 57.60, respectively, for females. The samples consisted of 10 males and 10 females. Do these data support the research hypothesis that female undergraduates' self-disclosure scores are more variable than male undergraduates' scores? Use $\alpha = .01$.

9.6 · PARAMETRIC VERSUS NONPARAMETRIC
STATISTICAL INFERENCE

As we have noted, the parametric statistical tests discussed in sections 9.3 and 9.4 are used with experimental situations that closely resemble those described in chapter 6. The experiments in that chapter were used to illustrate the application of various nonparametric tests. For example, the Mann-Whitney U test was employed to compare two populations using the independent sampling design and the Wilcoxon rank sum test was employed to compare two populations using the matched pairs design. In this chapter we compared two populations by using a t statistic for *both* test situations. Since the type of experiment does not in itself dictate whether a parametric or a nonparametric test is appropriate, some additional comments regarding when to use one or the other type of test are given here.

The major consideration in deciding between a parametric and a nonparametric test is the nature of the measurements involved. If we are dealing with a behavioral attribute or a trait that can be meaningfully measured only by rank ordering, only a nonparametric test is appropriate. If observations can be measured on a quantitative scale and the parametric distribution assumptions are satisfied, either a parametric or a nonparametric test may be validly applied.

Where the parametric assumptions are true and both types of tests are appropriate, parametric tests are usually preferred. They are applied to numerical score data (rather than to ranks) and thus more of the available information is used. As a result, parametric tests tend to be more likely to detect a disagreement with the null hypothesis, particularly when the sample sizes are small. This means that a nonparametric statistical test requires a sample that is larger than that needed for the corresponding parametric test in order to detect a disagreement with the null hypothesis.

These comments concerning parametric and nonparametric tests apply only if the parametric distribution assumptions are reasonably well satisfied. If the necessary assumptions are obviously untrue, a parametric test may not be appropriate. For example, an application of the t statistic where two independent samples are drawn from populations with markedly skewed distributions, or grossly unequal variances, or both, could result in a test for which α is actually much larger than assumed.

On the other hand, it has been shown that, for some parametric tests, moderate departures from the parametric assumptions do not seriously disturb the distribution of the test statistic. In particular, moderate departures from normality do not affect the validity of the t test. In the case of two independent samples, unequal population variances do not seriously affect the validity of the t test for comparing two population means if the sample sizes n_1 and n_2 are equal. Furthermore, we may use the F test in section 9.5 to detect large differences in population variances.

To conclude the comments of this section, the choice between a parametric or a nonparametric statistical test depends on a familiarity with the kind of measurements involved, or it may be based on an inspection of the data. If the measurements are such that the necessary distribution assumptions are reasonable or are not apt to be seriously violated, a parametric test is usually preferred, especially if sample sizes are small. If the measurements are such that parametric distribution assumptions are obviously unreasonable or highly questionable, a nonparametric test is the appropriate choice.

SUMMARY

When we wish to make parametric inferences about population means by using small samples, the Student's t distribution is often appropriate. In actual experimental situations, the formula for the t statistic changes depending on (1) the number of populations involved (one or two) and (2) the type of experimental design employed (independent sampling or matched pairs).

When we use the t statistic for an independent sampling design with two populations, we must assume that the variances of the populations are equal. The F statistic allows us to compare the variances in this case and to test this assumption.

It is important to note that the t statistic and the F statistic employed in the small-sample statistical methods discussed in this chapter are based on the assumption that the sampled populations possess a normal probability distribution. This requirement is reasonably well satisfied for many types of experimental measurements.

You may have observed the very close relationship connecting the Student's t and the z statistic. Because of this close relationship, the methods used with both statistics for testing hypotheses and constructing confidence intervals are very similar. The F statistic, employed in making comparisons about population variances, does not, of course, follow this pattern. However, the reasoning used in the construction of the F test is identical to the reasoning used with the other methods we have presented.

A summary of the confidence intervals and statistical tests described in chapters 8 and 9 is presented in appendix I.

SUPPLEMENTARY EXERCISES

1. In a perception judgment task, 6 subjects were asked to estimate the elapsed time between two presentations of an auditory stimulus. The 6 estimates, in seconds, were 7.5, 4.8, 8.1, 7.8, 5.9, and 6.7. Given that the elapsed time was actually 8.0 seconds, do these data indicate that subjects tend to underestimate the time interval between the two stimuli? Test at an $\alpha = .05$ level.
2. Construct a 90 percent confidence interval for the population mean estimate of the elapsed time in exercise 1.
3. Refer to exercises 1 and 2. How large should the sample be so that the width of the confidence interval is reduced to approximately 1 second?

4. Nine therapists were rated on a 12-point scale designed to assess clinical effectiveness. The resulting scores were

$$5, 11, 7, 7, 2, 10, 8, 4, 9$$

Do the data present sufficient evidence to indicate that the average rating differed from 6 points? Test at the 10 percent level of significance.

5. Construct a 90 percent confidence interval for the mean clinical effectiveness rating in exercise 4.

6. A comparison of reaction times (in seconds) for two different stimuli in a psychological word-association experiment produced the following results when applied to a random sample of 16 people.

Stimulus 1	1	3	2	1	2	1	3	2
Stimulus 2	4	2	3	3	1	2	3	3

Do the data present sufficient evidence to indicate a difference in population mean reaction time for the two stimuli? Test at the $\alpha = .05$ level of population significance.

7. Refer to exercise 6. Suppose that the word-association experiment had been conducted by using a matched pairs design and by making a comparison of reaction time within each person; that is, each person would be subjected to both stimuli in a random order. The data for the experiment are as follows (values in seconds).

Person	1	2	3	4	5	6	7	8
Stimulus 1	3	1	1	2	1	2	3	1
Stimulus 2	4	2	3	1	2	3	3	3

Do the data present sufficient evidence to indicate a difference in mean reaction time for the two stimuli? Test at the $\alpha = .05$ level of significance.

8. Construct a 90 percent confidence interval for $(\mu_1 - \mu_2)$ in exercise 6.

9. Construct a 95 percent confidence interval for $(\mu_1 - \mu_2)$ in exercise 7.

10. Analyze the data in exercise 7 as though the experiment had been conducted in an unpaired manner. Construct a 95 percent confidence interval for $(\mu_1 - \mu_2)$ and compare it with your answer to exercise 9. Does it appear that using a matched pairs design increases the amount of information available in the experiment?

11. Tresselt and Mayzner (1965) were interested in how individual difference factors relate to the ability to solve a problem. Twenty subjects were given anagrams to solve and the solution time was recorded. Half of the subjects were high (subscript 1) in stored digram frequency and half were low (subscript 2). The data for the experiment are presented below.

High	184.5	24.0	83.5	55.0	144.0	17.5	12.5	133.5	83.5	44.0
Low	240.0	71.5	143.5	240.0	143.0	28.5	29.0	143.5	80.5	91.0

$$\bar{y}_1 = 78.2 \qquad\qquad \bar{y}_2 = 121.05$$

$$\sum_{i=1}^{10} (y_i - \bar{y}_1)^2 = 31{,}390.1 \qquad \sum_{i=1}^{10} (y_i - \bar{y}_2)^2 = 51{,}829.225$$

Test the research hypothesis that the mean solution times differ for the two populations represented by the high and low stored digram frequencies. Use $\alpha = .05$.

12. Construct a 90 percent confidence interval for the difference in population mean solution times in exercise 11.

13. The test you conducted in exercise 11 requires the assumption of equal population variances. Test the research hypothesis that the variances are not equal. Use $\alpha = .10$.

14. Suppose that the two groups of subjects in Exercise 11 had been matched on intelligence, age, sex, and socioeconomic status. Reanalyze the data as if it were a matched pairs experiment.

15. Paivio (1963) tested the notion that social isolation is a deprivation which arouses social drives, just as physical deficits arouse primary appetitive drives. Children either were exposed or were not exposed to a period of social isolation, after which they told stories to an adult. Below are the ratings given the story by the experimenter, with a higher rating implying a better-told story. (The subscript 1 is used for the isolated condition and the subscript 2 is for the nonisolated condition.)

Isolated	56.0	56.4	106.8	84.3	95.5	56.2
Nonisolated	133.4	85.0	118.1	74.0	96.1	109.2

$$\bar{y}_1 = 75.9 \qquad\qquad \bar{y}_2 = 102.6$$

$$\sum_{i=1}^{6} (y_i - \bar{y}_1)^2 = 2573.9 \qquad \sum_{i=1}^{6} (y_i - \bar{y}_2)^2 = 2402.4$$

(a) Test for equality of the two population variances.

(b) Test to see if the data provide sufficient evidence to indicate a difference in mean ratings for the two populations. Use a two-tailed test, with $\alpha = .05$.

(c) Construct a 90 percent confidence interval for the difference between the two population means.

16. To validate a measure of social dominance, an experiment was conducted to compare two groups, extroverts and introverts. These concepts come from Jung's psychological type theory which states that, under stress, extroverts are likely to lose themselves in people and are in general very sociable, while introverts draw into themselves under stress and in general are shy and are likely to work alone. On the basis of prior tests, 9 subjects were identified as extroverts (A) and 9 subjects were identified as introverts (B). Each subject was administered a scale which measures social dominance, and the scores were as follows.

A	25	16	33	15	23	20	32	28	21
B	9	21	17	15	14	22	18	26	18

$$A: \sum_{i=1}^{9} y_i = 213 \qquad B: \sum_{i=1}^{9} y_i = 160$$

$$\bar{y}_1 = 23.7 \qquad \bar{y}_2 = 17.8$$

$$\sum_{i=1}^{9} y_i^2 = 5373 \qquad \sum_{i=1}^{9} y_i^2 = 3040$$

Do the data provide sufficient evidence to indicate that the mean social dominance score for extroverts exceeds the mean social dominance score for introverts?

17. One method of measuring drive in psychological research is to measure general activity level. Rats, for instance, can be placed in an activity cage and measurements can be obtained on their speed of running or on an amount of restless activity. This can be studied in the relation to such things as hours of food deprivation.

    Suppose a matched pairs experiment is conducted by matching preexperimental activity levels of 14 rats from a single litter, thereby forming 7 pairs. Then one rat in each pair is deprived of food for 1 hour while the other is deprived for 4 hours. At the end of the respective deprivation periods, activity scores are recorded for each rat. The scores are presented below.

Pair	4-hour Deprivation	1-hour Deprivation
1	63	56
2	83	78
3	80	81
4	68	61
5	68	61
6	91	92
7	86	79

Do the data present sufficient evidence to indicate a population difference in mean activity level for the two deprivation states at the $\alpha = .10$ level?

18. Construct a 90 percent confidence interval for $(\mu_1 - \mu_2)$ in exercise 17.
19. Analyze the data in exercise 17 as though it had been conducted in an unpaired manner. Construct a 90 percent confidence interval for $(\mu_1 - \mu_2)$ and compare it with your answer for exercise 18.

REFERENCES

Anderson, R. L., and Bancroft, T. A. 1952. *Statistical theory in research.* New York: McGraw-Hill. Chapter 7.

Dutton, D. G., and Avon, A. P. 1974. Some evidence for heightened sexual attraction under conditions of anxiety. *Journal of Personality and Social Psychology* 30:510–517.

Fontaine, G. 1974. Social comparison and some determinants of expected personal control and expected performance in a novel task situation. *Journal of Personality and Social Psychology* 29:487–496.

Jourard, S. M., and Lasakow, P. 1958. Some factors in self-disclosure. *Journal of Abnormal and Social Psychology* 59:91–98.

Li, J. C. R. 1961. *Introduction to statistical inference.* Ann Arbor, Mich.: J. W. Edwards, Publisher. Chapter 10.

Millar, S. 1974. Tactile short-term memory by blind and sighted children. *British Journal of Psychology* 65:253–263.

Paivio, A. 1963. Audience influence, social isolation and speech. *Journal of Abnormal and Social Psychology* 67:247–253.

Schachter, S., and Wheeler, L. 1962. Epinephrine, chlorpromazine and amusement. *Journal of Abnormal and Social Psychology* 65:121–128.

Sheppard, C.; Ricca, E.; Fracchia, J.; and Merlis, S. 1974. Psychological needs of suburban male heroin addicts. *Journal of Psychology* 87:123–128.

Tresselt, M. E., and Mayzner, M. S. 1965. Anagram solution times: A function of individual differences in stored digram frequencies. *Journal of Experimental Psychology* 70:606–610.

Williams, J. S. 1975. Aspects of Dependence-Independence Conflict in Children with Asthma. *Journal of Child Psychology and Psychiatry and Applied Disciplines* 16:199–218.

10·The Design of Psychological Experiments

INTRODUCTION

The basic elements of a psychological experiment and some elementary concepts of experimental design were presented in chapter 6. In particular, we presented the independent sampling design and the matched pairs design, both necessary for a discussion of nonparametric methods for comparing two treatments. In this chapter we will briefly review and expand on the material of chapter 6; this is done in sections 10.1 through 10.3.

We will explain in greater detail how we can directly increase the amount of information in psychological experiments (volume-increasing designs, section 10.4). We will show how to increase the information available from a sample by reducing the variation in an experiment (noise-reducing designs, section 10.5). In particular, in sections 10.4 and 10.5 we will present experimental designs that are appropriate for comparing more than two treatments and for investigating the effects of two or more variables on a response measurement.

In section 10.6 we will discuss a method for increasing the information in an experiment by reducing the variability of a response due to the variations within a given subject. Then in section 10.7 we will review the notion of random sampling, and we will discuss some ways you can use the random number table to obtain your sample.

Much of the material presented in this chapter is in the nature of a brief introduction. In chapters 11 and 12 we will learn how to analyze the data generated by the experimental designs presented here.

10.1 • THE ELEMENTS OF A PSYCHOLOGICAL EXPERIMENT: SOME NEW IDEAS

The basic elements of a psychological experiment, presented in chapter 6, are defined as follows.

1. The objects upon which measurements are taken are called **experimental units.** For example, if we are interested in the reaction time of a subject exposed to a particular stimulus, each subject is an experimental unit.
2. A measurement made on an experimental unit is called a **response.** In the reaction time experiment (see item 1 above), the reaction time for a given subject is the response.
3. Whatever is done to experimental units that makes them differ from one population to another is called a **treatment.** For example, in the reaction time experiment, we may be interested in studying the effects of the length of time the stimulus is applied and of the sex of the subject on the reaction time response. A particular combination of ''length of time of stimulus application'' and ''sex of subject'' would represent a treatment.

Most experiments involve a study of the effect of one or more *independent variables* on a response.

Definition 10.1

Independent experimental variables are called **factors.**

Factors can be *quantitative* or *qualitative*.

Definition 10.2

A **quantitative factor** is one that can take values corresponding to points on a real number line. Factors that are not quantitative are said to be **qualitative.**

In our reaction time experiment there are two factors: length of time of stimulus application and sex of subject. Since time is measured on a scale whose values correspond to points on a real number line, length of time of stimulus application is a quantitative factor. Sex of subject is a qualitative factor.

Definition 10.3

The intensity setting of a factor is called a level.

The word "level" is usually used to denote the intensity setting for a quantitative independent variable. We use it here to refer to the settings for either quantitative or qualitative independent variables.

If we are interested in investigating the three stimulus application times of 5, 10, and 15 seconds, we will vary this factor over *three levels*. Of course, the factor "sex of subject" is varied over two levels, "female" and "male."

When planning a psychological experiment, you should identify these five elements of the experiment. That is, you should describe and list the following:

1. the experimental units
2. the response of interest
3. the factor(s)
4. the levels for each factor
5. the treatments.

For our reaction time experiment, the elements are summarized below.

1. Experimental units: Human subjects.
2. Response: Reaction time.
3. Factors: Length of time of stimulus application (quantitative); sex (qualitative).
4. Levels: Three levels of time of stimulus application—5, 10, and 15 seconds; two levels of sex of subject—female and male.
5. Treatments: The six factor-level combinations shown below.

Treatments	Length of Time of Stimulus (seconds)	Sex of Subject
1	5	female
2	10	female
3	15	female
4	5	male
5	10	male
6	15	male

EXERCISES

1. What is a factor?
2. What is meant by the levels of a factor?

3. An experiment is designed to determine the effect of room temperature and emotional state on blood pressure of adults. Two room temperatures, 70°F and 80°F, are used. The experimenter also will induce one of three emotional states in each subject—anger, calm, or happiness—before taking a subject's blood pressure. List the basic elements of this experiment.

10.2 • THE STRATEGY TO USE IN DESIGNING GOOD PSYCHOLOGICAL EXPERIMENTS

As we noted in earlier chapters, the objective of statistics is to make an inference about a population based on information contained in a sample. More generally, we may wish to compare two or more populations with regard to their frequency distributions or their corresponding parameters—for example, the means of the populations—based on information contained in samples selected from each of the populations. As noted earlier (chapter 6), the populations will correspond to the treatments the experimenter wishes to compare.

Before studying the strategy to use in designing good experiments, you must understand that experimentation, which generates the sample measurements, costs time and money. And what does this time and money buy? The answer is *information*, information that is used in making inferences about the population(s) of interest.

An experimental design is a plan for collecting the response measurements of an experiment. This plan involves two major steps: (1) selecting the treatments to be employed in the experiment and (2) deciding how the treatments will be applied to the experimental units.

Definition 10.4

An experimental design is a plan for collecting the response measurements in an experiment.

For example, in section 6.2 we presented two experimental designs for comparing two populations (two treatments): the independent sampling design and the matched pairs design. In succeeding sections of chapter 6, we discussed how these designs differ and the advantages associated with each. Knowing the differences and advantages associated with various designs helps in deciding how the treatments will be applied to the experimental units.

Finally, let us consider the problem of selecting a good experimental design for a particular research objective. To develop a strategy for designing good experiments, we must first be able to measure the amount of information (relative to one or more of the population parameters) that is contained in a sample. Then we can see how changes in the design will increase or decrease the quantity of information in a sample and, at that point, we can develop a strategy for planning an experiment.

The information in a sample available for making an inference about a population parameter can be measured by the width (or half-width) of the confidence interval that can be constructed from the sample data. A large-sample confidence interval for a population mean is

$$\bar{x} \pm \frac{2\sigma}{\sqrt{n}}$$

and this confidence interval can be used, with appropriate modifications, to measure the amount of information in a sample.

The widths of almost all the commonly employed confidence intervals are, like the confidence interval for a population mean, dependent on the population variance σ^2 and the sample size n. The less the variation in the population, as measured by σ^2, the smaller is the confidence interval. Similarly, the width of the confidence interval decreases as n increases. This interesting phenomenon leads us to believe that two factors affect the quantity of information in a sample about a parameter: the variation of the data and the sample size n. We will see that this deduction is slightly oversimplified but essentially true.

A strong similarity exists between the audio theory of communication and the theory of statistics. Both are concerned with the transmission of a message (signal) from one point to another and consequently both are theories of information. For example, a telephone engineer is responsible for transmitting a verbal message that might originate in New York City and be received in New Orleans. Or, as another example, a speaker may wish to communicate with a large and noisy audience. If static or background noise is sizable in either situation, the receiver may get only a sample of the complete signal and from this partial information must infer the nature of the complete message.

Similarly, scientific experimentation is conducted to verify certain theories about natural phenomena. Or, it is conducted simply to explore some aspect of nature and then to find, exactly or with a good approximation, the relationships of certain natural variables. Thus we might think of experimentation as the communication between nature and a scientist. The message about the natural phenomenon is contained, in garbled form, in the experimenter's sample data. Imperfections in the measuring instruments, nonhomogeneity of experimental material, and many other factors contribute background noise (or static). This static tends to obscure nature's signal and cause the observed response to vary in a random manner.

For both the communications engineer and the statistician, two things affect the quantity of information in an experiment: the magnitude of the background noise (or the variation) and the volume of the signal (or sample size). The greater the noise or, equivalently, the variation, the less is the information contained in the sample. Likewise, the louder the signal, the greater is the amplification, and hence the more likely the message is to penetrate the noise and be received.

The design of experiments is a very broad subject concerned with methods of sampling to reduce the variation in an experiment, to amplify nature's signal, and thereby to acquire a *specified quantity* of information at minimum cost. Despite the complexity of the subject, some of the important considerations in the design of good experiments can be easily understood by the beginner.

EXERCISES

1. How can you measure the quantity of information in a sample that is pertinent to a specific population parameter?
2. What two things affect the quantity of information in an experiment?

10.3 • THE PROCESS OF DESIGNING AN EXPERIMENT

As we stated in section 10.2, two things affect the quantity of information in a sample that is pertinent to one or more population parameters: the volume of the signal and the extent of the background noise. To understand how these variables can be controlled, we must identify the steps involved in designing an experiment. Then we can see which of these affect the volume of the signal and which affect the background noise.

The steps used in designing an experiment are given in the box.

Steps Employed in Designing an Experiment

1. Identify the experimental units.
2. Identify the response of interest.
3. Select the factors to be included in the experiment and the specific population parameter(s) of interest.
4. Decide how much information is desired about the parameter(s) of interest. (For example, how accurately do you wish to estimate the parameters?)
5. Select the treatments (combinations of factor levels) to be employed in the experiment and decide the number of experimental units to be assigned to each.
6. Decide how the treatments should be applied to the experimental units.

You will note that the identification of the elements of an experiment, presented in section 10.1, is an essential part of the design of an experiment. And it goes without saying that a prerequisite to this process is a careful specification of the research objective.

Besides the selection of the factors to be included in the experiment, which is a choice dictated by the researcher's objective, two other steps imply action and permit control. They are (1) selecting the treatments (accomplished by a specification of factor levels) and (2) deciding how the treatments should be applied to the experimental units. As we will subsequently show, the first step affects the volume of the signal that we wish to receive. The second affects the extent of the background noise. How to select treatments in order to increase the volume of the signal is discussed in section 10.4. Then in section 10.5 we explain how the background noise is affected by the way we assign the treatments to the experimental units.

EXERCISE

1. State the steps involved in designing an experiment.

10.4 • VOLUME-INCREASING EXPERIMENTAL DESIGNS

Designing an experiment to increase the volume of a signal, that is, to increase the information about one or more population parameters, depends on the selection of treatments and the number of (experimental units as- [*is subjects*] signed to each (step 5 in designing an experiment). The treatments (the combinations of factor levels) identify the points at which one or more response measurements will be made—they indicate the general location in which the experimenter is focusing his attention.

As you will see, some designs contain more information about specific population parameters than others for the same number of observations. And some very costly experiments contain *no* information concerning certain population parameters. No single design is best for obtaining information about all types of population parameters. Indeed, the problem of finding the best design for focusing information on a specific population parameter has been solved in only a few specific cases.

Our purpose in this section is not to present a general theory or to find the best selection of factor-level combinations for a given experiment. Rather, we wish to present a few examples to illustrate the principles involved. For both of the following two examples, we will give the design that provides the maximum amount of information about the parameter(s) of interest (for a fixed sample size n).

The simplest example of an information-focusing experiment is the problem of estimating the difference between a pair of population means ($\mu_1 - \mu_2$), based on independent random samples. In this instance, the two treatments have already been selected and the question concerns the allocation of experimental units to the two samples. If we plan to invest enough money to sample a total of n experimental units, how many units should we select from populations 1 and 2 so as to maximize the information in the data about ($\mu_1 - \mu_2$)?

Let n_1 be the number of measurements in the sample from population 1, n_2 the number in the sample from population 2, and let $n = (n_1 + n_2)$, the total number of sample measurements. Then for $n = 10$, should we select $n_1 = n_2 = 5$ observations from each population? Or would an allocation of $n_1 = 4$ and $n_2 = 6$ be better?

You will recall that the estimator $(\bar{y}_1 - \bar{y}_2)$ of $(\mu_1 - \mu_2)$ has a standard deviation

$$\sigma_{(\bar{y}_1-\bar{y}_2)} = \sqrt{\frac{\sigma_1^2}{n_1} + \frac{\sigma_2^2}{n_2}}$$

The smaller the $\sigma_{(\bar{y}_1-\bar{y}_2)}$, the smaller is the corresponding error of estimation and the greater is the quantity of information in the sample pertinent to $(\mu_1 - \mu_2)$. If, as we frequently assume, $\sigma_1^2 = \sigma_2^2 = \sigma^2$, then

$$\sigma_{(\bar{y}_1-\bar{y}_2)} = \sigma\sqrt{\frac{1}{n_1} + \frac{1}{n_2}}$$

It can be verified that this quantity is a minimum when $n_1 = n_2$. Consequently, the sample contains a maximum of information on $(\mu_1 - \mu_2)$ when the n experimental units are equally divided between the two treatments. We illustrate (but do not prove) our point with an example.

Example 10.1

Calculate the standard deviation for $(\bar{y}_1 - \bar{y}_2)$ when $\sigma_1^2 = \sigma_2^2 = \sigma^2$ and the number of measurements are as follows.

(a) $n = 10$, $n_1 = n_2 = 5$.
(b) $n = 10$, $n_1 = 4$, $n_2 = 6$.

Solution:

$$\sigma_{(\bar{y}_1-\bar{y}_2)} = \sigma\sqrt{\frac{1}{n_1} + \frac{1}{n_2}}$$

(a) When $n_1 = n_2 = 5$,

$$\sigma_{(\bar{y}_1-\bar{y}_2)} = \sigma\sqrt{\frac{1}{5} + \frac{1}{5}} = \sigma\sqrt{.4}$$

(b) When $n_1 = 4$ and $n_2 = 6$,

$$\sigma_{(\bar{y}_1-\bar{y}_2)} = \sigma\sqrt{\frac{1}{4} + \frac{1}{6}} = \sigma\sqrt{.42}$$

Note that $\sigma_{(\bar{y}_1-\bar{y}_2)}$ is smaller for an equal allocation, that is, $n_1 = n_2 = 5$.

Equal allocation of experimental units to the two treatments is *not* best when $\sigma_1^2 \neq \sigma_2^2$. In this case an *unequal* allocation of the n experimental units gives the maximum information about $(\mu_1 - \mu_2)$. It can be proved that the optimal allocation assigns values to n_1 and n_2 that are proportional to σ_1 and σ_2.

As a second example of an experiment that increases the quantity of information about a population parameter, suppose we wish to investigate the relationship between age and the ability to comprehend the concept of volume. We suspect that boys and girls differ in their rate of development of the concept of volume. This leads us to examine both age and sex as factors that relate to the comprehension of volume, the dependent variable. Note that age is a quantitative factor and sex is qualitative.

Two strategies are available to us. We might examine the relationship between age and the comprehension of volume separately for boys and for girls. Or we might examine the combined effect of age and sex on the comprehension of volume.

Suppose we suspect that both sex and age affect a child's ability to comprehend the concept of volume. What kind of experimental design would best explore the relationships? Photo by Mimi Forsyth, Monkmeyer Press Photo Service.

The second strategy has a distinct advantage over the first. Using the first strategy, we would most likely find that both boys' and girls' comprehension of volume increases with age, but we would be unable to determine whether boys and girls differ in their rate of development of the concept. Using the second strategy, we would be able to examine, in a single experiment, the effect of age, the effect of sex, and the combined effect of both age and sex. The second strategy, then, should yield more information on the dependent variable, the ability to comprehend the concept of volume.

This second strategy, which permits examination of the combined effect of two factors, age and sex, utilizes a **factorial experiment.**

Definition 10.5

A **complete factorial experiment** is one that includes all combinations of the levels of the factors.

For example, suppose that in the age–volume comprehension example, the age range of interest is from four years to nine years. The experimenter defines the levels of the age factor as follows: four years, five years, . . . , nine years (six levels in all). There are, of course, two levels of the sex factor: boys and girls. So for this example, a factorial experiment, which includes all combinations of the levels of the two factors "age" and "sex," would involve $(6)(2) = 12$ combinations.

Let y represent a measure of the ability to comprehend the concept of volume. A factorial experiment might yield any of the results shown in figure 10.1. Figure 10.1(a) indicates that the ability to comprehend the concept of volume increases

Figure 10.1 • Examples of some possible outcomes of a factorial experiment to investigate the relationship between age, sex, and the rate of development of the concept of volume

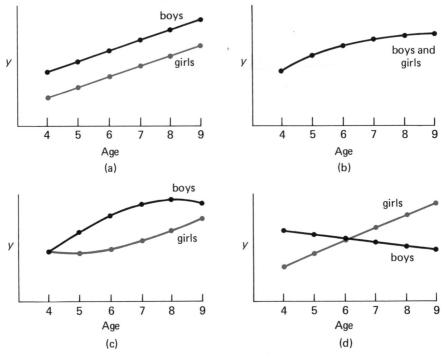

with age and at the same rate for both boys and girls. However, boys differ from girls by a constant amount at all age levels. In figure 10.1(b), the two curves for boys and girls are superimposed, indicating that both sexes develop the concept of volume at the same rate and achieve the same degree of development at each age level. In contrast, figure 10.1(c) indicates that boys show a higher degree of development of the concept at each age level except age four and that the two sexes differ in rate of development. Thus figure 10.1(c) depicts an *interaction* of the two factors age and sex in their effect on ability to comprehend the concept of volume.

Definition 10.6

insdep. variables

An interaction between two or more factors occurs when the effect of one factor is not the same for all levels of the other factor(s).

To amplify our point, let us stretch our imagination and suppose that the ability to comprehend the concept of volume increases with age for girls but decreases for boys. Then a graph of the volume comprehension scores might appear as shown in figure 10.1(d). Again we see a case of interaction between age and sex. That is, the effect of age on volume comprehension depends on sex. The graphs in figures 10.1(c) and 10.1(d) tell us that we must discuss the effect of age on volume comprehension separately for boys and for girls.

Interactions between the independent variables in an experiment are extremely important. If present, they tell us that we cannot study the effect of one variable on the response independent of the other variable. Furthermore, the effect of a single variable cannot be meaningfully interpreted. The response must be investigated at each factor-level combination.

Examples of the factorial experiment will be given in chapter 11, where the design and analysis of several experiments will be discussed in detail.

To summarize, we have presented the optimal designs for comparing a pair of means and for investigating the interaction between two factors. These two simple designs illustrate how the information in an experiment can be increased or decreased by selecting the factor-level combinations that represent treatments and by changing the allocation of observations to treatments. Thus we have demonstrated that factor-level selection and the allocation of experimental units to treatments can greatly affect the information in an experiment about a particular population parameter and, thereby, can amplify nature's signal. Thus step 5 in section 10.3 is an important consideration in the design of good experiments.

EXERCISES

1. Suppose you wish to compare the means for two populations. If $\sigma_1^2 = \sigma_2^2$, what is the optimal allocation of n_1 and n_2 (where $n_1 + n_2 = n$) for a fixed sample size n? Does this operation use the principle of noise reduction or signal amplification?

2. Refer to exercise 1. Suppose that $\sigma_1^2 = 9, \sigma_2^2 = 25$, and $n = 90$. What allocation of $n = 90$ to the two samples will result in the maximum amount of information on $(\mu_1 - \mu_2)$?

3. Refer to exercise 2. Suppose that you allocate $n_1 = n_2$ observations to each sample. How large must n_1 and n_2 be to obtain the same amount of information as that implied by the solution to exercise 2?

4. McConville and Hemphill (1966) conducted research on the effect of communication restraints on problem-solving behavior in groups. They wished to compare the means for the population allowed free communication and the population limited in communication. Suppose that $\sigma_1^2 = 15.4$, $\sigma_2^2 = 27.9$, and $n = 20$. What allocation of $n = 20$ to the two samples will result in the maximum amount of information about $(\mu_1 - \mu_2)$?

5. What is a factorial experiment?

6. What is the objective of a factorial experiment?

7. In what sense does a factorial experiment increase the quantity of information in an experiment?

8. Why is it important to locate factor interactions?

10.5 · NOISE-REDUCING EXPERIMENTAL DESIGNS

Noise-reducing experimental designs increase the information in an experiment by decreasing the background noise (variation) caused by uncontrolled nuisance variables. Thus by serving as filters to screen out undesirable noise, they permit nature's signal to be received more clearly. Reduction of noise can be accomplished in step 6 of the design of an experiment—that is, in the method used for assigning treatments to the experimental units.

Designing for noise reduction is based on a single principle; making all the comparisons of the treatments within relatively homogeneous groups of experimental units. The more homogeneous the experimental units, the easier it is to detect a difference in the treatments. Because noise-reducing or filtering designs work with groups (or blocks) of relatively homogeneous experimental units, they are called block designs.

Up to this point, we have presented only two ways to assign treatments to the experimental units: the independent sampling design and the matched pairs design, both introduced in chapter 6. The matched pairs design for the reading age example of section 9.4 employed the block design to achieve a very sizable reduction in noise and a large increase in information about the difference in treatment means.

As another example, consider an experiment for making an inference about the difference in mean age at which preschool children begin reading. Some of the children are subjected to an educational program (A) and others are assigned to a control group receiving no program (B). Because the experimenter anticipated large individual differences in IQ and home environment, measurements of primary reading age were obtained from paired identical twins, one twin assigned to the A group, the other to the B group. Six pairs of twins were used in the experiment, with twins of each pair randomly assigned to the two conditions.

By matching subjects preexperimentally, the variability due to differences in IQ and home environment was prevented from obscuring any differences in primary reading age that were actually due to the experimental treatment. The resulting increase in information about $(\mu_A - \mu_B)$ can be seen by comparing the width of the confidence intervals generated by the paired and unpaired analyses. The paired analysis, with subjects matched genetically and environmentally, should produce a considerably narrower confidence interval for $(\mu_A - \mu_B)$ than that generated by an unpaired analysis with the same number of subjects.

The matched pairs design is a special case of the most elementary noise- or error-reducing design, the randomized block design. The randomized block design, discussed in detail in sections 11.7 and 11.8, is used to compare the means of any number of treatments, say p, within relatively homogeneous blocks of p experimental units. Any number of blocks may be employed, but each treatment must appear exactly once in each block. Thus the matched pairs experiment is a randomized block design containing $p = 2$ treatments.

Definition 10.7

A randomized block design containing b blocks and p treatments consists of b blocks of p experimental units each. The treatments are randomly assigned to the units in each block, with each treatment appearing exactly once in every block.

A randomized block design for the beginning reading age experiment is illustrated below.

Block 1			Block 2		. . .	Block b	
Twin	Program		Twin	Program		Twin	Program
1	A		3	B	. . .	$n - 1$	A
2	B		4	A		n	B

A more extensive discussion of block designs and their analyses is presented in chapter 11 and in the references at the end of this chapter. The objective of this section is to make you aware of the existence of block designs, how they work, and how they can produce substantial increases in the quantity of information in an experiment by reducing nuisance variation.

EXERCISES

1. What is a randomized block design?
2. In what sense does a randomized block design decrease the noise or error in an experiment?

10.6 · USING REPEATED MEASUREMENTS

Another rather indirect way of increasing the volume of nature's signal is to take repeated measurements on the experimental units. Indeed, many psychological researchers take repeated measurements on the subjects who participate in an experiment. How and by what amount a repeated measures design increases the information in an experiment will be explained in this section.

In all the preceding material in this text, we have implied that the researcher takes one (and only one) response measurement on each experimental unit. By a repeated measures design, we mean any design that employs multiple response measurements on each experimental unit.

Definition 10.8

A repeated measures design is one that employs multiple response measurements on each experimental unit. subject

---

For example, suppose that an experiment is conducted to investigate the effect of three stimuli on the tension level of a subject. An experimental unit is a subject. The response is the tension level of a subject as measured by the subject's diastolic blood pressure. The single quantitative factor is the type of stimuli, which would be set at three levels (corresponding to the three types of stimuli). Finally, suppose that 4 subjects are randomly assigned to each of the treatments (12 subjects in all) and that the stimuli are applied and the blood pressures measured in an independent manner. Thus far we have described an independent sampling design which might appear diagrammatically as shown in figure 10.2. Note that the 12 subjects have been randomly assigned, 4 to each treatment.

Figure 10.2 • Diagrammatic illustration of the random assignment of 4 subjects to each of 3 treatments

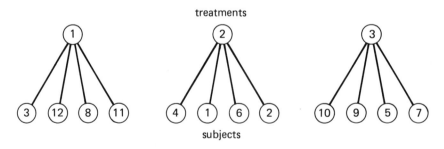

It is clear from figure 10.2 that the object of the experiment is to compare the mean tension levels corresponding to the three stimuli. Now let us examine the sources of variation that tend to obscure the differences.

First and foremost, the differences in mean blood pressures corresponding to the three stimuli will be obscured by the variation in blood pressure *between* subjects. That is, the blood pressures of the subjects will vary widely even if the subjects are exposed to the *same* stimulus. To this we add a *second* source of variation, the variation of blood pressure *within* a given subject. That is, if we were to apply a given stimulus to a single subject on 10 different occasions and then measured the subject's blood pressures on each occasion, we might obtain 10 different blood pressure readings. In other words, the blood pressure induced in a subject as a result of a stimulus will not only vary from subject to subject but will also vary within the same subject when repeated blood pressure measurements are made.

To reduce the first source of variation, we can employ some kind of block design, as described in section 10.5. The second source of variation can be reduced by employing repeated measurements.

The logic of repeated measurements is simple. Suppose we know that the blood pressure measurements vary from one time to another when a subject is treated with a specified stimulus. Then we can reduce the error of measurement of a subject's response by taking repeated measurements on each subject. For example, we might more accurately estimate the effects of the stimuli on the subjects by exposing each subject to his or her assigned stimulus on three different occasions. This would produce three blood pressure measurements for each subject, thereby reducing the error in estimating the effect of a given stimulus on that subject. Such a design is shown diagrammatically in figure 10.3.

Figure 10.3 • An independent sampling design with repeated measurements

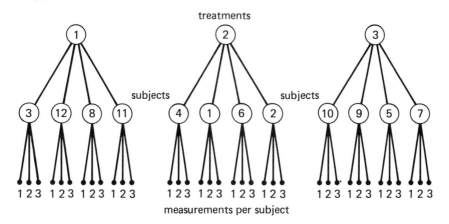

An analysis of the data (see figure 10.3) associated with a repeated measurements design will show an increase in information over the independent sampling design, which uses one measurement per subject (see figure 10.2). (The statistical analyses of these designs will be given in chapter 11.) The increase in information gained by repeated sampling will be substantial if the variation in repeated measurements on the *same subject* is large. This enables you to obtain a more accurate estimate of each subject's response to a stimulus. Usually it is much less costly to take repeated measurements on a single subject than it is to add more subjects. When the cost of each repeated observation is low, and when repeated measurements in the same subject vary greatly, you should employ a repeated measurements design. As you will subsequently see (in chapter 11), the analysis is simplified if you take the same number of repeated measurements on each subject.

Be careful not to misuse repeated measurements. That is, do not think that a repeated measurement is equivalent to the addition of a new experimental unit and hence that repeated measurements can be substituted for a needed increase in sample size. Repeated measurements do not compensate for the variation between experimental units. Although the repeated measurements design of figure 10.3 yields three times as many observations per stimulus as the design in figure 10.2, both involve only four sampling units per treatment. To reduce the person-to-person variation in blood pressure for a given stimulus, you must increase the number of subjects. No amount of measurements on one subject can substitute for an increase in the subject sample size.

EXERCISES

1. What is a repeated measures design?
2. How does a repeated measures design increase the information in an experiment?

10.7 · RANDOM SAMPLING AND RANDOMIZATION BY USING A RANDOM NUMBER TABLE

The notion of random sampling and the definition of a random sample were presented in section 4.7. Now that we have encountered a further need for randomization—for example, when using the randomized block design—we will review our earlier discussion. Also, we will expand our explanation of how to draw a random sample and how to randomly assign treatments to experimental units.

The simplest way to select a random sample of *n* elements from a large population is to use a table of random numbers, such as that shown in table 11 of appendix II. Random number tables are constructed so that integers occur randomly and with equal frequency. For example, suppose that the population contains $N = 1000$ elements. Number the elements from 1 to 1000. Then turn to a table of random numbers, such as the excerpt shown below in table 10.1. Select *n* of the random numbers in order. The population elements to be included in the random sample are given by the first three digits of the random numbers (the three digits 000 correspond to the element numbered 1000). Thus for $n = 5$, we would include the elements numbered 155, 450, 32, 882, and 350.

To avoid using the same sequence of random numbers over and over again, we should select different starting points in table 11, appendix II, to begin the selection of random numbers for different samples.

Table 10.1 • Portion of a table of random numbers

15574	35026	98924
45045	36933	28630
03225	78812	50856
88292	26053	21121

Example 10.2

Draw a random sample of $n = 10$ experimental units from a population containing 5000 experimental units.

Solution: Turn to table 11, appendix II, and randomly select a starting point. To make it easy to locate, suppose we select the number in line 7, column 9, which is 44013. We begin our count with 44013 and proceed down column 9. We use only the last four digits (we drop the digit in the 10,000 column) and we discard numbers in excess of 5000. This gives us the following numbers for our random sample.

$$
\begin{array}{l}
44013 \\
69014 \\
25331 \\
08158 \\
90106 \\
52180 \\
30015 \\
01511 \\
97735 \\
49442 \\
01188 \\
71585 \\
23495 \\
51851 \\
59193 \\
58151 \\
35806 \\
46557 \\
50001
\end{array}
$$

To summarize our results, we would include as experimental units the elements of the population which are numbered 4013, 106, 2180, 15, 1511, 1188, 1585, 3495, 1851, and 1 in our sample.

Example 10.3

Suppose you wish to use an independent sampling design by randomly assigning 40 experimental units, 10 to each of four treatments, A, B, C, and D. How would you use the table of random numbers to make your assignments?

Solution: Refer to table 11, appendix II, and randomly select a starting point. Again, to make it easy to follow, suppose we select the number in line 5, column 6, which is 91782. Use only the last two digits of the number, that is, delete 917 leaving the number 82. Then discard all numbers over 40. If a number appears more than once, discard it after its first occurrence. Continue in this way until you have obtained the numbers 1 through 40.

Now assign the elements which correspond to the first ten numbers you drew from the table to Treatment A, the next ten to Treatment B, and so on.

For example, starting with the random numbers 91782, we would have

~~82~~	08
~~98~~	~~85~~
16	~~46~~
22	13
03	~~91~~
33	~~68~~
36	06
~~45~~	05
~~88~~	~~56~~
~~67~~	20
~~16~~ (appeared earlier)	

Then we would assign the experimental units numbered 16, 22, 3, 33, 36, 8, 13, 6, 5, and 20 to Treatment A. We would continue the procedure to obtain the experimental units to be assigned to the treatments B, C, and D.

EXERCISES

1. What is a random sample?
2. A political analyst wishes to select a sample of $n = 20$ people from a population of 2000. Use the random number table to identify the people to be included in the sample.
3. Two drugs, A and B, are to be applied to each of 5 rats. The rats are numbered 1 to 10. Use the random number table to randomly assign the rats to the two treatments.
4. Refer to exercise 3. Suppose that the experiment involved three drugs, A, B, and C, with 5 rats assigned to each. Use the random number table to randomly assign the 15 rats to the three treatments.
5. A population contains 50,000 voters. Use the random number table to identify the voters to be included in a random sample of $n = 15$.
6. Give two reasons for using random samples.
7. Sheppard and his colleagues (1974) administered the Edwards Personal Preference

Schedule to a random sample of 51 male heroin addicts. Suppose the population from which they drew the sample consisted of 400 male heroin addicts. Use the random number table to identify the people to be included in the sample.

8. Schachter and Wheeler (1962) gave subjects injections of epinephrine, chlorproma-zine, and a placebo. Use the random number table to assign 10 subjects to each of the three treatments.

SUMMARY

The design of experiments is a very broad subject that cannot be condensed into a single chapter in an introductory text. In contrast, the philosophy underlying a design, the methods for varying information in an experiment, and the desirable strategies for a design are easily explained. Thus the objective of this chapter was to identify the factors that affect the quantity of information in an experiment and to use this knowledge to design better experiments.

Two factors affect the quantity of information in an experiment; the volume of nature's signal and the magnitude of the variation caused by uncontrolled variables. The volume of the information pertinent to a parameter of interest depends on the selection of the factor-level combinations (treatments) to be included in the experiment and on the allocation of the total number of experi-mental units to the treatments. This choice determines the focus of attention of the experimenter.

The second method for increasing the information in an experiment concerns the way we assign treatments to the experimental units. A block design, which compares treatments within relatively homogeneous blocks of experimental material, can be used to eliminate block-to-block variation when comparing treatments. As such, it serves as a filter to reduce the unwanted variation that tends to obscure nature's signal.

Thus factor and factor-level selection are important considerations in shifting information in an experiment to amplify the information on a population parame-ter. The use of blocking in assigning treatments to experimental units reduces the noise created by uncontrolled variables and consequently increases the informa-tion in an experiment.

Repeated measures designs also increase the quantity of information in an experiment. Repeated measurements on experimental units reduce the error in estimating the mean response for the experimental units by reducing the within-subject variation. Although the use of repeated measurements greatly increases the number of response measurements, it does not increase the number of experimental units. Consequently, it does not reduce the portion of the error of estimation caused by the variation *between* experimental units.

The analysis of some elementary experimental designs will be given in chapter 11. A more extensive treatment of the design and analysis of experiments is a course in itself. The reader interested in exploring this subject is directed to the references at the end of this chapter.

SUPPLEMENTARY EXERCISES

1. If you were to design an experiment, what part of the design procedure would result in signal amplification?
2. Refer to exercise 1. What part of the design procedure would result in noise reduction?
3. Could an independent variable be a factor in one experiment and a nuisance variable (a noise contributor) in another?
4. Suppose that you wish to study the effect of two stimulants, A and B, on the blood pressure of rats over a dosage range of $x = 2$ to $x = 5$ units. Eight rats are to be used in the experiment, one each at dosages of 2, 3, 4, and 5 units, for both stimulants A and B. What type of experiment is this? What type of variable is "dosage"? "Stimulants"?
5. Refer to exercise 4. Suppose that blood pressure is linearly related to dosage. Draw a graph of blood pressure versus dosage for the two stimulants if no interaction exists between "dosage" and "stimulants." Now draw a graph for the case where interaction does exist.
6. An experiment is conducted to compare the effect of digitalis on the contraction of the heart muscles of a rat. The experiment is performed by removing the heart from a live rat, slicing the heart into thin layers, and treating the layers to a dosage of digitalis. The muscle contraction is then measured. If four dosages (A, B, C, and D) are used, what advantage might be derived by applying A, B, C, and D to a slice of tissue from each rat heart? What principle of design is illustrated by this example?
7. Describe the factors that affect the quantity of information in an experiment and the design procedures that control these factors.
8. Seitz (1969) hypothesized that mentally retarded subjects would perform better at a task if they were paced at a rate that was slower than the rate they would have established for themselves. Such information has applications for the education of the mentally retarded. Shown below are the error scores for subjects in three different conditions: self-paced, paced at two seconds before the presentation of the next item in a discrimnation task, and paced at four seconds. The two-second pacing is the same amount of time as the mean interval that self-paced subjects allowed between items.

Self-paced	2.4	5.0	4.8	1.8	
Two-second Pacing	4.0	1.8			
Four-second Pacing	1.2	.8	.6	1.7	.7

(a) List the basic elements in the experiment. (See section 10.1.)
(b) What type of experimental design is this?
(c) What are the merits of this design?

9. It is commonly thought that certain colors impart apparent warmth and coolness, and, in fact, that physiology has something to do with this phenomenon. Morgan, Goodson, and Jones (1975) conducted a study to see whether it is physiology or cultural norms that causes associations between certain colors and certain temperatures. Subjects were presented with different color stimuli and were asked to state whether each reminded them of hot, warm, cold, or cool. Within a series of trials of

presentations of the colors, the number of times a particular color was matched with the same temperature stimulus was recorded. The data obtained were as follows.

Color Stimuli	Subjects							
	1	2	3	4	5	6	7	8
A	3	1	1	5	3	8	2	3
B	6	5	7	4	5	3	7	6
C	3	2	2	1	1	4	3	2
D	8	1	1	6	2	2	1	3

(a) List the basic elements in the experiment. (See section 10.1.)
(b) What type of experimental design is this?
(c) What are the merits of this design?

10. Koch and Arnold (1972) studied the effects of early social deprivation on emotionality. Since it is not possible to conduct controlled research on this issue among humans (due to ethical problems), the subjects were infant rats. Each subject was either reared by its mother or reared in an incubator, and it was reared either with or without its peers. The response was latency of emergence into a lighted field, that is, the elapsed time until the subject emerged into a lighted field. Since rats are nocturnal animals, this represented an emotional experience for them. A sample of 10 infant rats was selected for each of these four combinations:

> mother-reared, with peers
> mother-reared, without peers
> incubator-reared, with peers
> incubator-reared, without peers

(a) List the basic elements in the experiment.
(b) What type of experimental design is this?
(c) What are the merits of this design?

11. Dreistadt (1969) studied creative problem solving in students to examine the effect of presentation of pictorial analogy and incubation. Subjects either were given a pictorial analogy to their problem or were not. In addition, they either were instructed to stop working and rest for a few minutes (incubation) or were not given this opportunity. Thus there were four conditions. The number of problems, out of 5, that were successfully solved was recorded for each subject. The data for the experiment are shown at the top of page 296.
(a) List the basic elements in the experiment.
(b) What type of experimental design in this?
(c) What are the merits of this design?

12. The autokinetic effect refers to perceived movement of a stationary light in a dark room. Glick (1971) conducted an experiment to study the effects of eye fatigue and "report" condition (what the experimenter reported to the subject) on perception. Three levels of eye fatigue were used, with two different "report" conditions.

Suppose you conducted a similar study as follows: You have 12 subjects available and you randomly assign 2 subjects to each of the six eye fatigue–"report" condition combinations. Each subject will tell you how far to move the light to keep it in a certain position, although the light will be stationary. The measurement of

No Analogy		Analogy	
No Incubation	Incubation	No Incubation	Incubation
2	2	2	5
3	2	5	5
2	1	2	4
2	3	2	5
2	2	5	5
3	4	3	2
5	2	2	5
3	2	4	5
4	5	3	5
2	1	5	4

interest is the distance (in centimeters) from the final position of the light to its initial position. You take three measurements on each subject, obtaining the following data (positive measurements refer to rightward deviations, negative measurements to leftward deviations).

	Report I		Report II	
	subject 1	subject 2	subject 3	subject 4
Eye Fatigue I	20	16	18	20
	23	14	22	23
	19	17	19	20
	subject 5	subject 6	subject 7	subject 8
Eye Fatigue II	−9	−11	−13	−7
	−13	−8	−10	−11
	−12	−11	−10	−10
	subject 9	subject 10	subject 11	subject 12
Eye Fatigue III	0	−2	0	−2
	−1	1	−1	1
	3	−2	0	−2

(a) List the basic elements in the experiment.
(b) What type of experimental design is this?
(c) What are the merits of this design?

REFERENCES

Cochran, W. G., and Cox, G. M. 1957. *Experimental design.* 2d ed. New York: John Wiley and Sons. Chapter 5.

Dreistadt, R. 1969. The use of analogies and incubation in obtaining insights in creative problem solving. *Journal of Psychology* 71:159–175.

Glick, J. 1971. Is autokinetic motion related to experienced displacement? *American Journal of Psychology* 84:210–217.

Koch, M. D., and Arnold, W. J. 1972. Effects of early social deprivation on emotionality in rats. *Journal of Comparative and Physiological Psychology* 78:391–399.

McConville, C. B., and Hemphill, J. K. 1966. Some effects of communication restraint on problem solving behavior. *Journal of Social Psychology* 64:265–276.

Mendenhall, W. 1968. *Introduction to linear models and the design and analysis of experiments.* N. Scituate, Mass.: Duxbury Press. Chapters 4 and 5.

Morgan G. A.; Goodson, F. E.; and Jones, T. 1975. Age differences in the associations between felt and color choices. *American Journal of Psychology* 88:125–130.

Schachter, S., and Wheeler, L. 1962. Epinephrine, chlorpromazine and amusement. *Journal of Abnormal and Social Psychology* 65:121–128.

Seitz, S. 1969. Pacing effects on performance of an automated task. *Psychological Reports* 25:204–206.

Sheppard, C.; Ricca, E.; Fracchia, J.; and Merlis, S. 1974. Psychological needs of suburban male heroin addicts. *Journal of Psychology* 87:123–128.

11·The Analysis of Variance

INTRODUCTION

Broadly speaking, investigation in the behavioral sciences is directed toward establishing the existence or clarifying the nature of a relationship between behavior and its determinants. Or, using a terminology that is particularly useful in this case, the behavioral scientist seeks to examine the relationships between various *dependent variables* (particular behaviors of behavioral traits) and the relevant *independent variables* (factors).

As the terms "dependent variable" and "independent variable" imply, the former is presumed to be a function of the latter. That is, the dependent variable is regarded as being determined or influenced by the independent variable. For example, in a study designed to compare several different methods of teaching reading to see which is most effective, the independent variable would be the teaching method and the dependent variable would very likely be some aspect of reading achievement, such as reading speed or comprehension. Or, a social psychologist might wish to determine whether an adolescent's sex and age are related to his or her ability to resist peer group pressure. In this case there would be two independent variables, sex and age, and the dependent variable would be a measure of the ability to resist group pressure.

In most experiments the dependent variable is that property or behavior that we seek to understand and explain. To do so, we presume it to be a function of one or more factors—the independent variables—that we can manipulate or control in the experiment. As noted in chapter 10, these independent variables may be one of two types, qualitative or quantitative.

In this chapter we develop a very general procedure for exploring the relationship between a dependent variable and one or more independent variables, either qualitative or quantitative. This procedure, called the *analysis of variance*, is designed to break down the variation in a dependent variable by assigning portions of such variation to each independent variable selected for study. Since an experimenter will rarely, if ever, include all the relevant independent variables, a portion of the total variation is unexplained and is attributed to experimental error. The effect of each independent variable is then evaluated by comparing its contribution to total variability with that attributed to error.

To begin our discussion, in sections 11.1 and 11.2 we introduce you to some of the basic and fundamental ideas contained in the procedure of an analysis of variance. Then in the remaining sections of the chapter, we discuss some of the ways an analysis of variance can proceed, depending on the design of the experiment.

We point out one caution before we begin our discussion of an analysis of variance. You may, at times, be somewhat overwhelmed by the number of computations and formulas needed. For your convenience, we have summarized these in boxes and set them apart from the text. We hope that by doing this you will be able to concentrate on the *concept* of the analysis of variance and thus avoid getting bogged down in the formulas. It is more important for you to know how to interpret the results of your computations than it is for you to know and memorize all the formulas which give the results.

11.1 · PARTITION OF A SUM OF SQUARES

An operation that is basic to the analysis of variance and that indicates the underlying rationale is the operation of *partitioning a sum of squares*. You will recall that the variability in a set of n measurements is proportional to the sum of the squares of the deviations,

$$\sum_{i=1}^{n} (y_i - \bar{y})^2$$

This quantity is used to calculate the sample variance. In an analysis of variance, this sum, called the *total sum of the squares of the deviations,* or, simply, *the total sum of squares,* is partitioned into components. Each component is attributed to one of the independent variables in the experiment, plus a remainder that is associated with random error. This may be shown diagrammatically, as indicated in figure 11.1 for three independent variables.

Figure 11.1 • Partitioning of the total sum of the squares of the deviations

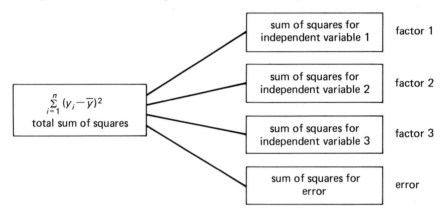

If the sum of the squares of the deviations for a particular factor is large, it may indicate a difference in the means for the levels of the factor. This would tell us that the factor is important in predicting the response y. How large is large? That is, how can we tell whether a sum of the squares of the deviations associated with a factor is larger than might be expected (due to chance) even if the factor were unrelated to the response? The answer is that we compare the sum of squares for the factor with the sum of squares for the error. The logic behind this comparison is explained in section 11.2.

11.2 • THE LOGIC BEHIND AN ANALYSIS
OF VARIANCE TEST

To understand how an analysis of variance works, suppose we wish to investigate the behavior of a response variable, say reading achievement, as a function of

one qualitative independent variable, teaching methods. An experiment is conducted using three teaching methods with 5 students randomly assigned to each
method. Thus the elements of the experiment are as follows:

1. Experimental units: Students.
2. Response: Achievement test score.
3. Factors: A single factor, teaching methods.
4. Levels of factor: A, B, and C, corresponding to the three teaching methods.
5. Treatments: The three teaching methods, A, B, and C.

Because the students are independently selected and randomly assigned to the
three treatments, we have used an independent sampling design.

Now suppose that we have collected achievement score data for the 15
students and plotted the scores on graph paper, as shown in figure 11.2. The
graph shows a plot of the response for each of the 15 students. The first 5
students (numbered 1 to 5) received Teaching Method A, the second 5 (6 to 10)
received Method B, and the last 5 (11 to 15) received Teaching Method C. The
location of the mean response for each of the three treatments is indicated by a
horizontal line.

Figure 11.2 • Plot of the data for the hypothetical experiment to investigate teaching methods and reading achievement, case I

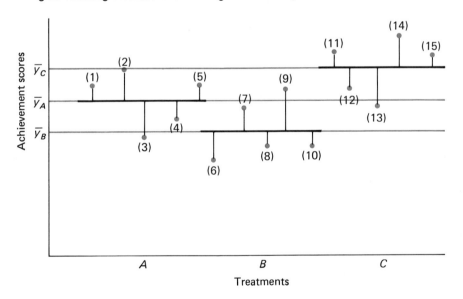

Now examine the plotted points on the graphs and the location of the sample
means for the three teaching methods. What does your intuition tell you? Do you

think the data present sufficient evidence to indicate differences in the mean achievement for the three teaching methods?

Before we answer that question, let's consider another situation. Suppose that, instead of the data appearing as they do in the plot of figure 11.2, they appear as shown in figure 11.3.

Figure 11.3 • Plot of the data for the hypothetical experiment to investigate teaching methods and reading achievement, case II

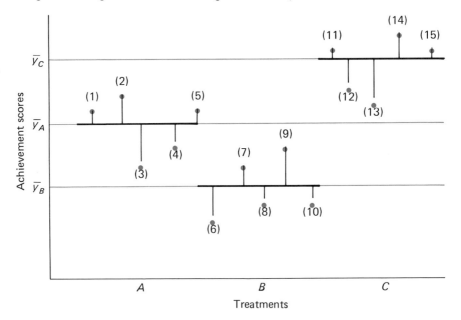

Once again, use your intuition. Do the data present sufficient evidence to indicate differences in mean achievement for the three teaching techniques?

Extend this game one step further. Suppose the data appear as shown in figure 11.4. Now what can be said about the difference in mean achievement for the three teaching techniques? Which data, figure 11.2, figure 11.3, or figure 11.4, provide the greatest evidence supporting the research hypothesis that mean achievement varies for the three teaching techniques? How did you reach your conclusion?

For the data of figure 11.2, we see little evidence of differences in achievement for the three teaching techniques. We see greater evidence for the data of figure 11.3 and what appears to be conclusive evidence in figure 11.4. Did you notice that the variation between measurements *within* each of the three samples is identical for all three figures? In fact, the only distinction in the data shown in

Figure 11.4 • Plot of the data for the hypothetical experiment to investigate teaching methods and reading achievement, case III

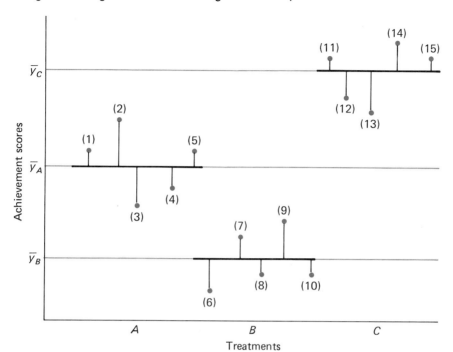

figures 11.2, 11.3, and 11.4 is that the difference *between* the sample means increases as you move from figure 11.2 to figure 11.4.

Figures 11.2 to 11.4 graphically demonstrate the logic behind an analysis of variance. The greater the variation *between* the sample means in comparison with the variation within the samples, the greater the evidence to indicate differences among the population treatment means. The sample means in figure 11.4 differ so much in comparison with the variation of the measurements within the samples that we are led immediately to the conclusion that the population means differ.

Examine figure 11.2 again. The means differ only slightly in comparison with the variation within the samples. Now suppose the sample means differ by exactly the same amount as in figure 11.2 but the variation within the samples is much less. This case is shown in figure 11.5.

Now what do you conclude about the differences in means for the three teaching techniques? We think you will now conclude that the samples provide evidence to indicate a difference in mean achievement for the three teaching techniques. By reducing the variation within the samples (in comparison with figure 11.2), the difference among the sample means appears to be substantial.

Figure 11.5 • Plot of the data for the hypothetical experiment to investigate teaching methods and reading achievement, case IV

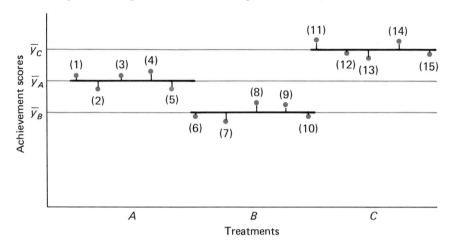

11.3 • THE ANALYSIS OF VARIANCE F TEST

It is easy to convert our eyeball comparison of *between*-sample variation and *within*-sample variation to a comparison of statistical quantities. The variation of a set of measurements $y_1, y_2, \ldots, y_n$ is measured by their variance (chapter 2), that is,

$$s^2 = \sum_{i=1}^{n} \frac{(y_i - \bar{y})^2}{n - 1}$$

So all we need to do is to compare the variance of the sample means, s_m^2,

$$s_m^2 = \sum_{i=1}^{3} \frac{(\bar{y}_i - \bar{y})^2}{2}$$

with the variance s^2 of the measurements within the individual samples. Note that we are using $\bar{y}$ to represent the mean of all the measurements and $\bar{y}_i$ to represent the mean of the measurements for treatment i.

The estimate s^2 of the within-sample variation is the same as the pooled estimate given in section 9.3 for the independent sampling design for two populations, except that we now pool the sum of the squares of the deviations within the three samples. Thus

$$s^2 = \frac{\sum_{i=1}^{5} (y_{i1} - \bar{y}_1)^2 + \sum_{i=1}^{5} (y_{i2} - \bar{y}_2)^2 + \sum_{i=1}^{5} (y_{i3} - \bar{y}_3)^2}{(5 - 1) + (5 - 1) + (5 - 1)}$$

Now that we have these two measures of variation, how can we compare them? If the treatment samples have been drawn from identical normal populations, then the ratio of the two variances, multiplied by an appropriate constant, will possess the F distribution of section 9.5. (In fact, you will remember that we used the F statistic in section 9.5 to test the hypothesis that two population variances are equal.)

If the population treatment means actually differ, s_m^2 will be larger than expected. Thus the ratio

$$F = \frac{s_m^2}{s^2} \times \text{(constant)}$$

will be larger than expected, and F will fall in the upper tail of the F distribution (see figure 11.6). Hence we reject the null hypothesis of no difference in population treatment means when the calculated F-value falls in the upper tail of the F distribution. We will use this result in section 11.4 to test an hypothesis that a set of population treatment means are equal, and we will give a numerical example to illustrate the procedure.

Figure 11.6 • The F distribution

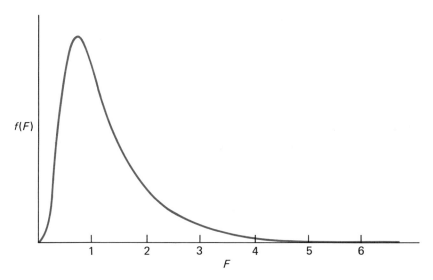

Note: We use "treatment" and "population" interchangeably, not to confuse the reader, but rather as a constant reminder that in experimental design terminology, each population is associated with a treatment of the experiment.

11.4 • THE ANALYSIS OF VARIANCE FOR COMPARING MORE THAN TWO POPULATIONS

In comparing more than two population means, our objective is to test the null hypothesis

H_0: All p population means are equal, or, equivalently,
$$\mu_1 = \mu_2 = \cdots = \mu_p$$

against the research hypothesis

H_a: At least two of the population means are different

As we discussed in section 11.3, we will compare the between-sample variation to the within-sample variation by using the F test statistic.

$$\text{Test statistic: } F = \frac{\text{MST}}{\text{MSE}}$$

where

MST = a measure of the variation between treatment means

MSE = the pooled estimate of σ^2, a measure of the variation within the samples

The formulas for computing MST and MSE are given later in this section.

Recall that in sections 8.5 and 9.3 we used an independent sampling design to compare two population means. In section 8.5 we used large samples and a z statistic; in section 9.3 we used the t statistic with small samples. In this section we again use the independent sampling design to compare more than two population means. But in contrast to our comparisons in sections 8.5 and 9.3, our F test statistic is valid for *both* large samples and small samples (with certain assumptions to be discussed later). This design, the independent sampling design used with more than two treatments, is often called a **completely randomized design**.

Assume that we have p populations with means $\mu_1, \mu_2, \ldots, \mu_p$ and a common variance σ^2. We draw independent random samples, one sample from each population, and compute the mean and variance of each sample. We summarize this procedure in table 11.1. Note that the sample sizes do not have to be equal. We will denote the total sample size by $n(n = n_1 + n_2 + \cdots + n_p)$.

The estimate MST of the variation *between* the treatment means, called the mean square for treatments, is equal to the sum of the squares for treatments (abbreviated SST) divided by the appropriate number of degrees of freedom (the number of treatments minus 1). The formula for computing SST is given in table 11.2.

The estimate MSE of the variation *within* the samples, called the mean square

Table 11.1 • Summary of notation for completely randomized designs

	Treatment 1	Treatment 2	$\cdots$	Treatment p
Population Mean	μ_1	μ_2	$\cdots$	μ_p
Population Variance	σ^2	σ^2	$\cdots$	σ^2

	Sample 1	Sample 2	$\cdots$	Sample p	Total Sample
Sample Size	n_1	n_2	$\cdots$	n_p	n
Sample Total	T_1	T_2	$\cdots$	T_p	$\sum\limits_{i=1}^{n} y_i$
Sample Mean	$\overline{T}_1$	$\overline{T}_2$	$\cdots$	$\overline{T}_p$	$\overline{y}$
Sample Variance	s_1^2	s_2^2	$\cdots$	s_p^2	—

$$\text{sum of squares of all observations: } \sum_{i=1}^{n} y_i^2$$

for error, is equal to the sum of the squares for error (SSE) divided by the appropriate number of degrees of freedom (the total sample size minus the number of treatments). MSE is obtained by pooling the sample variances $s_1^2, s_2^2, \ldots, s_p^2$. However, you will note in table 11.2 that we calculate SSE by subtracting the sum of squares for treatments (SST) from the total sum of squares (Total SS). We are using the partitioning of the total sum of squares introduced in section 11.1 to simplify our calculations. When comparing p treatment means, this partitioning is as shown in figure 11.7.

The formulas for calculating all the quantities in a completely randomized design are given in table 11.2.

We illustrate the calculations needed for the analysis of variance for the completely randomized design in example 11.1.

Figure 11.7 • Partition of the total sum of squares for completely randomized designs

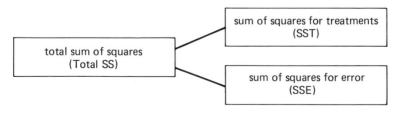

Table 11.2 • Formulas for the calculations in the completely randomized design

CM = correction for mean

$$= \frac{\text{(total of all observations)}^2}{\text{total number of observations}} = \frac{\left(\sum\limits_{i=1}^{n} y_i\right)^2}{n}$$

Total SS = total sum of squares

$$= \text{(sum of squares of each observation)} - CM = \sum\limits_{i=1}^{n} y_i^2 - CM$$

SST = sum of squares for treatments

$$= \left(\begin{array}{c}\text{sum of squares of treatment totals with} \\ \text{each square divided by number of} \\ \text{observations for that treatment}\end{array}\right) - CM$$

$$= \frac{T_1^2}{n_1} + \frac{T_2^2}{n_2} + \cdots + \frac{T_p^2}{n_p} - CM$$

SSE = sum of squares for error

$$= \text{(total sum of squares)} - \text{(sum of squares for treatments)}$$

$$= \text{Total SS} - \text{SST}$$

MST = mean square for treatments

$$= \frac{\text{sum of squares for treatments}}{\text{(number of treatments) minus 1}} = \frac{\text{SST}}{p - 1}$$

MSE = mean square error

$$= \frac{\text{sum of squares for error}}{\text{(total number of observations) minus (number of treatments)}} = \frac{\text{SSE}}{n - p}$$

F = test statistic for research hypothesis that at least

two population means differ

$$= \frac{\text{MST}}{\text{MSE}}$$

Example 11.1

From tape recordings made during therapy, volunteers who participated in one of four different therapy programs were scored for the number of words spoken over a given period of time. Because of recording difficulties, the number of individuals who were scored varied from program to program. The data are presented in table 11.3, and some necessary calculations are given below.

Table 11.3 • Number of words spoken over a given time period by each volunteer in a therapy program

	Therapy Program			
	1	**2**	**3**	**4**
	30	50	18	88
	74	38	56	78
	46	66	34	60
	58	62	24	76
	62	44	66	
	38	58	52	
		80		
n_i	6	7	6	4
T_i	308	398	250	302
$\overline{T}_i$	51.33	56.86	41.67	75.50

$$n = 23$$

$$\sum_{i=1}^{23} y_i = 1258$$

$$\sum_{i=1}^{23} y_i^2 = 76{,}444$$

Calculate the F statistic for testing the research hypothesis that the treatment (therapy program) means differ.

Solution: We follow table 11.2 in performing the calculations.

$$CM = \frac{\left(\sum_{i=1}^{23} y_i\right)^2}{n} = \frac{(1258)^2}{23} = 68{,}807.1$$

$$\text{Total SS} = \sum_{i=1}^{23} y_i^2 - CM = 76{,}444 - 68{,}807.1 = 7636.9$$

$$SST = \frac{T_1^2}{n_1} + \frac{T_2^2}{n_2} + \frac{T_3^2}{n_3} + \frac{T_4^2}{n_4} - CM$$

$$= \frac{(308)^2}{6} + \frac{(398)^2}{7} + \frac{(250)^2}{6} + \frac{(302)^2}{4} - 68{,}807.1$$

$$= 71{,}657.5 - 68{,}807.1 = 2850.4$$

$$SSE = \text{Total SS} - SST = 7636.9 - 2850.4 = 4786.5$$

$$MST = \frac{SST}{p-1} = \frac{2850.4}{4-1} = 950.1$$

$$MSE = \frac{SSE}{n-p} = \frac{4786.5}{23-4} = 251.9$$

$$F = \frac{MST}{MSE} = \frac{950.1}{251.9} = 3.77$$

As we have seen in section 11.3, we will reject the hypothesis that the treatment means are equal when the F statistic is large. Large values of F imply great variation among the p sample means, as measured by MST. Thus if we have fixed the α-value for our test, we will reject the null hypothesis of no difference between population means for

$$\text{Rejection region: } F > F_\alpha$$

F_α is the table value (from tables 6 and 7 in appendix II) with degrees of freedom given by

$$\nu_1 = \text{degrees of freedom associated with MST}$$
$$= \text{denominator of MST} = p - 1$$
$$\nu_2 = \text{degrees of freedom associated with MSE}$$
$$= \text{denominator of MSE} = n - p$$

The rejection region is shown in figure 11.8.

Figure 11.8 • Rejection region for a test of no difference in p population means; $\nu_1 = p - 1$ and $\nu_2 = n - p$

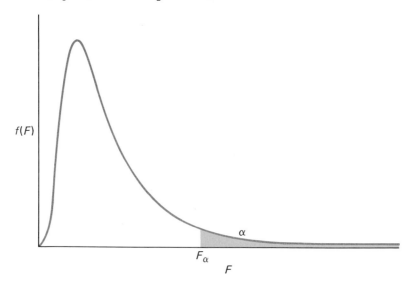

Two assumptions are necessary to make the F test valid for the completely randomized design.

Assumptions: 1. The p populations are normally distributed.
2. The p populations have equal variances.

These assumptions are pictorially depicted in figure 11.9. Of course, the actual location of the five means may be different than shown in figure 11.9.

Figure 11.9 • Assumptions for the F test of equal population means using a completely randomized design with $p = 5$ treatments

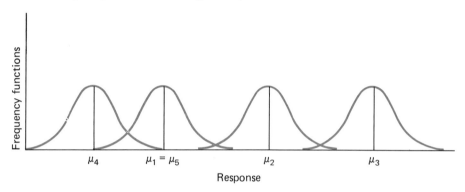

A summary of the procedure for testing the null hypothesis that p treatment means are equal is given in the box.

Test of the Hypothesis that Treatment Means Are Equal for a Completely Randomized Design

Null hypothesis H_0: All treatment means are equal.

Research hypothesis H_a: At least two treatment means differ.

Test statistic: $F = \dfrac{\text{mean square for treatments}}{\text{mean square for errors}} = \dfrac{\text{MST}}{\text{MSE}}$.

Assumptions: 1. All populations are approximately normal.
2. All populations possess a common variance.

Rejection region: Reject H_0 at the α-level of significance when $F > F_\alpha$, where F_α is the table value with degrees of freedom

$\nu_1 = $ (number of treatments) minus $1 = p - 1$

$\nu_2 = $ (total number of observations) minus (number of treatments)

$= n - p$

Example 11.2

Refer to example 11.1. We recorded the number of words spoken over a given period of time for each volunteer participating in one of four therapy programs. Do the data in table 11.3 present sufficient evidence to reject the null hypothesis that the four treatment (therapy program) means are equal? Use $\alpha = .05$.

Solution: We first construct the test.

Null hypothesis H_0: All four therapy programs have the same population mean number of words spoken in the given time interval.

Research hypothesis H_a: At least two of the therapy program means differ.

Test statistic: $F = \dfrac{\text{mean square for treatments}}{\text{mean square for error}} = \dfrac{MST}{MSE}$.

Assumptions: 1. The "words spoken" scores for each therapy program form a normal distribution.
2. The populations of scores for the four therapy programs have equal variances.

Rejection region: $F > F_{.05} = 3.13$, where we use

$$\nu_1 = (\text{number of treatments}) \text{ minus } 1$$
$$= p - 1 = 4 - 1 = 3$$
$$\nu_2 = (\text{total number of observations}) \text{ minus}$$
$$(\text{number of treatments})$$
$$= n - p = 23 - 4 = 19$$

The $F_{.05}$-value for 3 and 19 degrees of freedom, respectively, is found in table 6 to be 3.13.

The calculation of the test statistic F was given in example 11.1, where we found that

$$F = 3.77$$

Since the computed F statistic exceeds $F_{.05} = 3.13$, we reject the null hypothesis. We conclude that the evidence is sufficient to indicate, at the .05 level, that at least two of the therapy programs possess different mean scores for the number of words spoken in a given time period.

EXERCISES

1. State the assumptions underlying the analysis of variance of a completely randomized design.
2. Seitz (1969) hypothesized that mentally retarded subjects would perform better at a task if they were paced at a rate that was slower than the rate they would have paced for themselves. Such information has applications for the education of the mentally retarded. Shown below are the error scores for subjects in three different conditions: self-paced, paced at two seconds before presentation of the next item in a discrimination task, and paced at four seconds before presentation of the next item.

Self-paced	2.4	5.0	4.8	1.8	
Two-second Pacing	4.0	1.8	3.2	3.2	
Four-second Pacing	1.2	.8	.6	1.7	.7

Do these data support the research hypothesis that the population mean error scores differ for at least two of the pacing levels? Use $\alpha = .05$.

11.5 • THE ANALYSIS OF VARIANCE SUMMARY TABLE

The calculations of the analysis of variance are usually displayed in an analysis of variance (ANOVA or AOV) summary table. The summary table for the design of section 11.4 involving p treatment means is shown in table 11.4. The first column shows the source of each sum of squares of the deviations. The second column gives the respective degrees of freedom. The third and fourth columns give the corresponding sums of squares and mean squares, respectively. A calculated value of F, comparing MST and MSE, is usually shown in a fifth column. Note that the degrees of freedom and the sums of squares add to their respective totals.

Table 11.4 • ANOVA summary table for a comparison of means

Source	d.f.	SS	MS	F
Treatment	$p - 1$	SST	$MST = SST/(p - 1)$	MST/MSE
Error	$n - p$	SSE	$MSE = SSE/(n - p)$	
Total	$n - 1$	$\sum_{i=1}^{n} (y_i - \bar{y})^2$		

The ANOVA summary table for the data in examples 11.1 and 11.2 is shown in table 11.5.

Table 11.5 • ANOVA summary table for examples
11.1 and 11.2

Source	d.f.	SS	MS	F
Treatment	3	2850.4	950.1	3.77
Error	19	4786.5	251.9	
Total	22	7636.9		

EXERCISE

1. Refer to exercise 2 in section 11.4. Construct an ANOVA table for the experiment.

11.6 • PAIRWISE COMPARISONS AMONG MEANS IN A COMPLETELY RANDOMIZED DESIGN

If the F test statistic for comparing p treatments in a completely randomized design supports the research hypothesis that a difference exists among the treatment means, the experimenter will probably want to know which of the means are different. That is, the experimenter will want to compare all the pairs of treatment means to determine which pairs are different and which are similar.

Perhaps the simplest method of comparing all the pairs of the p sample means is to use the two-sample t statistic for independent sampling designs (section 9.3). Unfortunately, there is a rather serious drawback in the repeated use of the t statistic for this purpose. Since there will be $[p(p-1)/2]$ pairs of means, we will have to conduct $[p(p-1)/2]$ t tests to compare all the pairs. If we use an α-level of significance for each comparison, the probability of a type I error (rejecting the null hypothesis of no difference between treatments when, in fact, no difference exists) is α for *each* test. However, it can be shown that the probability of making *one or more* type I errors in a series of $[p(p-1)/2]$ such tests will be greater than α. That is, the more tests we conduct, the greater our chance of incorrectly concluding *at least* once that identical treatment means differ. Thus repeated t tests increase the risk of seeing treatment differences which do not exist. What is worse, we do not even know what this overall risk (the probability of making at least one type I error in the series of tests) is for the experiment. Consequently, we seek a test for which we know the overall probability of incorrectly rejecting at least one null hypothesis of no difference between a pair of treatments.

Various multiple-comparison test procedures have been developed to control this sort of cumulative type I error probability. We will limit our discussion to only one of these, the Newman-Keuls pairwise comparison test procedure. This procedure, which is designed to test the significance of all $[p(p-1)/2]$ sample mean differences, is selected for several reasons. It is relatively powerful, yields results that are easily interpreted, and is becoming more and more frequently used in behavioral research. The interpretation of α for the Newman-Keuls procedure is not in terms of the individual tests but in terms of a *protection level* that applies to the entire collection of tests. More specifically, the Newman-Keuls test provides a protection level of $(1-\alpha)$, which implies that the probability of incorrectly rejecting one or more of the null hypotheses does not exceed α.

To conduct the Newman-Keuls pairwise comparison test, we first rank the treatment means in order of magnitude, from smallest to largest. For example, in a completely randomized design with four treatments, we might obtain the ranking

$$\bar{T}_3 < \bar{T}_1 < \bar{T}_4 < \bar{T}_2$$

Then we calculate the Newman-Keuls test statistic.

The Newman-Keuls test statistic for comparing a particular pair of treatment means, μ_i and μ_j, is calculated as shown in the box.

Newman-Keuls Test Statistic

$$q_{r\ (ij)} = \frac{\bar{T}_i - \bar{T}_j}{\sqrt{MSE/\tilde{n}}}$$

when $\bar{T}_i > \bar{T}_j$ and where

$$\tilde{n} = \frac{p}{\dfrac{1}{n_1} + \dfrac{1}{n_2} + \cdots + \dfrac{1}{n_p}}$$

and

r = the number of means spanned from $\bar{T}_i$ to $\bar{T}_j$ in the ranked set of p treatment means

---

The test statistic $q_{r\ (ij)}$ will always be positive since we always subtract the smaller mean from the larger mean in the numerator of $q_{r\ (ij)}$.

We determine the value of r by locating $\bar{T}_i$ and $\bar{T}_j$ in the set of ranked means and counting the number of means spanned, or encompassed, by this pair, including the pair itself. In figure 11.10, r-values are shown for a hypothetical set of $p = 4$ ranked means. Note that r will always be two or more, but it will not exceed p.

Figure 11.10 • Values of r for a set of $p = 4$ ranked means; the vertical lines indicate the pairs being compared

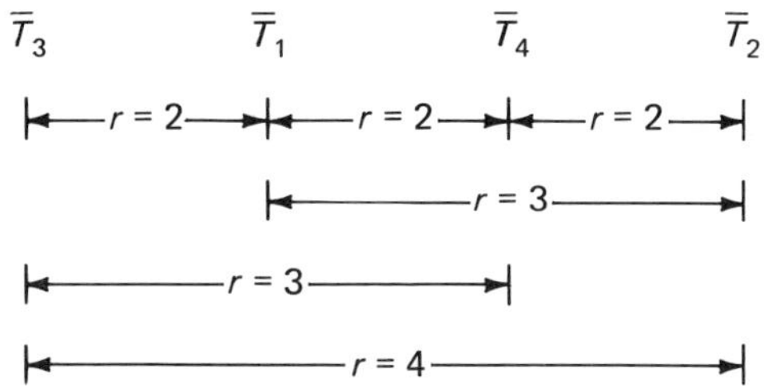

The numbers in parentheses following r in the subscript of $q_{r\ (ij)}$ refer to the treatment numbers $(1, 2, \ldots, p)$ of the pair being compared.

Probably the best way to see how the Newman-Keuls test statistic is computed and used is by working through an example.

Example 11.3

Refer to examples 11.1 and 11.2. We compared the average (mean) number of words spoken for four different therapy programs using a completely randomized design. Recall from example 11.2 that we concluded, on the basis of our F test, that at least two of the population means associated with the therapy programs differed. We are now interested in comparing the pairs of therapy program means to determine specifically which of the programs differ. As a first step, compute the Newman-Keuls test statistic for all $[4(3)/2] = 6$ possible pairs of treatment (therapy program) means. The data are repeated in table 11.6 for your convenience.

Table 11.6 • Number of words spoken over a given time period by each volunteer in a therapy program

	Therapy Program			
	1	2	3	4
	30	50	18	88
	74	38	56	78
	46	66	34	60
	58	62	24	76
	62	44	66	
	38	58	52	
		80		
n_i	6	7	6	4
T_i	308	398	250	302
$\bar{T}_i$	51.33	56.86	41.67	75.50

Solution: We first rank the treatment means in ascending order.

$$\bar{T}_3 \qquad \bar{T}_1 \qquad \bar{T}_2 \qquad \bar{T}_4$$
$$41.67 \qquad 51.33 \qquad 56.86 \qquad 75.50$$

Next, we calculate

$$\tilde{n} = \frac{p}{\dfrac{1}{n_1} + \dfrac{1}{n_2} + \dfrac{1}{n_3} + \dfrac{1}{n_4}} = \frac{4}{\dfrac{1}{6} + \dfrac{1}{7} + \dfrac{1}{6} + \dfrac{1}{4}} = \frac{4}{.726} = 5.51$$

The denominator of all the test statistics is

$$\sqrt{\frac{MSE}{\tilde{n}}} = \sqrt{\frac{251.9}{5.51}} = 6.76$$

We now calculate the Newman-Keuls test statistic for each pair of treatment means. We begin with the most extreme pair and work our way into the middle.

$$q_{4(43)} = \frac{\bar{T}_4 - \bar{T}_3}{\sqrt{MSE/n}} = \frac{75.50 - 41.67}{6.76} = 5.00$$

Note that the subscript of the test statistic $q_{r(\ \ )}$ is 4, because $r = 4$ means are encompassed (spanned) by the pair $(\bar{T}_3, \bar{T}_4)$.

Now we move to the pairs which encompass $r = 3$ means.

$$q_{3(23)} = \frac{\bar{T}_2 - \bar{T}_3}{\sqrt{MSE/n}} = \frac{56.86 - 41.67}{6.76} = 2.25$$

$$q_{3(41)} = \frac{\bar{T}_4 - \bar{T}_1}{\sqrt{MSE/n}} = \frac{75.50 - 51.33}{6.76} = 3.58$$

The rest of the comparisons span only two means ($r = 2$).

$$q_{2(13)} = \frac{\bar{T}_1 - \bar{T}_3}{\sqrt{MSE/n}} = \frac{51.33 - 41.67}{6.76} = 1.43$$

$$q_{2(21)} = \frac{\bar{T}_2 - \bar{T}_1}{\sqrt{MSE/n}} = \frac{56.86 - 51.33}{6.76} = .82$$

$$q_{2(42)} = \frac{\bar{T}_4 - \bar{T}_2}{\sqrt{MSE/n}} = \frac{75.50 - 56.86}{6.76} = 2.76$$

This completes our calculation of the Newman-Keuls test statistic for all six pairs of therapy program means.

The test statistic $q_{r\,(ij)}$ will increase as the difference $(\bar{T}_i - \bar{T}_j)$ increases. Thus large values of $q_{r\,(ij)}$ support the research hypothesis that the population means μ_i and μ_j differ. How large must $q_{r\,(ij)}$ be before we accept this research hypothesis? The answer depends on the table value of the **studentized range statistic** given in table 8 of appendix II. Use of this table requires that we know the three quantities given in the box.

Rejection Region for Newman-Keuls Test

$$q_{r\,(ij)} > q_\alpha$$

where q_α is the studentized range statistic with ν degrees of freedom and where

α = the significance level

r = the number of sample means encompassed by those

being compared

ν = the degrees of freedom associated with MSE = $n - p$

Note that we have only given an upper-tail rejection region since $q_{r\,(ij)}$ will always be positive. As we mentioned before, table values of the studentized range statistic are given in table 8 of appendix II.

Suppose in the hypothetical example depicted in figure 11.10 we are comparing $\bar{T}_1$ and $\bar{T}_2$. Figure 11.10 shows that $r = 3$. Further suppose that we want an *overall* (all comparisons) α-level of .05 and that we have $\nu = 10$ degrees of freedom associated with MSE. We now determine our rejection region by referring to table 8, appendix II, part of which is reproduced in table 11.7.

Table 11.7 • Partial reproduction of table 8 in appendix II

Percentage points of the studentized range, q(r, v)

Upper 5% points

ν \ r	2	3	4	5	6	7	8	9	10
1	17·97	26·98	32·82	37·08	40·41	43·12	45·40	47·36	49·07
2	6·08	8·33	9·80	10·88	11·74	12·44	13·03	13·54	13·99
3	4·50	5·91	6·82	7·50	8·04	8·48	8·85	9·18	9·46
4	3·93	5·04	5·76	6·29	6·71	7·05	7·35	7·60	7·83
5	3·64	4·60	5·22	5·67	6·03	6·33	6·58	6·80	6·99
6	3·46	4·34	4·90	5·30	5·63	5·90	6·12	6·32	6·49
7	3·34	4·16	4·68	5·06	5·36	5·61	5·82	6·00	6·16
8	3·26	4·04	4·53	4·89	5·17	5·40	5·60	5·77	5·92
9	3·20	3·95	4·41	4·76	5·02	5·24	5·43	5·59	5·74
10	3·15	3·88	4·33	4·65	4·91	5·12	5·30	5·46	5·60
11	3·11	3·82	4·26	4·57	4·82	5·03	5·20	5·35	5·49
12	3·08	3·77	4·20	4·51	4·75	4·95	5·12	5·27	5·39
13	3·06	3·73	4·15	4·45	4·69	4·88	5·05	5·19	5·32
14	3·03	3·70	4·11	4·41	4·64	4·83	4·99	5·13	5·25
15	3·01	3·67	4·08	4·37	4·59	4·78	4·94	5·08	5·20
16	3·00	3·65	4·05	4·33	4·56	4·74	4·90	5·03	5·15
17	2·98	3·63	4·02	4·30	4·52	4·70	4·86	4·99	5·11
18	2·97	3·61	4·00	4·28	4·49	4·67	4·82	4·96	5·07
19	2·96	3·59	3·98	4·25	4·47	4·65	4·79	4·92	5·04
20	2·95	3·58	3·96	4·23	4·45	4·62	4·77	4·90	5·01
24	2·92	3·53	3·90	4·17	4·37	4·54	4·68	4·81	4·92
30	2·89	3·49	3·85	4·10	4·30	4·46	4·60	4·72	4·82
40	2·86	3·44	3·79	4·04	4·23	4·39	4·52	4·63	4·73
60	2·83	3·40	3·74	3·98	4·16	4·31	4·44	4·55	4·65
120	2·80	3·36	3·68	3·92	4·10	4·24	4·36	4·47	4·56
∞	2·77	3·31	3·63	3·86	4·03	4·17	4·29	4·39	4·47

Notice that the α-level is given in italics at the top of the table: "*Upper 5% points.*" The *r*-values are the columns of the table, and the ν values are the rows. We find the column corresponding to $r = 3$ and the row corresponding to $\nu = 10$. The value in this row and column is $q_{.05} = 3.88$, shown by the shading in table 11.7. If the test statistic $q_{3(21)}$ exceeds 3.88, the data supports the research hypothesis that the population mean associated with treatment 2 exceeds that associated with treatment 1. We can similarly test every pair of means in our hypothetical example, and our overall protection level is $\alpha = .05$. However, the *r*-value and thus the rejection region will vary from test to test. We summarize the Newman-Keuls pairwise comparison test in the box.

Summary of the Newman-Keuls Pairwise Comparison Test of Treatment i with Treatment j for a Completely Randomized Design

Null hypothesis H_0: The population mean associated with treatment i equals the population mean for treatment j $(\mu_i - \mu_j = 0)$.

Research hypothesis H_a: The population mean associated with treatment i exceeds that for treatment j $(\mu_i - \mu_j > 0)$.

Test statistic:

$$q_{r\,(ij)} = \frac{\overline{T}_i - \overline{T}_j}{\sqrt{MSE/\tilde{n}}}$$

where $\overline{T}_i > \overline{T}_j$ and

$$\tilde{n} = \frac{p}{\dfrac{1}{n_1} + \dfrac{1}{n_2} + \cdots + \dfrac{1}{n_p}}$$

Rejection region: $q_{r\,(ij)} > q_\alpha$, where q_α is a table studentized range value corresponding to the α-level of significance, with

$\nu =$ the degrees of freedom for MSE $= n - p$

$r =$ the number of means encompassed by $\overline{T}_i$ and $\overline{T}_j$

The assumptions necessary for the Newman-Keuls procedure are identical to those made for the F test of equal treatment means in the completely randomized design. All p populations must be normal with equal variances. Since the F test will have preceded the Newman-Keuls in any experiment, we do not repeat the assumptions each time the Newman-Keuls procedure is applied.

One important point remains to be considered: the sequence in which we test the pairs of means. We summarize the sequence of application for the Newman-Keuls test in the box.

Sequence of Application for the Newman-Keuls Test

1. Begin by testing the most extreme pair of means in the ranking.
   (a) If a nonrejection of the null hypothesis is indicated, draw a solid line under *all* p means and stop. The data do not indicate that *any* pair of population means differ. (This will rarely occur if the F test supports the research hypothesis of different treatment means.)
   (b) If a rejection of the null hypothesis results, proceed to step 2.
2. Test the two pairs which span $(p - 1)$ means. *From this point on, underline all pairs which result in a nonrejection, and do not test any other pairs spanned by such lines.*

If either or both of these tests result in a rejection, we proceed to test, at the next r-level ($p - 2$), any pairs which are not yet connected by a single solid line. This is continued until *every* pair is *either* connected by a single solid line or has been determined to be different.

3. Our conclusion is that all pairs of treatment means *unconnected* by a single solid line are different in the population. The data *do not* indicate that pairs connected by a line are different. The *entire* conclusion is made at the chosen level of significance, α.

This procedure will be made clearer by working an example.

Example 11.4

Refer to examples 11.1 through 11.3. We are analyzing a completely randomized design comparing four therapy programs. We have determined that at least two of the four programs differ with respect to the average number of words spoken in a given time period.

Now compare the pairs of treatment means by conducting the Newman-Keuls test procedure. Use $\alpha = .05$.

Solution: The proper sequence of application begins with a comparison of the two most extreme means in the ranking of the sample means.

$$\begin{array}{cccc} \overline{T}_3 & \overline{T}_1 & \overline{T}_2 & \overline{T}_4 \\ 41.67 & 51.33 & 56.86 & 75.50 \end{array}$$

Our test setup is as follows:

Null hypothesis H_0: The population mean associated with Therapy Program 4 is equal to the mean associated with Therapy Program 3 ($\mu_4 - \mu_3 = 0$).

Research hypothesis H_a: The population mean associated with Therapy Program 4 exceeds that for Therapy Program 3 ($\mu_4 - \mu_3 > 0$).

Test statistic: $q_{4(43)} = \dfrac{\overline{T}_4 - \overline{T}_3}{\sqrt{MSE/n}}$

Rejection region: $q_{4(43)} > q_{.05} = 3.98$, where $r = 4$ and the degrees of freedom for MSE are

$$\nu = n - p = 23 - 4 = 19$$

From example 11.3, where all the Newman-Keuls test statistics were calculated, we have

$$q_{4(43)} = 5.00$$

Thus the data support the research hypothesis that $\mu_4 > \mu_3$. We therefore proceed to the next step of the procedure *without* connecting any of the means by a line.

The next step is to test the means for which $r = 3$, that is, the pairs of means which span a total of three sample means. These tests are conducted side by side below.

H_0: $\mu_2 - \mu_3 = 0$

H_a: $\mu_2 - \mu_3 > 0$

T.S.: $q_{3(23)} = \dfrac{\bar{T}_2 - \bar{T}_3}{\sqrt{MSE/\tilde{n}}}$

R.R.: $q_{3(23)} > q_{.05} = 3.59$

$(r = 3, \nu = 19)$

From example 11.3,

$q_{3(23)} = 2.25$

H_0: $\mu_4 - \mu_1 = 0$

H_a: $\mu_4 - \mu_1 > 0$

T.S.: $q_{3(41)} = \dfrac{\bar{T}_4 - \bar{T}_1}{\sqrt{MSE/\tilde{n}}}$

R.R.: $q_{3(41)} > q_{.05} = 3.59$

$(r = 3, \nu = 19)$

From example 11.3,

$q_{3(41)} = 3.58$

Neither test presents sufficient evidence at the .05 level to support the research hypothesis that the pair of treatment means differ. Thus we connect each pair by a separate solid line.

$$\bar{T}_3 \quad \bar{T}_1 \quad \bar{T}_2 \quad \bar{T}_4$$

$$\underline{\phantom{\bar{T}_3 \quad \bar{T}_1 \quad \bar{T}_2 \quad \bar{T}_4}} \quad (41)$$

$$(23) \quad \underline{}$$

Note that each pair of means which remains to be tested [(42), (21), (13)] is now connected by one of the two lines. We therefore need not conduct further tests.

The only unconnected pair (by a *single* line) is $\bar{T}_3$ and $\bar{T}_4$ (because $q_{4(43)} > q_{.05}$). So our final conclusion is that the true average number of words spoken using Therapy Program 4 exceeds that for Therapy Program 3. There is insufficient evidence to conclude that any other pair of therapy program means differ. This conclusion has an overall significance level of $\alpha = .05$.

EXERCISES

1. Refer to exercise 2 in section 11.4. You tested the research hypothesis that the mean error scores for mentally retarded subjects would differ for three different task-pacing rates. The data are repeated below.

Self-paced	2.4	5.0	4.8	1.8	
Two-second Pacing	4.0	1.8	3.2	3.2	
Four-second Pacing	1.2	.8	.6	1.7	.7

Use the Newman-Keuls procedure to conduct a pairwise comparison of the $[3(2)/2] = 3$ pairs of means. Present your results by showing a ranking of the three means, underscoring those that the data do not indicate as different. Follow this by a written conclusion. (See example 11.4 for a sample of this format.)

2. To compare the effects of four dosage levels of a central nervous system stimulant on avoidance response latency, an experiment is conducted using 12 rats of a particular

strain. Three are selected at random from the 12 and are used as controls; that is, they are administered a simple saline solution. Three are taken at random from the remaining 9 rats and are administered a 5-mg/kg dose of the stimulant. Of the remaining 6, 3 are assigned randomly to a 10-mg/kg treatment condition and the last 3 are administered a 20-mg/kg dose of the stimulant. A measurement of latency of avoidance response to a shock stimulus is then taken for each of the 12 animals and the following results obtained.

Control	5 mg/kg	10 mg/kg	20 mg/kg
15.0	5.9	3.9	2.8
13.3	6.2	4.8	3.5
18.2	4.7	3.9	4.2

Assuming that the requirements for a completely randomized design are met, analyze the data. State whether there is statistical support, at the $\alpha = .05$ level of significance, for the conclusion that two or more of the four dosage levels have different effects on avoidance response latency.

3. Refer to exercise 2. Use the Newman-Keuls pairwise comparison procedure to test the significance of all $[(4)(3)/2] = 6$ pairs of sample mean differences. Present your results as described in exercise 1. Use $\alpha = .05$.

11.7 · THE RANDOMIZED BLOCK DESIGN

The randomized block design is a generalization of the matched pairs design, section 9.4. The purpose of the randomized block design is to compare two or more treatments within blocks of relatively homogeneous material. Thus in section 9.4, two treatments (program versus control) were compared for their effects on beginning reading age within blocks consisting of identical twins.

The major reason for using a randomized block design is to reduce the standard deviation of the experimental error. The confidence interval for comparing means increases or decreases as the value of s increases or decreases, where s is the estimated standard deviation of the experimental error. Therefore, a reduction in σ would be expected to lead to a decrease in the value of s and to a narrower confidence interval, indicating an increase in information from the experiment. Thus the randomized block design is, in the terminology of chapter 10, a noise-reducing design, because its use tends to produce a reduction in sample variability, or noise.

Experimental error arises from a number of sources, including differences between subjects, within-subject variations in physical and emotional state, failure to reproduce exactly a given stimulus in repeated administrations, and errors of measurement. Reduction of any of these causes of error will increase the information in an experiment.

We illustrate how subject-to-subject variation can be reduced by using subjects as blocks and also demonstrate the difference between the completely randomized and a randomized block design by considering this experiment. Four stimulus intensities (treatments) are compared for their effects on a given response. We will denote the treatments as S_1, S_2, S_3, and S_4.

Suppose that 10 subjects are randomly assigned to each of the four treatments. Random assignment of subjects to treatments (or vice versa) randomly distributes errors due to person-to-person variability to the four treatments. This yields four samples that are, for all practical purposes, random and independent. This is a completely randomized experimental design and requires the analysis of sections 11.3 and 11.4.

If, instead, we use a randomized block design with subjects as blocks, each subject would receive each of the four treatments assigned in a random sequence. The resulting design is shown in figure 11.11. Now only 10 subjects are required to get 10 response measurements per treatment. Note that each treatment occurs exactly once in each block.

Figure 11.11 • Randomized block design: 10 blocks (subjects) and 4 treatments (stimulus intensities, S_1, S_2, S_3, S_4)

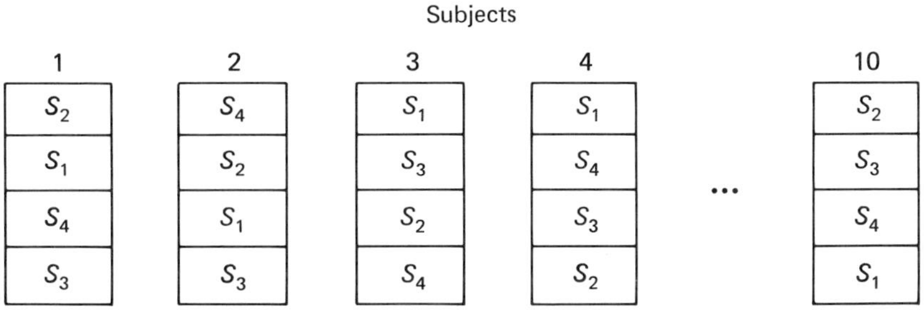

Subjects

1	2	3	4		10
S_2	S_4	S_1	S_1		S_2
S_1	S_2	S_3	S_4	...	S_3
S_4	S_1	S_2	S_3		S_4
S_3	S_3	S_4	S_2		S_1

The word "randomized" in the name of the design implies that the treatments are randomly assigned within a block. For our experiment, the position in the block would pertain to the position in the sequence when assigning the stimuli to a given subject. The purpose of the randomization (that is, the position in the block) is to eliminate bias caused by such carry-over effects as practice or fatigue.

As indicated in section 9.4, the purpose of blocking is to control "nuisance" variables, those which influence the dependent variable but whose effects are not of primary interest. Thus blocks may represent time, location, or experimental material—any source of variation in the dependent variable that is not associated with the independent variables of interest. We wish to use an experimental design that removes this component of experimental error variation. The objective of the randomized block design is to reduce the experimental error attributable to nuisance variables.

11.8 • THE ANALYSIS OF VARIANCE FOR A RANDOMIZED BLOCK DESIGN

Although we are now employing a randomized block design instead of a completely randomized design, our objective remains the same. We wish to compare the means of the populations associated with the p treatments. As you might expect, the calculations are affected by the change of experimental design. However, the structure of our hypothesis test and the form of our test statistic are the same, regardless of which experimental design is employed.

Suppose we conduct a randomized block design experiment with p treatments and b blocks. This design is shown in figure 11.12, with the treatments shown in numerical order, rather than in randomized order, for convenience of presentation. The treatments are denoted by the letter C as a reminder that each treatment is a combination of factor levels.

Figure 11.12 • Randomized block design with p treatments and, b blocks (the treatments are denoted by the letter C)

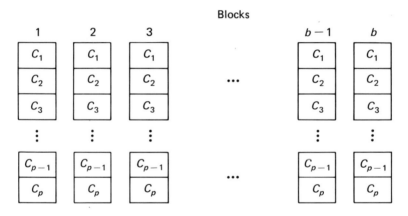

Note that one experimental unit is assigned to each of the $p \times b$ treatment block combinations, so that we have $p \times b$ total observations. Thus if we have 3 treatments in 4 blocks, we get a total of $3 \times 4 = 12$ observations. Also note that each treatment is observed exactly b times, once in each block, and that each block contains exactly p observations, one for each treatment.

We summarize the notation used for randomized block designs in table 11.8. Our primary objective is to test the null hypothesis

H_0: All p treatment population means are equal

against the research hypothesis

H_a: At least two of the treatment means are different

Table 11.8 • Summary of notation for randomized block designs

	Treatment 1	Treatment 2	. . .	Treatment p
Sample Size	b	b	. . .	b
Sample Total	T_1	T_2	. . .	T_p
Sample Mean	$\overline{T}_1$	$\overline{T}_2$	. . .	$\overline{T}_p$
	Block 1	**Block 2**	. . .	**Block b**
Sample Size	p	p	. . .	p
Sample Total	B_1	B_2	. . .	B_p
Sample Mean	$\overline{B}_1$	$\overline{B}_2$	. . .	$\overline{B}_p$

total of all observations: $\sum_{i=1}^{n} y_i$

total number of observations: $n = bp$

mean of all observations: $\overline{y}$

sum of squares of all observations: $\sum_{i=1}^{n} y_i^2$

The appropriate test statistic is identical in form to that used with the completely randomized design.

$$\text{Test statistic: } F = \frac{\text{mean square for treatments}}{\text{mean square for error}} = \frac{\text{MST}}{\text{MSE}}$$

The calculation formula of MST is unchanged from the completely randomized design. Also unchanged is the fact that in order to calculate MSE, we must first compute SSE. Recall that in section 11.4 we found SSE by subtracting the sum of squares for treatments (SST) from the total sum of squares (Total SS) for the completely randomized design. We are now employing the randomized block design to reduce SSE by separating the variability due to blocks from the variability due to random error, and this is reflected in our calculations. We now subtract *both* the sum of squares for treatments (SST) *and* the sum of squares for blocks (SSB) from the total sum of squares. The partitioning of the total sum of squares is shown in figure 11.13.

The increase in information (due to a reduction in the error sum of squares) obtained by using the randomized block design instead of a completely randomized design is accompanied by a corresponding loss. **The degrees of freedom for the randomized block SSE will be less than for the corresponding completely randomized design. Usually the gain in information obtained by blocking will more than compensate for the loss in the degrees of freedom.**

Figure 11.13 • Partitioning the total sum of squares for the randomized block design

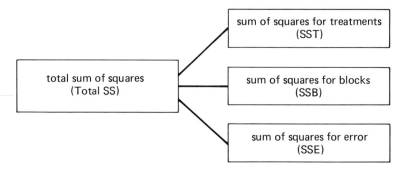

The formulas for calculating all the quantities in the randomized block design are given in table 11.9.

We illustrate the calculations for the randomized block design with an example.

Example 11.5

A researcher wishes to compare mean reaction times for three different visual stimuli. She decides to control subject-to-subject variability by using only 4 subjects in a randomized block design. Each subject (block) is administered the three stimuli in a random order and the reaction time is recorded for each stimulus. The design and the data are shown in figure 11.14.

Figure 11.14 • Reaction times to three visual stimuli: A randomized block design

Subjects

1	2	3	4
S_1 1.7	S_3 2.1	S_1 .1	S_2 2.2
S_3 2.3	S_1 1.5	S_2 2.3	S_1 .6
S_2 3.4	S_2 2.6	S_3 .8	S_3 1.6

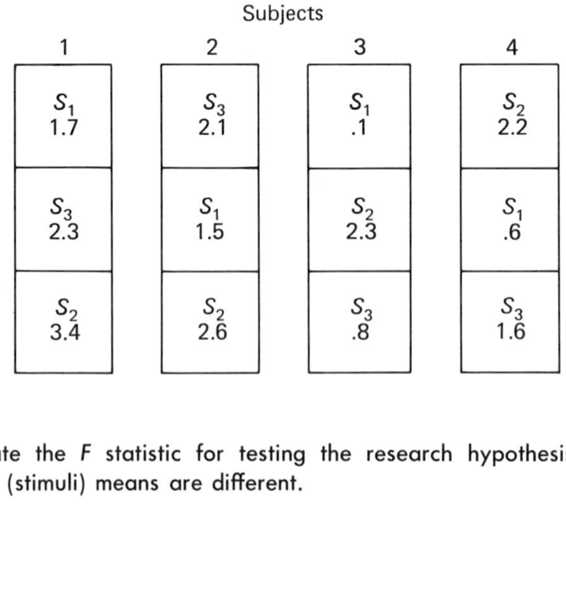

Calculate the F statistic for testing the research hypothesis that the treatment (stimuli) means are different.

Table 11.9 • Formulas for the calculations in the randomized block design

---

$$\text{CM} = \text{correction for mean} = \frac{(\text{total of all observations})^2}{\text{total number of observations}} = \frac{\left(\sum\limits_{i=1}^{n} y_i\right)^2}{n}$$

Total SS = total sum of squares

$$= \text{sum of squares of all observations} - \text{CM} = \sum_{i=1}^{n} y_i^2 - \text{CM}$$

SST = sum of squares for treatments

$$= \left(\begin{array}{c}\text{sum of squares of treatment totals with each square divided} \\ \text{by } b, \text{ the number of observations for each treatment}\end{array}\right) - \text{CM}$$

$$= \frac{T_1^2}{b} + \frac{T_2^2}{b} + \cdots + \frac{T_p^2}{b} - \text{CM}$$

SSB = sum of squares for blocks

$$= \left(\begin{array}{c}\text{sum of squares for block totals with each square divided} \\ \text{by } p, \text{ the number of observations in each block}\end{array}\right) - \text{CM}$$

$$= \frac{B_1^2}{p} + \frac{B_2^2}{p} + \cdots + \frac{B_b^2}{p} - \text{CM}$$

SSE = sum of squares for error

$$= (\text{total sum of squares}) - (\text{sum of squares for treatments})$$
$$- (\text{sum of squares for blocks})$$

$$= \text{Total SS} - \text{SST} - \text{SSB}$$

MST = mean square for treatments

$$= \frac{\text{sum of squares for treatments}}{(\text{number of treatments}) \text{ minus } 1} = \frac{\text{SST}}{p - 1}$$

MSB = mean square for blocks

$$= \frac{\text{sum of squares for blocks}}{(\text{number of blocks}) \text{ minus } 1} = \frac{\text{SSB}}{b - 1}$$

MSE = mean square for error

$$= \frac{\text{sum of squares for error}}{\left(\begin{array}{c}\text{total number} \\ \text{of observations}\end{array}\right) \text{minus} \left(\begin{array}{c}\text{number of} \\ \text{treatments}\end{array}\right) \text{minus} \left(\begin{array}{c}\text{number of} \\ \text{blocks}\end{array}\right) \text{plus } 1}$$

$$= \frac{\text{SSE}}{n - p - b + 1}$$

F = test statistic for research hypothesis that at least
two population means differ

$$= \frac{\text{MST}}{\text{MSE}}$$

Solution: Table 11.10 shows the results of computing the basic quantities for the randomized block design.

Table 11.10 • Basic calculations for the visual stimuli experiment in example 11.5

	Treatments		
	Stimulus 1	**Stimulus 2**	**Stimulus 3**
Totals	3.9	10.5	6.8
Means	$3.9/4 = .975$	$10.5/4 = 2.625$	$6.8/4 = 1.700$

	Blocks			
	Subject 1	**Subject 2**	**Subject 3**	**Subject 4**
Totals	7.4	6.2	3.2	4.4
Means	$7.4/3 = 2.467$	$6.2/3 = 2.067$	$3.2/3 = 1.067$	$4.4/3 = 1.467$

total of all observations: 21.2
total of squares of all observations: 46.86
mean of all observations: $21.2/12 = 1.767$

Using tables 11.9 and 11.10 we can proceed as follows through the calculations necessary to compute the F statistic.

$$CM = \frac{\left(\sum_{i=1}^{12} y_i\right)^2}{12} = \frac{(21.2)^2}{12} = 37.45$$

$$\text{Total SS} = \sum_{i=1}^{12} y_i^2 - CM = 46.86 - 37.45 = 9.41$$

$$SST = \frac{T_1^2}{4} + \frac{T_2^2}{4} + \frac{T_3^2}{4} - CM$$

$$= \frac{(3.9)^2}{4} + \frac{(10.5)^2}{4} + \frac{(6.8)^2}{4} - 37.45$$

$$= 42.93 - 37.45 = 5.48$$

$$SSB = \frac{B_1^2}{3} + \frac{B_2^2}{3} + \frac{B_3^2}{3} + \frac{B_4^2}{3} - CM$$

$$= \frac{(7.4)^2}{3} + \frac{(6.2)^2}{3} + \frac{(3.2)^2}{3} + \frac{(4.4)^2}{3} - 37.45$$

$$= 40.93 - 37.45 = 3.48$$

$$SSE = \text{Total SS} - SST - SSB = 9.41 - 5.48 - 3.48 = .45$$

$$MST = \frac{SST}{p-1} = \frac{5.48}{3-1} = 2.74$$

$$MSB = \frac{SSB}{b - 1} = \frac{3.48}{4 - 1} = 1.16$$

$$MSE = \frac{SSE}{n - p - b + 1} = \frac{.45}{12 - 3 - 4 + 1} = .075$$

The required F statistic is

$$F = \frac{MST}{MSE} = \frac{2.74}{.075} = 36.53$$

Large values of F support the research hypothesis that the treatment means differ. If we choose α as our significance level, we establish the rejection region as follows:

$$\text{Rejection region: } F > F_\alpha$$

F_α is the table value corresponding to α, with the following degrees of freedom:

$$\nu_1 = \text{denominator of MST} = p - 1$$

$$\nu_2 = \text{denominator of MSE} = n - p - b + 1$$

The assumptions for this test are unchanged from the completely randomized design. A summary of the test is given in the box.

Test of the Hypothesis that Treatment Means Are Equal for a Randomized Block Design

Null hypothesis H_0: All treatment means are equal.

Research hypothesis H_a: At least two treatment means differ.

Test statistic: $F = \dfrac{\text{mean square for treatments}}{\text{mean square for error}} = \dfrac{MST}{MSE}$.

Assumptions: 1. All populations are approximately normal.
2. The variances of all the populations are equal.

Rejection region: Reject H_0 at the α-level of significance when $F > F_\alpha$, where F_α is the table value with degrees of freedom

$$\nu_1 = (\text{number of treatments}) \text{ minus } 1 = p - 1$$

$$\nu_2 = (\text{total number of observations}) \text{ minus}$$
$$(\text{number of treatments}) \text{ minus}$$
$$(\text{number of blocks}) \text{ plus } 1$$

$$= n - p - b + 1$$

Example 11.6

Refer to example 11.5. An experimenter used a randomized block design to compare mean reaction times to three visual stimuli. Do the data in that example provide sufficient evidence to reject the null hypothesis that the true mean reaction time is the same for all three stimuli? Use $\alpha = .01$.

Solution: The test construction is our first task.

Null hypothesis H_0: The population mean reaction times are the same for the three stimuli.

Research hypothesis H_a: At least two of the stimuli have different population mean reaction times.

Test statistic: $F = \dfrac{\text{mean square for treatments}}{\text{mean square for error}} = \dfrac{MST}{MSE}$.

Assumptions: 1. The reaction times form normal populations.
2. The variances of the reaction time populations corresponding to all subject-stimulus combinations are equal.

Rejection region: $F > F_{.01} = 10.92$, where we use

$$\nu_1 = p - 1 = 3 - 1 = 2$$
$$\nu_2 = n - p - b + 1$$
$$= 12 - 3 - 4 + 1 = 6$$

Table 7 in appendix II shows that the $F_{.01}$-value for 2 and 6 degrees of freedom, respectively, is 10.92. The calculation of our F test statistic was performed in example 11.5.

$$F = 36.53$$

Our computed value greatly exceeds the $\alpha = .01$ F-value of 10.92. There is overwhelming evidence that the population mean reaction times are *not* the same for the three stimuli.

You may have noticed that we gave the formula for the mean square for blocks (MSB) in table 11.9, although we have not used this value in any of our calculations. This quantity is a measure of the variation among the block means, and it may be of interest to examine this measure more closely. If the data indicate that block-to-block variability is large, then designing a randomized block experiment was worth the effort, having significantly reduced the error of variability. On the other hand, if MSB is small, we may wonder whether blocking is necessary in future similar experiments, since the data indicate that not much reduction in error variability is obtained by employing a randomized block design.

A test of the research hypothesis that the block population means differ is constructed exactly like that for treatments, except that we now switch the roles of blocks and treatments. A summary of this test is given in the box.

Test of the Hypothesis that Block Means Are Equal for a Randomized Block Design

Null hypothesis H_0: All block means are equal.

Research hypothesis H_a: At least two block means differ.

Test statistic: $F = \dfrac{\text{mean square for blocks}}{\text{mean square for error}} = \dfrac{\text{MSB}}{\text{MSE}}$.

Assumptions: 1. All populations are approximately normal.
2. The variances of all populations are equal.

Rejection region: Reject H_0 at the α-level of significance when $F > F_\alpha$, where F_α is the table value with degrees of freedom

$$\nu_1 = (\text{number of blocks}) \text{ minus } 1 = b - 1$$
$$\nu_2 = n - p - b + 1$$

Example 11.7

Refer to examples 11.5 and 11.6. A randomized block design was used to compare mean reaction times to three visual stimuli. Test to see if the data support the research hypothesis that population mean reaction times differ for the 4 subjects, that is, that the 4 block means differ. Use $\alpha = .05$.

Solution: Our test is constructed as follows.

Null hypothesis H_0: The population mean reaction times are the same for the four subjects.

Research hypothesis H_a: At least two subjects have different mean reaction times.

Test statistic: $F = \dfrac{\text{mean square for blocks}}{\text{mean square for error}} = \dfrac{\text{MSB}}{\text{MSE}}$.

Assumptions: Same as in example 11.6.

Rejection region: $F > F_{.05} = 4.76$, where we use

$$\nu_1 = b - 1 = 4 - 1 = 3$$
$$\nu_2 = n - b - p + 1$$
$$= 12 - 4 - 3 + 1 = 6$$

In example 11.5, we calculated MSB $= 1.16$ and MSE $= .075$, so that

$$F = \frac{\text{MSB}}{\text{MSE}} = \frac{1.16}{.075} = 15.47$$

The data support the research hypothesis of different subject mean reaction times at the $\alpha = .05$ level. In fact, the $F_{.01}$-value is found to be 9.78 in Table 7 of appendix II. So the significance level P associated with this result is less than .01 ($P < .01$).

There is strong evidence of subject-to-subject variability. Our decision to use the randomized block design was well founded.

The analysis of variance (ANOVA) table provides a convenient summary of the calculations for a randomized block design. It is shown for the general case in table 11.11.

Table 11.11 • ANOVA summary table for a randomized block design

Source	d.f.	SS	MS	F
Treatment	$p - 1$	SST	$SST/(p - 1)$	MST/MSE
Blocks	$b - 1$	SSB	$SSB/(b - 1)$	MSB/MSE
Error	$n - p - b + 1$	SSE	$SSE/(n - p - b + 1)$	
Total	$n - 1$	Total SS		

For our reaction time example, the ANOVA table would appear as in table 11.12.

Table 11.12 • ANOVA summary table for the reaction time experiment of examples 11.5, 11.6, and 11.7

Source	d.f.	SS	MS	F
Treatments	2	5.48	2.74	36.53
Blocks	3	3.48	1.16	15.47
Error	6	.45	.075	
Total	11	9.41		

We end our discussion of randomized block designs with several important comments. The experimenter should be very wary of concluding that blocking is unimportant for a certain type of experiment just because the F test for blocks proved nonsignificant at some α-level on one particular occasion. This is equivalent to accepting a null hypothesis, which we have carefully avoided in all our hypothesis testing. To repeat a point made several times before, our data either support the research hypothesis at some specified α-level or they do not. If the data do not support the research hypothesis, we do not conclude that our research hypothesis is untrue or that the null hypothesis is true. We conclude only that the data do not provide sufficient evidence to decide whether or not the research hypothesis is true.

Our final comment concerns the assumptions necessary for the analysis of both completely randomized and randomized block designs. We have previously mentioned that empirical evidence collected over the decades lends support to the assumption of normality. It is a fact that many measured variables possess mound-shaped distributions. However, the assumption of equal variances is more critical. When data exhibit very different within-sample variances, the use of the F statistic may lead to erroneous conclusions. There are various methods for coping with such situations, but, unfortunately, these are beyond the scope of this text.

EXERCISES

1. It is commonly thought that certain colors impart apparent warmth and coolness and, in fact, that physiology has something to do with this phenomenon. Morgan, Goodson, and Jones (1975) conducted a study to see whether it is physiology or cultural norms that causes associations between certain colors and certain temperatures. Subjects were presented with different color stimuli and were asked to state whether each reminded them of hot, warm, cold, or cool. Within a series of trials of presentations of the colors, the number of times a particular color was matched with the same temperature stimulus was recorded. The data obtained were as follows.

Color Stimuli	Subjects							
	1	2	3	4	5	6	7	8
A	3	1	1	5	3	8	2	3
B	6	5	7	4	5	3	7	6
C	3	2	2	1	1	4	3	2
D	8	1	1	6	2	2	1	3

   (a) Give the type of design employed for this experiment and justify your diagnosis.
   (b) Do the data provide sufficient evidence to reject the null hypothesis that the mean matching score is the same for the four color stimuli? Test using $\alpha = .05$.
   (c) Summarize your calculations in an ANOVA table.

2. Refer to exercise 1. Do the data support the research hypothesis that blocking was worthwhile in this experiment? That is, is there evidence that mean matching scores vary from subject to subject? Use $\alpha = .05$.

3. A questionnaire was constructed to enable judges to evaluate a certain aspect of observed classroom teaching. Four films portraying teaching performances, and differing markedly in the teaching characteristic under study, were viewed by each of 8 judges. The order of viewing the four films was assigned in a random manner to each judge. The data obtained were scores given the films by the judges; the data are presented below.

Films	Judges							
	1	2	3	4	5	6	7	8
1	9	10	7	5	12	7	8	6
2	4	9	3	0	6	8	2	4
3	12	16	10	9	11	10	10	14
4	9	11	7	8	12	7	7	8

   (a) Do the data provide sufficient evidence to indicate that the mean questionnaire score varies from film to film? Test using $\alpha = .05$.
   (b) Summarize your calculations in an ANOVA table.
   (c) Suppose that the data did provide sufficient evidence to indicate differences among the mean questionnaire scores for the four films. Would this imply that the

questionnaire was able to detect a difference in the teaching characteristic exhibited in the four films?

4. Refer to exercise 3. Do the data support the decision to employ a randomized block design rather than a completely randomized design? Test to see whether the mean scores vary from judge to judge. Use $\alpha = .05$.

11.9 • PAIRWISE COMPARISONS AMONG MEANS IN A RANDOMIZED BLOCK DESIGN

Just as with the completely randomized design, if the randomized block design yields data which indicate that the treatment means are different, we will probably want to conduct pairwise comparisons to determine specifically which pairs of treatments are different. The Newman-Keuls procedure is again appropriate, providing a pairwise comparison procedure with an overall risk α of finding one or more differences when, in fact, those differences do not exist.

As before, we first rank the p treatment (sample) means in ascending order. Then if we wish to compare the pair of population means (μ_i, μ_j), we use the test structure summarized in the box.

Summary of the Newman-Keuls Pairwise Comparison Test for a Randomized Block Design

Null hypothesis H_0: The population mean associated with treatment i equals the population mean associated with treatment j ($\mu_i - \mu_j = 0$).

Research hypothesis H_a: The population mean associated with treatment i exceeds that associated with treatment j ($\mu_i - \mu_j > 0$).

Test statistic: $q_{r\,(ij)} = \dfrac{\bar{T}_i - \bar{T}_j}{\sqrt{MSE/b}}$, when $\bar{T}_i > \bar{T}_j$, and where r is the number of means spanned by $\bar{T}_i$ and $\bar{T}_j$, and b is the number of observations for each treatment (also, b is the number of blocks).

Assumptions: 1. All treatment response populations are normally distributed.
2. The populations have equal variances.

Rejection region: $q_{r\,(ij)} > q_\alpha$, where q_α is a table value corresponding to a significance level of α and ν is the number of degrees of freedom for MSE, or

$$\nu = n - p - b + 1$$

The sequence of the test application is also identical to that for the completely randomized design. We first test the most extreme means, moving from there to the next most extreme pairs, and so on. Each time a test results in a nonrejection of the null hypothesis of equality of means, we connect the two means by a solid line and test no other pair which is connected by this line.

Example 11.8

Refer to examples 11.5 and 11.6. We used a randomized block design to test the research hypothesis that at least two of the population mean reaction times corresponding to the three visual stimuli would differ. We were able to decisively conclude that this research hypothesis was supported by the data.

Use the Newman-Keuls pairwise comparison procedure to decide which of the visual stimuli produce different mean reaction times. Use $\alpha = .01$.

Solution: We first rank the treatment means. (Refer to table 11.10.)

$$\overline{T}_1 \qquad\qquad \overline{T}_3 \qquad\qquad \overline{T}_2$$
$$.975 \qquad\qquad 1.700 \qquad\qquad 2.625$$

Our first test is of the most extreme pair.

Null hypothesis H_0: The population mean reaction times corresponding to visual stimuli 1 and 2 are equal ($\mu_2 - \mu_1 = 0$).

Research hypothesis H_a: The population mean reaction time for visual stimulus 2 exceeds that for visual stimulus 1 ($\mu_2 - \mu_1 > 0$).

Test statistic: $q_{3(21)} = \dfrac{\overline{T}_2 - \overline{T}_1}{\sqrt{MSE/b}}$.

Rejection region: $q_{3(21)} > q_{.01} = 6.33$, using

$$r = 3$$
$$\nu = n - p - b + 1$$
$$= 12 - 3 - 4 + 1 = 6$$

We now calculate

$$q_{3(21)} = \frac{\overline{T}_2 - \overline{T}_1}{\sqrt{MSE/b}} = \frac{2.625 - .975}{\sqrt{.075/4}} = \frac{1.65}{.137} = 12.04$$

The data support the research hypothesis that the true mean reaction time for visual stimulus 2 exceeds that for stimulus 1.

We proceed to the next (and last) level of the test, testing all the pairs spanning $r = 2$ means (neighbors).

$H_0: \mu_3 - \mu_1 = 0$	$H_0: \mu_2 - \mu_3 = 0$
$H_a: \mu_3 - \mu_1 > 0$	$H_a: \mu_2 - \mu_3 > 0$
T.S.: $q_{2(31)} = \dfrac{\overline{T}_3 - \overline{T}_1}{\sqrt{MSE/b}}$	T.S.: $q_{2(23)} = \dfrac{\overline{T}_2 - \overline{T}_3}{\sqrt{MSE/b}}$
R.R.: $q_{2(31)} > q_{.01} = 5.24$	R.R.: $q_{2(23)} > q_{.01} = 5.24$
$(r = 2, \nu = 6)$	$(r = 2, \nu = 6)$

Our calculations are as follows:

$$q_{2(31)} = \frac{\bar{T}_3 - \bar{T}_1}{\sqrt{MSE/b}} \qquad\qquad q_{2(23)} = \frac{\bar{T}_2 - \bar{T}_3}{\sqrt{MSE/b}}$$

$$= \frac{1.700 - .975}{\sqrt{.075/4}} \qquad\qquad = \frac{2.625 - 1.700}{\sqrt{.075/4}}$$

$$= \frac{.725}{.137} = 5.29 \qquad\qquad = \frac{.925}{.137} = 6.75$$

Both test statistics exceed $q_{.01} = 5.24$, so the data support both research hypotheses. That is, we conclude that the population means are ranked exactly as we ranked the sample means: the mean reaction time to visual stimulus 1 is exceeded by that for visual stimulus 3, and both are exceeded by the population mean reaction time of stimulus 2. The conclusion is made at the $\alpha = .01$ level of significance.

EXERCISES

1. Refer to exercise 1 in section 11.8. We compared the mean matching scores of four colors with four corresponding temperatures using a randomized block design with 8 subjects (blocks).

    Use the Newman-Keuls procedure to conduct pairwise comparisons of the $[4(3)/2] = 6$ pairs of mean matching scores for the four treatments. Use $\alpha = .05$.

2. Refer to exercise 3 of section 11.8. A randomized block design was employed to see whether mean ratings of the judges would differ for four different films. Eight judges viewed each film and then completed a questionnaire designed to evaluate the film.

    Use the Newman-Keuls procedure for making pairwise comparisons of the $[4(3)/2] = 6$ pairs of average scores corresponding to the four films. Use $\alpha = .01$.

11.10 · SELECTING THE SAMPLE SIZE

Selecting the sample size for the completely randomized or the randomized block design is an extension of the procedure of section 8.8. We confine our attention to the case of equal sample sizes, $n_1 = n_2 = \cdots = n_p$, for the p treatments of the completely randomized design. The number of observations per treatment is equal to b for the randomized block design. The problem is to select n_i (if a completely randomized design) or b (if a randomized block design).

The selection of the sample size follows a similar procedure for both designs; hence we will outline a general method. First we decide on the parameter (or parameters) of major interest. Usually we will be interested in the differences between treatment means. Second, a bound on the error of estimation must be specified. Once this is determined, we select the n_i (the number of observations in a treatment mean) or, correspondingly, the b (the number of blocks in the randomized block design) that will reduce the half-width of the confidence interval for the parameter. We wish this half-width to be less than or equal to the specified bound on the error of estimation.

It should be emphasized that the sample size solution will *always* be an approximation, since the common population variance σ^2 is unknown, and the pooled sample variance s^2 (MSE) is also unknown until the data is collected. The best available value will be used for s to produce an approximate solution.

We illustrate the procedure of selecting the sample size with some examples.

Example 11.9

A completely randomized design is conducted to compare five teaching techniques on classes of equal size. Estimation of the difference in mean response to an achievement test is desired correct to within 30 test-score points, with a probability of .95. It is expected that the test scores for a given teaching technique will have a range of approximately 240. Find the approximate number of observations required for each sample in order to acquire the specified information.

Solution: Recall from section 9.3 that the confidence interval for the difference between a pair of treatment means is

$$(\bar{T}_i - \bar{T}_j) \pm t_{\alpha/2}s\sqrt{\frac{1}{n_i} + \frac{1}{n_j}}$$

Therefore, we wish to select n_i and n_j so that

$$t_{\alpha/2}s\sqrt{\frac{1}{n_i} + \frac{1}{n_j}} \le 30$$

The value of σ is unknown and s is a random variable. However, an approximate solution for $n_i = n_j$ can be obtained by guessing s to be roughly equal to one-fourth of the range. Thus $s \approx 240/4 = 60$. The value of $t_{\alpha/2}$ will be based on $(n_1 + n_2 + \cdots + n_5 - 5)$ degrees of freedom, and for even moderate values of n_i, $t_{.025}$ will be approximately equal 2. (See table 5 in appendix II.) Then

$$t_{.025}s\sqrt{\frac{1}{n_i} + \frac{1}{n_j}} \approx (2)(60)\sqrt{\frac{2}{n_i}} \le 30$$

$$\sqrt{\frac{2}{n_i}} \approx \frac{30}{(2)(60)} = \frac{1}{4}$$

$$\frac{2}{n_i} \approx \frac{1}{16}$$

$$n_i \approx 32 \qquad i = 1, 2, \ldots, 5$$

Thus about 32 subjects will be needed for each sample to obtain the specified information.

Example 11.10

An experiment is conducted to compare three tone frequencies for their effects on sound localization. Since large individual differences in ability to localize sound are expected, each subject is tested with all three frequencies, thereby blocking out subject-to-subject variability.

The standard deviation of the experimental error is unknown. However, prior experimentation, in which the same subject was tested several times with a given tone frequency, suggests a range of response measurements of 5 units.

Find a value for b such that the error of estimating the difference between a pair of treatment means is less than 1 unit, with a probability of .95.

Solution: A very approximate value for s would be one-fourth the range, or $s \approx 1.25$. Then we wish to select b so that the half-width of a confidence interval for the difference in mean response between any pair of frequencies is less than 1 unit. That is,

$$t_{.025}s\sqrt{\frac{1}{b} + \frac{1}{b}} = t_{.025}s\sqrt{\frac{2}{b}} \leq 1$$

Since $t_{.025}$ will depend upon the degrees of freedom associated with s^2, which will be $(n - b - p + 1)$, we will guess $t_{.025} \approx 2$. Then

$$(2)(1.25)\sqrt{\frac{2}{b}} \leq 1 \qquad \text{or} \qquad b \approx 13$$

Thus approximately 13 subjects will be needed to obtain the required information.

The degrees of freedom associated with s^2 will be 24 based on this solution. Therefore, the guessed value of t would seem to be adequate for this approximate solution.

The sample size solutions for examples 11.9 and 11.10 are very approximate and are intended to provide only a rough estimate of size and consequent cost of the experiment. Information about σ will be obtained as the data are being collected and a better approximation to n can be calculated as the experiment proceeds.

EXERCISES

1. Refer to exercise 2 in section 11.6. Approximately how many rats would be required in each treatment to estimate the difference in mean latency of avoidance response correct to within 1.5 seconds? Assume knowledge of the data given in exercise 2, section 11.6.

2. Refer to exercise 3 of section 11.8. About how many judges should be used to allow estimation of the difference in mean questionnaire scores for a preselected pair of films to within 1 unit? Assume knowledge of the data given in exercise 3, section 11.8.

11.11 • THE ANALYSIS OF VARIANCE FOR TWO-WAY CLASSIFICATIONS

A two-way classification of the data originates from a factorial experiment involving two independent variables, or factors, which may be either quantitative or qualitative. The factorial experiment was defined in section 10.4 as one which includes all combinations of factor levels. If a response is measured for all combinations of levels of the two factors exactly the same number of times, the experiment is one that produces a two-way classification of the data with an equal number of observations per treatment (combinations of factor levels).

You should recall (section 10.4) that in addition to examining the effect each factor has on the response population mean, we are also interested in knowing whether or not this effect is the same at each level of the other factor, that is, whether or not the factors interact. To explore the possibility of interaction, *more than one* observation per treatment must be made.

In section 10.4 we used the example of a volume comprehension experiment in which the researcher wished to examine the effects of two factors, age and sex, on the ability to comprehend volume. There were six levels of the factor "age" (4 through 9) and two of "sex" (boys and girls), resulting in twelve treatments (age-sex combinations). This, then, is a two-way classification. The researcher should assign more than one experimental unit (child) to each of the twelve treatments in order to investigate interaction between the age and sex factors.

More generally, consider a factorial experiment consisting of two factors A and B, with factor A having p levels and factor B having q levels. The experiment therefore consists of pq treatments, and it is often called a p × q factorial experiment. We assume that the same number of observations are taken on each treatment and that this number exceeds 1. A summary of the notation for such an experiment is given in table 11.13.

Note that the treatment total for the treatment consisting of the combination of level i from factor A and level j from factor B is written $(AB)_{ij}$. This total consists of the sum of all n_{AB} observations in this (i, j) factor-level combination. The total for all the observations in level i of factor A is A_i, having sample size $n_A = q n_{AB}$. The total for all observations for level j of factor B is B_j, with sample size $n_B = p n_{AB}$.

There are three related sets of hypotheses we might wish to test in a two-way classification. These are shown in the box.

Hypotheses Set 1 for a Two-way Classification

Null hypothesis H_0: There is no interaction between factors A and B, or, equivalently, the effect of factor A on the population mean response is unrelated to the effect of factor B.

Research hypothesis H_a: The factors A and B interact. The effect of factor

A on the population mean response depends on the level of factor B.

Hypotheses Set 2 for a Two-way Classification

Null hypothesis H_0: Factor A does not affect the population mean response, that is, the mean response is the same at all levels of A.

Research hypothesis H_a: The population mean response is different for at least two levels of factor A.

Hypotheses Set 3 for a Two-way Classification

Null hypothesis H_0: Factor B does not affect the population mean response, that is, the mean response is the same at all levels of B.

Research hypothesis H_a: The population mean response is different for at least two levels of factor B.

Table 11.13 • Summary of notation for a two-way classification (two-factor factorial)

Factor A	Factor B				Totals for Factor A
	Level b_1	Level b_2	. . .	Level b_q	
Level a_1	$(AB)_{11}$	$(AB)_{12}$	. . .	$(AB)_{1q}$	A_1
Level a_2	$(AB)_{21}$	$(AB)_{22}$	. . .	$(AB)_{2q}$	A_2
$\vdots$	$\vdots$	$\vdots$		$\vdots$	$\vdots$
Level a_p	$(AB)_{p1}$	$(AB)_{p2}$	. . .	$(AB)_{pq}$	A_p
Totals for Factor B	B_1	B_2	. . .	B_q	

sample sizes: each treatment: n_{AB}

each level of factor A: $n_A = qn_{AB}$

each level of factor B: $n_B = pn_{AB}$

total sample: $n = pqn_{AB}$

total of all observations: $\sum_{i=1}^{n} y_i$

total of squares of all observations: $\sum_{i=1}^{n} y_i^2$

The test statistic for all three tests is an F statistic, although the form differs for each. The three forms are given in the box.

Test Statistic for Hypotheses Set 1

$$F = \frac{\text{mean square for } AB \text{ interaction}}{\text{mean square for error}} = \frac{MS(AB)}{MSE}$$

Test Statistic for Hypotheses Set 2

$$F = \frac{\text{mean square for factor } A}{\text{mean square for error}} = \frac{MSA}{MSE}$$

Test Statistic for Hypotheses Set 3

$$F = \frac{\text{mean square for factor } B}{\text{mean square for error}} = \frac{MSB}{MSE}$$

By now it should be no surprise that each of the mean squares is calculated by dividing the corresponding sum of squares by an appropriate number of degrees of freedom. Each of the sums of squares is computed directly with the exception of the sum of squares for error (SSE), which is again computed by subtraction. We make use of the partitioning of the total sum of squares shown in figure 11.15.

Figure 11.15 • Partitioning the total sum of squares for a two-way classification

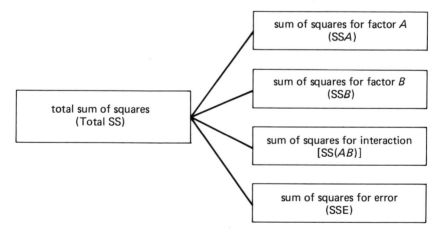

The formulas for the calculation of all the necessary quantities are given in table 11.14.

Table 11.14 • Formulas for the calculations in the two-way classification

CM = correction for mean

$$= \frac{\text{(total of all observations)}^2}{\text{total number of observations}} = \frac{\left(\sum\limits_{i=1}^{n} y_i\right)^2}{n}$$

Total SS = total sum of squares

$$= \text{(sum of squares of all observations)} - \text{CM} = \sum_{i=1}^{n} y_i^2 - \text{CM}$$

SSA = sum of squares for factor A

$$= \left(\begin{array}{c}\text{sum of squares of totals for each level of}\\ \text{factor A with each square divided by } n_A, \text{ the}\\ \text{number of observations for each level of A}\end{array}\right) - \text{CM}$$

$$= \frac{A_1^2}{n_A} + \frac{A_2^2}{n_A} + \cdots + \frac{A_p^2}{n_A} - \text{CM}$$

SSB = sum of squares for factor B

$$= \left(\begin{array}{c}\text{sum of squares of totals for each level of}\\ \text{factor B with each square divided by } n_B, \text{ the}\\ \text{number of observations for each level of B}\end{array}\right) - \text{CM}$$

$$= \frac{B_1^2}{n_B} + \frac{B_2^2}{n_B} + \cdots + \frac{B_q^2}{n_B} - \text{CM}$$

SS(AB) = sum of squares for interaction

$$= \left(\begin{array}{c}\text{sum of squares of treatment totals with}\\ \text{each square divided by } n_{AB}, \text{ the number}\\ \text{of observations for each treatment}\end{array}\right) - \text{SSA} - \text{SSB} - \text{CM}$$

$$= \frac{(AB_{11})^2}{n_{AB}} + \frac{(AB_{12})^2}{n_{AB}} + \cdots + \frac{(AB_{pq})^2}{n_{AB}} - \text{SSA} - \text{SSB} - \text{CM}$$

SSE = sum of squares for error = Total SS − SSA − SSB − SS(AB)

MSA = mean square for factor A

$$= \frac{\text{sum of squares for factor A}}{\text{(number of levels of factor A) minus 1}} = \frac{\text{SSA}}{p-1}$$

MSB = mean square for factor B

$$= \frac{\text{sum of squares for factor B}}{\text{(number of levels of factor B) minus 1}} = \frac{\text{SSB}}{q-1}$$

MS(AB) = mean square for interaction

$$= \frac{\text{sum of squares for interaction}}{\left[\left(\begin{array}{c}\text{number of}\\ \text{levels of}\\ \text{factor A}\end{array}\right)\text{minus 1}\right]\left[\left(\begin{array}{c}\text{number of}\\ \text{levels of}\\ \text{factor B}\end{array}\right)\text{minus 1}\right]}$$

Table 11.14 • Formulas for the calculations in the two-way classification (*Cont.*)

$$= \frac{SS(AB)}{(p-1)(q-1)}$$

MSE = mean square for error

$$= \frac{\text{sum of squares for error}}{(\text{total number of observations}) \text{ minus } (\text{number of treatments})}$$

$$= \frac{SSE}{n - pq}$$

Interaction F statistic: $F = \dfrac{MS(AB)}{MSE}$

Factor A F statistic: $F = \dfrac{MSA}{MSE}$

Factor B F statistic: $F = \dfrac{MSB}{MSE}$

Example 11.11

Computer assisted instruction (CAI) has become a very popular device for teaching material that is high in factual content. A researcher wishes to evaluate four different CAI programs designed to transmit the same material. Each program will be examined at three different study times: 30 minutes, 60 minutes, and 90 minutes. Achievement tests will be given to each subject at the end of the program to measure the program's effectiveness. The basic elements of the experiment are as follows.

Experimental units: Students.

Response: Achievement test scores.

Factors: Two factors: the CAI program (qualitative) and study time (quantitative).

Levels of factors: 4 levels of CAI programs (types of program) and 3 levels of study time (30, 60, 90 minutes).

Treatments: The 12 CAI program–study time combinations.

Suppose the researcher conducts a factorial experiment with 24 randomly selected students, 2 students being randomly assigned to each treatment. The data generated by this factorial experiment are given in table 11.15.

We have arbitrarily let factor A be the study time and factor B be the CAI program. Note that b_1, b_2, b_3, and b_4 represent the four different CAI programs being studied.

Calculate the F test statistics for the following:

(a) interaction of factor A and B;

(b) factor A;

(c) factor B.

Table 11.15 • Data for the CAI program–study time factorial experiment of example 11.11

Study Time (Factor A)	CAI Program (Factor B)			
	b_1	b_2	b_3	b_4
30 min (a_1)	61	72	54	59
	49	65	53	63
60 min (a_2)	77	84	69	96
	61	72	53	83
90 min (a_3)	90	109	78	110
	86	100	79	95

Solution: Table 11.16 shows the results of computing the basic quantities for this two-way classification.

Table 11.16 • Basic calculations for the CAI program–study time experiment

Study Time (Factor A)	CAI Program (Factor B)				Factor A Totals
	b_1	b_2	b_3	b_4	
30	$(AB)_{11}$ 110	$(AB)_{12}$ 137	$(AB)_{13}$ 107	$(AB)_{14}$ 122	$A_1 = 476$
60	$(AB)_{21}$ 138	$(AB)_{22}$ 156	$(AB)_{23}$ 122	$(AB)_{24}$ 179	$A_2 = 595$
90	$(AB)_{31}$ 176	$(AB)_{32}$ 209	$(AB)_{33}$ 157	$(AB)_{34}$ 205	$A_3 = 747$
Factor B Totals	$B_1 = 424$	$B_2 = 502$	$B_3 = 386$	$B_4 = 506$	1818

sample sizes: each treatment: $n_{AB} = 2$

each level of factor A: $n_A = (4)(2) = 8$

each level of factor B: $n_B = (3)(2) = 6$

total sample size: $n = (3)(4)(2) = 24$

total of all observations: $\sum_{i=1}^{n} y_i = 1818$

total of squares of all observations: $\sum_{i=1}^{n} y_i^2 = 145,098$

We follow the order of calculations given in table 11.14 to get the appropriate F statistics.

$$CM = \frac{\left(\sum_{i=1}^{24} y_i\right)^2}{24} = \frac{(1818)^2}{24} = 137{,}713.5$$

$$\text{Total SS} = \sum_{i=1}^{24} y_i^2 - CM = 145{,}098 - CM = 7384.5$$

$$SSA = \frac{A_1^2}{n_A} + \frac{A_2^2}{n_A} + \frac{A_3^2}{n_A} - CM$$

$$= \frac{(476)^2}{8} + \frac{(595)^2}{8} + \frac{(747)^2}{8} - CM = 4612.8$$

$$SSB = \frac{B_1^2}{n_B} + \frac{B_2^2}{n_B} + \frac{B_3^2}{n_B} + \frac{B_4^2}{n_B} - CM$$

$$= \frac{(424)^2}{6} + \frac{(502)^2}{6} + \frac{(386)^2}{6} + \frac{(506)^2}{6} - CM = 1755.2$$

$$SS(AB) = \frac{(AB_{11})^2}{n_{AB}} + \frac{(AB_{12})^2}{n_{AB}} + \cdots + \frac{(AB_{34})^2}{n_{AB}} - SSA - SSB - CM$$

$$= \frac{(110)^2}{2} + \frac{(137)^2}{2} + \cdots + \frac{(205)^2}{2} - SSA - SSB - CM$$

$$= 337.5$$

$$SSE = \text{Total SS} - SSA - SSB - SS(AB)$$

$$= 7384.5 - 4612.8 - 1755.2 - 337.5 = 679.0$$

$$MSA = \frac{SSA}{p-1} = \frac{4612.8}{2} = 2306.4$$

$$MSB = \frac{SSB}{q-1} = \frac{1755.2}{3} = 585.1$$

$$MS(AB) = \frac{SS(AB)}{(p-1)(q-1)} = \frac{337.5}{(3-1)(4-1)} = \frac{337.5}{6} = 56.3$$

$$MSE = \frac{SSE}{n-pq} = \frac{679.0}{24-12} = 56.6$$

The F statistics of interest, then, are as given below.

(a) Interaction:

$$F = \frac{MS(AB)}{MSE} = \frac{56.3}{56.6} = .99$$

(b) Factor A:

$$F = \frac{MSA}{MSE} = \frac{2306.4}{56.6} = 40.75$$

(c) Factor B:

$$F = \frac{MSB}{MSE} = \frac{585.1}{56.6} = 10.34$$

Large values of the F statistics support their respective research hypotheses. Thus for an α significance level, each test would have this rejection region:

Rejection region: $F > F_\alpha$

where F_α is the table value corresponding to α. The MSE degrees of freedom ν_2 will be the same for each test:

$\nu_2 = $ denominator of MSE

$= $ (total number of observations) minus (number of treatments)

However, the numerator degrees of freedom ν_1 will depend on the test.

1. Interaction:

$\nu_1 = $ denominator of MS(AB)

$= $ [(number of levels of A) minus 1][(number of levels of B) minus 1]
$= (p - 1)(q - 1)$

2. Factor A:

$\nu_1 = $ denominator of MSA $= $ (number of levels of A) minus 1 $= (p - 1)$

3. Factor B:

$\nu_1 = $ denominator of MSB $= $ (number of levels of B) minus 1 $= (q - 1)$

The assumptions for these tests are identical to those for the completely randomized and the randomized block designs. Summaries of the three pertinent tests for a two-way classification are given in the boxes.

Test for the Effect of Interaction in a Factorial Experiment

Null hypothesis H_0: There is no interaction between factors A and B.

Research hypothesis H_a: Factors A and B interact.

Test statistic: $F = \dfrac{\text{mean square for interaction}}{\text{mean square for error}} = \dfrac{MS(AB)}{MSE}$.

Assumptions: 1. The populations associated with the treatments are normally distributed.
2. The variances of all the populations are equal.

Rejection region: $F > F_\alpha$, where F_α is the table value corresponding to the α-level of significance, with degrees of freedom

$$\nu_1 = [(\text{number of levels for factor A}) \text{ minus } 1]$$
$$\times [(\text{number of levels for factor B}) \text{ minus } 1]$$
$$= (p - 1)(q - 1)$$
$$\nu_2 = (\text{total number of observations}) \text{ minus}$$
$$(\text{number of treatments})$$
$$= n - pq$$

Test for the Effect of Factor A in a Factorial Experiment

Null hypothesis H_0: The population mean response is the same at all levels of factor A.

Research hypothesis H_a: The population mean response differs for at least two levels of factor A.

Test statistic: $F = \dfrac{\text{mean square for factor A}}{\text{mean square for error}} = \dfrac{MSA}{MSE}$.

Assumptions: Same as for the test for interaction.

Rejection region: $F > F_\alpha$, where F_α is the table value corresponding to the α-level of significance, with degrees of freedom

$$\nu_1 = (\text{number of levels of factor A}) \text{ minus } 1$$
$$= p - 1$$
$$\nu_2 = (\text{total number of observations}) \text{ minus}$$
$$(\text{number of treatments})$$
$$= n - pq$$

Test for the Effect of Factor B in a Factorial Experiment

Null hypothesis H_0: The population mean response is the same at all levels of factor B.

Research hypothesis H_a: The population mean response differs for at least two levels of factor B.

Test statistic: $F = \dfrac{\text{mean square for factor B}}{\text{mean square for error}} = \dfrac{MSB}{MSE}$.

Assumptions: Same as for the test for interaction.

Rejection region: $F > F_\alpha$, where F_α is the table value corresponding to the α-level of significance, with degrees of freedom

$$\nu_1 = \text{(number of levels of factor } B) \text{ minus } 1$$
$$= q - 1$$

$$\nu_2 = \text{(total number of observations) minus}$$
$$\qquad\qquad\qquad\qquad \text{(number of treatments)}$$

$$= n - pq$$

You may have noted that we consistently list the test of interaction before the tests of the individual factors. The reason is that we will always conduct the test of interaction first. If the data support the research hypothesis that the factors interact, there is usually little to be gained by conducting the tests for the individual factor effects. If we conclude that the factors interact, we are inferring that both factors affect the response and that they do so in a dependent way. That is, the effect of factor A on the population mean response depends on the level of B. This implies that there is evidence to indicate a difference in the means of various factor-level combinations. You should proceed to use various statistical techniques to compare these means.

On the other hand, if the data do not support the research hypothesis of interaction, we will be interested in knowing whether the data support the hypotheses that factors A and B separately affect the population mean response. This requires conducting a separate hypothesis test for factor A and for factor B, as summarized above. Our testing strategy for two-way classifications is summarized, then, as in the box.

Testing Strategy for Two-way Classifications

1. Test the research hypothesis that the two factors interact.
    (a) If the data support the research hypothesis at the specified α-level, conclude that both factors affect the response mean in a dependent fashion. At this point you will usually proceed to a comparison of the individual treatment means.
    (b) If the data do *not* support the research hypothesis, proceed to step 2.
2. Test the following research hypotheses separately.
    (a) The mean response differs for at least two levels of factor A.
    (b) The mean response differs for at least two levels of factor B.

Example 11.12

Refer to example 11.11. We performed calculations for a two-way classification involving a study of the effects of different computer assisted instruction programs and different lengths of study time on achievement test scores. Recall that the qualitative factor "CAI programs" was examined at four levels, and the quantitative factor "study time" was set at three levels.

Conduct the pertinent tests of hypotheses for this experiment and state your conclusions. Use $\alpha = .05$.

Solution: We first construct the test for interaction between CAI programs and study time.

Null hypothesis H_0: The factors "CAI program" and "study time" do not interact to affect achievement test means.

Research hypothesis H_a: The factors do interact to affect achievement test means.

Test statistic: $F = \dfrac{MS(AB)}{MSE}$.

Assumptions: 1. The populations of achievement test scores associated with the CAI program–study time combinations are approximately normally distributed.
2. The variances of the populations of achievement test scores are the same for all treatments (factor-level combinations).

Rejection region: $F > 3.00$, the $F_{.05}$ table value, with degrees of freedom

$$\nu_1 = \text{denominator of } MS(AB) = 6$$

$$\nu_2 = \text{denominator of } MSE = 12$$

From our calculations in example 11.11, we have

$$F = \frac{MS(AB)}{MSE} = .99$$

Thus our data do not support the research hypothesis that the two factors interact to affect achievement scores. We therefore proceed to test the factors separately.

Null hypothesis H_0: The population mean achievement score is the same for the three levels of study time (30, 60, and 90 minutes).

Research hypothesis H_a: The population mean achievement score differs for at least two of the study times.

Test statistic: $F = \dfrac{MSA}{MSE}$.

Assumptions: Same as for the test for interaction.

Rejection region: $F > 3.89$, the $F_{.05}$ table value with degrees of freedom

$$\nu_1 = \text{denominator of } MSA = 2$$

$$\nu_2 = \text{denominator of } MSE = 12$$

Again from example 11.11, we have

$$F = \frac{MSA}{MSE} = 40.75$$

There is very strong evidence that mean achievement test score depends upon study time. To determine the nature of this dependence would require pairwise comparisons of the means, using a procedure like the Newman-Keuls.

What about the effect of "CAI program" on mean achievement score?

Null hypothesis H_0: The population mean achievement score is the same for the four types of CAI programs.

Research hypothesis H_a: The population mean achievement score differs for at least two of the CAI programs.

Test statistic: $F = \dfrac{MSB}{MSE}$.

Assumptions: Same as for the previous two tests.

Rejection region: $F > 3.49$, the $F_{.05}$ table value with degrees of freedom

$$\nu_1 = \text{denominator of } MSB = 3$$
$$\nu_2 = \text{denominator of } MSE = 12$$

The computations in example 11.11 produced

$$F = \frac{MSB}{MSE} = 10.34$$

Thus the evidence is quite strong that the population mean of the achievement test scores varies with the CAI program used. Again, to obtain more specific information about the differences, pairwise comparisons of the CAI program means could be made.

In summary, the data do not indicate any interactive effect of CAI program with study time. But they strongly indicate (with both the F-values significant at the .01 level, although we used only the .05 level) that both study time and CAI program separately affect the mean of the achievement test scores.

The results of a two-way classification are conveniently displayed in an ANOVA table. The form of the general table is shown in table 11.17. The ANOVA table for our CAI program–study time example is given in table 11.18 p. 351.

Table 11.17 · Analysis of variance summary table for a $p \times q$ factorial experiment

Source	d.f.	SS	MS	F
Factor A	$p - 1$	SSA	$SSA/(p - 1)$	MSA/MSE
Factor B	$q - 1$	SSB	$SSB/(q - 1)$	MSB/MSE
$A \times B$	$(p - 1)(q - 1)$	SS(AB)	$SS(AB)/(p - 1)(q - 1)$	MS(AB)/MSE
Error	$n - pq$	SSE	$SSE/(n - pq)$	
Total	$n - 1$	Total SS		

EXERCISES

1. Koch and Arnold (1972) studied the effects of early social deprivation on emotionality. Since it is not possible to conduct controlled research on this issue among humans (due to ethical problems), the subjects were infant rats. The subjects were either reared by

Table 11.18 • Analysis of variance summary table for the data of the CAI program–study time experiment

Source	d.f.	SS	MS	F
Study time, A	2	4612.8	2306.4	40.75
CAI Program, B	3	1755.2	585.1	10.34
A × B	6	337.5	56.3	.99
Error	12	679.0	56.6	
Total	23	7384.5		

their mother or reared in incubators. Also, they were reared with or without their peers, introducing a second factor into the experiment. The dependent measure was latency of emergence into a lighted field. Since rats are nocturnal animals, this emergence represents an emotional experience for the rats. The emergence latency scores for the four groups of rats, 3 to a treatment, are presented below.

Mother-reared		Incubator-reared	
With Peers	Without Peers	With Peers	Without Peers
56	55	72	86
65	48	65	95
72	40	80	81

Compute the analysis of variance for this two-way classification. Display the results in a summary table and conduct the pertinent tests of hypotheses. Conduct your tests according to the strategy outlined in this section.

2. A 2 × 2 factorial experiment was conducted by Fuller and Forrest (1973) to study the relationship between arousal and smoking. Subjects either viewed a stressful film (arousal condition) or spent time alone relaxed on a couch (nonarousal). Subjects were further divided into light smokers and heavy smokers. One dependent variable was the interval between cigarette puffs while participating in the experiment. A lower rate of smoking was predicted for high-arousal subjects, since their arousal already was high. It was further conjectured that unaroused subjects would use the stimulant properties of the nicotine to raise their arousal levels. A total of 40 subjects participated, with 10 in each treatment. Given the results below (interval between cigarette puffs, in seconds), conduct the pertinent tests of hypotheses. Summarize your calculations in an ANOVA table.

Arousal Condition				Nonarousal Condition			
Heavy Smokers		Light Smokers		Heavy Smokers		Light Smokers	
37	17	31	30	29	27	27	16
29	42	33	42	23	21	28	24
46	39	47	28	33	25	34	19
30	37	18	35	15	27	10	30
40	49	49	47	32	26	36	28

3. Interpret the interaction between the factors "rearing" and "peer" in exercise 1. That is, what does the presence of interaction between these factors mean?

11.12 • ANALYSIS OF VARIANCE FOR THE REPEATED MEASURES DESIGN

In section 10.6 we defined the *repeated measures design* as one which employs multiple response measurements on each experimental unit. For example, we may wish to compare three treatments by assigning 4 different subjects to each treatment and then obtaining three separate response measurements on each subject. This design is shown in figure 11.16.

Figure 11.16 • Repeated measures design: 3 treatments, 4 subjects, and 3 measurements per subject

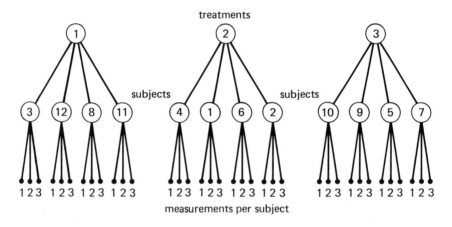

In this section we consider the analysis of variance for the repeated measures design. We assume that we are comparing p treatments, with n_1 subjects (experimental units) randomly assigned to each treatment. We use the term "subjects" for "experimental units" for the sake of brevity. Also, most behavioral science experiments use subjects (human or animal) as their experimental units. Next, we assume that n_2 repeated measurements are obtained for each subject. The notation for the repeated measures design is summarized in table 11.19.

Our objective is to compare the population means corresponding to the p treatments. We will test the null hypothesis

H_0: The p treatment means are equal

against the research hypothesis

H_a: At least two of the p treatment means differ

Table 11.19 • Summary of notation for repeated measures designs

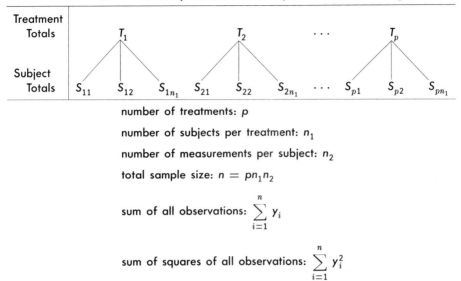

number of treatments: p

number of subjects per treatment: n_1

number of measurements per subject: n_2

total sample size: $n = pn_1n_2$

sum of all observations: $\sum_{i=1}^{n} y_i$

sum of squares of all observations: $\sum_{i=1}^{n} y_i^2$

As we stressed in section 10.6, there are three sources of variation in the repeated measures design. The first is the variation between treatments; the second is the variation between subjects; and the third is the variation within subjects. The total sum of squares is thus partitioned into three components: the *treatment* sum of squares, the *between-subject* sum of squares, and the *within-subject* sum of squares. This partitioning is shown in figure 11.17.

Figure 11.17 • Partition of the total sum of squares for a repeated measures design

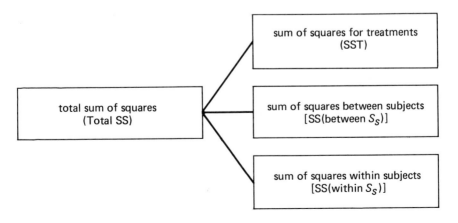

The statistic used for testing the null hypothesis that the treatment means are equal is again an *F* ratio, comparing the mean square for treatments to the mean square between subjects.

$$\text{Test statistic: } F = \frac{\text{MST}}{\text{MS(between } S_s)}$$

The formulas for the calculations in the repeated measures design are given in table 11.20. We illustrate the use of these calculations with an example.

Table 11.20 • Formulas for the calculations in the repeated measures design

CM = correction for mean

$$= \frac{(\text{total of all observations})^2}{n} = \frac{\left(\sum\limits_{i=1}^{n} y_i\right)^2}{n}$$

Total SS = total sum of squares

$$= (\text{sum of squares of all observations}) - CM = \sum\limits_{i=1}^{n} y_i^2 - CM$$

SST = sum of squares for treatments

$$= \frac{\text{sum of squares of treatment totals}}{\left(\begin{array}{c}\text{number of subjects}\\\text{per treatment}\end{array}\right)\left(\begin{array}{c}\text{number of repeated}\\\text{measures per subject}\end{array}\right)} - CM$$

$$= \frac{T_1^2 + T_2^2 + \cdots + T_p^2}{n_1 n_2} - CM$$

SS(between S_s) = sum of squares between subjects

$$= \frac{\text{sum of squares of subject totals}}{\text{number of repeated measures per subject}} - SST - CM$$

$$= \frac{(S_{11}^2 + S_{12}^2 + \cdots + S_{1n_1}^2) + \cdots + (S_{p1}^2 + S_{p2}^2 + \cdots + S_{pn_1}^2)}{n_2} - SST - CM$$

SS(within S_s) = sum of squares within subjects

$$= (\text{total sum of squares}) - (\text{sum of squares for treatments}) - (\text{sum of squares between subjects})$$

$$= \text{Total SS} - SST - SS(\text{between } S_s)$$

MST = mean square for treatments

$$= \frac{\text{sum of squares for treatments}}{(\text{number of treatments}) \text{ minus } 1} = \frac{SST}{p-1}$$

Table 11.20 • Formulas for the calculations in the repeated measures design (*Cont.*)

MS(between S_s) = mean square between subjects

$$= \frac{\text{sum of squares between subjects}}{\left(\begin{array}{c}\text{number of}\\\text{treatments}\end{array}\right)\left[\left(\begin{array}{c}\text{number of subjects}\\\text{per treatment}\end{array}\right)\text{minus } 1\right]}$$

$$= \frac{\text{SS(between } S_s)}{p(n_1 - 1)}$$

MS(within S_s) = mean square within subjects

$$= \frac{\text{sum of squares within subjects}}{\left(\begin{array}{c}\text{number of}\\\text{treatments}\end{array}\right)\left(\begin{array}{c}\text{number of}\\\text{subjects per}\\\text{treatment}\end{array}\right)\left[\left(\begin{array}{c}\text{number of}\\\text{repeated measures}\\\text{per subject}\end{array}\right)\text{minus } 1\right]}$$

$$= \frac{\text{SS(within } S_s)}{pn_1(n_2 - 1)}$$

$$F = \frac{\text{mean square for treatments}}{\text{mean square between subjects}} = \frac{\text{MST}}{\text{MS(between } S_s)}$$

$$F = \frac{\text{mean square between subjects}}{\text{mean square within subjects}} = \frac{\text{MS(between } S_s)}{\text{MS(within } S_s)}$$

Example 11.13

An experiment is conducted to compare reaction times to three visual stimuli. In examples 11.5 and 11.6 a randomized block experiment was used for this purpose. Now, however, the researcher decides to employ a repeated measures design to obtain an estimate of both between-subject and within-subject variation. She selects 12 subjects and randomly assigns 4 subjects to each treatment (visual stimulus). She then records the reaction time of each subject on three occasions, obtaining three repeated measures of each subject's reaction time. The data are presented in table 11.21.

Calculate the F statistic for testing the research hypothesis that the treatment (stimulus) means differ.

Solution: Table 11.22 gives the basic elements needed in the computations.

We now follow Table 11.20 to perform the calculations necessary to obtain the F statistic.

$$CM = \frac{\left(\sum_{i=1}^{36} y_i\right)^2}{36} = \frac{(60.9)^2}{36} = 103.02$$

$$\text{Total SS} = \sum_{i=1}^{36} y_i^2 - CM = 124.05 - 103.02 = 21.03$$

$$\text{SST} = \frac{T_1^2 + T_2^2 + T_3^2}{n_1 n_2} - CM$$

Table 11.21 • Reaction times to three visual stimuli: A repeated measures design for example 11.13

	Stimulus 1			
	Subject 1	Subject 2	Subject 3	Subject 4
Measure 1	.9	1.5	.5	.8
Measure 2	1.2	1.1	.8	1.3
Measure 3	.7	.8	.5	.9

	Stimulus 2			
	Subject 5	Subject 6	Subject 7	Subject 8
Measure 1	2.4	1.9	2.9	2.4
Measure 2	2.8	2.4	3.3	2.8
Measure 3	2.1	2.2	2.7	2.9

	Stimulus 3			
	Subject 9	Subject 10	Subject 11	Subject 12
Measure 1	1.5	2.1	1.1	1.6
Measure 2	1.2	1.9	1.5	1.8
Measure 3	1.9	2.2	1.0	1.3

Table 11.22 • Basic computations for the visual stimuli experiment of example 11.13

	Stimulus 1	Stimulus 2	Stimulus 3
Treatment Totals	$T_1 = 11.0$	$T_2 = 30.8$	$T_3 = 19.1$
Subject Totals	$S_{11} = 2.8$ $S_{12} = 3.4$ $S_{13} = 1.8$ $S_{14} = 3.0$	$S_{21} = 7.3$ $S_{22} = 6.5$ $S_{23} = 8.9$ $S_{24} = 8.1$	$S_{31} = 4.6$ $S_{32} = 6.2$ $S_{33} = 3.6$ $S_{34} = 4.7$

sum of all observations: 60.9

sum of squares of all observations: 124.05

number of treatments: $p = 3$

number of subjects per treatment: $n_1 = 4$

number of repeated measures per subject: $n_2 = 3$

$n = p n_1 n_2 = 36$

$$= \frac{(11.0)^2 + (30.8)^2 + (19.1)^2}{(4)(3)} - 103.02$$

$$= 119.54 - 103.02 = 16.52$$

$$\text{SS(between } S_s) = \frac{S_{11}^2 + S_{12}^2 + \cdots + S_{33}^2 + S_{34}^2}{n_2} - \text{SST} - \text{CM}$$

$$= \frac{(2.8)^2 + (3.4)^2 + \cdots + (3.6)^2 + (4.7)^2}{3}$$

$$- 16.52 - 103.02$$

$$= 122.22 - 119.54 = 2.68$$

$$\text{SS(within } S_s) = \text{Total SS} - \text{SST} - \text{SS(between } S_s)$$

$$= 21.03 - 16.52 - 2.68 = 1.83$$

$$\text{MST} = \frac{\text{SST}}{p-1} = \frac{16.52}{3-1} = 8.26$$

$$\text{MS(between } S_s) = \frac{\text{SS(between } S_s)}{p(n_1 - 1)} = \frac{2.68}{(3)(4-1)} = .30$$

$$\text{MS(between } S_s) = \frac{\text{SS(within } S_s)}{pn_1(n_2 - 1)} = \frac{1.83}{(3)(4)(3-1)} = .076$$

The F statistic, then, is

$$F = \frac{\text{MST}}{\text{MS(between } S_s)} = \frac{8.26}{.30} = 27.53$$

As in the case of a completely randomized block design, if the treatment means differ, we expect the variation between treatments to exceed the variation between subjects by a substantial amount. That is, we expect the ratio of the mean square for treatments (MST) to the mean square between subjects [MS(between S_s)] to be much greater than 1. We therefore use the following rejection region:

Rejection region: $F > F_\alpha$

where F_α is the table value corresponding to the α-level of significance, with degrees of freedom

$$\nu_1 = \text{denominator of MST} = p - 1$$

$$\nu_2 = \text{denominator of MS(between } S_s) = p(n_1 - 1)$$

The assumptions necessary for the validity of this test are the same as the assumptions for previous analyses of variances. We must assume that the populations of responses are normally distributed, that the between-subject variances are constant across all treatments, and that the within-subject variances are the same for all subjects.

A summary of the test to compare treatment means using a repeated measures design is given in the box.

Test of the Hypothesis that Treatment Means Are Equal for a Repeated Measures Design

Null hypothesis H_0: All p treatment means are equal.

Research hypothesis H_a: At least two treatment means differ.

Test statistic: $F = \dfrac{\text{mean square for treatments}}{\text{mean square between subjects}} = \dfrac{\text{MST}}{\text{MS(between } S_s)}$.

Assumptions: 1. All populations are normally distributed.
2. Between-subjects variances are equal for all treatments.
3. Within-subject variances are the same for all subjects.

Rejection region: Reject H_0 at the α-level of significance when $F > F_\alpha$, where F_α is the table value with degrees of freedom

$$\nu_1 = \text{denominator of MST} = p - 1$$

$$\nu_2 = \text{denominator of MS(between } S_s)$$
$$= p(n_1 - 1)$$

Example 11.14

Refer to example 11.13. We used a repeated measures design to compare three visual stimuli. Do the data in table 11.21 present sufficient evidence to support the research hypothesis that the true mean reaction times to the three visual stimuli differ? Use $\alpha = .05$.

Solution: We first construct the test.

Null hypothesis H_0: The population mean reaction times to the three stimuli are the same.

Research hypothesis H_a: At least two of the visual stimuli have different mean reaction times.

Test statistic: $F = \dfrac{\text{MST}}{\text{MS(between } S_s)}$.

Assumptions: 1. The populations of reaction times form normal distributions for each visual stimulus.
2. The variance of reaction times between subjects is the same for all three stimuli.
3. The variance of reaction times within subjects is the same for all subjects.

Rejection region: $F > F_{.05} = 4.26$, where

$$\nu_1 = p - 1 = 3 - 1 = 2$$
$$\nu_2 = p(n_1 - 1) = 3(4 - 1) = 9$$

In example 11.13 we calculated the test statistic $F = 27.53$. The data supports, at the $\alpha = .05$ level, the research hypothesis that the mean reaction time differs for the three visual stimuli. Indeed, our calculated F is so large that this hypothesis is strongly supported by the data at a lower significance level. We are extremely confident that the treatment means differ.

You may be wondering whether the within-subject calculations were necessary, since we have not yet used MS(within S_s) to make inferences about the populations. Recall that a primary reason for employing a repeated measures design is to estimate two sources of variation: between-subject variation and within-subject variation. We may use our estimates of these sources of variation to make inferences about their true relationship in the population.

A research hypothesis of interest, then, is that the between-subject variation exceeds the within-subject variation. That is, we wish to know whether responses vary more between subjects than they do within subjects. This test is summarized in the box.

Test of the Hypothesis that Between-Subject and Within-Subject Variances Are Equal

Null hypothesis H_0: The population variance of the response measurements between subjects equals the population variance within subjects.

Research hypothesis H_a: The variance between subjects exceeds the variance within subjects.

Test statistic: $F = \dfrac{MS(\text{between } S_s)}{MS(\text{within } S_s)}$.

Assumptions: Same as for the test of treatment means using the repeated measures design.

Rejection region: Reject H_0 at the α-level of significance when $F > F_\alpha$, where F_α is the table value with degrees of freedom

$$\nu_1 = \text{denominator of MS(between } S_s) = p(n_1 - 1)$$
$$\nu_2 = \text{denominator of MS(within } S_s) = pn_1(n_2 - 1)$$

Example 11.15

Refer to examples 11.13 and 11.14. We compared the mean response time to three visual stimuli using a repeated measures design. Do the data from this experiment support the research hypothesis that the population variance of response time between subjects exceeds that within subjects? Use $\alpha = .05$.

Solution: We construct the test as shown below.

Null hypothesis H_0: The population variance of response time between subjects equals that within subjects.

Research hypothesis H_a: The response time variance between subjects exceeds that within subjects.

Test statistic: $F = \dfrac{MS(\text{between } S_s)}{MS(\text{within } S_s)}$.

Assumptions: Same as for the test of treatment means in example 11.14.

Rejection region: $F > F_{.05} = 2.30$, where

$$\nu_1 = p(n_1 - 1) = 3(4 - 1) = 9$$
$$\nu_2 = pn_1(n_2 - 1) = (3)(4)(3 - 1) = 24$$

We calculated the mean squares in example 11.13. We now determine the F statistic.

$$F = \frac{MS(\text{between } S_s)}{MS(\text{within } S_s)} = \frac{.30}{.076} = 3.95$$

The calculated F exceeds $F_{.05} = 2.30$. We conclude, at the $\alpha = .05$ level, that the response time variance between subjects exceeds the response time variance within subjects. Note that our inference applies to all three visual stimuli, since we are assuming that both the between-subject and the within-subject variances are constant for all three stimuli.

As for the other designs we have discussed, an ANOVA table summarizes the calculations for the repeated measures design. This is shown in table 11.23.

Table 11.23 • ANOVA table for the repeated measures design

Source	d.f.	SS	MS	F
Treatment	$p - 1$	SST	$SST/(p - 1)$	$MST/MS(\text{between } S_s)$
Between S_s	$p(n_1 - 1)$	$SS(\text{between } S_s)$	$SS(\text{between } S_s)/p(n_1 - 1)$	$MS(\text{between } S_s)/MS(\text{within } S_s)$
Within S_s	$pn_1(n_2 - 1)$	$SS(\text{within } S_s)$	$SS(\text{within } S_s)/pn_1(n_2 - 1)$	
Total	$n - 1$	Total SS		

The ANOVA table for the reaction time experiment of examples 11.13 through 11.15 is given in table 11.24.

Table 11.24 • ANOVA table for the reaction time experiment of examples 11.13, 11.14, and 11.15

Source	d.f.	SS	MS	F
Treatment	2	16.52	8.26	27.53
Between S_s	9	2.68	.30	3.95
Within S_s	24	1.83	.076	
Total	35	21.03		

We conclude this section on the analysis of repeated measures designs with a note of caution. **Do not confuse the randomized block design with the repeated measures design.** Compare examples 11.5 and 11.13. Both involve taking more than one measurement on each subject (experimental unit). However, in the randomized block experiment, each subject is exposed to all p treatments so that each subject yields p measurements, one for each treatment. Each subject in a repeated measures experiment is assigned to a *single* treatment, and the n_1 repeated measurements are taken on that subject for that treatment only. Thus n_1 measurements are obtained for a subject, but all of them correspond to only one treatment.

The objective of the randomized block design is to compare treatments by removing between-subject variation. On the other hand, the objective of the repeated measures design is to isolate and estimate both the between-subject variation and the within-subject variation so that both the treatment means and the sources of error variation may be compared.

EXERCISES

1. A study was conducted on the development of motor skills in children (Connolly, Brown, and Bassett, 1968). Three age groups—6, 8, and 10 year olds—performed a target task, with each child repeating the task four times.

   Suppose we randomly select 9 female subjects, 3 from each age group, and perform the experiment described above. A score is obtained for each task performance, indicating the degree to which the task is successfully completed. The scores are given below.

	6 year olds			8 year olds			10 year olds		
Subject									
Trial	1	2	3	1	2	3	1	2	3
1	13	10	10	15	16	14	22	21	23
2	12	11	10	16	14	18	25	23	22
3	13	12	12	16	17	15	20	20	19
4	14	13	11	18	14	17	23	21	22

   (a) List the basic elements of this experiment.
   (b) Do the data provide sufficient evidence to conclude that the mean task score differs for the three age groups? Use $\alpha = .05$.
2. Refer to exercise 1. Form the ANOVA summary table for the repeated measures experiment.
3. Refer to exercise 1. Do the data provide sufficient evidence to indicate that between-subject variation in task performance score exceeds the variation within subjects? Use $\alpha = .05$.
4. What are the differences between the randomized block design and the repeated measures design?

SUMMARY

Analysis of variance refers generally to the comparison of variability attributable to a factor (or factor interaction) with the variability attributable to error (or to unknown sources of variation). The objective of making such a comparison is to make a parametric inference about the treatment (factor level) means. The F statistic is formed by taking the ratio of the two appropriate mean squares, with large F-values implying a difference in treatment means. It is important to remember that the assumptions of normality and constant response variance across treatments are necessary for this parametric test.

The few types of experimental designs we discussed are basic and important, but a thorough coverage of all experimental designs would fill several volumes. However, the objective of maximizing information and the idea of partitioning the total sum of squares into its components are common to all designs. A more complete coverage of other designs and the rationale behind them can be found in the references at the end of the chapter.

SUPPLEMENTARY EXERCISES

1. A completely randomized design is conducted to compare the effect of five different stimuli on reaction time. Twenty-seven people are employed in the experiment. Regardless of the results of the analysis of variance, it is desired to compare stimuli A and D. The results of the experiment are as follows.

			Stimulus		
	A	B	C	D	E
	.8	.7	1.2	1.0	.6
	.6	.8	1.0	.9	.4
	.6	.5	.9	.9	.4
	.5	.5	1.2	1.1	.7
		.6	1.3	.7	.3
		.9	.8		
		.7			
Totals	2.5	4.7	6.4	4.6	2.4
Means	.625	.671	1.067	.920	.48

   (a) Conduct an analysis of variance and test for a difference in mean reaction time due to the five stimuli.
   (b) Compare stimuli A and D to see if there is a difference in mean reaction time.
2. The experiment in exercise 1 might have been more effectively conducted using a randomized block design, with people as blocks, since we would expect mean reaction time to vary from one person to another. Hence 4 people are used in a new experiment and each person is subjected to each of the five stimuli in a random order. The results of this experiment are as follows.

	Stimulus				
Subject	A	B	C	D	E
1	.7	.8	1.0	1.0	.5
2	.6	.6	1.1	1.0	.6
3	.9	1.0	1.2	1.1	.6
4	.6	.8	.9	1.0	.4

Conduct an analysis of variance and test for differences in treatments (stimuli).

3. Refer to exercise 2. Use the Newman-Keuls pairwise comparison procedure of section 11.9 to test the significance of all $(5)(4)/2 = 10$ sample treatment mean differences. Present your results by ranking the treatment means and underscoring those which are *not* significantly different at the (overall) $\alpha = .05$ level.

4. What is the proper sequence of tests in the analysis of a two-factor factorial experiment?

5. Tomasin (1973) tested the effect of peer-induced anxiety in a problem-solving task in both high-anxiety and low-anxiety subjects. Some subjects from each group performed the task alone (not in an anxiety-inducing situation). The other subjects performed the task in the presence of a person who had finished the task (an anxiety-inducing situation). The response was the number of errors made in performing the task. Six subjects were selected for each of the 2×2 factorial combinations. The data are presented below.

Low Anxiety				High Anxiety			
Alone		Anxiety-induced		Alone		Anxiety-induced	
4	66	7	9	2	3	14	10
4	7	8	10	5	2	9	6
9	5	11	4	6	0	15	44

(a) List the basic elements of the experiment.

(b) Analyze the 2×2 factorial experiment, conducting the appropriate test(s) at the $\alpha = .05$ level of significance.

(c) Display the results of the analysis in an ANOVA summary table.

6. Weber and Bach (1969) studied the imagery involved in processing information. Subjects were divided into three groups: visual imagery, speech imagery, and control. For all groups, the task was to recite the alphabet as fast as possible without skipping letters. Prior to the task performance, the visual imagery group was told to visualize the letters appearing one at a time while the speech imagery group was told to say the letters silently. The control group was given no preparation. The response was the time taken to complete the task.

Suppose we were to conduct this experiment using a repeated measures design, with 4 subjects assigned to each group and each subject repeating the task five times. The data are given below.

Conduct an analysis of variance and test for a difference in mean task performance time among the three groups.

Trial \ Subject	Visual Imagery				Speech Imagery				Control			
	1	2	3	4	5	6	7	8	9	10	11	12
1	25	28	18	20	8	9	6	8	10	9	13	8
2	22	32	18	22	7	11	7	10	9	8	9	10
3	20	26	13	17	10	7	6	8	8	12	9	7
4	22	20	20	14	6	8	6	6	7	11	8	11
5	18	23	14	16	7	9	8	9	8	8	9	7

7. Refer to exercise 6. Test to see whether the data provide evidence that between-subject variation exceeds the within-subject variation in task performance time.

8. To compare three books designed to teach preschool children to associate objects with words, the following experiment is conducted. Twelve children are randomly assigned to three experimental conditions representing the three books; 4 children are taught from Book A, 4 from Book B, and 4 from Book C. Each child spends approximately the same period of time each day in a teaching session using his or her particular book. After one month, a standaridzed object–word association test is administered to each child and the following results obtained.

A	B	C
34	37	34
21	25	20
13	18	17
8	16	9

Do these data present sufficient evidence to indicate a difference in mean test score for the three books? Use $\alpha = .05$.

9. Refer to exercise 8. Suppose that each row of the data table in exercise 8 represents three children matched preexperimentally on the basis of having similar vocabulary test scores. The children within each group of three are randomly assigned to the three experimental conditions. Analyze the data, assuming that the requirements for a randomized block design are met, with four blocks corresponding to the four rows of the data table in exercise 8.

(a) At the $\alpha = .05$ level, is there evidence to indicate a difference in mean object–word association test score for the three books?

(b) Does the conclusion of part (a) contradict the conclusion obtained in exercise 8?

10. Refer to exercise 9. Use the Newman-Keuls pairwise comparison procedure of section 11.9 to test the significance of all $(3)(2)/2 = 3$ sample treatment mean differences. Present your results by ranking the treatment means and underscoring those which are *not* significantly different at the (overall) $\alpha = .05$ level.

11. There is some evidence that the hormone MSH helps animals maintain a response that is necessary for escape or avoidance. Sandman, Miller, Kastin, and Schally (1972) conducted a study on rats to get further information on this phenomenon. Rats were trained to escape shock by going to a lighted ("safe") door. Then the rats were administered either an MSH compound or a control. Finally, for half the rats in each group, the "safe" door was the lighted door, but for the other half, the "safe" door

was the dark door. The latter group could escape shock by going to the door that was opposite the door they had been trained to approach. This change required an adaptive response on the part of the rats, that is, the trained behavior should not be maintained.

Suppose we run an experiment like the one described above. We have trained 18 rats, so we randomly assign 3 rats to each of the following six treatments.

1. Control, Lighted
2. Control, Dark
3. MSH (Dose A), Lighted
4. MSH (Dose A), Dark
5. MSH (Dose B), Lighted
6. MSH (Dose B), Dark

"Lighted" and "Dark" refer to the "safe" door for each rat. We record the number of trials to criterion and obtain the data below.

Control		MSH A		MSH B	
Lighted	Dark	Lighted	Dark	Lighted	Dark
75	53	40	58	53	56
60	40	55	32	62	70
84	68	36	40	38	62

Perform the analysis of variance for this 3×2 factorial experiment.

12. An experiment is conducted to investigate the toxic effect of three chemicals, A, B, and C, on the skin of rats. One-inch squares of skin are treated with the chemicals and then scored from 0 to 10, depending on the degree of irritation. Three adjacent 1-inch squares are marked on the backs of 8 rats and each of the three chemicals applied to each rat. Thus the experiment was blocked on rats to eliminate the variation in skin sensitivity from rat to rat. The data are as follows.

				Rat			
1	2	3	4	5	6	7	8
B	A	A	C	B	C	C	B
5	9	6	6	8	5	5	7
A	C	B	B	C	A	B	A
6	4	9	8	8	5	7	6
C	B	C	A	A	B	A	C
3	9	3	5	7	7	6	7

Do the data provide sufficient evidence to indicate a difference in the toxic effect of the three chemicals? Use $\alpha = .05$.

13. Refer to exercise 12. Is there evidence to indicate that the mean degree of irritation differs among rats (blocks)? Use $\alpha = .05$.

14. A repeated measures experiment is conducted to compare the adult human sleep-wakefulness pattern for several age groups. The age groups of interest are 20–29, 30–39, 40–49, and 50–59. Four subjects are randomly selected from each age group, and the duration of sleep per day is measured for each subject on four randomly selected days during the experimental period. The results (in hours of sleep) are presented below.

		20–29				30–39		
Subject Day	1	2	3	4	1	2	3	4
1	7.2	8.3	7.5	8.1	7.3	8.0	7.1	7.8
2	8.3	7.9	7.7	7.7	7.7	7.4	7.5	7.2
3	8.2	8.5	7.2	7.8	7.8	7.7	7.4	6.8
4	7.6	8.3	7.6	8.3	7.5	7.6	7.0	7.3

		40–49				50–59		
Subject Day	1	2	3	4	1	2	3	4
1	6.9	7.6	7.3	7.3	6.5	5.8	7.1	5.5
2	7.3	7.2	6.5	8.0	6.8	6.7	7.3	6.2
3	6.5	7.0	6.8	7.6	6.0	6.5	6.6	6.0
4	7.4	7.2	6.4	7.2	6.1	5.9	6.9	5.6

Do these data provide sufficient evidence to support the research hypothesis that the mean number of sleeping hours per day differs for the age groups? Use $\alpha = .05$.

15. Refer to exercise 14. Is there evidence that the variability in sleeping hours per day between subjects exceeds that within subjects? Use $\alpha = .01$.

16. A study was conducted to investigate the effects of background noise and task complexity on subjects' performance of a visual-matching task. Five levels of background noise and three levels of task complexity were employed. Forty-five subjects were selected at random from a large group of volunteers and 3 were assigned to each of the fifteen noise-complexity combinations. Subjects within each task complexity level were given a series of matching tasks of equal complexity and were scored for the number of errors made. The data obtained are given below.

Task Complexity	Background Noise (increasing from 1 to 5)				
	b_1	b_2	b_3	b_4	b_5
(high) a_1	10	19	16	32	21
	18	8	21	19	24
	8	18	20	21	30
(med) a_2	5	14	16	20	14
	13	3	7	15	24
	9	7	10	13	19
(low) a_3	2	6	5	9	4
	0	3	7	2	12
	7	3	0	7	8

Compute the analysis of variance for this 3×5 factorial experiment. Display the results in a summary table and conduct the appropriate tests at the $\alpha = .05$ level.

REFERENCES

Cochran, W. G., and Cox, G. M. 1957. *Experimental design.* 2d ed. New York: John Wiley and Sons. Chapter 5.

Connolly, K.; Brown, K.; and Bassett, E. 1968. Developmental changes in same components of a motor skill. *British Journal of Psychology* 59:305–314.

Dreistadt, R. 1969. The use of anatogies and incubation in obtaining insights in creative problem solving. *Journal of Psychology* 71:159–175.

Fuller, R. C. G., and Forrest, D. W. 1973. Behavioral aspects of cigarette smoking in relation to arousal level. *Psychological Reports* 33:115–121.

Koch, M. D., and Arnold, W. J. 1972. Effects of early social deprivation on emotionality in rats. *Journal of Comparative and Physiological Psychology* 78:391–399.

McConville, C. B., and Hemphill, J. K. 1966. Some effects of communication restraint on problem-solving behavior. *Journal of Social Psychology* 64:265–276.

Mendenhall, W. 1968. *Introduction to linear models and the design and analysis of experiments.* N. Scituate, Mass.: Duxbury Press. Chapters 4 and 5.

Morgan, G. A.; Goodson, F. E.; and Jones, T. 1975. Age differences in the associations between felt and color choices. *American Journal of Psychology* 88:125–130.

Sandman, C. A.; Miller, L. H.; Kastin, A. J.; and Schally, A. V. 1972. Neuroendocrine influence on attention and memory. *Journal of Comparative and Physiological Psychology* 80:54–58.

Schachter, S., and Wheeler, L. 1962. Epinephrine, chlorpromazine and amusement. *Journal of Abnormal and Social Psychology* 65:121–128.

Seitz, S. 1969. Pacing effects on performance of an automated task. *Psychological Reports* 25:204–206.

Sheppard, C.; Ricca, E.; Fracchia, J.; and Merlis, S. 1974. Psychological needs of suburban male heroin addicts. *Journal of Psychology* 87:123–128.

Siegel, S. 1956. *Nonparametric statistics.* New York: McGraw-Hill.

Tomasin, J. 1973. Effect of peer-induced anxiety on a problem solving task. *Psychological Reports* 33:355–358.

Weber, R. J., and Bach, M. 1969. Visual and speech imagery. *British Journal of Psychology* 60:199–202.

12·Linear Regression and Correlation

INTRODUCTION

In chapter 3 we introduced some techniques for describing relationships between two variables. In this chapter we will employ these and other techniques to accomplish the objective which constitutes the theme of this text and statistics in general: inference making. In particular, we are interested in making inferences about the nature of the population relationship, assuming that one exists, between variables. If we can establish that a relationship exists between variables, we may then exploit this relationship to accomplish another inferential objective: prediction.

For both theoretical and practical reasons, *prediction* is one of the ultimate objectives of the behavioral scientist. For example, he or she wishes to know how a patient will respond to therapy, how an expectant mother will react to childbirth, if a child will develop unusual language or social skills, or whether a college student will successfully complete an academic program.

Answers to such questions require that (1) the behavior of interest be measurable in some fashion and (2) the factors that determine or influence the criterion behavior be indentifiable and measurable and that their relationship to the criterion be a stable one. **Then the problem of prediction may be stated as one in which a random variable y, the criterion, is functionally related to a number of independent variables, or predictors, x_1, x_2, x_3, ...** This idea is discussed in section 12.1. The method used to determine the prediction equation—called the method of least squares—is presented in section 12.2. Of course, once having determined the prediction equation, we would like to have a measure of its goodness. Thus in section 12.3 we discuss the error of prediction. And in section 12.4 we test the adequacy of the prediction model we have hypothesized.

Given measurements of x_1, x_2, x_3, . . . for a particular individual, we would like to substitute these values into a prediction equation and thereby predict that individual's standing on the criterion variable y. There are two ways of doing this: estimating the average value of y for a given x and predicting a particular value of y for a given x. These ideas are presented in sections 12.5 through 12.7.

The correlation coefficient, first discussed in chapter 3, is also a measure of the linear relationship between x and y. In section 12.8 we return to this idea and its use in linear regression. Then in section 12.9 we present an example that combines and illustrates all the concepts discussed in the chapter.

In this chapter we will be primarily concerned with the *reasoning* involved in acquiring a prediction equation based on one or more independent variables. Thus we will restrict our attention to the simple problem of predicting y as a *linear function* of a *single variable*. We will observe that the solution for the multivariate problem consists of a generalization of our technique (section 12.10). The methodology for the multivariate predictor is fairly complex, as will be apparent later, and is therefore omitted from our discussion.

12.1 • A LINEAR PROBABILISTIC MODEL

We introduce our topic by considering the problem of predicting a student's final grade in an introductory psychology course based on his or her score on a verbal ability test administered before college entrance. We wish to determine first whether the ability test is really worthwhile as a predictor; that is, whether the verbal ability test score is related to a student's introductory psychology grade. Second, we wish to obtain an equation that can be used for prediction purposes. The evidence, presented in table 12.1, represents a sample of the test scores and the introductory psychology grades for 10 students. We assume that these 10 students represent a random sample drawn from the population of students who have already taken the introductory psychology course or will do so in the immediate future.

Table 12.1 • Verbal ability test scores and final introductory psychology grades for 10 students

Student	Verbal Ability Test Scores	Final Introductory Psychology Grades
1	39	65
2	43	78
3	21	52
4	64	82
5	57	92
6	47	89
7	28	73
8	75	98
9	34	56
10	52	75

In section 3.1 we presented a very basic and very useful technique for graphically describing a set of data on two variables: the scattergram. Recall that the scattergram consists of a two-dimensional plot of each sample measurement, with one variable represented on each of the two axes. For our example in table 12.1, we let the x-axis represent verbal ability test scores and the y-axis represent the psychology grade. Then the scattergram is as shown in figure 12.1. Note the general tendency of y (psychology grade) to increase as x (verbal ability score) increases.

One method of obtaining a prediction equation relating y to x is to place a ruler on the graph and move it about until it seems to pass through most of the points, thus providing what we might regard as the "best fit" to the data. In fact, if we were to draw a line through the points, it would appear that our prediction problem is solved. That is, we could use the graph to predict a student's psychology grade on the basis of his or her score on the verbal ability test. Furthermore, note that we have chosen a *mathematical model* that expresses the supposed functional relation between y and x.

You should recall several facts concerning the graphing of mathematical functions. The mathematical equation of a straight line can be written as

$$y = \beta_0 + \beta_1 x$$

where β_0 is the y-intercept and β_1 is the slope of the line. The y-intercept β_0 is the value of y when $x = 0$. The slope β_1 is the change in y for a 1-unit change in x.

The line that we graph corresponding to a linear equation is unique. Each equation corresponds to only one line, and each line corresponds to only one equation. Thus when we draw a line through the points, we have automatically chosen a mathematical equation,

Figure 12.1 • Plot of the data in table 12.1

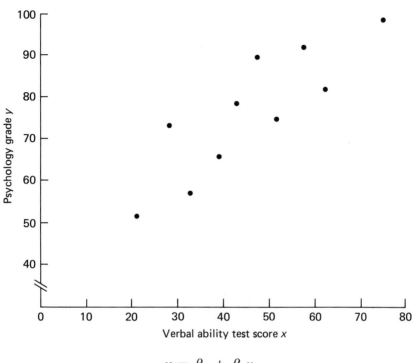

$$y = \beta_0 + \beta_1 x$$

where β_0 and β_1 have unique numerical values.

A linear model $y = \beta_0 + \beta_1 x$ is said to be a *deterministic mathematical model* because when a value of x is substituted into the equation, the value of y is determined and no allowance is made for error. Deterministic models are quite suitable for explaining physical phenomena and predicting when the error of prediction is negligible, for all practical purposes. Thus many examples of deterministic mathematical models may be found by leafing through the pages of elementary chemistry, physics, or engineering textbooks. For example, Newton's second law of motion expresses the relation between the force F imparted by a moving body with mass m and acceleration a. This relationship is given by the deterministic model

$$F = ma$$

This model predicts force with very little error and is suitable for most practical applications.

"Very little" is, of course, a relative concept. An error of 1 minute can be tolerated when giving the arrival time for a transatlantic airplane flight but might be financially disastrous when estimating the finishing time for a horse in the Kentucky Derby. Likewise, for many situations in the behavioral sciences, the error of prediction cannot be ignored. We would be hesitant to place much confidence in a prediction unaccompanied by a measure of its goodness. For this reason, we would be reluctant to accept a line as a mathematical model to relate introductory psychology grade and verbal ability test score, because it would be more difficult to measure the goodness of the resulting predictions.

Rather than adopting a deterministic model, we might employ a probabilistic mathematical model to explain a behavioral phenomenon. As you might suspect, probabilistic mathematical models contain one or more random terms which allow for an error of prediction. For our example, we could relate introductory psychology grade to verbal ability test score by the equation

$$y = \beta_0 + \beta_1 x + \varepsilon$$

By including the random error term ε (Greek epsilon) in the model, we are recognizing the fact that behavioral variables are rarely, if ever, predictable with perfect accuracy.

In our example, we know that it is possible for two subjects to have identical verbal ability test scores but different psychology grades. Thus psychology grades are not *deterministically* related to verbal ability scores. However, they may very well be *probabilistically* related. The random error could account for the difference in psychology grades for two students having the same verbal ability scores, as shown in figure 12.2. Note that students A and B have identical verbal ability scores but different psychology grades because the random errors differ. However, the deterministic part of the model in figure 12.2, $\beta_0 + \beta_1 x$, shows that the psychology grades have a general tendency to increase as verbal ability scores increase.

Figure 12.2 • Hypothetical probabilistic model relating verbal ability scores and psychology grades: Students A and B have equal verbal ability scores but different psychology grades

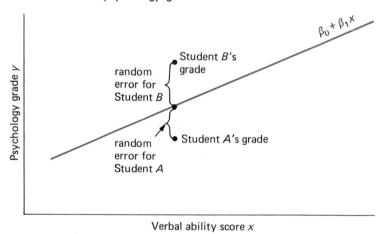

Once we have hypothesized the probabilistic model

$$y = \beta_0 + \beta_1 x + \varepsilon$$

as one which describes the relationship between y and x, we have four distinct statistical tasks to accomplish.

1. We use the sample data to find the best estimate of the deterministic part of the model, $\beta_0 + \beta_1 x$.
2. We use the sample data to describe the random error part of the model, ε.
3. We use our results from the first two steps to infer the utility of our model.
4. Assuming our model passes the test of utility, we use the model to make predictions of unknown y-values from known x-values.

We will consider each step separately in the following sections. In the next section we consider step 1, that of estimating $\beta_0 + \beta_1 x$. This estimate, our prediction equation, is often called a *regression line* in statistics.

EXERCISES

1. Graph the line corresponding to the equation $y = 2x + 1$ by locating the points corresponding to $x = 0$, 1, and 2.
2. Given the linear equation $2x + 3y + 6 = 0$.
   (a) Find the y-intercept and the slope of the line.
   (b) Graph the line corresponding to the equation.
3. Follow the instructions given in exercise 2, using the linear equation $2x - 3y - 5 = 0$.
4. Follow the instructions given in exercise 2, using the linear equation $x/y = \frac{1}{2}$.

12.2 • THE METHOD OF LEAST SQUARES

The statistical procedure for finding the "best-fitting" straight line for a set of points would seem to be, in many respects, a formalization of the procedure employed when we fit a line by eye. For instance, when we visually fit a line to a set of data, we move the ruler until we think that we have minimized the *deviations* of the points from the prospective line. If we denote the predicted value of y obtained from the fitted line as $\hat{y}$, then the prediction equation will be as given in the box.

Prediction Equation

$$\hat{y} = \hat{\beta}_0 + \hat{\beta}_1 x$$

where $\hat{\beta}_0$ and $\hat{\beta}_1$ represent sample estimates of β_0 and β_1.

Note that our prediction equation does not contain a random error component, since we are fitting a deterministic straight line through the data points, even though we know they were generated by a probabilistic model. We really have no alternative, because the random error component of the model is literally ''unpredictable.''

Our prediction line for the data of table 12.1 is shown in figure 12.3. The vertical lines drawn from the prediction line to each point represent the deviations of the points from the predicted value of y. Thus the deviation of the point with coordinates (x_i, y_i) from the predicted value $\widehat{y}$ is

$$\text{deviation} = y_i - \widehat{y}_i$$

where $\widehat{y}_i$ is computed by substituting x_i into the prediction equation

$$\widehat{y} = \widehat{\beta}_0 + \widehat{\beta}_1 x$$

These deviations represent the errors between the actual observation y_i and the predicted value $\widehat{y}_i$.

Figure 12.3 • Linear prediction equation

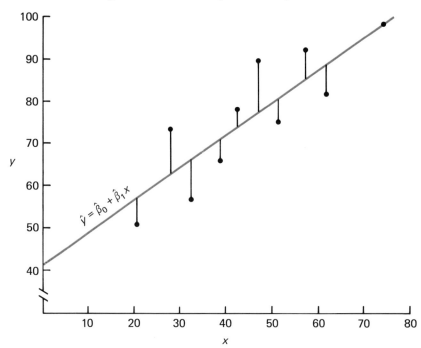

Having decided that somehow we will attempt to minimize the deviations of the points in choosing the best-fitting line, we must now define what we mean by ''best.'' That is, we wish to define a criterion for ''best fit'' which will seem intuitively reasonable, which is objective, and which under certain conditions will give the best prediction of y for a given value of x.

We will employ a criterion of goodness that is known as the principle of least squares and which may be stated as follows. Choose as the best-fitting line that line which minimizes the sum of squares of the deviations of the observed values of y from those predicted.

Expressed mathematically, we wish to minimize the sum of squares for error, as shown in the box.

Term to Be Minimized in Regression Analysis

SSE = sum of squares of vertical deviations of
observed y-values minus predicted y-values

$$= \sum_{i=1}^{n} (y_i - \hat{y}_i)^2$$

Recall that SSE was used in chapter 11 to denote the sum of squares for error in an analysis of variance. Its connotation is unchanged here, except that it now represents the sum of squares for error in a regression analysis.

It can be proved that the slope $\hat{\beta}_1$ and the y-intercept $\hat{\beta}_0$ which minimize SSE are as given in the box.

Least Squares Estimators of β_0 and β_1

$$\hat{\beta}_1 = \frac{SS_{xy}}{SS_{xx}} \quad \text{and} \quad \hat{\beta}_0 = \bar{y} - \hat{\beta}_1 \bar{x}$$

where

$$SS_{xx} = \sum_{i=1}^{n} (x_i - \bar{x})^2 = \sum_{i=1}^{n} x_i^2 - \frac{\left(\sum_{i=1}^{n} x_i \right)^2}{n}$$

$$SS_{xy} = \sum_{i=1}^{n} (x_i - \bar{x})(y_i - \bar{y}) = \sum_{i=1}^{n} x_i y_i - \frac{\left(\sum_{i=1}^{n} x_i \right)\left(\sum_{i=1}^{n} y_i \right)}{n}$$

Recall that we used the notation SS_{xx} and SS_{xy} in chapter 3 to denote the same quantities as those given above. You will recall that the cross product summation SS_{xy} played a key role in calculating the *correlation coefficient* (section 3.2). It is no accident that SS_{xy} appears again in determining the slope β_1 of the least squares line, since both the slope and the correlation coefficient are measures of the linear relationship between x and y. We will investigate this similarity between slope and correlation later in the chapter.

Once the y-intercept $\hat{\beta}_0$ and the slope $\hat{\beta}_1$ have been computed, we simply substitute them for β_0 and β_1 in the deterministic part of our model to get the least squares prediction equation.

Least Squares Prediction Equation

$$\hat{y} = \hat{\beta}_0 + \hat{\beta}_1 x$$

where $\hat{\beta}_0$ and $\hat{\beta}_1$ are the least squares estimators of β_0 and β_1.

Example 12.1

Let us hypothesize a probabilistic linear relationship between the final grade in an introductory psychology course (y) and a verbal ability test score (x).

$$y = \beta_0 + \beta_1 x + \varepsilon$$

Using the data given in table 12.1, find the least squares prediction equation which estimates the deterministic part of the model, $\beta_0 + \beta_1 x$.

Solution: In table 12.2 we again present the data for the 10 students, along with several other columns of squares and the cross product which will be useful in our calculations. The sum of each column is given at the bottom of the table.

Table 12.2 • Calculations for the data of table 12.1 and example 12.1

Student	y_i	x_i	x_i^2	$x_i y_i$	y_i^2
1	65	39	1,521	2,535	4,225
2	78	43	1,849	3,354	6,084
3	52	21	441	1,092	2,704
4	82	64	4,096	5,248	6,724
5	92	57	3,249	5,244	8,464
6	89	47	2,209	4,183	7,921
7	73	28	784	2,044	5,329
8	98	75	5,625	7,350	9,604
9	56	34	1,156	1,904	3,136
10	75	52	2,704	3,900	5,625
Totals	760	460	23,634	36,854	59,816

Substituting the appropriate values into the shortcut formulas for SS_{xx} and SS_{xy}, we obtain

$$SS_{xx} = \sum_{i=1}^{n} x_i^2 - \frac{\left(\sum_{i=1}^{n} x_i\right)^2}{n} = 23,634 - \frac{(460)^2}{10} = 2474$$

$$SS_{xy} = \sum_{i=1}^{n} x_i y_i - \frac{\left(\sum_{i=1}^{n} x_i\right)\left(\sum_{i=1}^{n} y_i\right)}{n} = 36,854 - \frac{(460)(760)}{10}$$

$$= 1894$$

Then

$$\widehat{\beta}_1 = \frac{SS_{xy}}{SS_{xx}} = \frac{1894}{2474} = .76556 \approx .77$$

$$\widehat{\beta}_0 = \overline{y} - \widehat{\beta}_1 \overline{x} = 76 - (.76556)(46) = 40.78424 \approx 40.78$$

According to the principle of least squares, the best-fitting line relating introductory psychology grade to verbal ability test score is

$$\widehat{y} = \widehat{\beta}_0 + \widehat{\beta}_1 x$$

or

$$\hat{y} = 40.78 + .77x$$

The graph of this equation is shown in figure 12.3.

We may now predict y for a given value of x by referring to figure 12.3 or by substituting into the prediction equation. Note that the estimated slope of $\hat{\beta}_1 = .77$ implies that the predicted psychology grade increases by .77 units for every 1-unit increase in verbal ability test score. For example, if a student scored $x = 50$ on the ability test, the predicted psychology grade for that student is

$$\hat{y} = \hat{\beta}_0 + \hat{\beta}_1 x = 40.78 + (.77)(50) = 79.28$$

As in other statistical procedures we have used, we will wish to place a bound on the prediction error. But before we can do that, we must use the sample data to describe the random error term ε in our model. This topic is discussed in the next section.

EXERCISES

1. Given five points whose coordinates are as shown below.

y	0	0	1	1	3
x	−2	−1	0	1	2

(a) Find the least squares line for the data.
(b) As a check on the calculations in part (a), plot the five points and graph the line.
2. Given the following data for corresponding values of two variables, y and x. Follow the instructions of exercise 1.

y	2	1.5	1	2.5	2.5	4	5
x	−3	−2	−1	0	1	2	3

3. Newman and Grice (1965) conducted research on albino rats in which the response measures were the speed of first test response and the percentage of extinction responses. These two measures were seen as reflecting a common underlying variable. So the data were submitted to a linear regression equation to see if a straight-line function described the relationship. The data are given below. Follow the instructions of exercise 1.

Speed (y)	50	200	325	325	400	525
Extinction Response (x)	15	22	30	28	30	50

4. Consider the following data for corresponding values of entrance examination scores and freshman grades. Follow the instructions of exercise 1.

Entrance Test (x)	71	67	65	63	59
Freshman Grades (y)	92	88	89	80	72

12.3 • THE RANDOM ERROR TERM ε

Since the error component ε of our model is a random variable, we must describe it by using a frequency distribution. As you know, we could only be certain of the nature of this frequency distribution if we could obtain a very large number of data values, that is, if we could actually collect a population of ε's. Since it is very unlikely that we can obtain such a large number of values, we must make certain assumptions about the frequency distribution of ε. Then we use our data to check the reasonableness of these assumptions.

Before listing the basic assumptions about ε, we present a pictorial summary of the assumptions in figure 12.4. Figure 12.4 will be used as a reference for each of the assumptions listed below.

Figure 12.4 • Summary of assumptions about ϵ

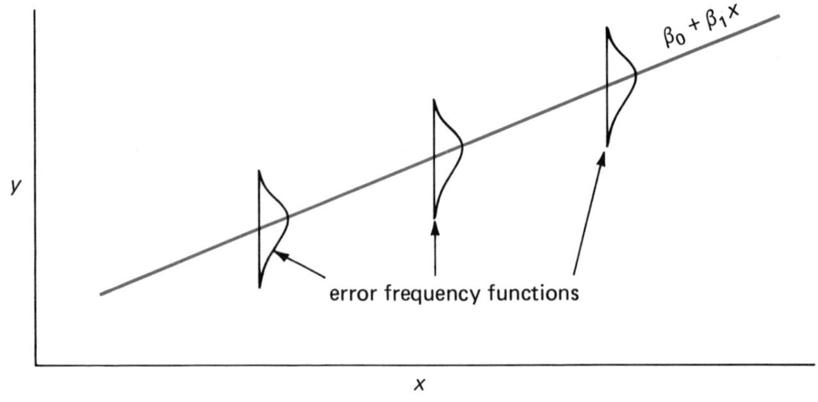

error frequency functions

Assumption 1

We assume that the average value of ε is zero. That is, we assume that in repeated sampling the positive and negative random errors associated with the observations will tend to cancel. In the long run we will have

$$\text{average of } y = \beta_0 + \beta_1 x$$

Figure 12.4 reflects this assumption, since each of the pictured error frequency distributions is centered on $\beta_0 + \beta_1 x$, implying that the average of ε is zero.

Assumption 2

We assume that the variance of ε is constant, no matter what the value of x. Thus we are assuming that the variations in the random errors are the same no matter where the observations fall in the two-dimensional plane. Note in figure 12.4 that each error frequency distribution has the same amount of variation around $\beta_0 + \beta_1 x$, that is, the same variance. We denote the constant error variance by σ^2. The value of σ^2 will almost always be unknown, but we will show how to use the data to estimate σ^2 at the end of this section.

Assumption 3

The random error term in the model is assumed to have a *normal frequency distribution*. Thus in figure 12.4 you will note that each of the pictured frequency distributions for ε has the familiar bell shape of the normal distribution.

Assumption 4

We assume that the error terms are independent of one another from observation to observation. That is, the error associated with one observation should not in any way affect the error of the next observation or any other past or future observation. There is no convenient way of picturing this final assumption.

Much time and space could be devoted to describing checks of these assumptions and to prescribing remedies when one or several of them are not found to be reasonable for a certain data set. However, like many of the topics we have covered, regression analysis is a course (or more) in itself. Our purpose will be accomplished if you understand that these assumptions about ε are those which are made in *standard* regression analysis and if you understand the basic idea behind each assumption.

Suppose, as we will from now on, that the four assumptions are satisfied. Then we need only calculate an estimate of the error variance σ^2 in order to be able to make inferences about the model's utility and to place bounds on the error of prediction. The data provide a quantity well-suited to use in estimating the error variance, namely, the sum of the squared deviations between the actual and the predicted y-values from our least squares model in section 12.2. This is

$$SSE = \sum_{i=1}^{n} (y_i - \hat{y}_i)^2$$

The estimator of σ^2, then, is as given in the box.

Estimator of the Variance of ε

$$\hat{\sigma}^2 = s^2 = \frac{SSE}{n-2}$$

where $(n - 2)$ is the degrees of freedom for the sample variance s^2.

A shortcut formula for SSE is given below.

Shortcut Formula for SSE

$$SSE = SS_{yy} - \frac{(SS_{xy})^2}{SS_{xx}}$$

Example 12.2

Refer to example 12.1. We calculated the least squares prediction line for a sample of 10 students' introductory psychology grades (y) and verbal ability test scores (x). Calculate an estimate of the error variance σ^2 for this model.

Solution: Referring to table 12.2, we calculate the following:

$$SS_{yy} = \sum_{i=1}^{n} y_i^2 - \frac{\left(\sum_{i=1}^{n} y_i\right)^2}{n} = 59{,}816 - \frac{(760)^2}{10}$$

$$= 59{,}816 - 57{,}760 = 2056$$

$$SSE = SS_{yy} - \frac{(SS_{xy})^2}{SS_{xx}} = 2056 - \frac{(1894)^2}{2474} = 606.03$$

Then our estimate of σ^2 is

$$s^2 = \frac{SSE}{n-2} = \frac{606.03}{8} = 75.754$$

Note that "least squares" means that *any other* straight-line fit to this set of data with a y-intercept or a slope different from

$$\hat{y} = 40.78 + .77x$$

will possess a larger SSE than 606.03.

EXERCISES

1. Calculate s^2 for the data in exercise 1 of section 12.2.
2. Calculate s^2 for the data in exercise 2 of section 12.2.
3. Calculate s^2 for the data in exercise 3 of section 12.2.
4. Calculate s^2 for the data in exercise 4 of section 12.2.

12.4 • INFERENCES CONCERNING THE SLOPE OF THE REGRESSION LINE: A CHECK OF MODEL UTILITY

We now wish to make an inference concerning the suitability of our hypothesized probabilistic model

$$y = \beta_0 + \beta_1 x + \varepsilon$$

That is, do the data present sufficient evidence to indicate that y and x are linearly related over the region of observation? Or is it possible that a scattergram will appear like that shown in figure 12.1, even when, in reality, y and x are completely unrelated?

The test of model utility which we consider here involves an hypothesis about the slope β_1. If $\beta_1 = 0$, there is no change in the average value of y for a 1-unit change in x, or for any change in x. Thus x is not useful in predicting y using the linear model. That is, our linear model is inadequate. On the other hand, if the slope is not zero ($\beta_1 \neq 0$), then y changes (on the average) as x changes, and our linear model is of some use in predicting y.

Thus we test the null hypothesis

H_0: There is no linear relationship between x and y over the region of observation; that is, $\beta_1 = 0$

against the research hypothesis

H_a: There exists a linear relationship between x and y over the region of observation; that is, $\beta_1 \neq 0$

As you would expect, the test statistic involves $\widehat{\beta}_1$, the slope of our least squares prediction line. We make the four assumptions about ε listed in section 12.3. Then we can find the frequency distribution of $\widehat{\beta}_1$ obtained by repeatedly sampling n data points and each time calculating $\widehat{\beta}_1$ according to the least squares formula. It can be shown that this repeated sampling distribution would appear as in figure 12.5.

Figure 12.5 • Repeated sampling distribution of $\widehat{\beta}_1$

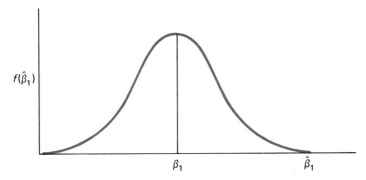

Note that $\widehat{\beta}_1$ is an *unbiased* estimator of β_1, since the mean of its repeated sampling distribution is β_1. It is also true that the standard deviation of $\widehat{\beta}_1$

$$\sigma_{\widehat{\beta}_1} = \frac{\sigma}{\sqrt{SS_{xx}}}$$

is smaller than that of any other unbiased slope estimator. We are therefore satisfied that $\widehat{\beta}_1$ is the best estimator of β_1.

The normal distribution of $\widehat{\beta}_1$ implies that one of the two test statistics given in the box will be appropriate for testing the hypotheses about β_1.

Test Statistic for Testing H_0: $\beta_1 = 0$

1. If σ is known (very unlikely) or n is large enough (say $n > 30$) so that $s \approx \sigma$, use (0 is the null hypothesis value of β_1)

$$z = \frac{\widehat{\beta}_1 - 0}{\sigma_{\widehat{\beta}_1}} = \frac{\widehat{\beta}_1}{\sigma/\sqrt{SS_{xx}}} \approx \frac{\widehat{\beta}_1}{s/\sqrt{SS_{xx}}}$$

2. If σ is unknown *and* n is small, use

$$t = \frac{\widehat{\beta}_1 - 0}{s/\sqrt{SS_{xx}}}$$

with degrees of freedom equal to the denominator of s^2, or $(n-2)$.

The rejection region for the test will be determined in the usual way (see chapters 8 and 9), using either the z or t tables for the desired significance level α.

Example 12.3

Refer to examples 12.1 and 12.2. We fit a least squares prediction line

$$\widehat{y} = 40.78 + .77x$$

to a sample of 10 students' verbal ability test scores (x) and psychology grades (y). Do the data provide sufficient evidence to indicate that the variables x and y are linearly related over the region of observation? Use $\alpha = .05$.

Solution: Our test setup is as follows.

Null hypothesis H_0: $\beta_1 = 0$.

Research hypothesis H_a: $\beta_1 \neq 0$.

Test statistic: Since $n = 10$, we use

$$t = \frac{\widehat{\beta}_1}{s/\sqrt{SS_{xx}}}$$

Rejection region: For our two-tailed research hypothesis, we use the table t-value for $\alpha/2 = .025$ with $(n - 2) = 8$ degrees of freedom, that is,

$$t_{.025} = 2.306$$

We will reject H_0 if

$$t > 2.306 \qquad \text{or} \qquad t < -2.306$$

The rejection region is shown in figure 12.6.

Figure 12.6 • Two-tailed rejection region for the test in example 12.3

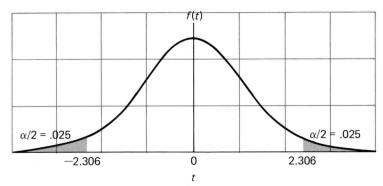

In example 12.2 we found that $s^2 = 75.754$; so $s = 8.70$. And in example 12.1 we found $SS_{xx} = 2474$. We now calculate t:

$$t = \frac{\hat{\beta}_1}{s/\sqrt{SS_{xx}}} = \frac{.77}{8.70/\sqrt{2474}} = 4.40$$

Since the t statistic exceeds 2.306, we conclude that the data support at the .05 level, the research hypothesis that the verbal ability test scores and the psychology grades are linearly related. Furthermore, we infer from the fact that $\hat{\beta}_1$ is positive that the true relationship is positive in nature. The average psychology grade increases as the verbal ability score increases, at least over the range of observation represented by our sample.

Several points concerning the interpretation of our results deserve particular attention. As we have noted, β_1 is the slope of the assumed line over the region of observation and indicates the *linear* change in y for a 1-unit change in x. If we do not reject the null hypothesis $\beta_1 = 0$, it *does not* mean that x and y are unrelated.

In the first place, we must be concerned with the possibility of accepting the null hypothesis when it is false.

Second, it is possible that x and y might be perfectly related in some curvilinear manner. For example, figure 12.7 shows a curvilinear relationship between y and x over the domain of x, $a \le x \le f$. We note that a straight line would provide a good predictor of y if fitted over a small interval in the x domain, say $b \le x \le c$. The resulting line is line 1 in figure 12.7. On the other hand, if we attempt to fit a line over the region $b \le x \le d$, β_1 is zero and the best fit to the data is the horizontal line 2. Thus we must take care in drawing conclusions if we do not find evidence to indicate that β_1 differs from zero. Perhaps we have chosen the wrong type of probabilistic model for the physical situation.

Note that these comments contain a second implication. If the data provide values of x in an interval $b \le x \le c$, then the calculated prediction equation is appropriate only *over this region*. As you can see, extrapolation in predicting y for values of x outside the region $b \le x \le c$ for the situation indicated in figure 12.7 would result in a serious prediction error.

Figure 12.7 • A curvilinear relation between x and y

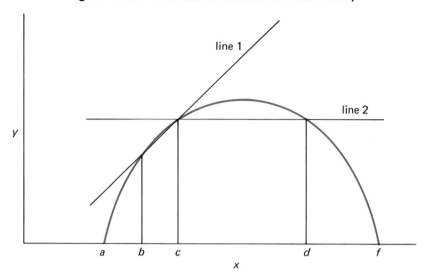

Finally, if the data present sufficient evidence to indicate that β_1 differs from zero, as they did in our example, we do not conclude that the *true* relationship between y and x is linear. Thus in our conclusion to example 12.3, we were careful to state only that the *true* relationship was an increasing or positive relationship over the region of experimentation; we did not state that the relationship was necessarily linear.

Undoubtedly, y is a function of several variables, which are accounted for, at least to some degree, by the random error ε which appears in the model. This, of course, is why we have been obliged to use a probabilistic model in the first place. Large errors of prediction imply either curvatures in the true relation between y and x, or the presence of other important variables which do not appear in the model, or, as most often is the case, both. All we can say is that we have evidence to indicate that y changes as x changes and that we may obtain a better prediction of y using x and the linear predictor than simply using $\bar{y}$ and ignoring x. Note that this *does not* imply a *causal* relationship between x and y. A third variable may have caused the change in both x and y, thus producing the relationship that we have observed.

EXERCISES

1. Do the data in exercise 3 of section 12.2 present sufficient evidence to indicate that y and x are linearly related? (Test the hypothesis that $\beta_1 = 0$, using $\alpha = .05$.)
2. Do the data in exercise 4 of section 12.2 present sufficient evidence to indicate that y and x are linearly related? (Test the hypothesis that $\beta_1 = 0$, using $\alpha = .05$.)
3. Schailble (1975) administered the Thematic Apperception Test to subjects to study the

relationship between age and the number of words used, the silence interval before response, and achievement. Below are some data on age (x) and total words used (y) for 11 subjects. Note that there were 2 subjects aged 11.5, 1 aged 12, 2 aged 13.5, and so on.

Age (x)	11.5	12	13.5	14.5	16	17.5
Total Words (y)	55 60	60	61 63	63 64	70 71	74 79

(a) Write a simple linear probabilistic model relating total words to age.
(b) Use the least squares method to estimate the deterministic part of the linear model.
(c) Write down the usual assumptions about the frequency distribution of the random error component. Estimate the error variance σ^2 by calculating s^2.
(d) Test the model adequacy by testing the null hypothesis that the slope $\beta_1 = 0$. Use $\alpha = .10$.

12.5 • TWO TYPES OF PREDICTIONS

We have now accomplished the first three goals listed at the end of section 12.1: we have used least squares to estimate the deterministic part of our model; we have made assumptions and inferences about the random error component; and we have tested the model's utility. Assuming that we are satisfied that a linear relationship exists between x and y, it remains for us to use the model for prediction.

There are two distinct types of prediction in which we may be interested. The first type involves predicting (in actuality, estimating) the average value of y for a given value of x. That is, we want to predict the average value of all the y-values we would observe if we were to experiment a very large number of times at the same value of x.

For example, suppose we want to know the average value of y when $x = x_p$. Then our least squares prediction equation would yield

$$\hat{y} = \hat{\beta}_0 + \hat{\beta}_1 x_p$$

as an estimate of this average value. This is shown in figure 12.8. Note that the error of estimation is the vertical distance between the estimated and the true average value of y. In the next section we will place bounds on this error of estimation.

The second type of prediction involves predicting a *particular value of y* for a given value of x. That is, rather than estimating the average value of y in repeated experimentation at $x = x_p$, we want to predict the result of a single experiment, say the next experiment, at $x = x_p$. This value will be represented as

$$\text{particular } y = \beta_0 + \beta_1 x_p + \varepsilon \qquad Y = a + b(x)$$

Note that the particular value of y, unlike the average value of y, includes the

Figure 12.8 • Estimating the average value of y when $x = x_p$

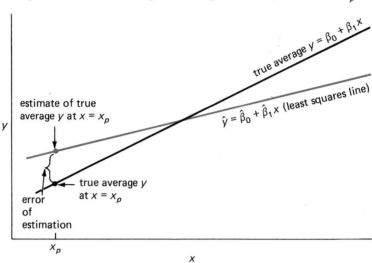

random error component. This is necessary for the particular value, since our use of a probabilistic model implies that some random error will be associated with each observation.

We again use our prediction equation to obtain precisely the same predicted value as before,

$$\widehat{y} = \widehat{\beta}_0 + \widehat{\beta}_1 x_p$$

But as figure 12.9 shows, the error of prediction for predicting a particular value of y will in general be different than that for estimating an average value of y.

Figure 12.9 • Predicting a particular value of y when $x = x_p$

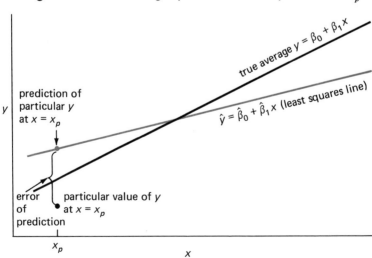

Now the prediction error is the distance between the *predicted* $\hat{y}$ and the particular value of y that occurs on a single experimental trial. In section 12.7 we will consider bounds on the error for this type of prediction.

As you may already have surmised, we will have more success predicting average values of y than particular values of y, simply because we can be more certain of the *average* outcome of a very large number of experiments than we can be of the *particular* outcome of a single experiment. Thus our error estimates will be smaller when estimating average values than when predicting particular values.

Example 12.4

Referring to our previous examples, suppose we wish to predict the psychology grade for a student whose verbal ability score is 50. Which type of prediction should be used, estimation of an average value of y or prediction of a particular value of y?

Solution: The fact that we wish to predict the psychology grade for one student whose verbal ability score is 50 is the key. That is, we are interested in a *particular* value of y. Only if we were interested in estimating the average psychology grade of *all* the students who score 50 on the verbal ability test would we want to estimate an average value of y.

EXERCISES

1. Refer to exercise 3 of section 12.4. We hypothesized and fit a linear probabilistic model to relate total words used (y) to age (x). If we wish to predict the average number of words used by all fourteen year olds, would we be estimating an average value of y or predicting a particular value of y at x = 14?
2. Refer to exercise 1. Susan Smith is 14, and we wish to use our linear model to predict the total number of words she will use in our experiment. Are we estimating an average value of y or predicting a particular value of y at x = 14?

12.6 • ESTIMATING THE AVERAGE VALUE OF Y FOR A GIVEN VALUE OF X

In this section we pursue the idea of estimating an average value of y for a given value of x, say x_p. The concept was pictured in figure 12.8. We are trying to estimate the

$$\text{average value of } y = \beta_0 + \beta_1 x_p$$

Our estimator is

$$\hat{y} = \hat{\beta}_0 + \hat{\beta}_1 x_p$$

Making the four assumptions about ε listed in section 12.3, we have the repeated sampling properties for $\widehat{y}$ as given in the box.

Summary of Properties of $\widehat{y}$, the Estimator of an Average Value of y

1. The estimator $\widehat{y}$ has a mean value of $\beta_0 + \beta_1 x_p$ in repeated sampling and thus is unbiased.
2. The average squared distance between $\widehat{y}$ and $\beta_0 + \beta_1 x_p$ in repeated sampling, that is, the variance of $\widehat{y}$, is

$$\sigma^2_{\widehat{y}} = \sigma^2 \left[\frac{1}{n} + \frac{(x_p - \bar{x})^2}{SS_{xx}} \right]$$

3. The repeated sampling frequency distribution of $\widehat{y}$ is normal.

Note that the farther x_p lies from $\bar{x}$, the larger will be the variance of $\widehat{y}$, $\sigma^2_{\widehat{y}}$. We will use the variance of $\widehat{y}$ to place bounds on the error of estimation. Assuming σ^2, the variance of our random error ε, is unknown, we will substitute s^2 for σ^2. We form the $(1 - \alpha)$ confidence interval given in the box for the true average value of y.

A $(1 - \alpha)$ Confidence Interval for the Average Value of $y = \beta_0 + \beta_1 x_p$

$$\widehat{y} \pm t_{\alpha/2} s \sqrt{\frac{1}{n} + \frac{(x_p - \bar{x})^2}{SS_{xx}}} \qquad \widehat{y} \pm t \sigma_{\widehat{y}}$$

where the t statistic has $(n - 2)$ degrees of freedom (the denominator of s^2).

Example 12.5

For the verbal ability score and psychology grade example, form a 95 percent confidence interval for the average psychology grade of all students who score 50 on the verbal ability test.

Solution: First, we estimate our average value of y (psychology grade) when x (verbal ability score) is 50.

$$\widehat{y} = \widehat{\beta}_0 + \widehat{\beta}_1(50) = 40.78 + .77(50) = 79.28$$

To form a 95 percent confidence interval, we calculate

$$\widehat{y} \pm t_{.025} s \sqrt{\frac{1}{10} + \frac{(50 - \bar{x})^2}{SS_{xx}}}$$

$$= 79.28 \pm (2.306)(8.70) \sqrt{\frac{1}{10} + \frac{(50 - 46)^2}{2474}}$$

$$= 79.28 \pm 6.55$$

We therefore are 95 percent confident that the average psychology grade for all students who score 50 on the verbal ability test is between 72.73 and 85.83. This confidence interval is shown in figure 12.10.

Figure 12.10 • 95 percent confidence interval for the average psychology grade (y) when the verbal ability score (x) is 50

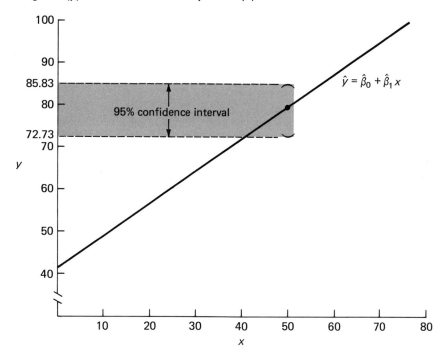

EXERCISES

1. Refer to exercise 3 of section 12.2. What is the estimated average speed of first test response for all albino rats whose extinction response is 35? Place a 95 percent confidence interval on the true average.
2. Refer to exercise 4 of section 12.2. Place a 90 percent confidence interval on the average freshman grades for all incoming students with an entrance test score of 70.
3. Refer to exercise 3 of section 12.4. Using a 95 percent confidence interval, estimate the average number of words used by all 14-year-old subjects.

12.7 • PREDICTING A PARTICULAR VALUE OF Y FOR A GIVEN VALUE OF X

We now turn to the prediction of a single observation when $x = x_p$. The observation we are trying to predict may be represented by

$$\text{particular value of } y = \beta_0 + \beta_1 x_p + \varepsilon$$

The presence of the error term reflects the fact that we are predicting the outcome of a single experiment at $x = x_p$ (see figure 12.9).

Our predictor remains

$$\hat{y} = \hat{\beta}_0 + \hat{\beta}_1 x_p$$

since we have no better predictor of the error term ε than its average value, zero. The repeated sampling properties of $\hat{y}$ were summarized in section 12.6. However, we are now interested in the prediction error of $\hat{y}$ when predicting a particular y-value, that is, the distance between $\hat{y}$ and $\beta_0 + \beta_1 x_p + \varepsilon$.

The Average Squared Distance Between $\hat{y}$ and $\beta_0 + \beta_1 x_p + \varepsilon$

$$\sigma^2_{error} = \sigma^2 \left[1 + \frac{1}{n} + \frac{(x_p - \bar{x})^2}{SS_{xx}} \right]$$

Comparing this variance with the variance of $\hat{y}$ when estimating an average value, we note the addition of an extra σ^2 in the above expression. This is the error added by the presence of ε in the formula for the predicted value. Note also that the farther x_p lies from $\bar{x}$, the larger will be σ^2_{error} and the larger will be the corresponding $(1 - \alpha)$ prediction interval. The $(1 - \alpha)$ prediction interval is formed as given in the box.

A $(1 - \alpha)$ Prediction Interval for a Particular Value of y at $x = x_p$

$$\hat{y} \pm t_{\alpha/2} s \sqrt{1 + \frac{1}{n} + \frac{(x_p - \bar{x})^2}{SS_{xx}}}$$

with degrees of freedom of $(n - 2)$.

Example 12.6

Mike Jones has scored 50 on the verbal ability test. Form a 95 percent prediction interval for the grade Mike will receive in the introductory psychology course.

Solution: We want to predict a particular psychology grade, namely Mike's. Our prediction is

$$\hat{y} = \hat{\beta}_0 + \hat{\beta}_1 x_p = 40.78 + (.77)(50) = 79.28$$

A 95 percent prediction interval for his grade is

$$79.28 \pm t_{\alpha/2} s \sqrt{1 + \frac{1}{10} + \frac{(50 - \bar{x})^2}{SS_{xx}}}$$

$$= 79.28 \pm (2.306)(8.70) \sqrt{1 + \frac{1}{10} + \frac{(50 - 46)^2}{2474}}$$

$$= 79.28 \pm 21.10$$

Thus we are 95 percent confident that Mike's final grade in the introductory psychology course will be between 58.18 and 100 (the upper value actually exceeds 100, but we exclude impossible scores from our interval). This interval is shown in figure 12.11.

Figure 12.11 • 95 percent prediction interval for a particular student's psychology grade when his or her verbal ability score is 50

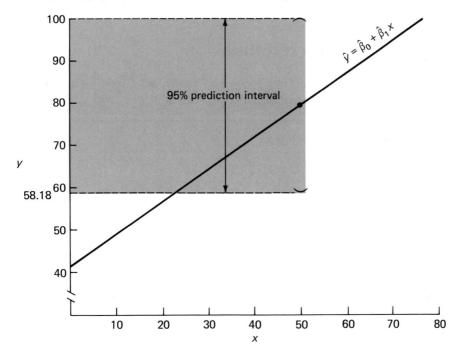

Note that the prediction interval for predicting a particular value of y is much wider than the interval for estimating an average value of y. In fact, in our example the interval for a particular value of y is so wide that it is virtually useless. Predicting that Mike Jones will score between 58 and 100 in his psychology course is not earthshaking. One way of reducing the width of both intervals is to increase our sample size. Certainly we would sample many more than 10 students if we were interested in establishing an accurate predictive relationship between verbal ability test scores and psychology grades.

EXERCISES

1. Refer to exercise 3 of section 12.2. Suppose you find that a particular albino rat has a 35 percent extinction response. Predict the speed of the first test response for this rat, using a 95 percent prediction interval. Compare your result with the confidence

interval obtained in exercise 1, section 12.6, for the average first test response of all rats having a 35 percent extinction response.

2. Refer to exercise 4 of section 12.2. Predict the freshman grade of an incoming student whose entrance test score is 70. Use a 90 percent prediction interval.

3. Refer to exercise 3 of section 12.4. Susan Smith is fourteen years old. Predict the number of words she will use in the experiment, using a 95 percent prediction interval. How does this compare with the confidence interval obtained in exercise 3, section 12.6, for the average number of words used by all fourteen year olds?

12.8 · THE CORRELATION COEFFICIENT

In section 3.2 we introduced the correlation coefficient r as a measure of the strength of the linear relationship between two variables x and y.

The Correlation Coefficient

$$r = \frac{\sum_{i=1}^{n}(x_i - \bar{x})(y_i - \bar{y})}{\sqrt{\sum_{i=1}^{n}(x_i - \bar{x})^2 \sum_{i=1}^{n}(y_i - \bar{y})^2}} = \frac{SS_{xy}}{\sqrt{SS_{xx}SS_{yy}}}$$

In this chapter we have developed another measure of the strength of the linear relationship between x and y, the slope $\widehat{\beta}_1$ of our least squares prediction equation. Although the correlation coefficient r and the slope $\widehat{\beta}_1$ measure the same characteristic (in fact, $r = \sqrt{SS_{xx}/SS_{yy}} \times \widehat{\beta}_1$), they will have different numerical values, and both are useful.

As we have seen, the least squares slope $\widehat{\beta}_1$ estimates the average increase in y for a 1-unit increase in x. For this reason it is useful both for testing the existence of a linear relationship and for predicting y-values.

On the other hand, the correlation coefficient r is scaleless, always lying between -1 and $+1$. Therefore, values of r may be compared from experiment to experiment even though the scale of measurement may change. The sign of r will always agree with the sign of $\widehat{\beta}_1$, signifying whether the *sample* linear relationship is positive or negative.

Perhaps the biggest difference between $\widehat{\beta}_1$ and r is the nature of the data for which each may be meaningfully used. The slope $\widehat{\beta}_1$ may be calculated for any pair of variables so long as y, the dependent variable, is random. The independent variable may either be random or be controlled by the experimenter. However, the correlation coefficient r is meaningful only when both x and y are random variables. For example, for psychology grades (y) and verbal ability scores (x), neither variable can be controlled by the experimenter; thus both are random variables. Here, then, the correlation coefficient between x and y has a meaning.

However, if we were performing an experiment to relate learning time (y) to study time (x), we could control the value of x by setting specific lengths of study time for each subject. Only learning time would be random. The calculation of r would be inappropriate for this experiment, but we could still establish a prediction equation between y and x.

If both x and y are random, they will possess a true, or population, correlation coefficient which we denote by ρ (Greek letter rho). We have seen in section 12.4 that we may test the null hypothesis of no linear relationship by testing $H_0 : \beta_1 = 0$. However, in some experimental situations we will not be interested in predicting y from x. Instead, we will only be interested in knowing whether x and y are linearly related. In this case, calculation of the correlation coefficient will be more convenient than fitting the least squares prediction line.

We determine whether a linear relationship exists by testing the null hypothesis

H_0: The population correlation coefficient is 0 ($\rho = 0$)

against the research hypothesis

H_a: The population correlation coefficient is not 0 ($\rho \neq 0$)

The test statistic is the *exact* equivalent of that in section 12.4 for H_0: $\beta_1 = 0$, but it is written in terms of r rather than $\hat{\beta}_1$.

$$\text{Test statistic: } t = \frac{r}{\sqrt{(1 - r^2)/(n - 2)}}$$

where the degrees of freedom are $(n - 2)$, as before.

The assumptions which make this test valid are the same as those stated for ε in section 12.3, plus one additional assumption. The random variables y and x are assumed to be jointly normally distributed. Note that this is not necessary for testing the slope hypothesis, since x need not be random.

The rejection region for this test of an hypothesis will be identical to that for the test of the slope.

Example 12.7

Refer again to the verbal ability score and psychology grade data. Test the null hypothesis of no linear relationship using the correlation coefficient r. Use $\alpha = .05$.

Solution: We set up our test in terms of the population correlation coefficient between verbal ability score and psychology grade.

Null hypothesis H_0: $\rho = 0$.

Research hypothesis H_a: $\rho \neq 0$.

Test statistic: $t = \dfrac{r}{\sqrt{(1 - r^2)/(n - 2)}}$.

Assumptions: The same four assumptions about ε as listed in section 12.3.

Also, the verbal ability scores and the psychology grades are jointly normal.

Rejection region: This is a two-tailed test, with d.f. $= n - 2 = 8$ and $t_{\alpha/2} = t_{.025} = 2.306$. We will reject H_0 if

$$t > 2.306 \qquad \text{or} \qquad t < -2.306$$

We first calculate the correlation coefficient, then t.

$$r = \frac{SS_{xy}}{\sqrt{SS_{xx}SS_{yy}}} = \frac{1894}{\sqrt{(2474)(2056)}} = .84$$

$$t = \frac{r}{\sqrt{(1 - r^2)/(n - 2)}} = \frac{.84}{\sqrt{[1 - (.84)^2]/8}} = \frac{.84}{.19} = 4.42$$

Note that this is essentially the same t-value we obtained when testing the null hypothesis $\beta_1 = 0$ in example 12.3. The slight difference is due to roundoff errors. Our conclusion is identical to the conclusion we made in example 12.3. Our data provide sufficient evidence to conclude, at the .05 level, that a linear relationship exists between verbal ability score and psychology grade, at least over the range of observation. In the above test, the fact that r is positive allows the further inference that the relationship is a positive one.

We have seen that the information contained in the slope $\widehat{\beta}_1$ and the correlation coefficient r is somewhat redundant, since both measure the strength of the linear relationship between x and y. However, the square of the correlation coefficient contains some additional information about the sample linear relationship.

The value of the squared correlation coefficient r^2 is in the interval

$$0 \leq r^2 \leq 1$$

In fact, with a little algebra, we can show that r^2 can be determined as shown in the box.

$$r^2 = \frac{\displaystyle\sum_{i=1}^{n} (y_i - \bar{y})^2 - \sum_{i=1}^{n} (y_i - \widehat{y}_i)^2}{\displaystyle\sum_{i=1}^{n} (y_i - \bar{y})^2} = \frac{SS_{yy} - SSE}{SS_{yy}} = 1 - \frac{SSE}{SS_{yy}}$$

The verbal interpretation of the above formula is important. The value of r^2 represents the fraction by which the sample variance of the criterion variable y is reduced when the linear prediction model is used instead of just $\bar{y}$. In other words, r^2 represents the fraction of the total variation of y which is accounted for by linear x. Thus r^2 would seem to give a more meaningful interpretation of the strength of the relation between y and x than would the correlation coefficient r.

A better understanding of the meaning of r^2 can be obtained by considering an illustration. Suppose the data suggest a linear relationship between y and x. You fit a least squares line through the data as shown in figure 12.12(a). Note the deviations shown by the vertical line segments between the fitted line and the data points and imagine the magnitude of SSE, the sum of squares of these deviations.

Figure 12.12 • Two models fit to the same data

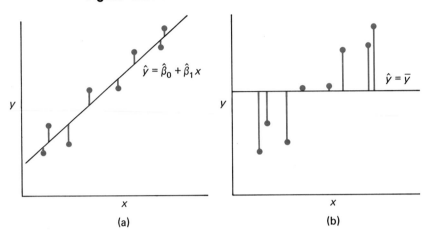

(a)   (b)

Now suppose that you do not assume that

$$y = \beta_0 + \beta_1 x + \varepsilon$$

but rather that x contributes no information for predicting y. Then the slope is zero, dropping the term $\beta_1 x$ out of the model. Then we would have

$$y = \beta_0 + \varepsilon$$

As you might suspect, the least squares prediction of some new value of y for this model is the sample mean, $\hat{y} = \bar{y}$. This prediction line is shown in figure 12.12(b) along with the vertical lines representing the errors of prediction.

Compare the magnitude of the deviations of the data points from the line

$$\hat{y} = \hat{\beta}_0 + \hat{\beta}_1 x$$

for figure 12.12(a) with those about the line

$$\hat{y} = \bar{y}$$

of figure 12.12(b). This subjective comparison can be expressed in a more objective way by comparing the sums of squares for error for the two models (prediction equations); that is,

$$\text{SSE} = \sum_{i=1}^{n} (y_i - \hat{y}_i)^2$$

$$SS_{yy} = \sum_{i=1}^{n} (y_i - \bar{y})^2$$

This comparison appears as a ratio in the expression for r^2; thus

$$r^2 = 1 - \frac{\sum\limits_{i=1}^{n}(y_i - \hat{y}_i)^2}{\sum\limits_{i=1}^{n}(y_i - \bar{y})^2} = 1 - \frac{SSE}{SS_{yy}}$$

Example 12.8

Interpret the value of r^2 for the verbal ability score and psychology grade data.

Solution: We previously computed $r = .84$, so that $r^2 = .71$. The implication for this sample of 10 students is that the sum of squared deviations about the prediction line $\hat{y}$ is 71 percent smaller than the sum of squared deviations about $\bar{y}$. That is, the use of verbal ability score to predict psychology grades results in a 71 percent decrease in the total sample variation which would exist if the verbal ability scores were not used.

Since r^2 indicates the amount of variability in y accounted for by linear regression on x, we should use restraint in interpreting low or even intermediate values of r. It is not uncommon for researchers in some fields to treat sample correlation coefficients in the neighborhood of .5 as indicative of a "strong" relationship between y and x. However, a value $r = .5$ would imply that the use of x in predicting y reduced the sample sum of squares of deviations about the prediction line by only $r^2 = .25$, or 25 percent. A correlation coefficient $r = .1$ would imply only an $r^2 = .01$ or 1 percent reduction in the total sum of squares of deviations that could be explained by x in the sample.

A further caution concerning the interpretation of r involves the use of two or more predictors. If the linear coefficient of correlation between y and each of two variables, x_1 and x_2, were calculated to be .4 and .5, respectively, it does not follow that a predictor using both variables would account for a $[(.4)^2 + (.5)^2] = .41$ or a 41 percent reduction in the sum of squares of deviations. Actually, x_1 and x_2 might be highly correlated and therefore contribute the same information for the prediction of y.

Finally, we remind you that r is a measure of *linear* correlation and that x and y could be perfectly related by some curvilinear function even though the observed value of r is close to zero.

EXERCISES

1. How does the coefficient of correlation measure the strength of the linear relationship between two variables y and x?

2. Describe the significance of the algebraic sign and the magnitude of r.
3. Suppose all the sample points fall on the same straight line.
   (a) What value does r assume if the line has a positive slope?
   (b) What value does r assume if the line has a negative slope?
4. What are the differences and similarities of the least squares slope $\hat{\beta}_1$ and the correlation coefficient r?
5. What additional assumption is necessary for using the correlation coefficient r to make inferences about the population correlation coefficient ρ that is *not* necessary for tests concerning the slope β_1?
6. Calculate the correlation coefficient r for the data in exercise 3 of section 12.2.
7. Calculate the correlation coefficient r for the data in exercise 4 of section 12.2. Test the null hypothesis that the population correlation coefficient ρ is zero. Compare your test results with those obtained in testing $H_0: \beta_1 = 0$ in exercise 2, section 12.4.
8. Refer to exercise 3 of section 12.4. Calculate the correlation coefficient between age and number of words used for the sample of 11 subjects. Test the null hypothesis that the population correlation coefficient is zero, using $\alpha = .10$. Compare your results with the results of part (d) of exercise 3, section 12.4.
9. By what percentage was the sum of squares of deviations reduced by using the least squares predictor, $\hat{y} = \hat{\beta}_0 + \hat{\beta}_1 x$, rather than $\bar{y}$ as a predictor of y for the data in exercise 3, section 12.4?

12.9 • SIMPLE LINEAR REGRESSION: AN EXAMPLE

Our objective in this section is to collect all the concepts from the previous eight sections and illustrate them in an example. The example we consider is one in which we wish to determine the relationship, if any, between flexibility and creativity in high school students. We will measure flexibility by recording the number of tasks completed in a fixed time interval. There are six tasks, each calling for different motor coordination and intellectual skills. The subject's score on a test instrument designed to measure creativity will also be recorded. In particular, we want to know whether the creativity score is a good predictor of flexibility.

A random sample of 16 high school students is selected, and the creativity score (x) and flexibility (y) is recorded for each. The data (and some calculations) are presented in table 12.3. A scattergram of the data is shown in figure 12.13.

The scattergram seems to indicate a positive relationship between the two variables. So we hypothesize a simple linear probabilistic model between the flexibility and creativity scores for the *population* of high school students. This model is

$$y = \beta_0 + \beta_1 x + \varepsilon$$

where $\beta_0 + \beta_1 x$ is the deterministic part of our model and ε is the random error component.

Before beginning our statistical analysis of the data, we compute three key quantities.

Table 12.3 • Flexibility (y) and creativity (x) score data for 16 high
school students (section 12.9)

Student	y_i	x_i	x_i^2	$x_i y_i$	y_i^2
1	2.2	17	289	37.4	4.84
2	2.0	18	324	36.0	4.00
3	3.3	28	784	92.4	10.89
4	3.0	24	576	72.0	9.00
5	2.2	35	1,225	77.0	4.84
6	4.8	44	1,936	211.2	23.04
7	1.2	19	361	22.8	1.44
8	2.8	33	1,089	92.4	7.84
9	2.7	14	196	37.8	7.29
10	1.4	21	441	29.4	1.96
11	3.5	26	676	91.0	12.25
12	3.6	22	484	79.2	12.96
13	1.6	15	225	24.0	2.56
14	2.6	23	529	59.8	6.76
15	5.2	48	2,304	249.6	27.04
16	2.5	20	400	50.0	6.25
Totals	44.6	407	11,839	1,262.0	142.96

Figure 12.13 • Scattergram of flexibility (y) and creativity (x) scores for
16 high school students (section 12.9)

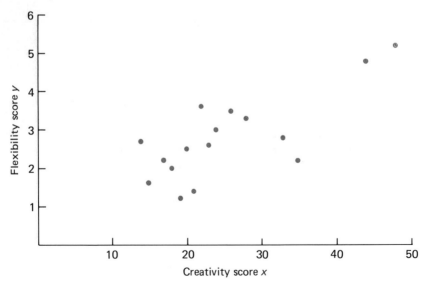

$$SS_{xx} = \sum_{i=1}^{16} (x_i - \bar{x})^2 = \sum_{i=1}^{16} x_i^2 - \frac{\left(\sum_{i=1}^{16} x_i\right)^2}{16}$$

$$= 11{,}839 - \frac{(407)^2}{16} = 1485.94$$

$$SS_{yy} = \sum_{i=1}^{16} (y_i - \bar{y})^2 = \sum_{i=1}^{16} y_i^2 - \frac{\left(\sum_{i=1}^{16} y_i\right)^2}{16}$$

$$= 142.96 - \frac{(44.6)^2}{16} = 18.638$$

$$SS_{xy} = \sum_{i=1}^{16} (x_i - \bar{x})(y_i - \bar{y}) = \sum_{i=1}^{16} x_i y_i - \frac{\left(\sum_{i=1}^{16} x_i\right)\left(\sum_{i=1}^{16} y_i\right)}{16}$$

$$= 1262 - \frac{(407)(44.6)}{16} = 127.49$$

We now proceed with the four steps of a regression analysis.

1. The first step is to use least squares to estimate the deterministic part of our model, $\beta_0 + \beta_1 x$. The least squares calculations yield

$$\hat{\beta}_1 = \frac{SS_{xy}}{SS_{xx}} = \frac{127.49}{1485.94} = .0858$$

$$\hat{\beta}_0 = \bar{y} - \hat{\beta}_1 \bar{x} = \frac{44.6}{16} - (.0858)\left(\frac{407}{16}\right) = .605$$

Our prediction line is therefore

$$\hat{y} = \hat{\beta}_0 + \hat{\beta}_1 x = .605 + .0858x$$

The least squares line is shown in figure 12.14.

Note the small slope of the prediction line. Is this a clue that the linear relationship between x and y is weak? The answer is "not necessarily." Since the slope β_1 is dependent on the scales of y and x, the numerical value has no absolute meaning. About all we can say at this stage is that flexibility increases .0858 of a point for every 1-point increase in creativity score, according to the least squares prediction line for our 16 sampled high school students.

2. We next wish to describe the random error component ε. First, the assumptions we make about ε are reviewed below. (For a more complete discussion of these assumptions, see section 12.3.)

Assumption 1: The average error is zero.

Figure 12.14 • Least squares prediction line for the flexibility-creativity data of section 12.9

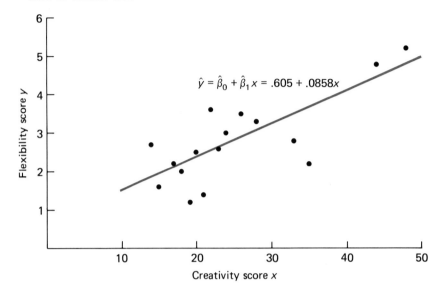

Assumption 2: The variance of the error term ε is the same no matter what the creativity score is.

Assumption 3: The frequency distribution of the random error is normal.

Assumption 4: The random errors for different high school students are independent.

Our remaining task in describing ε is to estimate its variance σ^2. For this we first calculate SSE.

$$\text{SSE} = \sum_{i=1}^{n} (y_i - \hat{y}_i)^2 = \text{SS}_{yy} - \frac{(\text{SS}_{xy})^2}{\text{SS}_{xx}}$$

$$= 18.638 - \frac{(127.49)^2}{1485.94} = 7.700$$

Then we estimate σ^2 by s^2.

$$s^2 = \frac{\text{SSE}}{n-2} = \frac{7.7}{16-2} = .55$$

Then

$$s = \sqrt{.55} = .742$$

3. Our third step in the regression analysis is to test the utility of our hypothesized linear model. We set up the test as follows.

Null hypothesis H_0: $\beta_1 = 0$ (there is no *linear* relationship between the flexibility and the creativity scores in the population of high school students).

Research hypothesis H_a: $\beta_1 \neq 0$ (there is a linear relationship between the flexibility and the creativity scores).

Test statistic: For our small sample we use

$$t = \frac{\widehat{\beta}_1 - 0}{s_{\widehat{\beta}_1}}$$

Assumptions: The four stated assumptions about ε are necessary for the validity of our t test.

Rejection region: Using $\alpha = .01$, we use table 5 to find $t_{\alpha/2} = t_{.005}$ with $(16 - 2) = 14$ degrees of freedom. This is $t_{.005} = 2.977$. Thus we will reject H_0 if

$$t > 2.977 \qquad \text{or} \qquad t < -2.977$$

To compute the t statistic, we first need

$$s_{\widehat{\beta}_1} = \frac{s}{\sqrt{SS_{xx}}} = \frac{.742}{\sqrt{1485.94}} = .0192$$

Then

$$t = \frac{\widehat{\beta}_1}{s_{\widehat{\beta}_1}} = \frac{.0858}{.0192} = 4.469$$

Since the computed t statistic exceeds 2.977, we conclude that the data provide sufficient evidence, at the .01 level, to support the research hypothesis that the flexibility and the creativity scores are linearly related for the population of high school students. Furthermore, the positive slope indicates that this linear relationship is a positive one: as the creativity score increases, the flexibility score increases.

4. Now that the probabilistic linear model has proven to be an adequate description of the relationship between flexibility and creativity scores, we may wish to use our model to predict a flexibility score for a given creativity score. For example, suppose a student has a creativity score of 40. What is the predicted flexibility score for this student?

You should recognize that we are predicting a *particular value* of y, because we wish to know the flexibility score for a single high school student. Our predicted value is

$$\widehat{y} = \widehat{\beta}_0 + \widehat{\beta}_1(40) = .605 + .0858(40) = 4.0$$

That is, we predict the student will have a flexibility score of 4.0. We can obtain a 95 percent prediction interval for the student's true flexibility score as follows. [Note that the degrees of freedom for t are $(n - 2) = (16 - 2) = 14$.]

$$\hat{y} \pm t_{.025}s\sqrt{1 + \frac{1}{n} + \frac{(40 - \bar{x})^2}{SS_{xx}}}$$

$$= 4.0 \pm (2.145)(.742)\sqrt{1 + \frac{1}{16} + \frac{(40 - 25.438)^2}{1485.94}}$$

$$= 4.0 \pm (2.145)(.742)(1.098) = 4.0 \pm 1.748$$

Thus we predict that the student will have a flexibility score between 2.3 and 5.7 (rounding to the nearest tenth). This prediction interval is shown in figure 12.15.

Figure 12.15 • 95 percent prediction interval for the flexibility score of a student whose creativity score is 40

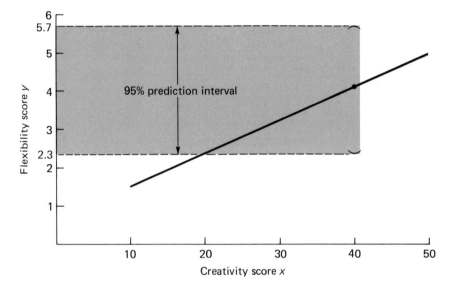

If we are interested in estimating the *average* flexibility score for *all* high school students whose creativity score is 40, our estimate is still

$$\hat{y} = \hat{\beta}_0 + \hat{\beta}_1(40) = 4.0$$

However, since we are estimating an average rather than predicting an individual flexibility score, our confidence interval will be narrower.

$$\hat{y} \pm t_{.025}s\sqrt{\frac{1}{n} + \frac{(40 - \bar{x})^2}{SS_{xx}}}$$

$$= 4.0 \pm (2.145)(.742)\sqrt{\frac{1}{16} + \frac{(40 - 25.438)^2}{1485.94}}$$

$$= 4.0 \pm (2.145)(.742)(.453) = 4.0 \pm .721$$

Then we are 95 percent confident that the average flexibility score of all high school students whose creativity score is 40 is between 3.3 and 4.7 (rounding to the nearest tenth). The confidence interval is shown in figure 12.16.

Figure 12.16 • 95 percent confidence interval for the average flexibility score of all high school students whose creativity score is 40

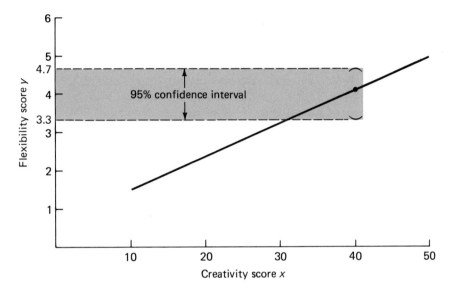

To complete the analysis, we can compute the sample correlation coefficient between the two random variables y and x.

$$r = \frac{SS_{xy}}{\sqrt{SS_{xx}SS_{yy}}} = \frac{127.49}{\sqrt{(1485.94)(18.638)}} = .77$$

There is no need to test the null hypothesis that $\rho = 0$, that is, that the population correlation coefficient is zero. This would result in precisely the same conclusion we reached in testing $\beta_1 = 0$.

However, if we calculate

$$r^2 = (.77)^2 = .59$$

we gain the information that the use of creativity scores in a linear model to predict flexibility scores resulted in a 59 percent decrease in the sample variation of flexibility scores about their mean. In other words, for this sample of 16 students, the use of the linear x yields a sum of squared deviations 59 percent smaller than the sum of deviations for the use of $\bar{y}$ alone as a predictor of flexibility.

12.10 • A MULTIVARIATE PREDICTOR

A prediction equation based on a number of independent variables, x_1, $x_2, \ldots, x_k$, could be obtained by the method of least squares in exactly the same manner as that employed for the simple linear model. For example, we might wish to fit the model

$$y = \beta_0 + \beta_1 x_1 + \beta_2 x_2 + \beta_3 x_3 + \varepsilon$$

where y is the final (numerical) grade in introductory psychology, x_1 is the verbal ability test score, x_2 is the score on a measure of test anxiety, and x_3 is the score on a "need for achievement" scale. (Note that we could add other variables, as well as the squares, cubes, and cross products of x_1, x_2, and x_3.)

We would require a random sample of n students selected from the population of interest. We would record the values of y, x_1, x_2, and x_3, which, for each student, could be regarded as coordinates of a point in a four-dimensional space. Then, ideally, we would like to possess a multidimensional "ruler" that we could visually move about among the n points until the deviations of the observed values of y from the predicted values would be a minimum in some ways. Although we cannot graph points in four dimensions, you will readily recognize that this device is provided by the method of least squares, which performs the task for us mathematically.

The sum of squares of deviations of the observed values of y from the fitted model is

$$SSE = \sum_{i=1}^{n} (y_i - \hat{y}_i)^2 = \sum_{i=1}^{n} [y_i - (\hat{\beta}_0 + \hat{\beta}_1 x_{1i} + \hat{\beta}_2 x_{2i} + \hat{\beta}_3 x_{3i})]^2$$

where $\hat{y} = \hat{\beta}_0 + \hat{\beta}_1 x_1 + \hat{\beta}_2 x_2 + \hat{\beta}_3 x_3$ is the fitted model and $\hat{\beta}_0$, $\hat{\beta}_1$, $\hat{\beta}_2$, and $\hat{\beta}_3$ are estimates of the model parameters. We would then use calculus to find the estimates $\hat{\beta}_0$, $\hat{\beta}_1$, $\hat{\beta}_2$, and $\hat{\beta}_3$ that make SSE a minimum. The estimates would be obtained as the solution of a set of four simultaneous linear equations known as the least squares equations.

Having obtained $\hat{\beta}_0$, $\hat{\beta}_1$, $\hat{\beta}_2$, and $\hat{\beta}_3$, we could also calculate the coefficient of correlation between y and $\hat{y}$, the weighted sum of the three predictor variables. This coefficient, called the **multiple correlation coefficient**, would be computed as was r in section 12.8 with $\hat{y}$ substituted for x in the computing formula. When squared, the resulting coefficient would have the same interpretation as r^2; that is, it would indicate the reduction in the total sum of squares of deviations attributable to using $\hat{y}$ instead of the sample mean $\bar{y}$ as a predictor of y.

While the reasoning employed in obtaining the least squares multivariate predictor is identical to the procedure developed for the simple linear model, a description of the least squares equations, their solution, and related methods of inference become quite complex. These topics are omitted from this elementary discussion. Our primary objective in this chapter has been to indicate the generality and usefulness of the method of least squares as well as its role in prediction.

SUMMARY

The objective of many experiments in the behavioral sciences is to determine how variables are related. Often probabilistic models are hypothesized to describe such relationships. We have presented four steps to follow in examining a probabilistic model, which we briefly summarize below.

1. We use least squares techniques to obtain the deterministic prediction equation with the smallest sum of squared errors.
2. We describe the random error component of the probabilistic model by making assumptions about its frequency distribution and estimating the error variance.
3. We test the utility of our hypothesized probabilistic model.
4. Assuming the model proves to be useful, we use the model to predict average values or particular values (or both) of the dependent variable for specific values of the independent variable. We place bounds on the error of prediction to obtain a measure of precision for the predictors.

SUPPLEMENTARY EXERCISES

1. For what configurations of data points will s^2 be zero?
2. For what parameter is s^2 an unbiased estimator? Explain how this parameter enters into the description of the probabilistic model $y = \beta_0 + \beta_1 x + \varepsilon$.
3. After hypothesizing the probabilistic model $y = \beta_0 + \beta_1 x + \varepsilon$, the experimenter collects a sample on y and x. List the four steps of the statistical analysis.
4. Shand (1970) studied the relationship between undergraduate grade point averages (GPA) and Graduate Record Examination advanced psychology test scores (GRE). Below are the data for a sample of 12 undergraduates.

Student	GRE Score (y)	GPA (x)	Student	GRE Score (y)	GPA (x)
1	513	2.72	7	520	3.25
2	590	2.90	8	600	3.45
3	640	3.25	9	550	3.00
4	560	3.40	10	670	3.75
5	410	2.46	11	500	2.80
6	440	2.27	12	555	2.96

(a) Hypothesizing a probabilistic model relating GRE and GPA, use least squares to estimate the deterministic part of the model, $\beta_0 + \beta_1 x$.
(b) Describe the random error component by listing assumptions about its frequency distribution and estimating its variance.

(c) Test the model adequacy by testing the research hypothesis $H_a: \beta_1 > 0$ (i.e., a positive linear relationship exists between GRE and GPA), using $\alpha = .05$.

(d) Predict the GRE score of Joe Johnson, an undergraduate whose GPA is 2.70. Use a 90 percent prediction interval.

5. Refer to exercise 4. Calculate the correlation coefficient r and use it to test the research hypothesis that the population correlation coefficient ρ is greater than 0, (i.e., a positive linear relationship exists between GRE and GPA). Compare your results with the results of exercise 4(c). What additional assumption is necessary for the validity of the correlation coefficient test?

6. Refer to exercises 4 and 5. Compute r^2, and interpret its meaning.

7. Refer to exercise 4. Estimate the average GRE score of all undergraduates whose GPA is 2.70. Use a 90 percent confidence interval, and compare your result with that for exercise 4(d).

8. Kidd (1964) investigated the possibility of dysfunction in monocular depth perception in schizophrenics. Subjects had to align images at different distances from the light. Below is a hypothetical sample of 10 schizophrenics, with the distance and perception score for each. High perception scores reflect good perception.

Subject	1	2	3	4	5	6	7	8	9	10
Distance (in ft) from Light (x)	4	4	6	6	8	8	10	10	12	12
Perception Score (y)	25	26	22	18	17	22	16	16	13	19

(a) Hypothesizing a linear probabilistic model to relate x and y, use least squares to estimate the deterministic part of the model, $\beta_0 + \beta_1 x$.

(b) What assumptions must you make about the random error component before making inferences about the model? Estimate the error variance σ^2 by calculating s^2.

(c) Test the adequacy of the model by testing the research hypothesis that the slope β_1 is negative, that is, that the average perception score decreases as the distance of the subject from the light increases. Use $\alpha = .05$.

(d) Estimate the average perception score for schizophrenic subjects placed at a 5-foot distance from the light. Use a 90 percent confidence interval.

9. Refer to exercise 8. Why is it inappropriate to compute the correlation coefficient for this set of data with the purpose of making inferences about the population correlation coefficient? (Hint: Recall the additional assumption necessary for such inferences.)

10. Refer to exercise 8. Compute the square of the correlation coefficient, r^2. What is the interpretation of this number? Note that even though r may not be appropriately used to make inferences about ρ, the meaning of r^2 is unchanged.

11. In psychological studies using the judgments of raters, it is important to determine if raters' agreements are close enough to be reliable. When raters are used, the inter-rater reliability is calculated. The following data represent judgments of two raters of the number of times 10 subjects smiled in a four-minute period.

Rater 1	28	17	10	38	31	4	26	41	34	27
Rater 2	25	20	10	40	34	3	21	48	32	28

Note that the prediction model is not pertinent for this data, since we do not wish to use one variable to predict the other. Rather, we are only interested in whether the raters' scores are *correlated* or not.

(a) Calculate the *linear* correlation coefficient r for this data.

(b) Test the research hypothesis that the population correlation coefficient between raters' scores is positive. Use $\alpha = .01$.

12. The Myers-Briggs Type Indicator was developed to assess Jung's typologies of personality. An underlying assumption of the typological approach is that a person's type does not change over time. Stricker and Ross (1964) tested this assumption by computing test-retest correlation for results of the indicator. College students took the indicator twice, with a fourteen-month interval between the two administrations. Below are the scores for the Extraversion-Introversion scale.

Test	0	27	−22	−5	17	5	19	22	26	−22	−10
Retest	−6	19	−17	5	15	10	23	16	17	−11	0

(a) Calculate the correlation coefficient r for this data.

(b) Test the research hypothesis that the population correlation coefficient ρ between test and retest scores is positive. Use $\alpha = .10$.

REFERENCES

Kidd, A. H. 1964. Monocular distance perception in schizophrenics. *Journal of Abnormal and Social Psychology* 68:100–103.

Mendenhall, W. 1975. *Introduction to probability and statistics.* 4th ed. N. Scituate, Mass.: Duxbury Press. Chapter 10.

Newman, J. R., and Grice, G. R. 1965. Stimulus generalization as a function of drive level and the relation between two measures of response strength. *Journal of Experimental Psychology* 69:357–362.

Schailble, M. 1975. An analysis of noncontent TAT variables in a longitudinal sample. *Journal Of Personality Assessment* 39:480–483.

Shand, J. 1970. The GRE advanced test in psychology in relation to undergraduate academic standing. *Journal of Psychology* 76:85–90.

Stricker, L. J., and Ross, J. 1964. An assessment of some structural properties of the Jungian personality typology. *Journal of Abnormal and Social Psychology* 68:62–71.

Walker, H. M., and Lev, J. 1953. *Statistical inference.* New York: Holt, Rinehart and Winston. Chapters 10 and 11.

13•The Analysis of Enumerative Data

INTRODUCTION

Many experiments, particularly in the social sciences, result in enumerative (or count) data. Placing each member of a sample of employed people into one of five income brackets would result in an enumeration or count corresponding to each of the five income classes. Or suppose we were interested in studying the reaction of a mouse to a particular stimulus in a psychological experiment. If a mouse will react in one of three ways when the stimulus is applied and if a large number of mice are subjected to the stimulus, the experiment would yield three counts, indicating the number of mice falling in each of the reaction classes.

Similarly, an attitude survey might require a count and classification of the number of individuals favoring or opposing a particular issue. An educational research project might classify children in categories corresponding to gifted, average, and slow learners. A student of the arts might classify paintings in one of k categories according to style and period in order to study trends in style over time. We might wish to classify ideas in a philosophical study or styles in literature. The results of an advertising campaign would yield count data indicating a classification of consumer reaction. Indeed, many observations in the behavioral sciences cannot be measured on a continuous scale and hence result in enumerative or classificatory data.

Enumerative data are often generated by a multinomial experiment, and we discuss the characteristics of multinomial experiments in section 13.1. Then in section 13.2 we present the most important test of an hypothesis about enumerative data, the chi-square test. Specific applications of the chi-square test are the subject of sections 13.3 through 13.6.

13.1 • THE MULTINOMIAL EXPERIMENT

As we pointed out in the Introduction, many experiments resulting in enumerative data have the characteristics of a multinomial experiment. These characteristics are outlined in the box.

Characteristics of a Multinomial Experiment

1. The experiment consists of n identical trials.
2. The outcome of each trial falls into one of k classes, or cells.
3. The probability that the outcome of a single trial will fall in a particular cell, say cell i, is $p_i (i = 1, 2, \ldots, k)$ and remains the same from trial to trial. Note that

$$p_1 + p_2 + p_3 + \cdots + p_k = 1$$

4. The trials are independent.
5. We are interested in $n_1, n_2, n_3, \ldots, n_k$, where n_i $(i = 1, 2, \ldots, k)$ is the number of trials in which the outcome falls in cell i. Note that $n_1 + n_2 + n_3 + \cdots + n_k = n$.

A multinomial experiment is analogous to tossing n balls at k boxes, where each ball must fall in one of the boxes. The boxes are arranged so that the probability that a ball will fall in a box varies from box to box but remains the same for a particular box in repeated tosses. Finally, the balls are tossed in such a way that the trials are independent. At the conclusion of the experiment, we observe n_1 balls in the first box, n_2 in the second, and n_k in the kth. The total number of balls is equal to

$$\sum_{i=1}^{k} n_i = n$$

Note the similarity between the binomial and the multinomial experiments. In particular, note that the binomial experiment represents the special case for the multinomial experiment when $k = 2$. The single parameter p of the binomial experiment is replaced by the k parameters, $p_1, p_2, \ldots, p_k$, of the multinomial.

In this chapter we will discuss inferences about $p_1, p_2, \ldots, p_k$. In particular, we will consider a statistical test of an hypothesis concerning their specific numerical values or the relationships among them.

If we were to proceed as in chapter 5, we would try to obtain the probability of the observed sample $(n_1, n_2, \ldots, n_k)$ for use in calculating the probability of the type I error associated with a statistical test. Fortunately, we have been relieved of this chore by the British statistician Karl Pearson, who proposed a very useful test statistic for testing hypotheses about $p_1, p_2, \ldots, p_k$ and gave an approximate probability distribution for this test statistic in repeated sampling. This test statistic is discussed in the next section.

13.2 · THE CHI-SQUARE TEST

Suppose that $n = 100$ balls are tossed at k cells (or boxes) and suppose we know that p_1 (the probability that a ball falls in cell 1) is equal to .1. How many balls would fall in the first cell, on the average, if we repeated the experiment many times?

If we are only interested in the number of balls falling in cell 1, we can treat this as a binomial experiment (chapter 5). Here a "success" is a ball falling into cell 1 and a "failure" is a ball falling into any other cell. If p_1 is the probability of success, that is, the probability of a ball falling into cell 1, we can calculate the average number of success when n balls are tossed. We use the formula given in section 5.3 for the mean of a binomial random variable. In our example $n = 100$ and $p_1 = .1$. Thus

$$\left\{\begin{array}{l}\text{average number of balls falling} \\ \text{in cell 1 in repeated sampling}\end{array}\right\} = np_1 = (100)(.1) = 10$$

In like manner, the average number of balls falling in each of the remaining cells may be calculated by the formula

$$\text{average number of balls in cell } i = np_i \qquad (i = 1, 2, \ldots, k)$$

Now suppose that we hypothesize values for $p_1, p_2, \ldots, p_k$ and calculate the average value for each cell. Certainly if our hypothesis is true, the cell counts n_i should not deviate greatly from their average values np_i $(i = 1, 2, \ldots, k)$. Hence it would seem intuitively reasonable to use a test statistic involving the k deviations

$$\text{(observed value) minus (average value)} = (n_i - np_i)$$
$$(i = 1, 2, \ldots, k)$$

In 1900, Karl Pearson proposed the following test statistic, which is a function of the squares of the deviations of the observed counts from their average values, weighted by the reciprocals of their average values.

Pearson's χ^2 Test Statistic

$$X^2 = \sum_{i=1}^{k} \frac{[n_i - np_i]^2}{np_i}$$

$\frac{\Sigma(0-E)^2}{E}$

We are interested in the frequency distribution of X^2 in repeated sampling. Pearson showed that X^2 will possess, approximately, a *chi-square distribu-*

tion. The chi-square (χ^2) distribution is one we have not yet encountered in this text, so we will describe it below.

The shape of the χ^2 distribution is, like the *t* distribution, dependent on the number of degrees of freedom associated with it. Several χ^2 density functions with different degrees of freedom are shown in figure 13.1.

Figure 13.1 • χ^2 distributions for 1, 4, and 6 degrees of freedom

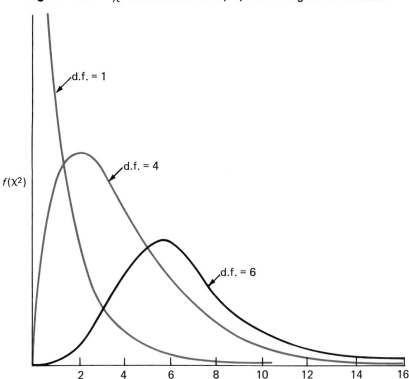

When we use the chi-square distribution for making inferences, we are interested in the tail areas of the distribution, as we have been with the normal, *t*, and *F* distributions. The tail values are given in table 9 of appendix II. Note that the table is constructed much like that for the *t* distribution (table 5), with degrees of freedom (d.f.) on the sides and tail areas across the top. Part of table 9 is reproduced in table 13.1.

Suppose we want to locate the value in a χ^2 distribution with 4 degrees of freedom which has a tail area of .05. That is, we want to find a value $\chi^2_{.05}$ such that

$$P\{\chi^2 > \chi^2_{.05}\} = .05$$

We consult table 9, locate the row corresponding to d.f. = 4 and the column labeled $\chi^2 0.050$. At the intersection of this row and column is the desired value,

Table 13.1 • Partial reproduction of table 9, appendix II

Values of χ^2

$\chi^2 0.100$	$\chi^2 0.050$	$\chi^2 0.025$	$\chi^2 0.010$	$\chi^2 0.005$	$d.f.$
2.70554	3.84146	5.02389	6.63490	7.87944	1
4.60517	5.99147	7.37776	9.21034	10.5966	2
6.25139	7.81473	9.34840	11.3449	12.8381	3
7.77944	9.48773	11.1433	13.2767	14.8602	4
9.23635	11.0705	12.8325	15.0863	16.7496	5
10.6446	12.5916	14.4494	16.8119	18.5476	6
12.0170	14.0671	16.0128	18.4753	20.2777	7
13.3616	15.5073	17.5346	20.0902	21.9550	8
14.6837	16.9190	19.0228	21.6660	23.5893	9
15.9871	18.3070	20.4831	23.2093	25.1882	10
17.2750	19.6751	21.9200	24.7250	26.7569	11
18.5494	21.0261	23.3367	26.2170	28.2995	12
19.8119	22.3621	24.7356	27.6883	29.8194	13
21.0642	23.6848	26.1190	29.1413	31.3193	14
22.3072	24.9958	27.4884	30.5779	32.8013	15
23.5418	26.2962	28.8454	31.9999	34.2672	16
24.7690	27.5871	30.1910	33.4087	35.7185	17
25.9894	28.8693	31.5264	34.8053	37.1564	18
27.2036	30.1435	32.8523	36.1908	38.5822	19

$\chi^2_{.05} = 9.48773$. This value is shown by the shading in table 13.1. We show the area to the right of $\chi^2_{.05}$ with 4 degrees of freedom in figure 13.2.
Let us return to our discussion of the statistic

$$X^2 = \sum_{i=1}^{k} \frac{[n_i - np_i]^2}{np_i}$$

for the hypothesized probabilities $p_1, p_2, \ldots, p_k$. We will doubt these hypothesized values if the observed cell counts n_i are too far from their hypothesized values, that is, if X^2 is too large. Since X^2 has a frequency distribution which is approximately a χ^2 distribution, we will use table 9 to determine the exact upper-tail rejection region for X^2.

Experience has shown that the cell counts n_i should not be too small in order for the χ^2 distribution to provide an adequate approximation to the distribution of X^2. As a rule of thumb, we will require that all average cell counts $n_i p_i$ equal or exceed 5. [Cochran (see the references) has noted that this value may be as small as 1 for some situations.]

If we are satisfied that the cell counts are large enough to justify the X^2 approximation, our next task is to determine the appropriate degrees of freedom. However, the determination of the appropriate number of degrees of freedom to

Figure 13.2 • The $\chi^2_{.05}$ table value for a χ^2 distribution with d.f. $= 4$

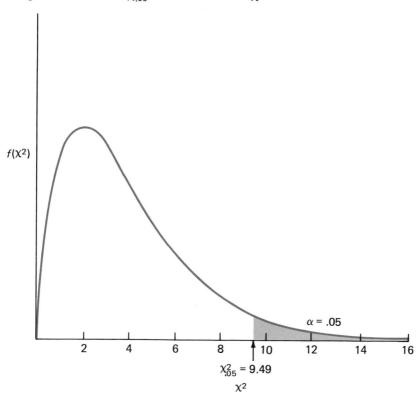

be used for the test can be rather difficult. Therefore, the degrees of freedom will be *specified* for the physical applications described in the following sections. In addition, we now state the principle involved (which is fundamental to the mathematical proof of the approximation) so that you may understand why the number of degrees of freedom changes with various applications. This principle states that the appropriate number of degrees of freedom will equal the number of cells k minus one degree of freedom for each independent linear restriction placed upon the observed cell counts. For example, one linear restriction is *always* present, because the sum of the cell counts must equal n. That is,

$$n_1 + n_2 + n_3 + \cdots + n_k = n$$

Other restrictions will be introduced for some applications because of the necessity for estimating unknown parameters that are needed in the calculation of the average cell frequencies or because of the way in which the sample is collected. These will become apparent as we consider various practical examples in the following sections.

13.3 · A TEST OF AN HYPOTHESIS ABOUT SPECIFIED CELL PROBABILITIES

The simplest hypothesis concerning the cell probabilities is one that specifies a numerical value for each probability. For example, let us consider a simple experiment in which one or more rats proceed down a ramp to one of three doors. We wish to test the null hypothesis that the rats have no preference about the choice of a door. If the rats have no preference for any of the doors, the probabilities of their choosing the doors will be equal. Thus we test

$$H_0: p_1 = p_2 = p_3 = \tfrac{1}{3}$$

where p_i is the probability that a rat will choose door i ($i = 1, 2, 3$). The research hypothesis is

H_a: The rats have a preference for at least one of the three doors; that is, at least one of p_1, p_2, and p_3 exceeds $\tfrac{1}{3}$

Suppose that $n = 90$ rats are sent down the ramp and that the three observed cell frequencies are $n_1 = 23$, $n_2 = 36$, and $n_3 = 31$. Assuming the null hypothesis to be true, the average cell frequency would be the same for each cell: $np_i = 90(\tfrac{1}{3}) = 30$. The observed and the average cell frequencies are presented in table 13.2. Noting the discrepancy between the observed and the average cell frequencies, we wonder whether the data present sufficient evidence to warrant rejection of the hypothesis of no preference.

Table 13.2 · Observed and average cell counts for the rat experiment of choosing one of three doors

	Door		
	1	2	3
Observed Cell Frequency	$n_1 = 23$	$n_2 = 36$	$n_3 = 31$
Average Cell Frequency (H_0)	30	30	30

Our test statistic X^2 will measure the difference between the observed values and the hypothesized average values.

$$\text{Test statistic: } X^2 = \sum_{i=1}^{3} \frac{[n_i - (np_i)_0]^2}{(np_i)_0} = \sum_{i=1}^{3} \frac{[n_i - 30]^2}{30}$$

where $(np_i)_0$ is the null hypothesized average count for cell i.

The chi-square test statistic for our example has $(k - 1) = 2$ degrees of freedom since the only linear restriction on the cell frequencies is that

$$n_1 + n_2 + \cdots + n_k = n$$

or, for our example, that

$$n_1 + n_2 + n_3 = 90$$

Thus we have the following rejection region.

Rejection region: For $\alpha = .05$, we will reject the null hypothesis of no preference when

$$X^2 > \chi^2_{.05} \text{ [d.f.} = 2] = 5.991$$

The rejection region is shown in figure 13.3.

Figure 13.3 • Rejection region for the rat experiment of choosing one of three doors; $\alpha = .05$ and d.f. $= 2$

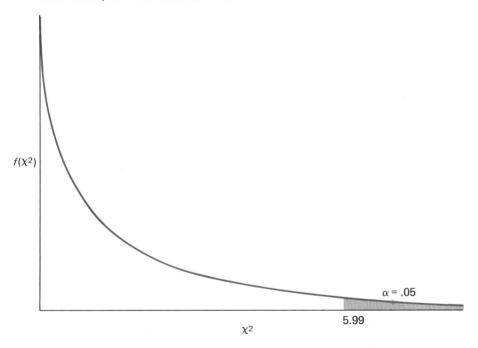

Substituting into the formula for X^2, we obtain

$$X^2 = \sum_{i=1}^{k} \frac{(n_i - np_i)^2}{np_i}$$

$$= \frac{(23 - 30)^2}{30} + \frac{(36 - 30)^2}{30} + \frac{(31 - 30)^2}{30} = 2.87$$

Since X^2 is less than the table value of χ^2, the null hypothesis is not rejected. We conclude that the data do not present sufficient evidence, at the $\alpha = .05$ level, to indicate that the rats have a preference for a particular door or doors.

Referring again to table 9, we note that the $\chi^2_{.10}$ value with d.f. $= 2$ is 4.605. Since our test statistic $X^2 = 2.87$ does not exceed this $\chi^2_{.10}$ either, we see that the significance level P is greater than .10 ($P > .10$).

EXERCISES

1. List the characteristics of a multinomial experiment.
2. A personality test item has four alternative responses, only one of which may be selected. To determine whether some responses are generally more popular or more "socially desirable" than others, 1000 subjects were administered the item and their responses recorded. The results were as given below.

Response	1	2	3	4
Observed Count	294	276	238	192

   Do the data present sufficient evidence to indicate that some responses are more popular than others? (Test the hypothesis that $p_1 = p_2 = p_3 = p_4 = \frac{1}{4}$, using $\alpha = .05$.)
3. Goodale and Aagaard (1975) gave 400 subjects a scale asking their reactions to the four-day work week. Each subject could respond in one of five ways, ranging from "highly favorable" (1) to "highly unfavorable" (5). The experimenters conducted a test to see if the probabilities of responses falling in each category were equal. The data for one item on the scale are presented below. Is there evidence that the probabilities differ for the five categories? Use $\alpha = .01$.

Response	1	2	3	4	5
Observed Count	89	113	98	55	45

4. After inspecting the data in exercise 3, we might wish to test the hypothesis that the probability of response 4 is .20 against the alternative that this probability is less than .20.
   (a) Carry out the above test, using $\alpha = .05$.
   (b) What tenet of good statistical practice is violated in the test of part (a)?

13.4 · CONTINGENCY TABLES

A problem frequently encountered in the analysis of count data concerns the dependence of the two methods used to classify the observed events. For example, suppose we wish to classify birth defects according to both the type of defect and the age of the mother. What we really are investigating here is a contingency—a dependence between the two classifications. Do the proportions of the various types of defects vary from one age range to another?

A total of $n = 309$ birth defects is recorded and the defects classified according to one of four types, A, B, C, or D. At the same time, each birth defect is associated with one of three maternal age ranges. These counts are presented in table 13.3, which is known as a contingency table.

Let p_A be the probability that a defect will be of Type A. Similarly, define p_B, p_C, and p_D as the probabilities of observing the three other types of defects. Then these probabilities, which we will call the column probabilities of table 13.3, will satisfy the requirement

Table 13.3 • Contingency table for birth defects and age range

Age Range	Type of Defect				Totals
	A	**B**	**C**	**D**	
1 : Below 25	51	46	25	15	137
2 : 25 to 40	33	17	49	20	119
3 : Over 40	4	11	35	3	53
Totals	88	74	109	38	309

$$p_A + p_B + p_C + p_D = 1$$

In like manner, let $p_i (i = 1, 2, 3)$ be the row probability that a defect will have occurred at age range i, where

$$p_1 + p_2 + p_3 = 1$$

Then if the two classifications are independent of each other, a cell probability is equal to the product of its respective row and column probabilities. (The proof for this statement is beyond the scope of this test.)

For example, the probability that a particular defect will occur in age range 1 and be of Type A is $(p_1)(p_A)$. Thus we observe that the numerical values of the cell probabilities are unspecified in the problem under consideration. The null hypothesis specifies only that each cell probability is equal to the product of its respective row and column probabilities, which, in turn, implies independence of the two classifications. Thus the null hypothesis is

H_0: The two classifications (rows and columns) are independent

The research hypothesis is

H_a: The two classifications are dependent

The test statistic for a contingency table differs from the problem discussed in section 13.3. Here we must estimate the row and column probabilities in order to estimate the average cell frequencies (cell counts) under the null hypothesis that the row and column classifications are independent.

If proper estimates of the cell probabilities are obtained, the estimated average cell frequencies may be substituted in X^2, and X^2 will continue to possess a distribution in repeated sampling that is approximated by the chi-square probability distribution. The proof of this statement as well as a discussion of the methods for obtaining the estimates are beyond the scope of this text. Fortunately, the procedures for obtaining the estimates, known as the method of maximum likelihood and the method of minimum chi-square, yield estimates that are intuitively obvious for our relatively simple applications.

It can be shown that the appropriate estimator of a column probability is equal to the column total divided by n. If we denote the total of column j as c_j, then for our example ($n = 309$),

$$\widehat{p}_A = \frac{c_1}{n} = \frac{88}{309}$$

$$\widehat{p}_B = \frac{c_2}{n} = \frac{74}{309}$$

$$\widehat{p}_C = \frac{c_3}{n} = \frac{109}{309}$$

$$\widehat{p}_D = \frac{c_4}{n} = \frac{38}{309}$$

Likewise, the row probabilities, p_1, p_2, and p_3, may be estimated using the row totals r_1, r_2, and r_3.

$$\widehat{p}_1 = \frac{r_1}{n} = \frac{137}{309}$$

$$\widehat{p}_2 = \frac{r_2}{n} = \frac{119}{309}$$

$$\widehat{p}_3 = \frac{r_3}{n} = \frac{53}{309}$$

We denote the observed frequency of the cell in row i and column j of the contingency table as n_{ij}. Then the estimated average value of n_{11} can be shown to be, assuming independence of row and column classifications,

$$\left\{ \begin{array}{l} \text{estimated average } n_{11} \text{ under the} \\ \text{null hypothesis of independence} \end{array} \right\} = n(\widehat{p}_1 \cdot \widehat{p}_A) = n\left(\frac{r_1}{n}\right) \cdot \left(\frac{c_1}{n}\right)$$

$$= \frac{r_1 \cdot c_1}{n} = \frac{(137)(88)}{309} = 39.02$$

where $(\widehat{p}_1 \cdot \widehat{p}_A)$ is the estimated cell probability. Likewise, we may find the estimated average value for any other cell, say row 2, column 3.

$$\left\{ \begin{array}{l} \text{estimated average } n_{23} \text{ under the} \\ \text{null hypothesis of independence} \end{array} \right\} = n(\widehat{p}_2 \cdot \widehat{p}_C) = n\left(\frac{r_2}{n}\right) \cdot \left(\frac{c_3}{n}\right)$$

$$= \frac{r_2 c_3}{n} = \frac{(119)(109)}{309} = 41.98$$

In other words, the estimated average value of the observed cell frequency n_{ij} for a contingency table is equal to the product of its respective row and column totals divided by the total frequency.

Estimated Average n_{ij} Under the Null Hypothesis of Independence

$$\frac{r_i c_j}{n}$$

Our test statistic is then given by the formula shown below.

$$X^2 = \sum \frac{\left[(\text{observed cell count}) - \left(\begin{array}{c}\text{estimated average cell count}\\\text{assuming independence}\end{array}\right)\right]^2}{\text{estimated average cell count assuming independence}}$$

$$= \sum_{i,j} \frac{[n_{ij} - (r_i c_j/n)]^2}{r_i c_j/n}$$

where $\sum_{i,j}$, refers to the summation over all rows and columns of the contingency table.

Before calculating the numerical value of X^2, we specify the rejection region. This requires specifying the α-level of the test and determining the appropriate number of degrees of freedom associated with the test statistic.

The degrees of freedom associated with a contingency table possessing r rows and c columns will always equal $(r - 1)(c - 1)$. Thus for our example, we will compare X^2 with the table χ^2-value whose degrees of freedom are $(r - 1)(c - 1) = (3 - 1)(4 - 1) = 6$. The details of the justification of this formula for the degrees of freedom are omitted. We only note again that the number of cells minus the number of linear restrictions equals the degrees of freedom.

Rejection region: For $\alpha = .05$, we reject the null hypothesis if

$$X^2 > \chi^2_{.05}[\text{d.f.} = 6] = 12.5916$$

To calculate the value of X^2 for the birth defects example, we must first calculate the estimated average cell counts under the null hypothesis of independence. These are shown in parentheses following the observed value in each cell in table 13.4.

Table 13.4 • Observed and (estimated average) cell counts for the birth defect example

Age Range	Type of Defect				Totals
	A	**B**	**C**	**D**	
1: Below 25	51 (39.02)	46 (32.81)	25 (48.33)	15 (16.85)	137
2: 25 to 40	33 (33.89)	17 (28.50)	49 (41.98)	20 (14.63)	119
3: Over 40	4 (15.09)	11 (12.69)	35 (18.70)	3 (6.52)	˙53
Totals	88	74	109	38	309

Then

$$X^2 = \sum_{i=1}^{12} \frac{[(\text{observed cell count}) - (\text{estimated average cell count})]^2}{\text{estimated average cell count}}$$

$$= \frac{(51 - 39.02)^2}{39.02} + \frac{(33 - 33.89)^2}{33.89} + \cdots + \frac{(3 - 6.52)^2}{6.52}$$

$$= 52.74$$

Since the test statistic $X^2 = 52.74$ exceeds 12.5916, we conclude, at the $\alpha = .05$ level, that the proportion of the various types of birth defects depends on maternal age.

We summarize the contingency table test procedure in the box.

Summary of the Contingency Table Test Procedure

Null hypothesis H_0: The rows and columns are independent.

Research hypothesis H_a: The rows and columns are dependent.

Test statistic: $X^2 = \dfrac{\sum(O-E)^2}{E}$

$$X^2 = \sum \frac{\left[(\text{observed cell count}) - \left(\begin{array}{c}\text{estimated average cell count}\\\text{assuming independence}\end{array}\right)\right]^2}{\text{estimated average cell count assuming independence}}$$

$$= \sum_{i,j} \frac{[n_{ij} - (r_i c_j/n)]^2}{r_i c_j/n}$$

Rejection region: For an α-level test, we reject the null hypothesis when

$$X^2 > \chi_\alpha^2$$

with degrees of freedom equal to $(r - 1)(c - 1)$.

Example 13.1

A survey is conducted to determine whether participation in college athletics is related to birth order. A survey of 1000 male college students on three different campuses provided the information in table 13.5. Do the data present sufficient evidence to indicate that participation in college athletics is related to birth order? Use $\alpha = .10$.

Table 13.5 • Data and calculations for example 13.1; observed and (estimated average) cell counts

	Firstborn	Secondborn	Third- or Laterborn	Totals
Participate	13 (26.6)	24 (14.4)	9 (5.0)	46
Do Not Participate	565 (551.4)	289 (298.6)	100 (104.0)	954
Totals	578	313	109	1000

Solution: The question asks whether the data provide sufficient evidence to indicate a dependence between the birth order classification and participation or nonparticipation in college athletics. Thus our test is set up as follows.

Null hypothesis H_0: Birth order and participation in college athletics are independent.

Research hypothesis H_a: Participation or nonparticipation in college athletics depends on birth order.

Test statistic: $X^2 = \sum_{i,j} \dfrac{[n_{ij} - (r_i c_j/n)]^2}{r_i c_j/n}$.

Rejection region: For $\alpha = .10$, we use table 9 to determine the $\chi^2_{.10}$ value with d.f. $= (r - 1)(c - 1) = (1)(2) = 2$. This is $\chi^2_{.10} = 4.605$. So we will reject the null hypothesis if

$$X^2 > 4.605$$

Our calculation of X^2 begins by calculating the estimated average cell counts under the null hypothesis of independent rows and columns. We use the row and column totals in table 13.5 to compute them.

$$\text{estimated average of } n_{11} = \frac{r_1 c_1}{n} = \frac{(46)(578)}{1000} = 26.6$$

$$\text{estimated average of } n_{12} = \frac{r_1 c_2}{n} = \frac{(46)(313)}{1000} = 14.4$$

The remaining estimated average cell counts are similarly computed. All are shown in parentheses in table 13.5 next to the observed cell counts. Now we calculate X^2.

$$X^2 = \frac{(13 - 26.6)^2}{26.6} + \frac{(24 - 14.4)^2}{14.4} + \cdots + \frac{(100 - 104.0)^2}{104.0}$$

$$= 17.35$$

Observing that X^2 falls in the rejection region, we reject the null hypothesis of independence of the two classifications at the $\alpha = .10$ level.

A comparison of the percentage of participation for each of the three categories would suggest that firstborns are less likely to participate in college athletics. Further analysis of the data could be obtained by deleting one of the three categories, the third column, for example, to compare firstborns with secondborns. This could be done either by using a 2×2 contingency table or by treating the two categories as two binomial populations and using the methods of section 8.7. Or we might wish to analyze the data by comparing firstborns with the combined second-, third-, and laterborns. That is, we could combine the last two columns of the 2×3 table into one.

EXERCISES

1. In the area of conformity research, one important factor is whether a person states his or her position in public or in private. Gerard (1964) conducted research to see if subjects would yield to an incorrect majority by conforming to the majority judgment. The two conditions were "anonymous," in which subjects indicated their response privately, and "face-to-face," in which subjects indicated their response in public. Based on their responses to several items, subjects were divided into three groups: those that made no errors (did not conform to incorrect majority opinion), those that made 1 to 4 errors, and those that made 5 or more errors. Do the following data indicate that conformity is dependent upon experimental condition? Use $\alpha = .10$.

	No Errors	1-4 Errors	5 or More Errors
Anonymous	8	50	16
Face-to-face	18	22	36

2. A sociologist conducted a survey to determine whether the incidence of various types of crime varied from one part of a particular city to another. The city was partitioned into three regions and the crimes classified as homicide, car theft, grand larceny, and others. An analysis of 1599 cases produced the following results.

	Homicide	Auto Theft	Grand Larceny (Omitting Auto Theft)	Petty Larceny	Other
Region 1	12	239	191	122	47
Region 2	17	163	278	201	54
Region 3	7	98	109	44	17

Do these data present sufficient evidence to indicate that the occurrence of various types of crime is dependent upon city region? Use $\alpha = .05$.

13.5 • $r \times c$ TABLES WITH FIXED ROW OR COLUMN TOTALS

In the previous section we described the analysis of an $r \times c$ contingency table by using examples which, for all practical purposes, fit the multinomial experiment described in section 13.1. Although the methods of collecting data in many surveys may satisfy the requirements of a multinomial experiment, other methods may not. For example, we might not wish to sample randomly the population described in example 13.1 because we might find that, owing to chance, one category is completely missing. For example, third- or laterborns might fail to appear in the sample. Thus we might decide beforehand to sample a specified number of people in each column category, thereby fixing the column totals in advance. While these restrictions tend to disturb somewhat our visualization of the experiment in the multinomial context, they have no effect on the analysis of the data. As long as we wish to test the hypothesis of independence of the two classifications and none of the row probabilities are specified in advance, we may analyze the data as an $r \times c$ contingency table. It can be shown that the resulting test statistic X^2 will possess a probability distribution in repeated sampling that is approximated by a chi-square distribution with $(r - 1)(c - 1)$ degrees of freedom.

To illustrate this idea, we test an hypothesis concerning the equivalence of four binomial populations in the following example.

Example 13.2

An attitude survey is conducted on four college campuses to compare the fraction of students favoring legislation establishing more stringent emission standards for automobiles. Random samples of 200 students are polled in each of the four colleges, with the results shown in table 13.6.

Table 13.6 • Data and calculations for example 13.2; observed and (estimated average) cell counts

	College				
	1	**2**	**3**	**4**	**Totals**
Favor	124 (141)	147 (141)	141 (141)	152 (141)	564
Do Not Favor	76 (59)	53 (59)	59 (59)	48 (59)	236
Totals	200	200	200	200	800

Do the data present sufficient evidence, at the $\alpha = .05$ level, to indicate that the fraction of students favoring stronger emission standards differ from college to college?

Solution: You will observe that the test of an hypothesis concerning the equivalence of the parameters of the four binomial populations corresponding to the four colleges is identical to an hypothesis implying independence of the row and column classifications. We denote the fraction of students favoring stronger emission standards by p and hypothesize that p is the same for all four colleges. Then we imply that the first-row and second-row probabilities are equal to p and $(1 - p)$, respectively.

We set up our test as follows.

Null hypothesis H_0: The true fraction of students favoring legislation establishing more stringent emission standards for automobiles is the same at the four sampled colleges; that is, the fraction of students favoring stronger emission standards is *independent* of the college.

Research hypothesis H_a: The true fraction of students favoring stronger emission standards varies for the four sampled colleges; that is, the fraction of students favoring stronger emission standards *depends* on the college.

Test statistic: $X^2 = \sum\limits_{i,j} \dfrac{[n_{ij} - (r_i c_j/n)]^2}{r_i c_j/n}$.

Rejection region: For $\alpha = .05$, we consult table 9, appendix II, for $\chi^2_{.05}$ with

$$\text{d.f.} = (r - 1)(c - 1) = (1)(3) = 3$$

We will reject the null hypothesis if

$$X^2 > \chi^2_{.05} = 7.815$$

Our calculations proceed as in the previous example. We first calculate each estimated average.

$$\text{estimated average } n_{11} = \frac{r_1 c_1}{n} = \frac{(564)(200)}{800} = 141$$

$$\text{estimated average } n_{12} = \frac{r_1 c_2}{n} = \frac{(564)(200)}{800} = 141$$

and so forth. Note in table 13.6 that since the column totals are equal, the estimated average cell counts across each row are also equal, assuming the null hypothesis is true. This is consistent with the null hypothesis that the fractions favoring stronger emission standards will be the same for the four colleges.

The test statistic is

$$X^2 = \frac{(124 - 141)^2}{141} + \frac{(147 - 141)^2}{141} + \cdots + \frac{(48 - 59)^2}{59}$$

$$= 10.72$$

Since the computed X^2 exceeds 7.815, we conclude that the contingency table data provide sufficient evidence, at the .05 level, to support the research hypothesis. The data indicate that the fraction of students favoring stronger emission standards differs for at least two of the four sampled colleges.

EXERCISES

1. Researchers have hypothesized that the social status position of a psychiatric patient is a determinant of the kind of treatment the patient will receive (Robinson, Redlich, and Myers, 1954). A study was conducted to test this hypothesis. A sample of cases being treated by psychiatrists was obtained and each person was classified according to social class. It was determined whether the patients' treatment types were psychotherapy, organic treatment (physical-chemical), or no treatment (those patients who were receiving custodial care in an institution but were not receiving either of the above treatments). Given the data shown below, is the research hypothesis supported at the $\alpha = .10$ level? Social classes are listed in descending order.

	Class I	Class II	Class III	Class IV
Psychotherapy	79	53	31	16
Organic	12	29	37	33
No Treatment	9	18	32	51

2. An experiment is designed to determine whether the relative accuracies of three expert judges differ. All three judges are shown a film, and then each judge is questioned separately about 50 specific aspects of the film. The number of correct responses each judge makes is recorded. The data are given below.

	Judge 1	Judge 2	Judge 3
Correct Responses	38	34	40
Incorrect Responses	12	16	10

Do these data provide evidence to indicate a difference in the three judges' abilities? Use $\alpha = .05$.

13.6 • OTHER APPLICATIONS

We have presented several applications of the chi-square test for analyzing enumerative data in sections 13.3, 13.4, and 13.5. These represent only a few of the interesting classificatory problems which may be approximated by the multinomial experiment and for which our method of analysis is appropriate. By and large, these applications are complicated to some degree because the numerical values of the cell probabilities are unspecified and hence require the estimation of one or more population parameters. Then, as in sections 13.4 and 13.5, we can estimate the cell probabilities. Although we omit the mechanics of the statistical tests, several additional applications of the chi-square test are worth mention as a matter of interest.

Suppose that we wish to test an hypothesis that a population possesses a normal probability distribution, an assumption we have often needed for small-sample inference making. The cells of a sample frequency histogram (for example, figure 2.1) would correspond to the k cells of the multinomial experiment. The observed cell frequencies would be the number of measurements falling in each cell of the histogram. Given the hypothesized normal probability distribution for the population, we could use the areas under the normal curve to calculate the theoretical cell probabilities and hence the average cell frequencies. The difficulty arises when μ and σ are unspecified for the normal population and these parameters must be estimated in order to obtain the estimated cell probabilities. This difficulty, of course, can be surmounted.

The construction of a two-way table to investigate dependency between two classifications can be extended to three or more classifications. For example, if we wish to test the mutual independence of three classifications, we would employ a three-dimensional "table" or rectangular parallelepiped. The reasoning and methodology associated with the analysis of both the two- and three-way tables are identical, although the analysis of the three-way table is a bit more complex. The interested reader should consult the article by Sutcliffe listed at the end of the chapter.

A third and interesting application of our methodology is its use in the investigation of the rate of change of a multinomial (or binomial) population as a function of time. For example, we might study the decision-making ability of a human (or any animal) as he is subjected to an educational program and tested over time. Suppose he is tested at prescribed intervals of time and the test is of the yes or no type, yielding a number of correct answers y that follow a binomial probability distribution. Then we would be interested in the behavior of the probability p of a correct response as a function of time. If the number of correct responses were recorded for c time periods, the data would fall in a $2 \times c$ table similar to that in example 13.2 (section 13.5). We would then be interested in testing the null hypothesis that p is equal to a constant, that is, that no learning has occurred, against the research hypothesis that the data present sufficient evidence to indicate a gradual (say linear) change over time as opposed to an abrupt change at some point in time. The procedures we have described could be extended to decisions involving more than two alternatives.

You will observe that our learning example is similar to many other applications in the behavioral sciences. For example, we might wish to study the rate of change in the proportion favoring a particular social issue as a function of time. Or we might wish to study the divorce rate in a particular state over a time period spanning a revision of divorce legislation. Both of these examples, as well as many others, require a study of the behavior of a binomial (or multinomial) process as a function of time.

The examples that we have just described are intended to suggest the relatively broad application of the chi-square analysis of enumerative data, a fact that should be borne in mind by the experimenter concerned with this type of data. The statistical test employing X^2 as a test statistic is often called a *goodness-of-fit test*. Its application for some of these examples requires care in the determination of the appropriate estimates and the number of degrees of freedom for X^2, which may be rather complex for some of these problems.

SUMMARY

In this chapter we introduced tests of hypotheses regarding the cell probabilities associated with a multinomial experiment. When the number of observations n is large, the test statistic X^2 can be shown to possess an approximate chi-square probability distribution in repeated sampling, the number of degrees of freedom being dependent upon the particular application. In general, we assume that n is large and that the minimum average cell frequency is at least 5.

Several words of caution are appropriate concerning the use of the X^2 statistic as a method of analyzing enumerative data. The determination of the correct number of degrees of freedom associated with the X^2 statistic is very important in locating the rejection region. If the number is incorrectly specified, erroneous conclusions might result.

Also, note that nonrejection of the null hypothesis does not imply that the null hypothesis should be accepted, a caution we have repeated throughout our coverage of hypothesis testing. For example, we hypothesize that the two classifications of a contingency table are independent. Our research hypothesis states that they are dependent. As we have seen in the examples, the data may support the research hypothesis of dependence at some significance level.

However, lack of such support should *not* be interpreted as showing independence of the classifications. If we were to accept the null hypothesis, we would risk making the error of accepting the null hypothesis when the research hypothesis is true. We do not know the probability of making such an error. As we have noted many times, making an inference without a measure of its goodness is a poor statistical technique. Unfortunately, there is no convenient way of calculating the probability of accepting the null hypothesis of independence when, in fact, the classifications are dependent. We must therefore be content with a "no decision" decision when the test statistic X^2 does not fall in the rejection region.

Finally, if parameters are missing and the average cell frequencies must be estimated, the estimators of missing parameters should be of a particular type for the test to be valid. In other words, the application of the chi-square test for other than the simple applications outlined in sections 13.3, 13.4, and 13.5 will require experience beyond the scope of this introductory presentation of the subject.

SUPPLEMENTARY EXERCISES

1. A study to assess the effectiveness of a new drug treatment for ulcers involved a comparison of two groups, each consisting of 200 patients diagnosed as having ulcers. One group received the experimental treatment while the other was treated using a more standard method. After a period of time, each person in the study was examined to determine whether the ulcer condition was improved. The observed results are shown below.

	Treatment	
	Experimental	**Standard**
Improved	117	74
Not Improved	83	126

Do these data present sufficient evidence to indicate that the experimental treatment was more effective than the standard treatment in improving the condition of ulcer patients?
(a) Test by using the X^2 statistic. Use $\alpha = .05$.
(b) Test by using the z test to compare two binomial populations (chapter 8). Again use $\alpha = .05$.

2. Four hundred essay exams were independently graded, "satisfactory" or "unsatisfactory," by three different teachers. The number of exams graded as unsatisfactory by each teacher is given below.

Teacher	1	2	3
No. Exams Graded "Unsatisfactory"	16	24	9

Do these data present sufficient evidence to indicate that the fraction of unsatisfactory grades varies from one teacher to another? Use $\alpha = .05$ to test.

3. In research about the treatment of alcoholism, social isolation is an important variable. Singer, Blane, and Kasschau (1964) obtained information of diagnosed alcoholics, undiagnosed alcoholics, and nonalcoholics to test the notion that alcoholics are socially isolated. One item measuring social isolation was whether the person was married or not. Do the data below indicate a dependence between classifications? Use $\alpha = .01$.

	Diagnosed Alcoholics	Undiagnosed	Nonalcoholics
Married	20	40	58
Not Married	60	60	42

4. Refer to exercise 3.
   (a) Another question asked in the study was this: "Of those who are married, how many have a stable marriage?" Do the data below indicate a dependence between the stated stability classification and the alcoholic classification? Use $\alpha = .05$.

	Diagnosed	Undiagnosed	Nonalcoholic
Stable Marriage	11	30	52
Unstable Marriage	9	10	6

   (b) Another question concerned whether or not the subjects were employed. Do the data below indicate that alcoholics are less likely to be employed than nonalcoholics?

	Diagnosed	Undiagnosed	Nonalcoholic
Employed	48	70	85
Not Employed	32	30	15

5. In a study of the relationship between children's ethnic classification and their ability to conceptualize space, 230 first-grade schoolchildren from a large metropolitan area were selected in such a way that five ethnic groups were represented. Each child was administered a test of space conceptualization. The results obtained are shown below.

Ethnic Group	Space Conceptualization Test Score		
	Below 20	Between 20 and 30	Above 30
A	17	19	7
B	14	7	9
C	6	21	12
D	33	44	19
E	7	9	6

Do these data present sufficient evidence to indicate a relationship between children's ethnic classification and their performance on the space conceptualization test? Choose any α-value that you think is suitable (and for which you have tables).

6. Voting behavior may be affected by personality traits. The F scale might relate to voting behavior, as it is a measure of authoritarianism and it correlates with attitudes of political and economic conservatism. Leventhal, Jacobs, and Kudirka (1964) divided college students into three groups based on their responses to the F scale. In addition, subjects stated their preference between Kennedy and Nixon. Do the data below indicate any relationship between F-scale responses and voting preference?

	Kennedy	Nixon
High F	6	18
Medium F	7	12
Low F	15	8

7. Refer to exercise 6. Subjects also indicated their political party preference, as shown in the data below. Is there a relationship between party preference and F-scale response?

	Republican	Democrat
High F	18	6
Medium F	10	9
Low F	9	14

8. Refer to exercise 6. In a further extension of the relationship between the F scale and voting behavior, the researchers conducted a laboratory experiment. Subjects were presented with bogus descriptions of candidates whose views were in line with the Republican or Democratic party. Subjects then indicated their preference. Do the data below indicate a dependence between these classifications?

	Republican Candidate	Democratic Candidate
High F	33	31
Medium F	27	29
Low F	32	36

9. A social psychologist uses in his research a competitive game that is played by a subject against an experimenter. Five different strategies can be used by a subject, although Strategy A is considered optimal. The following data were collected after 100 subjects had played the game.

Strategy	A	B	C	D	E
Frequency	27	17	15	22	19

Do these data present sufficient evidence to indicate a preference for one or more of the strategies over the others?

10. Researchers who send out questionnaires want a high percentage of people to return the questionnaire so that the sample will not be biased. Anderson and Bendie (1975) did research on the effects of different follow-up techniques on response rate. Four types of groups at universities were sent hand-addressed follow-up letters. Do the data below indicate that any group was more likely to return the questionnaire than the others? Use $\alpha = .05$.

	Returned	Not Returned
Faculty	32	168
Undergraduates	107	321
Graduate Assistants	310	690
Administration	36	81

11. Refer to exercise 10. Another mailing to different subjects was made, this time using a formal letter with a typed address label. Do the data below indicate a dependence between the type of group and the return rate? Use $\alpha = .05$.

	Returned	Not Returned
Faculty	23	77
Undergraduates	13	87
Graduate Assistants	31	69
Administration	15	35

12. A survey was conducted to investigate the interest of middle-aged adults in physical fitness programs in Rhode Island, Colorado, California, and Florida. The objective of the investigation was to determine whether adult participation in physical fitness programs varies from one region of the United States to another. A random sample of people was interviewed in each state. The data shown below were recorded.

	Rhode Island	Colorado	California	Florida
Participate	46	63	108	121
Do Not Participate	149	178	192	179

Do the data indicate a difference in adult participation in physical fitness programs from one state to another?

13. A survey was conducted to determine student, faculty, and administration attitudes on a new university parking policy. The distribution of those favoring or opposed to the policy is given below.

	Student	Faculty	Administration
Favor	252	107	43
Opposed	139	81	40

Do the data provide sufficient evidence to indicate that attitudes regarding the parking policy are dependent on student, faculty, or administration status? Use $\alpha = .10$.

14. A crisis intervention center conducted a study to determine whether single versus repeated telephone calls for assistance in dealing with a problem were related to the nature of the problem. Three major types of problems had previously been defined, and a random sample of 346 callers were classified according to the type of problem. The data obtained are shown below.

	Problem Type		
	A	B	C
Single Caller	67	26	16
Repeated Caller	128	63	46

Do the data indicate that the frequency of single call versus repeated calls is related to problem type?

REFERENCES

Anderson, J. F., and Bendie, D. R. 1975. Effects on response rates of formal and informal questionnaire follow-up techniques. *Journal of Applied Psychology* 60:255–257.

Cochran, W. G. 1952. The χ^2 test of goodness of fit. *Annals of Mathematical Statistics* 23:315–345.

Gerard, H. B. 1964. Conformity and commitment to the group. *Journal of Abnormal and Social Psychology* 68:209–211.

Goodale, J. G., and Aagaard, A. K. 1975. Factors relating to varying reactions to the four day work week. *Journal of Applied Psychology* 60:33–38.

Leventhal, H.; Jacobs, R. L.; and Kudirka, N. Z. 1964. Authoritarianism, ideology and political candidate choice. *Journal of Abnormal and Social Psychology* 69:372–389.

Mendenhall, W. 1975. *Introduction to probability and statistics.* 4th ed. N. Scituate, Mass.: Duxbury Press. Chapter 11.

Robinson, H. A.; Redlich, F. C.; and Myers, J. K. 1954. Social structure and psychiatric treatment. *American Journal of Orthopsychiatry* 24:307–316.

Siegel, S. 1956. *Nonparametric statistics.* New York: McGraw-Hill.

Singer, E.; Blane, H. T; and Kasschau, R. 1964. Alcoholism and social isolation. *Journal of Abnormal and Social Psychology* 69:681–685.

Sutcliffe, J. P. 1957. A general method of analysis of frequency data for multiple classification designs. *Psychology Bulletin* 54 (no. 2):134–137.

14·Nonparametric Analysis of Variance

14.1
* The Kruskal-Wallis *H* Test for the Completely Randomized Design
14.2
* The Friedman Test for Randomized Block Designs

INTRODUCTION

In chapter 11 we introduced a method for comparing *p* population means: the analysis of variance. You will recall that we must assume that the *p* populations are normally distributed for this method to be valid. For many experiments this assumption may be unreasonable, because the data may not possess a normal distribution.

Consider these examples: the performance of *p* therapists is filmed and then ranked on a scale from 1 to 5 by several observers; the number of trials required to extinguish a learned response for rats subjected to *p* different reinforcement schedules is recorded; the number of correct responses in six trials is recorded for subjects under *p* different levels of stress. In each example we are interested in comparing *p* populations, but the data are measured on scales that are not continuous, yielding only integer values in a rather small range. Such scores could not possess a normal distribution because the normal distribution applies to a continuous random variable and is a smooth curve. Thus we would be wary of using analysis of variance in the situations described here.

In this chapter we present two nonparametric techniques for comparing *p* populations (sections 14.1 and 14.2). Like the nonparametric methods for comparing two populations (chapter 6), these methods will be free of any assumption about the frequency distributions of the *p* populations. The ranks of the data rather than the actual numerical values are analyzed. The result of using ranks instead of actual measurements is a loss of information, but we are willing to sacrifice some information to be rid of an assumption we think is unwarranted for the data at hand.

432

14.1 • THE KRUSKAL-WALLIS H TEST FOR THE COMPLETELY RANDOMIZED DESIGN

We first consider a nonparametric procedure for comparing p treatments in a completely randomized design. You will recall that the completely randomized design is one for which the experimenter selects independent random samples from each of the p populations. The notation for this design is summarized in the box.

Summary of Notation for a Completely Randomized Design

	Sample 1	Sample 2	$\cdots$	Sample p
Sample size	n_1	n_2	$\cdots$	n_p
Rank sum	R_1	R_2	$\cdots$	R_p

Total sample size: n

Note that instead of computing sample means and variances, we compute only the rank sum for each of our p samples. The rank of each observation is determined by its position in the *entire* collection of measurements, that is, all p samples. If two or more measurements are tied, they each receive the average of the ranks which would have been assigned had they been slightly different. We will use these rank sums to test the null hypothesis

H_0: The p population frequency distributions are identical

Figure 14.1 depicts the null hypothesis for p populations. Of course, figure 14.1 shows only one possible shape of the infinitely many possible shapes the frequency distribution may possess. For example, if the response is an integer between 1 and 5, the frequency function would be a relative frequency histogram with five classifications.

We are interested in knowing whether the data support the research hypothesis

H_a: At least two of the p population frequency distributions differ

One example of this research hypothesis is shown in figure 14.2.

The test statistic is a function of the rank sums $R_1, R_2, \ldots, R_p$. The statistic, known as the **Kruskal-Wallis H statistic**, is computed as shown in the box.

The Kruskal-Wallis H Statistic

$$H = \frac{12}{n(n+1)} \sum_{j=1}^{p} \frac{R_j^2}{n_j} - 3(n+1)$$

We show how H is calculated in the following example.

Figure 14.1 • Null hypothesis of identical frequency distributions for p populations

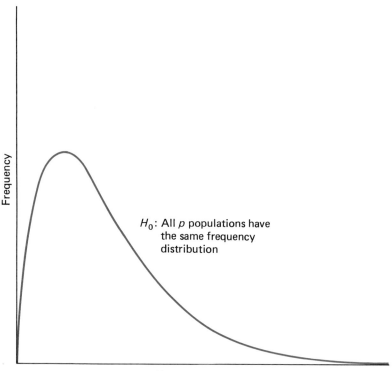

H_0: All p populations have the same frequency distribution

Measurement scale

Example 14.1

Three lists of words, representing three levels of abstractness, are randomly assigned to 24 experimental subjects so that 8 subjects receive each list. Subjects are then asked to respond to each word on their list with as many associated words as possible within a given period of time. Each subject is scored for his or her total number of associates by summing over all the words in the list. The measurements and their corresponding ranks are shown in table 14.1.

Compute the Kruskal-Wallis H statistic for these data.

Solution: The essential elements of this experiment are shown below.

Experimental units: Human subjects.

Response: Total number of word associations over a list of words.

Factor: Degree of abstractness represented by the various word lists (qualitative).

Levels: Three levels of abstractness, each represented by a list of words.

Treatments: The three levels of abstractness, List 1, List 2, and List 3.

We use the rank sums and the sample sizes $n_1 = n_2 = n_3 = 8$ and $n = 24$ to calculate H.

Figure 14.2 • Research hypothesis that the population frequency distributions differ for $p = 3$

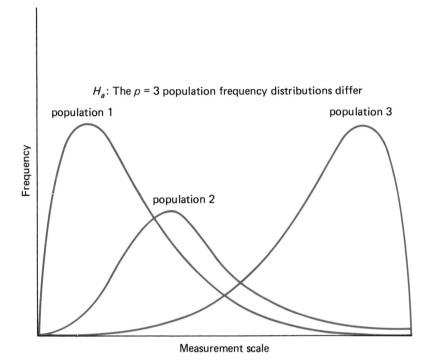

H_a: The $p = 3$ population frequency distributions differ

population 1

population 3

population 2

Frequency

Measurement scale

Table 14.1 • Data for the word association experiment: the measurements and their ranks

List 1		List 2		List 3	
Measurement	**Rank**	**Measurement**	**Rank**	**Measurement**	**Rank**
35	10	21	3	31	6
32	7.5	39	13	15	1
41	15	44	18	28	4
29	5	43	17	33	9
50	22	57	23	32	7.5
36	11	47	20	18	2
40	14	48	21	42	16
45	19	58	24	38	12
Rank Sums	$R_1 = 103.5$		$R_2 = 139$		$R_3 = 57.5$

$$H = \frac{12}{n(n+1)} \sum_{j=1}^{3} \frac{R_j^2}{n_j} - 3(n+1)$$

$$= \frac{12}{24(25)} \left[\frac{(103.5)^2}{8} + \frac{(139.0)^2}{8} + \frac{(57.5)^2}{8} \right] - 3(25) = 8.35$$

Note that if the rank sums $R_1, R_2, \ldots, R_p$ are very much different from each other, the implication is that the frequency distributions are also quite different. Thus we look for large variation among the rank sums to support the research hypothesis that the population frequency distributions differ. The amount of variation among rank sums is measured by the Kruskal-Wallis H statistic, with large values of H reflecting large variation and thus supporting the research hypothesis.

To determine the rejection region for H, we use the large-sample approximation to the repeated sampling distribution of H. When the null hypothesis is true, this approximation is a χ^2 distribution, with $(p - 1)$ degrees of freedom. We assume this approximation is adequate as long as each of the p sample sizes exceeds 5. We thus can form our rejection region as follows:

Rejection region: For an α-level of significance, we reject the null hypothesis when

$$H > \chi_\alpha^2$$

where the degrees of freedom are $(p - 1)$.

A summary of the Kruskal-Wallis test is given in the box.

Summary of the Kruskal-Wallis Nonparametric Comparison of p treatments for the Completely Randomized Design

Null hypothesis H_0: The p treatments possess identical population frequency distributions.

Research hypothesis H_a: At least two of the p population frequency distributions differ.

Test statistic: $H = \dfrac{12}{n(n + 1)} \sum_{j=1}^{p} \dfrac{R_j^2}{n_j} - 3(n + 1)$.

Rejection region: For a significance level α, reject H_0 if

$$H > \chi_\alpha^2$$

with degrees of freedom $(p - 1)$.

Example 14.2

Refer to example 14.1. A completely randomized design was used to compare three levels of abstractness in a word association experiment. Use the Kruskal-Wallis H test to test the null hypothesis that the frequency distributions corresponding to the three treatments are identical. Use $\alpha = .05$.

Solution: The nonparametric Kruskal-Wallis test concerns the frequency distributions corresponding to the treatments. In this case the treatments are the three lists of words which were designed to represent three levels of abstractness. The number of word associations made by the population of subjects constitutes the frequency distribution for each treatment. The setup for the test is given below.

Null hypothesis H_0: The frequency distributions corresponding to the number of word associations are identical for the three treatments (levels of abstractness).

Research hypothesis H_a: At least two of the word association populations possess different frequency distributions.

Test statistic: $H = \dfrac{12}{n(n-1)} \sum_{j=1}^{3} \dfrac{R_j^2}{n_j} - 3(n+1).$

Rejection region: For $\alpha = .05$, we reject the null hypothesis if

$$H > \chi_{.05}^2 = 5.99$$

where the degrees of freedom equal the number of treatments minus one; that is, d.f. $= p - 1 = 3 - 1 = 2$.

In example 14.1, we calculated $H = 8.35$. Since this value exceeds 5.99, we conclude that at least two of the frequency distributions corresponding to the three levels of abstraction differ.

We could compare the pairs of frequency distributions by means of the Mann-Whitney U test presented in section 6.5. This would allow us to make inferences about the relative ordering of the distributions. We omit the specific details of these paired comparisons.

EXERCISE

1. An investigator wishes to compare four methods of instruction, A, B, C, and D, for their effects on subjects' performances on a complex problem-solving task. (Method D is a "no instruction" control.) Twenty subjects are selected and randomly assigned to the four experimental conditions (methods) in such a way that 5 subjects are instructed by each method. Following the instruction period, the test problem is presented and the number of minutes to reach a solution is recorded for each subject. If a subject does not reach a solution within 60 minutes, he or she is assigned a score of 60. The following results are obtained.

A	B	C	D
12.3	22.6	42.3	51.1
23.2	29.7	44.9	58.6
21.6	32.4	38.6	60.0
16.4	28.6	52.2	60.0
15.9	41.6	43.3	39.4

(a) Why would the assumption of normality be inappropriate for this data?

(b) What are the basic elements of this experiment? That is, name the experimental units, the response, the factors, the factor levels, and the treatments.

(c) Use the Kruskal-Wallis test to compare the frequency distributions corresponding to the four methods of instruction. Use $\alpha = .05$.

14.2 · THE FRIEDMAN TEST FOR RANDOMIZED BLOCK DESIGNS

The randomized block design first introduced in section 10.5 uses relatively homogeneous blocks of experimental units to compare treatments. In this section we present a nonparametric analysis, the Friedman test, of the randomized block design.

Like the nonparametric Kruskal-Wallis test for completely randomized designs, the nonparametric Friedman test for randomized block designs uses the ranks of the measurements rather than their actual numerical values. However, the computation of the ranks is different for the two procedures. Whereas the Kruskal-Wallis ranks are computed with respect to the entire data set, the Friedman ranks are computed within each block. That is, we compare each measurement only to the other measurements in the same block when determining its rank. Tied measurements are given the average of the corresponding ranks. We illustrate this ranking procedure in an example.

Example 14.3

A randomized block experiment is designed to compare the effects of four different stress conditions (an electric shock preceded by a tone signal of varying duration) on water-intake suppression in rats. The homogenous blocks of experimental units are 9 sets of litter mates, each set consisting of 4 rats. One rat from each litter is assigned to each treatment (stress condition). An index of water-intake suppression is calculated by recording total water intake during the experimental session and computing the ratio of this measure to one obtained preexperimentally over a comparable time period. The resulting measurements, shown as percentages, are given in table 14.2.

Rank each measurement within the block (litter) in which it is contained.

Solution: Since we are ranking measurements within the blocks, we consider the litters separately. The smallest measurement in Litter 1 is that corresponding to Stress Condition A, which is 32. It receives the rank of (1). The measurement 35, corresponding to Stress Condition B, is next and thus receives rank (2). Next is 43, the measurement for Stress Condition D. The rank of (3) is assigned to that measurement. Finally, the largest measurement in this first block, 49, corresponding to Stress Condition C, receives rank (4). The ranks for Litter 1 are shown below in parentheses.

Stress Condition

	A		B		C		D	
	Meas.	Rank	Meas.	Rank	Meas.	Rank	Meas.	Rank
Litter 1	32	(1)	35	(2)	49	(4)	43	(3)

Table 14.2 • Data for the water-intake suppression experiment in example 14.3

	Stress Condition			
Litter	A	B	C	D
1	32	35	49	43
2	36	39	52	48
3	46	41	54	62
4	37	32	55	36
5	28	36	44	38
6	40	46	60	44
7	48	51	45	40
8	31	37	48	42
9	30	35	41	46

We proceed to rank all the other measurements *within* their respective blocks. The results are summarized in table 14.3.

As with the completely randomized experiment, we use the rank sums for each of the p treatments to compare their frequency distributions. The hypotheses are the same, regardless of which experimental design is employed.

Table 14.3 • Data and their within-block ranks for the water-intake suppression experiment

	Stress Condition							
	A		B		C		D	
Litter	Meas.	Rank	Meas.	Rank	Meas.	Rank	Meas.	Rank
1	32	1	35	2	49	4	43	3
2	36	1	39	2	52	4	48	3
3	46	2	41	1	54	3	62	4
4	37	3	32	1	55	4	36	2
5	28	1	36	2	44	4	38	3
6	40	1	46	3	60	4	44	2
7	48	3	51	4	45	2	40	1
8	31	1	37	2	48	4	42	3
9	30	1	35	2	41	3	46	4

Null hypothesis H_0: The p treatments have identical population frequency distributions.

Research hypothesis H_a: At least two of the p treatments have different frequency distributions.

The test statistic for the randomized block design, the Friedman test statistic, uses the sums of the within-block ranks for the p treatments. We denote these p rank sums by $R_1, R_2, \ldots, R_p$. The Friedman test statistic is given in the box.

The Friedman F_r Statistic

$$F_r = \frac{12}{bp(p + 1)} \sum_{j=1}^{p} R_j^2 - 3b(p + 1)$$

where p is the number of treatments, b is the number of blocks, and $R_1, R_2, \ldots, R_p$ are the rank sums of the p treatments.

Example 14.4

Refer to the water-intake suppression experiment introduced in example 14.3. Calculate the Friedman F_r statistic for this data.

Solution: The data and the ranks are repeated in table 14.4. The rank sums are computed for each of the four stress conditions (treatments).

Table 14.4 • Data, the within-block ranks, and the rank sums for the water-intake suppression experiment

	Stress Condition							
	A		**B**		**C**		**D**	
Litter	Meas.	Rank	Meas.	Rank	Meas.	Rank	Meas.	Rank
1	32	1	35	2	49	4	43	3
2	36	1	39	2	52	4	48	3
3	46	2	41	1	54	3	62	4
4	37	3	32	1	55	4	36	2
5	28	1	36	2	44	4	38	3
6	40	1	46	3	60	4	44	2
7	48	3	51	4	45	2	40	1
8	31	1	37	2	48	4	42	3
9	30	1	35	2	41	2	46	4
Rank Sums	$R_1 = 14$		$R_2 = 19$		$R_3 = 32$		$R_4 = 25$	

The number of treatments is $p = 4$ and the total sample size is $n = 36$. We now compute Friedman's statistic.

$$F_r = \frac{12}{bp(p+1)} \sum_{j=1}^{p} R_j^2 - 3b(p+1)$$

$$= \frac{12}{(9)(4)(5)}[(14)^2 + (19)^2 + (32)^2 + (25)^2] - (3)(9)(5)$$

$$= 12.067$$

Like the Kruskal-Wallis H statistic, the Friedman F_r statistic has a repeated sampling distribution which is approximately a chi-square distribution, with $(p-1)$ degrees of freedom, *when the null hypothesis is true.* We will assume this approximation is adequate as long as either p or b exceeds 5.

When the treatments possess different frequency distributions, the research hypothesis is true, and we expect the rank sums to vary considerably from sample to sample. This will inflate the F_r statistic. Thus we will reject H_0 when the F_r statistic is larger than we "expect" a χ^2 statistic with $(p-1)$ degrees of freedom to be.

Rejection region: For an α-level of significance, we reject the null hypothesis if

$$F_r > \chi_\alpha^2$$

where the degrees of freedom are $(p-1)$.

A summary of the Friedman test is given in the box.

Summary of the Friedman Nonparametric Comparison of p Populations for Randomized Block Designs

Null hypothesis H_0: The p treatments possess identical population frequency distributions.

Research hypothesis H_a: At least two of the p population frequency distributions differ.

Test statistic: $F_r = \frac{12}{bp(p+1)} \sum_{j=1}^{p} R_j^2 - 3b(p+1)$.

Rejection region: For a significance level α, reject H_0 if

$$F_r > \chi_\alpha^2$$

with degrees of freedom equal to $(p-1)$.

Example 14.5

Refer to examples 14.3 and 14.4. We introduced a water-intake suppression experiment, with the objective of comparing the effects of four different stress conditions on the water-intake of rats. Use the computed Friedman statistic from example 14.4 to see whether the data support the research hypothesis that the effects of the four different treatments differ. Test at the $\alpha = .10$ level of significance.

Solution: We are interested in comparing the frequency distributions corresponding to the water-intake suppression index of the four stress conditions. The test setup is as follows.

Null hypothesis H_0: The four stress condition frequency distributions are the same for the water-intake suppression index.

Research hypothesis H_a: At least two of the stress conditions produce different frequency distributions of the water-intake suppression index.

Test statistic: $F_r = \dfrac{12}{bp(p + 1)} \displaystyle\sum_{j=1}^{p} R_j^2 - 3b(p + 1).$

Rejection region: For $\alpha = .10$, we reject the null hypothesis if

$$F_r > \chi^2_{.10} = 6.25$$

where d.f. $= p - 1 = 3$.

In example 14.4 we calculated $F_r = 12.067$, which exceeds the rejection value 6.25. We therefore conclude that the data support the research hypothesis at the $\alpha = .10$ level. There is evidence that the suppression index frequency distributions corresponding to the four stress conditions differ.

We could compare pairs of stress conditions by using the Wilcoxon rank sum test of section 6.6. This would permit us to make inferences about the relative ordering of the four frequency distributions.

EXERCISE

1. Each of 8 educators was asked to rate four children's television shows using a 40-item scale designed to assess the show's educational value. The resulting ratings were as given below.

Educator	Television Show			
	A	B	C	D
1	17	25	6	2
2	23	13	16	9
3	32	27	14	18
4	28	26	15	10
5	24	29	11	19
6	30	7	22	12
7	21	8	5	3
8	20	31	4	1

Using the Friedman test for randomized block designs, test the hypothesis that the four television shows are considered equal in educational value. Use $\alpha = .05$.

SUMMARY

In general, nonparametric analysis of variance techniques are employed when we are uncomfortable with the assumptions necessary for parametric methods. Specifically, the assumption that the data are normally distributed is often unreasonable for behavioral science experiments. In these situations, then, we analyze the ranks of the data, sacrificing a portion of the information in order to eliminate the necessity of making unwarranted assumptions.

The Kruskal-Wallis test is appropriate for completely randomized experiments, and the Friedman test is used for randomized block experiments. Both tests are designed to make inferences about the differences between the frequency distributions of the treatments based on a comparison of the treatment rank sums.

SUPPLEMENTARY EXERCISES

1. What is the most common reason for using a nonparametric method instead of a parametric method of analysis of variance?
2. A study is undertaken to compare three food deprivation schedules (A, B, and C) for their effect on hoarding behavior in rats. Twenty-one rats are used in the study, 7 being subjected to each of the three deprivation conditions. At the end of the deprivation period, subjects are allowed free access to food pellets, and the number of pellets hoarded (taken but not eaten) during a given period is recorded for each. The data obtained are as follows.

A	5	1	2	8	2	3	2
B	15	10	5	7	4	9	11
C	9	6	13	5	11	8	9

  Can it be concluded that the three deprivation schedules differ in their effect on hoarding behavior as measured in this experiment? Use $\alpha = .05$.
3. The experiment in exercise 2 might have been designed somewhat more carefully. If, for example, some rats characteristically take more pellets than others even though never deprived, this kind of subject-to-subject variation could obscure actual treatment effects. An alternate design, using matched rather than independent samples, might be preferable. That is, prior to the actual experiment, the investigator might record the pellet intake for each potential subject; form groups of $p = 3$ subjects with similar intake records; and then, within each group, randomly assign each subject to one of the three deprivation conditions. Such a design would permit a comparison of the effects of the three deprivation conditions within relatively homogeneous groups of subjects.

  Suppose that a subsequent experiment is conducted in this fashion and the results below on the number of pellets hoarded are obtained. Do these data provide sufficient evidence to indicate that the three deprivation schedules differ in their effect on hoarding behavior? Use $\alpha = .05$.

	Schedule		
Group	**A**	**B**	**C**
1	2	7	5
2	3	8	12
3	7	6	10
4	4	11	14
5	3	6	8
6	2	7	6
7	6	10	13

4. To assess the relative sales appeal of four new products, a toy manufacturer conducted a small-sample study. Six mothers of infant boys were randomly selected and asked to rank the four new toys (A, B, C, and D) in order of probable appeal to their own children. The rank orderings shown below were obtained.

	Toys			
Mother	**A**	**B**	**C**	**D**
1	3	2	4	1
2	2	4	3	1
3	2	3	4	1
4	1	3	4	2
5	2	4	3	1
6	1	3	4	2

Do the data provide sufficient evidence to indicate a difference in the appeal of the four toys? Use $\alpha = .05$.

5. Refer to supplementary exercise 8 in chapter 11. We compared the mean object–word association test scores for groups of preschool children using three different books. Suppose the design is expanded to include 18 children, 6 using each book. The data for this expanded experiment are given below.

A	34	21	13	8	14	26
B	37	25	18	16	17	30
C	34	20	17	9	15	22

Suppose the researcher is concerned that the assumption that the test scores are normally distributed is unwarranted for this data and thus does not wish to conduct a parametric comparison of the test scores. Is there nonparametric evidence that the frequency distributions corresponding to the three books differ? Use $\alpha = .05$.

6. Refer to supplementary exercise 12 in chapter 11. We used a randomized block design to compare the mean degree of skin irritation corresponding to three chemicals applied to rats. The fact that skin irritation is measured on a scale from 0 to 10 makes

the assumption of normality questionable. So a nonparametric comparison of the three chemicals may be more suitable than a parametric comparison. Do the data, repeated below, provide evidence to support the research hypothesis that the frequency distributions of skin irritation scores corresponding to the three chemicals differ? Use $\alpha = .05$.

				Rat				
	1	2	3	4	5	6	7	8
	B	A	A	C	B	C	C	B
	5	9	6	6	8	5	5	7
	A	C	B	B	C	A	B	A
	6	4	9	8	8	5	7	6
	C	B	C	A	A	B	A	C
	3	9	3	5	7	7	6	7

REFERENCES

Hajek, J. 1969. *Nonparametric statistics.* San Francisco: Holden-Day.

Kirk, R. 1968. *Experimental design procedures for the behavioral sciences.* Belmont, Calif.: Wadsworth Publishing Company (Brooks/Cole).

Siegel, S. 1956. *Nonparametric statistics.* New York: McGraw-Hill.

15 • A Summary and Conclusion

The preceding fourteen chapters present a picture of statistics centered about the dominant feature of the subject, statistical inference. Inference, the objective of statistics, runs as a thread through the entire book, from the phrasing of the inference through the discussion of the probabilistic mechanism and the presentation of the reasoning involved in making the inference, to the formal elementary discussion of the concepts of statistical inference presented in chapters 6 and 8.

What is statistics, what is its purpose, and how does it accomplish its objective? If we have answered these questions to your satisfaction, if each chapter and section seems to fulfill a purpose and to complete a portion of the picture, we have in some measure accomplished our instructional objective.

Chapter 1 presented statistics as a scientific tool utilized in making inferences, a prediction, or a decision about a population of measurements based upon information contained in a sample. Thus statistics is employed in the evolutionary process known as the scientific method—which, in essence, is the observation of nature—in order that we may form inferences or theories concerning the structure of nature and test the theories against repeated observations. Inherent in this objective is the sampling and experimentation that purchase a quantity of information which will be employed to provide the best inferences about the population from which the sample was drawn.

The method of phrasing the inference, that is, describing a set of measurements, was presented in chapter 2 in terms of a frequency distribution and associated numerical descriptive measures. In particular, we noted that the frequency distribution is subject to a probabilistic interpretation and that the numerical descriptive measures are more suitable for inferential purposes because we can more easily associate with them a measure of their goodness. A secondary but extremely important result of our study of numerical descriptive measures involved the notion of variation, its measurement in terms of a standard deviation, and its interpretation using the Empirical Rule. We introduced the z score to provide a measure of relative standing for a member of a population. This concept later provided the basis for describing the relative position of a test statistic in an hypothesized sampling distribution.

In chapter 3 we extended our descriptive techniques to encompass samples of two variables. We developed methods for describing relationships between variables, with the correlation coefficient representing the primary numerical descriptive measure.

The mechanism involved in making an inference concerning the parameters of a population of die throws was introduced in chapter 4. We hypothesized that husbands and wives were equally likely to be first in seeking marital counseling (that is, $p = .5$). Observing that no wives first sought counseling in a random sample of 20 help-seeking couples, we concluded that the observed sample was highly improbable, assuming our hypothesis to be true, and we therefore rejected the hypothesis. We concluded that wives are less likely to seek marital counseling first. Thus we noted that the theory of probability assumes that the population is known and reasons from the population to the sample.

Statistical inference, using probability, observes the sample and attempts to make inferences concerning the population. Fundamental to this procedure is a probabilistic model for the frequency distribution of the population. The reasoning of chapter 4 was employed in chapter 5, where we presented a probability distribution, that is, a model for the population frequency distribution for a discrete random variable generated by the binomial experiment. The binomial experiment was chosen as an example because of its simplicity and its utility, which was exemplified by the marriage counseling and the rat maze experiments. Particularly, the inferential aspects of these problems were noted, with emphasis placed upon the reasoning involved. The structure of hypothesis testing and the notion of significance level were first introduced using binomial experiments. These concepts formed the basis of many important inferential techniques in later chapters.

Chapter 6 introduced two important concepts: the design of experiments and nonparametric hypothesis tests. The importance of the method by which sample information is obtained was stressed, and the effect of the experimental design on the inferential process was demonstrated. We showed that nonparametric tests are a simple flexible method for comparing two populations.

Study of a useful continuous random variable in chapter 7 centered about the Central Limit Theorem, its suggested support of the Empirical Rule, and its use in describing the probability distribution of sample means and sums. Indeed, we used the Central Limit Theorem to justify the use of the Empirical Rule and the normal probability distribution as an approximation to the binomial probability distribution when the number of trials n is large. Through examples we attempted to reinforce the probabilistic concept of statistical inference introduced in preceding chapters and induce you, as a matter of intuition, to employ statistical reasoning in making inferences.

Chapter 8 discussed statistical inference, estimation and tests of hypotheses, the methods of measuring the goodness of the inference, and presented a number of estimators and test statistics which, because of the Central Limit Theorem, possess approximately a normal probability distribution in repeated sampling. These notions were carried over to the discussion of the small-sample tests and estimators in chapter 9.

Chapters 1 through 9 dealt with the philosophy and the methodology for making inferences and for measuring the quantity of information in a sample. Thus they formed a necessary foundation for understanding how and why noise and volume affect the quantity of information in an experiment and set the stage for a discussion of experimental design in chapter 10.

The analysis of variance, chapter 11, extended the comparison of treatment means in the completely randomized and the randomized block designs (chapter 8) to more than two treatments. Simultaneously, it introduced a completely new way to view the analysis of data through the analysis (or partitioning) of variance.

Chapters 12, 13, and 14 were primarily intended to broaden the view of the beginner by presenting some interesting and useful solutions to inferential problems. In chapter 12 we expanded our treatment of variable relationships first introduced in chapter 3. The inferential methodology for detecting predictive relationships was developed. In chapter 13 we discussed methods for analyzing enumerative data. Finally, we presented nonparametric analysis of variance in chapter 14, so that populations could be compared even when they do not satisfy the assumptions necessary for the parametric methods of chapter 11.

In conclusion, we note that the methodology presented in this introduction to statistics represents a very small sample of the population of statistical methodology that is available to the researcher. It is a bare introduction and nothing more. The design of experiments—an extremely useful topic—was barely touched. Indeed, the methodology presented, although very useful, is intended primarily to serve as a vehicle suitable for conveying to you the philosophy of statistics.

Appendix I • Useful Statistical Tests and Confidence Intervals

I. Inferences concerning the mean of a population.

1. Sample size n is large ($n > 30$).

   A. Two-tailed test:

   Null hypothesis: $\mu = \mu_0$.
   Research hypothesis: $\mu \neq \mu_0$.
   Test statistic:

   $$z = \frac{\bar{y} - \mu_0}{\sigma/\sqrt{n}}.$$

   If σ is unknown and the sample is large, use

   $$s = \sqrt{\frac{\sum_{i=1}^{n}(y_i - \bar{y})^2}{n - 1}}$$

   as an estimate of σ.
   Rejection region: For $\alpha = .05$, reject if z is greater than 1.96 or if z is less than -1.96.

   B. $(1 - \alpha)$ confidence interval:

   $$\bar{y} \pm z_{\alpha/2} \frac{\sigma}{\sqrt{n}}$$

2. Small samples, $n < 30$, and the observations are nearly normally distributed.

   A. Two-tailed test:

   Null hypothesis: $\mu = \mu_0$.
   Research hypothesis: $\mu \neq \mu_0$.
   Test statistic:

   $$t = \frac{\bar{y} - \mu_0}{s/\sqrt{n}}.$$

   Rejection region: See t tables.

   B. $(1 - \alpha)$ confidence interval:

   $$\bar{y} \pm t_{\alpha/2} \frac{s}{\sqrt{n}}$$

II. Inferences concerning the difference between the means of two populations.

1. Large samples.

A. Assumptions:

(a) Population I has mean equal to μ_1 and variance equal to σ_1^2.
(b) Population II has mean equal to μ_2 and variance equal to σ_2^2.

B. Some results:

(a) Let $\bar{y}_1$ be the mean of a random sample of n_1 observations from population I and $\bar{y}_2$ be the mean of an independent and random sample of n_2 observations from population II. Consider the difference $(\bar{y}_1 - \bar{y}_2)$.
(b) It can be shown that the mean of $(\bar{y}_1 - \bar{y}_2)$ is $(\mu_1 - \mu_2)$ and its variance is $(\sigma_1^2/n_1) + (\sigma_2^2/n_2)$. Furthermore, for large samples, $(\bar{y}_1 - \bar{y}_2)$ will be approximately normally distributed.

C. Two-tailed test:

Null hypothesis: $(\mu_1 - \mu_2) = D_0$. (Note: We are usually testing the hypothesis that $(\mu_1 - \mu_2) = 0$, i.e., $\mu_1 = \mu_2$.)
Research hypothesis: $(\mu_1 - \mu_2) \neq D_0$.
Test statistic:

$$z = \frac{(\bar{y}_1 - \bar{y}_2) - D_0}{\sqrt{\dfrac{\sigma_1^2}{n_1} + \dfrac{\sigma_2^2}{n_2}}}.$$

If the null hypothesis is that $\mu_1 = \mu_2$, then $D_0 = 0$ and

$$z = \frac{\bar{y}_1 - \bar{y}_2}{\sqrt{\dfrac{\sigma_1^2}{n_1} + \dfrac{\sigma_2^2}{n_2}}}$$

If σ_1^2 and σ_2^2 are unknown and n is large, use s_1^2 and s_2^2 as estimates.
Rejection region: For $\alpha = .05$, reject if $z > 1.96$ or if $z < -1.96$.

D. $(1 - \alpha)$ confidence interval:

$$(\bar{y}_1 - \bar{y}_2) \pm z_{\alpha/2} \sqrt{\frac{\sigma_1^2}{n_1} + \frac{\sigma_2^2}{n_2}}$$

2. Small samples.

A. Assumptions: Both populations approximately normally distributed and $\sigma_1^2 = \sigma_2^2$.

B. Two-tailed test:

Null hypothesis: $(\mu_1 - \mu_2) = D_0$.
Research hypothesis: $(\mu_1 - \mu_2) \neq D_0$.

Test statistic:
$$t = \frac{(\bar{y}_1 - \bar{y}_2) - D_0}{s\sqrt{\dfrac{1}{n_1} + \dfrac{1}{n_2}}}$$

where s is a pooled estimate of σ:

$$s = \sqrt{\frac{(n_1 - 1)s_1^2 + (n_2 - 1)s_2^2}{n_1 + n_2 - 2}}$$

Rejection region: See t tables.

C. $(1 - \alpha)$ confidence interval:

$$(\bar{y}_1 - \bar{y}_2) \pm t_{\alpha/2}s\sqrt{\frac{1}{n_1} + \frac{1}{n_2}}$$

III. Inferences concerning a probability p.

1. Assumptions for a binomial experiment:

   A. Experiment consists of n identical trials, each resulting in one of two outcomes, say success and failure.
   B. The probability of success is equal to p and remains the same from trial to trial.
   C. The trials are independent of each other.
   D. The variable measured is $y =$ (number of successes observed during the n trials).

2. Results:

   A. The estimator of p is $\hat{p} = y/n$.
   B. The average value of $\hat{p}$ is p.
   C. The variance of $\hat{p}$ is equal to pq/n.
   D. For large n, $\hat{p}$ is approximately normally distributed.

3. Two-tailed test (n large):

   Null hypothesis: $p = p_0$.
   Research hypothesis: $p \neq p_0$.
   Test statistic:

   $$z = \frac{\hat{p} - p_0}{\sqrt{\dfrac{p_0 q_0}{n}}}.$$

   Rejection region: Reject if $|z| \geq 1.96$. Note: $\alpha = .05$.

4. $(1 - \alpha)$ confidence interval (n large):

   $$\hat{p} \pm z_{\alpha/2}\sqrt{\frac{\hat{p}\hat{q}}{n}}$$

IV. Inferences comparing two probabilities p_1 and p_2.

1. Assumption: Independent random samples are drawn from each of two binomial populations.

	Pop. I	Pop. II
Probability of success	p_1	p_2
Sample size	n_1	n_2
Observed successes	y_1	y_2

2. Results:

A. The estimated difference between p_1 and p_2 is

$$(\widehat{p}_1 - \widehat{p}_2) = \frac{y_1}{n_1} - \frac{y_2}{n_2}$$

B. The average value of $(\widehat{p}_1 - \widehat{p}_2)$ is $(p_1 - p_2)$.
C. The variance of $(\widehat{p}_1 - \widehat{p}_2)$ is

$$\frac{p_1 q_1}{n_1} + \frac{p_2 q_2}{n_2}$$

D. For large n, $(\widehat{p}_1 - \widehat{p}_2)$ is approximately normally distributed.

3. Two-tailed test (n_1 and n_2 large):

Null hypothesis: $p_1 = p_2$.
Research hypothesis: $p_1 \neq p_2$.
Test statistic:

$$z = \frac{(\widehat{p}_1 - \widehat{p}_2)}{\sqrt{\dfrac{\widehat{p}_1 \widehat{q}_1}{n_1} + \dfrac{\widehat{p}_2 \widehat{q}_2}{n_2}}}$$

Rejection region: Reject if $|z| \geq 1.96$. Note: $\alpha = .05$.

4. $(1 - \alpha)$ confidence interval (n_1 and n_2 large):

$$(\widehat{p}_1 - \widehat{p}_2) \pm z_{\alpha/2} \sqrt{\frac{\widehat{p}_1 \widehat{q}_1}{n_1} + \frac{\widehat{p}_2 \widehat{q}_2}{n_2}}$$

V. Tests concerning the equality of two population variances.

1. Assumptions:

A. Population I has a normal distribution with mean μ_1 and variance σ_1^2.
B. Population II has a normal distribution with mean μ_2 and variance σ_2^2.
C. Two independent random samples are drawn, n_1 measurements from population I, n_2 from population II.

2. Two-tailed test:

Null hypothesis: $\sigma_1^2 = \sigma_2^2$.
Research hypothesis: $\sigma_1^2 \neq \sigma_2^2$.
Test statistic:

$$F = \frac{s_1^2}{s_2^2} \qquad \text{(assuming } s_1^2 > s_2^2\text{)}.$$

Rejection region: Reject if F is greater than or equal to $F_{\alpha/2}(n_1 - 1, n_2 - 1)$.

Appendix II·Tables

Table 1 • Binomial probability tables

Tabulated values are $\sum_{y=0}^{a} p(y)$. (Computations are rounded at the third decimal place.)

(a) $n = 5$

P

a	0.01	0.05	0.10	0.20	0.30	0.40	0.50	0.60	0.70	0.80	0.90	0.95	0.99	a
0	.951	.774	.590	.328	.168	.078	.031	.010	.002	.000	.000	.000	.000	0
1	.999	.977	.919	.737	.528	.337	.188	.087	.031	.007	.000	.000	.000	1
2	1.000	.999	.991	.942	.837	.683	.500	.317	.163	.058	.009	.001	.000	2
3	1.000	1.000	1.000	.993	.969	.913	.812	.663	.472	.263	.081	.023	.001	3
4	1.000	1.000	1.000	1.000	.998	.990	.969	.922	.832	.672	.410	.226	.049	4

(b) $n = 10$

P

a	0.01	0.05	0.10	0.20	0.30	0.40	0.50	0.60	0.70	0.80	0.90	0.95	0.99	a
0	.904	.599	.349	.107	.028	.006	.001	.000	.000	.000	.000	.000	.000	0
1	.996	.914	.736	.376	.149	.046	.011	.002	.000	.000	.000	.000	.000	1
2	1.000	.988	.930	.678	.383	.167	.055	.012	.002	.000	.000	.000	.000	2
3	1.000	.999	.987	.879	.650	.382	.172	.055	.011	.001	.000	.000	.000	3
4	1.000	1.000	.998	.967	.850	.633	.377	.166	.047	.006	.000	.000	.000	4
5	1.000	1.000	1.000	.994	.953	.834	.623	.367	.150	.033	.002	.000	.000	5
6	1.000	1.000	1.000	.999	.989	.945	.828	.618	.350	.121	.013	.001	.000	6
7	1.000	1.000	1.000	1.000	.998	.988	.945	.833	.617	.322	.070	.012	.000	7
8	1.000	1.000	1.000	1.000	1.000	.998	.989	.954	.851	.624	.264	.086	.004	8
9	1.000	1.000	1.000	1.000	1.000	1.000	.999	.994	.972	.893	.651	.401	.096	9

(c) $n = 15$

	0.01	0.05	0.10	0.20	0.30	0.40	0.50	0.60	0.70	0.80	0.90	0.95	0.99	
a														*a*
0	.860	.463	.206	.035	.005	.000	.000	.000	.000	.000	.000	.000	.000	0
1	.990	.829	.549	.167	.035	.005	.000	.000	.000	.000	.000	.000	.000	1
2	1.000	.964	.816	.398	.127	.027	.004	.000	.000	.000	.000	.000	.000	2
3	1.000	.995	.944	.648	.297	.091	.018	.002	.000	.000	.000	.000	.000	3
4	1.000	.999	.987	.836	.515	.217	.059	.009	.001	.000	.000	.000	.000	4
5	1.000	1.000	.998	.939	.722	.403	.151	.034	.004	.000	.000	.000	.000	5
6	1.000	1.000	1.000	.982	.869	.610	.304	.095	.015	.001	.000	.000	.000	6
7	1.000	1.000	1.000	.996	.950	.787	.500	.213	.050	.004	.000	.000	.000	7
8	1.000	1.000	1.000	.999	.985	.905	.696	.390	.131	.018	.000	.000	.000	8
9	1.000	1.000	1.000	1.000	.996	.966	.849	.597	.278	.061	.002	.000	.000	9
10	1.000	1.000	1.000	1.000	.999	.991	.941	.783	.485	.164	.013	.001	.000	10
11	1.000	1.000	1.000	1.000	1.000	.998	.982	.909	.703	.352	.056	.005	.000	11
12	1.000	1.000	1.000	1.000	1.000	1.000	.996	.973	.873	.602	.184	.036	.000	12
13	1.000	1.000	1.000	1.000	1.000	1.000	1.000	.995	.965	.833	.451	.171	.010	13
14	1.000	1.000	1.000	1.000	1.000	1.000	1.000	1.000	.995	.965	.794	.537	.140	14

P

(d) $n = 20$

							P							
	0.01	0.05	0.10	0.20	0.30	0.40	0.50	0.60	0.70	0.80	0.90	0.95	0.99	
a														a
0	.818	.358	.122	.002	.001	.000	.000	.000	.000	.000	.000	.000	.000	0
1	.983	.736	.392	.069	.008	.001	.000	.000	.000	.000	.000	.000	.000	1
2	.999	.925	.677	.206	.035	.004	.000	.000	.000	.000	.000	.000	.000	2
3	1.000	.984	.867	.411	.107	.016	.001	.000	.000	.000	.000	.000	.000	3
4	1.000	.997	.957	.630	.238	.051	.006	.000	.000	.000	.000	.000	.000	4
5	1.000	1.000	.989	.804	.416	.126	.021	.002	.000	.000	.000	.000	.000	5
6	1.000	1.000	.998	.913	.608	.250	.058	.006	.000	.000	.000	.000	.000	6
7	1.000	1.000	1.000	.968	.772	.416	.132	.021	.001	.000	.000	.000	.000	7
8	1.000	1.000	1.000	.990	.887	.596	.252	.057	.005	.000	.000	.000	.000	8
9	1.000	1.000	1.000	.997	.952	.755	.412	.128	.017	.001	.000	.000	.000	9
10	1.000	1.000	1.000	.999	.983	.872	.588	.245	.048	.003	.000	.000	.000	10
11	1.000	1.000	1.000	1.000	.995	.943	.748	.404	.113	.010	.000	.000	.000	11
12	1.000	1.000	1.000	1.000	.999	.979	.868	.584	.228	.032	.000	.000	.000	12
13	1.000	1.000	1.000	1.000	1.000	.994	.942	.750	.392	.087	.002	.000	.000	13
14	1.000	1.000	1.000	1.000	1.000	.998	.979	.874	.584	.196	.011	.000	.000	14
15	1.000	1.000	1.000	1.000	1.000	1.000	.994	.949	.762	.370	.043	.003	.000	15
16	1.000	1.000	1.000	1.000	1.000	1.000	.999	.984	.893	.589	.133	.016	.000	16
17	1.000	1.000	1.000	1.000	1.000	1.000	1.000	.996	.965	.794	.323	.075	.001	17
18	1.000	1.000	1.000	1.000	1.000	1.000	1.000	.999	.992	.931	.608	.264	.017	18
19	1.000	1.000	1.000	1.000	1.000	1.000	1.000	1.000	.999	.988	.878	.642	.182	19

(e) $n = 25$

P

a	0.01	0.05	0.10	0.20	0.30	0.40	0.50	0.60	0.70	0.80	0.90	0.95	0.99	a
0	.778	.277	.072	.004	.000	.000	.000	.000	.000	.000	.000	.000	.000	0
1	.974	.642	.271	.027	.002	.000	.000	.000	.000	.000	.000	.000	.000	1
2	.998	.873	.537	.098	.009	.000	.000	.000	.000	.000	.000	.000	.000	2
3	1.000	.966	.764	.234	.033	.002	.000	.000	.000	.000	.000	.000	.000	3
4	1.000	.993	.902	.421	.090	.009	.000	.000	.000	.000	.000	.000	.000	4
5	1.000	.999	.967	.617	.193	.029	.002	.000	.000	.000	.000	.000	.000	5
6	1.000	1.000	.991	.780	.341	.074	.007	.000	.000	.000	.000	.000	.000	6
7	1.000	1.000	.998	.891	.512	.154	.022	.001	.000	.000	.000	.000	.000	7
8	1.000	1.000	1.000	.953	.677	.274	.054	.004	.000	.000	.000	.000	.000	8
9	1.000	1.000	1.000	.983	.811	.425	.115	.013	.000	.000	.000	.000	.000	9
10	1.000	1.000	1.000	.994	.902	.586	.212	.034	.002	.000	.000	.000	.000	10
11	1.000	1.000	1.000	.998	.956	.732	.345	.078	.006	.000	.000	.000	.000	11
12	1.000	1.000	1.000	1.000	.983	.846	.500	.154	.017	.000	.000	.000	.000	12
13	1.000	1.000	1.000	1.000	.994	.922	.655	.268	.044	.002	.000	.000	.000	13
14	1.000	1.000	1.000	1.000	.998	.966	.788	.414	.098	.006	.000	.000	.000	14
15	1.000	1.000	1.000	1.000	1.000	.987	.885	.575	.189	.017	.000	.000	.000	15
16	1.000	1.000	1.000	1.000	1.000	.996	.946	.726	.323	.047	.000	.000	.000	16
17	1.000	1.000	1.000	1.000	1.000	.999	.978	.846	.488	.109	.002	.000	.000	17
18	1.000	1.000	1.000	1.000	1.000	1.000	.993	.926	.659	.220	.009	.000	.000	18
19	1.000	1.000	1.000	1.000	1.000	1.000	.998	.971	.807	.383	.033	.001	.000	19
20	1.000	1.000	1.000	1.000	1.000	1.000	1.000	.991	.910	.579	.098	.007	.000	20
21	1.000	1.000	1.000	1.000	1.000	1.000	1.000	.998	.967	.766	.236	.034	.000	21
22	1.000	1.000	1.000	1.000	1.000	1.000	1.000	1.000	.991	.902	.463	.127	.002	22
23	1.000	1.000	1.000	1.000	1.000	1.000	1.000	1.000	.998	.973	.729	.358	.026	23
24	1.000	1.000	1.000	1.000	1.000	1.000	1.000	1.000	1.000	.996	.928	.723	.222	24

Table 2 • Distribution function of U

$P(U \leq U_0)$; U_0 is the argument; $n_1 \leq n_2$; and $3 \leq n_2 \leq 10$.

$n_2 = 3$

n_1	1	2	3
0	.25	.10	.05
1	.50	.20	.10
U_0 2		.40	.20
3		.60	.35
4			.50

$n_2 = 4$

n_1	1	2	3	4
0	.2000	.0667	.0286	.0143
1	.4000	.1333	.0571	.0286
2	.6000	.2667	.1143	.0571
3		.4000	.2000	.1000
U_0 4		.6000	.3143	.1714
5			.4286	.2429
6			.5714	.3429
7				.4429
8				.5571

$n_2 = 5$

n_1	1	2	3	4	5
0	.1667	.0476	.0179	.0079	.0040
1	.3333	.0952	.0357	.0159	.0079
2	.5000	.1905	.0714	.0317	.0159
3		.2857	.1250	.0556	.0278
4		.4286	.1964	.0952	.0476
5		.5714	.2857	.1429	.0754
U_0 6			.3929	.2063	.1111
7			.5000	.2778	.1548
8				.3651	.2103
9				.4524	.2738
10				.5476	.3452
11					.4206
12					.5000

$$n_2 = 6$$

n_1	1	2	3	4	5	6
0	.1429	.0357	.0119	.0048	.0022	.0011
1	.2857	.0714	.0238	.0095	.0043	.0022
2	.4286	.1429	.0476	.0190	.0087	.0043
3	.5714	.2143	.0833	.0333	.0152	.0076
4		.3214	.1310	.0571	.0260	.0130
5		.4286	.1905	.0857	.0411	.0206
6		.5714	.2738	.1286	.0628	.0325
7			.3571	.1762	.0887	.0465
8			.4524	.2381	.1234	.0660
U_0 9			.5476	.3048	.1645	.0898
10				.3810	.2143	.1201
11				.4571	.2684	.1548
12				.5429	.3312	.1970
13					.3961	.2424
14					.4654	.2944
15					.5346	.3496
16						.4091
17						.4686
18						.5314

$$n_2 = 7$$

n_1	1	2	3	4	5	6	7
0	.1250	.0278	.0083	.0030	.0013	.0006	.0003
1	.2500	.0556	.0167	.0061	.0025	.0012	.0006
2	.3750	.1111	.0333	.0121	.0051	.0023	.0012
3	.5000	.1667	.0583	.0212	.0088	.0041	.0020
4		.2500	.0917	.0364	.0152	.0070	.0035
5		.3333	.1333	.0545	.0240	.0111	.0055
6		.4444	.1917	.0818	.0366	.0175	.0087
7		.5556	.2583	.1152	.0530	.0256	.0131
8			.3333	.1576	.0745	.0367	.0189
9			.4167	.2061	.1010	.0507	.0265
10			.5000	.2636	.1338	.0688	.0364
11				.3242	.1717	.0903	.0487
U_0 12				.3939	.2159	.1171	.0641
13				.4636	.2652	.1474	.0825
14				.5364	.3194	.1830	.1043
15					.3775	.2226	.1297
16					.4381	.2669	.1588
17					.5000	.3141	.1914
18						.3654	.2279
19						.4178	.2675
20						.4726	.3100
21						.5274	.3552
22							.4024
23							.4508
24							.5000

460 · **Appendix II**

$$n_2 = 8$$

n_1	1	2	3	4	5	6	7	8
0	.1111	.0222	.0061	.0020	.0008	.0003	.0002	.0001
1	.2222	.0444	.0121	.0040	.0016	.0007	.0003	.0002
2	.3333	.0889	.0242	.0081	.0031	.0013	.0006	.0003
3	.4444	.1333	.0424	.0141	.0054	.0023	.0011	.0005
4	.5556	.2000	.0667	.0242	.0093	.0040	.0019	.0009
5		.2667	.0970	.0364	.0148	.0063	.0030	.0015
6		.3556	.1394	.0545	.0225	.0100	.0047	.0023
7		.4444	.1879	.0768	.0326	.0147	.0070	.0035
8		.5556	.2485	.1071	.0466	.0213	.0103	.0052
9			.3152	.1414	.0637	.0296	.0145	.0074
10			.3879	.1838	.0855	.0406	.0200	.0103
11			.4606	.2303	.1111	.0539	.0270	.0141
12			.5394	.2848	.1422	.0709	.0361	.0190
13				.3414	.1772	.0906	.0469	.0249
14				.4040	.2176	.1142	.0603	.0325
15				.4667	.2618	.1412	.0760	.0415
U_0 16				.5333	.3108	.1725	.0946	.0524
17					.3621	.2068	.1159	.0652
18					.4165	.2454	.1405	.0803
19					.4716	.2864	.1678	.0974
20					.5284	.3310	.1984	.1172
21						.3773	.2317	.1393
22						.4259	.2679	.1641
23						.4749	.3063	.1911
24						.5251	.3472	.2209
25							.3894	.2527
26							.4333	.2869
27							.4775	.3227
28							.5225	.3605
29								.3992
30								.4392
31								.4796
32								.5204

$n_2 = 9$

n_1	1	2	3	4	5	6	7	8	9
0	.1000	.0182	.0045	.0014	.0005	.0002	.0001	.0000	.0000
1	.2000	.0364	.0091	.0028	.0010	.0004	.0002	.0001	.0000
2	.3000	.0727	.0182	.0056	.0020	.0008	.0003	.0002	.0001
3	.4000	.1091	.0318	.0098	.0035	.0014	.0006	.0003	.0001
4	.5000	.1636	.0500	.0168	.0060	.0024	.0010	.0005	.0002
5		.2182	.0727	.0252	.0095	.0038	.0017	.0008	.0004
6		.2909	.1045	.0378	.0145	.0060	.0026	.0012	.0006
7		.3636	.1409	.0531	.0210	.0088	.0039	.0019	.0009
8		.4545	.1864	.0741	.0300	.0128	.0058	.0028	.0014
9		.5455	.2409	.0993	.0415	.0180	.0082	.0039	.0020
10			.3000	.1301	.0559	.0248	.0115	.0056	.0028
11			.3636	.1650	.0734	.0332	.0156	.0076	.0039
12			.4318	.2070	.0949	.0440	.0209	.0103	.0053
13			.5000	.2517	.1199	.0567	.0274	.0137	.0071
14				.3021	.1489	.0723	.0356	.0180	.0094
15				.3552	.1818	.0905	.0454	.0232	.0122
16				.4126	.2188	.1119	.0571	.0296	.0157
17				.4699	.2592	.1361	.0708	.0372	.0200
18				.5301	.3032	.1638	.0869	.0464	.0252
19					.3497	.1942	.1052	.0570	.0313
U_0 20					.3986	.2280	.1261	.0694	.0385
21					.4491	.2643	.1496	.0836	.0470
22					.5000	.3035	.1755	.0998	.0567
23						.3445	.2039	.1179	.0680
24						.3878	.2349	.1383	.0807
25						.4320	.2680	.1606	.0951
26						.4773	.3032	.1852	.1112
27						.5227	.3403	.2117	.1290
28							.3788	.2404	.1487
29							.4185	.2707	.1701
30							.4591	.3029	.1933
31							.5000	.3365	.2181
32								.3715	.2447
33								.4074	.2729
34								.4442	.3024
35								.4813	.3332
36								.5187	.3652
37									.3981
38									.4317
39									.4657
40									.5000

$$n_2 = 10$$

n_1	1	2	3	4	5	6	7	8	9	10
0	.0909	.0152	.0035	.0010	.0003	.0001	.0001	.0000	.0000	.0000
1	.1818	.0303	.0070	.0020	.0007	.0002	.0001	.0000	.0000	.0000
2	.2727	.0606	.0140	.0040	.0013	.0005	.0002	.0001	.0000	.0000
3	.3636	.0909	.0245	.0070	.0023	.0009	.0004	.0002	.0001	.0000
4	.4545	.1364	.0385	.0120	.0040	.0015	.0006	.0003	.0001	.0001
5	.5455	.1818	.0559	.0180	.0063	.0024	.0010	.0004	.0002	.0001
6		.2424	.0804	.0270	.0097	.0037	.0015	.0007	.0003	.0002
7		.3030	.1084	.0380	.0140	.0055	.0023	.0010	.0005	.0002
8		.3788	.1434	.0529	.0200	.0080	.0034	.0015	.0007	.0004
9		.4545	.1853	.0709	.0276	.0112	.0048	.0022	.0011	.0005
10		.5455	.2343	.0939	.0376	.0156	.0068	.0031	.0015	.0008
11			.2867	.1199	.0496	.0210	.0093	.0043	.0021	.0010
12			.3462	.1518	.0646	.0280	.0125	.0058	.0028	.0014
13			.4056	.1868	.0823	.0363	.0165	.0078	.0038	.0019
14			.4685	.2268	.1032	.0467	.0215	.0103	.0051	.0026
15			.5315	.2697	.1272	.0589	.0277	.0133	.0066	.0034
16				.3177	.1548	.0736	.0351	.0171	.0086	.0045
17				.3666	.1855	.0903	.0439	.0217	.0110	.0057
18				.4196	.2198	.1099	.0544	.0273	.0140	.0073
19				.4725	.2567	.1317	.0665	.0338	.0175	.0093
20				.5275	.2970	.1566	.0806	.0416	.0217	.0116
21					.3393	.1838	.0966	.0506	.0267	.0144
22					.3839	.2139	.1148	.0610	.0326	.0177
23					.4296	.2461	.1349	.0729	.0394	.0216
24					.4765	.2811	.1574	.0864	.0474	.0262
U_0 25					.5235	.3177	.1819	.1015	.0564	.0315
26						.3564	.2087	.1185	.0667	.0376
27						.3962	.2374	.1371	.0782	.0446
28						.4374	.2681	.1577	.0912	.0526
29						.4789	.3004	.1800	.1055	.0615
30						.5211	.3345	.2041	.1214	.0716
31							.3698	.2299	.1388	.0827
32							.4063	.2574	.1577	.0952
33							.4434	.2863	.1781	.1088
34							.4811	.3167	.2001	.1237
35							.5189	.3482	.2235	.1399
36								.3809	.2483	.1575
37								.4143	.2745	.1763
38								.4484	.3019	.1965
39								.4827	.3304	.2179
40								.5173	.3598	.2406
41									.3901	.2644
42									.4211	.2894
43									.4524	.3153
44									.4841	.3421
45									.5159	.3697
46										.3980
47										.4267
48										.4559
49										.4853
50										.5147

Computed by M. Pagano, Department of Statistics, University of Florida.

Table 3 • Critical values of *T* in the Wilcoxon matched pairs, signed rank test

$$n = 5(1)50$$

One sided	Two-sided	n = 5	n = 6	n = 7	n = 8	n = 9	n = 10
P = .05	P = .10	1	2	4	6	8	11
P = .025	P = .05		1	2	4	6	8
P = .01	P = .02			0	2	3	5
P = .005	P = .01				0	2	3

One-sided	Two-sided	n = 11	n = 12	n = 13	n = 14	n = 15	n = 16
P = .05	P = .10	14	17	21	26	30	36
P = .025	P = .05	11	14	17	21	25	30
P = .01	P = .02	7	10	13	16	20	24
P = .005	P = .01	5	7	10	13	16	19

One-sided	Two-sided	n = 17	n = 18	n = 19	n = 20	n = 21	n = 22
P = .05	P = .10	41	47	54	60	68	75
P = .025	P = .05	35	40	46	52	59	66
P = .01	P = .02	28	33	38	43	49	56
P = .005	P = .01	23	28	32	37	43	49

One-sided	Two-sided	n = 23	n = 24	n = 25	n = 26	n = 27	n = 28
P = .05	P = .10	83	92	101	110	120	130
P = .025	P = .05	73	81	90	98	107	117
P = .01	P = .02	62	69	77	85	93	102
P = .005	P = .01	55	68	68	76	84	92

One-sided	Two-sided	n = 29	n = 30	n = 31	n = 32	n = 33	n = 34
P = .05	P = .10	141	152	163	175	188	201
P = .025	P = .05	127	137	148	159	171	183
P = .01	P = .02	111	120	130	141	151	162
P = .005	P = .01	100	109	118	128	138	149

One-sided	Two-sided	n = 35	n = 36	n = 37	n = 38	n = 39	
P = .05	P = .10	214	228	242	256	271	
P = .025	P = .05	195	208	222	235	250	
P = .01	P = .02	174	186	198	211	224	
P = .005	P = .01	160	171	183	195	208	

One-sided	Two-sided	n = 40	n = 41	n = 42	n = 43	n = 44	n = 45
P = .05	P = .10	287	303	319	336	353	371
P = .025	P = .05	264	279	295	311	327	344
P = .01	P = .02	238	252	267	281	297	313
P = .005	P = .01	221	234	248	262	277	292

One-sided	Two-sided	n = 46	n = 47	n = 48	n = 49	n = 50	
P = .05	P = .10	389	408	427	446	466	
P = .025	P = .05	361	379	397	415	434	
P = .01	P = .02	329	345	362	380	398	
P = .005	P = .01	307	323	339	356	373	

From "Some Rapid Approximate Statistical Procedures" (1964), 28, F. Wilcoxon and R. A. Wilcox. Reproduced with the kind permission of R. A. Wilcox and the Lederle Laboratories.

Table 4 • Normal curve areas

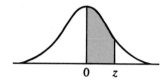

z	.00	.01	.02	.03	.04	.05	.06	.07	.08	.09
0.0	.0000	.0040	.0080	.0120	.0160	.0199	.0239	.0279	.0319	.0359
0.1	.0398	.0438	.0478	.0517	.0557	.0596	.0636	.0675	.0714	.0753
0.2	.0793	.0832	.0871	.0910	.0948	.0987	.1026	.1064	.1103	.1141
0.3	.1179	.1217	.1255	.1293	.1331	.1368	.1406	.1443	.1480	.1517
0.4	.1554	.1591	.1628	.1664	.1700	.1736	.1772	.1808	.1844	.1879
0.5	.1915	.1950	.1985	.2019	.2054	.2088	.2123	.2157	.2190	.2224
0.6	.2257	.2291	.2324	.2357	.2389	.2422	.2454	.2486	.2517	.2549
0.7	.2580	.2611	.2642	.2673	.2704	.2734	.2764	.2794	.2823	.2852
0.8	.2881	.2910	.2939	.2967	.2995	.3023	.3051	.3078	.3106	.3133
0.9	.3159	.3186	.3212	.3238	.3264	.3289	.3315	.3340	.3365	.3389
1.0	.3413	.3438	.3461	.3485	.3508	.3531	.3554	.3577	.3599	.3621
1.1	.3643	.3665	.3686	.3708	.3729	.3749	.3770	.3790	.3810	.3830
1.2	.3849	.3869	.3888	.3907	.3925	.3944	.3962	.3980	.3997	.4015
1.3	.4032	.4049	.4066	.4082	.4099	.4115	.4131	.4147	.4162	.4177
1.4	.4192	.4207	.4222	.4236	.4251	.4265	.4279	.4292	.4306	.4319
1.5	.4332	.4345	.4357	.4370	.4382	.4394	.4406	.4418	.4429	.4441
1.6	.4452	.4463	.4474	.4484	.4495	.4505	.4515	.4525	.4535	.4545
1.7	.4554	.4564	.4573	.4582	.4591	.4599	.4608	.4616	.4625	.4633
1.8	.4641	.4649	.4656	.4664	.4671	.4678	.4686	.4693	.4699	.4706
1.9	.4713	.4719	.4726	.4732	.4738	.4744	.4750	.4756	.4761	.4767
2.0	.4772	.4778	.4783	.4788	.4793	.4798	.4803	.4808	.4812	.4817
2.1	.4821	.4826	.4830	.4834	.4838	.4842	.4846	.4850	.4854	.4857
2.2	.4861	.4864	.4868	.4871	.4875	.4878	.4881	.4884	.4887	.4890
2.3	.4893	.4896	.4898	.4901	.4904	.4906	.4909	.4911	.4913	.4916
2.4	.4918	.4920	.4922	.4925	.4927	.4929	.4931	.4932	.4934	.4936
2.5	.4938	.4940	.4941	.4943	.4945	.4946	.4948	.4949	.4951	.4952
2.6	.4953	.4955	.4956	.4957	.4959	.4960	.4961	.4962	.4963	.4964
2.7	.4965	.4966	.4967	.4968	.4969	.4970	.4971	.4972	.4973	.4974
2.8	.4974	.4975	.4976	.4977	.4977	.4978	.4979	.4979	.4980	.4981
2.9	.4981	.4982	.4982	.4983	.4984	.4984	.4985	.4985	.4986	.4986
3.0	.4987	.4987	.4987	.4988	.4988	.4989	.4989	.4989	.4990	.4990

This table is abridged from Table I of *Statistical Tables and Formulas,* by A. Hald (New York: John Wiley & Sons, Inc., 1952). Reproduced by permission of A. Hald and the publishers, John Wiley & Sons, Inc.

Table 5 • Critical values of *t*

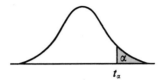

t_α

d.f.	$t_{.100}$	$t_{.050}$	$t_{.025}$	$t_{.010}$	$t_{.005}$	d.f.
1	3.078	6.314	12.706	31.821	63.657	1
2	1.886	2.920	4.303	6.965	9.925	2
3	1.638	2.353	3.182	4.541	5.841	3
4	1.533	2.132	2.776	3.747	4.604	4
5	1.476	2.015	2.571	3.365	4.032	5
6	1.440	1.943	2.447	3.143	3.707	6
7	1.415	1.895	2.365	2.998	3.499	7
8	1.397	1.860	2.306	2.896	3.355	8
9	1.383	1.833	2.262	2.821	3.250	9
10	1.372	1.812	2.228	2.764	3.169	10
11	1.363	1.796	2.201	2.718	3.106	11
12	1.356	1.782	2.179	2.681	3.055	12
13	1.350	1.771	2.160	2.650	3.012	13
14	1.345	1.761	2.145	2.624	2.977	14
15	1.341	1.753	2.131	2.602	2.947	15
16	1.337	1.746	2.120	2.583	2.921	16
17	1.333	1.740	2.110	2.567	2.898	17
18	1.330	1.734	2.101	2.552	2.878	18
19	1.328	1.729	2.093	2.539	2.861	19
20	1.325	1.725	2.086	2.528	2.845	20
21	1.323	1.721	2.080	2.518	2.831	21
22	1.321	1.717	2.074	2.508	2.819	22
23	1.319	1.714	2.069	2.500	2.807	23
24	1.318	1.711	2.064	2.492	2.797	24
25	1.316	1.708	2.060	2.485	2.787	25
26	1.315	1.706	2.056	2.479	2.779	26
27	1.314	1.703	2.052	2.473	2.771	27
28	1.313	1.701	2.048	2.467	2.763	28
29	1.311	1.699	2.045	2.462	2.756	29
inf.	1.282	1.645	1.960	2.326	2.576	inf.

From "Table of Percentage Points of the *t*-Distribution." Computed by Maxine Merrington, *Biometrika*, Vol. 32 (1941), p. 300. Reproduced by permission of Professor E. S. Pearson.

Table 6 • Percentage points of the F distribution ($\alpha = .05$)

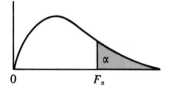

$$0 \qquad F_\alpha$$

Degrees of Freedom $\qquad \alpha = .05$

ν_1

ν_2	1	2	3	4	5	6	7	8	9
1	161.4	199.5	215.7	224.6	230.2	234.0	236.8	238.9	240.5
2	18.51	19.00	19.16	19.25	19.30	19.33	19.35	19.37	19.38
3	10.13	9.55	9.28	9.12	9.01	8.94	8.89	8.85	8.81
4	7.71	6.94	6.59	6.39	6.26	6.16	6.09	6.04	6.00
5	6.61	5.79	5.41	5.19	5.05	4.95	4.88	4.82	4.77
6	5.99	5.14	4.76	4.53	4.39	4.28	4.21	4.15	4.10
7	5.59	4.74	4.35	4.12	3.97	3.87	3.79	3.73	3.68
8	5.32	4.46	4.07	3.84	3.69	3.58	3.50	3.44	3.39
9	5.12	4.26	3.86	3.63	3.48	3.37	3.29	3.23	3.18
10	4.96	4.10	3.71	3.48	3.33	3.22	3.14	3.07	3.02
11	4.84	3.98	3.59	3.36	3.20	3.09	3.01	2.95	2.90
12	4.75	3.89	3.49	3.26	3.11	3.00	2.91	2.85	2.80
13	4.67	3.81	3.41	3.18	3.03	2.92	2.83	2.77	2.71
14	4.60	3.74	3.34	3.11	2.96	2.85	2.76	2.70	2.65
15	4.54	3.68	3.29	3.06	2.90	2.79	2.71	2.64	2.59
16	4.49	3.63	3.24	3.01	2.85	2.74	2.66	2.59	2.54
17	4.45	3.59	3.20	2.96	2.81	2.70	2.61	2.55	2.49
18	4.41	3.55	3.16	2.93	2.77	2.66	2.58	2.51	2.46
19	4.38	3.52	3.13	2.90	2.74	2.63	2.54	2.48	2.42
20	4.35	3.49	3.10	2.87	2.71	2.60	2.51	2.45	2.39
21	4.32	3.47	3.07	2.84	2.68	2.57	2.49	2.42	2.37
22	4.30	3.44	3.05	2.82	2.66	2.55	2.46	2.40	2.34
23	4.28	3.42	3.03	2.80	2.64	2.53	2.44	2.37	2.32
24	4.26	3.40	3.01	2.78	2.62	2.51	2.42	2.36	2.30
25	4.24	3.39	2.99	2.76	2.60	2.49	2.40	2.34	2.28
26	4.23	3.37	2.98	2.74	2.59	2.47	2.39	2.32	2.27
27	4.21	3.35	2.96	2.73	2.57	2.46	2.37	2.31	2.25
28	4.20	3.34	2.95	2.71	2.56	2.45	2.36	2.29	2.24
29	4.18	3.33	2.93	2.70	2.55	2.43	2.35	2.28	2.22
30	4.17	3.32	2.92	2.69	2.53	2.42	2.33	2.27	2.21
40	4.08	3.23	2.84	2.61	2.45	2.34	2.25	2.18	2.12
60	4.00	3.15	2.76	2.53	2.37	2.25	2.17	2.10	2.04
120	3.92	3.07	2.68	2.45	2.29	2.17	2.09	2.02	1.96
∞	3.84	3.00	2.60	2.37	2.21	2.10	2.01	1.94	1.88

ν_1

10	12	15	20	24	30	40	60	120	∞	ν_2
241.9	243.9	245.9	248.0	249.1	250.1	251.1	252.2	253.3	254.3	1
19.40	19.41	19.43	19.45	19.45	19.46	19.47	19.48	19.49	19.50	2
8.79	8.74	8.70	8.66	8.64	8.62	8.59	8.57	8.55	8.53	3
5.96	5.91	5.86	5.80	5.77	5.75	5.72	5.69	5.66	5.63	4
4.74	4.68	4.62	4.56	4.53	4.50	4.46	4.43	4.40	4.36	5
4.06	4.00	3.94	3.87	3.84	3.81	3.77	3.74	3.70	3.67	6
3.64	3.57	3.51	3.44	3.41	3.38	3.34	3.30	3.27	3.23	7
3.35	3.28	3.22	3.15	3.12	3.08	3.04	3.01	2.97	2.93	8
3.14	3.07	3.01	2.94	2.90	2.86	2.83	2.79	2.75	2.71	9
2.98	2.91	2.85	2.77	2.74	2.70	2.66	2.62	2.58	2.54	10
2.85	2.79	2.72	2.65	2.61	2.57	2.53	2.49	2.45	2.40	11
2.75	2.69	2.62	2.54	2.51	2.47	2.43	2.38	2.34	2.30	12
2.67	2.60	2.53	2.46	2.42	2.38	2.34	2.30	2.25	2.21	13
2.60	2.53	2.46	2.39	2.35	2.31	2.27	2.22	2.18	2.13	14
2.54	2.48	2.40	2.33	2.29	2.25	2.20	2.16	2.11	2.07	15
2.49	2.42	2.35	2.28	2.24	2.19	2.15	2.11	2.06	2.01	16
2.45	2.38	2.31	2.23	2.19	2.15	2.10	2.06	2.01	1.96	17
2.41	2.34	2.27	2.19	2.15	2.11	2.06	2.02	1.97	1.92	18
2.38	2.31	2.23	2.16	2.11	2.07	2.03	1.98	1.93	1.88	19
2.35	2.28	2.20	2.12	2.08	2.04	1.99	1.95	1.90	1.84	20
2.32	2.25	2.18	2.10	2.05	2.01	1.96	1.92	1.87	1.81	21
2.30	2.23	2.15	2.07	2.03	1.98	1.94	1.89	1.84	1.78	22
2.27	2.20	2.13	2.05	2.01	1.96	1.91	1.86	1.81	1.76	23
2.25	2.18	2.11	2.03	1.98	1.94	1.89	1.84	1.79	1.73	24
2.24	2.16	2.09	2.01	1.96	1.92	1.87	1.82	1.77	1.71	25
2.22	2.15	2.07	1.99	1.95	1.90	1.85	1.80	1.75	1.69	26
2.20	2.13	2.06	1.97	1.93	1.88	1.84	1.79	1.73	1.67	27
2.19	2.12	2.04	1.96	1.91	1.87	1.82	1.77	1.71	1.65	28
2.18	2.10	2.03	1.94	1.90	1.85	1.81	1.75	1.70	1.64	29
2.16	2.09	2.01	1.93	1.89	1.84	1.79	1.74	1.68	1.62	30
2.08	2.00	1.92	1.84	1.79	1.74	1.69	1.64	1.58	1.51	40
1.99	1.92	1.84	1.75	1.70	1.65	1.59	1.53	1.47	1.39	60
1.91	1.83	1.75	1.66	1.61	1.55	1.50	1.43	1.35	1.25	120
1.83	1.75	1.67	1.57	1.52	1.46	1.39	1.32	1.22	1.00	∞

From "Tables of Percentage Points of the Inverted Beta (F) Distribution," *Biometrika,* Vol. 33 (1943), pp. 73–88, by Maxine Merrington and Catherine M. Thompson. Reproduced by permission of Professor E. S. Pearson.

Table 7 • Percentage points of the F distribution ($\alpha = .01$)

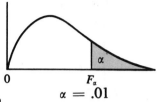

$$\alpha = .01$$

Degrees of Freedom

ν_1

ν_2	1	2	3	4	5	6	7	8	9
1	4052	4999.5	5403	5625	5764	5859	5928	5982	6022
2	98.50	99.00	99.17	99.25	99.30	99.33	99.36	99.37	99.39
3	34.12	30.82	29.46	28.71	28.24	27.91	27.67	27.49	27.35
4	21.20	18.00	16.69	15.98	15.52	15.21	14.98	14.80	14.66
5	16.26	13.27	12.06	11.39	10.97	10.67	10.46	10.29	10.16
6	13.75	10.92	9.78	9.15	8.75	8.47	8.26	8.10	7.98
7	12.25	9.55	8.45	7.85	7.46	7.19	6.99	6.84	6.72
8	11.26	8.65	7.59	7.01	6.63	6.37	6.18	6.03	5.91
9	10.56	8.02	6.99	6.42	6.06	5.80	5.61	5.47	5.35
10	10.04	7.56	6.55	5.99	5.64	5.39	5.20	5.06	4.94
11	9.65	7.21	6.22	5.67	5.32	5.07	4.89	4.74	4.63
12	9.33	6.93	5.95	5.41	5.06	4.82	4.64	4.50	4.39
13	9.07	6.70	5.74	5.21	4.86	4.62	4.44	4.30	4.19
14	8.86	6.51	5.56	5.04	4.69	4.46	4.28	4.14	4.03
15	8.68	6.36	5.42	4.89	4.56	4.32	4.14	4.00	3.89
16	8.53	6.23	5.29	4.77	4.44	4.20	4.03	3.89	3.78
17	8.40	6.11	5.18	4.67	4.34	4.10	3.93	3.79	3.68
18	8.29	6.01	5.09	4.58	4.25	4.01	3.84	3.71	3.60
19	8.18	5.93	5.01	4.50	4.17	3.94	3.77	3.63	3.52
20	8.10	5.85	4.94	4.43	4.10	3.87	3.70	3.56	3.46
21	8.02	5.78	4.87	4.37	4.04	3.81	3.64	3.51	3.40
22	7.95	5.72	4.82	4.31	3.99	3.76	3.59	3.45	3.35
23	7.88	5.66	4.76	4.26	3.94	3.71	3.54	3.41	3.30
24	7.82	5.61	4.72	4.22	3.90	3.67	3.50	3.36	3.26
25	7.77	5.57	4.68	4.18	3.85	3.63	3.46	3.32	3.22
26	7.72	5.53	4.64	4.14	3.82	3.59	3.42	3.29	3.18
27	7.68	5.49	4.60	4.11	3.78	3.56	3.39	3.26	3.15
28	7.64	5.45	4.57	4.07	3.75	3.53	3.36	3.23	3.12
29	7.60	5.42	4.54	4.04	3.73	3.50	3.33	3.20	3.09
30	7.56	5.39	4.51	4.02	3.70	3.47	3.30	3.17	3.07
40	7.31	5.18	4.31	3.83	3.51	3.29	3.12	2.99	2.89
60	7.08	4.98	4.13	3.65	3.34	3.12	2.95	2.82	2.72
120	6.85	4.79	3.95	3.48	3.17	2.96	2.79	2.66	2.56
∞	6.63	4.61	3.78	3.32	3.02	2.80	2.64	2.51	2.41

ν_1

10	12	15	20	24	30	40	60	120	∞	
										ν_2
6056	6106	6157	6209	6235	6261	6287	6313	6339	6366	1
99.40	99.42	99.43	99.45	99.46	99.47	99.47	99.48	99.49	99.50	2
27.23	27.05	26.87	26.69	26.60	26.50	26.41	26.32	26.22	26.13	3
14.55	14.37	14.20	14.02	13.93	13.84	13.75	13.65	13.56	13.46	4
10.05	9.89	9.72	9.55	9.47	9.38	9.29	9.20	9.11	9.02	5
7.87	7.72	7.56	7.40	7.31	7.23	7.14	7.06	6.97	6.88	6
6.62	6.47	6.31	6.16	6.07	5.99	5.91	5.82	5.74	5.65	7
5.81	5.67	5.52	5.36	5.28	5.20	5.12	5.03	4.95	4.86	8
5.26	5.11	4.96	4.81	4.73	4.65	4.57	4.48	4.40	4.31	9
4.85	4.71	4.56	4.41	4.33	4.25	4.17	4.08	4.00	3.91	10
4.54	4.40	4.25	4.10	4.02	3.94	3.86	3.78	3.69	3.60	11
4.30	4.16	4.01	3.86	3.78	3.70	3.62	3.54	3.45	3.36	12
4.10	3.96	3.82	3.66	3.59	3.51	3.43	3.34	3.25	3.17	13
3.94	3.80	3.66	3.51	3.43	3.35	3.27	3.18	3.09	3.00	14
3.80	3.67	3.52	3.37	3.29	3.21	3.13	3.05	2.96	2.87	15
3.69	3.55	3.41	3.26	3.18	3.10	3.02	2.93	2.84	2.75	16
3.59	3.46	3.31	3.16	3.08	3.00	2.92	2.83	2.75	2.65	17
3.51	3.37	3.23	3.08	3.00	2.92	2.84	2.75	2.66	2.57	18
3.43	3.30	3.15	3.00	2.92	2.84	2.76	2.67	2.58	2.49	19
3.37	3.23	3.09	2.94	2.86	2.78	2.69	2.61	2.52	2.42	20
3.31	3.17	3.03	2.88	2.80	2.72	2.64	2.55	2.46	2.36	21
3.26	3.12	2.98	2.83	2.75	2.67	2.58	2.50	2.40	2.31	22
3.21	3.07	2.93	2.78	2.70	2.62	2.54	2.45	2.35	2.26	23
3.17	3.03	2.89	2.74	2.66	2.58	2.49	2.40	2.31	2.21	24
3.13	2.99	2.85	2.70	2.62	2.54	2.45	2.36	2.27	2.17	25
3.09	2.96	2.81	2.66	2.58	2.50	2.42	2.33	2.23	2.13	26
3.06	2.93	2.78	2.63	2.55	2.47	2.38	2.29	2.20	2.10	27
3.03	2.90	2.75	2.60	2.52	2.44	2.35	2.26	2.17	2.06	28
3.00	2.87	2.73	2.57	2.49	2.41	2.33	2.23	2.14	2.03	29
2.98	2.84	2.70	2.55	2.47	2.39	2.30	2.21	2.11	2.01	30
2.80	2.66	2.52	2.37	2.29	2.20	2.11	2.02	1.92	1.80	40
2.63	2.50	2.35	2.20	2.12	2.03	1.94	1.84	1.73	1.60	60
2.47	2.34	2.19	2.03	1.95	1.86	1.76	1.66	1.53	1.38	120
2.32	2.18	2.04	1.88	1.79	1.70	1.59	1.47	1.32	1.00	∞

From "Tables of Percentage Points of the Inverted Beta (F) Distribution," *Biometrika*, Vol. 33 (1943), pp. 73–88, by Maxine Merrington and Catherine M. Thompson. Reproduced by permission of Professor E. S. Pearson.

Table 8 • Percentage points of the studentized range, q(r, ν)

Upper 5% points

ν \ r	2	3	4	5	6	7	8	9	10
1	17·97	26·98	32·82	37·08	40·41	43·12	45·40	47·36	49·07
2	6·08	8·33	9·80	10·88	11·74	12·44	13·03	13·54	13·99
3	4·50	5·91	6·82	7·50	8·04	8·48	8·85	9·18	9·46
4	3·93	5·04	5·76	6·29	6·71	7·05	7·35	7·60	7·83
5	3·64	4·60	5·22	5·67	6·03	6·33	6·58	6·80	6·99
6	3·46	4·34	4·90	5·30	5·63	5·90	6·12	6·32	6·49
7	3·34	4·16	4·68	5·06	5·36	5·61	5·82	6·00	6·16
8	3·26	4·04	4·53	4·89	5·17	5·40	5·60	5·77	5·92
9	3·20	3·95	4·41	4·76	5·02	5·24	5·43	5·59	5·74
10	3·15	3·88	4·33	4·65	4·91	5·12	5·30	5·46	5·60
11	3·11	3·82	4·26	4·57	4·82	5·03	5·20	5·35	5·49
12	3·08	3·77	4·20	4·51	4·75	4·95	5·12	5·27	5·39
13	3·06	3·73	4·15	4·45	4·69	4·88	5·05	5·19	5·32
14	3·03	3·70	4·11	4·41	4·64	4·83	4·99	5·13	5·25
15	3·01	3·67	4·08	4·37	4·59	4·78	4·94	5·08	5·20
16	3·00	3·65	4·05	4·33	4·56	4·74	4·90	5·03	5·15
17	2·98	3·63	4·02	4·30	4·52	4·70	4·86	4·99	5·11
18	2·97	3·61	4·00	4·28	4·49	4·67	4·82	4·96	5·07
19	2·96	3·59	3·98	4·25	4·47	4·65	4·79	4·92	5·04
20	2·95	3·58	3·96	4·23	4·45	4·62	4·77	4·90	5·01
24	2·92	3·53	3·90	4·17	4·37	4·54	4·68	4·81	4·92
30	2·89	3·49	3·85	4·10	4·30	4·46	4·60	4·72	4·82
40	2·86	3·44	3·79	4·04	4·23	4·39	4·52	4·63	4·73
60	2·83	3·40	3·74	3·98	4·16	4·31	4·44	4·55	4·65
120	2·80	3·36	3·68	3·92	4·10	4·24	4·36	4·47	4·56
∞	2·77	3·31	3·63	3·86	4·03	4·17	4·29	4·39	4·47

ν \ r	11	12	13	14	15	16	17	18	19	20
1	50·59	51·96	53·20	54·33	55·36	56·32	57·22	58·04	58·83	59·56
2	14·39	14·75	15·08	15·38	15·65	15·91	16·14	16·37	16·57	16·77
3	9·72	9·95	10·15	10·35	10·52	10·69	10·84	10·98	11·11	11·24
4	8·03	8·21	8·37	8·52	8·66	8·79	8·91	9·03	9·13	9·23
5	7·17	7·32	7·47	7·60	7·72	7·83	7·93	8·03	8·12	8·21
6	6·65	6·79	6·92	7·03	7·14	7·24	7·34	7·43	7·51	7·59
7	6·30	6·43	6·55	6·66	6·76	6·85	6·94	7·02	7·10	7·17
8	6·05	6·18	6·29	6·39	6·48	6·57	6·65	6·73	6·80	6·87
9	5·87	5·98	6·09	6·19	6·28	6·36	6·44	6·51	6·58	6·64
10	5·72	5·83	5·93	6·03	6·11	6·19	6·27	6·34	6·40	6·47
11	5·61	5·71	5·81	5·90	5·98	6·06	6·13	6·20	6·27	6·33
12	5·51	5·61	5·71	5·80	5·88	5·95	6·02	6·09	6·15	6·21
13	5·43	5·53	5·63	5·71	5·79	5·86	5·93	5·99	6·05	6·11
14	5·36	5·46	5·55	5·64	5·71	5·79	5·85	5·91	5·97	6·03
15	5·31	5·40	5·49	5·57	5·65	5·72	5·78	5·85	5·90	5·96
16	5·26	5·35	5·44	5·52	5·59	5·66	5·73	5·79	5·84	5·90
17	5·21	5·31	5·39	5·47	5·54	5·61	5·67	5·73	5·79	5·84
18	5·17	5·27	5·35	5·43	5·50	5·57	5·63	5·69	5·74	5·79
19	5·14	5·23	5·31	5·39	5·46	5·53	5·59	5·65	5·70	5·75
20	5·11	5·20	5·28	5·36	5·43	5·49	5·55	5·61	5·66	5·71
24	5·01	5·10	5·18	5·25	5·32	5·38	5·44	5·49	5·55	5·59
30	4·92	5·00	5·08	5·15	5·21	5·27	5·33	5·38	5·43	5·47
40	4·82	4·90	4·98	5·04	5·11	5·16	5·22	5·27	5·31	5·36
60	4·73	4·81	4·88	4·94	5·00	5·06	5·11	5·15	5·20	5·24
120	4·64	4·71	4·78	4·84	4·90	4·95	5·00	5·04	5·09	5·13
∞	4·55	4·62	4·68	4·74	4·80	4·85	4·89	4·93	4·97	5·01

Upper 1% points

ν \ r	2	3	4	5	6	7	8	9	10
1	90·03	135·0	164·3	185·6	202·2	215·8	227·2	237·0	245·6
2	14·04	19·02	22·29	24·72	26·63	28·20	29·53	30·68	31·69
3	8·26	10·62	12·17	13·33	14·24	15·00	15·64	16·20	16·69
4	6·51	8·12	9·17	9·96	10·58	11·10	11·55	11·93	12·27
5	5·70	6·98	7·80	8·42	8·91	9·32	9·67	9·97	10·24
6	5·24	6·33	7·03	7·56	7·97	8·32	8·61	8·87	9·10
7	4·95	5·92	6·54	7·01	7·37	7·68	7·94	8·17	8·37
8	4·75	5·64	6·20	6·62	6·96	7·24	7·47	7·68	7·86
9	4·60	5·43	5·96	6·35	6·66	6·91	7·13	7·33	7·49
10	4·48	5·27	5·77	6·14	6·43	6·67	6·87	7·05	7·21
11	4·39	5·15	5·62	5·97	6·25	6·48	6·67	6·84	6·99
12	4·32	5·05	5·50	5·84	6·10	6·32	6·51	6·67	6·81
13	4·26	4·96	5·40	5·73	5·98	6·19	6·37	6·53	6·67
14	4·21	4·89	5·32	5·63	5·88	6·08	6·26	6·41	6·54
15	4·17	4·84	5·25	5·56	5·80	5·99	6·16	6·31	6·44
16	4·13	4·79	5·19	5·49	5·72	5·92	6·08	6·22	6·35
17	4·10	4·74	5·14	5·43	5·66	5·85	6·01	6·15	6·27
18	4·07	4·70	5·09	5·38	5·60	5·79	5·94	6·08	6·20
19	4·05	4·67	5·05	5·33	5·55	5·73	5·89	6·02	6·14
20	4·02	4·64	5·02	5·29	5·51	5·69	5·84	5·97	6·09
24	3·96	4·55	4·91	5·17	5·37	5·54	5·69	5·81	5·92
30	3·89	4·45	4·80	5·05	5·24	5·40	5·54	5·65	5·76
40	3·82	4·37	4·70	4·93	5·11	5·26	5·39	5·50	5·60
60	3·76	4·28	4·59	4·82	4·99	5·13	5·25	5·36	5·45
120	3·70	4·20	4·50	4·71	4·87	5·01	5·12	5·21	5·30
∞	3·64	4·12	4·40	4·60	4·76	4·88	4·99	5·08	5·16

ν \ r	11	12	13	14	15	16	17	18	19	20
1	253·2	260·0	266·2	271·8	277·0	281·8	286·3	290·4	294·3	298·0
2	32·59	33·40	34·13	34·81	35·43	36·00	36·53	37·03	37·50	37·95
3	17·13	17·53	17·89	18·22	18·52	18·81	19·07	19·32	19·55	19·77
4	12·57	12·84	13·09	13·32	13·53	13·73	13·91	14·08	14·24	14·40
5	10·48	10·70	10·89	11·08	11·24	11·40	11·55	11·68	11·81	11·93
6	9·30	9·48	9·65	9·81	9·95	10·08	10·21	10·32	10·43	10·54
7	8·55	8·71	8·86	9·00	9·12	9·24	9·35	9·46	9·55	9·65
8	8·03	8·18	8·31	8·44	8·55	8·66	8·76	8·85	8·94	9·03
9	7·65	7·78	7·91	8·03	8·13	8·23	8·33	8·41	8·49	8·57
10	7·36	7·49	7·60	7·71	7·81	7·91	7·99	8·08	8·15	8·23
11	7·13	7·25	7·36	7·46	7·56	7·65	7·73	7·81	7·88	7·95
12	6·94	7·06	7·17	7·26	7·36	7·44	7·52	7·59	7·66	7·73
13	6·79	6·90	7·01	7·10	7·19	7·27	7·35	7·42	7·48	7·55
14	6·66	6·77	6·87	6·96	7·05	7·13	7·20	7·27	7·33	7·39
15	6·55	6·66	6·76	6·84	6·93	7·00	7·07	7·14	7·20	7·26
16	6·46	6·56	6·66	6·74	6·82	6·90	6·97	7·03	7·09	7·15
17	6·38	6·48	6·57	6·66	6·73	6·81	6·87	6·94	7·00	7·05
18	6·31	6·41	6·50	6·58	6·65	6·73	6·79	6·85	6·91	6·97
19	6·25	6·34	6·43	6·51	6·58	6·65	6·72	6·78	6·84	6·89
20	6·19	6·28	6·37	6·45	6·52	6·59	6·65	6·71	6·77	6·82
24	6·02	6·11	6·19	6·26	6·33	6·39	6·45	6·51	6·56	6·61
30	5·85	5·93	6·01	6·08	6·14	6·20	6·26	6·31	6·36	6·41
40	5·69	5·76	5·83	5·90	5·96	6·02	6·07	6·12	6·16	6·21
60	5·53	5·60	5·67	5·73	5·78	5·84	5·89	5·93	5·97	6·01
120	5·37	5·44	5·50	5·56	5·61	5·66	5·71	5·75	5·79	5·83
∞	5·23	5·29	5·35	5·40	5·45	5·49	5·54	5·57	5·61	5·65

Table 9 • Critical values of chi-square

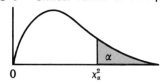

d.f.	$\chi^2 0.995$	$\chi^2 0.990$	$\chi^2 0.975$	$\chi^2 0.950$	$\chi^2 0.900$
1	0.0000393	0.0001571	0.0009821	0.0039321	0.0157908
2	0.0100251	0.0201007	0.0506356	0.102587	0.210720
3	0.0717212	0.114832	0.215795	0.351846	0.584375
4	0.206990	0.297110	0.484419	0.710721	1.063623
5	0.411740	0.554300	0.831211	1.145476	1.61031
6	0.675727	0.872085	1.237347	1.63539	2.20413
7	0.989265	1.239043	1.68987	2.16735	2.83311
8	1.344419	1.646482	2.17973	2.73264	3.48954
9	1.734926	2.087912	2.70039	3.32511	4.16816
10	2.15585	2.55821	3.24697	3.94030	4.86518
11	2.60321	3.05347	3.81575	4.57481	5.57779
12	3.07382	3.57056	4.40379	5.22603	6.30380
13	3.56503	4.10691	5.00874	5.89186	7.04150
14	4.07468	4.66043	5.62872	6.57063	7.78953
15	4.60094	5.22935	6.26214	7.26094	8.54675
16	5.14224	5.81221	6.90766	7.96164	9.31223
17	5.69724	6.40776	7.56418	8.67176	10.0852
18	6.26481	7.01491	8.23075	9.39046	10.8649
19	6.84398	7.63273	8.90655	10.1170	11.6509
20	7.43386	8.26040	9.59083	10.8508	12.4426
21	8.03366	8.89720	10.28293	11.5913	13.2396
22	8.64272	9.54249	10.9823	12.3380	14.0415
23	9.26042	10.19567	11.6885	13.0905	14.8479
24	9.88623	10.8564	12.4011	13.8484	15.6587
25	10.5197	11.5240	13.1197	14.6114	16.4734
26	11.1603	12.1981	13.8439	15.3791	17.2919
27	11.8076	12.8786	14.5733	16.1513	18.1138
28	12.4613	13.5648	15.3079	16.9279	18.9392
29	13.1211	14.2565	16.0471	17.7083	19.7677
30	13.7867	14.9535	16.7908	18.4926	20.5992
40	20.7065	22.1643	24.4331	26.5093	29.0505
50	27.9907	29.7067	32.3574	34.7642	37.6886
60	35.5346	37.4848	40.4817	43.1879	46.4589
70	43.2752	45.4418	48.7576	51.7393	55.3290
80	51.1720	53.5400	57.1532	60.3915	64.2778
90	59.1963	61.7541	65.6466	69.1260	73.2912
100	67.3276	70.0648	74.2219	77.9295	82.3581

X²0.100	X²0.050	X²0.025	X²0.010	X²0.005	d.f.
2.70554	3.84146	5.02389	6.63490	7.87944	1
4.60517	5.99147	7.37776	9.21034	10.5966	2
6.25139	7.81473	9.34840	11.3449	12.8381	3
7.77944	9.48773	11.1433	13.2767	14.8602	4
9.23635	11.0705	12.8325	15.0863	16.7496	5
10.6446	12.5916	14.4494	16.8119	18.5476	6
12.0170	14.0671	16.0128	18.4753	20.2777	7
13.3616	15.5073	17.5346	20.0902	21.9550	8
14.6837	16.9190	19.0228	21.6660	23.5893	9
15.9871	18.3070	20.4831	23.2093	25.1882	10
17.2750	19.6751	21.9200	24.7250	26.7569	11
18.5494	21.0261	23.3367	26.2170	28.2995	12
19.8119	22.3621	24.7356	27.6883	29.8194	13
21.0642	23.6848	26.1190	29.1413	31.3193	14
22.3072	24.9958	27.4884	30.5779	32.8013	15
23.5418	26.2962	28.8454	31.9999	34.2672	16
24.7690	27.5871	30.1910	33.4087	35.7185	17
25.9894	28.8693	31.5264	34.8053	37.1564	18
27.2036	30.1435	32.8523	36.1908	38.5822	19
28.4120	31.4104	34.1696	37.5662	39.9968	20
29.6151	32.6705	35.4789	38.9321	41.4010	21
30.8133	33.9244	36.7807	40.2894	42.7956	22
32.0069	35.1725	38.0757	41.6384	44.1813	23
33.1963	36.4151	39.3641	42.9798	45.5585	24
34.3816	37.6525	40.6465	44.3141	46.9278	25
35.5631	38.8852	41.9232	45.6417	48.2899	26
36.7412	40.1133	43.1944	46.9630	49.6449	27
37.9159	41.3372	44.4607	48.2782	50.9933	28
39.0875	42.5569	45.7222	49.5879	52.3356	29
40.2560	43.7729	46.9792	50.8922	53.6720	30
51.8050	55.7585	59.3417	63.6907	66.7659	40
63.1671	67.5048	71.4202	76.1539	79.4900	50
74.3970	79.0819	83.2976	88.3794	91.9517	60
85.5271	90.5312	95.0231	100.425	104.215	70
96.5782	101.879	106.629	112.329	116.321	80
107.565	113.145	118.136	124.116	128.299	90
118.498	124.342	129.561	135.807	140.169	100

From "Tables of the Percentage Points of the χ^2-Distribution." *Biometrika*, Vol. 32 (1941), pp. 188–189, by Catherine M. Thompson. Reproduced by permission of Professor E. S. Pearson.

Table 10 • Squares, cubes, and roots

Roots of numbers other than those given directly may be found by the following relations:

$$\sqrt{100n} = 10\sqrt{n}; \quad \sqrt{1000n} = 10\sqrt{10n}; \quad \sqrt{\tfrac{1}{10}n} = \tfrac{1}{10}\sqrt{10n};$$

$$\sqrt{\tfrac{1}{100}n} = \tfrac{1}{10}\sqrt{n}; \quad \sqrt{\tfrac{1}{1000}n} = \tfrac{1}{100}\sqrt{10n}; \quad \sqrt[3]{1000n} = 10\sqrt[3]{n};$$

$$\sqrt[3]{10,000n} = 10\sqrt[3]{10n}; \quad \sqrt[3]{100,000n} = 10\sqrt[3]{100n};$$

$$\sqrt[3]{\tfrac{1}{10}n} = \tfrac{1}{10}\sqrt[3]{100n}; \quad \sqrt[3]{\tfrac{1}{100}n} = \tfrac{1}{10}\sqrt[3]{10n}; \quad \sqrt[3]{\tfrac{1}{1000}n} = \tfrac{1}{10}\sqrt[3]{n}.$$

n	n^2	$\sqrt{n}$	$\sqrt{10n}$	n	n^2	$\sqrt{n}$	$\sqrt{10n}$
				30	900	5.477 226	17.32051
1	1	1.000 000	3.162 278	31	961	5.567 764	17.60682
2	4	1.414 214	4.472 136	32	1 024	5.656 854	17.88854
3	9	1.732 051	5.477 226	33	1 089	5.744 563	18.16590
4	16	2.000 000	6.324 555	34	1 156	5.830 952	18.43909
5	25	2.236 068	7.071 068	35	1 225	5.916 080	18.70829
6	36	2.449 490	7.745 967	36	1 296	6.000 000	18.97367
7	49	2.645 751	8.366 600	37	1 369	6.082 763	19.23538
8	64	2.828 427	8.944 272	38	1 444	6.164 414	19.49359
9	81	3.000 000	9.486 833	39	1 521	6.244 998	19.74842
10	100	3.162 278	10.00000	40	1 600	6.324 555	20.00000
11	121	3.316 625	10.48809	41	1 681	6.403 124	20.24846
12	144	3.464 102	10.95445	42	1 764	6.480 741	20.49390
13	169	3.605 551	11.40175	43	1 849	6.557 439	20.73644
14	196	3.741 657	11.83216	44	1 936	6.633 250	20.97618
15	225	3.872 983	12.24745	45	2 025	6.708 204	21.21320
16	256	4.000 000	12.64911	46	2 116	6.782 330	21.44761
17	289	4.123 106	13.03840	47	2 209	6.855 655	21.67948
18	324	4.242 641	13.41641	48	2 304	6.928 203	21.90890
19	361	4.358 899	13.78405	49	2 401	7.000 000	22.13594
20	400	4.472 136	14.14214	50	2 500	7.071 068	22.36068
21	441	4.582 576	14.49138	51	2 601	7.141 428	22.58318
22	484	4.690 416	14.83240	52	2 704	7.211 103	22.80351
23	529	4.795 832	15.16575	53	2 809	7.280 110	23.02173
24	576	4.898 979	15.49193	54	2 916	7.348 469	23.23790
25	625	5.000 000	15.81139	55	3 025	7.416 198	23.45208
26	676	5.099 020	16.12452	56	3 136	7.483 315	23.66432
27	729	5.196 152	16.43168	57	3 249	7.549 834	23.87467
28	784	5.291 503	16.73320	58	3 364	7.615 773	24.08319
29	841	5.385 165	17.02939	59	3 418	7.618 146	24.28992

n	n^2	$\sqrt{n}$	$\sqrt{10n}$	n	n^2	$\sqrt{n}$	$\sqrt{10n}$
60	3 600	7.745 967	24.49490	**100**	10 000	10.00000	31.62278
61	3 721	7.810 250	24.69818	101	10 201	10.04998	31.78050
62	3 844	7.874 008	24.89980	102	10 404	10.09950	31.93744
63	3 969	7.937 254	25.09980	103	10 609	10.14889	32.09361
64	4 096	8.000 000	25.29822	104	10 816	10.19804	32.24903
65	4 225	8.062 258	25.49510	105	11 025	10.24695	32.40370
66	4 356	8.124 038	25.69047	106	11 236	10.29563	32.55764
67	4 489	8.185 353	25.88436	107	11 449	10.34408	32.71085
68	4 624	8.246 211	26.07681	108	11 664	10.39230	32.86335
69	4 761	8.306 624	26.26785	109	11 881	10.44031	33.01515
70	4 900	8.366 600	26.45751	**110**	12 100	10.48809	33.16625
71	5 041	8.426 150	26.64583	111	12 321	10.53565	33.31666
72	5 184	8.485 281	26.83282	112	12 544	10.58301	33.46640
73	5 329	8.544 004	27.01851	113	12 769	10.63015	33.61547
74	5 476	8.602 325	27.20294	114	12 996	10.67708	33.76389
75	5 625	8.660 254	27.38613	115	13 225	10.72381	33.91165
76	5 776	8.717 798	27.56810	116	13 456	10.77033	34.05877
77	5 929	8.774 964	27.74887	117	13 689	10.81665	34.20526
78	6 084	8.831 761	27.92848	118	13 924	10.86278	34.35113
79	6 241	8.888 194	28.10694	119	14 161	10.90871	34.49638
80	6 400	8.944 272	28.28427	**120**	14 400	10.95445	34.64102
81	6 561	9.000 000	28.46050	121	14 641	11.00000	34.78505
82	6 724	9.055 385	28.63564	122	14 884	11.04536	34.92850
83	6 889	9.110 434	28.80972	123	15 129	11.09054	35 07136
84	7 056	9.165 151	28.98275	124	15 376	11.13553	35 21363
85	7 225	9.219 544	29.15476	125	15 625	11.18034	35.35534
86	7 396	9.273 618	29.32576	126	15 876	11.22497	35.49648
87	7 569	9.327 379	29.49576	127	16 129	11.26943	35.63706
88	7 744	9.380 832	29.66479	128	16 384	11.31371	35.77709
89	7 921	9.433 981	29.83287	129	16 641	11.35782	35.91657
90	8 100	9.486 833	30.00000	**130**	16 900	11.40175	36.05551
91	8 281	9.539 392	30.16621	131	17 161	11.44552	36.19392
92	8 464	9.591 663	30.33150	132	17 424	11.48913	36.33180
93	8 649	9.643 651	30.49590	133	17 689	11.53256	36.46917
94	8 836	9.695 360	30.65942	134	17 956	11.57584	36.60601
95	9 025	9.746 794	30.82207	135	18 225	11.61895	36.74235
96	9 216	9.797 959	30.98387	136	18 496	11.66190	36.87818
97	9 409	9.848 858	31.14482	137	18 769	11.70470	37.01351
98	9 604	9.899 495	31.30495	138	19 044	11.74734	37.14835
99	9 801	9.949 874	31.46427	139	19 321	11.78983	37.28270

n	n^2	$\sqrt{n}$	$\sqrt{10n}$	n	n^2	$\sqrt{n}$	$\sqrt{10n}$
140	19 600	11.83216	37.41657	**180**	32 400	13.41641	42.42641
141	19 881	11.87434	37.54997	181	32 761	13.45362	42.54409
142	20 164	11.91638	37.68289	182	33 124	13.49074	42.66146
143	20 449	11.95826	37.81534	183	33 489	13.52775	42.77850
144	20 736	12.00000	37.94733	184	33 856	13.56466	42.89522
145	21 025	12.04159	38.07887	185	34 225	13.60147	43.01163
146	21 316	12.08305	38.20995	186	34 596	13.63818	43.12772
147	21 609	12.12436	38.34058	187	34 969	13.67479	43.24350
148	21 904	12.16553	38.47077	188	35 344	13.71131	43.35897
149	22 201	12.20656	38.60052	189	35 721	13.74773	43.47413
150	22 500	12.24745	38.72983	**190**	36 100	13.78405	43.58899
151	22 801	12.28821	38.85872	191	36 481	13.82027	43.70355
152	23 104	12.32883	38.98718	192	36 864	13.85641	43.81780
153	23 409	12.36932	39.11521	193	37 249	13.89244	43.93177
154	23 716	12.40967	39.24283	194	37 636	13.92839	44.04543
155	24 025	12.44990	39.37004	195	38 025	13.96424	44.15880
156	24 336	12.49000	39.49684	196	38 416	14.00000	44.27189
157	24 649	12.52996	39.62323	197	38 809	14.03567	44.38468
158	24 964	12.56981	39.74921	198	39 204	14.07125	44.49719
159	25 281	12.60952	39.87480	199	39 601	14.10674	44.60942
160	25 600	12.64911	40.00000	**200**	40 000	14.14214	44.72136
161	25 921	12.68858	40.12481	201	40 401	14.17745	44.83302
162	26 244	12.72792	40.24922	202	40 804	14.21267	44.94441
163	26 569	12.76715	40.37326	203	41 209	14.24781	45.05552
164	26 806	12.80625	40.49691	204	41 616	14.28286	45.16636
165	27 225	12.84523	40.62019	205	42 025	14.31782	45.27693
166	27 556	12.88410	40.74310	206	42 436	14.35270	45.38722
167	27 889	12.92285	40.86563	207	42 849	14.38749	45.49725
168	28 224	12.96148	40.98780	208	43 264	14.42221	45.60702
169	28 561	13.00000	41.10961	209	43 681	14.45683	45.71652
170	28 900	13.03840	41.23106	**210**	44 100	14.49138	45.82576
171	29 241	13.07670	41.35215	211	44 521	14.52584	45.93474
172	29 584	13.11488	41.47288	212	44 944	14.56022	46.04346
173	29 929	13.15295	41.59327	213	45 369	14.59452	46.15192
174	30 276	13.19091	41.71331	214	45 796	14.62874	46.26013
175	30 625	13.22876	41.83300	215	46 225	14.66288	46.36809
176	30 976	13.26650	41.95235	216	46 656	14.69694	46.47580
177	31 329	13.30413	42.07137	217	47 089	14.73092	46.58326
178	31 684	13.34166	42.19005	218	47 524	14.76482	46.69047
179	32 041	13.37909	42.30829	219	47 961	14.79865	46.79744

n	n²	√n	√10n	n	n²	√n	√10n
220	48 400	14.83240	46.90416	**260**	67 600	16.12452	50.99020
221	48 841	14.86607	47.01064	261	68 121	16.15549	51.08816
222	49 284	14.89966	47.11688	262	68 644	16.18641	51.18594
223	49 729	14.93318	47.22288	263	69 169	16.21727	51.28353
224	50 176	14.96663	47.32864	264	69 696	16.24808	51.38093
225	50 625	15.00000	47.43416	265	70 225	16.27882	51.47815
226	51 076	15.03330	47.53946	266	70 756	16.30951	51.57519
227	51 529	15.06652	47.64452	267	71 289	16.34013	51.67204
228	51 984	15.09967	47.74935	268	71 824	16.37071	51.76872
229	52 441	15.13275	47.85394	269	72 361	16.40122	51.86521
230	52 900	15.16575	47.95832	**270**	72 900	16.43168	51.96152
231	53 361	15.19868	48.06246	271	73 441	16.46208	52.05766
232	53 824	15.23155	48.16638	272	73 984	16.49242	52.15362
233	54 289	15.26434	48.27007	273	74 529	16.52271	52.24940
234	54 756	15.29706	48.37355	274	75 076	16.55295	52.34501
235	55 225	15.32971	48.47680	275	75 625	16.58312	52.44044
236	55 696	15.36229	48.57983	276	76 176	16.61235	52.53570
237	56 169	15.39480	48.68265	277	76 729	16.64332	52.63079
238	56 644	15.42725	48.78524	278	77 284	16.67333	52.72571
239	57 121	15.45962	48.88763	279	77 841	16.70329	52.82045
240	57 600	15.49193	48.98979	**280**	78 400	16.73320	52.91503
241	58 081	15.52417	49.09175	281	78 961	16.76305	53.00943
242	58 564	15.55635	49.19350	282	79 524	16.79286	53.10367
243	59 049	15.58846	49.29503	283	80 089	16.82260	53.19774
244	59 536	15.62050	49.39636	284	80 656	16.85230	53.29165
245	60 025	15.65248	49.49747	285	81 225	16.88194	53.38539
246	60 516	15.68439	49.59839	286	81 796	16.91153	53.47897
247	61 009	15.71623	49.69909	287	82 369	16.94107	53.57238
248	61 504	15.74902	49.79960	288	82 944	16.97056	53.66563
249	62 001	15.77973	49.89990	289	83 521	17.00000	53.75872
250	62 500	15.81139	50.00000	**290**	84 100	17.02939	53.85165
251	63 001	15.84298	50.09990	291	84 681	17.05872	53.94442
252	63 504	15.87451	50.19960	292	85 264	17.08801	54.03702
253	64 009	15.90597	50.29911	293	85 849	17.11724	54.12947
254	64 516	15.93738	50.39841	294	86 436	17.14643	54.22177
255	65 025	15.96872	50.49752	295	87 025	17.17556	54.31390
256	65 536	16.00000	50.59644	296	87 616	17.20465	54.40588
257	66 049	16.03122	50.69517	297	88 209	17.23369	54.49771
258	66 564	16.06238	50.79370	298	88 804	17.26268	54.58938
259	67 081	16.09348	50.89204	299	89 401	17.29162	54.68089

n	n²	√n	√10n	n	n²	√n	√10n
300	90 000	17.32051	54.77226	**340**	115 600	18.43909	58.30952
301	90 601	17.34935	54.86347	341	116 281	18.46619	58.39521
302	91 204	17.37815	54.95453	342	116 964	18.49324	58.48077
303	91 809	17.40690	55.04544	343	117 649	18.52026	58.56620
304	92 416	17.43560	55.13620	344	118 336	18.54724	58.65151
305	93 025	17.46425	55.22681	345	119 025	18.57418	58.73670
306	93 636	17.49286	55.31727	346	119 716	18.60108	58.82176
307	94 249	17.52142	55.40758	347	120 409	18.62794	58.90671
308	94 864	17.54993	55.49775	348	121 104	18.65476	58.99152
309	95 481	17.57840	55.58777	349	121 801	18.68154	59.07622
310	96 100	17.60682	55.67764	**350**	122 500	18.70829	59.16080
311	96 721	17.63519	55.76737	351	123 201	18.73499	59.24525
312	97 344	17.66352	55.85696	352	123 904	18.76166	59.32959
313	97 969	17.69181	55.94640	353	124 609	18.78829	59.41380
314	98 596	17.72005	56.03570	354	125 316	18.81489	59.49790
315	99 225	17.74824	56.12486	355	126 025	18.84144	59.58188
316	99 856	17.77639	56.21388	356	126 736	18.86796	59.66574
317	100 489	17.80449	56.30275	357	127 449	18.89444	59.74948
318	101 124	17.83255	56.39149	358	128 164	18.92089	59.83310
319	101 761	17.86057	56.48008	359	128 881	18.94730	59.91661
320	102 400	17.88854	56.56854	**360**	129 600	18.97367	60.00000
321	103 041	17.91647	56.65686	361	130 321	19.00000	60.08328
322	103 684	17.94436	56.74504	362	131 044	19.02630	60.16644
323	104 329	17.97220	56.83309	363	131 769	19.05256	60.24948
324	104 976	18.00009	56.92100	364	132 496	19.07878	60.33241
325	105 625	18.02776	57.00877	365	133 225	19.10497	60.41523
326	106 276	18.05547	57.09641	366	133 956	19.13113	60.49793
327	106 929	18.08314	57.18391	367	134 689	19.15724	60.58052
328	107 584	18.11077	57.27128	368	135 424	19.18333	60.66300
329	108 241	18.13836	57.35852	369	136 161	19.20937	60.74537
330	108 900	18.16590	57.44563	**370**	136 900	19.23538	60.82763
331	109 561	18.19341	57.53260	371	137 641	19.26136	60.90977
332	110 224	18.22087	57.61944	372	138 384	19.28730	60.99180
333	110 889	18.24829	57.70615	373	139 129	19.31321	61.07373
334	111 556	18.27567	57.79273	374	139 876	19.33908	61.15554
335	112 225	18.30301	57.87918	375	140 625	19.36492	61.23724
336	112 896	18.33030	57.96551	376	141 376	19.39072	61.31884
337	113 569	18.35756	58.05170	377	142 129	19.41649	61.40033
338	114 244	18.38478	58.13777	378	142 884	19.44222	61.48170
339	114 921	18.41195	58.22371	379	143 641	19.46792	61.56298

n	n²	√n	√10n	n	n²	√n	√10n
380	144 400	19.49359	61.64414	420	176 400	20.49390	64.80741
381	145 161	19.51922	61.72520	421	177 241	20.51828	64.88451
382	145 924	19.54482	61.80615	422	178 084	20.54264	64.96153
383	146 689	19.57039	61.88699	423	178 929	20.56696	65.03845
384	147 456	19.59592	61.96773	424	179 776	20.59126	65.11528
385	148 225	19.62142	62.04837	425	180 625	20.61553	65.19202
386	148 996	19.64688	62.12890	426	181 476	20.63977	65.26868
387	149 769	19.67232	62.20932	427	182 329	20.66398	65.34524
388	150 544	19.69772	62.28965	428	183 184	20.68816	65.42171
389	151 321	19.72308	62.36986	429	184 041	20.71232	65.49809
390	152 100	19.74842	62.44998	**430**	184 900	20.73644	65.57439
391	152 881	19.77372	62.52999	431	185 761	20.76054	65.65059
392	153 664	19.79899	62.60990	432	186 624	20.78461	65.72671
393	154 449	19.82423	62.68971	433	187 489	20.80865	65.80274
394	155 236	19.84943	62.76942	434	188 356	20.83267	65.87868
395	156 025	19.87461	62.84903	435	189 225	20.85665	65.95453
396	156 816	19.89975	62.92853	436	190 096	20.88061	66.03030
397	157 609	19.92486	63.00794	437	190 969	20.90454	66.10598
398	158 404	19.94994	63.08724	438	191 844	20.92845	66.18157
399	159 201	19.97498	63.16645	439	192 721	20.95233	66.25708
400	160 000	20.00000	63.24555	**440**	193 600	20.97618	66.33250
401	160 801	20.02498	63.32456	441	194 481	21.00000	66.40783
402	161 604	20.04994	63.40347	442	195 364	21.02380	66.48308
403	162 409	20.07486	63.48228	443	196 249	21.04757	66.55825
404	163 216	20.09975	63.56099	444	197 136	21.07131	66.63332
405	164 025	20.12461	63.63961	445	198 025	21.09502	66.70832
406	164 836	20.14944	63.71813	446	198 916	21.11871	66.78323
407	165 649	20.17424	63.79655	447	199 809	21.14237	66.85806
408	166 464	20.19901	63.87488	448	200 704	21.16601	66.93280
409	167 281	20.22375	63.95311	449	201 601	21.18962	67.00746
410	168 100	20.24864	64.03124	**450**	202 500	21.21320	67.08204
411	168 921	20.27313	64.10928	451	203 401	21.23676	67.15653
412	169 744	20.29778	64.18723	452	204 304	21.26029	67.23095
413	170 569	20.32240	54.26508	453	205 209	21.28380	67.30527
414	171 396	20.34699	64.34283	454	206 116	21.30728	67.37952
415	172 225	20.37155	64.42049	455	207 025	21.33073	67.45369
416	173 056	20.39608	64.49806	456	207 936	21.35416	67.52777
417	173 889	20.42058	64.57554	457	208 849	21.37756	67.60178
418	174 724	20.44505	64.65292	458	209 764	21.40093	67.67570
419	175 561	20.46949	64.73021	459	210 681	21.42429	67.74954

n	n^2	$\sqrt{n}$	$\sqrt{10n}$	n	n^2	$\sqrt{n}$	$\sqrt{10n}$
460	211 600	21.44761	67.82330	**500**	250 000	22.36068	70.71068
461	212 521	21.47091	67.89698	501	251 001	22.38303	70.78135
462	213 444	21.49419	67.97058	502	252 004	22.40536	70.85196
463	214 369	21.51743	68.04410	503	253 009	22.42766	70.92249
464	215 296	21.54066	68.11755	504	254 016	22.44994	70.99296
465	216 225	21.56386	68.19091	505	255 025	22.47221	71.06335
466	217 156	21.58703	68.26419	506	256 036	22.49444	71.13368
467	218 089	21.61018	68.33740	507	257 049	22.51666	71.20393
468	219 024	21.63331	68.41053	508	258 064	22.53886	71.27412
469	219 961	21.65641	68.48957	509	259 081	22.56103	71.34424
470	220 900	21.67948	68.55655	**510**	260 100	22.58318	71.41428
471	221 841	21.70253	68.62944	511	261 121	22.60531	71.48426
472	222 784	21.72556	68.70226	512	262 144	22.62742	71.55418
473	223 729	21.74856	68.77500	513	263 169	22.64950	71.62402
474	224 676	21.77154	68.84766	514	264 196	22.67157	71.69379
475	225 625	21.79449	68.92024	515	265 225	22.69361	71.76350
476	226 576	21.81742	68.99275	516	266 256	22.71563	71.83314
477	227 529	21.84033	69.06519	517	267 289	22.73763	71.90271
478	228 484	21.86321	69.13754	518	268 324	22.75961	71.97222
479	229 441	21.88607	69.20983	519	269 361	22.78157	72.04165
480	230 400	21.90890	69.28203	**520**	270 400	22.80351	72.11103
481	231 361	21.93171	69.35416	521	271 441	22.82542	72.18033
482	232 324	21.95450	69.42622	522	272 484	22.84732	72.24957
483	233 289	21.97726	69.49820	523	273 529	22.86919	72.31874
484	234 256	22.00000	69.57011	524	274 576	22.89105	72.38784
485	235 225	22.02272	69.64194	525	275 625	22.91288	72.45688
486	236 196	22.04541	69.71370	526	276 676	22.93469	72.52586
487	237 169	22.06808	69.78539	527	277 729	22.95648	72.59477
488	238 144	22.09072	69.85700	528	278 784	22.97825	72.66361
489	239 121	22.11334	69.92853	529	279 841	23.00000	72.73239
490	240 100	22.13594	70.00000	**530**	280 900	23.02173	72.80110
491	241 081	22.15852	70.07139	531	281 961	23.04344	72.86975
492	242 064	22.18107	70.14271	532	283 024	23.06513	72.93833
493	243 049	22.20360	70.21396	533	284 089	23.08679	73.00685
494	244 036	22.22611	70.28513	534	285 156	23.10844	73.07530
495	245 025	22.24860	70.35624	535	286 225	23.13007	73.14369
496	246 016	22.27106	70.42727	536	287 296	23.15167	73.21202
497	247 009	22.29350	70.49823	537	288 369	23.17326	73.28028
498	248 004	22.31591	70.56912	538	289 444	23.19483	73.34848
499	249 001	22.33831	70.63993	539	290 521	23.21637	73.41662

n	n^2	$\sqrt{n}$	$\sqrt{10n}$	n	n^2	$\sqrt{n}$	$\sqrt{10n}$
540	291 600	23.23790	73.48469	**580**	336 400	24.08319	76.15773
541	292 681	23.25941	73.55270	581	337 561	24.10394	76.22336
542	293 764	23.28089	73.62065	582	338 724	24.12468	76.28892
543	294 849	23.30236	73.68853	583	339 889	24.14539	76.35444
544	295 936	23.32381	73.75636	584	341 056	24.16609	76.41989
545	297 025	23.34524	73.82412	585	342 225	24.18677	76.48529
546	298 116	23.36664	73.89181	586	343 396	24.20744	76.55064
547	299 209	23.38803	73.95945	587	344 569	24.22808	76.61593
548	300 304	23.40940	74.02702	588	345 744	24.24871	76.68116
549	301 401	23.43075	74.09453	589	346 921	24.26932	76.74634
550	302 500	23.45208	74.16198	**590**	348 100	24.28992	76.81146
551	303 601	23.47339	74.22937	591	349 281	24.31049	76.87652
552	304 704	23.49468	74.29670	592	350 464	24.33105	76.94154
553	305 809	23.51595	74.36397	593	351 649	24.35159	77.00649
554	306 916	23.53720	74.43118	594	352 836	24.37212	77.07140
555	308 025	23.55844	74.49832	595	354 025	24.39262	77.13624
556	309 136	23.57965	74.56541	596	355 216	24.41311	77.20104
557	310 249	23.60085	74.63243	597	356 409	24.43358	77.26578
558	311 364	23.62202	74.69940	598	357 604	24.45404	77.33046
559	312 481	23.64318	74.76630	599	358 801	24.47448	77.39509
560	313 600	23.66432	74.83315	**600**	360 000	24.49490	77.45967
561	314 721	23.68544	74.89993	601	361 201	24.51530	77.52419
562	315 844	23.70654	74.96666	602	362 404	24.53569	77.58866
563	316 969	23.72762	75.03333	603	363 609	24.55606	77.65307
564	318 096	23.74868	75.09993	604	364 816	24.57641	77.71744
565	319 225	23.76973	75.16648	605	366 025	24.59675	77.78175
566	320 356	23.79075	75.23297	606	367 236	24.61707	77.84600
567	321 489	23.81176	75.29940	607	368 449	24.63737	77.91020
568	322 624	23.83275	75.36577	608	369 664	24.65766	77.97435
569	323 761	23.85372	75.43209	609	370 881	24.67793	78.03845
570	324 900	23.87467	75.49834	**610**	372 100	24.69818	78.10250
571	326 041	23.89561	75.56454	611	373 321	24.71841	78.16649
572	327 184	23.91652	75.63068	612	374 544	24.73863	78.23043
573	328 329	23.93742	75.69676	613	375 769	24.75884	78.29432
574	329 476	23.95830	75.76279	614	376 996	24.77902	78.35815
575	330 625	23.97916	75.82875	615	378 225	24.79919	78.42194
576	331 776	24.00000	75.89466	616	379 456	24.81935	78.48567
577	332 929	24.02082	75.96052	617	380 689	24.83948	78.54935
578	334 084	24.04163	76.02631	618	381 924	24.85961	78.61298
579	335 241	24.06242	76.09205	619	383 161	24.87971	78.67655

n	n^2	$\sqrt{n}$	$\sqrt{10n}$	n	n^2	$\sqrt{n}$	$\sqrt{10n}$
620	384 400	24.89980	78.74008	**660**	435 600	25.69047	81.24038
621	385 641	24.91987	78.80355	661	436 921	25.70992	81.30191
622	386 884	24.93993	78.86698	662	438 244	25.72936	81.36338
623	388 129	24.95997	78.93035	663	439 569	25.74879	81.42481
624	389 376	24.97999	78.99367	664	440 896	25.76820	81.48620
625	390 625	25.00000	79.05694	665	442 225	25.78759	81.54753
626	391 876	25.01999	79.12016	666	443 556	25.80698	81.60882
627	393 129	25.03997	79.18333	667	444 889	25.82634	81.67007
628	394 384	25.05993	79.24645	668	446 224	25.84570	81.73127
629	395 641	25.07987	79.30952	669	447 561	25.86503	81.79242
630	396 900	25.09980	79.37254	**670**	448 900	25.88436	81.85353
631	398 161	25.11971	79.43551	671	450 241	25.90367	81.91459
632	399 424	25.13961	79.49843	672	451 584	25.92296	81.97561
633	400 689	25.15949	79.56130	673	452 929	25.94224	82.03658
634	401 956	25.17936	79.62412	674	454 276	25.96151	82.09750
635	403 225	25.19921	79.68689	675	455 625	25.98076	82.15838
636	404 496	25.21904	79.74961	676	456 976	26.00000	82.21922
637	405 769	25.23886	79.81228	677	458 329	26.01922	82.28001
638	407 044	25.25866	79.87490	678	459 684	26.03843	82.34076
639	408 321	25.27845	79.93748	679	461 041	26.05763	82.40146
640	409 600	25.29822	80.00000	**680**	462 400	26.07681	82.46211
641	410 881	25.31798	80.06248	681	463 761	26.09598	82.52272
642	412 164	25.33772	80.12490	682	465 124	26.11513	82.58329
643	413 449	25.35744	80.18728	683	466 489	26.13427	82.64381
644	414 736	25.37716	80.24961	684	467 856	26.15339	82.70429
645	416 025	25.39685	80.31189	685	469 225	26.17250	82.76473
646	417 316	25.41653	80.37413	686	470 596	26.19160	82.82512
647	418 609	25.43619	80.43631	687	471 969	26.21068	82.88546
648	419 904	25.45584	80.49845	688	473 344	26.22975	82.94577
649	421 201	25.47548	80.56054	689	474 721	26.24881	83.00602
650	422 500	25.49510	80.62258	**690**	476 100	26.26785	83.06624
651	423 801	25.51470	80.68457	691	477 481	26.28688	83.12641
652	425 104	25.53429	80.74652	692	478 864	26.30589	83.18654
653	426 409	25.55386	80.80842	693	480 249	26.32489	83.24662
654	427 716	25.57342	80.87027	694	481 636	26.34388	83.30666
655	429 025	25.59297	80.93207	695	483 025	26.36285	83.36666
656	430 336	25.61250	80.99383	696	484 416	26.38181	83.42661
657	431 649	25.63201	81.05554	697	485 809	26.40076	83.48653
658	432 964	25.65151	81.11720	698	487 204	26.41969	83.54639
659	434 281	25.67100	81.17881	699	488 601	26.43861	83.60622

n	n^2	$\sqrt{n}$	$\sqrt{10n}$	n	n^2	$\sqrt{n}$	$\sqrt{10n}$
700	490 000	26.45751	83.66600	**740**	547 600	27.20294	86.02325
701	491 401	26.47640	83.72574	741	549 081	27.22132	86.08136
702	492 804	26.49528	83.78544	742	550 564	27.23968	86.13942
703	494 209	26.51415	83.84510	743	552 049	27.25803	86.19745
704	495 616	26.53300	83.90471	744	553 536	27.27636	86.25543
705	497 025	26.55184	83.96428	745	555 025	27.29469	86.31338
706	498 436	26.57066	84.02381	746	556 516	27.31300	86.37129
707	499 849	26.58947	84.08329	747	558 009	27.33130	86.42916
708	501 264	26.60827	84.14274	748	559 504	27.34959	86.48699
709	502 681	26.62705	84.20214	749	561 001	27.36786	86.54479
710	504 100	26.64583	84.26150	**750**	562 500	27.38613	86.60254
711	505 521	26.66458	84.32082	751	564 001	27.40438	86.66026
712	506 944	26.68333	84.38009	752	565 504	27.42262	86.71793
713	508 369	26.70206	84.43933	753	567 009	27.44085	86.77557
714	509 796	26.72078	84.49852	754	568 516	27.45906	86.83317
715	511 225	26.73948	84.55767	755	570 025	27.47726	86.89074
716	512 656	26.75818	84.61678	756	571 536	27.49545	86.94826
717	514 089	26.77686	84.67585	757	573 049	27.51363	87.00575
718	515 524	26.79552	84.73488	758	574 564	27.53180	87.06320
719	516 961	26.81418	84.79387	759	576 081	27.54995	87.12061
720	518 400	26.83282	84.85281	**760**	577 600	27.56810	87.17798
721	519 841	26.85144	84.91172	761	579 121	27.58623	87.23531
722	521 284	26.87006	84.97058	762	580 644	27.60435	87.29261
723	522 729	26.88866	85.02941	763	582 169	27.62245	87.34987
724	524 176	26.90725	85.08819	764	583 696	27.64055	87.40709
725	525 625	26.92582	85.14693	765	585 225	27.65863	87.46428
726	527 076	26.94439	85.20563	766	586 756	27.67671	87.52143
727	528 529	26.96294	85.26429	767	588 289	27.69476	87.57854
728	529 984	26.98148	85.32292	768	589 824	27.71281	87.63561
729	531 441	27.00000	85.38150	769	591 361	27.73085	87.69265
730	532 900	27.01851	85.44004	**770**	592 900	27.74887	87.74964
731	534 361	27.03701	85.49854	771	594 441	27.76689	87.80661
732	535 824	27.05550	85.55700	772	595 984	27.78489	87.86353
733	537 289	27.07397	85.61542	773	597 529	27.80288	87.92042
734	538 756	27.09243	85.67380	774	599 076	27.82086	87.97727
735	540 225	27.11088	85.73214	775	600 625	27.83882	88.03408
736	541 696	27.12932	85.79044	776	602 176	27.85678	88.09086
737	543 169	27.14774	85.84870	777	603 729	27.87472	88.14760
738	544 644	27.16616	85.90693	778	605 284	27.89265	88.20431
739	546 121	27.18455	85.96511	779	606 841	27.91057	88.26098

n	n^2	$\sqrt{n}$	$\sqrt{10n}$	n	n^2	$\sqrt{n}$	$\sqrt{10n}$
780	608 400	27.92848	88.31761	**820**	672 400	28.63564	90.55385
781	609 961	27.94638	88.37420	821	674 041	28.65310	90.60905
782	611 524	27.96426	88.43076	822	675 684	28.67054	90.66422
783	613 089	27.98214	88.48729	823	677 329	28.68798	90.71935
784	614 656	28.00000	88.54377	824	678 976	28.70540	90.77445
785	616 225	28.01785	88.60023	825	680 625	28.72281	90.82951
786	617 796	28.03569	88.65664	826	682 726	28.74022	90.88454
787	619 369	28.05352	88.71302	827	683 929	28.75761	90.93954
788	620 944	28.07134	88.76936	828	685 584	28.77499	90.99451
789	622 521	28.08914	88.82567	829	687 241	28.79236	91.04944
790	624 100	28.10694	88.88194	**830**	688 900	28.80972	91.10434
791	625 681	28.12472	88.93818	831	690 561	28.82707	91.15920
792	627 264	28.14249	88.99428	832	692 224	28.84441	91.21403
793	628 849	28.16026	89.05055	833	693 889	28.86174	91.26883
794	630 436	28.17801	89.10668	834	695 556	28.87906	91.32360
795	632 025	28.19574	89.16277	835	697 225	28.89637	91.37833
796	633 616	28.21347	89.21883	836	698 896	28.91366	91.43304
797	635 209	28.23119	89.27486	837	700 569	28.93095	91.48770
798	636 804	28.24889	89.33085	838	702 244	28.94823	91.54234
799	638 401	28.26659	89.38680	839	703 921	28.96550	91.59694
800	640 000	28.28472	89.44272	**840**	705 600	28.98275	91.65151
801	641 601	28.30194	89.49860	841	707 281	29.00000	91.70605
802	643 204	28.31960	89.55445	842	708 964	29.01724	91.76056
803	644 809	28.33725	89.61027	843	710 649	29.03446	91.81503
804	646 416	28.35489	89.66605	844	712 336	29.05168	91.86947
805	648 025	28.37252	89.72179	845	714 025	29.06888	91.92388
806	649 636	28.39014	89.77750	846	715 716	29.08608	91.97826
807	651 249	28.40775	89.83318	847	717 409	29.10326	92.03260
808	652 864	28.42534	89.88882	848	719 104	29.12044	92.08692
809	654 481	28.44293	89.94443	849	720 801	29.13760	92.14120
810	656 100	28.46050	90.00000	**850**	722 500	29.15476	92.19544
811	657 721	28.47806	90.05554	851	724 201	29.17190	92.24966
812	659 344	28.49561	90.11104	852	725 904	29.18904	92.30385
813	660 969	28.51315	90.16651	853	727 609	29.20616	92.35800
814	662 596	28.53069	90.22195	854	729 316	29.22328	92.41212
815	664 225	28.54820	90.27735	855	731 025	29.24038	92.46621
816	665 856	28.56571	90.33272	856	732 736	29.25748	92.52027
817	667 489	28.58321	90.38805	857	734 449	29.27456	92.57429
818	669 124	28.60070	90.44335	858	736 164	29.29164	92.62829
819	670 761	28.61818	90.49862	859	737 881	29.30870	92.68225

n	n^2	$\sqrt{n}$	$\sqrt{10n}$	n	n^2	$\sqrt{n}$	$\sqrt{10n}$
860	739 600	29.32576	92.73618	**900**	810 000	30.00000	94.86833
861	741 321	29.34280	92.79009	901	811 801	30.01666	94.92102
862	743 044	29.35984	92.84396	902	813 604	30.03331	94.97368
863	744 769	29.37686	92.89779	903	815 409	30.04996	95.02631
864	746 496	29.39388	92.95160	904	817 216	30.06659	95.07891
865	748 225	29.41088	93.00538	905	819 025	30.08322	95.13149
866	749 956	29.42788	93.05912	906	820 836	30.09983	95.18403
867	751 689	29.44486	93.11283	907	822 649	30.11644	95.23655
868	753 424	29.46184	93.16652	908	824 464	30.13304	95.28903
869	755 161	29.47881	93.22017	909	826 281	30.14963	95.34149
870	756 900	29.49576	93.27379	**910**	828 100	30.16621	95.39392
871	758 641	29.51271	93.32738	911	829 921	30.18278	95.44632
872	760 384	29.52965	93.38094	912	831 744	30.19934	95.49869
873	762 129	29.54657	93.43447	913	833 569	30.21589	95.55103
874	763 876	29.56349	93.48797	914	835 396	30.23243	95.60335
875	765 625	29.58040	93.54143	915	837 225	30.24897	95.65563
876	767 376	29.59730	93.59487	916	839 056	30.26549	95.70789
877	769 129	29.61419	93.64828	917	840 889	30.28201	95.76012
878	770 884	29.63106	93.70165	918	842 724	30.29851	95.81232
879	772 641	29.64793	93.75500	919	844 561	30.31501	95.86449
880	774 400	29.66479	93.80832	**920**	846 400	30.33150	95.91663
881	776 161	29.68164	93.86160	921	848 241	30.34798	95.96874
882	777 924	29.69848	93.91486	922	850 084	30.36445	96.02083
883	779 689	29.71532	93.96808	923	851 929	30.38092	96.07289
884	781 456	29.73214	94.02127	924	853 776	30.39737	96.12492
885	783 225	29.74895	94.07444	925	855 625	30.41381	96.17692
886	784 996	29.76575	94.12757	926	857 476	30.43025	96.22889
887	786 769	29.78255	94.18068	927	859 329	30.44667	96.28084
888	788 544	29.79933	94.23375	928	861 184	30.46309	96.33276
889	790 321	29.81610	94.28680	929	863 041	30.47950	96.38465
890	792 100	29.83287	94.33981	**930**	864 900	30.49590	96.43651
891	793 881	29.84962	94.39280	931	866 761	30.51229	96.48834
892	795 664	29.86637	94.44575	932	868 624	30.52868	96.54015
893	797 449	29.88311	94.49868	933	870 489	30.54505	96.59193
894	799 236	29.89983	94.55157	934	872 356	30.56141	96.64368
895	801 025	29.91655	94.60444	935	874 225	30.57777	96.69540
896	802 816	29.93326	94.65728	936	876 096	30.59412	96.74709
897	804 609	29.94996	94.71008	937	877 969	30.61046	96.79876
898	806 404	29.96665	94.76286	938	879 844	30.62679	96.85040
899	808 201	29.98333	94.81561	939	881 721	30.64311	96.90201

n	n^2	$\sqrt{n}$	$\sqrt{10n}$	n	n^2	$\sqrt{n}$	$\sqrt{10n}$
940	883 600	30.65942	96.95360	**970**	940 900	31.14482	98.48858
941	885 481	30.67572	97.00515	971	942 841	31.16087	98.53933
942	887 364	30.69202	97.05668	972	944 784	31.17691	98.59006
943	889 249	30.70831	97.10819	973	946 729	31.19295	98.64076
944	891 136	30.72458	97.15966	974	948 676	31.20897	98.69144
945	893 025	30.74085	97.21111	975	950 625	31.22499	98.74209
946	894 916	30.75711	97.26253	976	952 576	31.24100	98.79271
947	896 809	30.77337	97.31393	977	954 529	31.25700	98.84331
948	898 704	30.78961	97.36529	978	956 484	31.27299	98.89388
949	900 601	30.80584	97.41663	979	958 441	31.28898	98.94443
950	902 500	30.82207	97.46794	**980**	960 400	31.30495	98.99495
951	904 401	30.83829	97.51923	981	962 361	31.32092	99.04544
952	906 304	30.85450	97.57049	982	964 324	31.33688	99.09591
953	908 209	30.87070	97.62172	983	966 289	31.35283	99.14636
954	910 116	30.88689	97.67292	984	968 256	31.36877	99.19677
955	912 025	30.90307	97.72410	985	970 225	31.38471	99.24717
956	913 936	30.91925	97.77525	986	972 196	31.40064	99.29753
957	915 849	30.93542	97.82638	987	974 169	31.41656	99.34787
958	917 764	30.95158	97.87747	988	976 144	31.43247	99.39819
959	919 681	30.96773	97.92855	989	978 121	31.44837	99.44848
960	921 600	30.98387	97.97959	**990**	980 100	31.46427	99.49874
961	923 521	31.00000	98.03061	991	982 081	31.48015	99.54898
962	925 444	31.01612	98.08160	992	984 064	31.49603	99.59920
963	927 369	31.03224	98.13256	993	986 049	31.51190	99.64939
964	929 296	31.04835	98.18350	994	988 036	31.52777	99.69955
965	931 225	31.06445	98.23441	995	990 025	31.54362	99.74969
966	933 156	31.08054	98.28530	996	992 016	31.55947	99.79980
967	935 089	31.09662	98.33616	997	994 009	31.57531	99.84989
968	937 024	31.11270	98.38699	998	996 004	31.59114	99.89995
969	938 961	31.12876	98.43780	999	998 001	31.60696	99.94999
				1000	1000 000	31.62278	100.00000

Abridged from *Handbook of Tables for Probability and Statistics*, 2d ed., edited by William H. Beyer (Cleveland: The Chemical Rubber Company, 1968). Reproduced by permission of the publishers, The Chemical Rubber Company.

Table 11 • Random numbers

Line/Col.	(1)	(2)	(3)	(4)	(5)	(6)	(7)	(8)	(9)	(10)	(11)	(12)	(13)	(14)
1	10480	15011	01536	02011	81647	91646	69179	14194	62590	36207	20969	99570	91291	90700
2	22368	46573	25595	85393	30995	89198	27982	53402	93965	34095	52666	19174	39615	99505
3	24130	48360	22527	97265	76393	64809	15179	24830	49340	32081	30680	19655	63348	58629
4	42167	93093	06243	61680	07856	16376	39440	53537	71341	57004	00849	74917	97758	16379
5	37570	39975	81837	16656	06121	91782	60468	81305	49684	60672	14110	06927	01263	54613
6	77921	06907	11008	42751	27756	53498	18602	70659	90655	15053	21916	81825	44394	42880
7	99562	72905	56420	69994	98872	31016	71194	18738	44013	48840	63213	21069	10634	12952
8	96301	91977	05463	07972	18876	20922	94595	56869	69014	60045	18425	84903	42508	32307
9	89579	14342	63661	10281	17453	18103	57740	84378	25331	12566	58678	44947	05585	56941
10	85475	36857	53342	53988	53060	59533	38867	62300	08158	17983	16439	11458	18593	64952
11	28918	69578	88231	33276	70997	79936	56865	05859	90106	31595	01547	85590	91610	78188
12	63553	40961	48235	03427	49626	69445	18663	72695	52180	20847	12234	90511	33703	90322
13	09429	93969	52636	92737	88974	33488	36320	17617	30015	08272	84115	27156	30613	74952
14	10365	61129	87529	85689	48237	52267	67689	93394	01511	26358	85104	20285	29975	89868
15	07119	97336	71048	08178	77233	13916	47564	81056	97735	85977	29372	74461	28551	90707
16	51085	12765	51821	51259	77452	16308	60756	92144	49442	53900	70960	63990	75601	40719
17	02368	21382	52404	60268	89368	19885	55322	44819	01188	65255	64835	44919	05944	55157
18	01011	54092	33362	94904	31273	04146	18594	29852	71585	85030	51132	01915	92747	64951
19	52162	53916	46369	58586	23216	14513	83149	98736	23495	64350	94738	17752	35156	35749
20	07056	97628	33787	09998	42698	06691	76988	13602	51851	46104	88916	19509	25625	58104
21	48663	91245	85828	14346	09172	30168	90229	04734	59193	22178	30421	61666	99904	32812
22	54164	58492	22421	74070	47070	25306	76468	26384	58151	06646	21524	15227	96909	44592
23	32639	32363	05597	24200	13363	38005	94342	28728	35806	06912	17012	64161	18296	22851
24	29334	27001	87637	87308	58731	00256	45834	15398	46557	41135	10367	07684	36188	18510
25	02488	33062	28834	07351	19731	92420	60952	61280	50001	67658	32586	86679	50720	94953

Abridged from *Handbook of Tables for Probability and Statistics*, 2d ed., edited by William H. Beyer (Cleveland: The Chemical Rubber Company, 1968). Reproduced by permission of the publishers, The Chemical Rubber Company.

Line/Col.	(1)	(2)	(3)	(4)	(5)	(6)	(7)	(8)	(9)	(10)	(11)	(12)	(13)	(14)
26	81525	72295	04839	96423	24878	82651	66566	14778	76797	14780	13300	87074	79666	95725
27	29676	20591	68086	26432	46901	20849	89768	81536	86645	12659	92259	57102	80428	25280
28	00742	57392	39064	66432	84673	40027	32832	61362	98947	96067	64760	64584	96096	98253
29	05366	04213	25669	26422	44407	44048	37937	63904	45766	66134	75470	66520	34693	90449
30	91921	26418	64117	94305	26766	25940	39972	22209	71500	64568	91402	42416	07844	69618
31	00582	04711	87917	77341	42206	35126	74087	99547	81817	42607	43808	76655	62028	76630
32	00725	69884	62797	56170	86324	88072	76222	36086	84637	93161	76038	63555	77919	88006
33	69011	65795	95876	55293	18988	27354	26575	08625	40801	59920	29841	80150	12777	48501
34	25976	57948	29888	88604	67917	48708	18912	82271	65424	69774	33611	54262	85963	03547
35	09763	83473	73577	12908	30883	18317	28290	35797	05998	41688	34952	37888	38917	88050
36	91567	42595	27958	30134	04024	86385	29880	99730	55536	84855	29080	09250	79656	73211
37	17955	56349	90999	49127	20044	59931	06115	20542	18059	02008	73708	83517	36103	42791
38	46503	18584	18845	49618	02304	51038	20655	58727	28168	15475	56942	53389	20562	87338
39	92157	89634	94824	78171	84610	82834	09922	25417	44137	48413	25555	21246	35509	20468
40	14577	62765	35605	81263	39667	47358	56873	56307	61607	49518	89656	20103	77490	18062
41	98427	07523	33362	64270	01638	92477	66969	98420	04880	45585	46565	04132	46880	45709
42	34914	63976	88720	82765	34476	17032	87589	40836	32427	70002	70663	88863	77775	69348
43	70060	28277	39475	46473	23219	53416	94970	25832	69975	94884	19661	72828	00102	66794
44	53976	54914	06990	67245	68350	82948	11398	42878	80287	88267	47363	46634	06541	97809
45	76072	29515	40980	07391	58745	25774	22987	80059	39911	96189	41151	14222	60697	59583
46	90725	52210	83974	29992	65831	38857	50490	83765	55657	14361	31720	57375	56228	41546
47	64364	67412	33339	31926	14883	24413	59744	92351	97473	89286	35931	04110	23726	51900
48	08962	00358	31662	25388	61642	34072	81249	35648	56891	69352	48373	45578	78547	81788
49	95012	68379	93526	70765	10592	04542	76463	54328	02349	17247	28865	14777	62730	92277
50	15664	10493	20492	38391	91132	21999	59516	81652	27195	48223	46751	22923	32261	85653
51	16408	81899	04153	53381	79401	21438	83035	92350	36693	31238	59649	91754	72772	02338
52	18629	81953	05520	91962	04739	13092	97662	24822	94730	06496	35090	04822	86774	98289
53	73115	35101	47498	87637	99016	71060	88824	71013	18735	20286	23153	72924	35165	43040
54	57491	16703	23167	49323	45021	33132	12544	41035	80780	45393	44812	12515	98931	91202
55	30405	83946	23792	14422	15059	45799	22716	19792	09983	74353	68668	30429	70735	25499
56	16631	35006	85900	98275	32388	52390	16815	69298	82732	38480	73817	32523	41961	44437
57	96773	20206	42559	78985	05300	22164	24369	54224	35083	19687	11052	91491	60383	19746
58	38935	64202	14349	82074	66523	44133	00697	35552	35970	19124	63318	29686	03387	59846
59	31624	76384	17403	53363	44167	64486	64758	75366	76554	31601	12614	33072	60332	92325
60	78919	19474	23632	27889	47914	02584	37680	20801	72152	39339	34806	08930	85001	87820
61	03931	33309	57047	74211	63445	17361	62825	39908	05607	91284	68833	25570	38818	46920
62	74426	33278	43972	10119	89917	15665	52872	73823	73144	88662	88970	74492	51805	99378
63	09066	00903	20795	95452	92648	45454	09552	88815	16553	51125	79375	97596	16296	66092
64	42238	12426	87025	14267	20979	04508	64535	31355	86064	29472	47689	05974	52468	16834
65	16153	08002	26504	41744	81959	65642	74240	56302	00033	67107	77510	70625	28725	34191

66	21457	40742	29820	96783	29400	21840	15035	34537	33310	06116	95240	15957	16572	06004
67	21581	57802	02050	89728	17937	37621	47075	42080	97403	48626	68995	43805	33386	21597
68	55612	78095	83197	33732	05810	24813	86902	60397	16489	03264	88525	42786	05269	92532
69	44657	66999	99324	51281	84463	60563	79312	93454	68876	25471	93911	25650	12682	73572
70	91340	84979	46949	81973	37949	61023	43997	15263	80944	43942	89203	71795	99533	50501
71	91227	21199	31935	27022	84067	05462	35216	14436	29891	68607	41867	14951	91696	85065
72	50001	38140	66321	19924	72163	09538	12151	06878	91903	18749	34405	56087	82790	70925
73	65390	05224	72958	28609	81406	39147	25549	48542	42627	45233	57202	94617	23772	07896
74	27504	96131	83944	41575	10573	08619	64482	73923	36152	05184	94142	25299	84387	34925
75	37169	94851	39117	89632	00959	16487	65536	49071	39782	17095	02330	74301	00275	48280
76	11508	70225	51111	28351	19444	66499	71945	05422	13442	78675	84081	66938	93654	59894
77	37449	30362	06694	54690	04052	53115	62757	95348	78662	11163	81651	50245	34971	52924
78	46515	70331	85922	38329	57015	15765	97161	17869	45349	61796	66345	81073	49106	79860
79	30986	81223	42416	58353	21532	30302	32305	86482	05174	07901	54339	58861	74818	46942
80	63798	64995	46583	09785	44160	78128	83091	42865	92520	83531	80377	35909	81250	54238
81	82486	84846	99254	67632	43218	50076	21361	64816	51202	88124	41870	52689	51275	83556
82	21885	32906	92431	09060	64297	51074	64126	62570	26123	05155	59194	52799	28225	85762
83	60336	98782	07408	53458	13564	59089	26445	29789	85205	41001	12535	12133	14645	23541
84	43937	46891	24010	25560	86355	33941	25786	54990	71899	15475	95434	98227	21824	19585
85	97656	63175	89303	16275	07100	92063	21942	18611	47348	20203	18534	03862	78095	50136
86	03299	01221	05418	38982	55758	92237	26759	86367	21216	98442	08303	56013	91511	75928
87	79628	06486	03574	17668	07785	76020	79924	25651	83325	88428	85076	72811	22717	50585
88	85636	68335	47539	03129	65651	11977	02510	26113	99447	68645	34327	15152	55230	93448
89	18039	14367	61337	06177	12143	46609	32989	74014	64708	00533	35398	58408	13261	47908
90	08362	15656	60627	36478	65648	16764	53412	09013	07832	41574	17639	82163	60859	75567
91	79556	29068	04142	16268	15387	12856	66227	38358	22478	73373	88732	09443	82558	05250
92	92608	82674	27072	32534	17075	27698	98204	63863	11951	34648	88022	56148	34925	57031
93	23982	25835	40055	67006	12293	02753	14827	23235	35071	99704	37543	11601	35503	85171
94	09915	96306	05908	97901	28395	14186	00821	80703	70426	75647	76310	88717	37890	40129
95	59037	33300	26695	62247	69927	76123	50842	43834	86654	70959	79725	93872	28117	19233
96	42488	78077	69882	61657	34136	79180	97526	43092	04098	73571	80799	76536	71255	64239
97	46764	86273	63003	93017	31204	36692	40202	35275	57306	55543	53203	18098	47625	88684
98	03237	45430	55417	63282	90816	17349	88298	90183	36000	78406	06216	95787	42579	90730
99	86591	81482	52667	61582	14972	90053	89534	76036	49199	43716	97548	04379	46370	28072
100	38534	01715	94964	87288	65680	43772	39560	12918	86537	62738	19636	51132	25739	56947

Glossary of Common Statistical Terms

Analysis of variance: Analysis of data based on a partitioning of the sum of squares of deviations of the y-values (response measurements) about their mean.

Biased estimator: Estimator whose probability distribution has a mean value that is not equal to the value of the estimated parameter.

Binomial experiment: Experiment involving n identical independent trials. (See chapter 5 for an exact and detailed description of a binomial experiment.)

Binomial random variable: Discrete random variable representing the number of successes y in n identical independent trials. (For an exact definition of a binomial experiment, see chapter 5.)

Central Limit Theorem: Theorem states that the probability distribution of the sample mean (or sum) will be approximately normal when certain conditions are satisfied. (See chapter 7.)

Chi-square: Test statistic used to test the null hypothesis of independence for the two classifications of a contingency table. Also has many other statistical applications not discussed in this text.

Class boundary: Dividing point between two cells in a frequency histogram.

Classes: Cells of a frequency histogram.

Class frequency: Number of observations falling in a class (referring to a frequency histogram).

Coefficient of linear correlation: Measure of linear dependence between two random variables.

Completely randomized design: Consider an experiment that involves k different ways of treating a set of experimental units so that k treatments can be compared. A completely randomized design assigns the experimental units to the treatments in such a way that any one allocation of experimental units to the treatments is just as probable as any other.

Confidence coefficient: Probability that an interval estimate (a confidence interval) will enclose the parameter of interest.

Confidence interval: Concerned with interval estimation. Two numbers, computed from sample data, that form an interval estimate for some parameter. (Naturally, we would like the interval to enclose the parameter of interest.)

Contingency table: Two-way table constructed for classifying count data. The entries in the table show the number of observations falling in the cells. The objective of an analysis is to determine whether the two directions of classification are dependent (contingent) upon one another.

Degrees of freedom: Parameter of Student's t and the chi-square probability distributions. Degrees of freedom measure the quantity of information available in normally distributed data for estimating the population variance σ^2.

Design of an experiment: Plan for collecting experimental data. The objective is to acquire a specified quantity of information (pertinent to a population parameter) at minimum cost.

Deviation from the mean: Distance between a sample observation and the sample mean $\bar{y}$.

Discrete random variable: Random variable that can assume only a finite number or a countable infinity of values.

Empirical Rule: Rule that describes the variability of data that possess a mound-shaped frequency distribution. (See chapter 2.)

Error of estimation: Distance between an estimate and the true value of the parameter estimated.

Estimate: Number computed from sample data used to approximate a population parameter.

Estimator: Rule that tells how to compute an estimate based on information contained in a sample. An estimator is usually given as a mathematical formula.

Event: Outcome of an experiment.

Experiment: Process of making an observation.

Experimental units: Objects upon which measurements are taken.

Factorial experiment: Experiment that includes all combinations of the levels of the factor.

Factors: Independent experimental variables that are related to a dependent response variable.

Frequency: Number of observations falling in a cell or classification category.

Friedman test: Extension of the matched pairs experiment to more than two populations. Design implies matching or, equivalently, blocking as described in chapter 10.

F statistic: Test statistic used to compare variances from two normal populations. Used in the analysis of variance.

Histogram: Graphical method for describing a set of data. (See chapter 2.)

Interaction (factor interaction): When the effect of one factor on a response depends on the level(s) of one (or more) other factors.

Interval estimate: Two numbers computed from the sample data. The interval formed by the numbers should enclose some parameter of interest. An interval estimate is usually called a *confidence interval*.

Interval estimator: A rule that explains how to calculate from sample data the two numbers required for an interval estimate.

Kruskal-Wallis H test: Rank sum test used to compare two or more populations.

Least squares: Method of curve fitting that selects as the best-fitting curve the one that minimizes the sum of the squares of deviations of the data points from the fitted curve. (See chapter 12.)

Level of a factor: Intensity setting.

Level of significance: Refers to the outcome of a specific statistical test of an hypothesis. The level of significance of the test is the probability of drawing a value of the test statistic that is as contradictory, or more contradictory, to the null hypothesis as the value observed.

Linear correlation: Dependence between two random variables.

Lower confidence limit: Smaller of the two numbers that form a confidence interval.

Mann-Whitney U test: Nonparametric test for comparing two populations based on independent random samples from each. Test statistics utilize the rank sum of the sample measurements.

Matched pairs test: Statistical test for the comparison of two population means. The test is based on paired observations, one from each of the two populations.

Mathematical model: Mathematical equation that characterizes (or models) the behavior of one or more variables associated with a natural phenomenon.

Mean: Average of a set of measurements. The symbols $\bar{y}$ and μ denote the means of a sample and a population, respectively.

Median: Middle measurement when a set is ordered according to numerical value. (See chapter 2.)

Multinomial experiment: Experiment that consists of n identical independent trials, where each trial can result in one of k (a fixed number) outcomes.

Newman-Keuls procedure: Method for making pairwise comparisons among means.

Nonparametric methods: Usually refers to statistical tests of hypotheses about population probability distributions—but not about specific parameters of the distributions. (See chapter 6.)

Normal distribution: Bell-shaped probability distribution. The curve possesses a specific mathematical formula.

Null hypothesis: Hypothesis under test in a statistical test of an hypothesis.

Parameter of a population: Numerical descriptive measure of a population.

Parametric methods: Statistical methods for estimating parameters or testing hypotheses about population parameters.

Percentiles: See chapter 2 for definition.

Point estimate: See **Estimate.**

Population: Set of measurements, actual or conceptual, that is of interest to the experimenter. Samples are selected from the population.

Probability: As a practical matter, we think of the probability of an event as a measure of one's belief that the event will occur when the experiment is conducted once. The exact definition, giving a quantitative measure of this belief, is subject to debate. The relative frequency concept is most widely accepted.

Probability distribution, continuous: Smooth curve that gives the theoretical frequency distribution for the continuous random variable. An area under the curve over an interval is proportional to the probability that the random variable will fall in the interval.

Probability distribution, discrete: Listing, mathematical formula, or histogram that gives the probability associated with each value of the random variable.

Qualitative factor: Factors that are not quantitative (see quantitative factor).

Quantitative factor: One that can take values corresponding to points on a real line.

Quartiles: See chapter 2 for definition.

Randomized block design (containing p treatments and b blocks of p experimental units each): The treatments are randomly assigned to the units in each block, with each treatment appearing exactly once in every block.

Random sample: Sample of n measurements selected in such a way that every different sample of n elements in the population has an equal probability of being selected.

Random variable: Random variable is associated with an experiment. Its values are numerical events that cannot be predicted with certainty.

Range of a set of measurements: Difference between the largest and smallest members of the set.

Regression line: Line fit to data points using the method of least squares.

Rejection region: Set of values of a test statistic that indicates rejection of the null hypothesis.

Relative frequency: Class frequency divided by the total number of measurements.

Research hypothesis: Hypothesis to be accepted if null hypothesis is rejected; sometimes called the alternative hypothesis.

Sample: Subset of measurements selected from a population.

Significance level: See **Level of significance.**

Sign test: Nonparametric statistical test used to compare two populations. (See chapter 6.)

Standard deviation: Measure of data variation. (See chapter 2.)

Standardized normal distribution: Normal distribution with mean and standard deviation equal to 0 and 1, respectively. The standardized normal variable is denoted by the symbol z.

Student's t: Test statistic used for small-sample tests of means.

Student's t distribution: Particular symmetric mound-shaped distribution that possesses more spread than the standard normal probability distribution.

Test statistic: Function of the sample measurements, used as a decision maker in a test of an hypothesis.

Treatment: Specific combination of factor levels.

Type I error: Rejecting the null hypothesis when it is true.

Unbiased estimator: Estimator that has a probability distribution with mean equal to the estimated parameter.

Upper confidence limit: Larger of the two numbers that form a confidence interval.

Variance: Measure of data variation. (See chapter 2.)

Wilcoxon rank sum test: Nonparametric test that utilizes the rank sum of the sample measurements.

z statistic: Standardized normal random variable that is frequently used as a test statistic.

Selected Answers to Exercises

CHAPTER 2

Section 2.5

1. median is 5; $\bar{y} = 6.25$
2. median is 5; $\bar{y} = 4.71$
3. No unique mode; median is 11,450; $\bar{y} = 15,325$. When highest measurement dropped: no unique mode; median is 11,400; $\bar{y} = 11,353$.
4. mode is 2.6; median is 2.6; $\bar{y} = 2.656$

Section 2.6

1. lower quartile is 73; upper quartile is 90; range = 44
2. $s^2 = 4.0$; $s = 2.0$
3. $s^2 = 7.6$; $s = 2.76$

Section 2.7

1. 42, 62, 32, 72, 23, 81

Section 2.8

1. $s^2 = 5.143$; $s = 2.27$
2. $\bar{y} = 2.1$; $s^2 = 1.779$; $s = 1.33$
3. $\bar{y} = 14.73$; $s^2 = 11.21$; $s = 3.35$

Section 2.9

1. (a) 2.0 (b) −1.0 (c) .6
2. (a) −1.67 (b) 3.33 (c) −.17

Supplementary Exercises

2. $\bar{y} = 3$; $s^2 = 6.8$; $s = 2.6$
5. 68% ($\frac{17}{25}$); 96% ($\frac{24}{25}$); yes
6. $\bar{y} = .149$; $s^2 = .0000425$; $s = .00652$
7. 80% ($\frac{4}{5}$); 100% ($\frac{5}{5}$); data not mound-shaped

9. Without feedback: $\bar{y} = 24.71$; $s^2 = 167.57$; $s = 12.94$. With feedback: $\bar{y} = 9.33$; $s^2 = 38.27$; $s = 6.19$
11. 81.5%
14. range is 55; ratio is 4.1
16. 2.8
18. 4.25
19. 45
20. $\bar{y} = 23.9$; $s^2 = 15.13$; $s = 3.89$

CHAPTER 3

Section 3.2

1. $r = -.879$
2. $r = .93$
5. $r = .885$

Supplementary Exercises

1. $r = .852$
3. $r = .302$
7. $r = -.580$

CHAPTER 4

Section 4.3

1. (a) discrete (b) continuous (c) discrete (d) discrete (e) continuous

Section 4.4

1. (b) $\frac{3}{10}$ (c) $\frac{4}{10}$ (d) $\frac{9}{10}$

Supplementary Exercises

6. (a) continuous (b) continuous
7. (a) $\frac{1}{10}$ (b) $\frac{4}{10}$ (c) $\frac{7}{10}$

CHAPTER 5

Section 5.2

2. (b) .1296 (c) .5248
3. (a) .033 (b) .967 (c) .376
   (d) .302

Section 5.3

1. $\mu = 500; \sigma = 21.21$
2. (a) $\mu = 1.0; \sigma = .975$
   (b) $\mu = 10.0; \sigma = 3.082$

Section 5.4

2. (b) $\alpha = .055$ (c) reject H_0
3. (b) $\alpha = .058$; (c) insufficient
   evidence to reject H_0

Section 5.5

2. (a) $P = .012$
3. (a) $P = .252$

Supplementary Exercises

1. (a) $p(0) = \frac{1}{8}$; $p(1) = \frac{3}{8}$; $p(2) = \frac{3}{8}$;
   $p(3) = \frac{1}{8}$ (c) $\mu = 1.5; \sigma = .866$
   (d) .634 to 2.366; $-.232$ to
   3.232
2. (a) $p(0) = .729$; $p(1) = .243$;
   $p(2) = .027$; $p(3) = .001$
   (c) $\mu = .3; \sigma = .520$ (d) $-.22$
   to .82; $-.74$ to 1.34
3. (a) .9606 (b) .9994
4. $\mu = .04; \sigma = .199$
5. (a) .387 (b) .651 (c) .264
8. (a) $\mu = 200$ (b) $\sigma = 10$
11. (a) $H_0: p = .2; H_a: p > .2$; test
    statistic: y; rejection region:
    $y = 9, 10, \ldots, 25$
    (b) $\alpha = .047$ (c) insufficient
    evidence to reject H_0

CHAPTER 6

Section 6.4

1. (a) number of plus signs is 7
   (b) $P = .344$

Section 6.5

1. (a) observed $U = 34$ (b) rejection
   region: $U \leq 28$; $\alpha = .0526$;
   insufficient evidence to reject H_0

Section 6.6

2. (a) rejection region: $T \leq 8$;
   $\alpha = .10$
   (b) observed $T = 10.5$; insufficient
   evidence to reject H_0

Supplementary Exercises

3. (c) observed $y = 4$; $P = .688$;
   insufficient evidence to reject H_0
5. (b) rejection region: $y \leq 3$ or
   $y \geq 12$; $\alpha \approx .05$
   (c) observed $y = 12$; reject H_0
6. (a) rejection region: $T \leq 25$;
   $\alpha = .05$; observed $T = 18.5$;
   reject H_0
7. (b) $U = 7.5$;
   $.0262 < P < .0378$; reject H_0
11. (b) $y = 5$; $P = .623$; insufficient
    evidence to reject H_0

CHAPTER 7

Section 7.4

1. (a) .4192 (b) .3315
2. (a) .3849 (b) .3159
3. (a) .4463 (b) .0948
5. (a) .3500 (b) .2358
8. (a) .5762 (b) .1936
10. (a) .95 (b) .0098
11. .7734
13. 0
15. .86
17. -1.19
19. -1.645
21. 2.575
22. .1596
24. .1056
27. .4481; .1056

Section 7.5

1. (a) .648 (b) .6527

3. .9554

5. .1814

Section 7.6

1. (b) rejection region: $z < -1.96$ or $z > 1.96$; $\alpha = .05$; calculated $z = 2.83$; reject H_0

3. (b) observed $z = 2.44$; $P = .0146$; reject H_0

Supplementary Exercises

1. 80.23

2. .0808

3. 706.3

4. 8.536

5. 15, 19

6. $\mu = 1000$; $\sigma = 24.49$; $z = -2.45$; $P = .0071$; reject H_0

9. 91.92%

11. rejection region: $z > 1.645$; calculated $z = 1.54$; insufficient evidence to reject H_0

13. (b) observed $z = -2.16$; $P = .0154$

CHAPTER 8

Section 8.2

1. $\bar{y} = 43.8$; bound is .75

2. $\bar{y} = 9.8$; bound is .56

Section 8.3

1. $9.8 \pm .72$

2. 78 ± 2.45

Section 8.5

1. 1.3; bound is .85

2. 1.3 ± 1.0

Section 8.6

1. .81; bound is .025

2. $.81 \pm .02$

Section 8.7

1. .16; bound is .121

2. $.16 \pm .118$

Section 8.8

1. 900 (using $z = 2$)

2. 2400

3. 72

4. $-.3 \pm .19$

Section 8.9

1. (a) rejection region: $z < -1.96$ or $z > 1.96$
   (b) calculated $z = -1.75$; insufficient evidence to reject H_0
   (c) $P = .0802$

3. (a) rejection region: $z > 1.645$
   (b) calculated $z = 2.98$; reject H_0
   (c) $P = .0014$

Supplementary Exercises

1. 27.9; bound is 1.74

3. .3300

5. 11.39; bound is .97

7. $-.04$; bound is .104

9. $-.42 \pm .027$

11. rejection region: $z < -1.96$ or $z > 1.96$; calculated $z = 11.93$; reject H_0

13. .27; bound is .028

15. (a) rejection region: $z > 1.28$ ($\alpha = .10$); calculated $z = 5.5$; reject H_0
    (b) P is close to 0

17. rejection region: $z > 1.645$ ($\alpha = .05$); calculated $z = 3.22$; reject H_0

19. 3.5; bound is .059

21. rejection region: $z > 1.645$; calculated $z = 4.47$; reject H_0

23. calculated $z = 3.73$; P is close to zero; reject H_0

25. .387; .651

CHAPTER 9

Section 9.2

3. (a) rejection region: $t < -1.711$; observed $t = -3.64$; reject H_0
   (b) rejection region: $t > 2.064$ or $t < -2.064$; observed $t = -1.18$; insufficient evidence to reject H_0
   (c) rejection region: $t > 1.711$; observed $t = 5.11$; reject H_0

Section 9.3

2. rejection region: $t > 1.313$; observed $t = 19.1$; reject H_0
4. $.89 \pm .48$

Section 9.4

1. rejection region: $t < -2.306$; observed $t = -12.09$; reject H_0
3. rejection region: $t > 2.015$; observed $t = 3.69$; reject H_0

Section 9.5

3. rejection region: $F > 2.46$; calculated $F = 4.0$; reject H_0
4. rejection region: $F > 5.35$; calculated $F = 2.55$; insufficient evidence to reject H_0

Supplementary Exercises

1. rejection region: $t < -2.015$; observed $t = -2.32$; reject H_0
2. 6.8 ± 1.04
4. rejection region: $|t| > 1.86$; observed $t = 1.03$; insufficient evidence to reject H_0
6. rejection region: $|t| > 2.145$; observed $t = -1.71$; insufficient evidence to reject H_0
7. rejection region: $|t| > 2.365$; observed $t = -2.5$; reject H_0
9. $-.875 \pm .828$
11. rejection region: $|t| > 2.101$; observed $t = -1.41$; insufficient evidence to reject H_0
13. rejection region: $F > 3.18$; calculated $F = 1.65$; insufficient evidence to reject H_0

15. (a) rejection region: $F > 5.05$; calculated $F = 1.07$; insufficient evidence to reject H_0
    (b) rejection region: $|t| > 2.228$; observed $t = -2.07$; insufficient evidence to reject H_0
    (c) -26.7 ± 23.34
17. rejection region: $|t| > 1.943$; observed $t = 3.10$; reject H_0
19. rejection region: $|t| > 1.782$; observed $t = .69$; insufficient evidence to reject H_0; 90% confidence interval is 4.43 ± 11.48

CHAPTER 10

Section 10.4

1. $n_1 = n_2 = n/2$
2. $n_1 = 34; n_2 = 56$
3. $n_1 = n_2 = 48$

CHAPTER 11

Section 11.4

2. rejection region: $F > 4.10$; calculated $F = 7.18$; reject H_0

Section 11.5

1.

Source	d.f.	SS	MS	F
treatment	2	16.33	8.165	7.18
error	10	11.37	1.137	
Totals	12	27.70		

Section 11.6

2. rejection region: $F > 4.07$; calculated $F = 49.68$; reject H_0

Source	d.f.	SS	MS
treatment	3	282.42	94.140
error	8	15.16	1.895
Totals	11	297.58	

Section 11.8

1. (a) randomized block design

(b) rejection region: $F > 3.07$;
calculated $F = 3.6$; reject H_0

(c)

Source	d.f.	SS	MS	F
treatment	3	43.1	14.4	3.6
block	7	23.2	3.3	.8
error	21	83.7	4.0	
Totals	31	150.0		

3. (a) rejection region: $F > 3.07$;
calculated $F = 23.57$; reject H_0

(b)

Source	d.f.	SS	MS	F
treatment	3	198.34	66.11	23.57
block	7	106.97	15.28	5.45
error	21	58.91	2.805	
Totals	31	364.22		

Section 11.10

1. $n = 7$
2. $n \geq 23$

Section 11.12

1. (b) rejection region: $F > 5.14$;
calculated $F = 112.56$;
reject H_0

2.

Source	d.f.	SS	MS	F
treatment	2	606.72	303.36	112.56
between S_s	6	16.17	2.695	1.25
within S_s	27	58.0	2.148	
Totals	35	680.89		

3. rejection region: $F > 2.46$;
calculated $F = 1.25$; insufficient
evidence to reject H_0

Supplementary Exercises

1. (a) rejection region: $F > 2.82$;
calculated $F = 11.65$; reject H_0
(b) rejection region: $|t| > 2.365$;
calculated $t = -2.73$;
reject H_0
6. rejection region: $F > 4.26$;
calculated $F = 31.41$; reject H_0

Source	d.f.	SS	MS	F
treatment	2	1927.63	963.815	31.41
between S_s	9	276.15	30.683	5.56
within S_s	48	264.80	5.517	
Totals		59	2468.58	

7. rejection region: $F > 2.12$;
calculated $F = 5.56$; reject H_0
9. (a) rejection region: $F > 5.14$;
calculated $F = 10.5$; reject H_0

Source	d.f.	SS	MS
treatment	2	56	28
block	3	966	322
error	6	16	2.667
Totals	11	1038	

12. rejection region: $F > 3.74$;
calculated $F = 5.76$; reject H_0
13. rejection region: $F > 2.76$;
calculated $F = 1.38$; insufficient
evidence to reject H_0
15. rejection region: $F > 2.66$;
calculated $F = 4.12$; reject H_0

CHAPTER 12

Section 12.1

1. $\beta_1 = 2;\ \beta_0 = 1$
3. $\beta_1 = \frac{2}{3};\ \beta_0 = -\frac{5}{3}$

Section 12.2

1. (a) $\hat{y} = 1 + .7x$
3. (a) $\hat{y} = -77.79 + 13.096x$

Section 12.3

1. $s^2 = .3667$
3. $s^2 = 4033.80$

Section 12.4

1. rejection region: $|t| > 2.776$;
observed $t = 5.41$; reject H_0
3. (a) $y = \beta_0 + \beta_1 x + \varepsilon$
(b) $\hat{y} = 21.167 + 3.083x$

(c) $s^2 = 5.467$

(d) rejection region: $|t| > 1.833$; observed $t = 9.19$; reject H_0

Section 12.6

1. 380.6 ± 82.0
3. 64.3 ± 1.6

Section 12.7

1. 380.6 ± 194.4
3. 64.3 ± 5.5

Section 12.8

6. $r = .938$
7. $r = .934$; rejection region: $|t| > 3.182$; observed $t = 4.53$; reject H_0

Supplementary Exercises

4. (a) $\hat{y} = 86.49 + 152.17x$
   (b) $s^2 = 1663.68$
   (c) rejection region: $t > 1.812$; observed $t = 5.28$; reject H_0
   (d) 497.3 ± 78.7
7. 497.3 ± 27.0
8. (a) $\hat{y} = 28.6 - 1.15x$
   (b) $s^2 = 6.825$
   (c) rejection region: $t < -1.860$; observed $t = -3.94$; reject H_0
   (d) 22.85 ± 2.24
11. (a) $r = .970$
    (b) rejection region: $t > 2.896$; observed $t = 11.29$; reject H_0

CHAPTER 13

Section 13.3

2. rejection region: $X^2 > 7.81$; calculated $X^2 = 24.48$; reject H_0
4. (a) rejection region: $z < -1.645$; calculated $z = -3.125$; reject H_0

Section 13.4

1. rejection region: $X^2 > 4.605$; calculated $X^2 = 22.40$; reject H_0

2. rejection region: $X^2 > 15.5$; calculated $X^2 = 53.92$; reject H_0

Section 13.5

1. rejection region: $X^2 > 10.64$; calculated $X^2 = 100.05$; reject H_0
2. rejection region: $X^2 > 5.99$; calculated $X^2 = 1.97$; insufficient evidence to reject H_0

Supplementary Exercises

1. (a) rejection region: $X^2 > 3.84$; calculated $X^2 = 18.527$; reject H_0
   (b) rejection region: $z > 1.645$; calculated $z = 4.41$; reject H_0
3. rejection region: $X^2 > 9.21$; calculated $X^2 = 20.175$; reject H_0
5. rejection region: $X^2 > 15.5$; calculated $X^2 = 12.91$; insufficient evidence to reject H_0
6. rejection region: $X^2 > 5.99$; calculated $X^2 = 8.08$; reject H_0
7. rejection region: $X^2 > 5.99$; calculated $X^2 = 6.22$; reject H_0
8. rejection region: $X^2 > 5.99$; calculated $X^2 = .29$; insufficient evidence to reject H_0

CHAPTER 14

Section 14.1

1. (c) rejection region: $H > 7.815$; calculated $H = 15.59$; reject H_0

Section 14.2

1. rejection region: $F_r > 7.815$; calculated $F_r = 14.55$; reject H_0

Supplementary Exercises

2. rejection region: $H > 5.99$; calculated $H = 9.60$; reject H_0
3. rejection region: $F_r > 5.99$; calculated $F_r = 8.86$; reject H_0
5. rejection region: $H > 5.99$; calculated $H = 1.196$; insufficient evidence to reject H_0

Index